"NOT BY FAITH ALONE"

"NOT BY FAITH ALONE"

The Biblical Evidence for the Catholic Doctrine of Justification

Robert A. Sungenis

Foreword by Scott Hann
Epilogue by Peter M.J. Stravinskas

Queenship
PUBLISHING COMPANY
P.O Box 42028 Santa Barbara, CA 93140-2028
(800) 647-9882 • (805) 957-4893 • Fax: (805) 957-1631

NIHIL OBSTAT
Monsignor Carroll E. Satterfield
Censor Librorum

IMPRIMATUR
Monsignor W. Francis Malooly
Vicar General of the Archdiocese of Baltimore

October 24, 1996

Library of Congress #: 97-69045

Published by:
Queenship Publishing
P.O. Box 42028
Santa Barbara, CA 93140-2028
(800) 647-9882 • (805) 957-4893 • Fax: (805) 957-1631

Printed in the United States of America

ISBN: 1-57918-008-6

Dedication

Scott and Kimberly Hahn, former Reformed Protestants, who by God's grace have seen the truth of the Catholic Church, and from this have inspired untold thousands to reexamine, appreciate, and embrace the historic Catholic faith.

Rev. Peter M. J. Stravinskas, for his tireless efforts as a Catholic priest, spokesman, apologist, and man of God.

Special Thanks to:

Mr. Bill Bora, for his unselfish concern and uplifting encouragement during the course of this entire project, especially in difficult times. **Mr. William Marshner**, for his help in translating the Latin and German texts of Martin Luther and other Reformed theologians. **Rev. Ronald Tecelli, Rev. Peter Stravinskas, Mr. John Collorafi, Dr. Art Sippo** for their tedious correcting of the manuscript. A very special thanks to **Mr. Steven Engle** in this regard, who did most of the editing. **Mr. Scott Butler**, for his promotion of the book and his daily encouragement. **Mr. Patrick Madrid**, for his suggestion to write this book. **Ms. Christiana Lange** for her daily help and encouragement. The staff at the **Catholic University of America** in Washington, D. C. for their personal help and access to the university library. And last but not least, my college freshmen English professor who told me I didn't know how to write.

About the Author

Robert Sungenis is the president of Catholic Apologetics International, a lay organization dedicated to teaching and defending the Catholic faith. Born into a Catholic family in 1955, Robert left the Church and became a Reformed Protestant at the age of 19. He served as an elder, itinerant preacher, adult education director, and radio bible teacher. He converted back to Catholicism in 1992. He was educated at George Washington University (Bachelors Degree, 1979), and Westminster Theological Seminary (Masters Degree, 1982). He is presently pursuing doctoral studies at the Maryvale Institute in Birmingham, England. Publications include: *Shockwave 2000* (New Leaf Press, 1994); contribution to *Surprised By Truth* (Basilica Press, 1994); editor: *Is The Bible Our Only Authority: A Critique of the Protestant Doctrine of Sola Scriptura* (to be published by Queenship Publishing, 1997), and various articles in Catholic Periodicals.

Author's Note to Readers:

This book is designed to be read by both layman and scholar. For the layman, the prose of the book is written in a simple, easy-to-read style. At the end of each chapter are short summary statements to help in focusing on the major points of discussion. For the scholar, all the technical points concerning sources, language, exegesis, and history, are contained in detailed footnotes and appendices within the body of the book. The book is designed so that the earlier chapters address and explain the more general areas of the doctrine of justification, while the latter chapters concentrate on the more specific and complex areas. Through all the chapters, the major arguments and themes of the book are continuously repeated so as to alert the reader to the simplest and most salient features of the doctrine of justification. Authors and works referenced in the footnotes are often listed without the name of the publisher, which can be found in the Selected Bibliography. The Selected Bibliography contains all the works referenced in the book, in addition to works that were consulted but not included in the body of the text. For those interested in first understanding the historical aspects of our topic, Chapter 9 contains a brief but penetrating critical analysis of past and current Protestant conceptions on Justification. Since this book makes extensive use of Scriptural references, and addresses most of the major Protestant spokesman on the topic of Justification, we have provided an Index for Scriptures and Authors in the back of the book for easy referencing.

Since Catholic Councils attribute the writings of the Epistle to the Hebrews to the apostle Paul, this book cites Paul as its author. For more information see *Decrees of the Ecumenical Councils,* Vol. 1, The Council of Florence, (London: Sheed and Ward, 1990) p. 572; and Denzinger's *Enchiridion Symbolorum*, The Council of Trent, trans., Roy J. Deferrari (St. Louis, MO: B. Herder Book Co., 1957), p. 245, #784.

Endorsements

Office of the Bishop

In proving from Sacred Scripture the veracity of the Catholic theology of justification, Robert Sungenis leaves nothing to chance, no stone unturned, no concession for any other reasonable argument. We know that an active faith in Christ Jesus presupposes corporal and spiritual works of mercy — that faith implies works. We know that the words we long to hear, "Well done, my good and faithful servant... come share your Master's joy" (Mt. 25:21), will be spoken to those who have *done well.* Faith alone is not enough. The Protestant Reformation sowed confusion about the biblical theology of faith and good works, and many today rely on this confusion to defend or excuse a failure to live holy lives of service and goodness. Robert Sungenis has systematically addressed the confusion and demonstrated what we have always known, namely that Sacred Scripture and the Catholic Deposit of Faith are in complete agreement about justification. I applaud this work, and recommend it for all who wish to know how and why the Bible teaches that we are not saved by faith alone.

The Most Reverend Fabian W. Bruskewitz
Bishop of Lincoln

"Only some books deserve to be called "seminal" and "revolutionary." This is surely one of them. The ecumenical enthusiasm following Vatican II led many of us to view our divisions as rooted in nothing more intractable than misunderstanding. But if Robert Sungenis is right, this optimistic view is itself the result of deep misunderstanding; a failure to face squarely and honestly the hard doctrines of the Reformation. *Not By Faith Alone* pays the reformers the ultimate compliment of taking them at their word; it also renders a real service to anyone who cares deeply about Christian unity. For there can be no such unity apart from the truth. By forcing Catholics and Protestants to take a long second look at the things that still divide us, Robert Sungenis deserves genuine gratitude — and undivided attention."

Ronald K. Tecelli, S.J.
Department of Philosophy, Boston College
Co-author: *A Handbook of Christian Apologetics*

"This study shows Robert Sungenis to be a theologian and scholar of the first rank. With objectivity, clarity and precision, the author sheds new light on one of the most subtle and difficult issues of the Christian faith. Making meticulous use of Scripture and the primary writings of the Protestant writers themselves, Robert Sungenis exposes the many weaknesses, problems and inconsistencies of the *sola fide* position. This book is a gold mine of historical detail and theological analysis. Anyone interested in what really is at stake in the Protestant/Catholic discussions over justification can only benefit from this illuminating and intelligent study."

Dr. Robert Fastiggi
Associate Professor of Religious Studies
St. Edwards University, Austin, Texas

"While this present work is clearly scholarly, it must be distinguished from many other efforts along these lines over the past five centuries. Previous volumes often exhibited an acerbic tone; yet others lacked passion because they had reduced the discussion to blandly academic. Robert Sungenis is not only a competent theologian but a convinced believer who, with the sacred author, holds that God wants all men to be saved, precisely by coming to know the truth (cf., 1 Timothy 2:4). But being an intelligent person and one desirous of fulfilling the Second Vatican Council's hope for Christian unity, he has refrained from polemics even while defending and explaining in the most articulate way possible the Church's position on this topic...Robert Sungenis has heard the invitation and responded to the challenge; in doing so, he paves the way for others to follow."

Rev. Peter M. J. Stravinskas
Author of *The Bible and the Mass*
Editor: The Catholic Encyclopedia

The notion of 'justification by faith alone' is so alluring that countless good people have been convinced by the (weak) arguments in favor of it. Robert Sungenis turns those arguments on their head and shows what the *real* biblical doctrine is. It may not have quite the pizazz of the position espoused by Martin Luther, but it has one great advantage: It's *true*.

Karl Keating
President of Catholic Answers
Author of: *Catholicism and Fundamentalism*

"*Not By Faith Alone* exposes the Reformation formula of *sola fide* for what it is: a legal fiction, a tragic misunderstanding of St. Paul. With relentless precision, Robert Sungenis examines *sola fide* in fine detail, showing that it cannot withstand careful biblical, linguistic, historical, and theological analysis."

Patrick Madrid
Editor: *Envoy* magazine & *Surprised By Truth*
Author: *Any Friend of God's is a Friend of Mine*

"*Not By Faith Alone* may well become the most significant contribution to ecumenical relations between Protestants and Catholics that has appeared in a long time. Robert Sungenis achieves exactly what is typically lacking in late 20th century ecumenism, a love for the Truth that doesn't belittle serious differences. As a former Presbyterian minister, I know traditional Protestants won't engage the ecumenical call of Vatican II unless they are convinced Catholics understand the Reformation doctrine of justification. As a Catholic, I know the Tridentine doctrine of justification cannot and will not ever be repudiated. But there's a lot of misunderstanding that needs to be cleared away. Robert Sungenis knowledgeably and charitably engages the classic Protestant sources and more recent interpretations of justification by faith. His knowledge is clearly at the service of love but a kind of love that recognizes how important are deeply held beliefs about how we find acceptance with God. Anyone who is serious about unity of faith must read this book."

Kenneth J. Howell, Ph.D.
Former Minister: Presbyterian Church in America
Professor: History & Philosophy, Indiana University

"...This work represents the first book-length response by an American Catholic to Protestant attacks against the Catholic Church's teaching on faith and justification in more than half a century — perhaps longer, since I am not familiar with a single title written in the 20th century!...If you are a Protestant, this book affords you today's greatest opportunity to judge fairly — for yourself — the solid scriptural grounds for the Church's teachings on justification, and how an informed Bible-Catholic would respond to standard anti-Catholic arguments put forth by many evangelicals today."

Scott Hahn, Ph.D.
Associate Professor, Steubenville University
Author of *Rome Sweet Home*

"Does the Bible teach justification by faith alone? Ever since the 16th century, the evangelical community has accepted this as fact. Now they have good reason to doubt it. Anyone who will make the effort to study carefully the details of Robert Sungenis' insightful work will make the rather remarkable discovery that open-minded, modern sons and daughters of the Protestant Reformation can no longer hold to both biblical clarity and justification by faith alone without being double-minded. With his characteristic sincerity and comprehensive intensity, Robert Sungenis details the bankruptcy of the man-made system of Protestant theology, especially the Reformed denominations."

Rev. Paul Rothermel
Former Evangelical
Pastor of Notre Dame Church

"Upon reading Robert Sungenis's book, one hopes most fervently that it will be very widely read and studied among those who have espoused Luther's doctrine — and most especially our brethren, the leaders of the evangelicals. This is a major document, noteworthy for its clarity, its exhaustive coverage of the topic, and its punctilious scholarship."

Thomas Howard, Ph.D.
Author: *Evangelical is Not Enough*

"Robert Sungenis's book is a thorough presentation of the Catholic doctrine of justification from the biblical perspective. It combines a keen knowledge of the original language texts with an historic perspective often lacking in discussions of this type. This book not only deals with the historic debates on the question of justification dating from the 16th century, it is also the first apologetic book to directly challenge the recent writings of Protestant critics of Catholicism such as McGrath, Sproul, Geisler, McCarthy, MacArthur, White, et al. This enlightening and readable book is accessible to both the scholar and the average believer. It is written with sufficient sensitivity and depth of scholarship that both Catholics and non-Catholics will benefit from a careful reading. Anyone interested in Catholic apologetics and sound biblical exegesis needs to read this book."

Dr. Arthur Sippo
Catholic Apologist

"There is no question that justification and salvation are hot topics in the Catholic-Protestant dialog. Proof texts are tossed about and heated words are exchanged. For many Protestants, this is the highest hurdle, not because Catholic teaching is difficult or unbiblical, but because Protestants have too often misrepresented, and therefore misunderstood the Catholic teaching — treating it as a mere caricature of its real substance. Robert Sungenis' book is just what the doctor ordered. It gives a lucid, organized, scholarly, and well-reasoned explanation of the biblical and Catholic view of justification. I find myself turning to this book frequently, not only for quick answers to burning questions, but also for a clear presentation of how "justification" has been understood for two thousand years of the Christian faith. Many deviations and corruptions (2 Peter 3:15) have sprouted through the centuries, but Robert Sungenis' book demonstrates the solid, biblical doctrine that has been sustained with unaltered clarity and faithfulness within the Catholic Church. I am grateful for this landmark achievement."

Steve Ray
Former Evangelical Protestant
Author of *Crossing the Tiber*

"Robert Sungenis has written a powerful essay in Catholic apologetics. With clarity and charity, he exposes the countless confusions and contradictions within and between the myriad Protestant theologies of faith and justification, as well as give a solid, biblical defense of the Catholic teaching on justification."

Professor John Saward
St. Charles Borromeo Seminary
Author of: *Redeemer in the Womb*

"*Not By Faith Alone* is a masterful biblical study which makes significant progress in two important areas. First, it advances the Catholic-Evangelical dialogue with its thorough presentation of the issue of justification. Second, it is a classic example of the "biblical theology" or "theological exegesis" that is so greatly needed in the Church today."

Rev. Pablo Gadenz
St. Ann's Church, Keansburg, NJ

"One of the most urgent needs among the various Christian traditions in our time is for an honest accounting of the sins and errors of judgment that converged to produce what Lutheran historian Jaraslov Pelikan has called the "tragic necessity" of the Reformation. By his meticulous analysis, Robert Sungenis contributes substantially to one of the most urgent needs among the various Christian traditions in our time — an honest sorting out of what was really "necessary" from what was truly "tragic" in the Protestant Reformation."

Professor Philip Blosser
Department of Philosophy
Lenoir-Rhyne College (Lutheran - ELCA)

"I am pleased that the important doctrine of Justification has received such a thorough *apologia* as this book offers. It is especially gratifying to read so clear an account of a matter which has often been sadly confused in the rush of polemics."

Rev. George W. Rutler
National Chaplain: *Legatus*

"Catholic Apologetics has rarely been in more flourishing condition, and this book is one of the foremost proofs of it."

William Marshner
Professor, Christendom College

Contents

Abbreviations

AC . . . . Augsburg Confession
AAC . . . . Apology of the Augsburg Confession
ARCIC . . . . Anglican/Roman Catholic International Commission
ASV . . . . American Standard Version, 1901
BHS . . . . Biblia Hebraica Stuttgartensia, 1967, 1977
CC . . . . Catholic Catechism, 1994
CSEL . . . . *Corpus Scriptorum Ecclesiasticorum Lantinorum*
CO . . . . Council of Orange, 529 AD
CT . . . . Council of Trent, 1545-1563
DR . . . . Douay-Rheims Version of the Bible
DS . . . . *Enchiridion Symbolorum* by Henry Denzinger, 1957 ed.
DSA . . . . *De Servo Arbitrio* by Martin Luther
DTC . . . . Dictionnaire de Theologie Catholique
ECT . . . . *Evangelical and Catholics Together*, 1994
FC . . . . Lutheran *Formula of Concord*, 1577
INT . . . . *Institutes of the Christian Religion* by John Calvin
JN . . . . Jena edition of Luther's Works
JD . . . . The Christian Faith: Doctrinal Documents of the Catholic Church
JR . . . . *Faith of the Early Fathers*, ed. William Jurgens
LCDa . . . . Lutheran/Catholic Dialogue, 1983
LCDb . . . . Lutheran/Catholic Dialogue, 1995
LG . . . . *Lumen Gentium* from Vatican II
LW . . . . *Luther's Works* (Philadelphia: Fortress Press, 1967)
MF . . . . Moffat's Version of the New Testament, 1922, 1935
NABa . . . . New American Bible, 1970
NABb . . . . New American Bible, 1993-1994
NEB . . . . New English Bible, 1976
NIV . . . . New International Version of the Bible, 1973, 1978, 1984
NKJV . . . . New King James Version of the Bible, 1979, 1980, 1982
NPNF . . . . Ante Nicene, Nicene and Post Nicene Fathers, 1896, 1994
NRSV . . . . New Revised Standard Version of the Bible, 1989
PG . . . . Abbe J. P. Migne, *Patrologiae Cursus Completus: Series graeca*
PL . . . . Abbe J. P. Migne, *Patrologiae Cursus Completus: Series latina*
RSV . . . . Revised Standard Version of the Bible, 1946, 1971
SCH . . . . Philip Schaff: *History of the Christian Church*
ST . . . . *Summa Theologica* by St. Thomas Aquinas
TDNT . . . . Theological Dictionary of the New Testament, ed. G. Kittel

TEV	Today's English Version of the Bible, 1976
TR	Textus Receptus
WA	*D. Martin Luthers Werke: Kritische Gesamtausgabe*, Weimar ed. 1888
WABr	*D. Martin Luthers Werke: Briefwechsel*, 1930ff
WATr	*D. Martin Luthers Werke: Tischreden*, 1912ff
WC	Westminster Confession, 1648
WL	Walch edition of Luther's Works
WT	Wittenberg edition of Luther's Works
WTJ	Westminster Theological Journal

Foreword

Controversy surrounding the issue of faith and justification has been raging for a long time now — about two thousand years to be exact, judging from what Paul wrote to the Romans and Galatians; nor is there any sign that the conflict is about to subside.

What *may* come as a surprise, however, is the fact that this work represents the first book-length response by an American Catholic to Protestant attacks against the Catholic Church's teaching on faith and justification in more than half a century — perhaps longer, since I am not familiar with a single title written in the 20th century! What makes the novelty even more striking is the fact that it is penned by a former Protestant who used to attack the Catholic view of justification as unbiblical. Thus, he knows very well — from the inside — what he writes about.

Robert Sungenis received his training at Westminster Theological Seminary, one of the finest evangelical schools in the country, and arguably the most anti-Catholic in its staunch Calvinistic teaching. Following graduation and several years of ministry as a Bible teacher on Protestant radio, Bob's study of the Scripture led him to question certain (mis) understandings about Catholicism which he was taught — and was himself teaching. After years of study and prayer, his heart was gradually opened to God's call to become a Roman Catholic, which he did in 1992.

What does this mean to you the reader? If you are a Protestant, this book affords you today's greatest opportunity to judge fairly — for yourself — the solid scriptural grounds for the Catholic Church's teachings on justification, and how an informed Bible-Catholic would respond to standard anti-Catholic arguments put forth by many evangelicals today. On the other hand, if you are a Catholic — practicing or otherwise — you will certainly come to a deeper appreciation of God's word and your own Church's proclamation of the gospel, and how badly both are often misunderstood and misrepresented by well-meaning folks outside the fold.

Faith alone — is it justifiable? Not biblically or personally, and Robert Sungenis shows why. I am very excited about this book.

Scott Hahn, Ph.D.
Steubenville University
December 1996

Introduction

How can I be saved? That is a question that has been asked thousands of times in the course of human history — but not always with the same answer. Many years ago a Philippian jailer asked that very question of Paul the apostle. Acts 16:31 records Paul's response, "Believe in the Lord Jesus and you shall be saved." Believe! That seems plain enough. In reading that simple statement one might wonder why someone would have to write a massive book, such as this one, to explain what it means. Then we read the rest of Acts 16:31: "...you and your household." Immediately, questions rush to our head. Did the jailer have children? If so, does this verse teach that the children were saved upon the belief of the jailer? More questions surface as we read verses 32-34 where we find Paul baptizing the jailer and his whole household sometime after midnight. Why, we wonder, did Paul insist on baptizing them, and so soon, in the middle of the night? Was the baptism a necessary part of being saved? What prompted the jailer to inquire about salvation? Did he do so of his own free will or did God predestinate him to do so, or both? And what happened to the jailer and his family afterward? Did they remain steadfast to the Christian faith or fall away? For that matter, what did Paul really mean when he said, "believe in the Lord Jesus"? What is it about Jesus we are supposed to believe? Are we required to do anything else? In fact, how do we explain Paul's simple answer to the Philippian jailer in light of the more involved answer to the Rich Young Man in Matthew 19:16-26 who, after inquiring how one obtains eternal life, was demanded, by Jesus, nothing concerning faith; rather, he told the young man to obey the commandments and give to the poor?

Perhaps now we are beginning to see why the question "how can I be saved?" has been asked so many times but not always with the same answer. It only takes the reading of a few biblical passages to discover that we have entered into a subject that is both complex and challenging. It cannot be completely addressed in one unadorned word or sentence. In fact, the rest of the Old and New Testaments were written precisely to provide us with a complete and definitive answer to that seemingly simple question, "how can I be saved." Hence, we must surmise that Paul's answer to the Philippian jailer was merely the *introduction* to the salvation offered in Jesus Christ.

Theology, by nature, can often be very complicated. When we add to this the limitations, biases, and false presuppositions of men and groups that are invariably brought to the study of Scripture, making sense out of theology can indeed be very perplexing, as history itself has proven. The early Fathers of the Church struggled for centuries to explain and define various doctrines of the faith that today we often take for granted. Even though we have their writings, men from every quarter still struggle with the question of salvation. In the last few hundred years alone, thousands of churches and denominations have been created from that seemingly simple yet paradoxically difficult question, "How can I be saved?"[1] Today there remains a cacophony of voices, each telling us something a little different.

Despite this confusion, this author believes, with all those who have held faithfully to the official teachings of the Catholic Church, that God did not leave his Church with a confusing assortment of competing answers. From the beginning of his dealings with men, we will show that God made it very plain how they could be saved. We reason that it is certainly not a stretch of the imagination to purpose that if God desired men to be saved he would have given, and still does give, the precise truth he wanted them to know and live out. If we can't depend on that premise, then Christianity certainly doesn't have much to offer the world — except the same confusion by which it is surrounded.

1 According to the *Oxford World Christian Encyclopedia*, in 1982 there existed 20,800 organized churches and denominations within Christendom, "...with a projected 22,190 by 1985." The authors attribute this to "...local disagreements in how to indigenize and inculturate the Christian faith. The inevitable result has been a vast increase in the number of distinct, discrete, separate and divergent Christian denominations in many countries of the world ... The present net increase is 270 denominations each year (5 new ones a week). In many countries this produces serious overlapping, competition, rivalries, clashes, violence, and even lawsuits and protracted litigation." (ed. David B. Barrett, Oxford University Press, 1982, pp. 15-18). If the projection rated continued since 1985, this would amount to over 28,000 churches and denominations at the present date.

Before he left the earth, Jesus told the apostles he would lead them into all truth (John 16:13). He told them that he would be with them and the Church till the end of the age (Matthew 28:20; John 14:16-17). Through Paul the apostle, he told us that these same truths should be passed down to other like-minded men (2 Timothy 1:13-2:2; 2 Thess. 2:15); that the Church would be "the pillar and ground of the truth" (1 Timothy 3:15). In light of these promises, we must start from the conviction that Jesus could not abandon his Church, leaving them in the dark groping for the truth of salvation that he said he would give them. It is Christ's Church, his bride, and he cherishes her as a loving husband cherishes his wife.

It is with this resolve that we begin the study into the details of the biblical and historical teaching of the Catholic Church on the subject of Justification. As one can readily sense from the title, *Not By Faith Alone*, we are attempting, on the one hand, to counter a theology prevalent in Christendom which believes that justification comes by *faith alone*. Although, as we shall see in the remainder of this study that justification by *faith alone* means different things to different people, it was a teaching originating and popularized in the 16th century among those who have been called the "Protestant Reformers." The seriousness of this issue is reflected by one highly-respected Evangelical theologian in this century who has candidly admitted that the teaching on the nature of justification given by these 16th century theologians was a "theological novum," never before believed or taught by the Church.[2] These men claimed to

[2] Alister McGrath writes: "A fundamental discontinuity was introduced into the western theological tradition where none had ever existed, or ever been contemplated, before. The Reformation understanding of the *nature* of justification — as opposed to its *mode* — must be regarded as a genuine theological *novum*" (*Iustitia Dei*, II, 1986, pp. 186-187). However, McGrath shows ambivalence in this assessment in a later work: "Although some polemical accounts of the reformation tend to suggest that the Reformers abandoned fifteen hundred years of Christian tradition in order to found what amounted to a new religion, this view rests upon a series of misunderstandings" (*ARCIC II and Justification*, 1987, p. 7). McGrath also states regarding Canon 11 of the Council of Trent (see **Appendix 20**): "Underlying this canon appears to be the view that Protestants denied that transformation and renewal was of the *esse* of Christian experience, an error primarily due to terminological confusion, but compounded by Luther's frequently intemperate (and occasionally obscure) statements on the matter" (*Iustitia Dei*, II, p. 85). McGrath also admits, however, that the "Protestant doctrines of justification have been subject to a process of continual modification from the time of the Reformation onwards..." (Ibid., p. 133).

have rediscovered the lost truth of the gospel, and in effect, they were accusing the time-honored Church of perpetuating a false gospel — a devilish deviation from what she had received from the apostles in the first century.[3] As was true among the groups who opposed the Church in the early centuries, those who assert such things today also claim that Scripture proves their case. However, as the Church has always done when challenged by Scripture, it is to Scripture she will go to prove that the challenger's claims are false. When all is said and done, we will be reassured that God did not leave his Church in doubt or obscurity for fifteen centuries on the most vital issue facing mankind, that is, how to be saved.

Current Attitudes Towards the Controversy

Of course, in any confrontation, there are two sides to the story. The history of Catholic and Protestant relations is no exception. Each side has produced a battery of accusations and complaints against the other, some exaggerated, some legitimate. Prior to Martin Luther, various events occurred that could, perhaps, make someone call into question where the Church of Jesus Christ was headed.[4] During the controversy, men on both sides took liberties with the intentions and desires of the other that in calmer times may have been deemed deplorable. To this effect, Vatican II states in its *Decree on Ecumenism*:

---

3 In 1538, Luther is quoted as saying: "The papists say: 'your doctrine is new and our ancestors knew nothing about it; therefore, if it is true, it must be that they are all damned.' Well, what does it matter to us what judgment was made against those who have already departed from this world? Today we preach the word of God; one must only listen and accept it without discussion. We shouldn't be like those who are always asking questions and demand of God why he has revealed pure doctrine to the present age but not to the former times" (cited in Herbert David Rix's *Martin Luther: The Man and the Image*, p. 83).

4 Catholic theologian Harry J. McSorely, C. S. P. writes: "The neglect by popes and bishops to attend to their chief function of feeding the flock of Christ with the word of God was one of the major causes not only of the widespread theological unclarity in Luther's time, but also of the emergence, in the Ockham-Biel school of late medieval Nominalism of a Catholicism that was not fully Catholic" (*Catholic Scholars Dialogue with Luther*, ed., Jared Wicks, 1970, p. 107).

> In this one and only Church of God from its very beginning there arose certain rifts, which the Apostle strongly censures as damnable. But in subsequent centuries much more serious dissensions appeared and large communities became separated from full communion with the Catholic Church — for which, often enough, men on both sides were to blame.[5]

In stating that "men of both sides were to blame," Vatican II admits that among human beings, including those in the Church, no one is perfect. All of us share the blame for the division that is upon us. With these words, and many others like them, the Council sought to open the doors to ecumenism that had been shut for virtually 450 years. Vatican II not only assigned to Catholic individuals their share of the blame for the divisions occurring in the 16th century and later, it also recognized the faults of the Church's current members:

> But their primary duty is to make a careful and honest appraisal of whatever needs to be renewed and done in the Catholic house-

[5] Vatican Council II: The Conciliar and Post Conciliar Documents, *Unitatis redintegratio 3*, ed. Austin Flannery, O.P., p. 455; CC, Section 817. In the same vein, evangelical Alister McGrath's thesis gives more insight into this problem: "Furthermore, the practices of the institutional church tended to deny what her theologians affirmed — the priority of God over human beings in justification...the sale of indulgences, for example, tended to suggest to credulous souls that forgiveness could be purchased...this is what this theology was *thought* to mean by the masses, and they were encouraged in this belief by avaricious clerics...his moral actions placed God under an obligation to justify him" (*ARCIC II and Justification,* p. 14-15). The entire forthcoming study of justification will spring from and be an answer to McGrath's objection concerning *obligation* and *merit*, for it is the quintessential theological truth that must be understood in order to have any comprehension and resolution of the biblical doctrine of justification. On the other hand, McGrath seems not to appreciate the dialectic between God's grace and man's necessary cooperation in salvation by concluding that medieval theology and practice held that "God forgives sins only if the individual performs certain (generally rather strenuous) good works, which lie within his power to perform" (Ibid., p. 11). This objection, too, will be answered in the following pages. We also hope to overturn the conclusion by Norman Geisler and Ralph MacKenzie that "while affirming the necessity of grace, Catholicism denies the exclusivity of grace as a condition for receiving the gift of eternal life. This, in the eyes of historic Protestantism, is a false gospel" *(Roman Catholics and Evangelicals*, p. 502).

hold itself...For although the Catholic Church has been endowed with all divinely revealed truth and with all means of grace, yet its members fail to live by them with all the fervor that they should.[6] As a result the radiance of the Church's face shines less brightly in the eyes of our separated brethren and of the world at large, and the growth of God's kingdom is retarded.[7]

Hence, in the quest to make herself more appealing to those of other faiths and the world at large, the Church must start with its own members. The Church has discovered that "the evangelical witness which the world finds most appealing is that of concern for people, and of charity towards the poor, the weak and those who suffer."[8] In addition, each person in the Church is required "to speak the truth in love" and become a vital part of the mission of God on earth: "The individual apostolate is everywhere and always in place; in certain circumstances it is the only one appropriate, the only one possible. Every lay person, whatever his condition, is called to it, is obliged to it..."[9]

On the other hand, Catholic theologian Paul Hacker gives us a worthy caution:

> Catholics are at present criticizing their own past and the present condition of their church with a zeal which to some extent is surely justified and healthy, though it often overshoots the mark. But is it only Catholicism that requires to be criticized? Is it not

6 Since Vatican II, many Catholics have given themselves license to reinterpret the Catholic faith, and as a result, have created extremes on both sides, liberal and conservative, that have put many of these groups on the brink of schism. Added to this is the internal deterioration occurring over the last 30 years, especially in American Catholicism, e.g., the large drop in Mass attendance, the rise of "nominal" Catholicism, the mass exodus of priests and nuns from religious life, the high rate of divorce and sexual promiscuity among Catholics, the acceptance of contraception, abortion, and homosexuality among some Catholics, paedophilia and promiscuity among priests, the spiritual decline of Catholic universities, the feminist influence among Catholic nuns and lay women, liberation theology, etc. For more details on this post-Vatican II phenomenon, see Kevin Perrota's "The U.S. Catholic Church" in *Evangelical Renewal in the Mainline Churches*, ed., Ronald Nash, 1987).

7 Vatican Council II, *Unitatis redintegratio 4.*

8 Ibid.

9 Vatican Council II, *Apostolicam actuositatem 16.*

> necessary that the principle underlying the separate existence of Protestant churches should also be critically examined?[10]

In the same vein, former Lutheran and now Catholic convert Richard John Neuhaus, in reference to the recent Lutheran/Catholic dialogues of the last two decades, points out other obstacles:

> The claim that reunion depends upon Rome's acknowledging that 'justification by faith' (or, as some prefer, justification by grace through faith) is the controlling norm or rule for everything else may constitute an upping of the ante on the part of the heirs of the Reformation.[11]

In arriving at a united Christendom, we must never compromise truth. Christ gave us one truth — a truth he said would be protected from the very gates of hell.[12] It is with this foundation of truth which must be the basis of our investigation into the history of the rift between Catholicism and Protestantism. We must lay aside all misconceptions, misunderstanding, exaggerations, and the like, as we seek to affirm that there is only one truth. There cannot be two ways of salvation — one Catholic and one Protestant. Someone is wrong, or at the least has misconceptions, and each side realizes that the issue of justification is a matter "upon which the

---

10 *The Ego in Faith: Martin Luther and the Origin of Anthropocentric Religion*, 1970, p. xii.

11 *The Catholic Moment: The Paradox of the Church in the Postmodern World*, 1987, p. 15. In spite of Neuhaus's experience, Lutherans are by no means settled on how they are to approach dialogue with Catholics. On September 30, 1996, the Council of the World Lutheran Federation, because of receiving over fifty recommendations from their member churches, postponed until late 1998, rather than 1997, the deadline for the final decision on their part in the joint declaration. This delay was said to be prompted by "the necessity to create structures for the churches associated in the Lutheran World Federation to formulate a consensus amongst themselves." In June 1996, Cardinal Cassidy, President of the Pontifical Council Promoting Christian Unity, sent the present draft to the Catholic bishops of the world and it is presently being studied.

12 The Catholic Catechism states: "Christ bestowed unity on his Church from the beginning. This unity, we believe, subsists in the Catholic Church as something she can never lose, and we hope that it will continue to increase until the end of time. Christ always gives his Church the gift of unity, but the Church must always pray and work to maintain, reinforce, and perfect the unity that Christ wills for her" (Section 820).

Church stands or falls." Hence, we seek in this critical study of the Protestant Reformation and present evangelical movements, to uncover, explain, and hopefully rectify those crucial points of theology which caused the initial separation from the historic Catholic Church. In this regard, Vatican II states:

> The manner and order in which Catholic belief is expressed should in no way become an obstacle to dialogue with our brethren. It is, of course, essential that the doctrine be clearly presented in its entirety. Nothing is so foreign to the spirit of ecumenism as a false irenicism which harms the purity of Catholic doctrine and obscures its genuine and certain meaning. Furthermore, in ecumenical dialogue, Catholic theologians, standing fast by the teaching of the Church yet searching together with separated brethren into the divine mysteries, should do so with love for the truth, with clarity, and with humility.[13]

---

13 Vatican Council II, *Unitatis redintegratio* 11. In the search for truth, the Catholic must also keep in mind the opening statement of Pope John XXIII at Vatican II: "...the certain and unchangeable doctrine, to which we must remain ever faithful...the teaching of the church as it still shines forth in the acts of the Council of Trent and the First Vatican Council." Many years ago, St. Augustine established the same sentiment and warning: "Still, doubt in inquiry ought not exceed the bounds of the Catholic faith...Many heretics try to twist the exposition of the divine Scriptures to their own opinion which stands apart from the faith of the Catholic discipline..." (*On the Literal Interpretation of Genesis,* PL 1, 1). Despite opinions both then and now that Trent did not deal with the Reformers' objections, evangelical Alister McGrath confirms that "The evangelical may rest assured that the theologians assembled at Trent really did wrestle with the crucial issues at stake. The competence and quality of the Tridentine proceedings on Justification allow us to conclude that the desire for theological integrity and competence far outweigh any temptation merely to indulge in ecclesiastical diplomacy..." (*ARCIC II and Justification*, p. 15). In light of this, we should note that it took the Council of Trent only five days to formulate its numerous "anathemas," but six months and twelve days to formulate its decrees on Justification. It was in 1981 that Pope John Paul II suggested that the anathemas of Trent be reexamined in light of various movements in Lutheranism away from its 16th century roots. Catholic consensus has stated that though the condemnations of Trent are, and always will be, valid, nevertheless the errors stipulated by Trent are, in large measure, not found in present Lutheran dogma. In contrast, the US Catholic bishops, "It could be that our different concepts of Church are not reconcilable simply by the mutual recognition of the legitimacy of each other's religious concerns and throught patterns" ("An Evaluation of the Lutheran-Catholic Statement Justification by Faith" *Lutheran Quarterly 5,* (1991) 63-71).

Along the same lines, Lutheran Carl Braaten warns against false fervor:

> The assumption seems to have prevailed that there is no church-dividing difference on justification, and that the cause of our separation lies elsewhere. Hans Küng's book on justification had an enormous impact, claiming to prove that there is no basic disagreement between Karl Barth and the Council of Trent on the doctrine of justification. Many people wanted to believe this bit of wishful thinking, and seemed to proceed in ecumenical dialogue on its precarious assumption.[14]

Although Protestantism understands the Church to be God-ordained and helpful, it also believes that the institutional Church is not an absolute necessity in order to know God or receive his grace. In fact, Protestantism suggests that the institutional church is often the very means by which the truth of the gospel is corrupted. Laying aside the pristine teachings of Christ and the Apostles which both Protestant and Catholic view as truth, divergence between the two faiths surfaces in a fundamental difference in understanding how truth is perpetuated by the Church and assimilated by the individual. Catholicism views the truth of the gospel as "deposited," once-for- all, in the Church, and all that comes forth in the centuries following is essentially a clarification or development but never a deviation of that original truth. Protestantism, because it believes the Church can be in error, necessarily views the truth of the gospel in a state of evolution — an evolution which supposedly reached its zenith in the 16th century. Since the individual cannot, then, put his complete confidence in the Church to provide truth, Protestantism places the burden on the individual, and from his search for truth it becomes his personal responsibility to become right with God.

Protestantism concludes that the individual's relationship with God is ultimately not to be judged by the Church. Hence, the battle cry of the 16th century was centered on the "aloneness" of the individual with God, exemplified best in the two Latin slogans, *sola*

---

14 *Justification:The Article Upon Which the Church Stands or Falls*, 1990, p. 10.

fide and *sola scriptura*, known respectively as "faith alone" and "Scripture alone." Though on the one hand this new ideal seemed to have brought a simplicity and openness to the Christian faith, on the other hand, it inadvertently complicated and obscured the picture of how God provides salvation to man. Since God is infinite and his working with man complex, the self-appointed mission of Protestantism left it with an extremely huge burden. It had to formulate how the infinite God came *directly* into the life of the individual, a formulation not dependent on the mediation of the Church's eons of tradition, teaching, authority, and sacraments. Protestantism had to reinvent the theological wheel, as it were. Unfortunately, since God's infiniteness is too vast for any one man to comprehend, many and varied conceptions of God and salvation were created by Protestant theologians, each claiming, ironically, to obtain their teachings from Scripture alone. Such men as Wycliffe, Luther, Melanchthon, Calvin, Zwingli, Bucer, Osiander, Arminius, Spener, Wesley, and many, many others, though agreeing on the basic premise that the individual did not require the Church's mediation to find God and be saved, nevertheless had wide ranging and sometimes diametrically opposed concepts of how to attain salvation. In short, they differed on what the phrase *faith alone* really meant, and they differed on whether the individual could be certain that his relationship with God was secure once he found him by such faith. The differences and uncertainties among the original Protestant theologians eventually filtered down through the next 475 years and created the thousands of denominations present today. As one leader or group found inadequacies in the previous one, the latter would formulate a new and supposedly better understanding of the infinite God and how salvation was attained from him. In the following pages we will examine those differences and uncertainties, their impact on the original formulators, the residual effect on the face of Protestantism today, and a forecast for the future. When all is said, we hope that all readers will agree with Vatican II:

> Certainly, such division openly contradicts the will of Christ, scandalizes the world, and damages that most holy cause, the preaching of the Gospel to every creature... Everywhere large

> numbers have felt the impulse of this grace, and among our separated brethren also there increases from day to day a movement, fostered by the grace of the Holy Spirit, for the restoration of unity among all Christians.[15]

Leading us into the third millenium the Council continues:

> The sacred Council now pleads with all to forget the past, and urges that a sincere effort be made to achieve mutual understanding; for the benefit of all men, let them together preserve and promote peace, liberty, social justice and moral values.[16]

Though we see unity in Christendom, this book does not gloss over the differences in our respective theologies. If anything, it endeavors to make them more evident. It does not seek or suggest a compromise solution between Catholics and Protestants. By the same token, however, this book gleans from Protestant thought those nuances in the Christian faith that will be beneficial for all. In the end, though the Catholic Church recognizes that the denominations that split from her all carried with them a certain degree of truth, and that thereby individuals within them can also be saved,[17] nevertheless the anathemas of Paul, and those later issued by the Council of Trent, are still alive and well for anyone who knowingly and deliberately distorts the truth of the historic gospel.[18] Consequently, this book insists, following official Catholic Church

---

15 Vatican Council II, *Unitatis redintegratio 1.*

16 Vatican Council II, *Nostra aetate 3.*

17 Catholic Catechism, Section 819: "Christ's Spirit uses these Churches and ecclesial communities as means of salvation, whose power derives from the fulness of grace and truth that Christ has entrusted to the Catholic Church. All these blessings come from Christ and lead to him, and are in themselves calls to 'Catholic unity.'" ... "The Church knows that she is joined in many ways to the baptized who are honored by the name of Christian, but do not profess the Catholic faith in its entirety or have not preserved unity or communion under the successor of Peter.' Those 'who believe in Christ and have been properly baptized are put in a certain, although imperfect, communion with the Catholic Church'" (CC, Section 838; see also Sections 1257- 1261 on Baptism).

18 See Galatians 1:6-8; Council of Trent, Session 6, Chapter 1. See **Appendix 17** regarding the edict of Pope Benedict VIII: 'extra ecclesiam nulla salus' ("outside the church there is no salvation").

teaching, that the goal of such a study is to convince our separated brethren to come back to the fold which they left and embrace the doctrines of the historic Church. As John Paul II has said:

> But it is ever more urgent that they work and bear witness together at this time when Christian and para-Christian sects are sowing confusion by their activity. The expansion of these sects represents a threat for the Catholic Church and for all the ecclesial communities with which she is engaged in dialogue. Wherever possible, and in the light of local circumstances, the response of Christians can itself be an ecumenical one.[19]

Obeying the marching orders given at Vatican Council II, this book attempts to explain the Catholic doctrine of justification in a *fresh and exciting way*, and, in order to persuade as many as possible, it does so *exclusively from Scripture*.[20] All the relevant passages of Scripture in regard to the topic of Justification are exegeted in terms and procedures familiar to most responsible Protestants.[21] The goal of this study is that:

> Catholic exegetes and other workers in the field of sacred theology should zealously combine their efforts. Under the watchful eye of the sacred Magisterium, and using appropriate techniques they should together set about examining and explaining the sacred texts in such a way that as many as possible of those who are ministers of the divine Word may be able to distribute fruitfully the nourishment of the Scriptures to the People of God.[22]

---

19 *Redemptoris missio* 50, 1990.

20 The Catholic Catechism states: "...Hence 'access to Sacred Scripture ought to be open wide to the Christian faithful.'... Therefore, the 'study of the sacred page' should be the very soul of sacred theology...The Church 'forcefully and specifically exhorts all the Christian faithful...to learn 'the surpassing knowledge of Jesus Christ,' by frequent reading of the divine Scriptures. 'Ignorance of the Scriptures is ignorance of Christ'" (Sections 131-133).

21 "At the same time, Catholic belief must be explained more profoundly and precisely, in such a way and in such terms that our separated brethren can also really understand it" (Vatican Council II, *Unitatis redintegratio 11*).

22 Vatican Council II, *Dei Verbum 23-24.*

To engage "other workers in the field of sacred theology," this book analyzes and critiques current arguments from popular Protestant spokesmen. The book offers critiques on the writings of the major Reformation personalities such as Martin Luther, John Calvin, Francis Turrentin, Philip Melanchthon, Martin Chemnitz, John Wycliffe, Huldreich Zwingli, Martin Bucer, Theodore Beza, Jacobus Arminius, Andreas Osiander, John Wesley, Jonathan Edwards, and many other individuals, as well as groups such as the Anabaptists and the Puritans. It also analyzes documents such as the Formulas of Concord, the Augsburg Confession and its Apology, and many of the Reformed confessions and catechisms. References and critiques are heavily concentrated on contemporary Evangelical and Fundamentalist representative spokesmen, especially those from the Reformed persuasion, including: Paul Althaus, John Armstrong, Karl Barth, Hermann Bavinck, Joel Beeke, Donald Bloesch, James M. Boice, James Buchanan, Lewis S. Chafer, Edmund Clowney, D. Clair Davis, Melvin Deiter, James Dunn, Sinclair Ferguson, Edward Fudge, Ronald Fung, Richard Gaffin, Norman Geisler, John Gerstner, W. Robert Godfrey, Glenn Hinson, Charles Hodge, Zane Hodges, Michael Horton, Philip E. Hughes, D. James Kennedy, George Eldon Ladd, R. C. H. Lenski, John MacArthur, J. Gresham Machen, Ralph MacKenzie, James G McCarthy, Alister McGrath, John Murray, J. I. Packer, John W. Robbins, Charles Ryrie, E. P. Sanders, Andrew Sandlin, Norman Shepherd, Henry Smith, Russell Spittler, R. C. Sproul, Kristar Stendahl, Robert Strimple, Alan Suggate, Peter Toon, D. O. Via, Roger Wagner, John F. Walvoord, James R. White, Lawrence Wood, William Wrede, Robert Zins, and many others. Protestants who have written on justification and were consulted, but who are not critiqued in this book because of lack of space or because their views are similar to those of the above authors, are included in the Selected Bibliography. An author's index is included in the back of the book.

Among other things, the footnotes cite official Catholic Church documents to verify the Church's historical understanding from Scripture. For easy reading, the *New International Version* (NIV) of the Old and New Testaments is used in most of this book, unless the Deutero-Canonical books are cited in which case the *New Revised Standard Version* (NRSV) is used. In instances which demand a more literal and precise translation from the Greek or Hebrew, the NIV is replaced by the author's rendering.[23]

It is my hope that if we let Scripture speak, it will reveal to us that the doctrine of Justification, and thus our salvation, never veered from the path originally set down for us by Christ and the Apostles, and has been preserved ever since by the Catholic Church. For Catholics, it is time for us to reeducate ourselves to the scriptural truth that supports our faith. Afterward, we must teach it to others. For Evangelicals, it is time to face squarely the confusion and contradictions evident in the thousands of denominations that dot the landscape of Christendom, each offering a different answer to the question: "How can I be saved?" You owe it to yourself and to all those who preceded you: take another look at the Catholic Church to see if we have something better to offer you. If we can agree on what Christ wants us to believe, then together we can conquer the world for Christ in the third millenium, otherwise, the world may conquer us. In short, it is time for Evangelicals to become Catholic and for Catholics to become evangelical.[24] The documents of Vatican II, the conciliar statements made by recent Popes, and teachings from the Catholic Church at large, all express a common theme, hope, and prayer: that in the third millenium all of Christendom will be united.

Robert Sungenis

---

23 *The New International Version* is chosen not because it is the most accurate translation but due to the fact that it is one of the more popular Protestant versions. Concerning questions about the accuracy of the NIV, consult: Robert P. Martin, *Accuracy of Translation and the New International Version: The Primary Criterion in Evaluating Bible Versions* (Carlisle, PA: Banner of Truth Trust, 1989).

24 Examples of this fervent evangelical mentality in Catholicism are becoming increasingly abundant. Work include: *Surprised By Truth: 11 Converts Give the Biblical and Historical Reasons for Becoming Catholic*, ed., Patrick Madrid, 1994; *House United?: Evangelicals and Catholics Together; A Winning Alliance for the 21st Century,* Keith Fournier, 1994; *Rome Sweet Home: Our Journey to Catholicism*, Scott and Kimberly Hahn, 1993; *Born Fundamentalist, Born Again Catholic*, David Currie, 1995; *Evangelical Is Not Enough: Worship of God in Liturgy and Sacrament*, Thomas Howard, 1984; *On Begin Catholic,* 1997, *Why Do Catholics Do That? A Guide to the Teachings and Practices of the Catholic Church,* Kevin Johnson, 1994; *By What Authority: An Evangelical Discovers Catholic Tradition*, by Mark Shea, 1996; "Saving Evangelical Catholicism Today" in *New Mercersburg Review* 6, 1989; and "Evangelical Catholicity" in *New Mercersburg Review* 8, Linden J. De Bie, 1990.

Chapter 1

Did Paul Teach Justification By Faith Alone?

Did the apostle Paul teach justification by *faith alone*? For those who propose that he did, a very haunting question remains: *Why didn't Paul use the specific phrase "faith alone" anywhere in his New Testament writings*? A thorough study of his epistles reveals that Paul used the word *faith* and its cognates over two hundred times in the New Testament, but not once did he couple them with the adjectival qualifiers *alone* or *only*. Are we to believe that though he intended to teach justification by *faith alone,* he was never convinced that he should employ the attributes of the word *alone* to express explicitly what he invariably meant? What would have curtailed him from such an important qualification if indeed the solitude of faith in regard to justification was on the forefront at his mind?

A second reason that leads us to pose this critical question is that Paul used the word *alone* more frequently than did any other New Testament writer. Many of these instances appear right alongside the very contexts that contain teachings on faith and justification.[1] Thus it is obvious that even while Paul was teaching about

[1] The word "alone" or "only" is from the Greek μόνον or μόνος. In contexts where he discusses justification, Paul uses the word in Romans 3:29 ("Is God the God of the Jews *only*"); in Romans 4:12 ("...the father of the circumcised who not *only* are circumcised"); in Romans 4:16 ("...not *only* to those who are of the law"); in Romans 4:23 ("The words, 'it was credited to him' were written not for him *alone*"); in Galatians 2:10 ("*Only* that we might remember the poor"); in Galatians 3:2 ("I would like to learn *only* one thing from you"); in Galatians 4:18 ("...and not *only* when I am present"); in Galatians 5:13 ("*only* do not use the freedom for an advantage to the flesh"). It is the same word James uses when he says "not by faith *alone*" (James 2:24).

the nature of justification he was keenly aware of the word *alone* and its qualifying properties. This would lead us to expect that if Paul, who is usually very direct and candid in his epistles, wanted to teach unambiguously and unequivocally that man was justified by *faith alone*, he would be compelled to use the phrase if he thought it would help make his point indisputable. Moreover, since Paul's writings were inspired, we must also acknowledge that the Holy Spirit likewise knew of the inherent qualifying properties of the word *alone* but had specific reasons for prohibiting Paul from using it in connection with faith.

Thirdly, although the Holy Spirit prohibited *Paul* from using the phrase *faith alone*, he intentionally allowed *James* to make a clear and forceful point to the contrary by inspiring him with the words "man is justified by works and ***not*** by faith alone" (James 2:24). This unambiguous negation comes at the precise point in the epistle where James questions whether faith, by itself, is sufficient for justification. Comparing Paul and James leads us to believe that Paul avoids using the phrase *faith alone* because: (1) Paul's use of the word *faith* is pregnant with theological meaning and implications that absolutely preclude it from being coupled with the word *alone*; and (2) it would have created an obvious and acute contradiction in holy writ for one author to say, "man is justified by faith alone," while another is saying the exact opposite, namely, "man is *not* justified by faith alone."

With these facts from Scripture in the background, we submit that the burden of proof rests upon those who insist that the doctrine of justification be taught by using language that Scripture itself does not use. Although Protestantism proposes that the qualifying language "justified by faith alone" is appropriate to use because of the specific nature of justification, it is painfully obvious that, irrespective of what the true understanding of justification should be, Scripture intentionally chooses not to use such language. Precedence should be given to this undeniable fact when attempts are made to resolve this controversy. Since Scripture deliberately uses the converse phrase ("*not by faith alone*") when the issue of the solitude of faith is interrogated, it apparently realizes and concludes that the expression "justified by faith alone" is not the correct way to teach the masses how man is justified before God. We are forced to reflect on this issue ever more seriously when we realize Scripture's own insistence that its words are chosen very carefully,[2] and that it makes such choices precisely because it "foresees" the impact and implication of its teaching.[3] Moreover, Scripture teaches that Paul "...wrote to you with the wisdom given to him..." (2 Peter 3:16). We propose that it was this God-given "wisdom" which prevented him from joining the word *alone* with *faith,* wisdom that is as good for us as it was for him.[4]

---

2 For example, in Galatians 3:16 Paul makes quite an issue out of Scripture's choice, in explaining redemptive truth, of the singular "seed," not the plural "seeds" — a relatively imperceptible distinction for the uninformed reader. Paul writes: "The promises were spoken to Abraham and his seed. The Scripture does not say 'and to seeds,' meaning many people, but 'and to your seed,' meaning one person, who is Christ." Scripture often appeals to its own precise language, which many times goes unnoticed by the average reader, to settle disputes and uncover nuances to divine revelation that are not immediately obvious (cf., Matt. 12:3-5; 22:29-32; 22:41-46; 24: 15; Luke 20:37; John 7:41-43; 10:34-36; 19:36-37; Rom. 9:13; 10:8-11; 1 Cor. 9:9-10; 14:21; Gal. 4:30; Eph. 4:8-9; Heb. 4:2,6; 7:14; Num. 25:9/1 Cor. 10:8; Exo. 12:41/Gal. 3:17; Gen. 46:26-27/Acts 7:14; Luke 10:7/1 Tim. 5:18). Obviously, Paul, and the other inspired writers, treat Scripture as one cohesive whole wherein one book or testament anticipates and clarifies another. Hence, we can reasonably assume that Paul avoided the word "alone" but that James added it in recognition and respect of the ubiquity of Scripture's teaching on justification. We hasten to add that this argument should not be dismissed by claiming, for example, that if it is legitimate to use non-biblical words such as "Trinity" or "homousios" to explain theological truth, then it is acceptable to add such words as "alone" to Paul's writings for theological clarification. The reason: since "faith" and "alone" ***are*** words used by Scripture, we are required to follow Scriptural guidelines on their respective use.

3 Since Scripture is inspired by God, in Galatians 3:8 Paul does not hesitate to personify it as a 'thinking' personality. He writes: "The Scripture *foresaw* that God would justify the Gentiles by faith, and announced the gospel in advance to Abraham: 'All nations will be blessed through you.'" The word "foresaw" is from the Greek προειδέω. The only other passage where this word appears, Acts 2:21, confirms this meaning in reference to David "foreseeing" the resurrection of Christ, thus showing its personal and cognitive quality.

4 The Council of Trent (1545-1563) specifically attacked the Protestant Reformer's teaching of justification by *faith alone.* The Council stated: "And so no one should flatter himself because of faith alone, thinking that by faith alone he is made an heir and will obtain the inheritance..." (Session 6, Chapter 11). "But neither is this to be asserted, that they who are truly justified without any doubt whatever should decide for themselves that they are justified, and that no one is absolved from sins and is justified, except him who believes with certainty that he is absolved and justified, and that by this faith alone are absolution and justification effected..." (Chapter 9).

But Do "Works" Justify?

If Paul did not intend to convey the concept of *faith alone,* then how do we explain his teaching in Romans 3:28, "that a man is justified by faith apart from works of the law"? Could one not argue that the phrase "*apart from*"[5] is in fact a synonym of the word *alone,* and thus conclude that Paul really did teach that faith was alone in justification? To answer this, we must first point out that "justified by faith alone" does not mean the same thing as "justified by faith apart from works of the law." On a purely grammatical basis, the phrase "faith alone" denotes that faith is the *only* instrument for justification, while the statement "faith apart from works of the law" merely means that "works of the law" — whatever they are — are the only thing that cannot be coupled with faith for justification. In other words, "faith alone" excludes anything from being added to faith, while "faith apart from works of the law" excludes only "works of the law" from being added to faith. From this distinction one may infer either that something may be added to faith that is not considered "works of the law," or that we could implicitly understand "faith" as being inseparably related to other virtues that are not technically associated with "works of the law."[6] For example, Paul never says, "a man is justified by faith apart from love," or "man is justified by faith apart from obedience," or "man is justified by faith apart from hope." In fact, in reference to

---

5 The Greek of Romans 3:28 reads: λογιζόμεθα γὰρ δικαιοῦσθαι πίστει ἄνθρωπον χωρὶς ἔργων νόμου. ("For we understand a man to be justified by faith apart from works of law"). The words "apart from" are from the Greek χωρὶς which is normally understood as "without" or "apart from." It is used frequently in Paul's epistles, appearing three times in the immediate context of Romans 3-4, e.g., Romans 3:28 noted above; Romans 3:21: "...a righteousness from God apart from the law..."; Romans 4:6: "...God credits righteousness apart from works..."

6 The Council of Trent held that "...he is ingrafted, receives in the said justification together with the remission of sins all these [gifts] are infused at the same time: faith, hope, and charity" (Session 6, Chapter 7, DS 800). The Council understood that the infusion of hope and charity at the point of justification shows that "faith without works is dead," in reference to James 2:24. This aspect of justification will be covered more fully in chapters 2 and 5. As Catholic theologian Michael Schmaus concludes: "The faith preached by Paul is complex. It includes the act of faith as well as its content, and the unity of content and act" (*Dogma: Justification and the Last Things*, p. 26)

justification, Paul in Galatians 5:6 seems to make an inseparable bond between faith and love by the statement "faith working through love." By the same token, Paul never says "faith working through works of the law." Moreover, in Romans 1:5 and 16:26 Paul suggests an intimate link between faith and obedience by the unique phrase, "the obedience of faith."[7] Hence, with regard to justification, according due justice to Paul's dictum that faith must be apart from "works of the law" does not imply that faith is completely alone, especially from other virtues like love and obedience.[8] According to certain Scriptures, there is something about the concept of "works of the law" which forces Paul to separate it from his concept of faith, yet dissimilar Scriptures allow, or even require, one to add other virtues which are not necessarily associated with "works of the law" in order to achieve justification.

Suppose one were to argue, however, that love cannot be coupled with faith in justification because love itself, or even obedience or hope, should be classified as a "work of the law." From this proposal one could make the claim that if love, obedience, and hope are not separated from faith in regard to justification there would be a contradiction between what Scripture says in one place and what it says in another. It is precisely on this particular point that Martin Luther decided to divorce love, hope, and obedience from faith in regard to justification, opting to use the phrase "faith alone" and subsequently putting the three virtues on the side of

[7] The Greek phrase Paul uses in Romans 1:5 and 16:26 is ὑπακοὴν πίστεως ("obedience of faith") in which the genitive πίστεως (indicates that obedience is intimately and inseparably connected to faith. We also see this connection in the genitive phrase of 2 Thess. 1:11, ἔργον πίστεως ("work of faith"). In light of this the Catholic Catechism states: "By faith, man completely submits his intellect and his will to God. With his whole being man gives his assent to God, the revealer. Sacred Scripture call this human response to God, the author of revelation, 'the obedience of faith'" (Section 143; 2087).

[8] Protestants invariably miss this distinction and thus treat Paul's statement in Romans 3:28 as equal to justification by faith alone. For example, apologist James R. White states: "Paul goes on to describe the means of justification — it is by faith, *and faith alone*. He writes, 'For we maintain that a man is justified by faith apart from works of the Law (Romans 3:28)'" (*The Roman Catholic Controversy*, p. 41, emphasis mine). Here we see that the phrase "faith alone" is surreptitiously used to interpret Paul's statement and the uneducated reader is thus programmed to see "faith alone" in every instance where Paul puts faith in opposition to works of the law.

"works of the law" that cannot justify. However, other Protestants disagreed with Luther and leaned more toward defining faith in terms of love and obedience. Therein lies the controversy — a controversy not only between Catholics and Protestants, but among Protestant denominations themselves.[9]

Even if one insists on using the language "justified by faith alone" to express the uniqueness of faith in justification, one must still admit that the individual who exercises faith in God, at least in one sense, is "doing something" in order to be justified, regardless of whether that "something" is classified as an act, a work, or a mere mental process. It cannot be denied that even faith requires some effort from the individual, despite how one wishes to classify that effort, or however large or small that effort may be. As we shall see in later chapters, one's understanding of faith, either as a "work" or a "non-work," "qualified" or "non-qualified," becomes a great source of contention among various Protestant denominations. Thus, even applying the most exclusive meaning to the phrase

---

9 See chapter 9 for a more detailed treatment of Luther's view of the relationship between faith and love, as well as the departures from his theology by other Protestant theologians. Regarding the multiplicity of Protestant views on the meaning of *faith alone*, Lutheran Carl Braaten, citing the landmark work *Iustitia Dei* by Anglican Alister McGrath, states: "McGrath's discussion of the history of the doctrine of justification in the periods of the Reformation, orthodoxy, and pietism makes it clear that those who have adhered to the formula "justification by faith alone" have sometimes understood opposite things by it. It seems ironic and even embarrassing that the very theological tradition which has affirmed the article by which the church stands or falls has been so confused and void of inner harmony on this doctrine...We cannot go into each of these controversies here, but all of them can be reduced ultimately to the question of the nature of the correlation between justification and faith. It is no wonder that, weary of all such controversies, theologians sought formulae of concord that only served to conceal a fatal flaw lurking in the understanding of justification" (Braaten, *Justification: The Article By Which The Church Stands or Falls*, pp. 21-23). See **Appendix 10** for further discussion on this issue. One example of the weight placed on the phrase *faith alone* is noted in Evangelical R. C. Sproul's statement: "For the Reformers the doctrine of justification by faith alone meant justification by Christ and his righteousness alone" (*Faith Alone*, p. 73). Here we see that *faith alone* becomes a "code word" for an even higher concept, yet Sproul's book does not even address the propriety for using a non-biblical phrase to support his theology. (The issue of "justification by Christ and his righteousness alone," or what Protestant theology calls "imputed" righteousness, will be covered more thoroughly in chapter 5. For now, we are concerned more with Scriptural terminology).

faith alone, that is, divorcing faith from every other virtue, the individual is still required to perform some volitional act in order to be justified. While some Protestant theologians may choose not to call faith a work, or some may claim that faith is given exclusively by God and is not volitional, as we shall see, they have not escaped the problem surrounding the relationship between faith and works.

And our problems are not over. Consider this: If the justification of the individual requires that faith be apart from observing the law, then what did Paul mean when he wrote, just one chapter earlier in Romans 2:13, "For it is not the hearers of the law that are just with God, but the *doers of the law* will be justified"? In this passage Paul says precisely that the *law* (not love or obedience) justifies, while in Romans 3:28 he says specifically that justification comes apart from the law. From reading these two passages Paul suggests that there is a particular sense in which works justify and another sense in which they do not. To say the least, these passages seem somewhat confusing.

We are beginning to see why the answer to the question posed above (i.e., "But do works justify?") lies neither in postulating a mere polarity between faith and works, nor in injecting a phrase such as "faith alone" into the discussion. In fact, if we fail to address this issue properly, a cursory study of Paul's teaching appears contradictory at some points and leads either to total confusion, or worse, leads to premature and erroneous conclusions as to what he actually taught on this subject.[10] However, despite what may appear to be a confusing assortment of facts and ideas regarding Paul's view of justification, Paul himself gives us a very simple rule that enables us easily to understand his teaching, which we will now introduce.

---

[10] Concerning problems of this nature in Paul's writings, Peter comments in 2 Peter 3:16: "His letters contain some things that are hard to understand, which ignorant and unstable people distort, as they do other Scriptures, to their own destruction." Responsible Protestants themselves recognize how difficult bible interpretation can be; admitting that Scripture has often been treated as a proverbial ragdoll. Almost any book addressing the topic of hermeneutics bears this out, e.g., Gerald Bray, *Biblical Interpretation: Past and Present* (1996); D. A. Carson, *Exegetical Fallacies* (1984); Moisés Silva, *Has The Church Misread The Bible*? (1987); Erwin Lutzer, *All One Body — Why Don't We Agree*? (1989); Bernard Ramm, *Protestant Biblical Interpretation* (1970); Frederic Farrar, *History of Interpretation* (1961); Milton Terry, *Biblical Hermeneutics* (1974).

Paul's Principle of "Obligation"

To begin to uncover the true relationship between faith and works, we need to understand one of the most fundamental principles in the theology of Paul. That principle concerns the matter of *obligation* or *debt*. We see this principle established in that most famous of passages, Romans 4:4: "*To the one working, the wage is not reckoned according to grace but according to obligation.*" To help us understand this indispensable principle, Paul uses the example of the employer who is obligated to pay his employee for work performed. In the manner Paul is using the term "obligation," it refers to a measured compensation which is legally owed by one party to another.[11] The party in debt is obligated to pay the party owed, or the party who performs work is legally entitled to be paid for his services from the party for whom the work is done. Since we understand work as something which requires the strenuous use of one's faculties (e.g., manual labor that involves expending time and energy, inconveniencing oneself, creating or maintaining something, and/or suffering pain or discomfort), the worker is someone who, within the common understanding of labor relations, must be remunerated or compensated, in some manner, equal to his efforts. Colloquially speaking, for an hour's work, he must be paid an hour's wage. Unless the employer is willing to break the law, he is legally required to pay the worker what is due him. It does not matter whether the employer loves or hates, likes or dislikes, the employee. He is under obligation to pay him.

Establishing the principle of *obligation*, Paul introduces the foundational rule regarding anyone who attempts to work his way to God. If the appeal to God is based on obligation, then the relationship between God and man becomes one in which the party who works (man) is legally *obligating* the party for whom the work is done (God) to pay for the services rendered. Hence, in regard to

---

11 The word translated "obligation" is a form of the Greek word ὀφείλημα and is used twice in the New Testament. The other occurrence appears in Matthew 6:12 in the Lord's prayer ("forgive us our tresspasses"). Its cognates, ὀφειλέτης and ὀφειλή, are translated either as "debt," "owed," or "due" (cf., Matt. 18:24; Rom. 13:7; Gal. 5:3). The verbal form ὀφείλω is used 36 times in the New Testament with the meaning "owed" (Matt. 18:28; Rom. 13:8) or "ought" (John 13:14; Acts 17:29).

justification, a man who approaches God expecting legal payment for his efforts thus puts God in a position of being "obligated" to deem him righteous and acceptable, worthy of living with God and being blessed by him for eternity. Since in this situation God would be forced to owe a *legal* debt to the man who works, then the relationship is one based on law, i.e., a legal contract. If it is based on law, then it cannot be based on the personal benevolence of God to man, otherwise known as *grace*. If the appeal to God were based on grace, man would not be placing God in the position of being legally obligated to pay him for the work he performed. God could repay out of the goodness of his heart, but he would not be contractually obligated to do so, unless, of course, God had obligated himself.[12] This is the foundational principle Paul uses to establish his thesis. Any proposed understanding of justification must first take into account the principle of *legal obligation* that stands as the primary distinction between grace and works. Paul reiterates this principle in general terms in Romans 11:6 by saying: "And if by grace, then it is no longer by works; if it were, grace would no longer be grace.[13]

---

[12] The dimension of justification in which God obligates himself will be covered in chapter 6.

[13] Using Paul's wording, the Council of Trent, Session 6, Chapter 8, states: "...because none of those things which precede justification, whether faith or works, merit the grace itself of justification; for, 'if it is a grace, it is not now by reason of works; otherwise (as the Apostle says) grace is no more grace.'" The Catholic Catechism, Section 604, states: "By giving up his own Son for our sins, God manifests that his plan for us is one of benevolent love, prior to any merit on our part." Again, "Our justification comes from the grace of God. Grace is favor, the free and undeserved help that God gives us to respond to his call to become children of God, adoptive sons, partakers of the divine nature and of eternal life" (CC, Section 1996). "The preparation of man for the reception of grace is already a work of grace" (CC, Section 2001). "Since the initiative belongs to God in the order of grace, no one can merit the initial grace of forgiveness and justification, at the beginning of conversion" (CC, Section 2010). As Catholic theologian Joseph Fitzmeyer reminds us: "The laborer working for pay has a strict right to it. Paul introduces this comparison to illustrate [Romans] 4:2. God was never in Abraham's debt, and uprightness is not a matter of something owed" (*The Jerome Biblical Commentary*, "The Letter to the Romans," 1968, p. 303). We also understand Paul's remaining statement in Romans 5:5, "However, to the one who does not work but trusts God who justifies the wicked...", as referring to one who recognizes that he must refrain from working under the system of obligation and submit himself to the system of grace. As regards entering into the system of grace through

To understand the contrast between grace and works a little better, we need a theological backdrop to the principle of *obligation* that Paul is establishing in Romans 4:4. What God possesses that everyone desires is to be like God and to live eternally. In the very beginning, Adam and Eve wanted to be like God and live in eternal bliss. Deceived by the devil, they became convinced that the easiest way to obtain this blessed state was to eat immediately of the tree of the knowledge of good and evil — a tree that God had forbidden. After they sinned by eating of the fruit, God, knowing that Adam and Eve might attempt again to gain eternal life by eating from the *tree of life*, placed an angel to guard it with a flaming sword (Genesis 3:22-24). God subsequently banished them from the Garden. Although God prohibited Adam and Eve from gaining eternal life the quick and easy way, in his gracious love God still made it possible for them to obtain heavenly bliss. He promised them a redeemer who would suffer for Adam's sin and once again open the pathway to God's kingdom (Genesis 3:15). Accordingly, the primary purpose for all God's work on earth is that man can one day receive the blessing of heaven and live with God eternally. Heaven is, or should be, the ultimate goal of every person.

As regards the terms Paul uses in Romans 4:4, he indicates two ways in which eternal life is obtained: (1) that which one receives as a *gift* from God, or (2) that which is *owed* to the individual for work performed. If heaven is a gift, then it comes by grace. Conversely, if heaven is given because it is owed, then it is no longer by grace, since the giver has been made *obligated* to bestow it on the one who works. In either case, whether by grace or by works, there must be a justifiable reason why an imperfect and untested creature can be permitted to enter the dwelling of a perfect, holy, and transcendent Creator. If by works, the person must work sufficiently to justify his entrance into heaven. If by grace, the person receives heaven as a gift — a gift that the giver is

---

13 cont. justification, the Catholic Catechism states: "The Paschal mystery has two aspects: by his death, Christ liberates us from sin; by his Resurrection, he opens for us the way to a new life. This new life is above all justification that *reinstates us in God's grace*, 'so that as Christ was raised from the dead by the glory of the Father, we too might walk in newness of life.' Justification consists in both victory over the death caused by sin and a *new participation in grace*" (CC, Section 654, emphasis mine).

not obligated to give but does so only because of his kindness and mercy. Of the two options before man, grace or obligation, Paul goes on to explain that the problem with attempting to attain heaven based on obligation is two-fold. First, since God is the transcendent Creator, and the heaven in which he dwells is perfect, then those who wish to work under the terms of a legal contract in order to justify their entrance into heaven must work perfectly.[14] Under a contractual arrangement, only when the work is perfect can man put God in a position of being *obligated* to pay him. Essentially, perfect work would earn a perfect payment.

The second problem with attempting to enter heaven based on obligation is the reality of sin.[15] This fact brings us back to Adam and Eve. Once Adam and Eve failed the test in the Garden of Eden, God's precepts required that they and all their progeny come under the curse of sin and death. Paul explains this principle in Romans 5:12: "Therefore, as through one man sin entered into the world, and through sin came death, and so death passed to all men, upon which all sinned."[16] Paul also says something similar in Romans 3:9-11: "...We have previously accused Jews and Gentiles of being all under sin. As it is written, 'There is not a righteous man, not even one. There is not one who understands, there is not one who seeks God.'" Again in Romans 3:19 and 23 Paul says: "...and the whole world is held accountable to God...for all have sinned and

---

14 See also the Catholic Catechism, Sections 578-579.

15 Ibid., Section 1963.

16 Council of Trent, Decree on Original Sin: Session 5, Chapter 2, states: "If anyone asserts that the transgression of Adam has harmed him alone and not his posterity, and that the sanctity and justice, received from God, which he lost, he has lost for himself alone and not for us also; or that he having been defiled by the sin of disobedience has transfused only death and the punishments of the body into the whole human race, but not sin also, which is the death of the soul, let him be anathema, since he contradicts the Apostle who says: 'By one man sin entered into the world, and by sin death, and so death passed upon all men, in whom all have sinned.' Chapter 4: "If anyone denies that infants newly born from their mother's wombs are to be baptized...but that they derive nothing of original sin from Adam...let him be anathema." Session 6, Chapter 1: "it is necessary that each one recognize and confess that, whereas all men had lost their innocence in the prevarication of Adam, "having become unclean" and (as the Apostle says), "by nature children of wrath, as it (the Synod) has set forth in the decree on original sin..." See also Catholic Catechism, Sections 402-409).

fall short of the glory of God." It is quite clear that Adam and Eve created a serious problem. They forced God to withdraw himself from the human race to the extent that everyone created had to come under the reign of sin and death. All of mankind would inherit the stain of sin from Adam and continue to sin by their own volition. They lost the complete protection of God from the forces of nature. They would also face physical death.[17] Hence, with the curse of sin and death as part of their very nature, trying to work their way to heaven by attempting to legally obligate God to bless them would be an impossible task. No one could ever perform the work required to constrain God to pay one with eternal life. In fact, under law, God's judgments are so penetrating and uncompromising that anyone attempting to work his way to heaven while in the state of sin and death would only obligate God to pay with eternal punishment.[18] As Paul says in Romans 6:23, "For the *wages* [i.e., legal payment] of sin is death..." Consequently, obligation can never serve as the basis upon which we gain entrance into heaven. Salvation can only come as a result of grace wherein God is not put in a position of being legally obligated to pay man. Because of the specific nature of God's relationship to man, God must bestow salvation upon man as a gift.[19]

Who Is This God Who Justifies?

God's Transcendence

In correlation with Paul's principle of wages and obligation, one of the other keys to understanding justification is to understand the God behind it. As noted above, God is a totally transcendent and perfect being. Because of his transcendent status, God owes nothing to anyone. Those who attempt to obligate God to

---

17 We can say, however, that God gave Adam and Eve a "suspended sentence" since he did not take their lives immediately.

18 "...the eyes of the Lord are ten thousand times brighter than the sun; they look upon every aspect of human behavior and see into hidden corners" (Ecclesiasticus 23:19).

19 Augustine writes: "What is grace? Something given gratis. What is given gratis? That which is bestowed rather than paid as owed. If it is owed, it is wages paid, not a gift graciously given" (*Homilies on the Gospel of John*, PL 35, 3, 9.)

favor them are woefully inadequate for the task. As Paul says in Romans 11:33-35:

> Oh, the depth of the riches of the wisdom and knowledge of God! How unsearchable his judgments, and his paths beyond tracing out! Who has known the mind of the Lord? Or who has been his counselor? *Who has ever given to God that God should repay him*? For from him and through him and to him are all things.

In the words, "Who has ever given to God that God should repay him" we have the most succinct statement of Paul's theology. God is not obligated to repay anyone for their work simply because no one has ever given anything to God that deserves payment. Paul is saying the same thing in Romans 11:35 that he said in Romans 4:4, that is, one cannot put God in a position of obligation to repay. Therefore, one cannot establish his relationship to God based on working. This was true of Adam and Eve and it is certainly true for us today.

Another instance that describes well God's transcendent nature is the frequent descriptions of his holiness. In Isaiah 6:3 the prophet records, "Holy, Holy, Holy is the Lord Almighty, the whole earth is full of his glory." We understand from statements like these that God is perfectly pure; with not the slightest presence of evil. The picture of God's holiness is seen, for example, when he is dealing with the Israelites at the giving of the Ten Commandments in Exodus 19. God is so holy he will not allow any of the people to even touch the mountain that Moses ascends to receive the commandments. In verse 12 God says to Moses, "Put limits for the people around the mountain and tell them, 'Be careful that you do not go up the mountain or touch the foot of it. Whoever touches the mountain shall surely be put to death.'" Similarly, in Isaiah 55:11 God compares his transcendence to man's sin with the words, "As the heavens are higher than the earth, so are my ways higher than your ways, and my thoughts than your thoughts."

God's Personal Nature

Right alongside God's transcendent status is his personal nature. God is an intensely personal being. He loves, he hates, he has joy, he has sorrow, he sings, he laughs, he is jealous, he is kind, he has pity, he has anger.[20] Sometimes we think of God as being so transcendent, so totally-other, that we forget how intensely personal he is. God's personality is not anthropomorphic. God really has these personal qualities and he consistently expresses them to us. His intense emotional and passionate qualities are not signs of impetuousness and capriciousness. They are all divine qualities and as such are perfect in God. Because we are made in his image, we get a glimpse of what God is like personally. All our personal qualities derive from him, except that his personal qualities are more dynamic, without sin, and perfectly suited to his divinity. In being such an intensely personal being, God desires that we relate to him very personally. God is not interested in a superficial, mechanical, "do this — don't do that" kind of relationship. He wants us to love him as intensely as he loves us. Not surprisingly, God is personally offended when men sin. God is not to be pictured as an unemotional courtroom judge who has no vested interest or has no personal feelings for or against the criminal brought before him. No, God is a Father who has lost his wayward sons and he is intensely jealous for their return. He has a personal stake in their salvation.[21]

As regards justification, Paul makes the personal nature of God and man a primary part of his teaching. We see this, for example, in Paul's stress on those who "boast" of their works before God, and who, in turn, think that God owes them something for their self-styled efforts. In the heart of his teaching, Paul repeatedly mentions "boasting" in reference to the Jew's attempt to assent to God, e.g., Romans 2:17, "you rely on the law and *boast*"; Romans 2:23, "You *boast* about the law"; Romans 3:27, "Where then is *boasting*? It is excluded"; and Romans 4:2, "If, in fact, Abraham was justified by works, he had something to *boast* about." By the

---

[20] The Scripture is replete with references to God's personal nature. The following are just a few of the many descriptions: sorrow and pain (Genesis 6:6; Matthew 26:38); love (Isaiah 43:4; John 3:35); hate (Psalm 5:5; 11:5; Romans 9:13); singing for joy (Zephaniah 3:17; Matthew 26:30); laughter (Psalm 2:4); jealousy (Deuteronomy 32:21; James 4:5); compassion (Psalm 86:15; Matthew 15:32); sadness and consternation (Ezekiel 18:23,32; John 11:35); anger (Exodus 32:10; Revelation 6:16); grief and vexation (Psalm 78:40; Ephesians 4:30); pity (Psalm 103:13; James 5:11); pleasure (1 Chronicles 29:17; Luke 12:32).

[21] The aspect of God's personal nature as "Father" as regards justification will be covered in chapter 6.

same token, Paul also warns the Gentiles about boasting. In reference to God's rejection of the Jews whom he compares to branches that had been cut off, Paul tells the Gentile believers in Romans 11:18-22, "do not *boast* over those branches...they were broken off because of unbelief, and you stand by faith. Do not be arrogant but be afraid...Otherwise you also will be cut off." Similarly, Paul mentions grace in opposition to "boasting" in Ephesians 2:8-9: "For it is by grace you have been saved, through faith — and this is not of yourselves, it is the gift of God — not of works so that no one can *boast*." Again, to the Corinthian Gentiles in 1 Corinthians 4:7 Paul says, "What do you have that you did not receive? And if you did receive it, why do you *boast* as though you did not."[22] "Boasting" about one's adherence to the law conveys a proud attitude of the mind and heart, one in which the individual fails to recognize his own faults, judges the faults of others, and, most of all, attempts to place God in a position of being obligated to give payment for the work performed. Such a self-righteous individual thinks that he has performed a sufficient quantity or quality of work to *require* God to save him. But no creature can put God in a position of being obligated to save him, least of all those who out of hubris demand his blessing. Men who do not acknowledge this are a personal affront to God. God is personally offended by their arrogance and he will not save them.[23]

Faith: The Beginning of Salvation

In contrast to works performed in an attempt to obligate God, Paul speaks of justification by God's grace through our faith. In Romans 3:22-24, Paul says:

---

22 1 Corinthians 4:7 is the verse that convinced the great Augustine of the primacy of God's grace (*De praedestinatione sanctorum*, PL 44, 3, 7). The Old Testament reveals similar truth, e.g., Ecclesiasticus 1:30: "Do not exalt yourself, or you may fall and bring dishonor upon yourself. The Lord will reveal your secrets and overthrow you before the whole congregation, because you did not come in the fear of the Lord, and your heart was full of deceit." Eccles. 7:5: "Do not assert your righteousness before the Lord."

23 As Michael Schmaus has concluded: "First of all, let it be emphasized that the council [Trent] has not, and could not, reject the element of trust or confidence in faith...What has been rejected is a presumptuous self-confidence before God" (*Dogma: Justification and the Last Things*, p. 33). See also P. Gregory Stevens, *The Life of Grace*.

> This righteousness from God comes through faith in Jesus Christ to all who believe. There is no difference because all have sinned and come short of the glory of God, and are justified freely by his grace through the redemption that came by Jesus Christ.

Paul often opposes *faith* to *works of law* in reference to being justified; yet we have also seen earlier from Romans 2:13 that Paul requires obedience to the law for justification. Hence we must understand what Paul intends by the word "faith," what he intends by the words "works of law," and why, in spite of his doctrine in Romans 2:13, he maintains the opposition between faith and works in Romans 3-4. Simply put, the terms "faith" and "works" become extremely important to Paul because they best represent how one's relationship with God is *grounded* or *established*.[24] As noted above, God is a personal being who wants man to relate to him on a personal level. He is not an impersonal, unemotional, unconcerned third party. Hence, because faith is intrinsically personal, it is the ideal word to describe one who recognizes God's identity; one who takes a sincere interest in God's purposes and plans; one who trusts that God is good and looking out for everyone's best interests; one who recognizes that because God is the Creator and perfect he does not owe anything to anyone; that everything comes from his personal

[24] The Council of Trent stated it this way: "But when the apostle says that man is justified 'by faith' and 'freely,' these words must be understood in that sense in which the uninterrupted consent of the Catholic Church has always held and expressed, namely, that we are therefore said to be justified by faith, because *'faith is the beginning of human salvation,' the foundation and root* of all justification, 'without which it is impossible to please God...' (Council of Trent, Session 6, Chapter 8, DS 801, emphasis mine). By referring to the "beginning," "foundation," and "root" the Council is teaching that faith must be the initiator of our relationship with God. The Council also recognizes the part God's personal nature plays in this relationship by the reference "to please God" taken from Hebrews 11:6. The Catholic Catechism portrays faith from another perspective: "...a gift of God, a supernatural virtue infused by him. 'Before this faith can be exercised, man must have the grace of God to move and assist him...Believing is possible only by grace and the interior helps of the Holy Spirit. But it is no less true that believing is an authentically human act...In faith, the human intellect and will cooperate with divine grace: 'Believing is an act of the intellect assenting to the divine truth by command of the will moved by God through grace" (CC, Sections 153-155). Here we see the Catechism teaching that faith is synergistic relationship between the divine and the human will. This aspect of justification will be covered thoroughly in chapter 7.

love and benevolence. Conversely, "works" or "works of law" are *contractual* terms connoting an impersonal employer/employee kind of relationship: someone who is under contract to do a job but has no interest in a personal relationship with his employer. He works for the sole purpose of remuneration but has no genuine regard for the goals and aspirations of his payer. He boasts of his accomplishments and expects to be paid handsomely for his work. Man can never approach God in this way. If he does, God will simply show him that, compared to God's perfection, all his work amounts to naught and subsequently he is owed nothing, except condemnation. As Isaiah 40:17 says, "Before him all the nations are as nothing; they are regarded by him as worthless and less than nothing."

To say it another way, with respect to his principle of obligation, Paul uses faith to represent the primary element of human volition that recognizes and submits to knowing and relating to God through his grace. Faith is an act performed within the mind and heart of one who willingly assents to understand truly the nature of God and what he requires of man. Again, faith is the product of a thinking personality who comes to recognize God's benevolent nature, man's weakness, and what must be done to rectify the problem of sin.[25] Because God is a personal being who must be approached personally, one who attempts to obligate God to pay him (as an employee does to an employer) but does not acknowledge who God really is and what he really desires, can neither please God nor establish a legitimate relationship with him. God's personal nature demands that man must first recognize who God really is and what God really desires before he can ever approach God. As God told Moses in Exodus 3:5,14: "Do not come any closer...Take off your sandals, for the place you are standing is holy ground...I am who I am." Consequently, we cannot come to God through legal obligation because if the efforts of man are thrust in the face of God without God first establishing the proper relationship with that person — a relationship of grace and benevolence given as a gift — the uncompromising principles of legal obligation will simply show, without grace, all the instances in which we have failed to measure up to God's perfect righteousness,

---

[25] As Catholic theologian Michael Schmaus says, "Faith points out the end in view" and "faith always furnishes the foundation for an enduring dialogue with God, just as the root always remains the source for the growth and life of the tree" (*Dogma: Justification and the Last Things*, pp. 19, 34).

and thus we will be condemned.[26] Hence, since the relationship between God and man requires man's acknowledgment and appreciation of its personal quality, the first condition of justification is faith, a faith which must recognize God's grace in order to be saved. Thus, we can paraphrase a passage like Ephesians 2:8 in this way: "For it is by grace you have been saved, grace which is recognized and acknowledged by your faith; you are not saved by your own self-righteous works which attempt to obligate God; rather, salvation is a gift of God's grace so that no one will be able to boast before God that he attained salvation through his own efforts."

What Does Paul Mean By "Works of the Law"?

One of the primary questions that surfaces in discussions concerning the relationship among the concepts of faith, works, grace, and justification, is the meaning of the phrase "works of the law." Although we have stipulated that Scripture is very careful to avoid saying that faith is alone in justification, we have also seen that Paul often places faith in opposition to works of the law. To add more balance to these two competing principles, it is imperative that we understand the meaning that Paul assigns to the works of the law, as well as the perspective from which he desires that we view them. Does Paul mean that works of the law refer to any kind of law (e.g., moral, civil, ceremonial), or does he intend only to refer to a specific law (e.g., the ceremonial law, which consisted of circumcision, dietary laws, feast days, etc)? Why is this important? Because, on the one hand, if works of the law are confined to the ceremonial law, then the explanation one gives as to why Paul opposes faith to works will claim that Paul is only interested in condemning the observance of obsolete religious practices. Suppose, for example, that in interpreting Paul in Romans 3:28, "For we maintain that a man is justified by faith apart from observing the law," one confines the "law" to a specific kind of law. Such an interpretation of the passage will conclude that Paul is saying only that a person cannot be justified by

[26] In this sense, John Calvin was quite correct in stating: "See how all our works are under the curse of law if they are measured by the standard of law!" (*Institutes* 3:19:5). For further discussion of Calvin's view of God's judgment of works, along with the contradictions in his view, see chapter 9.

observing the ceremonial law of Israel, and that he is not suggesting a person is not required to do moral works (e.g., obey the Ten Commandments) in order to be justified. Based on certain Scriptures, this certainly seems like an appropriate explanation. If, as we have already suggested, faith is connected with love and obedience in justification, then it would seem appropriate not to include the moral law within Paul's condemnation of the law, since these virtues are derived from the moral law.

On the other hand, if Paul means that the phrase "works of the law" applies to any kind of law, then the interpretation of Romans 3:28 must conclude that Paul is placing faith not only in opposition to the obsolete ceremonial law, but also in opposition to the moral law of the Decalogue. In other words, Paul is divorcing faith from the whole concept of law. Based on certain Scriptures, this also seems like an appropriate explanation. Obviously, depending on whether "works of the law" refers only to the ceremonial law, or both the ceremonial and moral law, we can arrive at two diametrically opposed explanations to the problem. Unfortunately, only one can be right, and only in choosing the right one will we be able to understand Paul and the real nature of justification before God.[27]

---

[27] The debate over this issue began as far back as Jerome and Augustine. Jerome held that the "works of law" which will not justify refers only to the ceremonial law, whereas Augustine held that "works of law" included both the ceremonial and the moral law. Today certain Catholic apologists are tempted to use Jerome's argumentation because of its apparent simplicity. Opposing Scriptures, however, make this position difficult to prove. The Protestant apologetic maintains, and rightly so, that Paul's condemnation of the law is all-inclusive with regard to justification (e.g., Geisler and Mackenzie, *Roman Catholics and Evangelicals*, pp. 234-235; James White, *The Roman Catholic Controversy*, p. 149). To settle this issue, Catholic apologists need to remember that the Council of Trent in its decree on justification posited no distinction between the ceremonial and moral law; rather, it made a firm declaration that the works Paul understood as those that do not justify refer to *all* and *any* works, not merely certain kinds of works. In its very first canon on Justification, the Council declared: "If anyone shall say that man can be justified before God by his own works which are done either by his *own natural powers*, or through the *teaching of the Law*, and without divine grace through Christ Jesus: let him be anathema" (Session 6, Canon 1; emphasis mine). This approach is binding on all Catholic apologists. See **Appendix 3** for further details on this question.

The Ceremonial Law

Since *works of law* is a phrase that Paul uses frequently in reference to the Jews, it would be logical to assume that at least one of its meanings concerns the Jewish religious laws specified in the Old Testament. Paul suggests this most clearly in Galatians 2:14-16 when, after rebuking Peter for not eating with Gentiles, he writes to the Jews, "How is it, then, that you force Gentiles to follow Jewish customs? We who are Jews by birth and not 'Gentile sinners' know that a man is not justified by observing the law, but by faith in Jesus Christ." Here Paul equates "Jewish customs" (e.g., kosher laws, Sabbath observance, priestly practices, etc.) with the things one does by "observing the law."[28] One of the most prominent ceremonial laws to which the Jews tenaciously adhered was the rite of circumcision. Paul mentions circumcision frequently in the Galatian epistle.[29] For example, in Galatians 5:3 Paul says, "Again I declare to every man who lets himself be circumcised that he is obligated to obey the whole law. You who are trying to be justified by law have been alienated from Christ; you have fallen away from grace." Here we see that Paul considers circumcision as part of the law, the same law we have noted earlier that was set in opposition to the grace of God. Paul also makes this clear in Romans 4:9-17 as he speaks of *circumcision* in verses 9-12 and refers to it as *law* in verses 13-17: "And he [Abraham] received the sign of circumcision...but it was not through the *law* that Abraham and his offspring received the promise."

---

28 The translation "observing the law" is the Greek ἔργων νόμου, (literally: "works of law"). The translation "Jewish customs" is from the word ἰουδαΐζειν, which is a Greek infinitive literally meaning "to Judaize." Paul also focuses on the ceremonial law in Galatians 4:10 when he says, "Do you wish to be enslaved by them all over again? You are observing special days and months and seasons and years!" Paul also attends to the ceremonial law in Colossians 2:16: "Therefore do not let anyone judge you by what you eat or drink, or with regard to a religious festival, a New Moon celebration or a Sabbath day."

29 Galatians 2:3-12; 5:2-11; 6:12-15.

The Moral Law

Although circumcision and other ceremonial observances are some of the more prominent aspects of the Mosaic law, Paul also uses *works of law* or *law* in reference to the moral laws of God, exemplified in the Ten Commandments.[30] We see this, for example, in Paul's usage of *law* in Romans 2:17: "Now you, if you call yourself a Jew; if you rely on the law." Paul specifies that he is referring to the *moral* laws as he focuses on the commandments of the Decalogue: "You who preach against stealing, do you steal? You say that people should not commit adultery. Do you commit adultery?" Paul also focuses on the moral law in distinction to the ceremonial law when he says in Romans 2:25: "For indeed circumcision profits you if you obey the [moral] law, but if you transgress the [moral] law your circumcision has become an uncircumcision." According to the context, the Jews would transgress the law by committing adultery, idolatry, and stealing. If they commit sins against the moral law, they make their circumcision (the ceremonial law) as if it were uncircumcision, i.e., it is just as if they had never been circumcised in God's eyes; and whatever the spiritual benefit of circumcision, it would not apply to them.

In Romans 7:6-8, Paul again refers specifically to the *moral law* when he affirms that one cannot be saved by law.[31] He writes, "...we have been released from the law...what shall we say, then? Is the law sin? Certainly not! Indeed I would not have known what sin was except through the law. For I would not have known what coveting really was if the law had not said, 'do not covet.'" The law that stipulated "do not covet" is taken from the Ninth and Tenth Commandments, which are part of the moral law, not of the cer-

---

[30] Catholic Catechism, Sections 1950-1960; 2052-2074. "Works of law," from the Greek ἔργων νόμου, appears seven times in the New Testament (cf., Romans 3:19- 20, 21, 28, 32; Galatians 2:16, 19, 21, but with a textual variant in Rom. 9:32 with Papyrus 46 supporting only ἔργων). "Works of law" is interchangeable with the word "law," as noted in Paul's free exchange of these terms in Rom. 3:19-20 and Gal. 2:16-21.

[31] Ibid., Sections 708, 2542.

emonial law. By indicating that he has been "released" from the law against coveting, Paul shows that the moral law, as representative of the system of law in itself, cannot save him, and is thereby antithetical to salvation by grace. Instead, Paul says that the law against coveting "actually brought death" (verses 10, 11, 13). In other words, the moral law showed Paul how sinful he was and convicted him of being a lawbreaker.

Paul also refers to the moral law as representative of law in Romans 3:19-20:

> But whatever things the law says it says to those under the law in order that every mouth may be shut and all the world may come under the judgment of God. Because by works of the law no flesh will be justified before him, for through the law is the full knowledge of sin.

Since the statement "through the law we become conscious of sin" is said in the context of judging "all the world," that is, both Jews and Gentiles, this means that the law to which it refers must encompass more than the ceremonial law of the Jews. Thus, we are certain Paul is including the Gentiles under the condemnation of the law since the Gentiles were not identified with or bound by the regulations of the ceremonial law. Paul's "charge" in Romans 3:9 that "Jews and Gentiles alike are all under sin" means that the law which convicts the Gentile of sin must be a law which is common to both Jew and Gentile, i.e., the moral law.

We see the same truth concerning the law in Galatians 3:19-22. Paul writes:

> What, then, was the purpose of the law? It was added because of transgressions...the Scripture declares that the whole world is a prisoner of sin..."

In language almost identical to Romans 3:19-20, we see again that it is the "whole world" which is convicted and condemned by the law. Gentiles as well as Jews comprise the whole world and thus, since the Gentiles were not under the requirements of the ceremonial law, the law to which Paul refers must be the entire law. Galatians 3:17 reinforces this understanding: "The law, introduced 430 years later, does not set aside the covenant previously established..." The "430 year" period to which Paul refers is the time between the entrance of the patriarch Jacob into Egypt, who was then the custodian of the covenant made with Abraham and Isaac, and the time when God spoke the Decalogue and other commandments to Moses, as recorded in Exodus 20-23. According to Exodus 12:40 and 19:1, the recording of the Decalogue was exactly 430 years, to the very day, from the time that Jacob entered Egypt.[32] Two major transgressions occurred among the Jews just prior to the giving of the law at Mt. Sinai, (viz., the murmuring against Moses for the lack of food (Exodus 16) and the murmuring for lack of water (Exodus 17)). In this specific way, the law was "added because of transgressions."

From a more global perspective, in Romans 5:12-14 Paul speaks of the necessity to add the law because of the transgressions of mankind. He writes:

> Therefore, just as sin entered the world through one man, and death through sin, and in this way death came to all men, because all sinned — for before the law was given, sin was in the world. But sin is not taken into account when there is no law. Nevertheless, death reigned from the time of Adam to the time of Moses, even over those who did not sin by breaking a command, as did Adam...

[32] The Israelites left Sinai in the 2nd year of the exodus (or the 431st year from Jacob's entrance into Egypt), according to Num. 10:11. The second law at the plains of Moab would then have been given in the 470th year, according to Deut. 1:3; 2:14. The Penteteuch refers to the "Ten Commandments" given at Sinai as "the covenant" (Ex. 19:5; Deut. 4:13, 23; 5:3; 9:7). The "angels" and the "mediator" of Galatians 3:19 refer to the issuance of the initial Decalogue. Exodus 23:20-23 mentions an angel sent to guard and lead the Israelites. Acts 7:38,53 specify that an angel "spoke to him [Moses] on Mount Sinai" and that the "law was put into effect by angels," respectively, while Hebrews 2:2 specifies "the message spoken by angels was binding." The "mediator," referring to Moses himself, is alluded to in Exodus 20:19; 24:2,12; Acts 7:20-38.

Here Paul teaches that because of the sin of Adam, death was given to all men.[33] Through the curse of death, men became sinners, both passively by inheriting original sin and actively by sinning of their own volition. More importantly, Paul says in Romans 7:8, "for apart from the law sin is dead," and again in Romans 5:13, "But sin is not taken into account when there is no law." From these statements we understand that even though men before the time of Moses sinned apart from a written law, eventually a codified law would be formally established to convict them of sin, for without a law there can be no sin against the law. Thus we can understand why Paul insists in Romans 3:20 that "through the law is the full knowledge of sin," and in Galatians 3:19 that the law was "added because of transgressions." One of the chief functions of law is to convict men of sin.[34]

---

33 In Romans 5:12, the clause "because all sinned" is from the Greek ἐφ' ᾧ πάντες ἥμαρτον which begins with the contracted form of ἐπί which can be translated as "at," "on," "upon," "for," "in the power of," whereas ᾧ is a relative pronoun normally translated as "who" or "which." Paul uses ἐφ' ᾧ only one other place, Philippians 3:12, and it is understood in the context as "for which" or "upon which." Thus, a more precise translation of Romans 5:12 could be "upon which all have sinned" or "upon whom all have sinned." The former would denote that the death transferred to men is the basis "upon which" they have sinned, whereas the latter would refer to the sin inherited from Adam. For both, the implication is that the spiritual and physical death passed on to men is the cause for their sinful condition (e.g., original sin), and the cause for their inclination to sin. The latter case is evident in Romans 3:23 in which we understand the aorist tense of ἥμαρτον in the clause "for all have sinned" (the same tense of ἥμαρτον used in Romans 5:12) as the sinning action of man rather than his sinful condition. Supporting the former case is 1 Corinthians 15:56 where Paul says, "the sting of death is sin," i.e., the effect or result of death is sin. Thus, as long as death is in the world, men will sin. In heaven, men will be divinized and death will no longer exist, thus, men will be free from sin's effects and the inclination to sin.

34 Catholic Catechism, Section 708: "But the Law's powerlessness to save man deprived of the divine 'likeness,' along with the growing awareness of sin that it imparts (f. 74, Cf. Rom. 3:20), enkindles a desire for the Holy Spirit." "According to St. Paul, its special function is to denounce and disclose sin, which constitutes the 'law of concupiscence' in the human heart" (CC, Section 1963). Extending the principle that law is "added because of transgressions," one could also make a case that many of the civil and ceremonial laws of Israel were multiplied due to their sin. Genesis 15-17 implies that the original law of circumcision was given to Abraham due to his lapse of faith in taking Hagar as a wife to produce a son — a view held by many Church Fathers and Thomas Aquinas. Similarly, numerous regulations and ceremonies of the Levitical

The natural opposition between grace and law is made no clearer than in Paul's statement in Galatians 3:10-13:

> For as many are of the works of the law they are under a curse, for it has been written: 'Accursed is everyone who does not continue to do all the things written in the book of the law.' That no one is justified before God by the law is clear, because the just man will live by faith, and the law is not of faith but the one doing them will live by them. Christ has redeemed us from the curse of the law having become a curse for us...

Again, Paul's reference to "law" in this passage refers to the *whole* Mosaic law. This is so because Paul is quoting from Deuteronomy 27:26 and Leviticus 18:5 whose contexts include *all* the ethical and religious laws of Israel. In the former passage, the curses stipulated for disobedience are all based on infractions of the Ten Commandments regarding idol worship, sexual sin, murder, stealing, lying, and even general warnings concerning withholding justice from the underprivileged of society. The latter passage is exclusively concerned with sexual immorality. Hence, in referencing the moral components of the Mosaic law, Paul is conclusively repudiating any attempt by man to justify himself before God by the law, in whatever form that law comes. Instead, Paul insists in Galatians 3:11 that "the just man will live by faith." In effect, by referring to the books of Deuteronomy and Leviticus, Paul shows that Israel's own *law*, i.e., the Old Testament Mosaic law, was the very document explicitly stating that the law could not justify them. Paul also stated this truth in Romans 10:5-8: "Moses writes of the righteousness of the law, 'The man doing it will live by it.'...but what does it [the law] say? 'The word is near you, in your mouth and in your heart.' This is the word of faith

---

[34 cont.] priesthood, purification rites, sabbath regulations, food laws, etc., were added immediately after the Israelites worshiped the golden calf (cf., Exodus 32ff; Leviticus 1-27). Many civil regulations regarding sex, marriage and divorce, property, social order, etc., were frequently added to counteract the sinful abuse and neglect of these aspects of life among the Israelites. For a full treatment of this dimension of the law, consult "Kinship By Covenant: A Biblical Theological Study of Covenant Types and Texts in the Old and New Testaments" by Dr. Scott Hahn (doctoral dissertation, Marquette University, 1995).

which we proclaim." Here Paul is again quoting from Leviticus 18:5 (and Deuteronomy 30:12f.) showing plainly that the law upon which the Jews prided themselves for justification is the very law that "said" one must live by faith; not attempt to obligate God by law.[35] Paul makes it clear that the essential message of Deuteronomy is that God is *near* to the person who lives by faith, but *far* from the one who bases his relationship with God on law.

Since Scripture condemns both the ceremonial and moral law as a means of justification before God, we must address the attempts of certain theologians to limit the phrase "works of law" to the Jewish ceremonial law.[36] From a reading of Romans 2-4 and Galatians 2-3, it is apparent that while Paul elevates the discussion concerning justification to an antithesis between law and grace, he intermittently focuses his attention on circumcision as that part of the law with which he is most concerned. This is because the Jews had mistakenly made circumcision the *sine qua non* of their faith, and thus Paul used circumcision as the best example of the Jew's attitude toward the entire law. In their zeal, the Jews were compelling new converts to the Christian faith to observe certain ceremonial laws of Israel in order to be saved, most notably, circumcision. Normally the New Testament portrays Paul as a conciliatory man, but on this topic he does not compromise. In Galatians 1:8 he does not mince words: "But even if we or an angel from heaven should preach a gospel other than the one we preached to you, let him be eternally condemned."

Paul often focuses on circumcision as the best example of the futility of the system of law in justifying one before God. For ex-

---

[35] Catholic Catechism, Sections 1961-1964.

[36] Representing current Protestant thought on this issue is James Dunn, in "The New Perspective on Paul" *Bulletin of the John Rylands Library* 65 (1983): 95-122; also in *Jesus, Paul and the Law: Studies in Mark and Galatians* (Louisville, KY: Westminster/John Knox, 1990); and James Dunn and Alan Suggate, *The Justice of God: A Fresh Look at the Old Doctrine of Justification by Faith* (Grand Rapids: Eerdmans Publishing, 1993); also E. P. Sanders, *Paul and Palestinian Judaism* (Philadelphia: Fortress Press, 1977); "The Covenant as a Soteriological Category and the Nature of Salvation in Palestinian and Hellenistic Judaism" in *Jews, Greeks, and Christians: Religious Cultures in Late Antiquity*, eds. Robert Hamerton-Kelly and Robin Scroggs (Leiden: E. J. Brill, 1976) pp. 11-44. For a thorough critique of these views by a qualified Protestant, see Mark A. Seifrid, *Justification By Faith* (Leiden: E. J. Brill, 1992), 42-65.

ample, in Galatians 5:3 he writes: "Every man who lets himself be circumcised...is obligated to obey the whole law." Here Paul makes his point by teaching that elevating one's favorite aspect of law in an effort to justify oneself before God inadvertently obligates one to obey the whole law. By implication, Paul reasons that since man cannot obey the whole law without a single fault, then law, in itself, cannot be used as a means of justification. Requiring circumcision would put one back into the system of law, obligating one to obey the rest of the law perfectly, and thus prohibit one from being justified by grace. Paul makes the same point in Romans 4:1-12. As we have outlined earlier, Paul first lays down the foundational rule in Romans 4:1-8 that by the principle of legal obligation works, any works, cannot justify an individual. Paul decides to illustrate his point by citing Abraham's circumcision in Romans 4:9-12. Using the premise established in 4:1-8, Paul first reasons with the Jews that the work of circumcision, in itself, could not justify Abraham because it would have put God in a position of obligation. Second, Paul reinforces his point by specifying that Abraham's circumcision was performed *after* he had already been justified by his faith, a justification that came by grace, not obligation. Thus, in all respects, Abraham's justification was not procured on the *basis* of law but by grace, as Paul concludes in 4:16: "Therefore, the promise comes by faith, so that it may be by grace..." We understand from this that while the law of circumcision was a law that Abraham had to obey (disobedience would require his condemnation), nevertheless it was not the basis of his justification. In so many words, Paul is telling the Jews that Abraham was justified when he was a *Gentile*, saved by grace, not when he became a Jew through law by circumcision! In this way, Abraham can rightly be called the "father of the uncircumcised" and that through him "the nations [Gentiles] would be blessed."

The general and all-inclusive antithesis Paul develops between law and grace is made even more relevant for the first century Jew. By this time, the advent of the New Testament Church had abolished for the Christian not only circumcision but the whole ceremonial law of Israel.[37] Hence not only was it wrong to claim that law could justify a man, it was absolutely absurd to make such a

[37] Council of Florence (1438-1445) contains the most comprehensive treatise on the abolition of the Jewish ceremonial law. See DS 712-714; Catholic Catechism, Sections 582, 1540, 2125.

claim by basing it on an obsolete religious law. Paul argues that even when circumcision was required by law it was not a basis for justification; how much less, then, was it a basis for justification once circumcision itself had been abolished. To force someone to submit to circumcision or claim that it was required for justification not only returned to a system of obligation which was devoid of grace, it also misconstrued the Old Testament's conception and chronological ordering of justification.

The Universal Law

In other passages, Paul uses the law to refer not to a *written* code of ethics and religious practices but to an *unwritten* law, a law written, as it were, on the heart of man. He notes this in his description of the Gentiles in Romans 2:14-15:

> For whenever the Gentiles, who do not have the law, do by nature the things of the law, these not having a law are a law unto themselves, who show the work of the law written in their hearts, their consciences witnessing with their thoughts, accusing or excusing them.

Paul also speaks of this unwritten law indirectly in Romans 1:19-20: "...because what is known of God is plain to them for God has made it plain. For the invisible things of him from the creation of the world are clearly seen, both his everlasting power and his divinity, so that they are without excuse."[38] Clearly, then, the law, in whatever form it comes, invariably convicts men of sin.

[38] "If anyone shall have said that the one true God, our Creator and our Lord, cannot be known with certitude by those things which have been made, by the natural light of human reason, let him be anathema" (Vatican Council I, DS 3026). "The Sacred synod declares that 'God, the first principle and last end of all things can be known with certainty from the created world, by the natural light of human reason (cf., Rom. 1:20)'" (Vatican Council II, *Dei Verbum* 6). "God, who creates and conserves all things by his Word (cf. John 1:3), provides men with constant evidence of himself in created realities (cf. Rom. 1:19-20)" (*Dei Verbum 3*). See also Catholic Catechism on *Moral Conscience* in Sections 1776-1794; and *Natural Moral Law*, Sections 1949- 1960). This teaching is in opposition to those of various Protestant persuasions who hold that no one of mature intelligence and reason can be saved without first hearing the gospel in oral or written form.

Although God established the system of grace to rescue us from the rigorous judgment of the law, he did not abrogate the law.[39] The law issues forth from God's attributes of righteousness and justice. These attributes do not disappear when God institutes the system of grace and mercy. In fact, grace and mercy are also attributes of God. In effect, to the degree that we do not accept God's grace and mercy, God's law must then evaluate and judge us.

Paul indicates that those who receive the grace of God are free from the condemnation of the law. In Romans 5:1 he states: "Therefore, since we have been justified through faith, we have peace[40] with God through our Lord Jesus Christ, through whom we have gained access by faith into this grace in which we now stand." Here Paul speaks of "gaining access...into grace," which agrees with the concept we mentioned earlier of entering into the *system of grace.* The *peace* of God is available because of the grace he has shed upon us. We can now live in the system of grace, rather than the system of law. In Romans 8:1-2, Paul states it another way: "Therefore, there is now no condemnation for those who are in Christ Jesus, because through Christ Jesus the law of the Spirit of life set me free from the law of sin and death." Paul speaks of one system replacing another. Those who are no longer under condemnation are in the system of grace, or, as Paul puts it, *"the law of the Spirit of life."*

For those who have not repented of their sins, the opposite is true. They are still under the full curse of sin and death, and thus

---

39 "The Law has not been abolished, but rather man is invited to rediscover it in the person of his Master who is its perfect fulfillment" (CC, Section 2053).

40 The translation "we have peace" (KJV, NIV, NASB, RSV, Moffatt, et al) takes the verb ἔχομεν as a present indicative because of the presence of the Greek omicron. Each of these translations has a marginal note that other Greek manuscripts contain ἔχωμεν which is a present subjunctive since the omega is used in place of the omicron, indicating that the verb could just as likely be translated as "let us have peace." The NEB has chosen the later manuscripts as authoritative and rendered the phrase, "let us continue to have peace," and the Douay-Rheims has "let us have peace." The NEB and Douay-Rheims, siding with ἔχωμεν, have more uncial and early patristic evidence, including the originals of Codices Sinaiticus (א), Vaticanus (B), Alexandrinus (A) and Ephraemi Rescriptus (C), while ἔχομεν has slightly more minuscule evidence, but only corrected versions of Sinaiticus and Vaticanus. Although the ramifications of this variation are negligible, we will address this question more thoroughly in chapter 5.

they are *presently* under the condemnation of the law. Jesus states this most succinctly in the gospel of John 3:18-19: "Whoever believes in him is not condemned, but whoever does not believe stands condemned already because he has not believed in the name of God's one and only Son." Here we find that the condemnation of the law persists for those who have not accepted God's grace in Christ.[41] At the final judgment, they will be arraigned before the judgment throne of God and convicted of sin by the uncompromising stipulations of the law. Without God's grace, the law will show no mercy and God's justice will require that they be eternally condemned. To the degree that they have sinned against the law, they will be punished accordingly.[42]

In the final analysis, what we understand from Paul is that law, *as a system in itself*, cannot justify the sinner before God.[43] If one

---

41 Catholic Catechism, Section 679: "By rejecting grace in this life, one already judges oneself, receives according to one's works, and can even condemn oneself for all eternity by rejecting the Spirit of love." Another important aspect of this principle is the distinction between *actual grace* and *sanctifying grace* in Catholic theology. *Actual grace* is the grace God distributes as he wishes, either prior to or after conversion, to each individual. This grace prompts man to seek for God and to do good works (Council of Trent, Session 6, Canon 7). Prior to his conversion and baptism, however, man is still under the condemnation of the law for his sins. It is not until he cooperates and responds to God's *actual grace* that the judgment of the law is removed (ibid., Canon 4). The correct response to *actual grace,* e.g., repentance and baptism, provides *sanctifying grace* which removes him from the system of law and makes him a child of God. Through the prompting of *actual grace,* in cooperation with the intellect and will of man, man can possess a rudimentary faith, hope and love of God. At baptism, these virtues are then infused into the soul by *sanctifying grace*, and it is this transformation of the soul that justifies, or makes righteous, the individual before God. If *sanctifying grace* is lost through the commission of mortal sin, God, at his discretion, uses *actual grace* to prompt the sinner to repentance (See the Catholic Catechism, Sections 1996-2005; Ludwig Ott, *Fundamentals of Catholic Dogma*, pp. 225-267). The Council of Trent, Session 6, Chapter 5, states: "...freely assenting to and cooperating with the same grace...nor on the other hand can he of his own free will without the grace of God move himself to justice before Him." These aspects of grace will be explained more in chapters 4, 5, and 7.

42 This topic will be covered in chapter 8, "The Final Justification."

43 Council of Orange (529), Canons 16, 21. Catholic theologian Joseph A. Fitzmeyer, S.J., rightly points out: "For centuries commentators have tried from time to time to establish a distinction between Paul's use of *ho nomos* (Mosaic law) and *nomos* (law in general, or even "natural law"). But such a distinction is without sound philological support (pace M. Zerwick, *GrBib*, 177; > Pauline Theology, 79:106)" in *The Jerome Biblical Commentary*, op. cit., p. 298.

attempts to use the system of law to make himself right with God, the law will actually show how far away he is from God by exposing all the times he has disobeyed the law. As we noted earlier, unless a person can keep the law perfectly, God is not obligated to pay him with eternal life for his work.

A simple analogy illustrates the futility of keeping the law in order to reach the perfection of God's standard. Suppose you set out to make a wooden box, but with one stipulation: it must be a perfect box, precisely equal on all sides. In accepting the challenge, you use the finest marking, measuring, and cutting tools available. You mark and measure all the sides, trying your best to make them equal. Then you use the finest saw to cut the sides for the box. After cutting, you carefully nail the pieces together. Finally, when you have finished, the person who gave you the project comes and measures the sides of the box. He finds that you did a decent job, but in calibrating the exact length of the sides he notices that side A is 1/32 of an inch shorter than side B, and side B is 1/64 of an inch longer than side C. Though they are close, he finds that each side is a little bit longer or shorter than an opposing side. The result: you did not make a perfect box as requested. In this analogy, the box is your life. The person who gave you the project is God. The measuring stick is the law. What you find in this analogy is that the very law that you thought would provide the means to achieve perfection is actually the very thing that shows you how imperfect you really are. Just as the measuring stick is exact and uncompromising in its standard, so is God's law. For the slightest deviation in length, the measuring stick will reveal a flawed box that must be discarded. Likewise, for the slightest sin, the law will reveal an imperfect being that God cannot accept into heaven. This is why the law had to be done away with. However, rather than discard us, God set aside the law. As we will investigate shortly, he did this by the atonement and resurrection of Christ. In place of a system of law, God gave us the system of grace. As Paul says in Colossians 2:13-14: "He forgave us all our sins, having *canceled the written code*, with its regulations, that was against us and that stood opposed to us; he took it away, nailing it to the cross." And again in Ephesians 2:15: "...by *abolishing in his flesh the law* with its commandments and regulations..."

Works in the Realm of Grace

Although Paul takes great pains to make the sharpest distinction possible between faith, on the one hand, and works performed under legal obligation, on the other hand, he nonetheless creates the most intimate connection between faith and obedience to God's law. This connection is so strong that it is quite biblical to state that without obedience to the law it is impossible to be justified and enter the kingdom of heaven.[44] Some may find this conclusion contradictory since we seem to be saying that law is both condemnatory and salvific. Nevertheless, once one understands the basis for Paul's distinction between 'works done under the principle of obligation' as opposed to 'works performed under the auspices of God's grace,' the apparent contradiction disappears. We have stressed above the basis for the distinction Paul makes between grace and works by pointing out that man cannot obligate God to pay him for his work. Once man recognizes that any reward or blessing he receives is given strictly from the grace of God, rather than as payment which is owed, he will then understand the relationship between faith and works from the proper perspective.[45]

---

[44] Catholic Catechism, Section 1963: "According to St. Paul, its [the law's] special function is to denounce and disclose sin...However, the Law remains the first stage of the way to the kingdom. It prepares and disposes the chosen people and each Christian for conversion and faith in the Savior God. It provides a teaching which endures for ever, like the Word of God." The Council of Trent, Canon 20 states: "If anyone shall say that a man who is justified and ever so perfect is not bound to observe the commandments of God and the Church, but only to believe, as if indeed the Gospel were a mere absolute promise of eternal life, without the condition of observation of the commandments: let him be anathema."

[45] The Council of Trent made it clear that nothing good can be done by man without the grace of God: "Justification must be derived from the predisposing grace of God through Jesus Christ...whereby without any existing merits on their part...through his stimulating and assisting grace are disposed to convert...nor on the other hand can he of his own free will without the grace of God move himself to justice...we confess that we are anticipated by the grace of God" (Session 6, Chapter 5); "Now they are disposed to that justice when, aroused and assisted by divine grace, receiving faith by hearing..." (Chapter 6); "...continually infuses His virtue into the said justified, a virtue which always precedes their good works, and which accompanies and follows them, and without which they could in no wise be pleasing and meritorious before God..." (Chapter 16). Pope Pius V condemned the proposition of Michael De Bay in 1567 which

To help understand the principle of works performed under the auspices of grace, or what we may now introduce as "gracious merit," we can borrow from Paul's analogy of the employer/employee relationship he used in Romans 4:4. On the one hand, if the employee contracts with the employer to be paid X amount of dollars for X amount of work, this arrangement is formalized in a written agreement and is made binding by law, i.e., it is a legal contract. Whether or not the employer likes or trusts his employee, he is nonetheless legally obligated to pay him for the work performed. If, on the other hand, the employer asks the employee to do some personal work for him outside of the legal contract — work that is "not on company time" or is "off the clock," as it were — and promises to pay the employee an appropriate sum, such an arrangement is not under the legal contract of employment. Although we can say that the employee has "merited" payment by the mere fact that he has worked, nevertheless, for work that is "not on company time" the employer is not contractually obligated to pay the employee. Yet because of the employer's personal integrity, and perhaps because of a personal relationship he has cultivated with the employee, he will gladly pay what he feels the extra work is worth even though he is not legally required to do so. The employer could very easily renege on his promise to pay for work performed "off the clock," yet because he is honest and just he will not stoop to such underhanded behavior. God's relationship to man is very similar. For reasons already stated, God cannot be put in a position of being legally obligated to pay

[45 cont.] stated: "The good works performed by the children of adoption are meritorious, not because they are done through the Spirit of adoption dwelling in the hearts of the children of God, but only because they conform to the law and because through them the person shows obedience to the law" (JD 1913). In Scripture and in Catholic doctrine, the initial faith that brings one to justification is confirmed and stimulated by Baptism, the sacrament of faith (CC, Section 1253). The early Fathers also taught that faith is the beginning of salvation (See Justin Martyr, *First Apology*, PL 6, 10; Cyril of Jerusalem, *Catechetical Lectures*, PG 33, 1, 3; John Chrysostom, *On John*, PG 59, 46, 1; *On Matthew*, PG 58, 77, 1; Augustine, *Letter to Sixtus*, JR1452. Though baptism is a required work for justification, it is a work done under the auspices of God's grace, not the system of law (as is any obedience in faith), and thus, it is not a work that "boasts" or places God in a position of obligation. The grace of baptism is a free gift; and a grace that its recipient's serious and unrepentant disobedience can nullify.

man for his work. Outside of the legal framework, however, God can pay man what God thinks his work is worth because God is honest and just. Because of his personal integrity, and because he has cultivated a personal relationship with the individual, God can repay out of his graciousness because for God it is the proper thing to do. This principle of God's dealing with man is stated no better than in Hebrews 6:10, "God is not unjust; he will not forget your work and the love you have shown him as you have helped his people and continue to help them."[46]

Before we move on to the specifics of the above principle, there is another aspect of the law/grace relationship that we need to address. We have stressed that when Paul condemns law he is condemning it from the perspective of contractual obligation. Yet we must remember that several times in his discourse, Paul says that justification by faith is stipulated in none other than the law! Thus Paul is not condemning the law as a guide to and part of faith and righteousness, for then he would be condemning the very precepts that tell one he is justified by grace through faith. For example, Paul says in Romans 3:30-31, "Since there is only one God, who will justify the circumcision by faith and the uncircumcision through the same faith. Do we, then, nullify the law by this faith? Not at all! Rather, we uphold the law." Did the law speak of faith, not law, as the means of justification? We can answer this quite simply by noting that Paul spends most of his time supporting the notion of faith by quoting the Old Testament! In regard to Abraham's justification, we have already seen him quote from Genesis, the first of Moses' five books. We see him quoting again from the Old Testament as he refers to the prophet Habakkuk's statement "the just shall live by faith" in Romans 1:17. Paul says the same thing in Hebrews 10:38. In fact, Paul, who is here speaking to present day Christians, says in Hebrews 4:2,6 "For we [Christians] also have had the gospel preached to us, just as they [the Jews] did; but the message they heard was of no value to them, because they who heard did not combine it with faith...those who formerly had the gospel preached to them did not go in..." Here the sacred writer tells us that the Jews were given the same gospel of faith that is

[46] See **Appendix 4** for further discussion on Hebrews 6:10 and the issue of merit.

now present in the Christian era. Paul gives us a dramatic example from the book of Deuteronomy, the second law of Moses. In Romans 10:6-8, picking up the passage at Deuteronomy 30:12, right after mentioning the clause "what I am commanding you today is not too difficult for you or beyond your reach" of Deuteronomy 30:11, Paul says:

> But the righteousness that is by faith says: "Do not say in your heart, 'Who will ascend into heaven?'" (that is, to bring Christ down) or "Who will descend into the deep?" (that is, to bring Christ up from the dead). But what does it say? "The word is near you; it is in your mouth and in your heart," that is, the word of faith we are proclaiming: That if you confess with your mouth, "Jesus is Lord" and believe in your heart that God raised him from the dead, you will be saved.

Since this is a direct quote from Deuteronomy 30:12-14, we understand that the identity of what is "not too difficult for you" of Deuteronomy 30:11 is precisely the righteousness of faith. In other words, no one has to travel great distances ("ascend into heaven") or overcome great obstacles ("who will cross the sea" in Deuteronomy 30:13) in order to know the truth and the means of righteousness. God has already given it to man, it is in his heart and in his mouth, and God is trying to draw it out from him. In Romans 10:9, it is drawn out when one confesses that Jesus is Lord and that God raised him from the dead. In the Old Testament, they also confessed with their mouth by believing in God as their Savior (e.g., Psalm 106:21; Isaiah 43:3,11) in anticipation of the death and resurrection of Christ. Thus, God expected his people to live out the way of faith, a way "not too difficult," In light of this, it is significant that Deuteronomy 30:14 finishes the statement "the word is very near you, it is in your mouth and in your heart" with the clause "*so you may obey it*," whereas Romans 10:8 finishes it with "*that is, the word of faith we are proclaiming*." Here Paul substitutes "faith" for "obedience" and it is apparent that he understands one as being intimately identified and in full compatibility with the other.

Hence, once we oblige ourselves to view these principles from the proper perspective, we must conclude that Paul does not understand the law as antithetical to justification. Faith is commanded by the law, but faith is not law. Likewise, love is commanded by the law, but love is not law. Faith in God is implicit in the Decalogue's command to love God for one cannot love God unless he believes in him. Thus, faith and love are derived from law but they supercede law. The law can never force one to love and have faith; it can only point one in the direction of these virtues. Hence, we maintain that Paul is condemning law only with respect to contractual obligation, that is, when man attempts to demand payment from God for his works. Outside of the realm of contractual obligation, however, the law, as expressed in virtue, fully cooperates with grace in justification.

Case in Point: Romans 2: 5-10

Eternal Life: The Reward of Good Works

Let us observe how Paul views the distinction between works performed under the principle of obligation as opposed to works performed under grace. He elaborates on this distinction in two ways: first, in the way he describes God's blessing for good works, and second, in the way he describes God's judgment for bad works. One of the first expressions of Paul's positive view of works in regard to salvation occurs in Romans 2:5-10:

> ...of the righteous judgment of God, who will give to each man according to his works. On the one hand, to those who persist in good work, seeking glory, honor and incorruption, [he will give] eternal life. To the others who are self-seeking and disobey the truth, who follow unrighteousness, [he will give] wrath and anger. Affliction and anguish on every soul of man who works evil, to the Jew first and also to the Greek. But [he will give] glory and honor and peace to everyone who works good, to the Jew first and also to the Greek.

Romans 2:5-10 shows that in Paul's view, God saves or condemns based on the works performed by the individual. We see this clearly in his remark, verse 7, that God will give "*eternal life*" to those who "*persist in good work*." This is quite a bold statement, tantamount to saying that one can obtain eternal life by his good works. Consequently, it must also be true that "*wrath and anger*" in the same passage refers to the opposite of eternal life, namely eternal damnation. Paul's couching of his view of good and bad works within the framework of eternal life and eternal damnation, assures us that he is speaking in a justification/ salvation context. This is the same soteriological context he uses in Romans 3-6 where he contrasts faith against works and concludes in Romans 6:23 with, "for the wages of sin is death but the gift of God is *eternal life* through Jesus Christ our Lord." Hence one may wonder after reading Romans 2:5-10 and then reading Romans 3-6:23 if there is a contradiction in Paul's thinking. Does God determine whether we receive eternal life based on our works as it seems in Romans 2, or is it by faith without works as it seems in Romans 3 through Romans 6?

How to regard Romans 2:5-10, with its explicit teaching that the individual receives eternal life as a reward for his work, has been one of the most difficult questions faced by Protestant theology. Since a *faith alone* theology would have inherent difficulty in incorporating works as a *criterion* for eternal life, a popular solution to this dilemma among many Protestant scholars is to claim that Romans 2:5-10 presents a mere *hypothetical* means of salvation.[47] By this they mean that in Romans 2 Paul presents a

---

[47] e.g., Charles Hodge, W.G.T. Shedd, R. Haldane. *The Interpreters Bible* states: "Paul, in these references to 'working good,' to 'being doers of the law,' and 'to doing by nature the things contained in the law,' is speaking largely hypothetically (as also in verses 26-27)" (*Romans*, Vol. IX (New York: Abingdon Press, 1954), 409). Claiming to speak for the classic Reformed position, Andrew Sandlin writes in reference to Romans 2:13: "Only by achieving the flawless standard of the law could they expect justification; and since none can adhere to that standard, they are driven to place faith in Christ whose impeccable conformity to the law is then credited to the sinner's account..." (Andrew Sandlin, "Deviations From Historic Solafideism in the Reformed Community," *The Chalcedon Report*, p. 23). Other evangelicals, however, have admitted the futility of relegating Romans 2:6-13 to the hypothetical, e.g., John Murray, Norman Shepherd, William Hendriksen, et al. In Murray's view, the New Testament is replete with similar passages that cannot be treated hypothetically (John Murray, The New International Commentary on the New Testament, *The Epistle to the Romans* (Grand Rapids: Eerdmans, 1959,1965), 62- 63). Ironically, Sandlin makes

possible scenario such that if man *could* do works to merit eternal life, then that way of salvation would be legitimate. But since man *cannot* do good works to merit eternal life, as Paul seems to say in Romans 3:28 ("For we reckon that a man is justified by faith without works of law"), they conclude that Paul is mentioning the works in Romans 2 merely to show us that we cannot obtain salvation by good works. In essence, Romans 2 is touted as a plausible means of salvation but a means that will inevitably fail for each person who tries it. What is hoped for by the Protestant logic is that once one sees how miserably the system of works fails, then the person will accept the fact that his works do not possess any merit, and subsequently be forced to throw himself on the mercies of God by *faith alone* without works. He will see that works done for the purposes of receiving salvation, as set forth in Romans 2, are just another way in which Paul teaches that the law "exposes sin" and thus will drive the seeker of salvation to Christ alone for his true redemption.

The Catholic Response

In answer to this we must first point out that Paul does not use the word "earn," or anything similar to that term, in Romans 2:5-10. We can dogmatically state that Paul does not hold that a man can "earn," in the strict sense of the word, the reward of eternal life. As we have learned earlier, Romans 4:4 makes it unquestionably clear that when one attempts to "earn" his salvation based on

[47 cont.] reference to this same source (Murray, pp. 71-72) for support of Sandlin's hypothetical view of Romans 2:13 (Sandlin, 23). But Murray says only, "It is quite unnecessary to find in this verse any doctrine of justification by works in conflict with the teaching of this epistle in later chapters." Often, Romans 2:4-10 is not even addressed by critics of Catholicism's view of merit. Such is the case with Geisler and MacKenzie in *Roman Catholics and Evangelicals*, pp. 221-248. In dealing with 1 Cor. 3:13-15 or 2 Cor. 5:10 which speak of recompense for work, Geisler and MacKenzie conveniently relegate these passages to the area of personal rewards in heaven, not as a condition for getting to heaven. This aspect of the discussion will be covered more thoroughly in chapter 8.

works he is in turn obligating God to "pay" him with eternal life. Because of man's condition, God cannot be obligated to pay any man for anything. Hence we must conclude that the works Paul requires in Romans 2:5-10 are not those performed with an eye to *obligate* God to pay the individual with eternal life. Rather, it is presumed that those who "persist in doing good" and who "seek glory, honor, and incorruption" are doing so under the auspices of God's grace and mercy.

That the works of Romans 2:5-10 are those which are performed under the auspices of God's grace is suggested just one verse prior in Romans 2:4 where Paul says: "Or do you despise the riches of his kindness and his forbearance and longsuffering, not realizing that the kindness of God leads you to repentance?" The divine qualities of "kindness," "forbearance," and "longsuffering" are virtues of God that flow from his grace. If God were not exhibiting his grace, the proper response would be to show no mercy to men and destroy them at the first sign of disobedience. Moreover, God is not obligated to "lead them to repentance," or tolerate their sin. It is God's grace that gives men the opportunity to and leads them to repent and do good works. As Peter says in 2 Peter 3:9: "The Lord...is longsuffering toward us not wishing any to perish but for all men to come to repentance."

Since Paul speaks of "repentance" in Romans 2:4, and follows this with God giving "eternal life" to the ones who have repented and "persist in doing good," but "wrath and anger" to the ones who have not repented, all the elements of the New Testament gospel are present in this passage. Paul confirms this himself in Romans 2:16 when he says in summary, "...as my gospel declares." In light of this, we must also understand that the good works of Romans 2:5-10, being done in the context of repentance from sin, are works which presuppose faith in God, as well as an acknowledgment of personal sin. One cannot repent to God and do good works (i.e., works that are done for the purpose of seeking immortality), without truly believing in God. Hence, the works of Romans 2:5-10, accompanied by faith and repentance, are ***not*** works done under the principle of debt or obligation that Paul repudiates in Romans 4:4, but works done under the auspices of God's grace which seek their recognition and reward from within that grace.[48]

We must further state that the remaining context of Romans 2 categorically denies the Protestant's proposed solution of classifying Romans 2:5-10 as a hypothetical means of salvation. Romans 2 is divided into two sections: verses 1-16 and verses 17-29. The two sections deal with the same subject material. In the first section, verse 1 opens with: "...for in what you judge of another, you condemn yourself, for you who judge do the same things." Similarly, in the second section, verse 21 opens with: "you therefore, who are teaching others, do you not teach yourself? You who say not to steal, do you steal?" The entire chapter is an indictment against the Jews for their hypocritical living. They boast of having God's written law, which the Gentiles do not have, yet they continually disobey that law by sinning and judging others. This takes an entire chapter for Paul to develop and in the midst of this he specifies the warning that God will judge the wicked and bless the good (Rom. 2:6-10).

In addition, when Paul uses a hypothetical argument elsewhere, he alerts us that he is indeed using such a format, and the example is short and to the point. We see a short hypothetical statement, for example, in Romans 3:5, "...what shall we say, that God is unjust because he inflicts us with wrath? I am speaking in a human form of argument." This is not the form of argumentation Paul uses in Romans 2.

---

48 Paul's treatment of works done under grace which are rewarded with eternal life serve as a refutation to the Protestant claim that, "the apostle Paul did not have such a high view of works, and neither did he wish to polish up works by saying they must be 'of grace' since God starts everything by this grace" (Robert Zins, *Theo~Logical,* (2nd quarter, 1996, p. 3). Similar to Zins, James White asserts: "Saving grace, by definition, excludes the entire concept of human works of merit. Grace cannot be merited, and cannot coexist with merit on the part of the one to whom it is given" (*The Roman Catholic Controversy*, p. 150). Contrary to such opinions, there cannot possibly be any "higher view of works" under the realm of grace than what Paul says in Romans 2:4-10. As long as Protestant apologists refuse to see a distinction between strict merit due from obligation and gracious merit provided by benevolence, there can be no resolution to this controversy.

We must also note that the principle in Romans 2 of being judged for bad works and blessed for good works within a context of eternal life and eternal damnation is not at all peculiar to the New Testament, especially in Paul's epistles. For example, in Romans 14:10-12 Paul says:

> And why do you judge your brother? Or, indeed, why do you despise your brother? For we shall all stand before the judgment seat of God. For it is written: 'As I live, says the Lord, every knee will bend and every tongue will confess to God. So then, each one of us will give an account concerning himself to God.

This passage is dealing with the same problem addressed in Romans 2 regarding judging and despising other people. Paul gives the same ominous warning against such behavior in both Romans 2:6-10 and Romans 14:10-12. Other passages which describe the same type of judgment after death are Matthew 16:27; John 5:28-29; 1 Corinthians 3:13-17; 2 Corinthians 5:10; Revelation 22:11-12. These passages speak about the judgment God will render to each individual based on his *good and bad works.* Ironically, *none* of these passages are considered "hypothetical" by Protestant interpreters. If these latter passages are not hypothetical, it is only fair to ask why they insist upon making Romans 2:5-10 hypothetical? Could it be that their theological presuppositions are constraining them to interpret it this way?[49] We

[49] One method in which Protestant theologians avoid a contradiction is to relegate 1 Cor. 3:13-17; 2 Cor. 5:10, and Rom. 14:10-12 to a future judgment for personal rewards only, (rather than a judgment which will determine whether one will be saved), e.g., John MacArthur, F.F. Bruce, Philip Hughes, Norman Geisler, Ralph MacKenzie, most Dispensationalists, and popular Evangelical thought. Conversely, some in the Reformed and Lutheran persuasion have seen the same verses as representative of a universal judgment for salvation, e.g., Alford, Barnes, Hendriksen, Lenski, et al. Calvin, C. Hodge, L. Berkhof, et al, refer to these judgments as issuing rewards to Christians but giving various degrees of punishment to the wicked. This issue will be covered in chapter 8.

will answer this question more completely in chapter 8: "The Final Justification."[50]

Many other considerations militate against viewing Romans 2:5-10 as a hypothetical text. One of the more obvious is the specific argument Paul is raising in Romans 2. As noted previously, the chapter is an indictment against the Jews for their hypocrisy. They who claim to have the written law do not live by that law. Paul contrasts the Jews that disobey the law with the Gentiles who obey the law even though they do not have the same *written code* of law as do the Jews. Romans 2:26-27 makes this clear:

> If the uncircumcised [Gentiles] keep the requirements of the law, will not his uncircumcision be reckoned as circumcision? Those who are by nature uncircumcised but keep the law will judge you who, even though you have the written law and circumcision, transgress the law.

Since Paul is presenting an argument that condemns Jewish hypocrisy, how can his argument have any weight if there are no Gentiles who fit into the category he is proposing to the Jews? In other words, in order for his indictment against the Jews to be legitimate, there must be at least some Gentiles who have obeyed the law and have been considered as "circumcised" in God's eyes in order for Paul to use them as an example of people who obey God without the written law in their possession. If there were no such Gentiles in this class, Paul's argument against the Jews would be superfluous. The Jews would not look so bad, since they could point out that there are no good Gentiles to which Paul could contrast their evil behavior. Hence, Paul's stipulation in Romans 2:7 that there are some who "do good work" and "seek glory, honor, and immortality" must have the necessary potential to be fulfilled

---

[50] Referring to Romans 2:6-7, Vatican II states: "After the fall, he buoyed them up with the hope of salvation by promising redemption (cf. Gen. 3:15) and he has never ceased to take care of the human race. For he wishes to give eternal life to all those who seek salvation by patience in well-doing (Rom. 2:6-7)" (Vatican Council II, *Dei Verbum 3*).

in order to substantiate Paul's indictment against the Jews. The proposition that they can "do good" and receive eternal life for that goodness, then, cannot be hypothetical.

A further indication that Romans 2 is not hypothetical is the way in which Paul has arranged the flow of thought from chapter 1 through chapter 5. Protestants maintain that Paul is organizing the chapters in a specific sequential arrangement such that what is proposed as a plausibility in Romans 2 is then negated by the chronological placement of Romans 3-4. In essence, Romans 3-4 corrects, in due time, the "false" view presented in Romans 2 on how to be saved. The problem with this assumption, among other things, is that Paul is not writing these chapters chronologically as much as he is topically. Paul shows this, for example, in his opening statement in Romans 3:9: "...We have already made the charge that Jews and Gentiles alike are all under sin..." We must conclude that somewhere within the first two chapters of Romans Paul "*already* made the charge that Jews and Gentiles alike are all under sin." The first indications of such a "charge" on mankind appear in Romans 1:18-32, in which Paul refers to "all the godlessness and wickedness of men" (v. 18); and "For although they knew God they neither glorified him as God nor gave thanks to him (v. 21); and, "they have become filled with every kind of wickedness, evil, greed, and depravity" (v. 29). In fact, Paul's description of mankind's sin in Romans 1:18-32 matches the very language of Romans 3:10-18, in which Paul states "there is no one righteous, not even one" (v. 10); and "their mouths are full of cursing and bitterness" (v. 14); and "there is no fear of God before their eyes" (v. 18). Hence we see that the "charge" against mankind is identical in Romans 1 and Romans 3. Paul also reiterates the "charge" more subtly in Romans 5:12 in which he says, "Therefore, just as sin entered the world through one man, and death through sin, and in this way death came upon all men, upon which all men sinned."

Since Romans 1, Romans 3 and Romans 5, all stipulate the same "charge" against sin, it is obvious that Paul has arranged the Roman epistle topically. This structure allows Paul to state the same problem three times and give the same solution, but with an added nuance in each instance. For example, while Paul is levying the "charge" in Romans 1 and 2 against the sin of both Jew and Gentile, he is also offering the solution for that sin in the same context. Paul indicates this solution in Romans 1:16-17:

> I am not ashamed of the gospel, because it is the power of God for the salvation of everyone who believes: first for the Jew, then for the Gentile. For in it a righteousness of God is revealed from faith to faith, as it is written: The just man will live by faith.

We note here that Paul presents the gospel in all its flower before he even levies the "charge" of sin against mankind. It is as if he is anticipating the solution before he gives the details of the problem. Presenting the gospel at such an early stage in the Roman epistle does not suggest an arrangement whereby Paul is setting up a hypothetical means of salvation in Romans 2 which is then followed up with the real solution in Romans 3-4. Rather, we understand from Paul's mentioning of the gospel in Romans 1:16-17 that he has already given us the solution prior to Romans 2 and 3. In effect, Romans 2 takes the next step by completing the instruction and giving the very means of attaining that salvation.

To confirm this interpretation, we must look at two facets of the relationship between Romans 1:16-17 and Romans 2:5-10. First, we notice that Paul specifies the recipients of the gospel in Romans 1:16: "for the Jew first and then for the Gentile." This is the identical language Paul uses in Romans 2:9-10: "There will be trouble and distress for every human being who does evil: for the Jew first, then for the Gentile; but glory, honor, and peace for everyone who does good: for the Jew first, then for the Gentile."[51] It would be strange indeed for Paul to use identical language in both these passages but intend one as real and the other as hypothetical. The two passages are speaking of the same reality, albeit in different ways. Romans 1:16 uses terms such as "gospel," "salvation" and "faith" whereas Romans 2:9-10 uses terms such as, "does good" and "does evil." From this we can understand that he who "does good" and receives "eternal life" in Romans 2:6-10 is the same as

[51] The Greek phrasing of Romans 1:16 is identical to that in Romans 2:9 and Romans 2:10 (Ἰουδαίῳ τε πρῶτον καὶ Ἕλληνι).

he who lives by the "faith" of the "gospel" unto "salvation" in Romans 1:16-17. The good works of Romans 2:5-10, then, are in the same salvific category as faith. This is another clear indication that Paul is not opposing works to faith when both are included under the auspices of God's grace.

As noted previously, Paul makes the connection between Romans 1:16-17 and Romans 2:9-10 even stronger by bridging these two contexts in Romans 2:4: "Or do you show contempt for the riches of his kindness, tolerance and patience, not realizing that God's kindness leads you toward repentance?" In this passage we see Paul introducing the aspect of repentance into his discourse. In stating that God's "kindness leads to repentance," Paul's usage of these terms reveals the essential elements of the gospel. "God's kindness" speaks of his grace. Rather than just obliterating us in his righteous wrath against sin, God shows grace by leading us to repentance from sin. That God is expecting "repentance" from this gracious leading conveys the essence of the gospel. After all, what is the gospel if it is not salvation through repentance from sin?

Right on the heels of this presentation of the gospel of grace and repentance in Romans 2:4, Paul issues the ultimatum in Romans 2:5-10. Those who do not repent will receive God's wrath. This is noted in verses 5,8,9:

> Because of your unrepentant heart you are storing up wrath against yourself...but for those who are self-seeking and who reject the truth and follow evil, there will be wrath and anger...there will be trouble and distress for every human being who does evil...

Next, the logical complement to those who are "unrepentant" would be those who actually do repent. Those who "persist in doing good work" and "seek for glory, honor, and immortality" in verses 7 and 10 must then be those who have first repented of their sins. Their "doing good" implies their repentance from sin, since one cannot do good in God's eyes unless he has repented of sin. That they "seek for immortality" shows, in addition, that their lives are not focused on this earth but upon the heavenly kingdom that provides immortality. One cannot have a belief in immortality if he is still in the blindness of sin and has not responded to the principles of the gospel. God's grace and the expected repentance of man in Romans 2:4 is followed by either of two responses, i.e., "doing good...seeking glory, honor, and immortality...[for] eternal life" or "self-seeking and who reject the truth and follow evil [will receive] wrath and anger" in Romans 2:7-8. Thus, it is only logical to conclude that the two responses to God's calling are indicative of two different responses to the gospel.

If Paul lifts the doing of works for obtaining eternal life to such a height as he does in Romans 2:6-10, what, then, can we conclude about Paul's understanding of works in relation to salvation? The conclusion must be that works are necessary for salvation, and, in fact, are one of the principle determining factors in whether or not one obtains salvation. We say this with the proviso that Paul outrightly condemns works done with a view toward *obligating* God to pay the worker with salvation. Man can never put God in the position of being in debt to an imperfect and sinful creature. The only way God can accept our works is through his grace. Works done under the auspices of God's grace, that is, works done that do not demand payment from God but are rewarded only due to the kindness and mercy of God, are the works that Paul requires for salvation.[52]

Paul's Other Writings

Do the rest of Paul's writings on the nature of works support this concept? We have already seen briefly that Paul holds the ne-

[52] The distinction between works done under obligation and works done under the grace of God was made clear in the writings of Augustine and delineated further by medieval Catholic theology as the difference between "strict" merit and "condign" or "congruent" merit (Thomas Aquinas, "Nature and Grace," *Summa Theologica*, Ia-IIae, Q.114, Art. 3; Ludwig Ott, *Fundamentals of Catholic Dogma,* pp. 264-269). The Council of Trent did not use the terms *condign* or *congruent* merit, however. It referred only to the general distinction between merit by obligation and merit under grace (Session 6, Chapter 5, 16; Catholic Catechism, sections 2006-2011; See also St Augustine's *Sermon* 298, 4-5). Many Protestant theologians distort this concept by making condign merit equal to strict merit and thereby concluding that the Catholic theology of merit obligates God to give salvation. See **Appendix 4** for a thorough refutation of this charge.

cessity of works in such high regard that in Romans 14:10-12 and 2 Corinthians 5:10 he states that all people must eventually face God's judgment throne based on their works. In the passage just prior, i.e., Romans 13, Paul specifies the basic commandments of the Decalogue as a guide for doing good works. He says in Romans 13:9-10:

> The commandments, "Do not commit adultery," "Do not murder," "Do not steal," "Do not covet," and whatever other commandment there may be, are summed up in this one rule: "Love your neighbor as yourself. Love does no harm to a neighbor." Therefore love is the fulfillment of the law.

Obviously, Paul does not downplay the commandments. He holds them up as the ideal for us to follow. What is striking about this passage, however, is that Paul speaks of love as "*the fulfillment of the law*." Paul maintains that a Christian has a duty to use the specifics of the law to accomplish the intent of the law. The intent of the law is to show love to one's neighbor. Which law is this? Is it the same law that he describes in Romans 3:28 in which Paul says, "We maintain that a man is justified by faith apart from observing the *law*"? Yes it is. The law is the law. There is grace, and there is law. The explanation is simple. We understand that, in the sense of *strict* merit, the law cannot save us nor can we fulfill it. However, since God has given us his grace, we are no longer under the rigid and uncompromising requirements or judgments of the *system of law.* As Paul said in Ephesians 2:15, "...by abolishing in his flesh the law with its commandments and regulations..." We are under a more lenient plan that allows us to please God with our obedience and in turn God rewards us purely from his benevolence. It is in this sense only that we "fulfill" the law.[53]

[53] As one theologian has stated: "They are not under a legal system administered according to the principles of retributive justice, a system which requires perfect obedience as the condition of acceptance with God, and which says, 'Cursed is every one that continues not in all things which are written in the book of the law to do them.' They are under grace, that is, under a system in which believers are not dealt with on the principles of justice, but on the principles of undeserved mercy in which God does not impute 'their trespasses unto them'

Just how adamant is Paul about keeping the law with a view toward salvation? To the Galatians he writes: "For in Christ Jesus neither circumcision nor uncircumcision has any value. The only thing that counts is faith expressing itself through love...The entire law is summed up in a single command: Love your neighbor as yourself" (5:6,14). Except for the preface showing circumcision to be obsolete, this statement concerning the relationship between law and love is identical to what Paul said in Romans 13:9-10 cited above. His statement becomes even more significant when we realize that it is said right in the midst of the faith and works controversy occurring in the Galatian church. In fact, almost the whole epistle to the Galatians addresses the problem between faith and works. Does Paul give the command "love your neighbor as yourself" merely as a salutary encouragement to the Galatians, or is there something far more serious going on here in regard to their very salvation? As we read further in Galatians 5, we see that Paul expressed the necessity of love because the Galatians were attacking each other. Just prior to his mentioning of loving one's neighbor in verse 14, Paul set up a contrast in verse 13 between "indulging in the sinful nature" and "serving one another in love." We understand from this contrast that those who were not loving their neighbor were indulging in sinful desires. Paul goes on to define what he means by "sinful nature" in Galatians 5:21:

The acts of the *sinful nature* are obvious: sexual immorality, impurity and debauchery, idolatry and witchcraft, hatred, discord, jealousy, fits of rage, selfish ambition, dissensions, factions and envy, drunkenness, orgies, and the like. I warn you, as I did before, that those who live like this will not inherit the kingdom of God.

Of the fifteen or more sins that Paul describes here, most involve hurting a neighbor or engaging the neighbor in an illicit ac-

---

[53 cont.] (2 Cor. 5:19). There is therefore to them no condemnation. They are not condemned for their sins, not because they are not sins and do not deserve condemnation, but because Christ has already made expiation for their guilt and makes continual intercession for them." No, this statement does not come from a Catholic theologian. It comes from one of the most lauded Reformed Protestant theologians of the past few hundred years, Charles Hodge (*Justification By Faith Alone*, ed. John W. Robbins (Hobbs, NM: The Trinity Foundation), p. 109). For the context and further explanation of Hodge's statement, see chapter 5 of this book.

tivity. Doing such evil things shows that one is not loving his neighbor. For these kinds of sins Paul says clearly that one "will not inherit the kingdom of God." Apparently, this was a major problem with the Galatians since Paul says, "I warn you, *as I did before...*" Thus, this is the second time (the first we have no record of) that Paul had warned them about such behavior. It is clear that for such bad works they will forfeit their heavenly inheritance. Yes, works are important to Paul, so important that he threatens the Galatians with the loss of their very salvation if they persist in such evil behavior.

Paul also threatened the Corinthians in the same manner. In 1 Corinthians 6:8-9 he writes: "Instead, you yourselves cheat and do wrong, and you do this to your brothers. Do you not know that the wicked will *not inherit the kingdom of God...*" As he did with the Galatians, Paul points out the specific sins of the Corinthians. They were cheating and doing other harmful acts to their Christian brothers, just as the Galatians were doing to their brothers. Consequently Paul gives the same warning to the Corinthians that he gave to the Galatians — that is, a loss of the inheritance of the kingdom of God. This is not just an idle threat. Paul is not the type to warn of the loss of the kingdom and not mean what he says. As Paul issues the ultimatum to the Galatians, he issues the same to the Corinthians — either show love and obedience, or suffer the eternal consequences.

Other evidence that the Corinthians were engaging in illicit behavior appears in the admonition of Paul's second letter. In 2 Corinthians 12:21, he says: "...when I come again...I will be grieved over many who have sinned earlier and have not repented of the impurity, sexual sin and debauchery in which they have indulged." That these sins directly call into question their eternal salvation is evident in the verses immediately following in 2 Corinthians 13:2,5:

> I already gave you a warning when I was with you the second time. I now repeat it while absent: On my return I will not spare those who sinned earlier or any of the others...Examine yourselves to see whether you are in the faith; do you not realize that Christ Jesus is in you — unless, of course, you are reprobates.

We must conclude, then, that works are a primary criterion in deciding whether or not the individual will be saved. We have also seen that though Paul condemns works done in an effort to obligate God to pay the individual with salvation, Paul is adamant that works, under the auspices of grace, are absolutely necessary for our salvation. Though God does not require us to fulfill the requirements of the law from a strict and contractual arrangement of obligation, he does require that we "*please*" him with our faith and works, an aspect of our relationship with God that we will develop momentarily. The mere fact that we can, by God's own estimation, please him, even though our actions are far from perfect, shows that God does not evaluate earnest seekers from the standard of legal perfection but from his mercy and grace.[54] Just as a father is pleased with the devotion and obedience of his children, so God is pleased with the efforts of his children. The father, if he were to use an uncompromising and strict measure of judgment, could pardon none of his children's disobedience, but through grace it is possible. (We will see this principle developed more fully in chapter 6).

One of the more prominent passages in Paul's writings that firmly distinguishes between faith and works is Philippians 3:9: "...and be found in him not having a righteousness of my own that comes from the law, but that which is through faith in Christ — the righteousness that comes from God and is by faith." Most Protestants assert that Philippians 3:9 clearly indicates that Paul is op-

---

[54] Protestants believe that they can "please" God in the area of "sanctification." Knowing that their works are imperfect, the basis upon which the pleasing of God is possible for them is the atonement of Christ which allows God to view and evaluate them based on grace rather than law. Catholicism just takes this principle back one step to include justification. God can accept our imperfect faith and works for justification because he looks at us through the eyes of grace as we diligently seek him. Since justification and sanctification are simultaneous and ongoing, the "pleasing" of God, under the auspices of his grace, occurs throughout our life and leads to final salvation. (Chapters 4-5 will cover this in more detail). If the Protestant objects to applying these principles to justification, we must remind him that he is required to appeal to God's grace to judge the quality of what he calls "saving faith" for his own justification. In other words, since Protestants stipulate that faith must be of a certain "quality" in order for the individual to apprehend the righteousness of Christ, and since God is the only one who can judge the quality of this faith, the criterion for judging the faith must derive solely from God's grace, not from his standard of perfection. Otherwise, no one's faith would be acceptable.

posing any and all work over against simply believing in Christ's righteousness, i.e., "the righteousness that comes from God." But this interpretation introduces a false dichotomy in Paul's thinking and fails to pinpoint the real distinction he is making. The wording "a righteousness of my own *that comes from the law*" shows that Paul is not speaking of God- honoring or God-pleasing righteousness done under grace, but rather that which is derived from the *system of law,* or as we have learned, a system which attempts to put God in a position of *obligation.* In other words, up until the time he encountered the grace of Christ on the Damascus road, Paul was just like many other Jews. He was seeking to be justified before God within the *system of law.* He valiantly performed his ritual laws, yet with an eye toward obligating God to reward him for his religiosity. This is made clear earlier in the same context. In Philippians 3:5-6, Paul writes of himself as one: "...circumcised on the eighth day of the people of Israel, of the tribe of Benjamin, a Hebrew of Hebrews; in regard to the law, a Pharisee; as for zeal, persecuting the church; as for legalistic righteousness, faultless."

In regard to the law, Paul likens himself to the typical Pharisee. It is common understanding, expressed in many of Jesus's contentions with them, that the Pharisees attempted to obey the *letter* of the law but did not understand the *intent* or the *purpose* of the law. They boasted to God that they were holy and righteous by keeping the law, and subsequently expected God to requite them for their self-styled efforts. Not only did they seek to obligate God, they also failed to consider all the times they disobeyed the law, nor did they sincerely seek forgiveness for those failures. Now we can see why, before his conversion, Paul says he was *"faultless"* in *"legalistic righteousness."*[55] Again, it is clear that Paul is not speaking of a *God- pleasing* righteousness performed under grace which takes account of personal sin and produces humility, but a

---

[55] The phrase, *legalistic righteousness* is from the Greek δικαιοσύνην τὴν νόμου (lit: "righteousness the one of law"). This is the same Greek phrase behind the translation *righteousness of my own that come from law* in Philippians 3:9. The literal rendering of Philippians 3:9 is *not having my righteousness* [being one] *of law*, whereas Philippians 3:6 reads *righteousness* [being one] *in the law*. The only difference between the two is the Greek preposition used in each verse.

rigid, legalistic adherence to law which seeks to obligate God to reward him. Since he thought of himself as "faultless," he no doubt considered himself worthy of God's blessing. As noted previously, Paul would be likened to someone who "boasts" of his performance before God.[56] To him, God owed him something for "faultless" obedience. He was "better" than everyone else and thus he thought he deserved more from God. Of such pharisaical attitudes, Jesus spoke quite plainly in Luke 16:15 & 18:9:

> You are the ones who *justify yourselves* in the eyes of men, but God knows your hearts. What is highly valued among men is detestable in God's sight...To some who were confident of their own righteousness and looked down on everybody else, Jesus told this parable...

Faith: The Obligation to God

In regard to the principle of obligation, let us reiterate another dimension of the faith/works relationship. It is clear that Paul condemns justification on the basis of works because through such a relationship man puts God in an obligatory position to bless him. Since God is the Creator and perfect but man is the creature and imperfect, such an obligatory relationship cannot exist. Conversely, justification by grace allows God to justify man from sheer benevolence. However, God does not shower man with grace for the purpose of justification without requiring any effort on man's part. The first thing God requires from man in order to receive salvation is faith. Faith is the beginning of salvation. Faith is the first contingency which will determine whether or not the grace of God is applied salvifically to the individual. But notice this. By an ironic twist of fate, the requirement of faith in order to receive God's grace *obligates man* to God. Whereas man would put God in a position of obligation if he based his appeal on works, God's requirement of faith puts man in a position of obligation to God. The roles are completely reversed. Man is obliged to believe everything that God has declared about himself, whether he wants to or

[56] cf., Rom. 2:17, 23; 3:27; 4:2; Eph. 2:8-9; 1 Cor. 4:7.

not. If faith were merely an option, then man would not be obligated to believe. He is obligated to believe to such an extent that if he does not believe he will be condemned by God. He cannot ask God to annihilate him out of existence so that he is not required to make the choice to believe. Man is stuck in God's universe and must accept the nature and duties of his existence whether he likes them or not. Having faith in God is not an option, it is a command — something that man must do in order to be saved.

Why does God choose faith as the primary vehicle to obligate man to himself? Because it was precisely for lack of faith in God that the original man fell. Adam came to the conclusion that God was not who he said he was. More specifically, Adam did not believe that God was looking out for man's best interest. He thought that God was deliberately hiding something from him. Instead, Adam believed the devil who convinced him that God was prohibiting him and his wife, Eve, from attaining divinity. Since God is a personal being, Adam's disbelief was a personal affront to God and an attack against God's veracity and character. Essentially, Adam insulted the integrity of God. Consequently, at the point where Adam succumbed to doubt, God would require that each man who came after Adam pass the test that Adam failed. In effect, each man would be placed at his own 'tree of the knowledge of good and evil' to pass the test to believe that God is who he says he is; that despite what we see on the surface, God, in his infinite wisdom, is looking out for our best interests. This, as we will see in the next section, is what God required of Abraham, the father of faith. Abraham had to believe God despite all the circumstantial evidence surrounding him that suggested God was not being honest with him or good to him. God *obligated* Abraham to believe in God, and all that God is, in order for Abraham to be saved. We will also see that God requires the same faith from us.

The Life Of Faith

Though faith begins our salvation, it is then tested and made stronger with the help of God's grace. In Galatians 3:11, Paul says: "Clearly no one is justified before God by the law, because 'The righteous will live by faith.'" The clause "The righteous shall live by faith" is a quote taken from the Old Testament prophet Habakkuk. Habakkuk 2:4 reads: "See, he is puffed up; his desires are not upright, but the righteous will live by his faith." The New Testament quotes this passage three times. The first, as we noted earlier, is in Romans 1:17. The second instance appears in Galatians 3:11 noted above. The third instance appears in Hebrews 10:38. In light of the principle proposed in this chapter of *pleasing* God by our faith and works, the prophet Habakkuk has much to say. The context of Habakkuk 2 contrasts the proud man whose thoughts are evil over against the righteous man who humbly lives by his faith. The faith in view is a continuing one, a faith that walks with God and pleases him. Habakkuk is illustrating a lifestyle of faith. We notice this also in the word that Habakkuk chooses for "faith," derived from the Hebrew word *emunah*. The normal connotation of this word is that of continued "faithfulness," rather than a one-time act of faith. The verse could easily be translated, "the just shall live by his faithfulness."[57]

We can also see the same principle of ongoing faithfulness within the various contexts that Paul chooses for this quote. For example, the use of Habakkuk's quote in Romans 1:17 is prefaced by the statement, "...is revealed from *faith to faith...*" The expression "from faith to faith" implies a continuing life of faith, one that proceeds from one act of faith to the next throughout the person's life.

Similarly, the third and last time that Habakkuk's quote is used, Hebrews 10:38, portrays the same kind of ongoing faithfulness. Here Paul says: "He who is coming will come and not delay. But my righteous one will live by faith [faithfulness], and if he shrinks back I will not be pleased with him." The context is one of warning Christians to persevere in trials in order to receive the promise of God. The promise is understood as the eternal inheritance. This shows that Habakkuk's quote is not speaking of one act of faith at the beginning of someone's life, but a faith that lasts till the end

---

[57] Of the 49 times this word is used in the Old Testament, over half of the passages refer to "faithfulness" (e.g., Psalm 89:1, 2, 5, 8, 24, 33; 119:75, 90; Pro. 28:20; Lam. 3:23, et al). Other passages refer to "truth" or "steadfastness" (e.g., Jer. 5:1, 3). It is also worthy of note that in many of these passages *emunah* (אמונה) is used in reference to the character of God as much as it is to men.

when God returns, i.e., if the faith is not present, he will not receive the promise. Again, this denotes an ongoing faithfulness in the person, a life of walking with God and pleasing him. We also notice that Hebrews 10:38 stresses the "*pleasing*" of God by faith, the same truth we witnessed earlier concerning the principal dimension of our gracious relationship with God.

Since Paul had used the quote from Habakkuk twice in reference to justification (i.e., Romans 1:17 and Galatians 3:11), then it would most likely carry the same meaning when used in Hebrew 10:38. Since Paul speaks of faith as that which endures to the end of one's life, the justification of the individual must then be reserved to the end. By the same token, we must also understand that when Paul is quoting Habakkuk 2:4 in Galatians 3:11, he is not merely teaching the Galatians about the theological categories of faith and law, he is speaking of a lifestyle of faithfulness to God as opposed to one that attempts to appeal to God by boasting in the minute details of the law, (e.g., circumcision). Those who do the latter would be described by Habakkuk 2:4 as "he [who] is puffed up, his desires are not upright." Anyone who attempts to make himself right with God by his own works is one who is "puffed up," one who "boasts" of his own goodness and is filled with his own self-importance and significance (cf., Luke 18:9). His attitude and lifestyle do not *please* God. As a consequence, the law by which he is attempting to make himself acceptable to God is the very law which will be fully employed against him.

Is this "puffed up" thinking about the law evident in the Galatian church? It certainly is. First, there is the attitude of ethnic superiority prevalent among the Jews. Probably still in shock over God's rejection of the Jewish nation, the Jews attempted to resurrect their national pride by other means. They hearkened back to the one feature that distinguished them from all the other nations, the Mosaic code of law. They were not ready to give up that heritage or identity. Consequently, the tension between Jew and Gentile permeates the Galatian epistle. To counteract this tension, Paul teaches that the inclusion of the Gentiles in salvation should be no big surprise to the Jews, since it was already prophesied in their own Scriptures (cf., Galatians 3:8, 14, 28). Second, the Jews sought to demonstrate their supposed superiority by requiring that the new converts, many of them Gentiles, be circumcised in order to be saved. This requirement is evident first in Galatians 2:3-5:

> Yet not even Titus, who was with me, was *compelled* to be circumcised, even though he was a Greek. This matter arose because some false brothers had infiltrated our ranks to spy on the freedom we have in Christ Jesus and to make us slaves. We did not give into them for a moment so that the truth of the gospel might remain with you.

The Jew's *compelling* the Gentiles to be circumcised is evident also in Galatians 6:12: "Those who want to make a good impression outwardly are trying to *compel* you to be circumcised. The only reason they do this is to avoid being persecuted for the cross of Christ." Why was Paul so upset? Because in *compelling* the Gentiles to be circumcised, the Jews were making an obsolete Old Testament law a requirement for justification.[58] Circumcision was not being done for health reasons; it was being forced upon them for soteriological reasons. Not only was requiring circumcision an infringement on the principle of grace Paul so zealously tried to establish, but the above verse reveals that their motivations for requiring it was to downplay the necessity and meaning of the cross of Christ. In other words, they repudiated the system of grace, especially since it was given to the Gentiles, and desired the system of law in its place. In Galatians 5:2-3, Paul reinforces his stance: "Mark my words! I, Paul, tell you that if you let yourselves be circumcised, Christ will be of no value to you at all. Again I declare to every man who lets himself be circumcised that he is *obligated to obey the whole law.*"

We notice here the same type of argumentation that Paul used in Galatians 3:10. There Paul stated that those who place themselves under one aspect of the system of law in order to be justified must then obey *everything* written in the law, without exception or

---

[58] Evangelicals N. Geisler and R. MacKenzie maintain that in the Galatian epistle Paul is dealing only with sanctification, not justification. Further, these authors insist that Paul not only teaches that one is justified by faith alone but is also *sanctified* by faith alone (op. cit., pp. 236-237). Chapters 4-5 present and critique more fully this view of Geisler and MacKenzie.

fault. In regards to law, one cannot have the part without having the whole. Hence, one little mistake would mean condemnation. Here in Galatians 5:2-3, Paul uses the word "*obligation*" to express that truth. The system of law will *obligate* one to keep the whole law. "*Obligate*" is the same word that Paul used in Romans 4:4 in which he contrasted grace with law. There it was evident that those who base their justification before God on works, without grace, put themselves under a system of "obligation" or "debt" in which they demand strict payment from God for their works. Since God is not obligated to pay anyone for anything, the system of law cannot be used to justify them. Men simply cannot fulfill the strict obligations of the law perfectly. Pleasing God by obeying the precepts of law under his grace is one thing, but reverting to a system of law as the *basis* for justification is totally antithetical to the gospel. The law could never serve as the master of the gospel; it could only be its slave. Of those who made law the master, Paul says in 1 Thessalonians 2:14-16:

> ...the same things those churches suffered from the Jews, who killed the Lord Jesus and the prophets and also drove us out. They displease God and are hostile to all men in their effort to keep us from speaking to the Gentiles so that they may be saved. In this way they always heap up their sins to the limit. The wrath of God has come upon them at last.

How Deep Should One's Faith Be?

The Faith of Abraham

In the Galatian epistle we learned that Paul taught that faith was the means of justification in the Old Testament. In his attempts to convince the Jews that this was God's intent from the beginning, Paul uses one of the most prominent personalities of the Old Testament to prove his case. He brings the person of Abraham to the fore. Since the Jews prided themselves in being children of Abraham, which because of circumcision set them apart from the Gentile world, Paul knows that he must probe the life of Abraham more deeply in order to expose the Jews' wrong thinking about

Abraham. Though we will later discover other aspects of the significance of Abraham in understanding the nature of justification, at this point we will concentrate on Paul's view of the *depth* of faith that Abraham had before God, faith that the typical Jew of Paul's day did not have.

In Romans 4:18-21, Paul writes:

> Against all hope, Abraham in hope believed and so became the father of many nations, just as it had been said to him, "So shall your offspring be." Without weakening in his faith, he faced the fact that his body was as good as dead — since he was about a hundred years old — and that Sarah's womb was also dead. Yet he did not waver through unbelief regarding the promise of God, but was strengthened in his faith and gave glory to God, being fully persuaded that God had power to do what he had promised.

One can see clearly from this account that Abraham's concept of God was not a superficial one. All the circumstantial evidence surrounding his life and culture suggested to Abraham that things could not possibly happen as God had told him. Moreover, Abraham had no one to encourage him or lift him up in weak moments. In spite of this, when we read such statements as, "against all hope," "without weakening," "did not waver" and "being fully persuaded," we see that Abraham had a very deep faith. Not only did Sarah prove to be infertile in her younger years, but by the time the account in Genesis 15 to which Paul refers was occurring, Sarah was already ninety years old, far too old in anyone's estimation to be bearing children. God is asking Abraham to believe in something that is virtually impossible to believe. In his one hundred years of life, Abraham knew that the things God was proposing just didn't happen. Life was too normal, nor had Abraham been a witness to any miracles prior to this meeting with God.

So what makes Abraham take that step of faith and believe despite all the circumstantial evidence against God? Abraham's decision to believe stems from an intimate relationship he had established with God long ago. The beginning of this relationship is recorded in Genesis 11-12. Abram, as he was called then, lived with his wife Sarai and his father Terah in Ur of the Chaldeans. On their way out of Ur toward the land of Canaan, they stopped in Haran. After Terah's death in Haran, God came to Abram and told him to leave his homeland. Genesis 12:1 records: "The Lord had said to Abram, 'Leave your country, your people, and your father's household and go to the land I will show you.'" Though we cannot be sure, even this instance may not have been the origin of Abram's faith-relationship with God. As far back as Genesis 4:26 it is said that "men began to call on the name of the Lord" many years before Terah and Abram existed. According to the best estimates, the time span from Genesis 4:26 to Genesis 12 encompasses thousands of years. It is likely that Abram knew the Lord prior to Genesis 12; otherwise the calling of Abram to leave Haran would be considered rather abrupt. In fact, the call is given as if Abram had encountered or had known of the Lord long before. Perhaps his father Terah taught him of the Lord. Whatever the truth of this matter, Abram had a strong enough belief and relationship with God that he acted promptly on God's command to leave Haran. Genesis 12:5 records: "So Abram left, as the Lord had told him; and Lot went with him. Abram was seventy-five years old when he set out from Haran." We can conclude from this account that Abram had a strong faith-relationship with God at least twenty-five years prior to his next major encounter with God in Genesis 15. We would assume that the faith of Abraham continued to grow uninterrupted for the next twenty-five years until the time of Genesis 15 when God told Abram he would give Sarai a son to fulfill the promise he had made to him in Genesis 12.

How deep must faith be to leave one's own country, people, and customs and go to a place about which one knows nothing? It must be very deep, indeed! The companion account in Hebrews 11:8, which establishes the theological underpinnings in the call of Abraham, assures us that he had a very deep faith. In this passage, Paul stipulates: "By faith Abraham, when called to go to a place he would later receive as his inheritance, obeyed and went, even though he did not know where he was going." We also notice that all the heroes of faith Paul describes from the Old Testament exhibit the same strong faith. Prior to citing Abraham's faith, Paul first gives remarks on the faith of Abel (11:4), Enoch (11:5), and Noah (11:7). We would surmise, then, that Abraham's faith was of the same order as these other men of God, and that all of them were included under the rubric of Hebrews 11:6: "And without faith it is impossible to please God." Hence, the passage leads us to conclude that the faith of Abraham in Genesis 12, twenty-five years before he directly encountered God again in Genesis 15, is the same faith, a faith that *pleased* God. In both Genesis 12 and 15, Abraham is asked to believe in the integrity of God, that is, that God can do what he promised to do, no matter how impossible it may seem. In Genesis 12, Abram is asked to leave his homeland to go to another land where God would bless him. He did this, according to Paul's perspective, "even though he did not know where he was going." He believed that God would not steer him wrong. When Abram entered the land, he saw the fierce Canaanites living there, yet he did not fear and turn back as his descendants would do years later (cf., Genesis 12:6; Deut. 2:26-36; Eccles. 16:7-8). Similarly, in Genesis 15 Abraham believed that God would give him a son even though it seemed impossible for this to occur. Both Genesis 12 and Genesis 15 prove that God keeps his word and that he can be trusted. All in all, Abram was required to believe that God's word was absolutely, positively, reliable, even though the circumstances suggested otherwise.[59]

After this, Paul gives additional information to show that the faith of Abraham in Genesis 12 was the same as the faith in Genesis 15. As mentioned above, Hebrews 11:8 speaks of the time in Genesis 12 in which God came to Abram and told him to leave his homeland to go to the promised land. Hebrews 11:9 states that when Abraham arrived in the Promised land, he lived there in tents like a stranger. Notice that Paul prefaces each of these instances with "By faith Abraham..." and then closes with the following statement in Hebrews 11:10: "For he was looking forward to the *city* whose architect and builder is God." Unlike the Genesis account which merely provides the rudimentary facts of Abraham's faith, Paul deliberately penetrates into the mind and motivation of

---

59 "Consider the generations of old and see: has anyone trusted in the Lord and been disappointed? Or has anyone persevered in the fear of the Lord and been forsaken?...Woe to timid hearts and to slack hands...Woe to the fainthearted who have no trust...Woe to you who have lost your nerve! What will you do when the Lord's reckoning comes?" (Ecclesiasticus 2:10-14).

Abraham, making us privy to an insight we would never have gleaned from the Genesis account alone. We learn an astounding truth. We discover that Abraham did not just blindly obey; rather, he had a vivid vision of the future heavenly kingdom and of the whole plan and purpose of God's dealing with him. Abraham's vision anticipated not merely owning a piece of land on earth, but also his ultimate entry in heaven in the future, "a *city* whose architect and builder is God." What kind of faith is required to envision one's entrance into the heavenly kingdom for eternity? Surely more than some crude or rudimentary understanding; rather, it is a faith that comprehends the whole purpose and meaning of existence, and that trusts God implicitly for its eventual fulfillment. According to Paul's viewpoint, Christians possess this same faith, since he says in 13:14, "For here we do not have an enduring city, but we are looking for the *city* that is to come" (cf., Heb. 11:39-40). Obviously, Paul is teaching us that Abraham already possessed this depth of faith in Genesis 12, long before Genesis 15 (which Paul recounts in Romans 4 as the time Abraham was justified for his faith).[60]

To stress that the faith of Abraham in Genesis 12 was the same kind of faith he had in Genesis 15, we notice Paul using identical language to describe both instances of faith. Beginning in Hebrews 11:11, Paul opens by recounting the incident of Genesis 15 in which Abraham believed that God was going to give him a son. As he had done in the previous verses (8-9), Paul again prefaces verse 11 with: "By faith Abraham..." to confirm that he is talking about the same faith. He goes on to say:

> By faith Abraham, even though he was past age, and Sarah herself was barren, was enabled to become a father because he

[60] It is not surprising that most Protestant books and commentaries addressing the subject of justification do not mention, let alone exegete, Genesis 12. R. C. Sproul's *Faith Alone,* for example, has no reference to Genesis 12 (yet it won the CBA Gold Medallion for the best book in theology in 1996) and neither does the follow up book *Justification By Faith Alone* by Sproul, MacArthur, Beeke, Gerstner and Armstrong. Ironically, Beeke references Hebrews 11:8 (which Paul cites in reference to the faith of Abraham in Genesis 12) in a paragraph in which Beeke is attempting to specify the *kind* of faith that justifies. Apparently Beeke doesn't realize that in citing this passage he is inadvertently admitting that Abraham already had saving faith and thus was already justified in Genesis 12. (Beeke, op. cit., p. 84).

> considered him faithful who had made the promise...All these people were still living by faith when they died. They did not receive the things promised; they only saw them and welcomed them from a distance. And they admitted they were aliens and strangers on earth.

He then continues in Hebrews 11:14-16 with the same wording he already used in Hebrews 11:10 to describe Abraham's faith in leaving his homeland and sojourning in the promised land. He writes:

> People who say such things show that they are looking for a *country of their own*. If they had been thinking of the country they had left, they would have had opportunity to return. Instead, they *were longing for a better country, a heavenly one*. Therefore, God is not ashamed to be called their God, for he has *prepared a city for them*.

We see here that Paul has incorporated the same vivid vision of the future kingdom that he used a few verses prior in Hebrews 11:10. Since in both instances Abraham is looking forward to the heavenly kingdom, the object and meaning of faith must be the same in both instances. We also notice that Paul stresses the *life* of faith in the individual. He adds in Hebrews 11:13, "all these people were *still living by faith when they died*." In this way, he confirms what we have already seen: The faith that saves is not merely a faith that begins salvation but a faith that lasts until one's last breath.

Paul also shows us that the faith of Abraham in Genesis 12 was the same justifying faith of which he speaks in other contexts. For instance, in Galatians 3:7-9 Paul writes:

> Understand, then, that those who believe are children of Abraham. The Scripture foresaw that God would justify the Gentiles by faith, and announced the gospel in advance to Abraham: 'All nations will be blessed through you.' So those who have faith are blessed along with Abraham, the man of faith.

Here Paul speaks of Abraham as "the man of faith," but adds that this faith is the same faith which the Gentiles now possess and which justifies them. The quote, "All nations will be blessed through you" is taken from Genesis 12:3, not Genesis 15:6. This shows that the faith Abraham possessed in Genesis 12:3 was the same justifying faith he had in Genesis 15:6, the same faith through which the Gentiles can now believe and be justified. It is "the gospel announced in advance," yet the gospel already exercised by Abraham in Genesis 12:3, the gospel of justification by faith. To make the link between the faith of Genesis 12:3 and the faith of Genesis 15:6 even stronger, Paul begins his argumentation in Galatians 3:6 by quoting from Genesis 15:6: "He believed God and it was credited to him as righteousness." To conclude, as Protestantism is forced to do, that the faith of Genesis 15:6 was not the same faith as Genesis 12:3 is to make a travesty of Paul's use of Old Testament Scripture. Paul consistently juxtaposes the Genesis narratives in his writings precisely to show that they are all speaking about the same justifying faith that he wishes to bring to the debate against his Jewish opponent.

Although we will visit Abraham several more times in this discourse, for now we have been introduced to the idea that when Paul says Abraham was justified by faith, he has in view a faith which incorporates the whole of Abraham's life, a faith that believes God in spite of the circumstantial evidence that militates against believing, and a faith that envisions the ultimate glory of the heavenly kingdom. We must understand, then, that when God asks Abraham to believe, he is not merely asking him to assent to God's existence, but to believe in nothing less than the full *integrity* of God to provide for him not only in this life but in the life to come. God could make it easy for Abraham to believe by changing the circumstances and allowing Abraham to see in actuality more of what God intended. Instead, God purposely frames the situation to test Abraham's inner faithfulness. God is trying to draw something out from very deep within Abraham's personality. It will take every ounce of will-power that Abraham possesses to believe a God who seems to be leading him down a wrong path. In contrast to our first father, Adam, who did not believe in the integrity of God, Abraham must become our new father of faith. Later, we will address the supreme test of Abraham in which God asks him to sacrifice the very son that God promised, a time when perhaps Abraham is wondering just what kind of a God he is dealing with. Is he a blood-thirsty murderer who has fiendishly led Abraham along so that he could have the blood of his son, or is he a loving, kind, and benevolent God who is seeking to give his treasures to faithful men and their progeny? Abraham must believe, as Paul says in Romans 4:17, "...the God who gives life to the dead and *calls things that are not as though they were*."

Paul assures us that those who believe as Abraham did will receive the same promises as he. Paul says in Romans 4:16: "Therefore, the promise comes by faith, so that it may be by grace and may be guaranteed to all Abraham's offspring — not only to those who are of the law *but also to those who are of the faith of Abraham.*" Earlier, in Romans 4:12, Paul said: "And he is also the father of the circumcised who not only are circumcised *but also walk in the footsteps of the faith that our father Abraham* had before he was circumcised." The faith Paul is seeking from those who come after Abraham is a "walk in the footsteps of the faith that our father Abraham had..." The expression "walk in the footsteps" denotes an ongoing life of faith, a strong robust faith that has been tested and refined, a faith similar to that of Enoch's and Noah's who also "walked with God." When the New Testament uses the metaphor of "walking," it refers to an ongoing process in someone's life (cf., Gal. 5:25; 6:16). The imagery is one in which Abraham has gone before us and left his footprints in the sand, as it were, and we come after and place our feet in the impressions he has made until we reach our destination. At each impression, Abraham was tested and at each impression we are likewise tested. Either our faith is made stronger, or we succumb to doubt.[61]

Is Paul really asking us to believe in the same way Abraham believed? Or, as some suggest, is Paul simply asking us to accept Jesus into our heart and think that from then onward we are inevitably guaranteed to enter the kingdom of heaven? Does Paul expect us

---

[61] Ecclesiasticus 44:19-21 records of Abraham: "Abraham was the great father of a multitude of nations and no one has been found like him in glory. He kept the law of the Most High and entered into a covenant with him; he certified the covenant in his flesh and when he was tested he proved faithful."

to believe in the same God who tests us with seemingly impossible promises like Abraham, or do we just believe in the "alien righteousness of Christ alone" and then let God take care of the rest? We sense that it would be superfluous for Paul to describe the faith of Abraham in such vivid and exacting detail in Romans 4:17-21, and require us to "walk in the footsteps" of Abraham's faith in Romans 4:12, if this were not what he expected us to practice as well.

Paul sheds more light on this in Romans 4:23-24: "The words 'it was credited to him' were written not for him alone, but also for us to whom God will credit righteousness —*for us who believe in him* who raised Jesus our Lord from the dead." We notice here that Paul's concept of faith is not merely believing in the historical fact of Jesus' resurrection. The resurrection is certainly a grand part of our belief system, but it is not what Paul is trying to point out here. Rather, Paul specifies the one who, even Jesus said, was more important: "for us who believe ***in him***..." Paul emphasizes belief "*in him*" (God) who raised Jesus; not only on the fact that Jesus was raised. This is a crucial difference.[62] In effect, we are believing in a God who, as Paul said earlier in Romans 4:17, "gives life to the dead and calls things that are not as though they were." Abraham believed so firmly in God that he reasoned that if God allowed Isaac to die, he would then raise him from the dead (Heb. 11:19); likewise, we believe so firmly in the integrity of God that if God made his Son to die, he would then raise him from the dead. From human standards, both the resurrection of Isaac and the resurrection of Christ seem impossible. The negative influences in life lead us to doubt that such stupendous things could happen. Yet like Abraham, we believe in the integrity of God; that he does what he says he will do. This is the kind of faith that *pleases* God and it is this faith that allows us to become righteous in God's eyes, i.e., "he credits us with righteousness." He credits us with righteousness because we have shown ourselves acceptable, under his grace, by believing in God despite the circumstantial evidence all around

---

[62] Greek: "τοῖς πιστεύουσιν ἐπὶ τὸν ἐγεὶραντα Ἰησοῦν" (literally: "to those believing on the one who raised Jesus..."). The Catholic Catechism states: "Faith is first of all a personal adherence of man to God. At the same time, and inseparably, it is a free assent to the whole truth that God has revealed" (Section 150).

us that induces us not to believe in him. As Paul says in 2 Corinthians 4:13-14, "It is written: 'I believed; therefore I have spoken.' With that same spirit of faith we also believe and therefore speak, because we know that the one who raised the Lord Jesus from the dead will also raise us with Jesus..." If we have this kind of faith, a faith that *pleases* God, he will bless us with the promise he gave to Abraham. He will apply to our lives the work of his Son who was "delivered over to death for our sins and was raised to life for our justification" (Romans 4:25).[63]

What tests of faith does God give us in our lives that may resemble God's tests of Abraham? The tests are many and varied. As the apostle says in 1 Peter 1:7-9:

> These [trials] have come so that your faith...may be proved genuine and may result in praise, glory, and honor when Jesus Christ is revealed. Though you have not seen him, you love him; and even though you do not see him now, you believe in him...for you are receiving the goal of your faith, the salvation of your souls.

The supreme test of faith, of course, is believing in the things of God which cannot be seen. This is a test of faith, however, that extends over one's whole lifetime. In the face of evil, disease, persecution, poverty, discouragement, and any other negative influence, the real test of faith is manifested as one persists in believing despite all the circumstantial evidence that tells one not to believe: more specifically, in not doubting that God is who he says he is. Many, for example, ask the question: if God is so powerful, why doesn't he just make everything nice right now so we don't have to go through all this tragedy on earth? The answer is that God has a plan, a plan that takes time to work out, a plan that respects our free will, a plan that is the best possible way to rid the world of evil and bring us to eternal life. We must wait, wait on God, believing that he can and will do what he says, and will do so in the best method and most suitable timing possible for everyone involved.

---

[63] See chapter 5 for a more thorough analysis of this principle, as well as a critique of Protestant views on this passage.

That is the way Abraham believed. It is believing in a God who "calls things that are not as though they were"; a believing that requires one's whole being for one's whole lifetime.[64]

Other Heroes of Faith

As noted in the biblical accounts of Abel, Enoch, and Noah, each of these Old Testament personalities received the grace of God. Their salvation through grace is confirmed by the New Testament in Hebrews 11 and other passages.[65] This raises an important theological question. How could the saints of the Old Testament receive salvation considering the fact that Christ did not accomplish the atonement till many years after they lived on earth? The New Testament provides the answer. Although the formal establishment of the system of grace was put in place at Christ's death and resurrection, the application of the system of grace was already active before Christ came. In Romans 3:25, for example, Paul says: "God presented him as a sacrifice of atonement, through faith in his blood. He did this to demonstrate his justice, *because in his forbearance he had left the sins committed beforehand unpunished...*" This passage speaks primarily of all those who existed prior to the coming of Christ. Since the system of grace was not formally established until Christ's death and resurrection, only the *principle* of its future accomplishment could be applied to those who died before Christ. In order to include them in the redemptive plan, God held their sins in abeyance and did not punish them ac-

[64] God does not require that our faith be absolutely perfect in order to be saved. Through his grace, God accepts imperfections in both our faith and our works. In regard to faith, the Council of Trent stated in Canon 13: "If anyone shall say that it is necessary for every man in order to obtain the remission of sins to believe for certain and without any hesitation due to his own weakness and indisposition that his sins are forgiven him: let him be anathema." On the other hand, Vatican Council I maintained the distinct challenge of faith for each individual. In chapter 3 it states: "we are bound by faith to give full obedience of intellect and will to God who reveals...believe that the things revealed by him are true not because the intrinsic truth of the revealed things has been perceived by the natural light of reason, but because of the authority of God himself who reveals them, who can neither deceive nor be deceived." Such was the faith of Abraham.

[65] Ecclesiasticus 44-50 is the Old Testament counterpart to Hebrews 11.

cording to the strict standards of the law (e.g., death or eternal damnation). God put them on the shelf, as it were, until the formal accomplishment of redemption could deal with them. The Old Testament anticipated the redemption provided by Christ and based its hope for salvation on the anticipated grace provided by that salvific act. The Old Testament prophets knew that Christ's atonement and resurrection was planned by God and that it was their only hope. As Peter writes in 1 Peter 1:10-11:

> Concerning this salvation, the prophets, who spoke of the grace that was to come to you, searched intently and with the greatest care, trying to find out the time and circumstances to which the Spirit of Christ in them was pointing when he predicted the sufferings of Christ and the glories that would follow.[66]

The Faith of Noah

We have cited earlier Noah's "walk with God," and that God himself called him "righteous." Yet Noah is important for another reason. He is another example of one who believed God in spite of circumstantial evidence casting doubt on God's integrity. Surrounded by the utter wickedness of his day, Noah is told to build an ark to save humanity. Facing Noah is the task of building a ship approximately the size of a contemporary football stadium, in the midst of

---

66 The Church also holds as dogma that the souls of most Old Testament saints were released from "Sheol" (Hebrew: שאול) or "Hades" (Greek: ᾅδης) when Christ visited this realm immediately after his death, in accord with the statement in the Apostles Creed "he descended into hell." The descent into Sheol or Hades corresponds to other Scriptures which refer to the conscious abode of the dead, both righteous and unrighteous, before the resurrection of Christ, e.g., "he went and preached to the spirits in prison" (1 Peter 3:19); "the gospel was preached even to those who are now dead" (1 Peter 4:6); "the heart of the earth" (Matthew 12:40); "Abraham's bosom" (Luke 16:22-26); "the dead will hear the voice of the Son of God...and live" (John 5:25); "the bodies of many holy people who had died were raised to life" (Matthew 27:52-53); "he also descended to the lower, earthly regions" (Ephesians 4:9); "you and your sons will be with me" (1 Samuel 28:19); "consign to the earth below...with those who go down to the pit" (Ezekiel 32:18ff); "he leads down to Hades" (Tobit 13:2); "the dominion of Hades" (Wisdom 1:14; 2:1; 16:13). These interpretations were upheld at the Council of Rome (745 AD; DS 587); the Council of Toledo (625 AD; DS 485). See Catholic Catechism, Sections 631-635.

a barren wasteland with not a drop of rain in sight. According to the Genesis record, Noah may have been building the ark for 120 years (Genesis 6:3). We can imagine the jeers and ridicule the people of his day must have heaped upon him. If it rained for short spans before the Flood, we can imagine the mockery that filled Noah's ears every time it stopped: "Was that the big flood, Noah?" At these times Noah could only take his solace in God. Year after year, the circumstantial evidence must have mounted against God. Genesis does not record that God ever spoke to Noah again until the 120 years were over. For Noah's enduring faith, God testified to Noah's righteousness, a continuation of the righteousness he must have displayed long before the Flood (Genesis 6:9).

The Faith of Habakkuk

One of the most important passages in Paul's writings concerning the type of faith God requires is Romans 1:17: "For in it [the gospel] a righteousness of God is revealed from faith to faith, as it is written, 'the just man by faith will live.'" Though we have earlier studied this passage, we need to revisit this text for a more thorough understanding of the faith God desires from us. Habakkuk 2:4, from which Paul quotes in Romans 1:17, asserts that "the just man by his faith [or faithfulness] will live." Since the verse is expressing the type of faith one must live by in order to be justified, Paul's sudden spotlighting of Habakkuk becomes very important in the whole discussion of justification. Habakkuk, however, is a somewhat obscure and small book of the Old Testament. On the surface it does not seem to have too much to say about justification by faith. Nowhere else does the Old Testament mention the prophet Habakkuk, his particular era of prophecy, his birthplace, or his parentage. One who has not been alerted to the relevance of Habakkuk in the discussion of faith and justification might skip right over the book without a second thought. In fact, one might wonder if indeed Habakkuk was the best book from which Paul should quote to support his teaching of the nature of faith. Yet as obscure as Habakkuk is, its significance is heightened in that he is quoted three times in the New Testament (Rom. 1:17; Gal. 3:11; Heb. 10:37-38). Only a handful of Old Testament passages share this distinction. We will understand its significance when we examine the whole context of what prompted Habakkuk to write such a simple yet powerful statement: "the just shall live by his faith."

The reason the book of Habakkuk is so important to the discussion of faith is that, in actuality, the prophet *himself* is the man of great faith spoken of in the biblical text. Habakkuk's faith was the type that continued from one moment to the next, i.e., from "faith to faith," did not seek to obligate God through law, and a faith that endured to the end. Similar to Abraham, it was a faith that had to believe in God despite the circumstantial evidence surrounding him that suggested that God really wasn't fair or didn't know what he was doing.

As the book opens, Habakkuk is complaining that God seems to ignore the evildoers of that day. Habakkuk complains that the Jews go on their merry way cutting a swath of destruction and violence in their path and persecuting the righteous (Hab. 1:1-4). After Habakkuk registers his complaint, God answers him. The Lord says that in a little while he is going to send the Babylonians to punish Israel. God remarks that the Babylonians are feared and dreaded as if to impress Habakkuk with the anticipated outcome (Hab. 1:5-11). Habakkuk retorts, however, that it seems unjust for God to use the Babylonians, who are themselves a wicked people, to punish wicked Israel. Why doesn't God punish the Babylonians, too? (cf., Hab. 1:12-2:1). Habakkuk waits for a reply. The Lord answers by enumerating all the sins and treachery of the Babylonians throughout the years. For their wickedness, God says that he will punish them too (Hab. 2:2-20). In the midst of his explanation to Habakkuk, chapter 2:4 (the verse in question), the Lord says, "see he is puffed up his desires are not upright...but the righteous will live by his faith." We understand that it is the Babylonians who are "puffed up" and "not upright," but that Habakkuk must "live by faith" in spite of their haughtiness. God will use the Babylonians to accomplish his purposes to punish Israel, but in the end he will destroy the Babylonians too. The challenge for Habakkuk is that he must wait on God's timing, however long it may seem, to punish *both* Israel and the Babylonians. He teaches Habakkuk this truth in 2:3: "For the revelation awaits an appointed time; it speaks of the end and will not prove false. Though it linger, wait for it; it will certainly come and will not delay."

This is the real test of faith for Habakkuk. He sees all the sin around him that at that very instant is worthy of severe punishment. He sees righteous people being killed, maligned, extorted, and afflicted by the wicked Israelites. The temptation is to think that God doesn't care; that he has given up on them; that he is insensitive to their plight; in short, that he is not the God he claims to be. Like Abraham, Habakkuk must not "weaken in his faith" nor "waver in unbelief regarding the promise of God" (Romans 4:19-20). Habakkuk must be "fully persuaded that God had power to do what he promised" (Romans 4:21). Habakkuk must realize that God has his reasons for holding back judgment. One reason for God's delay is a principle he established long ago in his dealing with man, one which holds God back from destroying man until his iniquity reaches its full measure (cf., Genesis 15:16; 2 Maccabees 6:14; 1 Thess. 2:16).

In the end, Habakkuk shows great faith in God. Habakkuk 3:1-19 records how he reminds himself of all that he knows of God from the past; of God's ancient fame and awesome deeds. He prays that God would bring these mighty deeds to his own day. To confirm that eventuality, God shows him a vision of his wonderful works. The vision, which Habakkuk describes in vivid detail, convinces him that God's wrath will surely come. The precise timing he does not know, but it will come. Until then he must live in faith, believing in God's integrity and that God does care for his righteous people.

From this assortment of personalities, we see that Paul picks examples of men (e.g., Abraham and Habakkuk), who believed God in spite of all the evidence that would cast doubt on God's integrity. Moreover, as with Abraham's faith recorded in Genesis 15:6, Habakkuk's faith in Habakkuk 2:4 does not represent the first time he believed in God. Habakkuk lived a life of faith. To use Paul's phrase in Romans 1:17, Habakkuk lived "from faith to faith," that is, from one moment or test of faith to the next, until his last breath.[67]

---

[67] Jerome: "Rather, he says the just man lives by faith. He implies thereby that whoever would be faithful and would conduct his life according to the faith can in no other way arrive at the faith or live in it except first he be a just man of pure life, coming to faith as it were by certain degrees" (PL 26, 2, 3, 11).

Other Descriptions of Faith by Paul

In what other ways does Paul describe how faith works in salvation? One of his more succinct teachings is found in Galatians 5:6: "For in Christ Jesus neither circumcision nor uncircumcision has any value. The only thing that counts is *faith expressing itself through love.*"[68] Here Paul defines and qualifies the faith he had described earlier in the epistle. Faith and love are coupled together in what seems to be an inseparable bond. In regard to justification, love is not portrayed as a mere appendage of faith but a necessary element and addition to faith. Paul supports this notion as he develops the theme of love just eight verses later in Galatians 5:14: "The entire law is summed up in a single command: "*Love* your neighbor as yourself."

Even more important regarding the intimate bond Paul creates between faith and love is that he describes this bond as the only way to obtain salvation. This is more apparent in Galatians 5:2-3 as Paul contrasts "faith working in love" with "law" which cannot save. Paul is not only clarifying the *negative* by pitting faith against law, he is also bringing forth the *positive* which is faith working in love. Since Paul is concerned in this context with how one is justified, this places the bond between faith and love as indispensable to salvation. Faith is a superlative virtue, but it is not supreme, nor is it alone in the salvation of man. It is no surprise, then, when Paul says in 1 Corinthians 13:2,13: "...and if I have faith that can move mountains, but have not love, I am nothing...of faith, hope, and love, the greatest of these is love."

An interesting characteristic of Paul's focus on the bond of faith and love is the way he introduces the pairing with the phrase, "...neither circumcision nor uncircumcision has any value..." He uses this wording several times in his epistles. Paul first used it in 1 Corinthians 7:19: "Circumcision is nothing and uncircumcision is nothing. Keeping God's commandments is what counts." This

---

[68] A more literal translation would be "but faith working through love." Moreover, translations denoting the middle voice of ἐνεργουμένη ("working") could just as well be passive since both have the same form in Greek. The passive would denote that faith is being formed or acted upon by love. The passive voice of ἐνεργουμένη however, is not frequently used in the New Testament.

language is identical to Galatians 5:6, except that *faith working in love* now becomes *keeping God's commandments*. This should be no surprise at all. As noted above, Paul mentions the commandments of God in Galatians 5:14 ("love your neighbor as yourself") right in the context of "faith working in love." To Paul, there is no better expression of love than keeping God's commandments. If we love our neighbor we will not kill him, steal from him, commit adultery against him, etc.

But Paul requires more than just *not* doing evil to our neighbor. If we refrain from harming our neighbor we have only loved him half-way. Love also seeks to help our neighbor in a positive way. Paul carries this concept through in other usages of the "neither circumcision nor uncircumcision" phrasing in Galatians 6:15: "Neither circumcision nor uncircumcision means anything; what counts is a *new creation*." In this passage, "*faith working through love*" from Galatians 5:6 and "*keeping God's commandment*" from 1 Corinthians 7:19 now becomes "*a new creation*." The phrase "new creation" appears one other place, in 2 Corinthians 5:17, which is a context prefaced by the statement, "...those who live should no longer live for themselves...", referring again to the principle of loving a neighbor as one loves himself. Moreover, Paul describes the "new creation" in Galatians 5:16 through 6:10 as being a "life by the Spirit." In other words, living by the Spirit is a new life of faith working in love and keeping God's commandments.

Paul couples faith and love in other epistles. In Ephesians 6:23 he writes: "Peace to the brothers, and love with faith from God the Father and the Lord Jesus Christ." The following passages show the same connection between faith and love: Colossians 1:4-5: "...because we have heard of your faith in Christ Jesus and of the love you have for all the saints — the faith and love that spring from the hope that is stored up for you in heaven...and in the word of truth, the gospel..."; 1 Thessalonians 1:3: "...your work produced by faith, your labor prompted by love..."; 1 Thessalonians 3:6: "But Timothy...has brought good news about your faith and love"; 1 Thessalonians 5:8: "putting on faith and love as a breastplate..."; 1 Timothy 1:14: "The grace of our Lord was poured out on me abundantly, along with the faith and love that are in Christ Jesus"; 2 Timothy 1:13: "...keep as the pattern of sound teaching, with faith and love in Christ Jesus." 2 Timothy 3:10: "You, however, know all about my teaching, my way of life, my purpose, faith, patience, love..." Titus 2:2: "...sound in faith, in love and in endurance." Philemon 5: "because I hear about your faith in the Lord Jesus and your love for all the saints." In witnessing the inseparable bond Paul creates between faith and love, we can understand why in Galatians 5:6 he insists that only faith working through love can justify an individual, not faith alone.

The Principles of the Law

Although Paul condemns living under the *system* of law for salvation, he does not condemn living by the *principles* of law for salvation. The phrases we are using ("under the *system* of law" and "by the *principles* of law") are significant, and thus they must be properly understood. The phrase "under the system of law" signifies that one is being judged by the strict demands of law, standards which will show no mercy and will eventually condemn him. In contrast, the phrase "by the *principles* of law" signifies that one is striving to live by the *intent* of the law and is doing so by the power of the Spirit that lives in him. The exacting standards of law will not judge him because God is viewing and judging him from within the realm of grace. We must understand, then, that Paul uses "law" from two perspectives. One way condemns, the other saves, depending upon the perspective from which law is viewed.

That Paul requires obedience to the law for salvation is noted in the context of Romans 8:4: "In order that the *righteous requirements of the law* might be fully met in us, who do not live according to the sinful nature but according to the Spirit." A Protestant might be predisposed to see the *fulfilling of the righteous requirements of the law* as applying only to the work of Christ, that is, Christ's work in the atonement fulfills all the requirements of law. The result of that work is said to be "imputed" to us so that we then fulfill the law simply by believing in Christ. This is at best a half-truth. Coupling the first half of Romans 8:4 with the second half, it should be obvious that Paul is not referring to an imputation of righteousness. On the contrary, Paul points out that the requirements of the law are met specifically by *those who live according to the Spirit.*[69] It is they who are doing the "*fulfilling*" in this verse, not Christ. How do they fulfill the requirements of the law and live according to the Spirit? This is answered in verse 7: "...the sinful mind is hostile to God. It does not submit to God's law, nor can it do so." Here we see that whether or not one "*submits to God's law*" is the criterion to judge if he is living by the sinful nature or living by the Spirit. Hence, one fulfills the requirements of the law by simply obeying the law.[70] Consequently, if one deliberately does not submit to obeying the principles of God's law, then he will come under the full weight of the law and be condemned by it. In effect, God takes him out of the system of grace and resubmits him to the system of law.

Pleasing God Under His Grace

Although God views the actions of those who seek him from the perspective of grace, nevertheless he expects a high degree of obedience that is *pleasing* to him.[71] The principle of pleasing God is no better stated than in Hebrews 11:6 — the very passage that speaks of faith: "And without faith it is impossible to *please* God,

---

69 The NIV translation of Romans 8:4: "the righteousness of the law *might be fully met* in us, who do not live..." can be more literally translated "the righteousness of the law *may be fulfille*d in us who do not live..." (ἵνα τὸ δικαίωμα τοῦ νόμου πληρωθῇ ἐν ἡμῖν). The NIV's translation of the subjunctive πληρωθῇ as "fully met," with a comma to set off "who do not live" from the subjunctive clause, implies that only Christ has a part in "fully meeting" the requirement of the law, and that "those who live by the Spirit" are mere receptacles of this accomplished fact.

70 Catholic Catechism, Section 782: "Its law is the new commandment to love as Christ loved us.' This is the 'new' law of the Holy Spirit (f. 205: Rom 8:2; Gal 5:25)." "The Law of the Gospel *fulfills the commandment* of the Law...The Gospel thus brings the Law to its fulness through imitation of the perfection of the heavenly Father...The New Law is called a *law of love* because it makes us act out of the love infused by the Holy Spirit, rather than from fear; a *law of grace*, because it confers the strength of grace to act, by means of faith and the sacraments; a *law of freedom*, because it sets us free from the ritual and juridical observances of the Old Law..." (CC, Sections 1968, 1972).

71 Thomas Aquinas, one of the major developers of this concept in Catholic soteriology, believed that man is righteous by means of grace, making him pleasing before God *(Summa Theologica*, I-II, Q. 111, Art 1). In addition, Aquinas defended logically the definition of faith given in Hebrews 11:6 (*Summa Theologica*, II-II, Q. 4, Art. 1).

because anyone who comes to him must believe that he exists and that he rewards those who earnestly seek him." Obviously, the focus of Paul is on what "pleases" God. While this is not a strict legal relationship, nevertheless, this passage denotes that God desires sincere and sustained effort from those who want to know him and please him. By the same token, however, God is not portrayed as an ogre to whom nothing is acceptable.

Just prior to enunciating the principle of *pleasing* God, Paul gives an illustration of one man that did this very thing. In Hebrews 11:5 he writes: "By faith Enoch was taken from this life, so that he did not experience death; he could not be found, because God had taken him away. For before he was taken, he was commended as one who *pleased* God." Ecclesiasticus 44:16; 49:14 records: "Enoch pleased the Lord and was taken up, an example of repentance to all generations...Few have ever been created on earth like Enoch"; and Genesis 5:24: "Enoch walked with God; then he was no more because *God took him away*." Clearly the "taking away" of Enoch is due directly to the fact that he "walked" with God, since the first statement is in immediate proximity to the second. According to Paul's view, his "walking" describes his lifestyle that "pleased God." It shows that God and Enoch had a daily and intimate relationship. Yes, Enoch was a sinner and had no claims on God. In fact, Sirach tells us that it was the *repentance* of Enoch that stood out as the example to all generations. Like everyone else, he was saved by grace. God was not obligated to bless Enoch. Yet Enoch lived such a life of faith and holiness that God, being the personal being that he is, was *so well-pleased* with Enoch that he couldn't resist taking him to himself, something that we do not find explicitly recorded of anyone one else in Scripture, except, perhaps, Elijah.

In this text Paul mentions two facets of the faith that pleases God: 1) One must believe that God exists, and 2) that he rewards those who diligently seek him. The former is the beginning; the latter is the continuation. Of the two descriptions, it is significant for our purposes that Paul specifies the faith which pleases God is the kind that believes God *rewards* those who seek him. This speaks implicitly of a gratuitous relationship between God and his followers. God is pleased by man's seeking and subsequently rewards him. Moreover, the "seeking" is not to be confined to those who already have become Christians. It can be applied to those initially seeking God. God is not obligated to reward them but does so because he loves them and has mercy on them.

Pleasing God is a concept taught throughout Scripture: "When a man's ways are *pleasing* to the Lord he makes even his enemies live at peace with him" (Proverbs 16:7); "...offer your bodies as living sacrifices, holy and *pleasing* to God...approve what God's will is — his good, *pleasing* and perfect will" (Romans 12:1-2); "So we make it our goal to *please* him, whether we are at home in the body or away from it. For we must all appear before the judgment seat of Christ..." (2 Cor. 5:9-10)[72]; "...and find out what *pleases* the Lord." (Ephesians 5:10); "...an acceptable sacrifice, *pleasing* to God." (Philippians 4:18); "And we pray this in order that you may live a life worthy of the Lord and may *please* him in every way: bearing fruit in every good work..." (Colossians 1:10); "Children, obey your parents in everything, for this *pleases* the Lord" (Colossians 3:20); "We are not trying to *please* men but God, who tests our hearts" (1 Thess. 2:4); "...Because we obey his commands and do what *pleases* him" (1 John 3:22); "And do not forget to do good and to share with others, for with such sacrifices God is *pleased*" (Hebrews 13:16); "...and may work in us what is *pleasing* to him" (Hebrews 13:21). The same language is also used in the negative sense to describe those who are evil: "Those controlled by the sinful nature *cannot please* God" (Romans 8:8), or, "Nevertheless, God was *not pleased* with most of them; their bodies were scattered over the desert" (1 Corinthians 10:5). "The thing that David had done *displeased* the Lord" (2 Sam. 11:27). "The one whose service is pleasing to the Lord will be accepted, and his prayer will reach to the clouds" (Ecclesiasticus 35:20; 45:19). "To the man who pleases him God gives wisdom, knowledge and happiness; but to the sinner he gives the task of gathering and storing up wealth to

72 In 2 Cor. 5:9-10, the "pleasing" of God is tied in with the "judgment seat of Christ" at which time our final salvation will be affirmed or denied. This underscores the connection between "pleasing" God and our final justification. See also Hebrews 12:28, "so worship God *acceptably* (Greek cognate of εὐαρέστως, i.e., "pleasing") with reverence and awe, for our God is a consuming fire." The dimension concerning our pleasing of God and his judgment of us will be covered in more detail in Chapter 8: "The Final Justification."

hand it over to the one who pleases God" (Ecclesiastes 2:26).

In all of these passages we notice that there is a high level of faith and obedience expected by God from those who seek him and decide to follow him. We must fight against the sinful nature, and in turn, live by the Spirit. As we move on in our walk with God, the more faith we exercise and the more good works we do, the more God is pleased with us. God evaluates us by how we are living by the law of the Spirit. If we live by the Spirit, repenting each time we sin; loving God and our neighbor with all diligence, God is pleased by such faith and good works, even as he was with Enoch. Such individuals are "just" before God.

To clarify and understand the necessity of faith sufficient to please God, yet a faith which, if it is outside of God's grace cannot provide justification, it would be beneficial at this point to address an opposing position. Representing the Protestant concept, John Calvin writes:

> James follows his practice and declares that Rahab was justified by works...For our part we deny that there is any question here of attaining righteousness. We agree that good works are required of righteousness, but we do not allow them the power of conferring it, *since at God's tribunal they must draw back.*[73]

[73] Calvin's New Testament Commentary, *The Epistle of James*, Vol. 3, 1972, p. 287. Similarly, Evangelical James White asserts: "No human merit, even that supposedly produced by human works performed in a state of grace, will ever stand before the judgment throne of God" *(The Roman Catholic Controversy*, p. 151). Evangelical Donald Bloesch continues the same argumentation as Calvin: "...no Christian can merit God's favor. Base motivations always accompany godly motivations and thereby render us unworthy in the sight of God on the basis of our own goodness" *(Roman Catholicism: Evangelical Protestants Analyze What Divides and Unites Us*, op. cit., p. 151). Bloesch's comments are typical of the trumpery Reformed Evangelicals use to save the last vestiges of *faith alone* theology, making it look as if Catholic theology teaches that God accepts us *based* (Bloesch's own word) on our own merit and goodness. The Catholic Church has never taught this. The acceptance of our goodness is *based* on God's grace, the grace provided by the atonement of Christ. Much of Bloesch's essay, which is an attempt to discredit Catholic soteriology by pointing out its supposed amalgamation with Hellenistic philosophy, is a perfect example of how a theologically biased position, a millennium and a half removed from history, can pick and choose what elements it will

Here Calvin specifies the Protestant opposition to the concept of justification by works. The main objection: works cannot stand before the tribunal of God, thus they cannot be included in justification. In other words, because Calvin assumes that God must judge works by his perfect standard of righteousness, all works will come short of his perfection and thus be unworthy for justification before a holy God. Yet it is here that Calvin inadvertently exposes a fundamental flaw in Protestant theology. We will grant that no work of man could ever withstand the *tribunal of God*, if by *tribunal* we mean God's perfect standard of righteousness. What Calvin fails to see, however, is that the same principle would have to be true of faith. Protestant theology holds that God does not just accept any kind of faith. But whether it is weak or strong, no degree of faith could ever withstand the tribunal of God. If God were to judge us by his perfect standards, our faith would never be acceptable to

73 cont. favor and what elements it will disregard. Bloesch makes one generalization after another, taking the speculations and complexities of Catholic theology and turning them into the official Catholic dogma of that period. In the end, Bloesch portrays the Church Fathers and the theologians of the medieval period as theological ignoramuses who had neither the intellectual capacity nor the guidance of the Spirit to separate Platonic or Aristotelian thought from the Christian gospel. As might be expected, Bloesch feels that the only intellectual and spiritual heroes were the Protestant Reformers. Ironically, however, he admits that their beaming light faded just a century later when he laments that Protestantism became "semi-Pelagian." This is where most Reformed Evangelicals end up, maintaining that only in the years of the high Reformation did men understand and teach the pure gospel (and that despite the major differences in soteriology among the original Reformers themselves). An additional irony is Bloesch's assertion that, in contrast to Catholic theology, "Reformation theology stressed the descent of God to the sinful human condition" (ibid., p. 151). Apparently, then, God did not *descend* until the Reformation period, despite Jesus' assurance from the beginning that the Holy Spirit would descend upon the Church, lead her into all truth, and be with her till the end of time (John 14:15-18; 16:13-15; Matt. 28:20). It is also puzzling that Bloesch refers to Søren Kierkegaard and Deitrich Bonhoffer as modern prophets who are to lead us back to "other-worldliness and grace-alone theology" (ibid., p. 154), even though these Protestant theologians were two of the chief leaders of the theological liberalism of their day which denied major soteriological teachings of the Reformation. Such conclusions are indicative of the total confusion within Evangelical thought, even among those who claim to advance its traditional ideas. See chapter 9 for more commentary on this issue.

him.[74] It is only when God looks at us through the eyes of grace that he can accept our faith. Similarly, works that justify are also looked upon through the eyes of God's grace. We have neither perfect works nor perfect faith, nevertheless, faith and works that justify are *pleasing* to God because God graciously accepts them, just as a father is pleased with the faith and works of his children even though they are imperfect. What kind of faith and works please God? The same faith and works that Abraham had. Though he sometimes faltered both in his faith and works, Abraham sufficiently "pleased" God, as did Habakkuk and many other heroes of the faith (Hebrews 11:1ff). Sincere and enduring faith is the faith that pleases God (Hebrews 10:36-38; 12:1-2). We have his promise, however, that he will not test our faith beyond our strength to endure (cf., 1 Cor. 10:13; 2 Pet. 2:9).

The Protestant may counter with the objection that the individual's faith only "apprehends the righteousness of Christ" and therefore he is not subject to the *tribunal of God.* Christ meets God at the tribunal for him. But such reasoning allows Protestantism no escape. Calvin, as well as the Protestantism that followed him, admit that the faith of the individual must be of a *sufficient quality* in order for God to allow the apprehension of Christ's righteousness.[75] Accordingly, Protestant interpretations of the Epistle of James conclude that works must play a primary role in determining what *kind* of faith is possessed by the individual. It is commonly called "*saving faith.*" If this is true, then who but God can judge whether this so-called "saving faith" is indeed sufficient to allow the apprehension of Christ's righteousness? Moreover, since there is no one else but God to judge faith's quality, would the Protestant say that God makes such a judgment from his "tribunal of perfection" or does he do so from his "gracious forbearance"? Surely, no one's faith is sufficiently perfect to satisfy the standards of God's tribunal. God must accept the imperfect quality of the

---

[74] This is why the Council of Trent goes beyond the claims of the Reformation by insisting that "*none* of those things which precede justification, whether faith, or works, merit the grace of justification." Session 6, Chapter 8. See chapter 5 of this book for additional critique on the Protestant view of faith.

[75] Calvin: *Acts of the Council of Trent*, 3:152. See also *Faith Alone*, Sproul, op. cit., Chapters 4-8.

faith based on his grace and mercy. However, the corollary must also be true. If God can accept faith by his grace and mercy, then he can also accept works in the same way. The Protestant may object further that faith is merely a "gift" of God and not subject to judgment. He is attempting to shift the burden away from the individual and place it on God alone.[76] This hypothesis, however, will allow no escape from the theological corner into which he has painted himself, since Scripture is clear that everything in salvation is a gift, including the mental capacity of faith and the power to do the works that please God (Philippians 2:12-13; Ephesians 2:8-9).[77] In light of this argument, we must conclude that there is no justifiable reason to deny that both faith and works are necessary for justification, without any contradiction whatsoever, since both must be evaluated under the auspices of God's grace. More details of these truths will be covered in chapter 5.

The Concept of "Gracious Merit" in Scripture

At this point, we will investigate other support Scripture supplies concerning the concept of *gracious merit* we have just introduced.[78] For evidence, we can start with Hebrews 11. It gives us the running commentary of the many Old Testament personalities

---

76 Beeke, *Justification By Faith Alone*, op. cit., p. 64.

77 Augustine: "What merit, then, does a man have before grace, by which he might receive grace, when our every good merit is produced in us only by grace, and, when God, crowning our merits, crowns nothing else but His one gift to us" (*Letter of Augustine to Sixtus*, JR 1452). See also, Council of Trent, Session 6, Chapter 16; Catholic Catechism, section 2001. We have also seen earlier in the exegesis of Ephesians 2:8 that the Greek neuter demonstrative pronoun "this" (Greek: τοῦτο) encompasses the whole of salvation, not only faith, as the gift of God.

78 "Let your works be as your deposited withholdings, so that you may receive the back-pay which has accrued to you" (Ignatius of Antioch, *Letter to Polycarp,* PG 5, 6, 2); "...good rewards are distributed according to the merit of each man's actions" (Justin Martyr, *First Apology*, PG 6, 43); "so that we may receive a crown, and so that we may regard as a precious crown that which we acquire by our own struggle, and which does not grow on us spontaneously..." (Irenaeus, *Against Heresies*, PG 7, 4, 37, 7). God "viewing through grace" may correspond to "uncreated grace" in scholastic theology. (See Avery Dulles, *Justification by Faith: Lutherans and Catholics in Dialogue* VII, p. 258f; Karl Rahner, "Some Implications of the Scholastic Concept of Uncreated Grace," p. 319f.

whose faith and works were accepted by God and rewarded with eternal life. For example, Hebrews 11:4 says of Abel: "By faith, Abel offered God a better sacrifice than Cain did. By faith he was commended as a righteous man, when God spoke well of his offerings." Genesis 4:4-5 specifies how God was able to speak well of Abel: "The Lord *looked with grace* on Abel and his offering, but on Cain and his offering he *did not look with grace*." Here we are introduced to the specific phrase "looked with grace." In effect, because of his gracious viewing of Abel's faith and work, God is personally pleased with Abel and states that he produced a "better sacrifice" than Cain. Apparently, Abel had built a strong relationship with God which allowed God to look with favor upon his sincere offering. God, in strict terms, certainly did not owe anything to Abel. Abel could never attain to the perfect righteousness demanded by the law and the standard of God's perfection. Yet within the realm of God's grace, which anticipates redeeming Abel from the curse of sin by the atonement of Christ, God can look upon the intent of Abel's heart and the subsequent manifestation of his good works, graciously making these the criteria which determine the degree to which Abel pleases God and therefore the kind of blessing God will give him.

As noted above, a significant feature of this account is the specific language chosen by the writer to describe how God views Abel. The words "looked with grace" are translated literally from the Hebrew text, thus we are certain that the issue at hand is the specific way God perceives Abel.[79] This denotes a specific *frame of reference* from which God evaluates and responds to Abel. Previously we had used the terms *system of grace* as opposed to *system of law*. Now we can see clearly that the system of grace corresponds to the way in which God graciously looks upon us or the gracious standards God uses to evaluate us. Through his grace, God can "look upon" our works as both pleasing to him and worthy of his blessing, since this particular system does not demand absolute perfection nor put God in a position of obligation.

---

[79] The words "looked with grace" are from the Hebrew word שׁעה which is used in the Hebrew Qal form twelve times with reference to "look at," "look with expectation," or "look with favor"[i.e., grace], in the Old Testament. It is as if God puts on the spectacles of grace before he looks upon man.

In the same text, Paul mentions another man of great faith, namely, Noah (Hebrews 11:7): "By faith, Noah, when warned about the things not yet seen, in holy fear built an ark to save his family. By faith he condemned the world and became heir of the righteousness that comes by faith." Genesis 6:8-9 reads: "But Noah *found grace in the eyes of the Lord*...Noah was a righteous man, blameless among the people of his time, and he walked with God." In Ecclesiasticus 44:17 it states: "Noah was found perfect and righteous; in the time of wrath he kept the race alive..." We notice here even more pertinent language regarding gracious merit. The context indicates that God, who was about to destroy the whole world because of its unrepentant wickedness, views Noah as a "a righteous man, blameless among the people of his time." Genesis 7:1 is even more direct: the sacred author quotes God directly as saying, "because I have found you righteous in this generation." It is God who claims to be making the judgment about Noah's righteousness, and it is clear that it was for *Noah's* righteousness that God saved him and his family. Noah pleased God sufficiently that God, by his grace, saved Noah and his family. Within the strict limits of law and perfection, Noah could never have merited God's favor. He, like everyone else in the human race, was born in sin. But in anticipation of his setting aside of the strict demands of the law through the atonement of Christ, God could look at Noah differently. The *system of grace* through which God can look favorably upon Noah, as it was with Abel, is implied in the phrasing "in the eyes of the Lord," which, again, is a literal translation of the Hebrew text. Noah could please God by his faith and works to the point that God, under the auspices of his grace, could reward Noah with salvation.

A Protestant may object at this point that though he sees no problem with Noah's meriting of God's grace, Noah was already "saved" and thus everything he did was just part of his sanctification, not of his justification. First, this form of argumentation merely begs the question, since one must first prove that justification and sanctification are not simultaneous and continuous events. We will address this matter later. Second, we can certainly agree that the context of the Genesis passage connotes that Noah's life prior to this incident was one of holiness and faith. Thus, we can assume that Noah had received justification prior to the Flood. This fact, however, only proves our point that much more powerfully. It is the entire righteous life of Noah that God is viewing through the eyes of grace, not just one incident in which to impute him with so-called alien righteousness. It is the whole life of Noah that is pleasing to God, which, in turn, motivates God to give Noah the continued grace of salvation rather than cast him off with the wicked (cf., 2 Peter 2:5; Ezekiel 14:14). If Noah had become a wicked man some years or months prior to the incident in Genesis 6, the Scriptures teach that such a person would not have been counted as righteous (cf., Ezekiel 18:24). In receiving God's grace, the contrast set up is between those that live righteous lives in the sight of God and those who do not. The former receive the continued grace of God, the latter do not. As we will see in more detail in Chapter 4, God's saving of Noah and his family from the Flood is just another instance of the *continuing* justification in his life and the lives of all the Patriarchs.

The Psalms present an even clearer picture of the concept of gracious merit. David declares in Psalm 18:20-24:

> The Lord has dealt with me according to my righteousness; according to the cleanness of my hands he has rewarded me. For I have kept the ways of the Lord; I have not done evil by turning away from my God. All his laws are before me; I have not turned away from his decrees. I have been blameless before him and have kept myself from sin. The Lord has rewarded me according to my righteousness; according to the cleanness of my hands in his sight.

Here David refers several times to "my righteousness." There is nothing in the text to suggest that this is a legally imputed righteousness; rather, it is a personal righteousness that God can recognize through his grace, even as a father does to a son. David speaks of his personal righteousness as "the cleanness of my hands," "I have kept the ways of the Lord," "I have not done evil," "I have been blameless," and "kept myself from sin." For all these things the Lord "rewards" him.[80] If we take this language at face value, rather than

[80] See also Psalm 7:8; 26:1; 118:112 (LXX)

imposing our own theology upon it, we can see clearly that God blesses and saves David because of David's personal righteousness.

We also see gracious merit in the very beginnings of Israel's history. Deuteronomy 6:25 states: "And if we are careful to obey all this law before the Lord our God, as he has commanded us, that will be our righteousness."[81] A similar portrayal appears in Deuteronomy 24:13: "Return his cloak to him by sunset so that he may sleep in it. Then he will thank you, and it will be regarded as a righteousness in the sight of the Lord your God." The people of Israel, like the rest of the human race, were sinners in Adam, nevertheless through the eyes of grace, God can view their obedient and merciful deeds as "righteousness." God calls the deeds "righteous" not because he enjoys speaking in spiritual platitudes, but because he truly recognizes the deeds as righteous. They are ontologically righteous acts, accepted by God as righteousness. Further, these two passages encapsulate the whole law. Deuteronomy 6:25 exemplifies love of God, while Deuteronomy 24:13 exemplifies love of neighbor. It is the same kind of righteousness that Jesus requires (Matt. 22:37-40), that Paul requires (Rom. 13:9-10; Gal. 5:14), and that James requires (James 1:27, 2:8).

Salvation as a Reward

That salvation itself is understood as a "reward' is clearly evident in the New Testament.[82] As quoted previously, Hebrews 11:6

---

[81] The word "righteousness" is from the Hebrew *tsedaqah* (צדקה). For a detailed discussion of the derivation, cognates and meaning of this word, see chapter 5.

[82] Council of Trent, Session 6, Chapter 11, stated: "...in those works, in order to stimulate their own sloth and to encourage themselves to run in the race, with this in view, that above all God may be glorified, they have in view also the eternal reward, since it is written: 'I have inclined my heart to do thy justifications on account of the reward' [Psalm 118:112], and of Moses the Apostle says, that he 'looked to the reward' [Heb. 11:26];" "And therefore to those who work well 'unto the end,' and who trust in God, life eternal is to be proposed, both as a grace mercifully promised to the sons of God through Christ Jesus, 'and as a recompense' which is according to the promise of God Himself to be faithfully given to their good works and merits" (Chapter 16). See also Canons 2, 26, 32 in **Appendix 20**. See also Matthew 5:12; 10:41-42; Colossians 3:24; Hebrews 10:35; 11:26; 2 John 8; Revelation 11:18; 22:12.

states: "And without faith it is impossible to please God, because anyone who comes to him must believe that he exists and that he *rewards* those who earnestly seek him."[83] The context of Hebrews 10-11 refers not only to the earthly blessing given to those who please God but also to heavenly blessing. This is confirmed in Hebrews 10:35, in which the "reward"[84] is that which is withheld until the very end when Christ returns to fulfill the long-awaited promise:

> So do not throw away your confidence; it will be richly *rewarded*. You need to persevere so that when you have done the will of God, you will receive what he has *promised*. For in just a little while, He who is coming will come and not delay...

The heavenly reward is also confirmed by Moses's expectation of the reward as described in Hebrews 11:26: "He regarded disgrace for the sake of Christ as of greater value than the treasures of Egypt, because he was looking ahead to his reward." Similarly, Hebrews 11:10,16 describes the same promise as "...the city with foundations whose architect and builder is God...a better country, a heavenly one...for he has prepared a city for them."

Regarding the criteria for God's reward, Hebrews 6:10 says: "God is *not unjust*; he will not forget your work and the love you have shown him as you helped his people and continue to help them." Thus we see that even in God's grace there is a certain degree of *justice* upon which he rewards us as a gift. In other words, God is benevolent because it is right for him to be so. We call this *gracious merit*. Conversely, based on *strict merit*, God owes nothing to no one.

---

83 Luther often left off the latter part of Hebrews 11:6 when he quoted the verse. He wrote: "For without faith it is impossible to please God but whoever would draw near to God must believe (Heb. 11:6)" (LW, 26, 68). See chapter 9 for more detail.

84 From the Greek words μισθαποδοσία or μισθαποδοτης of the root μίσθιος (Hebrews 10:35; 11:6, 26)

Living by the Spirit

The opposition between "Spirit" and "the sinful nature" is one of Paul's major contrasts in his epistles. In Galatians 5:16-17 he says, "So I say, live by the Spirit, and you will not gratify the desires of the sinful nature. For the sinful nature desires what is contrary to the Spirit, and the Spirit what is contrary to the sinful nature." Succumbing to the sinful nature is the way to be lost, living by the Spirit is the way to be saved. We know that Paul has salvation in view when he uses the word "Spirit" since in Galatians 6:8 he issues the ultimatum of eternal life or eternal destruction depending upon one's choice of living either by the Spirit or by the sinful nature: "The one who sows to please his sinful nature, from that nature will reap destruction; the one who sows to please the Spirit, from the Spirit will reap eternal life." In Galatians 5:19, 21 Paul issues the same ultimatum: "The acts of the sinful nature are obvious...I warn you, as I did before, that those who live like this *will not inherit the kingdom of God.*"

A similar passage is Romans 8:6: "Those who live according to the sinful nature have their minds set on what that nature desires, but those who live in accordance with the Spirit have their minds set on what the Spirit desires." In Romans 8:13, Paul again concludes with the same warning as in Galatians 5:21: "For if you live *by the sinful nature, you will die*; but if by the Spirit you put to death the misdeeds of the body, you will live..."

Paul introduced the theme of the Spirit versus our sinful nature with this opening in Romans 8:1-4:

> Therefore, there is now no condemnation for those who are in Christ Jesus, because through Christ Jesus the law of the Spirit of life set me free from the law of sin and death. For what the law was powerless to do in that it was weakened by the sinful nature, God did by sending his own Son in the likeness of sinful man, in order that the righteous requirements of the law might be fully met in us, who do not live according to the sinful nature but according to the Spirit.

We understand from all of these passages that as long as one follows the ways of the Spirit and does not live according to the sinful nature, he is "in Christ Jesus" and is not under condemnation. If he goes back to living in the sinful nature, he once again comes under condemnation. As Paul said in Galatians 5:18, "But if you are led by the Spirit, you are not under the law." This means that one who lives by the Spirit will not come under the condemnation of the law. As noted earlier, the atonement and resurrection of Christ sets one free from the uncompromising and exacting system of law and places one under the auspices of God's grace. This is why Paul says above, "through Christ Jesus the law of the Spirit of life *set me free* from the law of sin and death." One system is exchanged for the other. In God's grace, we live by the Spirit, a life in which God no longer holds the absolute perfection of law over our heads. For if one is under law then he is required to do "everything written in the book of the law" without fault (Gal. 3:10). One mistake and the law will condemn him. Under the Spirit, we strive to live by God's law but if we sin we can seek repentance. God, under the principle of grace, can forgive our sin. God can provide this grace because his own Son served as a "sin offering."

Paul's Critique of Jewish Works

As one can gather from just a cursory reading of Paul's epistles, the Jewish notion of righteousness features prominently in his critique. By the time of Paul's writing, the Jews had developed a system that was so out of touch with true righteousness that it had to be condemned. Instead of obeying the principles of the law from the heart and in the Spirit, the Jews developed a system of outward performance and appearance that in the end only made them substantially more unrighteous in God's eyes. There is nothing God detests more than someone who in reality is cruel and wicked but gives a pretense of obeying the law. This hypocrisy became the plight of many in Israel.

Paul begins his indictment of the Jews in Romans 2:17-18: "Now you, if you call yourself a Jew; if you rely on the law and brag about your relationship to God; if you know his will and approve of what is superior because you are instructed by the law..." Here Paul points out their "bragging" about God and the law. This self-righteous attitude may have developed far back in their history. Deuteronomy 4:6-7 records:

> Observe them carefully, for this will show your wisdom and understanding to the nations, who will hear about all these decrees and say, "Surely this great nation is a wise and understanding people." What other nation is so great as to have their gods near them the way the Lord our God is near us whenever we pray to him?

The problem with many of the Jews was that they forgot the operative words in the above command: "observe them carefully." Instead, they thought that the mere possession of the law would show wisdom to the nations.

Paul makes his major strike against them in Romans 2:21-24:

> ...you who preach against stealing, do you steal? You who say that people should not commit adultery, do you commit adultery? You who abhor idols, do you rob temples? You who brag about the law, do you dishonor God by breaking the law. As it is written: God's name is blasphemed among the Gentiles because of you.

Earlier in the chapter, Paul remarked about the Gentiles as he described their obedience to the precepts of the law though they did not possess a codified, written law (Romans 2:14-15). The Jews possessed the law, a law written with the very finger of God, yet they disobeyed it as much as, if not more so, than the Gentiles did. After disobeying the precepts of the written law, the Jews tried to cover up it up by performing outward rituals, thus making a religion of appearance and pretense rather than substance. The chief means was the rite of circumcision. Warning against this, Paul says in Romans 2:25-27:

> Circumcision has value if you observe the law, but if you break the law, you have become as though you had not been circumcised...The one who is not circumcised physically and yet obeys the law will condemn you who even though you have the written code and circumcision, are a lawbreaker.

Paul will not allow them to elevate circumcision to a place of importance when all the while they disobey both the principles of the Ten Commandments (i.e., "the written code") and misunderstand the significance of circumcision itself. The Jew had no excuse. His own Old Testament had explained the true meaning of circumcision, a meaning that was far from what the Jews had come to understand by Paul's time.[85] Paul will not allow them to have a mere outward show of religion by parading either circumcision or the Ten Commandments in front of the world. In this way, Paul is condemning their whole system of law, not just their ceremonial observances, as a means of righteousness. This agrees with what we have discovered previously. When Paul condemns the law as a means of justification before God, he condemns the whole law — *the system of law* — not just parts of it. In order to please God, law is of value only when it is subsumed under the realm of grace.

Paul also uses the phrase "written code" in Romans 7:6-7:

> But now, by dying to what once bound us, we have been released from the law so that we serve in the new way of the Spirit, and not in the old way of the *written code*. What shall we say, then? Is the law sin? Certainly not! I would not have known what sin was except through the law. For I would not have known what coveting really was if the law had not said, "Do not covet."

We see again that the phrase *written code* refers to the moral law of God. The command against "coveting" was part of the Decalogue and thus part of the written code of ethics. The moral law is good because it tells us what sin is. Though the law cannot save, at least it tells us from what we must be saved. But there is more here. Notice that Paul contrasts the "new way of the Spirit" with the "old way of the written code." This is a similar same truth to what we saw in Paul's letter to the Galatians. There Paul set in opposition the "way of the Spirit" against the "law and the sinful nature."

The phrase *written code* appears two other places in the New Testament, both usages displaying the same contrast between Spirit

[85] cf., Deut. 10:16; 30:6; Jer. 4:4; 9:24-25; Ezk. 44:9.

and law. In 2 Corinthians 3:6, Paul writes: "He has made us ministers of a new covenant — not of the letter but of the Spirit; for the *letter* [written code] kills, but the Spirit gives life."[86] The last usage occurs in Romans 2:29: "No, a man is a Jew if he is one inwardly; and circumcision is circumcision of the heart, by the Spirit, not by the *written code*. Such a man's praise is not from men, but from God." Again, the same opposition between "Spirit" and "written code" is evident, this time with the word "heart" added to the Spirit side of the equation. What is Paul saying? Nothing different from what we have discovered earlier. Those who live by a "written code" attempt to obey the outward symbols of law without understanding the principle behind the law. Through their insincere efforts to obey the law they also attempt to obligate God to bless them. They have gotten caught up in the routine and mechanics of performance but have forgotten the intent of the law. We might say colloquially that they "couldn't see the forest for the trees." But it might be better explained by a simple illustration.

The speed limit posted in front of a school is 25 mph. This represents the law. This is a good law because it protects children crossing the street from being run over by speeding cars, and it forces drivers to check their speedometers as they enter a school zone. As Paul says in Romans 7:12, "the law is righteous and good." But the key factor in this situation is not the law but one's attitude toward the law. Do I slow down to 25 mph and stop just to avoid being ticketed by the local policeman — showing him what a "good" citizen I am — but all the while sneering at the children as they cross the street because they have delayed me in getting to my destination? Or do I slow down to 25 mph and stop because I care for the lives of the children and don't want to see them harmed by my speeding car? The answer to this question is crucial. The law says slow down and stop, but the spirit behind the law says that the life of children is precious. Obeying the law without understanding the spirit behind the law is living merely by a "written code" without any sense of love and understanding. Those who live only by the "written code" God will condemn by the "written code." If

[86] The word "letter" in the NIV is from the Greek γράμμα which is used fifteen times in the New Testament but only four times in the sense of a "written code" encompassing the whole Mosaic law.

in the analogy, for example, I travel 26 mph into a 25 mph zone, I have broken the law and an unmerciful judge would condemn me. But if I am living in the spirit of the law, even though I may go a few miles over the speed limit, the judge will not condemn me because he knows my heart and my intentions. God works with us in the same way. Under his grace, he wants us to live not by law for law's sake but by the spirit of the law. If we do, he will not bring the uncompromising standards of law against us. God, who looks graciously into our heart, is now our judge.[87] To be sure, we must *please* him, but it is as a child who pleases his father, not as a defendant who must answer to a judge.

Throughout Paul's denunciation of the legalistic practices among the Jews, one hears a constant refrain that the Jews sought God by works, not by faith. One of the more succinct passages is in Romans 9:30-32:

> What then shall we say? That the Gentiles, who did not pursue righteousness, have obtained it, a righteousness that is by faith; but Israel, who pursued a law of righteousness had not attained it. Why not? Because they pursued it not by faith but as if it were by works. As it is written: "See, I lay in Zion a stone that causes men to stumble and a rock that makes them fall, and the one who trusts in him will never be put to shame."

What does Paul mean when he says they "pursued it not by faith but as if it were by works"? Did Israel not have some faith in God? With regard to believing that God existed, Israel did have faith. With regard, however, to trusting God from their hearts, Israel's faith failed utterly. In reference to the terms of faith described in Hebrews 11:6, the Jews believed that "he exists," but they did not "diligently seek him" through his grace.[88] Examples of their lack of faith abound in the Old Testament. Unlike Abraham, the Jews simply did not believe that God would do what he promised to do. This led to a perpetual doubt about the plan and purposes of God as well as a frequent submission to sin. Paul men-

[87] Council of Trent, Session 6, Chapter 11; Canon 23.
[88] Ibid., Chapter 6.

tions a few examples in his epistles, some of the more notable passages being 1 Corinthians 10:1-11 and Hebrews 3-4. In brief, Israel's problem of unbelief started as soon as they departed Egypt for the Promised Land. Israel's sins ranged from worshiping a golden calf, to grumbling over food, to outright rebellion over their leaders, to cowering in fear before their enemies. Consequently, they were punished and humiliated by God, but however much he did so, as a whole they never seemed to learn their lesson.

In addition to the two general requirements for faith mentioned in Hebrews 11:6, the faith that pleases God has three main ingredients, all three of which Israel did not have. It goes without saying that faith is believing in what one cannot see, as Hebrews 11:1 states: "Now faith is being sure of what we hope for and certain of what we do not see. This is what the ancients were commended for." In addition, faith that pleases God grows beyond this basic definition to become: (1) a faith that lasts, (2) a faith that still believes in spite of the circumstantial evidence that tells one to doubt, and, (3) a faith that leads to obedience. God gives us enough evidence to allow us to make an intelligent decision to believe him, but then, as always, he tests that faith, sometimes rather severely. During the exodus from Egypt, for example, God gave Israel plenty of evidence that he was powerful enough to take care of them (cf., Deut. 4:32-34; 8:2,16). One of the more prominent demonstrations was the plundering of the Egyptians with ten devastating plagues. After giving such evidence of his integrity, God tested the Israelites. He called Moses up to the mountain for forty days. In the interim, the Jews lost faith in God and Moses, claiming that they were left stranded in the wilderness with no one to protect them. As a result, they made their own god out of gold and began to appeal to it for protection. Hence, their faith did not last, it did not overcome the circumstantial evidence to doubt, and it did not produce obedience. At the time they were supposed to enter the Promise Land, in Deuteronomy 1:27 the Jews said of God: "The Lord hates us, so he brought us out of Egypt to deliver us into the hands of the Amorites to destroy us. Where can we go?" This is why Paul says in 1 Corinthians 10:5: "...God was *not pleased* with most of them; their bodies were scattered over the desert."

The Jews had a rudimentary faith in God, but it was not the faith that *pleased* God and thus it was not a faith that could receive his salvation. The faith of many Jews was a mere pretense. They filled this vacuum with a system of self-effort and self-aggrandisment. Most of them were very zealous. Ironically, the more emptiness they experienced from their self-made religion, the busier they became in practicing it. Paul sums it up best in Romans 10:1-3: "For I can testify about them that they are zealous for God, but their zeal is not based on knowledge. Since they did not know the righteousness that comes from God and sought to establish their own, they did not submit to God's righteousness." Or, as Acts 21:20 records:

> ...Then they said to Paul: 'You see, brother, how many thousands of Jews have believed, and all of them are zealous for the law. They have been informed that you teach all the Jews who live among the Gentiles to turn away from Moses, telling them not to circumcise their children or live according to our customs.'

The Jews got so caught up in their self-made religion that, having lost all understanding of true faith, they clung to the only thing they had left, their outward laws and customs. This was never God's intent for them. But more than that, God is not neutral towards one who seeks a religion of *form* over *substance*. The more they ignored true righteousness and chased after the outward performance of law, the more laws God gave them. In effect, they got a taste of their own medicine. As Psalm 81:11-12 records: "But my people would not listen to me, Israel would not submit to me. So I gave them over to their stubborn hearts to follow their own devices." Or, as the prophet says in Ezekiel 20:23-26:

> Also with uplifted hand I swore to them in the desert that I would disperse them among the nations and scatter them through the countries, because they had not obeyed my laws but had rejected my decrees and desecrated my Sabbaths, and their eyes lusted after their father's idols. I also gave them over to statutes that were not good and laws they could not live by; I let them become defiled through their gifts — the sacrifice of every first-

> born — that I might fill them with horror so they would know that I am the Lord.

Again we see that Israel's problems began during their sojourn in the desert. They had disobeyed God's simple laws. As noted earlier, when God called Moses up to the mountain it was for the purpose of giving Israel the Ten Commandments. These were good and wholesome laws. Nevertheless, even the prophet Ezekiel clarifies in Ezekiel 20:13 (the same chapter in which he says God gave them statutes they could not live by): "Yet the people of Israel rebelled against me in the desert. They did not follow my decrees but rejected my laws — although the man who obeys them will live by them — and they utterly desecrated my Sabbaths."

If Israel had obeyed God, they would have been blessed. The clause in the above quote, "although the man who obeys them will live by them" is taken from Leviticus 18:5, the same passage Paul had quoted in Galatians 3:12. There, with reference to the general antithesis between law and grace, Paul had used Leviticus 18:5 to show that unless one obeyed the law perfectly he could not be justified by law. In studying the Leviticus passage more closely, however, we do not see the same condemnation of the law as we see in Paul's writing. In fact, the passage implies that God expects obedience to the law and will bless them for it. The context of the passage implies this. Leviticus 18:1-5 records these words:

> Speak to the Israelites and say to them: I am the Lord your God. You must not do as they do in Egypt, where you used to live, and you must not do as they do in the land of Canaan, where I am bringing you. Do not follow their practices. You must obey my laws and be careful to follow my decrees...Keep my decrees and laws, *for the man who obeys them will live by them.* I am the Lord.

Here it is clear that in contrast to the evil ways of the nations, God really desires and expects Israel to obey his laws. God was always ready to bless those who lived by his laws. Moses, Joshua, Caleb and many others were all obedient to God's laws and thus they pleased God. The law itself stated that God would bless obedience. For example, in Deuteronomy 28, God specifies all the good things the Israelites would experience if they were faithful and obedient (Deut. 28:1-14). In giving his commands and blessings, God knows that men are not perfect. They will sin from time to time, but obedience to God's law presupposed that God was not going to strike them dead for every minor offense against the law. Even Moses, who, in Numbers 12:3 was deemed "more humble than anyone else on the face of the earth," and had shown God his righteous character throughout his life, was not allowed to enter the Promised Land because of an instance in not trusting God.[89] Hence, in the Old Testament, God gave his grace and mercy for those who trusted in him and humbly sought his ways, even though they were not absolutely perfect in doing so.

In Deuteronomy 4:40, Moses says: "Keep his decrees and commands, which I am giving you today, so that it may go well with you and your children after you and *that you may live long in the land* the Lord your God gives you for all time." (cf., Deut. 5:16,33; 6:3,18; 30:16; Eph 6:2-3). Accordingly, the basic laws that God expected them to live by were not too difficult for them to keep. As long as man is willing to obey, God does not give laws that man will not be able to obey. He does not ask man to do anything that man does not have the power to do.[90] Deuteronomy 30:9-11 records:

> The Lord will again delight in you and make you prosperous, just as he delighted in your fathers, if you obey the Lord your God and keep his commands and decrees that are written in this Book of the Law and turn to the Lord your God with all your heart and with all your soul. Now what I am commanding you today *is not too difficult for you or beyond your reach.*

On the one hand, Deuteronomy 30:9-11 tells us that the laws God gave Israel were "not too difficult." On the other hand, Ezekiel

---

89 cf., Numbers 20:9-13; 27:14; Psalm 106:32-33.

90 Council of Trent, Session 6, Chapter 11 states: "'For God does not command impossibilities, but by commanding admonishes you both to do what you can do, and to pray for what you cannot do, and assists you that you may be able,' 'whose commandments are not heavy,' 'whose yoke is sweet and whose burden is light.'" In contrast, Luther wrote: "the moral duties it enjoined were impossible of fulfillment and incited not love, but hatred of God." ["Lex summum odium Dei affert" that is, "the law brings the greatest hatred of God"]. Patrick O'hare, *Luther*, p. 108.

records of God: "I gave them over to statutes that...they could not live by" (Ezekiel 20:25). We see in these opposing principles the dynamic of God's dealing with his people. God is never sitting by the sidelines. If one does not obey the basic commandments of the Lord, (e.g., "love the Lord and your neighbor as yourself" as summed up in the Ten Commandments), but instead bases his life on a mere "written code" of law rather than faith and obedience, then God will give a more extensive written code; laws that are burdensome; laws that God never intended to exist. Soon the law becomes a spiraling trap, an endless accumulation of ordinances and regulations, and the Jew in his blindness makes a religion out of them.

We also see this dynamic relationship between God and his people in whether or not he opens one's understanding. Deuteronomy 29:4 states: "But to this day the Lord has not given you a mind that understands or eyes that see or ears that hear." In the face of deliberate or prolonged disobedience, God may blind one to the truth or withhold understanding. God will allow such offenders to pursue paths that are not good and things that are not productive. What they want, God will give them, and more of it as a punishment. The start of Israel's disobedience was in the murmuring over food and water in the Sinai desert (Exodus 16-17). The major rebellion occurred when they worshiped the golden calf (Exodus 32). Moses reminds them of their rebellion in Deuteronomy 9:7, 24 with the words: "From the day you left Egypt until you have arrived here, you have been rebellious against the Lord....you have been rebellious against the Lord ever since I have known you." However, they still have the power, through grace, to repent of sin and turn to God in faith. God will never take that power away. This power is evident in Deuteronomy 10:16 as Moses tells them: "Circumcise your hearts, therefore, and do not be stiff-necked any longer." At the same time, Moses assures them that the power to do so comes only from God in the words of Deuteronomy 30:6: "The Lord your God will circumcise your hearts...so that you may love him with all your heart and with all your soul, and live."[91] But until they do repent, God will blind them and force them to follow a religion of numerous laws and regulations.

---

[91] These passages show the dynamic relationship between God's grace and man's free will. This aspect of salvation will be covered more thoroughly in chapter 7.

As noted above, in Deuteronomy 30:11 God assures us that his laws are *"not too difficult for you or beyond your reach,"* because it is within everyone's grasp to repent of sin, live by faith, and obey God's simple commands to love him and our neighbor. These precepts are *not too difficult* to obey.[92] Ordinances and regulations are difficult, but obeying God's moral principles is not. Paul acknowledges this fact, and it is the reason he quotes this section of Deuteronomy in Romans 10:6-8. Picking up the passage at Deuteronomy 30:12, right after mentioning the clause "what I am commanding you today is not too difficult for you or beyond your reach" from Deuteronomy 30:11, Paul says:

> But the righteousness that is by faith says: "Do not say in your heart, 'Who will ascend into heaven?'" (that is, to bring Christ down) or "Who will descend into the deep?" (that is, to bring Christ up from the dead). But what does it say? "The word is near you; it is in your mouth and in your heart," that is, the word of faith we are proclaiming: That if you confess with your mouth, "Jesus is Lord" and believe in your heart that God raised him from the dead, you will be saved.

Since this is a direct quote from Deuteronomy 30:12-14, we understand that the identity of what is "not too difficult for you" is precisely the righteousness of faith. No one has to travel great distances ("ascend into heaven") or overcome great obstacles ("who will cross the sea" in Deuteronomy 30:13) in order to know the truth and the means of righteousness. God has already given it to man, it is in his heart and in his mouth, and God is trying to draw it out from him. In Romans 10:9, it is drawn out by confessing that Jesus is Lord and that God raised him from the dead, just as Paul had said earlier in Romans 4:24 ("to whom God will credit righteousness — for us who believe ***in him*** who raised Jesus our Lord from the dead"). In the Old Testament, they confessed with their mouth by believing "in him" as their Savior (Psalm 106:21; Isaiah 43:3,11), in anticipation of the death and resurrection of Christ.

Thus, the way of faith, a way "not too difficult," was expected to be lived out in the Old Testament as well as the New Testament.

---

[92] cf., 1 John 5:3; Matthew 11:30; Titus 2:12; John 14:23.

In light of this, it is significant that Deuteronomy 30:14 finishes "the word is very near you, it is in your mouth and in your heart" with the clause "*so you may obey it*," whereas Romans 10:8 finishes it with "*that is, the word of faith we are proclaiming*." Here Paul substitutes "faith" for "obedience" and it is apparent that he is treating them as one and the same.

The connection between faith and obedience is further proven in the way Paul continues in Romans 10:16-17: "But not all the Israelites accepted *the good news*..." We notice that Paul speaks of the Old Testament precepts as "*the good news*." This phrase comes from the same word translated as *gospel* throughout the New Testament.[93] It is the word Paul uses in Hebrews 4:2, 6 when he indicates that the Israelites had received the same gospel of salvation as those in the New Testament:

> For we also have had the gospel preached to us, *just as they did*; but the message they heard was of no value to them, because those who heard did not combine it with faith...those who *formerly had the gospel preached to them* did not go in...

It is clear, then, that Israel had the gospel of salvation delivered to them and could be saved by it just as those in the New Testament are saved. However, most of them did not accept it. Paul records this again in Romans 10:16, 21: "For Isaiah says, 'Lord, who has believed our message?' ...concerning Israel he says, 'All day long I have held out my hands to a disobedient and obstinate people.'"

Obviously their disobedience showed their lack of faith. They had the message, it was shouted at them, but they pretended not to hear it. This was also apparent in what Moses wrote in the remainder of Deuteronomy 30:15-18:

> See, I set before you today life and prosperity, death and destruction. For I command you today to love the Lord your God, to walk in his ways, and to keep his commandments, decrees

93 Greek: *euangelion* (εὐαγγελιον).

> and laws; then you will live and increase, and the Lord your God will bless you in the land you are entering to possess. But if your heart turns away and you are not obedient...you will not live long in the land...[94]

In comparing Deuteronomy 30, Romans 10, and Hebrews 4, we are seeing clearly that Moses and Paul have the same gospel. It is a gospel of faith and obedience. It is a gospel that teaches us to trust God in spite of all the evidence that would cast doubt on him, a gospel that teaches us to love him in spite of our wretched circumstances, a gospel that teaches us to love our neighbor with the same intensity that we love ourselves, a gospel that teaches us to repent of sin, to seek God's forgiveness, and then live as obediently as we can to please God. It is a gospel that is fulfilled not merely by saying a few words accepting Jesus, but living a life of faith and obedience that lasts till the end. This is the gospel of faith that Paul preaches, which is also the gospel of the New Testament.[95] It is all made possible by the grace that issues forth from the death and resurrection of Christ.

---

94 Some commentators have suggested that the faith and obedience to the law that allowed God to bless them with physical land is on a different level from the faith and obedience necessary to obtain eternal life. We must be careful not to posit two standards of faith and obedience in God. There is a distinction, however, as to why God gave the physical land to the Israelites: 1) the promise he made to Abraham, and 2) the wickedness of the inhabitants who lived there, **not** the obedience of the Israelites (cf., Deuteronomy 9:4-6). If Israel had truly believed and obeyed God, they could have possessed the land based on that righteousness and also obtained eternal life by the same faith and obedience.

95 As R. B. Hays has said: "In Paul we encounter a first century Jewish thinker who, while undergoing a profound disjuncture with his own religious tradition, grappled his way through to a vigorous and theologically generative reappropriation of Israel's Scriptures. However great the tensions between his heritage and his new Christian convictions, he insistently sought to show that his proclamation of the gospel was grounded in the witness of Israel's sacred texts. The trick lay in learning to read these texts aright" (*Echoes of Scripture in the Letters of Paul* (New Haven, CT: Yale University, 1989) p. 2). As Scott Hahn has masterfully argued: "...Paul (unlike many modern covenant theologians) does not explain the Old and New Covenants exclusively in temporal terms (i.e., before/after Christ). [f. 45: In Gal. 4:21-31, Paul presents the difference between the Old and New in terms of 'two covenants'...which he also links to Abraham via his 'two sons.'] In fact, he does almost the opposite: by linking the New Covenant with Abraham, and the Old Covenant with Moses,

In summary, we have seen that in Paul's understanding of faith and works there exists a dynamic relationship. On the one hand, Paul is adamant that neither works, the law, nor anything of the sort, can save mankind. The reason is that work which attempts to obligate God to pay us with salvation cannot be used in a relationship between the Creator who is perfect and the creature who is imperfect and sinful. The system of law must be replaced with an alternative system, that is, the system of grace. Within the system of grace, God can now look at us with mercy and love rather then through the exacting and uncompromising standards of the law. In the system of grace, God can forgive us our sins, hold our sins in abeyance until rectified, treat us with longsuffering, and many other wonderful things. However, within the system of grace, we must *please* God both by our faith, a faith that believes that God can do what he said he will do even though the circumstantial evidence may suggest otherwise; and our works, works that must be modeled on the Ten Commandments and summed up in the two greatest commandments: love God and your neighbor as yourself. God, who is the judge of our hearts, knows if we are truly seeking to please him. We can be confident, as Hebrews 11:6 states, that God is "the rewarder of those who diligently seek him." On the other hand, if we do not please God in the system of grace, either by falling into serious sin; not repenting; or not showing the love of the Spirit, God will again bring the exacting standards of law

[95 cont.] Paul shows how the New supersedes the Old — in one sense — precisely because it preceded it, in view of the promise and oath which God pledged to Abraham. However, at another level, Paul appears intent on showing how both Old and New Covenants are discernible in God's manifold dealings with Abraham regarding the blessing and the seed" ("Kinship By Covenant," op. cit., pp. 392-393). In contrast, Martin Luther wrote of Moses: "To the gallows with Moses...chase that stammering and stuttering Moses...Moses must ever be looked upon with suspicion, even as upon a heretic, excommunicated, damned, worse than the Pope and the devil...I will not have Moses with his law, for he is the enemy of the Lord Christ. If he appears with me before the judgment I'll turn him away in the name of the devil and say 'Here stands Christ.' In the last judgment Moses will look at me and say, 'You have known and understood me correctly' and he will be favorably disposed to me" (LW 54, 128). "Therefore it is inevitable that the papists, the Zwinglians, the Anabaptists, and all those who either do not know about the righteousness of Christ or who do not believe correctly about it should change Christ into Moses and the Law and change the Law into Christ" (LW 26, 143).

against us and condemn us for our sin. For Paul, then, works are a two-edged sword, depending upon the system in which they are viewed and applied. If done through grace they are graciously meritorious for salvation; if done under the law, they are absolutely condemnatory.[96]

Paul's Teaching on the Redemptive Work of Christ

As stated previously, the means of salvation that God has established is grace. First, grace denotes that we can do nothing of ourselves to initiate salvation. As Paul levied the "charge" that the whole world is in sin (cf. Romans 3:9; 4:15; Galatians 3:22), consequently all of mankind stands condemned before God. Since the system of law is insufficient to provide the means of returning us to God, then another system had to be put into place in order to save man. Simply put, out of his kindness and mercy God would save man because he personally desired to do so. But there was a huge obstacle for God to overcome. God is perfectly just. No matter how much he desired to save man, he could not excuse the sin of man without some satisfactory basis for doing so. As Paul says, for God to be "*just*, and the one who justifies..." (Romans 3:26), the matter of sin had to be rectified. God could neither side-step his divine character nor the moral principles he had previously put in place. Once these were satisfied, however, God could provide salvation by grace.

When God created the world, he set up certain inviolate principles. One of those principles was that of *representation* or *substitution*. This was a principle in which one person out of a group of persons would be held responsible for the good or bad that would come to the group. Paul outlines this principle of God in Romans 5:18-19:

> Consequently, just as the result of one trespass was condemnation for all men, so also the result of one act of righteousness was justification that brings life for all men. For just as through

[96] Council of Trent, Session 6, Chapter 16.

> the disobedience of the one man the many were made sinners, so also through the obedience of the one man many will be made righteous.

God applied this principle when he created Adam. Adam's decision to obey or disobey God would affect the whole human race. If he obeyed, all would receive eternal life. If he disobeyed, all would receive eternal death. It was very simple, yet very ominous. As noted previously, Paul states in Romans 5:12 that Adam sinned, and when he sinned he initiated the curse of sin and death that fell upon the rest of humanity. He states: "Therefore, just as sin entered the world through one man [Adam], and death through sin, and in this way death came to all men, because all sinned." Paul reiterates this truth in Ephesians 2:1-3 with the words, "As for you, you were dead in transgressions and sins in which you used to live...like the rest we were by nature children of wrath."[97]

Because God is righteous and just, he had to condemn the sinner. In order to save mankind, God had to bring the sinner out of condemnation. This was quite a difficult task, but God had a wonderful plan to resolve it. Using the same principle of *representation* he instituted when he created Adam, God planned the best possible solution. He himself would fulfill the necessary requirements for redemption, atoning for man's sin, and satisfying the demands of his own personal holiness. Simultaneously, through his divine power, he would be able to survive the ordeal so that he could live with man eternally. Jesus made satisfaction to God by his suffering and death; he triumphed over both sin and death by his resurrection. Though the law demanded death for sin, there is one thing it did not prohibit — rising from the dead. Resurrection is outside the realm of law. This is why Paul specifies both the death *and* resurrection in Romans 4:25: "He was delivered over to

---

[97] Many Protestants hold that the word "dead" in Ephesians 2:1, 5 indicates a condition in man of "total depravity" — the teaching which claims that after the fall of Adam, man was totally incapable of responding to God (e.g., Sproul, R. C., *Chosen By God*, 1986, pp. 112-120). This false concept will be dealt with intermittently throughout our book, but for an introduction to a critique of "total depravity" derived from the word "dead," see **Appendix 11.**

death for our sins and was *raised to life for our justification.*"[98] In order to accomplish this, God had to become a man. Man had sinned; thus, according to God's law of *representation* already established, a representative of man had to atone for the transgression and satisfy the divine principles.[99]

Another divine quality that allowed Christ to serve as our representative was sinlessness. Since God demanded a perfect sacrifice for sin, both in his person and in his life, no other man could measure up to this requirement. Only a divine being could fulfill it. As Paul says in 2 Corinthians 5:21: "God made him who knew no sin to be sin for us,[100] so that in him we might become the righteousness of God." Or as he says in Galatians 3:13: "Christ redeemed us from the curse of the law by becoming a curse for us, for it is written, Cursed is everyone who is hung on a tree." Or as he says in Romans 8:1-3:

> Therefore, there is now no condemnation for those who are in Christ Jesus, because through Christ Jesus the law of the Spirit of life set me free from the law of sin and death. For what the law was powerless to do in that it was weakened by the sinful nature, God did by sending his own Son in the likeness of sinful man to be a sin offering. And so he condemned sin in sinful man...

---

98 The Greek uses διὰ in the accusative case, which could be translated, "raised to life *because* of our justification." This suggests that justification was secured by the anticipation of Christ's resurrection. In light of Romans 3:25 which makes justification of Old Testament saints contingent on Christ's atonement and resurrection, the causal use of διὰ may be appropriate.

99 We should also note that the doctrine of the Incarnation, formulated in the early Councils of the Church, stipulated that the God-man had to be fully divine and fully human, without dilution or mixture of either nature. This is so because the Law required that the representative who would sustain God's wrath be fully human. The Law could not punish a representative that was only half human, for then he could not redeem our human nature. This is one of the reasons why the Nicene Creed refers to Christ as "true God and true man." (See Catholic Catechism, Sections 464-478).

100 Most commentators and translators recognize the word "sin" in 2 Cor. 5:21 as referring not to a sinful quality in Christ, (i.e., that Christ actually became the substance of sin that God judged), but that he became a "sin offering" for us. This is the way Catholic theology interprets 2 Cor. 5:21.

By becoming our representative in God's judgment upon sin, Christ takes away the curse imposed on us by the strict standards of the law. The law demands perfect obedience and if it does not receive perfection then it curses with sin and death. Hence, it is law as a *system* of rectifying relationships, i.e., our relationship with God, that must be set aside. In its place, Christ brings the system of grace whereby God can offer us salvation from sin and death based on a wholly different kind of relationship. Christ's atonement and resurrection provide the means by which God can fulfill his desire to save mankind while still remaining a just God who condemns sin. Christ's atonement and resurrection provided grace to the world, whereas before there was only law which had to condemn.[101] As John says in 1 John 2:2: "He is the atoning sacrifice for our sins, and not only for ours but also for the sins of the whole world."

How Does Christ's Suffering and Death Make Redemption Possible?

What did Christ's suffering and death actually accomplish that allowed the Father to provide the human race with salvation? Did Christ take within himself the sin and guilt of mankind and suffer the specific punishment for that sin and guilt, as Protestants contend? The answer is no. The punishment for sin is first physical death, but ultimately it is eternal damnation. Obviously, Christ did not undergo the punishment of eternal damnation; otherwise he

---

[101] Another aspect of the atonement involves the "covenant" God made with man. In Hebrews 9:11-18 the writer speaks of the new covenant in which Christ is the mediator. It required the death of the one who made the covenant in order to put it into effect, much like a "last will and testament" used today. For the old covenant under Moses, the death came in the form of animal sacrifices. For the new covenant, the death came upon Christ, who, representing God, became the covenant initiator or testator. In Genesis 15:9-21, God fulfills a prophetic element in the covenant with Abraham in which the death of the testator was symbolized by the slaughter of the animals Abraham brought before God. In Genesis 22:15-18, upon the supreme obedience of Abraham, God ratifies this covenant by a divine oath, affirming that the promise can never be abrogated. In order to put this covenant into effect, God himself would suffer the death that was necessary for its actualization. This occurred in the death of Christ.

would still be in hell suffering for sin. Further, there is no Scripture specifying that Christ suffered the eternal punishment of hell for sin. If Christ had paid the eternal consequence for everyone's sin, God would have no recourse to punish anyone because the sin would have already been adjudicated. God could not demand double payment for the same sin. We must conclude then, that Christ did not take upon himself the entire punishment required of man for sin. Rather, Scripture teaches only that Christ became a "propitiation," a "sin offering," or a "sacrifice" for sins.[102] Paul writes, for example, in Ephesians 5:2 that "Christ loved us and gave himself up for us as a fragrant offering and sacrifice to God," or, as 1 John 2:2 states, "He is the atoning sacrifice [viz., propitiation] for our sins, and not only for ours but also for the sins of the whole world."[103] Essen-

[102] Christ is called the "offering" (Ephesians 5:2; Hebrews 7:27; 9:28), a "sacrifice" (1 Cor. 5:7; Eph. 5:2; Heb. 9:28; 10:12), and a "propitiation" (Romans 3:25; 1 John 2:2; 4:10). In the Scriptural language "He himself *bore* our sins in his body on the tree..." in 1 Peter 2:24, the Greek word ἀναφέρω = "bore") is a sacrificial term referring to Christ as a "sin offering" to God. Ἀναφέρω appears ten times in the New Testament in contexts of "lifting up" or "offering sacrifice" (e.g., Hebrews 7:27; 9:28; 13:15; 1 Peter 2:5; Matt. 17:1; Mark 9:2; Luke 24:51). Old Testament sacrifices fell into five categories: 1) burnt offerings (e.g., Lev. 1:1-17; 6:8-13; 8:18-21; 16:24); 2) grain offerings (e.g., Lev. 2:1-16; 6:14-23); 3) fellowship offerings (e.g., Lev. 3:1-17; ; 7:11-34); 4) sin offerings (e.g., Lev. 4:1-5:13; 6:24-30; 8:14-17; 16:3-22); and 5) guilt offerings (Lev. 5:14-6:7; 7:1-6).

[103] The NIV translation "atoning sacrifice" is replaced here in favor of the more traditional "propitiation." The English word "propitiation," is understood from its derivation in the Latin word "propitiatus," meaning: "to appease and make favorable; conciliate; a synonym is "to pacify." Webster's Seventh New Collegiate Dictionary (Chicago: Donnelley and Sons, 1965), p. 683. The word "propitiation" is translated from the Greek word ἱλασμός which appears twice in the New Testament (1 John 3:2 and 1 John 4:10). A noun cognate, ἱλαστήριον appears twice in the New Testament, is likewise rendered as "propitiation" in Romans 3:25, but Hebrews 9:5 translates it as "mercyseat" in reference to the covering of the ark of the covenant. The verbal cognate ἱλάσκομαι, appearing twice in the New Testament, is understood as "merciful" in Luke 18:13 or as "to propitiate" in Hebrews 2:17. The Septuagint uses ἱλασμός seven times. It is understood as "atonement" or "propitiation" in Lev. 25:9, from the Hebrew בפרים which means "coverings;" and also in Numbers 5:8, from the Hebrew בפר which refers to a single covering; as "sin offering" in Ezekiel 44:27 from the Hebrew חטאה referring to the same; as "forgiveness" in Psalm 129:4; Dan. 9:9, both from the Hebrew סליחה which is the ordinary word for "forgiveness;" and a very obscure reference in Amos 8:14 which is translated as "sin" (KJV, ASV, Douay-Rheims), as "shame"

tially, this means that Christ, because he was guiltless, sin-free and in favor with God, could offer himself up as a means of persuading God to relent of his angry wrath against the sins of mankind.[104] Sin destroys God's creation. God, who is a passionate and sensitive being, is angry against man for harming the creation. Anger against sin shows the personal side of God, for sin is a personal offense against him.[105] We must not picture God as an unemotional courtroom judge who is personally unharmed by the sin of the offender brought before him. God is personally offended by sin and thus he needs to be personally appeased in order to offer a personal forgiveness. In keeping with his divine principles, his personal nature, and the magnitude of the sins of man, the only thing that God would allow to appease him was the suffering and death of the sinless representative of mankind, namely, Christ. A great satisfaction was necessary since man had sinned against a great and holy God. This dramatic plan is stated no better than in Isaiah 53:10-12:

> Yet it was the Lord's will to *crush* him and cause him to *suffer*, and though the Lord makes his life a guilt offering...After the

---

[103 cont.] (NIV), and as "guilt" (NASB), or "oath of Ashimah" (NEB, RSV) because of Hebrew text anomalies. The noun cognate ἱλαστήριον appears in the Septuagint 19 times, exclusively in reference to the "mercy seat" covering on the ark of the covenant. The verbal form ἱλάσκουαι appears 11 times: in reference to forgiveness and appeasing the Lord's anger (Ex. 32:14, from the Hebrew נחם meaning "to change one's mind, be penitent"); as "to pardon or forgive," 2 Kings 5:18; 24:4; 2 Chr. 6:30; Psalm 24:11; Lam. 3:42; Dan. 9:19, from the Hebrew סליחה meaning "to forgive"; Psalm 77:38; 78:9, from the Hebrew כפר meaning "to cover."

[104] "This sacrifice of Christ is unique; it completes and surpasses all other sacrifices. First, it is a gift from God the Father himself, for the Father handed his Son over to sinners in order to reconcile us with himself. At the same time it is the offering of the Son of God made man, who in freedom and love offered his life to his Father through the Holy Spirit in reparation for our disobedience" (Catholic Catechism, Section 614). "Jesus atoned for our faults and made satisfaction for our sins to the Father" (Ibid, Section 615).

[105] The personal and emotional anger of God against sin is a major theme in the Old Testament, (cf., Exodus 4:14; Numbers 11:1,10; 22:22; 25:3-4; 32:10,13,14; Deut. 6:15; 7:4; 13:17; 29:20-28; 31:17; 32:22; Joshua 7:1,26; Judges 2:14,20; 2 Samuel 6:7; 24:1; 2 Kings 13:3; 24:20; Psalms 6:1; 69:24; 85:5; Ecclesiasticus 39:28; 45:19; Isaiah 5:25; 63:3; 66:15; Jeremiah 4:8; 12:13; 25:37; Lamentations 1:12; Ezekiel 5:13; 20:8; Hosea 8:5; Micah 5:15; Nahum 1:2-3; 2 Maccabees 5:17; 7:33; Hebrews 3:3, et al.).

> *suffering* of his [Christ's] soul, he [God] will see the result of the suffering of his soul and be *satisfied*...For he bore the sin of many, and made *intercession* for the transgressors.[106]

In his mediatorial role, Christ, living a sinless life and dying a perfect death, obtains favor from God so that he can approach and beseech Him for mercy and forgiveness on behalf of sinful man. God is not required to offer forgiveness, yet Christ pleads and appeals to the intrinsic love and longsuffering of God. Christ, as the obedient son who sacrifices himself, intercedes to obtain the mercy of the Father and to abate his anger. From his paternal qualities of pity and love, the Father grants an avenue of forgiveness for mankind.

As noted previously, just as Scripture requires man to *please* God, so Christ, as a Son, was required to *please* his Father. This was evident first at Christ's baptism in which the Father states, "This is my Son, whom I love; with him I am *well pleased*" (Matthew 3:17). Christ maintains this posture as he says in John 8:29, "...for I always do what *pleases* him" or in John 5:30, "for I seek not to *please* myself but him who sent me." Christ's ultimate pleasing of the Father in regard to salvation was, as stated in Ephesians 5:2, his "sweet-smelling sacrifice" destined to appease the Father's anger against sin and provide grace for mankind.[107]

The Old Testament provides the historical precedent for the concept of *appeasing the anger of God* against sin. First, the ani-

---

106 This reading is from the Masoretic text and published in *Biblia Hebraica Stuttgartensia* by Deutsche Bibelstiftung Stuttgart, 1967, 1977, p. 760, and is followed by the KJV, ASV, RSV, et al. The LXX refers to Christ "seeing light" through his suffering which is followed by the NIV, NEB, NRSV. In reference to the satisfaction Christ gave to the Father, the Catholic Catechism states: "Jesus atoned for our faults and made satisfaction for our sins to the Father...It is love 'to the end' that confers on Christ's sacrifice its value as redemption and reparation, as atonement and satisfaction...No man, not even the holiest, was ever able to take on himself the sins of all men and offer himself as a sacrifice for all. The existence in Christ of the divine person of the Son, who at once surpasses and embraces all human persons and constitutes himself as the Head of all mankind, makes possible his redemptive sacrifice *for all*" (Sections 615-616).

107 St. Anselm, Archbishop of Canterbury (1033-1109), in *Cur Deus Homo?* ("Why the God-man?"), is generally credited with recognizing an important aspect of the atonement, which was introduced many years earlier in Tertullian's *De Poenitentia*. See **Appendix 18** for more detail.

mal sacrifices of the Old Testament, although typically pointing to the ultimate sacrifice of Christ, were intended to appease God's anger against sin for the people of that time. God would "smell the sweet savor of the sacrifice" and in turn he would relent of his wrath and forgive the individual for his sin. This is noted, for example, in Leviticus 5:5-10, 6:21:

> When anyone is guilty in any of these ways, he must confess in what way he has sinned...and the priest shall make atonement for him for his sin...it is a sin offering...The priest shall then offer the other as a burnt offering in the prescribed way and make atonement for him for the sin he has committed, *and he will be forgiven*...and burn the memorial portion on the altar as an aroma pleasing to the Lord.[108]

The appeasement motif is also evident in many Old Testament narratives which depict a righteous individual who is looked upon with favor by God. This favored individual is able to be a mediator or intercessor who persuades God to turn away his wrath from sinful people. One of the primary examples of this intercessory role is Moses. When Moses received the Ten Commandments, he remained on the mountain with God for forty days and nights. By this time the people thought that God and Moses had abandoned them, and they proceeded to make their own god out of gold and call upon it in an effort to secure protection in the hostile desert. In observing their apostasy, God says to Moses: "I have seen this people...and they are a stiff- necked people. Now leave me alone so that my *anger* may burn against them and that I may destroy them" (Exodus 32:9-10). In an attempt to appease God's anger and persuade him that this would not be the best course of action, Moses replies in Exodus 32:11-13:

> "O Lord, why should your anger burn against your people...Why should the Egyptians say, 'It was with evil intent that he brought them out, to kill them in the mountains and to wipe them off the face of the earth'? Turn from your fierce anger; relent and do not

[108] See also Leviticus 4:20,26,31,35; 6:7; 19:22; Numbers 15:25-28.

> bring disaster upon your people. Remember your servants, Abraham, Isaac and Israel, to whom you swore by your own self..."

After this impassioned and dramatic plea from Moses, Exodus 32:14 records God's astounding response: "Then the Lord relented and did not bring on his people the disaster he had threatened." This shows the virtual human-like quality of God, who can be persuaded to change his mind through the appeal of a worthy and significant person. In fact, Exodus 33:5 records that God remained so angry against the people for their sin that when he later tells Moses to lead them out of that place he says, "Tell the Israelites, 'You are a stiff-necked people. If I were to go with you even for a moment, I might destroy you." Apparently, God was on the verge of destroying all of them and only Moses's plea abated that occurrence.

The appeasement of God becomes even more pronounced in the remaining section of Exodus 32:30-32:

> The next day Moses said to the people, "You have committed a great sin. But now I will go up to the Lord; perhaps I can make atonement[109] for your sin." So Moses went back to the Lord and said, "Oh, what a great sin these people have committed! They have made themselves gods of gold. But now, please forgive their sin — but if not, then blot me out of the book you have written."

Even though God eventually destroyed and punished some of the people (as recorded in Exodus 32:27-35), he did not destroy all of Israel. This is similar to Christ offering himself as an atonement, appeasing the anger of God on behalf of the human race. In turn, God decides not to condemn all of mankind, yet he still punishes and destroys those within mankind that he has singled out for his retribution.

We see the extent of Moses's influence with God in Exodus 33:16-19. After Moses asks God to go with the Israelites through the desert, God replies, "I will do the very thing you have asked,

---

109 From the Hebrew כפר, which is the ordinary word for "atonement" used throughout the Old Testament (e.g., Exodus 30:10, 15, 16; Leviticus 1-23; Numbers 5-31). According to Hebrews 7-9, these atonements foreshadowed the once-for-all atonement of Christ for our redemption.

because I am *pleased* with you and I know you by name." Again, we see that it is because Moses has been pleasing to God that God relents of his anger and follows Moses's request. In verse 19 God then says, "...I will have mercy on whom I will have mercy, and I will have compassion on whom I will have compassion," showing that even God's election of individuals is based on his pleasure in them (cf., Romans 9:14-16).

Other examples in the Old Testament include Abraham's plea for the cities of Sodom and Gomorrah which God had intended to destroy (Genesis 18f). God's anger is temporarily stayed as Abraham, who pleads with God for mercy, attempts to find ten righteous people in those cities to satisfy God. God agreed that his anger would be appeased if ten righteous people could be found. God granted this request because he had respect for Abraham and looked with favor upon him.

Similarly, Job offered sacrifices to God for his children who perhaps may have sinned against him (Job 1:5). In light of Job's actions, the Old Testament prophets also recognize the mediatorial role of a righteous person in appeasing God's anger. At the height of Judah's apostasy, Ezekiel 14:14,20 states:

> Even if these three men — Noah, Daniel and Job — were in it, they could save only themselves by their righteousness, declares the Sovereign Lord...as surely as I live, declares the Sovereign Lord, even if Noah, Daniel and Job were in it, they could save neither son nor daughter. They would save only themselves by their own righteousness.

Here we see that after serious and continual transgression against God, none in the nation can appease God's anger. He is determined to destroy Judah because their sins have been continual and grave, without repentance. By posing the hypothetical example of Noah, Daniel, and Job who would, under more normal circumstances, be able to appease God's anger toward the people, Scripture shows the precedent for the mediatorial role of intercession accomplished by Christ in redeeming mankind. This same truth is evident in Jeremiah 15:1, which states: "Then the Lord said to me: 'Even if Moses and Samuel were to stand before me, my heart would not go out to this people. Send them away from my presence!'" Here again we see the possibility that, under more normal circumstances, God would have allowed the intercession of a Moses or a Samuel to appease his anger against sin. We also see the intense and passionate emotion displayed by God in his anger as he speaks of his "heart" that he would not allow to "go out to his people" which results in his sending them "out of his presence!" — as an angry father or king might do.

One could cite many more examples of the *appeasement* motif in Scripture. The important point to understand is that as a personal being who is personally offended by sin, God must receive a personal and satisfactory appeasement to persuade him to relent of his anger and wrath. To be appeased for the sin of man so that God could open an avenue of grace and forgiveness, it was God's desire to see an obedient and sinless representative of man, namely, Christ, suffer and die. Because of the infinite value that God placed on Christ's suffering and death, He is able to take away the punishment of eternal damnation for those who accept his gift of salvation. They will suffer the temporal punishment of sin, i.e., physical death, but will not undergo the eternal punishment of sin.

For each man there is a crucial element required in order to benefit from Christ's appeasement of God's wrath against sin. Each must show himself faithful and obedient to God in order to receive and maintain the turning away of God's wrath. Christ made it possible for God to turn away his wrath from every man who ever existed. In this sense, Christ's propitiation was global. As noted earlier, the apostle John states it this way in 1 John 2:1: "And he is the propitiation for our sins, and not ours only but also *for the whole world.*" Here we see that Christ is the *propitiation* for everyone in the world.[110] However, it is a fact that not everyone in the world escapes the wrath of God. Therefore, the propitiation was not received by them. The propitiation is global, but it is only applied to individuals who repent of their personal sins and show themselves faithful to God, a faithfulness God judges from his grace.

---

[110] "But because in his incarnate divine person he has in some way united himself to every man, 'the possibility of being made partners, in a way known to God, in the paschal mystery' is offered to all men" (Catholic Catechism, Section 618). "But although Christ died for all, yet not all receive the benefit of His death, but those only to whom the merit of His passion is communicated" (Council of Trent, Session 6, Ch. 3).

This truth is also confirmed in the usage of *propitiation* in Romans 3:25: "Whom God purposed to be a *propitiation*, through *faith* in his blood, to demonstrate his righteousness..." Paul says that God *purposed* Christ to be a propitiation but with the additional dimension that it is appropriated to the individual by "*faith* in his blood."[111] The "blood" does not, in itself, reconcile the individual with God. Faith is the necessary ingredient for the propitiation to be applied to him. As noted earlier, without faith it is "impossible to please God," that is, without faith God will not allow Christ's propitiation to be used by the individual. Hence, faithfulness to God is the personal way in which we appease God's wrath against our sin.[112] As we noted previously, though the death and resurrection of Christ had put the *system of grace* in place, this only made *possible* the salvation of all men.[113] Man now had to respond to the grace of God (John 6:40; 1 Tim. 2:4; Rom. 10:9). Although the strict standards of law would not condemn the sincere seeker of God any longer, man still had to seek and *please* God who in turn would save and bless him. Man first had to believe in God and what God said about man. As Paul says in Romans 3:21-22: "But now a righteousness from God, apart from the law, has been made known, to which the Law and the Prophets testify. This righteousness from God comes through faith in Jesus Christ to all who believe..."

---

[111] The word "purposed" is from the Greek word προέθετο which is used three times in the New Testament. The other two usages are in Rom. 1:13 and Eph. 1:9. It refers to the intention, determination or resolution offered or to be attained.

[112] The interrelatedness of our personal appeasement of God with the appeasement accomplished by Christ is noted in the connection between Ephesians 5:2, which speaks of Christ who "gave himself up for us as a fragrant offering and sacrifice to God" for our salvation, and Philippians 4:18, which refers to the personal gifts and sacrifices we give to God as "a fragrant offering, an acceptable sacrifice, pleasing to God" (cf, 2 Cor. 2:15). The language of "fragrant offering" or "sweet smelling savor" as in older translations is directly related to the same language in the Old Testament in which God is pacified or appeased by the sweet smell of sacrifices. For example, in Genesis 8:21 God promises to never again curse the ground based on the burnt sacrifices of Noah whose aroma God smelled. See also Exodus 29:18-25; Leviticus 1:9-17; 2:2-12; 4:31 in which the sin of the offender is forgiven based on the sweet smell of the burnt offering; Numbers 15:3-24; 28:2-27; 29:2-36; Ezek. 20:28, 41. "To keep from wickedness is pleasing to the Lord, and to forsake unrighteousness is an atonement...The offering of the righteous enriches the altar, and its pleasing odor rises before the Most High" (Ecclesiasticus 35:5).

[113] Council of Trent, Session 6, Chapter 5; Catholic Catechism, Sections 978, 2000, 2002, 2024.

Summary Points

1) Paul uses the word "alone" more than any other New Testament writer, many usages appearing in the very contexts which speak of faith and justification, but never as a qualifier or description of faith. For Paul, faith carries far too much meaning and implications to be limited by the word "alone." The only time Scripture couples the word "faith" with the word "alone" is in the Epistle of James (2:24) where it is specified that we are not justified by faith alone.

2) When Paul says that man cannot be justified by works or through the law, he is referring to any and all works done by man, not merely certain kinds of works. These works include moral, civil and ceremonial laws of the Old Testament as well as any such laws in the present age.

3) Paul teaches that because of the principle of obligation, man cannot be justified by works. Doing works, outside the realm of grace, attempts to obligate God to pay the worker. If God is obligated to pay the worker, then the relationship is one based on a strict, legal contract; not on grace. God, because he is the Creator and perfect, man, who is the creature and imperfect, cannot place God in a position of legal obligation.

4) Paul teaches that works, under the auspices of God's grace, do indeed justify the individual. Paul teaches that through God's grace he can accept the faith and works of the individual for the purposes of salvation. Passages in the New Testament that speak of works being judged with a view toward gaining eternal life are not hypothetical.

5) Faith is placed in opposition to works by Paul since faith is used to represent a personal, grace-based relationship with God whereas works are used to represent a contractual, non-grace relationship. Faith is the element of human volition which recognizes and acknowledges God's grace and thus it is the first element that establishes our relationship to God.

6) Paul teaches that we fulfill the law, and are justified through obedience to the law, by loving God and loving our neighbor as ourselves.

7) Although Paul tells us to model our behavior on the law, he has the intent of the law, or the higher purpose of the law, in view. On the other hand, he is adamant against legalistic obedience.

8) Scripture teaches that within the system of grace, the individual must please God by his faith and obedience. If he does not please God, then he cannot be saved. God is the sole judge of whether we have pleased him.

9) Scripture teaches that God gives gracious merit to individuals who have pleased him, and he will graciously reward them with eternal life for their faith and obedience — not from obligation but from his sheer benevolence to those who earnestly seek him.

10) Faith is the beginning of salvation. Each person that comes to God must first believe that he exists and is the source of all goodness and blessing.

11) All men are sinners in the eyes of God and in order to receive salvation it is necessary that all men be redeemed through the atoning work of Christ.

12) Christ did not take on himself the guilt and punishment required of man for sin, since hell itself is the ultimate punishment for sin. Rather, Christ became a propitiatory sacrifice in order to appease the wrath of God against sin. In this way, he opens the floodgates of grace and makes it possible for every man to attain salvation.

13) God's grace, through anticipation of the atonement of Christ in the New Testament, was made available to those in the Old Testament, and thus they could be saved in the same way as we may be today. As regards their relationship to God, those in the

Old Testament were to understand the ultimate purpose of the law in the same way we are to understand it today.

14) Through the measure of grace God gives each individual believer, he expects that the believer will exercise that grace by continuing to believe in God despite the circumstantial experiences of life that may cast doubt on God's integrity. In this regard, Abraham is one of the greatest examples of faith in the Scripture and one on whom we should model our own faith in order to be justified.

15) Paul teaches that faith must express itself through love in order to effectuate justification. The qualities and requirements for genuine love are specified throughout Scripture.

Chapter 2

Did James Teach Justification By Works?

The Epistle of James has been a thorn in the side of many a Protestant, but the calling-card for many a Catholic. Not surprisingly, the Council of Trent frequently quoted from the Epistle of James, but so do many contemporary Evangelicals who question and contradict the *faith alone* formulations of their Protestant forefathers. Martin Luther maintained there was a contradiction between Paul and James. He decided in favor of Paul and concluded that James was an "epistle of straw" and subsequently sought to "throw Jimmy into the stove."[1] His contemporaries, especially Philip Melanchthon, persuaded Luther not to reject the book of James from the accepted canon of Scripture. In giving this advice, however, Melanchthon and his colleagues now had to find a wholly different apologetic other than Luther's to deal with the book of James. Since the Reformation, Protestant theologians have given many and varied explanations in attempts to harmonize James with Paul. Doing so is certainly a difficult task, since James's words, "*a man is justified by works and not by faith alone*" (James 2:24) ring very clear and unequivocal to any ear. Any attempt to twist such a clear statement and make it say something that is not obvious is bound to receive a harsh critique, especially because the doctrine of justification is so important. Indeed, this task of explaining

1 Luther stated: "Therefore St. James' epistle is really an epistle of straw, compared to these others, for it has nothing of the nature of the gospel about it" (LW 35, 362); and "The epistle of James gives us much trouble, for the papists embrace it alone and leave out all the rest ... Accordingly, if they will not admit my interpretations, then I shall make rubble also of it. I almost feel like throwing Jimmy into the stove, as the priest in Kalenberg did" (LW 34, 317). See chapter 9 for further details into Luther's view of the Epistle of James.

James's clear statement becomes even more formidable for the Protestant challenger when he considers that the phrase "*faith alone*" appears only once in the New Testament — and there it is preceded by the words "*not by*." For Protestants to maintain that Paul teaches a *faith alone* justification, while James, also inspired by the Holy Spirit, explicitly denies that very doctrine, is indeed a very difficult undertaking. And, as we noted in chapter 1, Paul used the word *alone* more than any other New Testament writer, but he never used it in reference to faith.

To help formulate an initial understanding of James, Catholic commentators suggest he is correcting an error that seeped into the Church regarding Paul's teaching. Since Paul was adamant that works of the law could not justify the individual, it is possible that some in the church overreacted to Paul's teaching by propounding a doctrine of antinomianism, which held that one was not required to do any works in order to be justified. Since James refers to the life of Abraham, actually quoting from the same passage of Scripture that Paul did in Romans 4:3 (*viz*., Genesis 15:6), it is likely that James is aware of Paul's doctrine and wishes either to add to his teaching or to clarify Paul's intent. Unlike Paul, however, James refers to another incident in Abraham's life recorded in Genesis 22:9-12, the account of Abraham offering his son Isaac on the altar at God's command. James also adds the story of Rahab, who was saved in the conquest of Jericho many years after Abraham, which Paul does not address. These additions to the study of justification strongly suggest that James' purpose is to clear up any misunderstanding of Paul.

Protestant theologians may counter that though James might indeed be correcting false notions of Paul's teaching, this proposition cannot explain the apparent contradiction between James and Paul because scholarly efforts to date the New Testament epistles offer no conclusive proof that James wrote his book after Paul wrote the book of Romans. This line of argumentation, while it may have some merit, does not disprove that James was written after Paul, but merely casts doubt on it. However, the same commentators who suggest that Romans may have postdated James are not as willing to say the same about the book of Galatians, also written by Paul. Most scholarly literature recognizes that Galatians is one of the earliest books of the New Testament.[2] This is important because Galatians teaches the same doctrine of faith and works that the book of Romans does, even down to the very language and use of Old Testament citations. Paul also features Abraham prominently in the Galatian epistle. As he did in Romans 4:3, Paul in Galatians 3:6 quotes from Genesis 15:6, as well as from many other passages in the Genesis account of Abraham. Because Paul saturates his teaching on justification with references to Abraham in such an early epistle as Galatians, it seems logical to assume that James, which postdates Galatians and is addressing Abraham's justification, is a direct attempt to add to and clarify Paul's teaching about Abraham. In fact, if the book of James antedates the book of Romans yet postdates the book of Galatians, it may be safe to assume that each writer knows and takes into account the work of the other. In addition, since the book of Romans and the book of Galatians seem to be separated by considerable time and location, we can surmise that Paul's teaching on justification had spread over the whole Judean, Asian, and Mediterranean area. Perhaps it is not coincidental that James in his opening statement directs his teaching on justification to this entire global area, "To the twelve tribes *scattered among the nations*" (James 1:1).

Protestant Interpretations of James 2

Protestant theologians have tried in innumerable ways to downplay the significance of James's teaching regarding justification.[3] In short, their goal is to reduce James's writings to a mere

---

[2] The dating of Galatians, or any book in the New Testament, is by no means precise. One's acceptance of the "North Galatia" theory or the "South Galatia" theory regarding the destination of the epistle, is the chief determining factor in narrowing down the date of Galatians. One of the earliest accepted dates is 49 AD. The dating of James is also uncertain, but the majority accept that it was written at the end of James's life, prior to the most likely date of his martyrdom of 62 AD (see Donald Guthrie, *New Testament Introduction*, pp. 457-465; 761-764). Some make a case that James is written before Paul's epistle based on the "non-forensic" use of δικαιόω in James 2:24. (See Ronald Fung, *Right With God*, ed., D.A. Carson, "Justification in the Epistle of James" p. 160). We will address this proposal momentarily.

[3] R. C. Sproul attempts to minimize these by citing G. C. Berkouwer's summary of three options: (1) James was polemicizing against Paul, (2) James was polemicizing against antinomianism, 3) Paul and James have different problems in view and are not struggling with each other at all. Sproul opts for the third of these explanations (*Faith Alone*, op. cit., p. 162).

afterthought of Paul's, a sort of addendum to Paul's thought, but nothing monumental or in any way modifying Paul's teaching. The following are some of the ways they make these attempts:

1) Since Protestant theology views Paul's use of justification as a "declared righteousness,"[4] consistency in definition would suggest applying the same meaning to the epistle of James. Some Protestants have agreed with this line of thinking. A difficulty arises, however, since Paul and James are dealing with two different time periods in Abraham's life; hence, these theologians realize that in order to safeguard their theology they must distinguish the respective justifications in some way. Since the Protestant conception of "declared righteousness" in justification is a *one-time* act never to be repeated again, they must then place Abraham's justification in Genesis 22 into a different category than his justification in Genesis 15. To solve this problem, they classify the justification in Genesis 15:6 as Abraham's *actual* justification. Conversely, they propose that because James is confirming this prior justification of Abraham, and since God actually "speaks" to Abraham on that occasion about his deed,[5] God, in Genesis 22, is thus *declaring* that Abraham was previously justified in Genesis 15:6. Hence, they separate the general category of "declared righteousness" into an *actual* and *declared* righteousness.[6]

2) Another explanation of Abraham's justification in Genesis 22 is to view it as a justification before *men* rather than God. Being viewed and judged by men would eliminate any salvific meaning to James's use of justification, since only God can issue or determine justification. Hence, only the justification of Genesis 15:6 could be the salvific justification of Abraham while the justifica-

---

4 That is, God "declares" a person righteous even though intrinsically he is still unrighteous. Chapter 5 gives more detail on this aspect of the Protestant concept of justification.

5 Genesis 22:12: "Now I know that you fear God" and "because you have done this, I sware, says the Lord."

6 The 19th century Scottish theologian, James Buchanan, espoused this view (see *The Doctrine of Justification*, pp. 243-249). Buchanan maintained that declaratory justification was applicable to the second chapter of James despite, as we will see later, the extreme difficulties and tensions this view created.

tion in Genesis 22:12 would only demonstrate Abraham's previous justification. Protestants who support this view assert that the words *you see* in the sentence "you see that a person is justified by what he does and not by faith alone" in James 2:24 indicates that this passage is referring to what *people* see on the outside. The argument then states that although James uses the word *justified,* he does not intend to use this term in the same soteriological sense as Paul does, (i.e., as a one-time forensic imputation), but only in the demonstrative sense. Hence, in viewing his works, Abraham finally proved his justification to men when he offered Isaac on the altar, but he was already justified before God by *faith alone* in Genesis 15:6.[7] What men see in Genesis 22 is the *fruit* of Abraham's prior justification, but Genesis 22 was not the point at which Abraham was legally and actually justified.[8]

3) In an attempt to bolster this reasoning Protestant theologians postulate that James's use of the word *justified* is not the

---

7 Various Protestant apologists offer this explanation, in one form or another. Evangelical R. C. Sproul adds another spin. He claims that it is not necessary for God to view the works of men because he already knows what they believe in their heart (*Faith Alone*, op. cit., p. 165). We must insist that though it is true that God knows the heart of every individual, Scripture does not teach that God judges men merely on their good intentions or aspirations. Scripture treats this subject from a phenomenological perspective, as Genesis 22 expressly states when the angel, speaking for God, says, "*Now* I know that you fear God." God does not judge Abraham's faith from his foreknowledge but from the evidence Abraham displays. Likewise, Scripture gives no support to the notion that God does not require evidence of obedience because he sees into our heart. Rather, Scripture teaches that God's evaluation of the heart depends upon and is consequent with man's actions, e.g., "Forgive and deal with each man according to all he does, since you know his heart (for you alone know the hearts of men), so that they will fear you and walk in your ways..." (2 Chronicles 6:30-31). Conversely, if followed to its logical conclusion, Sproul's reasoning would make any act of obedience on the part of man superfluous. Chapter 5 deals more full with this problem.

8 While many hold this view, Protestant apologist James R. White, has expounded it repeatedly (debate with Fr. Mitchell Pacwa, 1991). Protestants use the word "legal" or "forensic" to characterize Abraham's justification, which we will take up in more detail in chapters 5-6. Suffice it to say that Protestant theology believes there is only one point in Abraham's life in which he was justified before God, that is, Genesis 15:6, when God "credits righteousness to Abraham for his faith." Most Protestants claim this is a one-time legal act of imputation in which God declares Abraham righteous and is not to be repeated.

same as Paul's. They say that Paul uses *justified* in the sense of Abraham having his sins forgiven through the righteousness of Christ but that James is using *justified* in the sense of Abraham being *vindicated* by his works.[9] The work of offering Isaac, then, is said only to *vindicate* Abraham's prior legal justification established in Genesis 15:6. In effect, these interpreters suggest that James 2:24 could read, "you see that a person is *vindicated* by what he does..."[10]

4) A related explanation of James' language postulates that James is not speaking of one who is striving for salvation, but only of the degree of *sanctification* one experiences in this life by doing good works.[11] This would mean that the justification mentioned in James 2:24 is not really a justification at all but some aspect of one's sanctification.

5) Also relevant to the above reasoning is the suggestion that James is concerned only with the *kind* of faith required for justification. This theory attempts to fuse faith with works so as to make one theological category in which to impute the individual with righteousness for justification. The work, then, becomes merely the *qualifier* of faith rather than a separate and independent *quality* to be added to faith in order to procure justification. In this way, one can maintain the language of *faith alone* since the issue of

---

9 E.g., Joel Beeke in *Justification By Faith Alone*, op. cit., p. 84; R. C. Sproul in *Faith Alone*, p. 166.

10 The highly respected Reformed theologian, J. Gresham Machen, faulted his Protestant brethren for assigning one meaning of justification to Paul and another to James. Machen appealed to Galatians 5:6 to balance Paul and James. (*Machen's Notes on Galatians*, "Faith and Works," ed. John Skilton, p. 220; Also, J. Gresham Machen, *The New Testament: An Introduction to its Literature and History*, pp. 238ff). The Dutch Reformed theologian, Hermann Bavinck, agreed: "It is indeed not right to say that Paul speaks only of the *justification of the sinner* and James the *justification of the just*." Historically, it was Calvin who first used Galatians 5:6 to depart from Luther's strict view of *faith alone* (see chapter 9 for further details).

11 The distinction between justification and sanctification is a major Protestant belief. Since justification is a one-time act of imputation, anything after justification must be placed in the category of sanctification, and thus not related to whether one is ultimately saved or not. This is a major fallacy in Protestant thinking that we will address in chapters 4-5.

justification is now limited to discussing the *quality* of faith in the individual rather than the quality or quantity of his works, which will be judged separately and for entirely different reasons.[12]

6) A more subtle attempt to downplay James's teaching on justification is to relegate his entire book to the category of *wisdom* literature. Such analysis postulates that, similar to Old Testament wisdom literature (e.g., Proverbs), James is not teaching *theory*, only *practice*. They conclude that James is not concerned with doctrinal matters, and thus one should not take his statements as dogmatic formulations of the doctrine of justification. In this view, Paul is the only teacher of soteriological doctrine.[13]

7) Finally, a somewhat novel argument, presented to prove that James is not referring to a salvific justification, maintains that after Abraham's willingness to sacrifice Isaac, God does not say, "I will surely *justify* you" or "I will surely *credit you with righteousness*"; rather, he limits his language in Genesis 22:17 to "I will surely *bless* you." Since the language of *crediting with righteousness* appears in Genesis 15:6 but is absent from Genesis 22, the argument concludes Genesis 15:6 is the only instance of Abraham's justification.[14]

The Catholic Rejoinder

Obviously each of the above explanations is attempting to minimize the soteriological import of James's treatment of the doctrine

[12] Protestant apologists often posit arguments of this kind, claiming that Paul and James are dealing with two entirely different definitions of faith (e.g., James White, *The Roman Catholic Controversy*, p. 254, n. 5). Protestant exegesis of James invariably seeks to create a distinction among Paul's and James's view of faith, works or justification, respectively. Different authors will attempt to create one or more of these distinctions in the reader's mind depending on which one seems to work best to downplay James's impact on the discussion of justification. Once separated from faith, the judgment of works is usually relegated to the matter of whether the individual will obtain a personal reward in heaven.

[13] E.g., John Armstrong, *Justification By Faith Alone*, pp. 162-163; James White, *The Roman Catholic Controversy*, pp. 147-148.

[14] E.g., James G. McCarthy in *The Gospel According to Rome: Comparing Catholic Tradition and The Word of God*, p. 48.

of justification. It becomes evident by the sheer variety of explanations offered that the Protestant apologetic is desperately trying to downplay James's impact on the subject while urging the teaching of Paul with regard to the meaning and extent of justification. In effect, they hold up Paul as the grid through which any understanding of the epistle of James must first pass. Paul's teaching becomes a "canon within the canon" that can overrule the teaching of James. Unfortunately, doing so needlessly distorts the teaching of James. In the end, the various explanations offered, though plausible on the surface, contradict both the context within which James writes, the teaching of Paul, and the remaining teaching of Scripture. Let us see how this happens.

Countering the Protestant interpretation that *"you see"* in James 2:24 refers to what *man* sees as the fruit of one's salvation as opposed to what *God* sees for justification, is the mere fact that at Abraham's attempt to sacrifice his son Isaac, no human beings witnessed the act. Even the two servants that Abraham took with him to the base of the mountain apparently had no knowledge concerning what Abraham was about to do. According to Genesis 22:5, Abraham told the two servants to wait in a designated area while he and Isaac went off privately to worship. Then, as Abraham is raising his knife to sacrifice Isaac, the only witnesses to the event are God and an angel. In fact, it is the angel who says, "Now I know that you fear God because you have not withheld from me your son, your only son." Hence, every indication in the account is that the sacrifice of Isaac was an act designed specifically for God, not men, to witness. Genesis 22:1 makes the reason for this clear at the outset: "Some time later God tested Abraham." Thus it is God who is waiting for the outcome of that test. Neither the context of Genesis 22 nor James 2 suggests that the witness of men is even remotely significant in the story.

Regarding the notion that James is referring to a *vindication* rather than a *justification* of Abraham, the context of James 2 does not support such argumentation. First, it would certainly be illogical for James to use a non-salvific sense of the word *justified* when he is trying to make a case that one is "not justified by faith alone." In other words, if James were teaching a concept of *vindication* he could have chosen a word that solely and clearly refers to vindication, rather than a word that is commonly understood to refer to salvific justification. Second, if James had vindication in mind he could have simply said, "you see, a person is *vindicated* by works" without the addendum "and not by faith alone." The addition of "and not by faith alone" introduces a specific element and direction to his argument, for it clearly shows that James is attempting to correct a false notion about the solitude of faith in justification, not suggest that Abraham was merely vindicated by his works. Third, if James was arguing for the vindication of Abraham, this line of argumentation would only make sense if one of James's opponents had claimed that Abraham was "*vindicated* by his faith alone." If so, James would have easily refuted the argument by saying, "you see, a person is vindicated by what he does and not by faith alone." Such refutation would have required James to use "vindicated" in the first part of his argument (verse 20-21) in order for him to use it in the latter part (verse 24); otherwise, the concept of vindication simply would have no referent in the context. If James meant to teach only vindication in verse 24, the syntactical structure of the sentence would require that the phrase "not by faith alone" have its referent in "is vindicated," and thus the text would have to read as "you see, a man is vindicated by works and not vindicated by faith alone." It would assert that one is vindicated not only by faith but also by works. We see, then, that by injecting the concept of *vindication* into James 2:24, Protestantism has actually done more damage to its case than would have otherwise occurred, for the concept of vindication must then apply to both faith and works, which then destroys faith itself as being salvific.

We can also attack this line of argumentation by examining the way the New Testament uses the word "justified."[15] Though it may be *possible* to construe the Greek word (*dikaioo)* as referring to a vindication, this is neither the normal sense of the word, nor is such a sense ever used in a soteriological context in the New Testament. This is significant, because if the meaning of *dikaioo* as referring to

[15] The word "justified" is from the Greek verb *dikaioo* (δικαιόω). It is the same word used by Paul and James when each refers to Abraham's justification (cf., Romans 4:2 and James 2:24). There are other cognates of *dikaioo*, such as δικαιοσύνη, δικαίωμα, δίκαιος and δικαίωσις that we will cover in later chapters.

a vindication is not used elsewhere in the New Testament in the context of salvation, then there is no precedent for using it as such in James. James makes it clear when he opens the discussion in James 2:14 that he is setting up a salvation context by asking the rhetorical questions, "What good is it, my brothers, if a man claims to have faith but has no deeds? Can such faith save him?"

Four, perhaps five, authors of the New Testament use the word *dikaioo:* Matthew, Luke, Paul, James, and John.[16] Matthew uses *dikaioo* in 12:37 ("for by your words you will be justified, and by your words you will be condemned"). It is clear that Matthew's context is one of salvation/damnation. Luke uses the word in his gospel and in the book of Acts. In Acts 13:39 he writes, "Through him everyone who believes is justified from everything you could not be justified from by the law of Moses." Obviously, Luke is using *justified* in reference to salvation. Paul uses *dikaioo* 27 times in his epistles but in only one place does he use it outside a soteriological context. However, in this single instance he is referring exclusively to God (i.e., Romans 3:4, "so that you may be justified in your sayings"). God is justified because he has the *quality* of justice within him, or because he is the subsisting source of all goodness and thus of all justice. Finally, James uses *dikaioo* three times, twice in reference to Abraham and once in reference to Rahab, both, as noted above, within the context of salvation or damnation. Hence, we must conclude from this evidence that in the New Testament, *dikaioo*, when used in reference to man, deals exclusively with man's justification before God and its outcome of salvation or damnation. To claim, then, that James is using the word *dikaioo* differently from Paul is simply to beg the question.

Advocates of the vindication theory commonly refer to one usage of *dikaioo* in particular to support their contention that James may not be using the word "justified" in the same sense as Paul. John Calvin used this single example and many modern evangelicals continue to use it. In Matthew 11:19, Jesus says, "And wisdom is

16 The fifth may be in Revelation 22:11. Here, though, there is a textual variant. A few Greek manuscripts contain the present imperative form of δικαιωθητω which is translated as "let him be righteous" whereas other manuscripts contain the noun δικαιοσύνη, followed by a predicate. This variant will be addressed more thoroughly in chapter 4.

justified [*dikaioo*] by her works." Similarly, Luke 7:35 reads, "And wisdom is justified by all her children."[17] The proposed argument is that these passages are using *dikaioo* in the sense of vindication or demonstration, not as a salvific justification.[18] We respond to this argument as follows: Matthew 11:19 and Luke 7:35 are not using *dikaioo* in a context that discusses the technical aspects of justification or the general category of salvation. In fact, it is only because the context of these verses does not concern itself with justification and salvation, not because *dikaioo* can normally be understood as demonstrative, that the meaning of *dikaioo* can be given a different nuance in these passages. A similar thing happens in poetry. Words that have a technical meaning in everyday speech suddenly take on a different nuance when put in a metaphorical or symbolic context. In such a case we should not misconstrue the metaphorical usage of a word with the technical or lexical meaning of the same word.[19] Obviously, "wisdom" cannot be justified in the soteriological sense because it is an abstract virtue, not a man who needs to be saved from sin. Hence, when the word "justified" refers to "wisdom," its meaning must change to accommodate the poetic context in which it is placed. Matthew 11:19 and Luke 7:35 are purely metaphorical contexts and thus they change the technical meaning of the word "justified." James 2:14-26 is not metaphorical. Thus, to assert that James is using *dikaioo* in the same sense as that used in Matthew and Luke requires valid linguistic reasons for doing so, not simply because one's theology demands that James must use *dikaioo* in the demonstrative sense. When applied to men, the New Testament always uses "justified" to mean forgiveness of sin, the maintaining of one's forgiven state (lest he fall from that state), the increase of

---

17 Greek: καὶ ἐδικαιώθη ἡ σοφία ἀπὸ τῶν ἔργων and καὶ ἐδικαιώθη ἡ σοφία ἀπὸ πάντων τῶν τέκνων αὐτῆς.

18 For example, R. C. Sproul, in citing Luke 7:35, explains that the children are demonstrating wisdom, not reconciling wisdom to God by having babies. Sproul admits, however, that this is a "figurative" use of *dikaioo* (*Faith Alone*, op. cit., p. 166).

19 For example, in the metaphorical expression "you are the apple of my eye," we certainly should not understand "apple" as a person who was transformed into a piece of fruit in someone's eye. The technical understanding of an apple is a piece of fruit, but the poetic context changes the connotation of *apple* to a term of endearment. In any case, we cannot define the technical meaning of words by appealing to their use in poetic contexts.

grace from God, and the receiving of eternal life. All in all, when James and Paul use the term "justified," they are referring to an *active* event, not a passive demonstration.[20]

That *vindication* cannot be James's meaning of the word *dikaioo* is seen even more clearly by his addition of Rahab to the discussion of justification. As James opens up the review of Rahab, he introduces her account by the phrase "In the same way..." (James 2:25). By this wording, James is connecting the justification of Abraham to the justification of Rahab and declaring that *they are the same*. We must conclude, then, that there is no theological difference in the way these two people were justified in the eyes of God. If there were a difference, then either James would be misleading us or God would have two systems of justification, one for the Jews and one for the Gentiles. The former is impossible: inspired Scripture could never mislead. According to many passages in the New Testament the latter is also impossible: God shows no favoritism between Jew and Gentile, and there is only one name under heaven by which men and women are saved. The importance of understanding the identical nature of Abraham's and Rahab's respective justifications becomes clear when we consider that James certainly does not view Rahab's justification as a *vindication.* Using Protestant terminology, we cannot say that Rahab was given a forensic imputation of justification *prior* to the meeting of the Israelite spies. Rahab was a prostitute who lived an immoral life until she encountered God through the Israelites. Her justification comes on the heels of her acceptance of the God of Israel and his laws, which would necessitate that she immediately

[20] Since the use of δικαιόω in Luke 7:35 is figurative, the only other possible reference for a demonstrative meaning is 1 Timothy 3:16, which speaks of Christ being "justified in the Spirit." Yet as Protestant Richard Gaffin points out, even in this instance the demonstrative application fails (*Resurrection and Redemption: A Study in Paul's Soteriology* (New Jersey: Presbyterian and Reformed, 1978, 1987) pp. 119-122). Gaffin insists that since "justified by the Spirit" refers to the resurrection, "nothing warrants a different sense for the verb than its virtually uniform meaning elsewhere in Paul." Though Gaffin concludes that *dikaioo* in 1 Timothy 3:16 must then have a declarative meaning in keeping with Reformation thought, we must insist, conversely, that 1 Tim. 3:16 is yet another proof of the *transformational* dimension of δικαιόω by the mere fact that Christ in his resurrection was literally transformed from a state of death to a state of life.

repented of her evil ways and decided to live righteously. An *active event* took place in Rahab's relationship with God, not a demonstration of a previous justification. Hence, if Rahab is not *vindicated* but is truly *justified* during her encounter with the Israelite spies, and since James insists that Abraham was justified "*in the same way,*" then we can only conclude that both Abraham in Genesis 22 and Rahab in Joshua 2 were salvifically *justified* before God, not *vindicated.*

We can critique the so-called "actual/declarative" model of Protestant James Buchanan in a similar fashion. Although it may be *theoretically* plausible to insert a two-stage justification — one actual, one declaratory — in Abraham's life, it is not possible to do so with Rahab. Rahab's justification is not divided into two phases as is Abraham's. Thus, using Buchanan's terms, if we are to understand Rahab's justification in James 2:25-26 as a *declared* justification, this leaves no room for her *actual* justification. On the other hand, if we are to understand the justification of Rahab in James 2:25-26 as her *actual* justification, then there is not only no room for her *declared* justification, there is also no *verbal* declaration from God in Joshua 2 that Rahab was justified. Moreover, if Rahab's justification in James 2:25-26 is an *actual* justification, then Abraham's justification in James 2:24 must also be an *actual* justification, since James states specifically that Rahab was justified "in the same way" as Abraham. This would of course mean that Abraham's justification in Genesis 22 was also an *actual* justification.

Another reason we must understand that Paul and James are using the same definition of the word *dikaioo* is that in clarifying the proper relation of faith and works, James 2:23 quotes from Genesis 15:6 ("Abraham believed God and it was credited to him as *righteousness*"). As noted above, this is the same Genesis passage from which Paul quotes in Romans 4:3. The Greek word for "righteousness" is *dikaiosune*. Since both James and Paul quote from Genesis 15:6, both must be using the same meaning and have the same understanding of the word *dikaiosune*.[21] That being the

[21] The word *dikaiosune* (δικαιοσύνη) translates the Hebrew word *tsedaqah* (צדקה) from Genesis 15:6, unless Paul and James were using the Septuagint translation, which already contained δικαιοσύνη.

case, it would be totally incongruous for both of them to have the same definition of *dikaiosune,* but for one of them suddenly to have a different definition of its cognate *dikaioo* ("justified"). Yet Protestants must accept this incongruity or conclude even more incongruously that James is using two different senses of the same root word within two verses (i.e., James 2:23 and 2:24).[22] In addition, it would be totally inconsistent for Paul and James to be appealing to the same Old Testament verse (i.e., Genesis 15:6) to prove their respective points, the former choosing a forensic model wherein Abraham is an ungodly man imputed with someone else's righteousness, and the latter choosing a demonstrative model wherein Abraham is a godly man who merely needs to demonstrate his justified state. What the Protestant position ends up saying is that the word *justified* for Paul means, "declared legally just" but for James means, "demonstrated to be declared legally just." Suffice it to say that even the most ardent advocate of the forensic model cannot demonstrate the latter usage of *dikaioo* in Scripture.

We can critique the use of the demonstrative/vindicative model to explain Abraham's justification in James 2:24 from a larger perspective. The demonstrative/vindicative model assumes that Abraham's salvation is a foregone conclusion after Genesis 15:6. In turn, his justification needs only to be verified by a measurable act of obedience.[23] The problem with this view is that the context

---

22 Protestant Ronald Fung proposes that very thing. He writes: "The above exegesis has revealed two senses of 'justification' in James: (1) imputed righteousness (dikaiosyne) or forensic justification is attained as a gift by faith ([verse] 23); (2) justification (dikaiousthai) in the sense of a demonstration of the possession of genuine faith is by works ([verses] 21, 24, 25)" (op. cit., p. 157).

23 Fung commandeers the adjectival cognate δίκαιος from James 5:16 and uses it to refer to a "devout member of the believing community so that for Abraham to be 'shown to be just' means for him to be shown by his action of offering up Isaac, to be a true believer." Fung continues that Abraham is "making good on the claim to have faith" that was put as a question in James 2:14, *viz.*, "can faith save him?" The problem with this view is that the context of James 2:13-26 is not concerned so much with how one will demonstrate his faith as with whether one will even be saved. To resolve this dilemma, Fung's demonstrative/vindicative model assumes that Abraham's salvation was already made absolute in Genesis 15:6 and that thus all Abraham needed to do was make that certainty evident in Genesis 22.

of James 2, as well as the surrounding context of James 1-5, is not so concerned with the demonstration of faith as it is with whether one, in the end, will be saved or not. The question posed by James 2:14 is "Can faith save him?" (pointing to the future), not "Can he demonstrate that he is already saved?" (pointing to the past).[24] Hence, if the person to whom James is speaking chooses not to perform the good works James details in 2:15 (e.g., feeding the hungry, clothing the naked), then the answer to the question posed in James 2:14 will be in the negative, that is, he will not be saved. The same must apply to Abraham and Rahab. A refusal from either to do the works of obedience required of them (i.e., not offering Isaac and not hiding the spies, respectively) would have put them in the same negative category in answer to the question posed in James 2:14, e.g., they would not be saved. Not applying the question of salvation to Abraham and Rahab with regard to their respective justifications would neutralize James 2:14 of its intent to probe and interrogate this very important area in their lives.

The Context of James 2

To prove that James is placing his material in a *soteriological* context as opposed to a mere *demonstrative* context, we need only observe how James opens up the matter for discussion. After admonishing Christians not to discriminate against the poor (James 2:1-9), and further encouraging them not to come under judgment by breaking the law (2:10-11), James warns in 2:12-13, "Speak and act as those who are going to be judged by the law that gives freedom, because judgment without mercy will be shown to anyone who has not been merciful..." Here is James's first reference to the coming judgment. It is a judgment that will show either mercy

[24] The word "save" is a Greek infinitive of purpose (σῶσαι) which is used to express the purpose of the action or state denoted by the principal verb. The aorist infinitive (used in James 2:14), when used in these cases to point to the future result of the main verb (in this case δύναται ("able")). New Testament examples of the aorist infinitive used to point to future results appear in Matthew 5:17; Luke 18:10; Acts 10:33, et al.

or no mercy to the one being judged; thus, the question of whether one will be saved or damned is clearly in view.[25]

As noted above, James continues to describe the context in which he is writing by the question he raises in James 2:14: "What is the profit, my brothers, if anyone says he has faith but does not have works? Can faith ***save*** him?" The question James poses is one of eternal importance. "Will he indeed be saved?" is the haunting question that begins the section on faith and works. James is not just speaking in spiritual platitudes when he warns them in the previous verses not to discriminate against the poor and not to fall into personal sin. In light of his rhetorical question in verse 14, the categorical consequence of such sinful actions are that one will *not* be saved. By extension, we must also understand that the one who may *not be saved* in James 2:14 is the same person who may *not be justified* in James 2:21-26.[26]

James also focuses on the same issue we have seen Paul cite so frequently in his epistles: the second greatest commandment. In James 2:8, he writes, "If you really keep the royal law found in

---

25 As we have seen of Paul's writing in chapter 1, James also uses the principle of *evaluation under grace* as opposed to *judgment under law*. James speaks of a *law of freedom* and a *law which shows no mercy*. The *law of freedom* is the same as Paul's teaching of living under God's grace and pleasing God by our faith and works. On the other hand, the *law which shows no mercy* is the system of law that requires 100% obedience or else it will condemn. We know this is James's intent from James 2:10 where he states in reference to the system of law, "For whoever keeps the whole law and yet stumbles at just one point is guilty of all of it." In the system of law, one fault will condemn the individual eternally.

26 Fung admits that giving "justified" the same sense as "to save" in James 2:14 would indeed fit the context but he objects that this usage is not paralleled in Scripture. It is hard to see any merit in Fung's argument, not only because the context demands such an association between "justified" and "save," but because the Scripture uses both words together and in connection with one another. For example, Paul uses the aorist indicative ἔσωσεν ("he saved") and the aorist participle δικαιωθέντες ("having been justified"), in Titus 3:5-7, showing that salvation is in view when justification is mentioned. In addition, Paul uses the aorist participle δικαιωθέντες with the future indicative σωθησόμεθα in Romans 5:9, showing the timely connection between the two. We can also add Matthew's use of the future indicative δικαιωθήσῃ in Matthew 12:37 in the context of being judged for one's works at the eschaton. Hence, the interchange of words and tenses in reference to both σῴζω and δικαιόω puts the burden of proof on anyone attempting to separate them in James 2:14-26.

Scripture, 'Love your neighbor as yourself,' you are doing right. But if you show favoritism, you sin and are convicted by the law as lawbreakers." "Love your neighbor as yourself" is the focal point of this section. It is interesting to note that James appeals to the "royal law found in Scripture" to reinforce this point. This law of love was recorded as far back as Leviticus 19:18. Things have not changed in that respect. James takes this "royal law" and opposes it to "showing favoritism," obviously teaching that one is not loving his neighbor when he favors one person over another.

In 2:15-16, James elaborates on how a person is to love his neighbor: "Suppose a brother or sister is without clothes and daily food. If one of you says to him, 'Go, I wish you well; keep warm and well fed,' but does nothing about his physical needs, what good is it?" This is another form of the discrimination against the poor to which James had first alluded to in 2:5: "Suppose a man comes into your meeting wearing a gold ring and fine clothes, and a poor man in shabby clothes also comes in..." By the use of the word "suppose" in both 2:5 and 2:15, James is presenting two hypothetical yet highly probable cases to his audience. In both cases the situation involves one who is not financially well-off, in the first with "shabby clothes," in the second "without clothes." In both cases, if one were to abide by the "royal law of Scripture" which is to "love your neighbor as yourself," then he would treat the poor man in the first case with the same respect as the rich man, and he would give the poor man in the second case some clothes and food. Hence, when James asks the all-important question "Can faith save him?," he is directing it to the person who is not abiding by the royal law to love one's neighbor. Not only would James say that his faith will not save him, but as 2:9 says, "if you show favoritism, *you sin* and are convicted by the law as lawbreakers." The emphasis on sin is very apparent. Thus we must understand that if one sees a brother or sister in physical need and deliberately chooses not to provide for them, it is not just a lack of works, it is also *sin*. As James says in 4:17, "Anyone, then, who knows the good he ought to do and doesn't do it, sins."[27] Or as John says in 1 John 3:17, "If anyone has

[27] This illustrates why the demonstrative/vindicative model cannot apply in James 2. If one deliberately refuses to do the required works, it is not merely that his faith is alone, but he has also sinned and is subject to judgment.

material possessions and sees his brother in need but has no pity on him, how can the love of God be in him? Dear children, let us not love with words or tongue but with actions and in truth."[28]

James had mentioned previously in 1:27, "Religion that God our Father accepts as pure and faultless is this: to look after orphans and widows in their distress and to keep oneself from being polluted by the world." Orphans and widows would indeed fit into the same class of destitution as the man dressed in shabby clothes in James 2:2 or the man with no clothes and food in James 2:15. Not taking care of their needs would be classed as sins of *omission*. In addition, James never tires of reminding his audience not to sin and thus includes a command to refrain from the world's influence. These "worldly" sins, which are later specified in James 2:10-11 as murder, adultery, etc., are sins of *commission.*

James says in 2:17, "Even so, faith, if it has not works, is dead by itself." By the words, "even so," James is connecting the previous two verses (15-16) concerning taking care of someone's physical needs with the principle that faith without works is dead (verse 17). In other words, a deliberate refusal to provide for the needs of the poor and destitute shows either that one's faith is already dead or that it died at the moment of refusal.[29] The concept of "dead faith" is a major theme in the chapter since James mentions it three times (verses 17, 20, 26).[30] In the last reference (verse 26, "the

---

28 "Even though incorporated into the Church, one who does not however persevere in charity is not saved. He remains indeed in the bosom of the Church, but 'in body' not 'in heart'" (Vatican Council II, *Lumen Gentium,* 14...); "therefore the first and most necessary gift is charity, by which we love God above all things and our neighbor because of him..." (*Lumen Gentium*, 42).

29 Catholic Catechism, Section 1033: "Our Lord warns us that we shall be separated from him if we fail to meet the serious needs of the poor and the little ones who are his brethren." (See also Sections 2443-2449).

30 From the Greek νεκρός which is the normal word for *dead* in the New Testament, here used as an adjective modifying faith. In verse 20, the wording could be "barren" or "unfruitful" due to a textual variant which contains the Greek ἀργόν rather than νεκρός. Ἀργόν appears in Codices Vaticanus (B) and Ephraemi Rescriptus (C) and four minuscules. This is in opposition to νεκρός which is used by the majority of uncials, including Sinaiticus (א) and Alexandrinus (A), along with twenty-two minuscules, the Byzantine lectionary and other versions. A curious solo variant κενή ("empty, without result or effect") appears in the Bodmer papyrus #74. (*The Greek New Testament*, ed. Kurt Aland, et al; 3rd ed., p. 783). In my opinion, νεκρός is the proper reading due to the majority of manuscript witnesses and the preponderant usage of it in the context of James.

body without the spirit is dead"), James makes it clear that he is using the word *dead* in the normal sense of physical death. The analogy of a dead body follows the reference to the justification of Rahab. In other words, faith that is not accompanied by work will not justify. James's analogy can be used in either of two senses. A whole life of dead faith (e.g., a body which has been dead a long time) is different from just one incident in which the faith is "killed" because a work was not done (e.g., a body that has just died).

James considered the people to whom he was writing as "believers in our Lord Jesus Christ" (James 2:1). This would mean that they had faith. The main question, then, is whether they will consistently add works to their faith.[31] On the one hand, if they have never chosen to add works to their faith, then they have always had a dead faith. On the other hand, if an incident occurs in which they choose not to add works to faith, then they have ruptured the relationship between faith and works at that instant. Any instance of separating works from faith is sin (e.g., not helping a brother in need is sin, as noted in James 4:17). This does not mean that faith is nonexistent, however. Just as a dead body exists by the mere fact that someone recognizes it as dead, by analogy dead faith can exist as faith. Hence, one should not misconstrue James's point in referring to "dead faith" to say that the faith is nonexistent; rather, James is referring to faith that has no capability to act even as a dead body without the spirit has no capability to act. As the spirit gives physical life to the body, so works give salvific life to faith. Only faith alive with consciously decided works pleases God. Christians, then, must make a decision every day to make their faith alive.

By adding the words "by itself" in 2:17, James is pointing out that his objection is to a faith that is alone. If James was not interested in objecting to the solitude of faith he could simply have

---

[31] The New Testament speaks directly to the aspect of "adding" to faith, e.g., "For this reason, make every effort to add to your faith goodness ... knowledge ... self-control ... perseverance ... godliness ... brotherly kindness ...love" (2 Peter 2:5-8). This is said in a context of striving to complete one's salvation, as noted in the final exhortation of the passage, "Therefore, my brothers, be all the more eager to make your calling and election sure. For if you do these things you will never fall and you will receive a rich welcome into the eternal kingdom..." See also Col. 1:4-5; 1 Tim. 1:14; 2 Tim. 1:13; 3:10; Tit. 2:2; Philem. 5; Rev. 2:19.

said, "Faith, if it does not have works, is dead" without the addendum of "by itself." Whatever one's conception of faith and works, James is making it clear that the best way to describe the rupture in the relationship is to say that it puts faith into a position of being "by itself"[32] (verse 17) or that faith "is alone" (verse 24). Apparently there is no better way to describe it. It is not called "unqualified faith" or "nonjustifying faith." Apparently James does not want to give the impression that as long as faith is of a sufficient quality then faith by itself can save. Faith and works are two separate entities: one believes, the other acts. Sin (bad work) does not necessarily destroy faith but it does make one ineligible for salvation. By analogy, faith that cannot be used in justification is a "dead faith." To balance this equation, one must also recognize that Scripture also speaks of "dead works."[33] Work, by itself, will not produce justification either. Faith and works, though separate entities, must be joined together for salvation to occur. Hence considering that James has chosen language which specifies not the quality of faith but the addition or subtraction of works to faith (e.g., 2:14: "you have faith but do not have works"; 2:17: "faith, by itself"; 2:24: "not by faith alone"), one should not understand the question "Can faith save him?" in 2:14 to read "Can *that kind* of faith save him?", but rather "Can faith *alone* save him?" or "Can faith, *by itself*, save him?" The answer is an unequivocal no.

This analysis introduces another category of explanations that Protestants offer as to the nature of James's argument. Many claim that the works which James has in view are those that inevitably, automatically, or necessarily flow from true faith. Consequently, it is not the works that are involved in the justification of the man but only his faith, since true faith will inevitably produce good works. In this framework, these Protestants consider works as merely a *by-product* or *result* of faith. Thus works themselves do

[32] The phrase "by itself" is from the Greek καθ' ἑαυτήν, in which κατα is a preposition meaning "by, in, according," etc., and the reflexive personal pronoun ἑαυτήν meaning, "himself, herself, or itself."

[33] cf., Hebrews 6:1: "repentance from dead works"; Hebrews 9:14: "will cleanse the conscience from dead works"; Rom. 9:32: "they sought it not by faith but as it were by works."

not determine salvation; they only prove that the faith is real.[34] The individual need only have a "saving faith" and his justification is secure.[35]

Although we grant that faith for justification must be genuine, this does not mean that we must consider the works which accompany faith as mere qualifiers or descriptions of faith, as though "quality faith" alone is all that James is requiring.[36] James is teaching that we must intentionally and categorically add works to faith in order to effectuate and complete justification. Protestant theol-

---

[34] Translations of key passages in James show this tendency. The Greek of James 2:14 literally translates as, "Is the faith able to save him?" Most translations opt for turning the article into a demonstrative pronoun, e.g., "Can *that* faith save him?" (ASV, NASB, NEB, TEV), but more deliberate is the rendering of the NIV: "Can *such* faith save him?" Translations that keep the article or treat it as superfluous are the RSV: "Can his faith save him?"; the NRSV: "Can faith save you?"; the KJV and Moffatt: "Can faith save him?"; and the Douay-Rheims: "Shall faith be able to save him?" Fung defends the use of the demonstrative "that" on the basis that it is anaphoric (op. cit., p. 278). Though this is possible, the major problem which develops from anaphora is the unproven assumption that James is concerned only about the quality of faith, which leads to the false conclusion that faith can act alone as long as it is the right kind of faith.

[35] Although "saving faith" has become a very popular phrase in Evangelical teaching on justification, Scripture never uses such terminology. Of the 125 times the Greek word σῶζω is used in the New Testament, it is never used as an adjectival participle in conjunction with the noun faith, or any other noun. It is only used in noun and verb form. On the other hand, faith is described in various ways, e.g., "I...delight to see how firm your faith in Christ is" (Col. 2:5); "a sincere faith" (1 Tim. 1:5; 2 Tim. 1:5); "rich in faith" (James 2:5); "standing firm in the faith" (1 Peter 5:9); "your most holy faith" (Jude 20).

[36] It is important to note here that Catholic theology distinguishes among three states: (1) one who has faith united with hope and love and thereby procures salvation (Council of Trent, Session 6, Chapter 7); (2) one who retains faith but has fallen into mortal sin and thereby loses the grace of salvation; (3) one who loses his faith, e.g., by heresy or apostasy, and thus loses the grace of justification (Council of Trent, Session 6, Chapter 15). In light of perspective #2, we should note that the distinction that is often made between "intellectual faith" and "heart faith," which concludes that the former is *not* salvific and the latter *is* salvific (i.e., what is commonly termed as "saving faith"), presents a false dichotomy within the total picture of justification. Although one who has "intellectual faith" is usually a callous, unrepentant person, by the same token, a person who has "heart faith" may fall into mortal sin and end up under eternal judgment. His faith may still be strong after he sins but if he were to die at that moment, his mortal sin would bring him under condemnation. Hence, whether it is "intellectual faith" or "heart faith," it still remains that faith alone cannot save. Defining faith in terms of "saving faith," then, merely begs the question.

ogy needs to emphasize the quality of faith, as opposed to separate categories of faith and works joining together, partly because of its theory of legal imputation. In essence, the Protestant conception of justification is that one is saved by a one-time act of faith. In that act of faith, God is said to impute the righteousness of Christ to the individual so that God can now consider him as legally, though not intrinsically, justified. Anything coming after the solitary act of faith which produced the one-time justification must be placed in another theological category — a non salvific category called "sanctification." In other words, the completed imputation seals the justification and the person is now out of the category of justification and into the category of sanctification. Since sanctification is the only category in which he can do works, works cannot be connected to the category of justification. Hence, Protestants reason that James's stress on works is only for the purpose of demonstrating the authenticity of the initial faith in which one accepted Christ. If the works are not of the expected quality, then this, in many Protestant views, shows that one never had true faith and therefore was never justified originally. We will address more of this notion in chapters 4 and 5. For the time being, let us examine more of James's description of faith and works to show the fallacy of Protestant thinking on this issue.[37]

James opens up his context in 2:1 by saying, "My *brothers*, as believers in our glorious Lord Jesus Christ..." He continues with this *brotherly* address in 2:5, "Listen, my *brothers*..." and uses it again in 2:14, "What good is it, my *brothers*..." (cf., James 1:16,19). Here we see that James is not addressing some amorphous collection of people who have merely assented to Christian principles of

---

[37] Not all Protestants hold this view. D.O. Via, for example, sees faith and works as true co-working factors both necessary for justification. ("The Right Strawy Epistle Reconsidered: A Study in Biblical Ethics and Hermeneutics" *Journal of Religion* 49 (1969), pp. 255-257). Others point out that while Reformed doctrine places regeneration prior to justifying faith, this would necessitate that works are a product of regeneration and thus equally as necessary as faith for justification. Martin Luther believed that faith preceded regeneration but John Calvin reversed the order. Some current Reformed theologians, such as Norman Shepherd, follow Calvin's *ordo salutis* to its logical conclusion and assert that works are salvific since they stem from the same regeneration that produced faith. See chapter 9 for a more thorough discussion of this issue.

conduct as if they possessed only a civil religion. These are people whom James knows very well, people who are in the Church, people who have been baptized, confessed their sins, and are already called "believers in our glorious Lord Jesus Christ" (2:1). James confirms this genuine state of belief by mentioning their intimate gatherings of worship in verse 2: "Suppose a man comes into your meeting (or "synagogue")." These people already have faith, but what is the problem? They are tempted to show favoritism to the rich man and to despise the poor man. Are the works of kindness and love just flowing naturally out of them? Indeed they are not. Apparently, they must be taught and trained to do good works, and they must be made aware that if they do not do them it is sin — sin that could result in damnation. They must make a decision not to discriminate — it does not merely flow from them naturally. Granted, once they have cultivated their faith they should possess a better spiritual disposition from which to perform good works, but this does not mean that at each moment when works are required that they will see them inevitably appear. Good works will not automatically flow from them any more than refraining from overt sin happens automatically without a conscious decision to abstain from it. The backdrop for James's teaching is the age-old battle between the spirit and the flesh. The spirit tells them to love the poor man but the flesh tells them to discriminate against him. To encourage them, James refers them to the "Royal Law found in Scripture — Love your neighbor as yourself."[38]

The Larger Context of James

In examining the context of the chapters surrounding the Epistle of James, we find the same evidence that good works do not inevitably or necessarily flow from the Christian. Rather, James teaches

---

38 We should also add that, because of *actual* grace, faith and love can be present in rudimentary form prior to justification. Then, through *sanctifying* grace, they are infused into the individual in a more profound way at initial justification. Thus, the individual possesses an inherent power to exhibit faith and love. When we speak of "adding" love to faith for the purposes of being justified we are referring to accessing the spirit of love already infused into the individual — a love that must be brought out by a conscious act of his will in cooperation with the grace of God.

that the individual must make a conscious decision not only to refrain from sin but also to do good works. James 1:4 states one of the major themes of the book: "*Perseverance* must finish its work so that you may be mature and complete, not lacking anything," and reiterates the theme in 1:12: "Blessed is the man who perseveres under trial..." In 1:20-22, James explains that man's sin, specifically his anger, does not produce the righteousness of God.[39] He commands them to "get rid of all moral filth and evil," demonstrating that they must make the conscious effort to attain the righteousness of God. Earlier, in 1:5-7, James had told them that if they lacked wisdom to do these good works, they should ask God, who gives generously to all. But he warns that one must ask God without doubting; otherwise, one will not receive God's divine help. Again, he places the burden on the individual to cooperate with the grace that God has given him.

In 1:21, James says that doing such things "can save you." He uses the word "save" five times in this epistle. We have already noted one of the most important in 2:14 where James asks the rhetorical question "Can faith save him?"[40] One other instance of "to save" occurs in 4:12. Here James says, "There is only one Lawgiver and Judge, the one who is able to *save* and destroy. But you — who are you to judge your neighbor?" This warning is quite ominous. Notice that James speaks of "judging your neighbor." He further develops the theme in 4:11 with the warning, "Brothers, do not slander one another. Anyone who speaks against his brother or judges him speaks against the law and judges it." This closely resembles what James said in 2:1-13 (the passage just prior to the controversy about faith and works in 2:14-26), where he faulted them for discriminating against the poor and committing adultery and murder against their brothers. James 2:13 specified a "judgment that will be shown without mercy" for those who do such

---

[39] This is one of ten places where the New Testament uses the phrase "righteousness of God." We will develop this theme more fully in chapter 5.

[40] The phrase "can save you" in James 1:21 is the almost identical verbal form used in James 2:14 (present participle δυνάμενον with the aorist infinitive σῶσαι), the former putting δύναται in the present participle, the latter in the present indicative. Both point to the potential of salvation rather than unquestioned security.

things. Similarly, 4:12 warns them that God is the one who "saves and destroys." Clearly, James wants to avoid giving the impression that their salvation is secured and guaranteed. If they persist in sin, they will be "judged without mercy" (2:13) and "destroyed" (4:12).

We can see James's serious intent by the way he opens up chapter 4. In 4:1, he specifies their "fights and quarrels." These come from the "desires that battle within" them (i.e., their sinful nature). In 4:2, he says they "murder and covet." In 4:4, he calls them "adulterous people" who are "friends of the world." In 4:8 he calls them "sinners" and "double-minded." But James is speaking not to the world, rather, to the Christians in the Church. We see this, for example, in 4:2 as he points out that they "do not ask God," and in 4:11 as he again calls them "brothers." Repeatedly, he places the burden on the Christian to choose right — to make a conscious decision to seek God — just as he told them in 1:2-6 to seek God's wisdom in knowing how to endure trials and not fall into sin. James emphasizes this responsibility in 4:7 when he commands them to:

> Submit yourselves, then, to God. Resist the devil and he will flee from you. Come near to God and he will come near to you. Wash your hands, you sinners, and purify your hearts...grieve, mourn, and wail. Change your laughter into mourning and your joy into gloom. Humble yourselves before the Lord, and he will lift you up.

Can anyone doubt from reading these passages, addressed specifically to Christians, that works of obedience do not just inevitably flow from believers but that they must recognize themselves to be in a constant daily struggle to resist the sinful nature? Indeed, James leaves them no room for doubt about this message. The text states that they are this way because they have chosen not to seek the Lord. If they had, God would have helped them.

Now we can see more clearly why James in 2:14 holds their salvation in abeyance with the haunting question "Can faith save him?" The issue is not merely whether or not the Christian's good works will justify him, but whether or not he has refrained from sin. "Good works" refer not only to doing something positive (e.g., feeding the hungry) but also to refraining from the negative, i.e., sin. Since sin can occur not only by commission (e.g., murder, adultery, coveting) but also by omission (e.g., James 4:17: "anyone who knows the good he ought to do and doesn't do it, sins"), then the potential for sin has a direct bearing on our understanding of the passage in question.

This is not all. In chapter 3, James again describes the bad works that will jeopardize one's salvation. James gives the most astounding treatise on the evil of the spoken word found in Scripture. Speaking to the same Christian audience in 3:9 (NB, the continual use of "my brothers" in 3:10, 12; cf., 1:16,19; 4:11), James points out that with the tongue they "praise the Lord and Father" but at the same time "curse men made in the likeness of God." This is the same accusation he made in 1:26, "If anyone considers himself religious and yet does not keep a *tight reign on his tongue*, he deceives himself and his religion is worthless," and in 4:11, "Brothers, do not *slander* one another..." In this pervasive context, two important points emerge. First, chapters 1, 3, and 4 of James, all of which warn against sin, especially sins of the tongue, surround chapter 2's discussion of faith and works. This positioning leads us to conclude that the potential for sin, especially sins of the tongue, is germane to the discussion of faith and works. In fact, in chapter 2 James consistently stresses what a brother "says" as he discriminates against the poor (e.g., James 2:3: "but *say* to the poor man...sit on the floor by my feet"). In this instance, James concludes that they have become "*judges* with evil thoughts" (2:4), which is the same language he uses in 4:11, "Anyone who speaks against his brother or *judges* him." In 2:16 he also points out what is "said": "one of you *says* to him, 'Go, I wish you well; keep warm and well fed.'" This person, like the one in 1:26, cannot keep a tight reign on his tongue but instead spills out spiritual platitudes that help no one. James could have taught the same truths without this hypothetical dialogue. He could simply have made a matter-of-fact statement such as "what good is it if one has faith but does not care for someone's physical needs?" The stress on the words the Christian *speaks*, however, illustrates an important theme in the book of James: *watch what you say — you may harm someone*. The tongue can give pretense of religiosity; it can judge another; in fact, "it is a world of iniquity" (3:6).[41]

Second, after James's treatise on the tongue in 3:1-12, he follows with "Who is wise and understanding among you? Let him show it by his good life, by *deeds* done in the humility that comes from wisdom." Clearly, controlling one's tongue is a matter of wisdom and understanding. In 3:1, James points out that they were all wishing to be "teachers." They all had *something to say*, as it were, things they thought were full of wisdom and understanding. In their teaching they "praised God" but "cursed man made in the image of God." They would sing God's praises with the tongue but then treat men, including their Christian brothers, with contempt. They would teach faith with their tongue but curse men both by the tongue and lack of good deeds. Thus, in so many words, James says in 3:13, "Do you really want to have wisdom and understanding? Then show it by deeds done in humility."[42] This is the same "wisdom" he told them to seek in 1:5-6. The opposite of this wisdom, as James goes on to say in 3:14-16, is "bitter envy" and "selfish ambition" and "every evil practice." Perhaps the teachers of 3:1 were prone to living by this double standard — teaching faith but doing evil. Again, we see that the contrast James develops throughout this epistle is good works versus bad works, obedience versus sin, "saying" you will do good versus actually doing good. When James says "let him show it" in 3:13, he is using the same word he used in 2:18 in the faith and works controversy, i.e., "I will show you."[43] The mind can be deceived into thinking it has done good but it cannot know for certain, yea, it cannot know at all, until it makes a conscious effort to do good and avoid sin. Goodness will not flow naturally; in fact, the believer's inner sinful nature will continually fight against the good. He must control his sinful desires and discipline himself to do good works. By the grace and wisdom of God, which he must

41 "If you blow on a spark, it will glow; if you spit on it, it will be put out; yet both come out of your mouth. Curse the gossips and the double-tongued, for they destroy the peace of many...Those who pay heed to slander will not find rest...Many have fallen by the edge of the sword, but not as many as have fallen because of the tongue" (Ecclesiasticus 28:12-18).

42 The word "deeds" in James 3:13 is the same Greek word for "works" in James 2:14- 26.

43 From the Greek δεῖξόν.

also consciously call on for help, he can be victorious. He *must* do this, for without holiness he will not see the Lord (Hebrews 12:14), or in James's words, he will not be "saved" or "justified."

James continues the stress on avoiding sins of the tongue in Chapter 5. In 5:1-6, the Christians are being persecuted and physically abused by the rich masters. In 5:7-12, James tells them to be patient in this trial until "the Lord's coming." Interspersed with this admonition is the admonition not to sin with one's tongue. In 5:9, James warns them: "Do not *grumble* against each other, brothers, or you will be judged. The Judge is standing at the door!" Perhaps in suffering under the strain of persecution they were beginning to take it out on their Christian brothers by verbally abusing one another. James reinforces his admonition by citing an example from the Old Testament: Job, who did not curse God or his neighbors with his tongue even though he was put through a terrible test. It was Job's very wife who told him, "Curse God and die" (Job 2:9). The most important statement in all of Job appears in Job 2:10: "In all this Job did not sin with his *lips*." James continues the same line of argument when in 5:12 he tells them not to *swear* by anything and to let their "yes" be "yes" and "no" be "no." Again the stress is on the possibility of sinning with the tongue. James recommends that for those who do not hold up under the persecution, either physically or spiritually, call for the presbyters of the Church who will pray over them and seek God's grace and healing. If one has sinned, either with the lips or in any other manner, the Lord will forgive him and raise him up (5:13-18). Those who bring the wayward brother to the presbyters[44] receive James's commendation for a good work (5:19-20).

James and Paul

At this point, it would be helpful to see the parallels between James and Paul. In Galatians 5:6, Paul speaks of "faith working through love." In this context, Paul includes the "Royal law" of James in Galatians 5:14 by the statement, "The entire law is summed

44 Versions such as the Douay-Rheims translate the word πεσβυτέρους in James 5:14 as "priests." This is appropriate since etymologically, "priest" is derived from the old English "presbys" or "presbyter" (see Webster's Dictionary).

up in a single command, 'Love your neighbor as yourself.'" In the same context, Paul also speaks about avoiding sin by not living in the sinful nature (Galatians 5:15-26); the same theme that James takes up in James 1:13 and 2:10-11. Finally, in Galatians 5:21, Paul warns of the consequences for disobedience as "those who live like this will not inherit the kingdom of God." James warns of the same consequences in 2:13 when he says, "because judgment without mercy will be shown to anyone who has not been merciful." The similarities between Paul and James are not mere coincidence. Faith requires the addition of love towards God and one's neighbor. Salvation is not by faith alone.

In the following verses of Galatians 5, Paul goes on to describe the same battle between the Spirit and the flesh that James repeats so often. In Galatians 5:16 Paul says, "So I say, live by the Spirit, and you will not gratify the desires of the sinful nature. For the sinful nature desires what is contrary to the Spirit, and the Spirit what is contrary to the sinful nature." Next, Paul's warning in 5:21 is that if one lives by the sinful nature he will lose his inheritance in the kingdom of God. Likewise, James makes it clear that he is just as serious, continuing in 2:9-13 that if one discriminates against a lower social class, then he will be judged by God "without mercy."

The analysis is important because it shows that for both Paul and James works are the ultimate factor in the salvation of the individual. If one decides not to follow the Spirit and instead to follow his sinful desires and discriminate against the poor, God will judge him. This is not just a judgment to determine how low his status will be in heaven; according to James 2:14 it is a judgment that allows James to ask the all important question, "Can faith *save* him?" This rhetorical question shows clearly that James is dealing with salvation and damnation within the context of works.

Back to James 2

We notice in James's hypothetical examples of the poor man walking into a meeting with shabby clothes in 2:1-5, and the poor man with no clothes in 2:15, that he wants his audience to think about what they would or should do if a situation like this ever presents itself to them. "What would you do if..." is the type of argumentation he is using. In this method, James forces the individual to examine himself and make a decision: "Will I discriminate or not discriminate?" "Will I help by giving clothing and food or will I not help?" The decision process is what James is trying to probe and establish here. "I say I believe in God and love God; I say I love my neighbor. Am I willing to make the physical effort to help my neighbor with whatever his needs are?" This decision process confronts any person who claims he has faith. According to James, it is a decision to which he must say "yes," or he will not be justified. His hypothetical example of helping someone with physical needs shows by its very nature that it is a daily decision, a decision to which the answer must be "yes" at any moment in a person's life when he is confronted with the possibility of doing good. If he does not answer affirmatively, he sins. If he does not repent of his sin, he will not be justified.

The distinction between the Protestant concept of works that inevitably flow out of true faith and the concept of James in which a person must make a conscious decision to help a brother in need is an important one to stress. Scripture does not teach a mechanical process in which faith automatically produces good works. It is not as if once the button of faith is pushed that the conveyor belt of works will begin to produce the desired product. In fact, as the individual confronts the decision to sin or not to sin each day of his life, so he also confronts the decision to do good works or not do good works, and the two are intimately interrelated. Merely having faith, even good-quality faith, does not mean one will refrain from sin in each situation; likewise, having faith does not mean one will necessarily decide to do good works. As Paul warned the Galatians, "Those who do such things will not inherit the kingdom of God" (Galatians 5:21), so it would be equally valid to warn those who say they have faith but do not do good works — they will not inherit the kingdom of God. Again, James is crystal clear about this ultimatum when he introduces his proposition with the question, "Can faith ***save*** him?" Otherwise, this question would have no real meaning or impact upon his hearers.

James continues this theme in 2:18 by picking up the hypothetical objector left over from 2:16: "But someone will say, You have faith; I have deeds. Show me your faith without deeds, and I will show you my faith by what I do."[45] In this verse James is again basing his argument on what someone *says* as opposed to what he does. Behind the challenge to "Show me your faith without works" is the assumption that someone can convince another by what he *says* that he indeed has faith. He can even do so without showing any works. Conversely, his opponent says that he can show faith by his works. That this incident is put in the form of a dialogue between two opponents would mean that both individuals are dealing from a theological basis, i.e., rather than observing the whole of each other's lives, they are conversing at a moment in time about who between them has the correct understanding of faith and works. Interpreting this verse within the context that James sets up, the first opponent, confronted with the destitute man that James describes in 2:15-16, would conclude that in order to be saved he does *not* need to provide for the poor man's needs. It is simply sufficient that he have faith in God. The second individual insists that one must add to faith by caring for someone's physical needs. James is not condemning the first opponent for giving verbal affirmation of faith. Faith is an act of the will. It puts one on the road to salvation. Faith is good. Having faith in God is much better than being an atheist.[46] James maintains, however, that if one is to be saved, having faith in God is not enough. One must also make a

---

[45] There is some question as to the identity of the opponents in the hypothetical match of wits. One suggestion is that the opening phrase of 2:18, "Someone will say, you have faith" should be in the form of an interrogative as if the opponent is challenging James. Thus it would read, "Someone will say, 'you have faith?'" The next statement, "and I have works" is the answer to the interrogative. The verb, though missing, is implied so as to make the passage mean: "and I will say, 'I have works.'" Lending support to the implied verb, "I will say" are other passages that assume its presence, e.g., Acts 25:22; 9:5; 9:10f. For arguments to this effect see Fung, op. cit., pp. 148-150.

[46] Paul speaks of those who do not have faith: "And pray that we may be delivered from wicked and evil men, for not everyone has faith" (2 Thess. 3:2). Regarding faith itself, Vatican Council I states: "Wherefore, 'faith' itself in itself, even if it 'worketh not by charity,' is a gift of God, and its act is a work pertaining to salvation, by which man offers a free obedience to God himself by agreeing to, and cooperating with his grace, which he could resist"... "Moreover, although the assent of faith is by no means a blind movement of the intellect, nevertheless, no one can 'assent to the preaching of the Gospel,' as he must to attain salvation, 'without the illumination and inspiration of the Holy Spirit, who gives to all a sweetness in consenting to and believing in truth'" (Vatican Council I, DS 1791; in reference to the Council of Orange, Canon 5).

conscious effort to join works with faith in order to show that he is willing to do all that God requires for righteousness. It is relatively easy for me to have faith in God's existence, and to believe that he may perhaps want me to do a *few* things to acknowledge him, but doing works of love for people who are lowly and despised is difficult. The world would pass the needy by without lifting a finger, just as Jesus pointed out in the parable of the Good Samaritan of Luke 10:30-32, the priest and the Levite who passed by the wounded man without helping him. Christians must rise above the mediocrity of the world and be like the Good Samaritan. When the Lord asks them at judgment day if they have fed the hungry and clothed the naked, they must be able to answer in the affirmative or he will condemn them (Matthew 25:31-46). If one refuses to add works of love to faith when the opportunity arises, then the rhetorical question of James 2:14, namely, "Can faith ['by itself'] save him?", must be answered in the negative.

In order to tone down the seriousness of this issue, some Protestants turn to the statement James makes in 2:19: "You believe that there is one God. Good! Even the demons believe that — and shudder." They propose that James's only concern is that someone not have faith like that of the demons. As long as he does not have "that kind" of faith, he can be assured of having "saving faith." This kind of interpretation is a total distortion of James's teaching. James has already established in his context the major tenet that faith and works must both be present in a working relationship, actively participating in caring for someone's physical needs (verses 15-17). Then why does James add the demons to the discussion? By the mere fact that demons are not often used as an example of someone who has faith, James's inclusion of them into the discussion serves as a hyperbolic example of his thesis in the face of continued opposition to James's thesis. In other words, if one does not accept James's opening argument that one must consciously add works to faith by actively participating in caring for the needs of the destitute, then James will take his opponent back to a truth that he cannot deny, namely that the demons have faith, too. As we discovered in Hebrews 11:6, faith has two basic components. First, one must believe that God exists. The demons have this component.[47] However, they do not have the second component, that is, they do not aspire to God as "the rewarder of those that *diligently* seek him." Diligently seeking God requires that they work to please him — something the demons will not do.[48]

As we noted above, James is presenting his point in the form of argumentative dialogue. This is evident in the way he refers to his hypothetical opponent in 2:18 by the clause "But someone will say..." The example of the demons is a powerful argument to convince the opponent because it takes the extreme negative case and makes it the background for the plausible positive case — like

---

[47] Catholic theology holds that just as a demon can believe in God's existence and power yet still be condemned, so a person in mortal sin can still believe in God and yet still be under eternal condemnation. In this sense, then, James's use of the demons is not strictly hyperbolic. The sins James mentions in James 2:11, e.g., murder and adultery, are mortal sins (cf., Cyprian, Ephraim, Theodore, Basil, Pacian, Augustine, Aphraates). If a Christian fell into such sin he would essentially be in the same situation as the demons in regard to faith, i.e., believing yet condemned. Unlike the demons, however, he still has time to repent and be restored to grace. In order to be restored to grace, and thus justified, the person must have the mortal sin forgiven. Sins of such serious nature must be forgiven by God through the instrumentality of the Church. Hence this is another reason why *faith alone* cannot justify. One must add repentance to his faith, along with works of penance (prayers and good works) and restitution (restoring or repairing the damage done by sin). Passages teaching both the Church's mediatorial role in the forgiveness of sins, and the distinction between mortal and venial sin, are plentiful. For the former, cf., Matt. 16:19; 18:18; John 20:23; 2 Cor. 2:7; 5:18; James 5:14-15; for the latter, cf., Matt. 12:39; 23:14-15; Luke 10:12; 12:47-48 (1 Tim. 1:13; Luke 23:34; 2 Pt. 2:21); John 5:14; 19:11; Acts 2:38; 5:3-5; 19:18; 1 Cor. 3:14-17; 6:9; Gal. 5:19-21; Eph. 5:5; 1 Thess. 2:16; 2 Tim. 3:5-6; Heb. 10:26-29; James 3:1; 1 John 5:16-17; Num. 15:27-36; Deut. 22:22; 29:19-21; Lam. 4:6. In the Old Testament, generally, sins punishable by death were mortal sins. See also Council of Trent, Canons on the Sacrament of Penance, e.g., Canons 4, 7, 9, 12-14; Catholic Catechism, Sections 980, 1395, 1440-1460, 1854-1864; as supported by the Church Fathers: Clement, Ignatius, Irenaeus, Tertullian, Cyprian, Lactantius, Hilary, Aphraates, Ambrose, Jerome, Augustine, Cyril, et al.)

[48] Luther attempts to explain James 2:19 by claiming that James is condemning the mere acknowledgment of facts as sufficient for salvation (Hacker, *The Ego in Faith*, p. 101, n. 44). First, James does not discountenance belief in or obedient assent to the facts of redemption. Neither does the New Testament suggest any condemnation of factual knowledge. That even the demons are moved to "shudder" over such knowledge shows the impact it can have. Most important, however, is that James censures the faith of the individual not because he fails to assent firmly to his own faith and salvation, as Luther held, but precisely because he refuses to supplement his faith with works.

putting a white dot on a piece of black paper. That being said, however, James's main argument is not the contrast between demon faith and Christian faith, but between a Christian who takes care of his brother's needs and a Christian who does not. "Can the mere faith of the latter save him?" is the question remaining for James to answer even more completely.

In the following verses (2:21-26), James goes into the third phase of his answer. The first phase concerned the hypothetical situation in which one must decide whether to care for his brother. The second phase used a hyperbolic contrast between Christian faith and demon faith. The third phase concentrates on two real-life examples of the principles James is attempting to illustrate. In this phase, James completes his argument.

Considering that the man with whom he is arguing is not yet convinced of his point, James opens in verse 20 with the address, "You foolish man..." This kind of introduction would be intended, perhaps, for some of the obstinate Jews of that day. Whether the Jew is the only member of James's audience is not known (James 1:1), but even if Gentiles were included, as they probably were, the church at this time contained many Jewish Christians. Ironically, James seems to be having the opposite problem from the one his brother Paul had. Paul was struggling to educate the Jew that the system of law/works could not save anyone, while James is arguing that works are necessary for salvation. The reason Paul and James have these different foci is that the Jew was clinging to his ceremonial rituals and attempting to elevate them as the works that God required, rather than performing works of love encapsulated in the command "love your neighbor as yourself." To be sure, Paul condemned the whole category of law as a means of salvation, but the primary dimension of the law used as a means of salvation for the typical Jew was the ceremonial law, e.g., circumcision, dietary ordinances, etc. For Paul, if one insists on being circumcised as a legal requirement for being a Christian, then one repudiates the system of grace and places himself in the system of law. One who is placed into the system of law will be condemned because one must then obey the whole law faultlessly, and for a single sin one will be held guilty. For James, the same principle is true (see James 2:10). The Jew could not cling to his ceremonial works and ignore the "royal law" of loving the Lord and his neighbor as himself. Although James does not explicitly present the argument as one of ritual law as opposed to royal law, his choice of Abraham as his prime example to prove his point implies this intent. Since the Jew sees Abraham as his godly mentor, James must attack the false notion of Abraham to which the Jew clings. As Paul argues in Romans 4, it was not mere ritual rites that justified Abraham, but a life of faith and obedience that pleased God. Later in the chapter, James presents an even stronger argument as he speaks of the Gentile harlot, Rahab, who was justified even though she knew nothing of Jewish ritual.

James begins the third phase of his argumentation in 2:21: "Was not our father Abraham justified when he offered his son Isaac on the altar."[49] Unlike Paul's quote of Genesis 15:6, which James references in 2:23, James's commentary on the offering of Isaac is significant, since Genesis 22 does not explicitly say that Abraham "was justified" or "credited with righteousness" at that moment in time. Only James's interpretation of the incident tells us that the attempted sacrifice of Isaac is considered a "justification" of Abraham. This tells us that the word "justification," or its cognates, does not have to appear in the original account for the concept of justification to be in view. This will become more important later when we discuss the *process* of justification in chapter 4.[50]

---

[49] The NIV translation, "Was not our ancestor Abraham *considered righteous* for what he did" may show a bias toward the Protestant view of imputation. The Greek aorist passive which literally reads "was justified" is the same word used in James 2:24 which the NIV translates as "you see a person *is justified* by what he does." The translation "considered righteous" may imply that Abraham was not personally or authentically righteous but was only "considered" as such, i.e., he did not possess it personally. In *Justification by Faith Alone,* Protestant Joel Beeke uses such argumentation in reference to the Greek word *logizomai* (λογίζομαι) which we will deal with at length in chapter 5.

[50] Paul and James exchange the verbal form "justified" (δικαιόω) and the noun form "righteous" or "just" (δικαισύνη). We see this in Paul's speaking of Abraham in the verbal form as "was justified" (ἐδικαιώθη, Romans 4:2) and in the noun form as "was credited to him as *righteousness*" (δικαιοσύη, Romans 4:3). As we noted above, James refers to the noun phrasing in James 2:23, which is a direct quote from Genesis 15:6. The Hebrew noun *tsadaqah* (צדקה) in Genesis 15:6 is the equivalent to the Greek δικαιοσύη. The interplay between the verb and noun forms of the root word shows us that the passive act whereby God justifies someone is intimately connected to the existence of a righteous act(s) in the individual.

James Continues His Argument

Next, James elaborates on the example of Abraham in James 2:22: "You see that his faith and his actions were working together, and his faith was made complete by what he did." James gives us two aspects of the relationship between Abraham's faith and works: (1) faith and deeds were working together, and (2) his works completed or perfected his faith. As we noted previously, Protestant interpreters tend to separate Abraham's faith from his works in order to compensate for the disjunction needed between the imputed justification and the ongoing sanctification. In doing so, they look upon the account in Genesis 15 as the decisive moment of faith which gives Abraham his actual justification, while they view Genesis 22 as illustrating the works that inevitably tagged along after the faith and justification of Genesis 15 were established. James, however, already concludes in 2:22, in reference to the offering of Isaac (before he addresses the account of Abraham's faith in 2:23 in reference to Genesis 15), that Abraham's faith and works were "working together."[51] This shows that Abraham's attempted sacrifice of Isaac was an act of faith, not merely a work following the faith he displayed in Genesis 15 a decade or so earlier. Hebrews 11:17, 19 confirm this analysis: "By *faith*, Abraham, when God tested him, offered Isaac as a sacrifice...Abraham reasoned that God could raise the dead, and figuratively speaking, he did receive Isaac back from death." Abraham's faith and works were "working together" in Genesis 22. Thus we should not think of Genesis 15 as merely establishing the faith of Abraham and of Genesis 22 as demonstrating the works of Abraham. James considers the faith and works of Genesis 22 as an indivisible unit. This likewise implies that we should not attempt to understand other instances of either faith or works that are highlighted in Abraham's life without considering their respective counterpart. Just as the account of Genesis 22 assumes Abraham's *faith* without explicitly mentioning it, so Genesis 15 must assume Abraham's *works* without explicitly mentioning them. In light of this new perspective,

[51] The verb συνήργει ("working together") in James 2:22 is in the Greek *imperfect* tense, which indicates the coexistence of faith and works in the life of Abraham over a period of time.

we must again go back to the accounts of Abraham's life in Genesis 12-21 to see how his faith and works always "worked together."

The "Working Together" of Abraham's Faith and Works

In Genesis 12:1-3, God calls Abram out of Haran and Abram sets out on his way to the Promised Land of Canaan. In this command God gives Abram certain promises: "I will make you into a great nation and I will bless you...and all the peoples of the earth will be blessed through you." Genesis 12:4 records Abram's response: "So Abram left, as the Lord had told him..." This passage does not specifically mention either "faith" or "works," yet both are implicit in the account. That Abram believed God had a special land in store for him is evident in Abram's departure from Haran; likewise, his work of obedience is equally obvious by the same departure. If anything is more prominent, it is the actual work of obedience displayed specifically by Abram's departure from Haran. The faith which convinces him to leave is implicit. Yet that faith, according to Paul's viewpoint, is obviously a major underlying feature of this account, as he states in Hebrews 11:8: "By *faith* Abraham, when called to go to a place he would later receive as his inheritance, obeyed and went, even though he did not know where he was going."

Paul's analysis of this event has two important characteristics. First, he defines Abraham's faith primarily in terms of his obedience. This shows the intrinsic synergism between faith and works. Second, he describes the cognitive aspect of Abraham's faith as "even though he did not know where he was going." As mentioned previously, the faith that God is trying to draw out of Abraham is more than an acknowledgment that God exists; rather, he is attempting to elicit a deep faith from Abraham; one that trusts implicitly in God's integrity to do what he says he will do; a faith that believes that God is looking out for Abraham's best interests even though the circumstances at the time do not dictate such assurance. As Hebrews 11:6 states, Abraham's faith allows him to wait to see God as "the rewarder of those who diligently seek him." Hence, the only way for Abraham to establish his faith is actually to leave Haran at God's command not knowing where he is going or what he will confront when he gets to his destination. In fact, Abram had sufficient cause to fear as soon as he entered the land of Canaan. Genesis 12:6 records the kind of people he or his descendants would eventually encounter: "Abram traveled through the land...At that time the Canaanites were in the land." According to Numbers 13:31-14:4, some of the people who inhabited Canaan were giants who seemed much fiercer and stronger than the average man. Later in their history, the Israelites would become so frightened of them that they would rebel against Moses and complain that God had taken them out of Egypt to destroy them at the hands of these giants. Hence, Abram, having only his wife Sarai and his nephew Lot with him, must have had very great faith in God to protect him.

From the account in Genesis 13 one might conclude that Abram had a momentary lapse of faith. A famine arises in the land of Canaan. Without seeking God's advice, Abram went to Egypt for food. Arriving in Egypt, Abram fears that the Egyptians will seize his wife due to her great beauty. He tells Sarai to say she is his sister so that the Egyptians do not kill him. Rather than trusting in God at this point, Abram lets the Egyptians believe that Sarai is only his sister and not his wife. (Actually, Sarai is Abraham's sister, so what he says is not totally false but rather a half-truth and consequently deceiving.) Though it may seem that Abram has a lapse of faith, the text does not give enough information to determine whether doubt is his state of mind or not, nor does it record that God warned Abram not to go down into Egypt, as he later warned Isaac in Genesis 26:2. On the contrary, God immediately comes to Abraham's rescue by inflicting "serious diseases" on Pharoah and his household for taking Sarai. This suggests that Abram's walk with God is sufficiently in order that God acts on his behalf, which is not necessarily what God does when someone sins.

As we move on in the Genesis account, we observe in Abram a very faithful and loving man. Genesis 13 describes a conflict between the herdsmen of Abram and the herdsmen of Lot. As the peacemaker, Abram suggests that he and Lot divide the land, giving first choice to Lot. Lot takes the more fertile land of Jordan which was "watered like the garden of the Lord." Abram is left with the land of Canaan. There, he erects an altar in honor of the Lord after God reiterates the promise he first made with him when he left Haran. This account shows his generosity to man and devotion to God.

In Genesis 14, invading armies rout the plain of Sodom and Gomorrah where Lot lives and take Lot captive. Not giving a second thought to his own life, Abram gathers 318 fighting men and pursues the kidnaping army. He rescues Lot, Lot's family, and his possessions. This shows his courage and love for his fellow man. Later in the same chapter, we read of Abram's meeting with Melchizedek, king of Salem, who is a priest of the Most High. Abram bows himself before Melchizedek and gives him a tenth of all his possessions, showing his humility and generosity. Next, the king of Sodom offers Abram possessions that were part of the spoil when they rescued Lot. Abram refuses to take the possessions, not wanting to appear as if he had benefitted by someone else's hand. This incident shows Abram's integrity and lack of greed.

The next major event in Abram's life is the encounter with God in Genesis 15. In the first verse, God tells Abram, "Do not be afraid, Abram. I am your shield, your very great reward." Abram has heard God's voice once before so it is not likely that he is fearful at this point. Living in a strange land among strange people can be very frightening, however. God assures Abram that despite these strangers he is his *shield*. Wherever Abram goes, God will be there to protect him.

Sensing the love that God is bestowing upon him, Abram perhaps wanting to save face for God politely mentions that God has not yet given him the son he had promised. God had spoken of being his reward, but there is as yet no reward of a son. Here God interjects and explains that Abram will indeed have a son by his own wife Sarai. The famous text of Genesis 15:6 states: "And Abram believed the Lord, and he credited it to him as righteousness." As we noted earlier, this was indeed a great step of faith for Abram. Though this text does not tell us explicitly, we understand from Paul's commentary in Romans 4 that Abram is one hundred years old at this time and Sarai is ninety. Sarai had proven to be barren all the years up to her ninetieth birthday, an age far beyond normal child-bearing years. Yet despite the circumstantial evidence that speaks against God's integrity, Abram believes. Abram does not believe, however, as a spur-of-the-moment decision to trust God.

He has built up a life of trusting God since the moment twenty-five years earlier when he, in a similar act of faith and obedience, answered the summon of God to leave Haran. The act of believing God in Genesis 15 is just one more step in the life of faith, hope, and love that Abram has already displayed many times in the past.

Regarding Abram's obedience which joins with his faith in Genesis 15, we must remember that the two spouses were almost a century old, and because of Sarai's known barrenness, Abram and Sarai most likely had not engaged in intimate relations for a long time prior to this event. In any case, we are obliged to recognize that the couples mere act of intimate relations in anticipation that God would produce the promised son from this union indicates both Abram's and Sarai's trust and obedience.

Second, Genesis 15 shows that Abram continued to obey in the period after God counted his belief as righteousness. In Genesis 15:7, God speaks to Abram and declares that he has called him out of Ur of the Chaldeans to give him the promised land. Abram inquires of the Lord how he can know that he will receive the promised possession. God commands Abram to bring various animals to a designated place. Abram obeys by killing the animals and separating them into halves. Through this, God makes a covenant with Abram and promises that his descendants would inherit the land. Abram's obedience in participating in the covenant ritual shows his trust and obedience in God.

As great as Abram's faith is in Genesis 15:6, a decade or so later the promise of God to give him a son begins to fade in Abram's mind. Such is the case described in Genesis 16 when Abram listens to Sarai's advice to take Hagar for a wife in an effort to produce the child that God has apparently not given to Abram. Abram's complicity with Sarai is surprising since he has previously inquired of God in Genesis 15:2 whether Eliezer his servant was to be the inheritor that God promised. God had assured him that Eliezer was not the recipient but that Abram would have his *own* child. Perhaps since God has not said specifically that Sarai would be the mother of the child, Abram may have been reasoning that God's general statement "but a son coming from your own body will be your heir" in Genesis 15:4 leaves room for taking Hagar as a wife. Whatever his reasoning, Abram listens to the advice of Sarai without consulting the Lord. This shows a retreat from the faith he exhibited in Genesis 15:6.

Genesis 17 records a dramatic instance of another retreat from faith. It is now thirteen years after Abram had first retreated from faith in Genesis 16 by taking Hagar as a wife. If Abram had doubted the promise of God in Genesis 16, we can imagine what thirteen more years of not seeing Sarai produce the promised child has done. Genesis 17:17 records Abraham's state of mind. After God promises once again that Sarah will bear the child, "Abraham fell face down and laughed and said to himself, 'Will a son be born to a man a hundred years old? Will Sarah bear a child at the age of ninety?'"[52] It is hard to believe this is the same man who a decade or so earlier had accepted God's words without question in Genesis 15:6. The nuances of language in the Hebrew version of Genesis 17:17 portray the scene as if Abraham is rolling on the floor in hysterical laughter and making snide comments under his breath about his and Sarah's old age. A decade and a half ago, the proposition of having a child had seemed at least probable. But with the passage of time, certainly a passage of time that Abraham had not expected, the prospect of having his own child becomes outright laughable, at least in human terms. Fortunately for Abraham, God does not become angry when Abraham virtually laughs in his face. Instead, God politely brings him to his senses by reiterating the promise. But God does not forget this lapse of faith, as we shall soon see.

Abraham's and Sarah's doubt produced several consequences. First, an unanticipated jealousy and hatred arises between Sarah and Hagar, causing Sarah to ask Abraham to send Hagar away. Second, the son born to Hagar, Ishmael by name, though blessed by God, eventually becomes the progenitor of the Arab nations, Israel's bitter enemies in the future (Genesis 16:12).

Abraham's next encounter with God occurs in Genesis 18:23f in the destruction of Sodom and Gomorrah. Because of the intimate relationship that Abraham has already established with the Lord, Abraham pleads with God not to destroy the city if he

---

[52] Genesis 17:5 is the point at which God changes Abram's name from "Abram" (meaning "exalted father") to "Abraham" (meaning "father of a multitude"). In Genesis 17:15 God changes Sarai's names from Sarai ("Jah is prince") to "Sarah" (meaning "princess").

finds only ten righteous people living there. Perhaps Abraham is concerned about his nephew Lot and his family who have made their home in Sodom. As it turns out, God takes Lot and his family out of Sodom before he destroys the city. The point we are making here is that in God's eyes Abraham is significant enough to be able to strike a compromise with God. This again is indicative of a long and abiding relationship of trust, understanding, and obedience. It is for Abraham's righteous relationship with God that God reconsiders, if only temporarily, his original assessment of Sodom and Gomorrah. Scripture reflects a common understanding that God will graciously honor the request of one who is righteous to benefit another (cf., Deut. 9:13-29; Ezek. 14:14; James 5:17).

This dimension of Abraham's relationship with God also appears in Genesis 20 when Abraham prays for the well-being of Abimelech after the latter has mistakenly taken Sarah for his own. In Genesis 20:7 God tells Abimelech to ask Abraham to pray for him, and verse 17 states that Abraham did pray and in turn God restored the fertility of Abimelech's household. Abraham's reputation is well-known in that place, for Abimelech admits to Abraham in Genesis 21:22 that "God is with you in everything you do." This kind of recognition comes only through an intimate walk with God in which Abraham's faith and obedience please God sufficiently that God can bless him in this way. Genesis 21:33 again expresses Abraham's faith and obedience to God: "...and there he called upon the name of the Lord, the Eternal God." Of course, we must not leave this incident without pointing out that Abraham has again made the same mistake he had made in Genesis 13 when he allowed Pharaoh to take Sarah under the pretense that she was only his sister, not his wife. Here we see that Abraham is an ordinary man — one with many doubts and fears in a frequently hostile world.

Finally in Genesis 21, Isaac, the long-awaited fulfillment of God's promise, is born. Some years later, God approaches Abraham for his supreme test of faith. Genesis 22 records that God commands Abraham to take Isaac and sacrifice him. Perhaps this is the third consequence of Abraham's retreat from faith noted earlier when in Genesis 16 he takes Hagar as a wife, and in Genesis 17:17 he laughs at God. Those moments of doubt and lack of consultation with the Lord may be the very reason God has to test him one more time. The doubts concerning God's integrity have retarded Abraham's faith to some degree and now Abraham, with God's help, must eradicate that doubt. To do so God will now subject Abraham to the severest test of faith in God's integrity ever given to man.

At this point we must interject that the Protestant demonstrative/vindicative model again meets a tough challenge in giving an adequate explanation of Abraham's works. As we noted previously, James has set up a context in which to answer the question "Can faith save him?" in reference to the works one must choose to do. In order to be the prime example of James's thesis, Abraham's salvation must have equal potential of being granted or of being denied, based on his works. Though Abraham had showed great faith a decade or so earlier in Genesis 15:6, God has not forgotten his lapse of faith in Genesis 16:1f and 17:17. Abraham has not only disappointed God, but has even personally affronted God by laughing in his face. After so much time since the original promise in Genesis 15:6, his fear and respect of God has subsided to a considerable degree. Hence, Abraham has opened himself up for another test — the harshest test he will ever face — the sacrifice of his own son.

If Abraham had not come to know God as well as he now does in the thirty or so years prior to the test in Genesis 22, he might be tempted to think God was a blood-thirsty murderer who has enticed him with promises of life but has really wanted death. Instead, the life of faith and obedience Abraham has cultivated with God help him decide at this point to trust God. Abraham has finally witnessed the birth of the promised child and this has restored his faith in God. God has kept his part of the bargain. God has also prepared Abraham for the final test by a marvelous display of fearful judgment in the destruction of Sodom and Gomorrah in Genesis 18f. Abraham knows that God means business. In light of this, the lingering doubt concerning Abraham's reverence and respect for God now has to be answered. There will be no more laughing in God's face. God will test Abraham's reverence by asking him to do something that seems totally absurd and, ironically, could even cause Abraham to laugh in God's face again. In more sublime moments, Abraham might be driven to say, "You mean you want me to kill the very son that I have agonized over for the last 25 years? You have got to be joking!" This would be an appropriate reply if the person addressed were not God Almighty. This time, though, Abraham, instead of laughing, raises the knife to kill Isaac, putting his complete trust in God. According to Hebrews 11:19, Abraham reasons that if Isaac dies, God would even raise him from the dead to fulfill the promise. As he raises the knife, God stops him and says, "Now I know that you *fear* God." God does not say, "Now I know that you have faith in me" or "Now I know that you are obedient to me," even though Abraham certainly possesses those virtues. At this point, God's concern is fear and reverence. No matter how foolish the circumstances have appeared, God literally wants to see the *fear* in Abraham's eyes, a fear which recognizes that God knows what he is doing. In short, it is no laughing matter. As Ecclesiasticus 25:10-11 states, "How great is the one who finds wisdom! But none is superior to the one who fears the Lord. Fear of the Lord surpasses everything; to whom can we compare the one who has it?"

This final test in Genesis 22 seals and confirms the covenant between God and Abraham. Abraham will undergo no more climactic tests but may now live his life out in the simple faith and obedience he had cultivated many years before. At each encounter with God, God has reiterated the promises to Abraham concerning the land.[53] What is most important to understand in the sequence of these promises is that the promise to bless Abraham and his descendants is not ultimately confirmed until the final test of Genesis 22. This means that the stipulations of the promise given in Genesis 12-17 cannot be fulfilled unless Abraham passes the final test of offering up Isaac as a sacrifice. Genesis 22:15-16 states:

> The angel of the Lord called to Abraham from heaven a second time and said, '*I swear by myself*, declares the Lord, that *because you have done this and have not withheld your son*, your only son, I will surely bless you and make your descendants as numerous as the stars in the sky...and through your offspring all nations on earth will be blessed because you have obeyed me.'

Of all the times that God has stipulated the components of the promise to Abraham in Genesis 12-22, this is the only time that

53 Genesis 12:2-3,7; 13:14-17; 15:16-21; 17:3-8; 22:17-18.

God has said "*I swear by myself*." This language denotes that God has confirmed and sealed the covenant promises. They would not be altered for any reason. This is such an important issue that the sacred writer refers to it in absolute terms in Hebrews 6:13-17:

> When God made his promise to Abraham, since there was no one greater for him to swear by, he swore by himself...Men swear by someone greater than themselves, and the oath confirms what is said and puts an end to all argument. Because God wanted to make the unchanging nature of his purpose very clear to the heirs of what was promised he confirmed it with an oath.

That this divine oath-swearing occurs at Genesis 22:16, (and not at Genesis 15:6), shows that without the obedience of Genesis 22 the righteousness previously credited to Abraham would become null and void. Prior to Genesis 22, God would not have had to honor the covenant he made with Abraham if Abraham had subsequently disobeyed. Genesis 22:16's wording, "because you have done this and have not withheld your son, your only son" implies this because God conditions his oath on the obedience of Abraham. His obedience is of such cosmic importance that the blessing to his seed, and to the nations, rests virtually on Abraham's shoulders alone. His act in Genesis 22 is the quintessential act of faith and obedience that has reverberations for the rest of the world into eternity.

We might ask at this point that if the oath-swearing in Genesis 22:16-17 is the most important exchange between God and Abraham as regards the promises, why does Paul not mention this event in Romans 4 when he speaks of Abraham? In fact, Paul either ignores or is oblivious to the lapses of faith that Abraham exhibited in Genesis, speaking of Abraham only in glowing terms, e.g., "Without weakening in his faith...yet he did not waver through unbelief regarding the promises of God..." (Romans 4:18-21). The key to understanding Paul's perspective in Romans 4 is to realize that here he is dealing with the issue of circumcision. Since the Jews had elevated circumcision to be their rite of passage into heaven, Paul must explain the chronological relationship between the establishment of circumcision as opposed to the establishment of Abraham's faith that was credited to him as righteousness. Paul argues that since the covenant of circumcision came chronologically *after* Abraham's faith and righteousness, then his circumcision could not have caused his justification or righteousness. In other words, Abraham had to have faith in God's grace before he did any works. Trying to do works without faith would have put Abraham in a situation that Paul describes in Romans 4:4 as, "when a man works his wages are not credited to him as a gift, but as an obligation." Works done without faith put one in the system of law and obligation. Works done in faith put one in the system of grace that seeks to please God. To be sure, Abraham's obedience to the covenant of circumcision was a good work that pleased God, but that is only because Abraham had already established a grace relationship with God. Paul understands circumcision positively as, "a seal of the righteousness that he had by faith" (Romans 4:11), and thus as a good and wholesome work. But because the Jews lack a faith like Abraham's — a faith that believes "that God has power to do what he has promised" (Romans 4:21) — whatever works they do only draw them further away from God. As Paul says in Romans 9:32, "Because they pursued it not by faith but as it were by works." Paul's point, then, is not to deny that works play a primary role in the justification of the individual, but rather, to prove by the chronological layout of the Genesis account that through grace Abraham had genuine faith in God before he set out to work for God. One must believe in God and be in the state of grace in order to do work that is pleasing to God. If not, one is still operating in the system of law. On the other hand, as we have seen in his Galatian epistle, Paul whole heartedly agrees with James that if the works done subsequent to the establishment of faith turn out to be disobedience instead of obedience, this makes one unacceptable for justification.

At this point someone may argue that Paul's chronological distinction between Abraham's faith and his circumcision merely proves that *faith alone*, as long as it is established prior to works, causes the crediting of righteousness. This cannot be Paul's meaning or intent. As we saw above, Paul picks the chronological distinction between the faith of Genesis 15 and the works of Genesis 17 only to show that one must have faith in the grace of God as Abraham did before he can expect God to recognize his works

(Romans 4:12). Paul recognizes Abraham's work of circumcision as a legitimate work that pleased God. Circumcision was indeed a sign of the covenant, but the Jews misinterpreted this to make circumcision the means of obtaining the promises of the covenant.

We must not misconstrue this understanding of Paul in Romans 4, however, to teach that Paul would have discounted any works done by Abraham prior to his expression of faith in Genesis 15:6. We have already seen from Genesis 12 that when God first commanded Abraham to leave Haran Abraham had faith and works that were pleasing to God. His faith in God had put him in a relationship of grace that allowed God to look with favor on his works. In Hebrews 11:8, Paul verified this faith and obedience: "By faith Abraham, when called to go to a place...obeyed and went." At each point in Abraham's life his faith and works were, as James says, "working together." In Romans 4, Paul is not faulting Abraham's concept of faith and works. He is faulting the Jews. He has to expose a glaring contradiction in their theology so they can see how spiritually bankrupt they are. To do this, he attacks the very practice in which they most take pride — circumcision. Works without faith will simply not pass muster with God. All in all, as James points out that faith without works is dead, Paul's point is that work without faith is dead.

We may infer that James understands a continual relationship between faith and works from the use of the plural "works" rather than the singular "work" in James 2:20-24. Though James is singling out the sacrifice of Isaac as the work of Abraham, this is only for the purpose of illustration. As we noted earlier in this chapter, James 2:15 also presents the situation where one sees a brother or sister in need of food and clothing. The individual must couple his faith with works by making a decision to help that needy person. Such situations are not isolated events in a person's life. On numerous occasions one becomes aware of another's physical needs, and, as James teaches, God expects him to answer each situation with the resources God has placed at his disposal. Hence, we speak of the plural "works" in the sense of a life of work. On the other hand, we do not speak of "faiths" since normally we cannot quantify faith, but rather, understand it as a quality or state of mind.

James Continues With Abraham

James continues in 2:23 with his analysis of Abraham: "And the Scripture was fulfilled that says, 'Abraham believed God, and it was credited to him as righteousness,' and he was called God's friend." The clause, "and the Scripture was fulfilled" is not a statement we would expect at this point, since the Bible normally uses such phrasing in the fulfillment of a prophecy pointing to an actual event in the future.[54] In fact, the Bible contains no instance of the clause "and the Scripture was fulfilled" which does not take into account the prophecy of a future event. The faith of Abraham, being an actual event in itself, is not really a prophecy as we normally understand the word. Nevertheless, according to James, the event of faith in Genesis 15:6 includes a prophetic element and as such the prophecy is waiting for an event in the future for its fulfillment.

Before we look more closely at how the faith of Genesis 15:6 was fulfilled, we must emphasize that James 2:23 does not imply that God had to wait a decade or more for Abraham to finally show works that fulfilled the faith of Genesis 15, or wait three decades for Abraham to fulfill the faith from Genesis 12.[55] Abraham demonstrated throughout his life the works that "work together" with faith by continually loving his neighbor, avoiding sin, worshiping God, and many other acts of obedience. We have already detailed many instances of these works that occurred prior to Genesis 15 and Genesis 22.[56] These are the same works that James requires of Christians in the chapter under discussion (James 2:8-11). Since Abraham had already accomplished works of love and obedience, there may be a much more profound reason why James is pointing

54 e.g., Mark 15:28; John 17:12.

55 Since Ishmael, who was born after God came to Abraham in Genesis 15, was thirteen years old when Abraham circumcised him in Genesis 17:25, at least thirteen years must have elapsed between the Genesis 15 encounter and the covenant of circumcision in Genesis 17. Abraham was ninety-nine at the circumcision. Isaac was born in Genesis 21, and since he was of a mature talking age in Genesis 22:7, this would make him about 5-10 years old at the time, which would thus be approximately two decades from Genesis 15. Since Abraham was 75 years old when he left Haran, this would make the time from Genesis 12 to Genesis 22 about thirty years or more.

56 Genesis 17:3, 23; 18:2, 32; 20:17; 21:11-14, 22, 27, 33.

to the sacrifice of Isaac in Genesis 22 as the "fulfillment" of the faith in Genesis 15:6.

Looking again at the event of faith in Genesis 15:6, we see two components to what Abraham is believing. The first is that Abraham's heir will not be Eliezer, his servant, but rather Abraham's own son. Second, God takes Abraham outside to look at the heavens and promises that his offspring will be as numerous as the stars of the sky. The first promise was fulfilled prior to Genesis 22 at the birth of Isaac recorded in Genesis 21. The second promise would not see fulfillment for many years to come, although it was potentially realized in the birth of Isaac. Thus, these events are not the direct "fulfillment of Scripture" to which James is pointing. James is more specific. He states that the Scripture of Genesis 15:6 has to be fulfilled in two ways. First, "Abraham believed God" and second, "and it was credited to him as righteousness." The sacrifice of Isaac fulfills both of these requirements. The final fulfillment of Abraham's belief in Genesis 15:6 comes when he believes again in Genesis 22. As Paul says in Hebrews 11:17, "By *faith* Abraham, when God tested him, offered Isaac as a sacrifice."

In both Genesis 15 and 22, God's integrity is on the line. Despite the circumstantial evidence, Abraham must believe that God can give him a child even though he is one hundred years old and Sarah is ninety and proven to be barren. He must also believe that God will preserve this child even if he happens to be killed by Abraham's knife. Abraham's faith is fulfilled because it is an enduring faith. Abraham possesses, to use Paul's phrase of Romans 1:17, "a righteousness that is revealed from faith to faith" — one instance of faith to another instance of faith.

The second part of Genesis 15:6 (i.e., "and it was credited to him as righteousness") is also fulfilled in Genesis 22 because one can also understand the faith Abraham manifested in Genesis 22 as a *crediting of righteousness*. Whenever Abraham exercises faith in God, he is credited with righteousness. It is not a one-time event in his life. In fact, in Genesis 22 the faith required to sacrifice Isaac is a much more mature and stronger faith than the faith in Genesis 15, especially since Abraham had later shown some doubts about the faith he exhibited in Genesis 15 when he laughed at God's promise in Genesis 17:17. If there is any faith that deserves the *crediting of righteousness,* it is the faith of Genesis 22 where only an angel from heaven stopped Abraham at the very last moment from plunging the knife into Isaac.[57] The crediting of righteousness in Genesis 22 does not infringe on the chronology Paul sets up in Romans 4:10-16, where he specifies that Abraham's crediting of righteousness in Genesis 15 came *before* his circumcision in Genesis 17. The crediting of righteousness in Genesis 22 merely extends that of Genesis 15.

The event of Genesis 22 is also more important than that of Genesis 15 as regards the crediting of righteousness because, unlike Genesis 15:6, Genesis 22 includes a high-profile event that once and for all will either establish Abraham's faith or negate his faith. Once Abraham ties Isaac on the altar and raises the knife, there is no turning back. If he unties him, he has lost faith in God and God will no longer be pleased with him. Fortunately, Abraham does not untie Isaac, and for this James says Abraham "was called God's friend" (James 2:23).

We must understand Genesis 22 as one event in many of Abraham's life in which he is "credited with righteousness," and this is the very reason why James concludes his remarks on Abraham by saying: "You see that a person is justified by what he does and *not by faith alone*." As we noted earlier in the chapter, James and Paul use the same word for *justified*. In reference to men who are pursuing salvation, *justified* has no usage other than in the sense of justification before God for righteousness. Hence, James's use of the word *justification* in reference to the faith and works of Genesis 22 means that James is borrowing the phrasing of Genesis 15:6 ("and it was credited to him as righteousness") and applying it to Genesis 22 by his conclusion, "a person is justified by what he does and not by faith alone." If righteousness was not credited to Abraham in Genesis 22, James could not have used the word *justified* in reference to that event. Supporting this analogy, as noted earlier, James in James 2:23 understands the noun cognate *dikaiosune* ("righteousness") in the same way that Paul does, which

[57] In chapter 4 we will investigate the event in which Phinehas (Psalm 106:30-31) is "credited with righteousness" for a supreme work of faith and obedience to God. This is the only other time the Old Testament uses the phrase "credited with righteousness."

then requires that he understand the verbal form *dikaioo* ("justified") that he uses in James 2:24 in the same way that Paul does. Thus, Abraham was truly and salvifically justified in Genesis 22.

The unique way James has crafted his language prohibits any misconstruing of what he wrote. James says two things in James 2:24 which reinforce each other: (1) that a person is justified by works, and (2) that he is not justified by faith alone. James is using the clearest form of argumentation: making an affirmation of his case and at the same time asserting a negation of the most important opposing case. If he had said only that a person was justified by works, one might possibly think that James is merely making an addendum to the teaching that faith justifies. But in adding the negation, James tells us the focus and reason for his affirmation. It is not only to advance the truth that works justify an individual, but it is to obliterate the opposite idea that one can be saved by faith alone. The negative statement is how we know James is using *justified* in the same sense that Paul used it, for if James was not concerned that someone would be misled by thinking that Abraham was justified by merely having faith, then he would have had no cause to add "*justified...not by faith alone.*" We see that James is quite aware of the possible interpretations of Abraham's faith precisely in his quotation from Genesis 15:6, the very passage that Paul uses. It is also likely that James knew of Paul's use of the same passage, having been the bishop of Jerusalem in full purview of church doctrine at the time (cf., Acts 15:13). Hence, it is only logical to assume that in giving his affirmation and negation about justification, James has taken into account that some would misconstrue Paul's teaching on Genesis 15:6 and say that one is justified by faith alone. James will simply not allow that option.

As noted above, we should understand the faith and works of Genesis 22 as the quintessential event that justifies and credits Abraham with righteousness, but not the only event that does so. James has chosen Genesis 22 because of its intimate connection with the promised seed and the multiplication of progeny from that seed. Abraham lived a whole life of faith and works stemming from his first walk of faith in Genesis 12, when God called him out of his own country. As we have seen earlier with Enoch and Noah, Abraham *walked with God*. James's final remark, "and he was called

God's friend," suggests such a life of faith in intimacy with God. The phrase is not a direct quote from Genesis but alludes to historical and prophetic writings dated more than a thousand years after Abraham. The two passages in view are 2 Chronicles 20:7 ("of Abraham your friend") and Isaiah 41:8 ("Abraham my friend"). These passages could be reiterating what was already known of the relationship between God and Abraham during the latter's lifetime. We have already seen a suggestion of this reputation in Abimelech's remark about Abraham in Genesis 21:22. Most likely, a tradition arose citing the patriarch as God's friend and was later put into writing by the Chronicler and Isaiah.[58] The contexts of 2 Chronicles 20:7 and Isaiah 41:8 appeal to the faithful relationship established between good king Jehoshaphat and the Lord, as God helps him defeat Moab and Ammon, as well as a reaffirmation of God's help in destroying other enemies. As noted earlier, these kinds of relationships speak of *lifelong* commitments to God. The closest thing in Scripture to being the "friend of God" is David's being called "a man after God's own heart" (cf., 1 Samuel 13:14; Acts 13:22). God had said this about David after he had observed him for some time. It was because of David's character that God chose him to replace Saul as king, passing up his seven brothers on the basis that "God looks into the heart" of those he chooses (1 Samuel 16:7-13). Once again, it is not just the beginning of faith or of works, but the whole life of faith and works, that God views in the individual.

The Justification of Rahab

To cap off his argument that faith and works "work together" in justification, James appeals to a very remote case — a case of justification that would really rub against a Jew's pride. James chooses Rahab, the Gentile prostitute, who showed faith in God by believing that he would destroy her city, and displayed works by hiding the Israelite soldiers who came to spy out the land (Joshua 1-2). James's use of the word *even* in the statement, "was not *even* Rahab...considered righteous..." is akin to saying, "yes, even Rahab,

---

[58] Although James uses φιλος rather than the Septuagint ἀγάπη translated from the Hebrew אהב ("to love"), his choice of words suffices for his intent which is to show the close *relationship* between God and Abraham.

who you would think could not obtain righteousness, did." Hebrews 11:31, in the statement "By *faith*, the prostitute Rahab..." confirms that Rahab's faith is necessary for God to accept her works. James may have used the example of Rahab for several reasons. First, the immediacy of her faith and works contrast sharply with the unbelief and disobedience characteristic of the Jews prior to the conquest of Canaan. As noted in Deuteronomy 9:5f, the taking of Canaan was due not to the righteousness of Israel but to the wickedness of the Canaanites and the promise by oath that God made to Abraham. Second, that she was a prostitute who made it to the kingdom of heaven hearkens back to the statement of Jesus in Matthew 21:31, "I tell you the truth...the prostitutes are entering the kingdom of God ahead of you." Third, that a Gentile understood the reign of God and her own sin adds another person to the class of Gentiles who, as Paul says in Romans 2:26, "are not circumcised but keep the law's requirements," and in Romans 2:10, "but glory, honor, and peace for everyone who does good...first for the Jew, then for the Gentile. For God does not show favoritism." As we will see in chapter 4 with the case of Cornelius, Rahab is one who, prompted by the drawing grace of God, cooperates with that grace and seeks him for salvation.[59]

The most significant aspect of Rahab's story in the discussion of justification is that there is no categorical or chronological distinction between her faith and works. James considers them as one unit. Perhaps anticipating that someone might try to divide the faith of Abraham recorded in Genesis 15:6 from his work recorded in Genesis 22 in order to make a case that the works were only fruits of Abraham's faith and not an integral part of his salvation, James adds the story of Rahab which has no such possible distinction. We see this first in the way the apostle Paul explains the faith of Rahab: "By faith the prostitute Rahab, because she welcomed the spies, was not killed with those who were disobedi-

---

[59] "The Church's message 'is true and solid, in which one and the same way of salvation appears throughout the whole world'" (CC, Section 174; Irenaeus, *Against Heresies*, 1, 10, 1-2).

[60] Council of Trent, Session 6, Canon 24: "If anyone shall say, that justice received is not preserved and also not increased in the sight of God through good works but that those same works are only the fruits and signs of justification received, but not a cause of its increase: let him be anathema."

ent."[60] Paul does not describe Rahab's faith as merely a state of mind, but in language which specifies her actions, i.e., "she welcomed the spies." Her faith is defined in terms of her works, or her faith and works were "working together" for her justification. Just as Paul had explained, James remarks and elaborates on the same actions of Rahab as he says in James 2:25, "she gave lodging to the spies" and "sent them off in a different direction." The addition of "sent them off..." shows that this was a deliberate plan of action, in two successive steps, devised by Rahab. James does not specifically mention the faith of Rahab in contrast to what Paul does, rather, he cites only the two phases of her works. As Paul's description explicitly mentions Rahab's faith, James's description leaves Rahab's faith implicit. When James mentions someone's good works, we must remember that faith is also included. As far as the New Testament writers are concerned, faith and works are inseparable in regard to justification.

In the account of Rahab in Joshua 2:9-11, Rahab's faith in God was prompted by her fear in his judgments. Rahab says to the Israelite soldiers:

> I know that the Lord has given this land to you and that a great fear of you has fallen on us...We have heard how the Lord dried up the water of the Red Sea for you when you came out of Egypt, and what you did to Sihon and Og...whom you completely destroyed...for the Lord your God is God in heaven above and earth below.

Though this description of Rahab's state of mind shows a great fear of God and an acknowledgment of his Lordship over the universe, one could not propose that Rahab was already justified by this fear. It is only when she pleads for mercy and barters to protect the spies in exchange for her and her family's lives that the New Testament writers consider her justified. This is why they describe her faith only from the vantage point of her works, not as her mental state of fear concerning God's judgments prior to meeting the spies. Rahab proves this when in Joshua 2:10-11 she acknowledges, by using the plural "we," that *everyone* in the city of Jericho is in a state of fear of God's destruction. All of them, however, were destroyed.

As we noted earlier, as James opens up the discussion of Rahab's justification, he introduces her account by the phrase, "*In the same way...*" By this wording, James is intimately connecting the justification of Abraham with the justification of Rahab. He is teaching that there is no appreciable difference in the way these two people were justified. If there were, then God would have two systems of justification, one for the Jews and one for the Gentiles, which according to Romans 2:10 cited above is impossible — God shows no favoritism between Jew and Gentile, and there is no name under heaven by which men can be saved other than that of Jesus Christ (Acts 4:12). We can conclude, then, that the inseparability of the faith and works that justified Rahab speaks of the same inseparable nature of the faith and works that justified Abraham. In Rahab, faith alone cannot justify because faith is only and specifically defined by her works of obedience. In addition, James's use of the word *justified* in reference to both Rahab and Abraham shows that he has the same understanding of how both people were justified before God.

We must also reiterate that one cannot say that Rahab's justification was merely a *vindication* (as some have tried to say of Abraham's justification in James 2:24), since she was not justified prior to her meeting with the Israelite spies. Rahab was a prostitute who lived an immoral life until she encountered God through the Israelites. We may assume, although Scripture does not explicitly state it, that once Israel destroyed Jericho, Rahab and her family became part of the Israelite community and continued to obey the laws of God. It is for her abiding faith and works that the New Testament writers can hold her up as an example of justifying faith and works. Hence, if Rahab is not merely vindicated but is truly justified, then James's use of the phrase "*in the same way*" in reference to Abraham proves once again that James's use of the word *justify* does not convey a mere vindication but a true justification in righteousness. It can work no other way.

James concludes this section by appealing in 2:26 to a simple biological fact: "As the body without the spirit is dead, so faith without deeds is dead." Faith without works is "dead" (Greek: νεκρός). In other words, without adding works, faith cannot be used for justification. Since everyone knows that a body without the spirit means the body is dead and cannot come back to life unless the spirit is restored, so faith cannot be included in justification unless it is infused with works. The works, then, become just as much a salvific part of the individual's justification as his faith. As James says in 3:13: "Who is wise and understanding among you? Let him show it by his good life, by deeds done in the humility that comes from wisdom."

Though many Protestants claim that *saving faith* is a faith that is accompanied by works, (i.e., what they term "the fruit of faith"), we will see in chapter 5 that while they do make at least this attempt to incorporate the language of James into their theology, it neither fits into the theology of Paul nor does justice to the teaching of James.

Summary Points

1) Protestants have devised many and varied explanations to neutralize the clear and unambiguous statement in James 2:24 that "man is justified by works and not by faith alone." Each of these explanations concludes that James is not teaching that man is justified by works in the same sense that Paul says man is justified by faith. Puzzled by James's language, Martin Luther even concluded that the epistle of James was a spurious book and should not be canonically authoritative for New Testament teaching.

2) Countering the Protestant explanation of the epistle of James which states that James means that "men" witness Abraham's works, the Genesis text (Genesis 22) does not include any men as witness to Abraham's works, but only God himself.

3) Countering the Protestant explanation of James which holds that the word "justified" as James uses the term refers to a "vindication," rather than to a salvific justification, as Paul uses the term, are the following arguments:

    a) If James were teaching a concept of "vindication," he would have said, with the proper Greek word, "you see, a person is vindicated by works." Moreover, since James adds the clause "and not by faith alone" we know that he is correcting a false notion concerning the solitude of faith in justification, not suggesting that Abraham was vindicated by works.

b) If James were attempting to teach a vindication of Abraham, the specific argumentation he used would make sense only if James's opponents had claimed that Abraham was "vindicated by faith alone." In other words, if the vindication hypothesis were true, syntactical requirements would have forced James to use the meaning of "vindicated" in the first part of his argument (2:20-21) in order also to use it in the latter part (2:24). Since the grammatical structure of the verse would then require that the phrase "not by faith alone" have its referent in the phrase "is vindicated," this would force the meaning of the verse to be, "a person is vindicated...not by faith alone" — a meaning that has no relevance to James's discussion.

c) The New Testament does not use the word "*justified*" in the sense of vindicated in contexts which are soteriological, i.e., contexts which discuss salvation or damnation. Moreover, such passages as Matthew 11:19 where one could plausibly interpret the Greek word *dikaioo* as referring to a vindication do so only in a metaphorical sense; therefore they do not use *dikaioo* in the same way that James, and even Paul, use the term, which is historical and literal.

d) James's discussion of the events surrounding the justification of Rahab preclude assigning the meaning of "vindicated" to the word justified. Rahab's justification, as described in James 2:25, is a salvific justification, not a vindication, yet James specifies that Rahab was justified "in the same way" that Abraham was justified. Therefore, one cannot understand Abraham's justification as a vindication.

e) Since James and Paul use the same Greek noun *dikaiosune* ("righteous") in reference to Abraham, and interpret the word in the same way (cf., Genesis 15:6, Romans 4:3, James 2:23), it would be totally incongruous for one of them to use a different meaning of its verbal cognate *dikaioo* in reference to Abraham.

f) The Protestant position assumes that Abraham's justification is a once-for-all event. James's all important question "Can faith save him?" (2:14), however, includes Abraham within its purview. Hence we must conclude that if Abraham's works were not of the quality that James prescribes in the context (2:15), then Abraham would not be justified. Abraham could not be justified in a "once-for-all" event in Genesis 15:6 and at the same time have that justification put in jeopardy by disobedience to James's requirement of works for justification. If this could happen, the question in 2:14 would have no meaning.

4) Abraham's acts in Genesis 12, 15, and 22 were acts of faith *and* works. We should not misconstrue Paul's stress on Abraham's faith in his view of Genesis 15:6 to say that Abraham performed no works of loving obedience to God at this time or prior, nor should we misconstrue James's view of works in Genesis 22 to say that Abraham's attempted sacrifice of Isaac was not a supreme act of faith. Similarly, Abraham's departure from his homeland in Genesis 12 also couples his faith and works in regard to justification. Throughout his life, in the periods recorded in Genesis 13-14, 16-21, and 23-25 which are between the times of his recorded faith and obedience in the New Testament, Abraham continued to live in faith and obedience, with only what we may call minor lapses along the way. Genesis 22's importance is its detailing of Abraham's quintessential act of the faith-and-works which allowed God to swear an oath of blessing to him and for all his future descendants. Abraham's act in Genesis 22, not Genesis 15:6, was the most important act in Abraham's life. The act in Genesis 22 was just as much a crediting of righteousness to Abraham as that in Genesis 15:6.

5) The entire context of the book of James concerns what one must do to be saved. He concentrates on obedience to the law as the means of salvation, and judgment for those who disobey that law.

6) James includes sins of commission as well as omission in his warning against disobedience to the law. The supreme law, or "royal law," that James has in view is the law of love.

7) James assumes that the audience to whom he writes already has faith in God. The main question that James poses to them is whether they have added works to their faith. James does not suggest that works will immediately or inevitably flow from one who has faith, even though he may have a greater disposition towards good works once he has faith. James teaches that one who has faith must make a daily, conscious decision to do good works, just as he must decide each day to refrain from sin. In fact, if he chooses not to do good works when the opportunity arises, he has sinned (James 4:17).

8) James does not support the Protestant concept that one can be saved as long as he has "saving faith." James is not so much attempting to qualify the faith needed for justification as he is saying that one must consciously add works to faith in order to be justified. A person, to be justified, must persevere to his last breath in this conscious decision to add works to faith.

9) One of the most heinous in the catalogue of sins that James specifies is sin of the tongue. What is "said" to God and man is of the utmost importance to James and a major criterion on how the individual will be judged.

10) Both Paul and James speak of the works of love that one must add to his faith in order to be justified.

11) Like Paul, James concludes that if one chooses the system of law and desires God to evaluate him on that basis without the benefit of grace, he must then obey the whole law without fault. For one fault, the law will utterly condemn him.

Chapter 3

What Did Jesus Teach About Justification?

One would think that in a study on the biblical basis for justification much of the time would be spent examining what Jesus said on the subject. Unfortunately, most Protestant literature makes a mere passing reference to the teachings of Jesus on the subject of justification. In fact, there is a saying among many Protestant apologists that those who spend too much time in the gospels seeking information on subjects like justification are "red letter" interpreters.[1] We posit, however, that if there is a question in the Protestant mind about reconciling Paul with James, there should also be a question about reconciling Paul with Jesus.[2]

---

1 The term "red letter" originates from Bibles that put the words of Jesus in red ink. An example of this mentality is noted in the approach of Protestant apologist James White. He writes: "Instead, we must allow the primary expositor of this issue, in this case, the Apostle Paul, to speak first; his epistles to the Romans and the Galatians must define the issues, for it is in them that we have direct discussions of exactly how justification takes place. Once we have consulted these sources, we can then move on to garner other elements of the biblical revelation that are found in *tangential* ways elsewhere" (*The Romans Catholic Controversy*, p. 147, emphasis his). Of Jesus's teaching on justification, White adds: "But he did not deem it proper to discuss the specifics of the issues prior to Calvary. In His sovereign will He left that to the Apostle Paul..." (Ibid, p. 148). Suffice it to say, this is precisely the problem with the Protestant approach to justification.

2 One of the only books on the current Protestant market to devote most of its attention to the teachings of Jesus in regards to justification is the recent book titled, *The Gospel According to Jesus* by John MacArthur. (Grand Rapids, Zondervan Publishing, 1988, 1994). However, MacArthur's extensive use of Jesus's teaching is for the sole purpose of countermanding the teachings of Zane Hodges, Charles Ryrie, and Lewis Sperry Chafer who, being "anti-Lordship salvation" proponents, do not believe that works play *any* role in the justification of the individual. See chapter 9 for more on this topic.

As we noted in chapters 1 and 2, Evangelicals tend to elevate Paul's writings to a status above the other biblical writers. They pass each biblical author, including the sayings of Jesus, through the grid of Paul's supposedly "Protestant" theology before interpreting them. By doing this, Protestants not only relegate the gospels to a secondary level of authority on justification, but they also do a horrible injustice to the teachings of Paul. Since they misunderstand Paul's teaching of faith and works, any teachings from Jesus or James that seem to contradict their understanding of Paul are quickly explained away, deemed hypothetical, or dismissed altogether. These mechanisms will be amply demonstrated in the following analysis.

The Rich Young Man

Faith alone theology has a most difficult time legitimizing itself when compared to the teachings of Jesus. In the story of the Rich Young Man in Matthew 19:17-21, for example, an earnest seeker approaches Jesus inquiring how one enters eternal life. Jesus answers, "...If you want to enter life, *obey the commandments*." After the man states that he has obeyed the commandments, he inquires what else he must do. Jesus tells him to sell what he has and *give the money to the poor*. Here is an instance in which a question of eternal importance is raised, that is, how is one justified before God in order to obtain eternal life. It would be the same question that Paul answers in Romans or James answers in his epistle. The answer Jesus gives, however, simply does not fit into the theory of justification Protestants understand. Nowhere in his answer to the Rich Young Man does Jesus mention accepting him by *faith alone*. Nowhere does Jesus shun the law or obedience to the law. He does just the opposite. He upholds the law as the very means of salvation. In fact, when approached for clarification on his initial answer, Jesus simply adds another requirement, "go sell all that you have and give to the poor."[3]

Protestants attempt to explain this story by elevating the teaching of Paul and toning down the teaching of Jesus. They do

[3] Catholic Catechism, Sections 2052-2053.

this by reiterating the theory of justification by *faith alone* and the condemnation of law, while at the same time treating Jesus's teaching as something impossible to do and therefore a hypothetical answer to the Rich Young Man.[4] In effect, they say that Jesus is giving a misleading answer to the Rich Young Man in an effort to show him that the law cannot save him. Evangelical John MacArthur, for instance, says the following:

> Strictly speaking, Jesus' answer was correct. If a person could keep the law all his life and never violate a single jot or tittle, he would be perfect, sinless (cf. James 2:10). But no one except the Savior alone is like that; we are born in sin (Ps. 51:5). To suggest that the law is a means to eternal life clouds the issue of faith.[5]
>
> Then he slammed the man up against the divine standard, not because keeping the law would merit eternal life, but that he would see how far he fell short.[6]
>
> But the emphasis in Jesus' teaching from the beginning had been to define all the law in such a way that no one — even those who adhered strictly to the law's external requirements — could look at the commandments and feel justified (cf. Matt 5:20-48; Rom. 3:20).[7]
>
> The commandment to love your neighbor as yourself has an inescapable internal application. There was no way he could honestly say he had always kept *that* law.[8]

From these statements, MacArthur alleges: (1) Jesus requires *faultless* obedience to the law for salvation; (2) that obedience to the law "clouds the issue of faith"; (3) that the law *only* shows him how far he has fallen short of perfection; (4) that no one can "feel

---

4 For an example of this method of interpretation, see the debate between Evangelical Dave Hunt and Catholic apologist Dr. Robert Fastiggi, June 17, 1995.
5 MacArthur, op. cit., p. 90.
6 Ibid., p. 91.
7 Ibid., p. 92.
8 Ibid., p. 92.

justified" by obeying the Sermon on the Mount (Matt. 5:20-48); and (5) that no one can claim to have kept the law to love his neighbor. The problem with these objections is that what little truths they contain are at best half-truths. As a result, they totally distort the real teaching of Jesus. Granted, law as a system in itself can never provide eternal life. But obedience to the law as representing the desires of one's heart toward God and neighbor is the issue Jesus is bringing to the fore. In this sense, law does not "cloud the issue of faith." It ***is*** the issue of faith. Jesus does not expect the Rich Young Man to obey the commandments without ever making a mistake. Scripture says clearly that all men have sinned (Rom. 3:20). It also speaks, however, about those who have lived blameless lives before God. Of Zachariah and Elizabeth, Luke 1:6 records: "Both of them were righteous in the sight of God, observing all the Lord's commandments and regulations blamelessly."

Scripture says the same of Enoch (Gen. 5:24; Heb. 11:5); Noah (Gen. 6:9; 7:1; 1 Pt. 3:20); Abraham (Gen. 17:1; Rom. 4:12); Job (Job 1:1); David (Acts 13:22); Daniel (Ezk. 14:14), and many more biblical personages. Apparently, these people obeyed God sufficiently to please him and for that obedience they are considered "blameless" and "righteous." How is this possible when all men are sinners? As we noted in chapter 1, if God views us under the uncompromising edicts of the system of law, all men are condemned; but if God views us under the auspices of his grace, men can lead sufficiently obedient lives to please the Lord and be considered righteous in his sight. Moreover, as in the case of the Rich Young Man, this obedience is necessary but also sufficient for salvation. Jesus, and all the biblical writers, profoundly desire us to do our utmost to abide by the principles of the Sermon on the Mount and to love our neighbor as ourselves. Those laws are ***not*** put there merely to show us how sinful we are. When Jesus says, "Blessed are the poor in spirit, for theirs is the kingdom of heaven," or "Blessed are the merciful, for they shall obtain mercy," he means what he says. Those who are not poor in spirit or who do not show mercy will be condemned.[9] James, as we have seen previously, taught us the same principle in James 2:13, "...because judgment

[9] See Catholic Catechism, Sections 1716-1729.

without mercy will be shown to anyone who has not been merciful." He taught us that those who do not take care of the physical needs of a brother or sister are not being merciful (James 2:14-15). We will recall that James's comments are right in the context of how one is *justified by works and not by faith alone*. In addition, it is Jesus himself in the parable of the Good Samaritan (Luke 10:25-37) who lays the precedent for James's teaching of caring for our neighbor's physical needs.

In the story of the Rich Young Man, faith is not the issue. He believes God exists and that he has a duty to God. As the scene begins, when Jesus refers to the "One who is good" (i.e., God), the Rich Young man does not disagree or argue. In the clearest language possible, Jesus teaches that the central issue involves whether he has combined his faith with works of love sufficiently to gain eternal life. To a certain degree, he has obeyed and Jesus acknowledges that prior obedience. In fact, after acknowledging his obedience, Mark 10:21 adds, "And looking at him, Jesus felt a *love* for him..." Jesus does not ridicule or shun his prior acquiescence to God's law. He feels a loving affinity toward this man for his previous obedience. The man is not the typical Pharisee who says one thing and does another; who takes advantage of widows and then for a pretense stands on the street corner praying (Matthew 23:14). No, the Rich Young Man was close to the kingdom of God, but he had not yet arrived. There was at least one more work he had to do.

A similar discussion of the nature of the law arises in Mark 12:28-34. One of the teachers of the law had heard Jesus give a remarkable answer to the Sadducees concerning the resurrection and felt inclined to inquire about something on his own heart. The text does not say he came to trap Jesus, as was so often true of the Pharisees. Perhaps this man, like Nicodemus the Pharisee in John 3, was a sincere inquirer who was intrigued by the teaching of Jesus. He asked Jesus which commandment was the most important. Jesus answered that he is to love the Lord with all his heart, mind, and strength, and to love his neighbor as himself. The teacher of the law agrees with Jesus. He even adds the remark that obeying these two commands is better "than all burnt offerings and sacrifices," showing his understanding that God is looking inwardly at men not outwardly, a clear teaching from the Old Testament (cf., 1

Samuel 15:22; Hosea 6:6; Micah 6:6-8; Hebrews 10:8). Jesus agrees with him and says, "You are *not far* from the kingdom of God." This statement shows us that in Jesus's view, the more one acknowledges and obeys the commandments of God, the *closer* he is to the kingdom of God. There is no discussion here about faith. Faith is presumed. The question is: has this man developed his faith into love? If he loves, then he has either entered into the kingdom or is *not far* from it. All this teacher of the law has to do is to practice continually what he already believes, and he too will enter the kingdom. As we summed up the teaching of Paul in chapter 1 from the statement he made in Romans 11:35 ("Who has ever given to God that God should repay him?"), we can likewise sum up the teaching of Jesus from one of his most succinct and penetrating teachings. In Matthew 12:7, Jesus quotes from Hosea 6:6 in the Old Testament and says, "I desire mercy, not sacrifice."

As for the Rich Young Man, he will now receive his greatest test, a test even like that of Abraham who was asked to offer his son Isaac, a test to see if he has cultivated his faith into a real love of God and neighbor. As Paul says, he can have faith great enough to move mountains or live by a written code of ethics, but if he does not have love from his heart, he is nothing. Faith works in love and love is the supreme work.[10]

We notice that Jesus says to him in Matthew 19:21, "If you want to be *perfect*..." This is the same word Jesus used in the Sermon on the Mount in Matthew 5:48: "Be *perfect*, therefore, as your heavenly Father is *perfect*." Jesus says this in a context about the nature of love. We must "love our enemies" and "bless those who persecute." We are not to love only those who love us; otherwise, we are no different from pagan people. Hence, we are perfect in God's eyes if we can love the unlovable. This is not an impossibility since God would not give us moral commands that we cannot not keep.[11] Granted, we will fall from our ideal on many occasions,

---

[10] In contrast, Luther wrote: "FAITH [sic] is the principle point and the highest commandment which includes all others in itself" (WA 36, 365, 8). "Rather, faith shall be the master over love, and love shall yield to it" (WA 39I, 23, 11-12). See chapter 9 for a comprehensive treatment of this aspect of Luther's teaching.

[11] Council of Trent, Session 6, Chapter 11.

but we repent, pick ourselves back up through the power of God's grace, and try again.

The final command to the Rich Young Man is, "...go, sell your possessions and give to the poor, and you will have treasure in heaven. Then come, follow me." This confirms Jesus's lifting up of the interior law as the very means of salvation,[12] not the system of law, or life by a written code, but the principle of God's laws expressed from the heart in the spirit of love and compassion. Essentially, Jesus is saying that if you want to enter the kingdom of heaven then you must act like those in the kingdom of heaven. In short, you must know how to love. This is not just a teaching tool to draw out a resignation to *faith alone* theology from the Rich Man. No, he must go beyond faith into a realm of being to which he probably had never given much thought. The way Jesus wants him to love his neighbor is not just by refraining from the negative, e.g., not stealing from him or not killing him, but by doing something positive, that is, taking care of his physical needs. As James says, when we see a brother or sister in physical need, we must take care of those needs (James 2:15). One must go beyond the written code of, "don't do this, don't do that." He must live a selfless life. James also says, "Anyone, then, who knows the good he ought to do and doesn't do it, sins" (James 4:17). As to who the recipients of our love should be, Jesus answered that question in the parable of the Good Samaritan; it is anyone who is in need that crosses our path (Luke 10:25-37). If we don't do these things, then we are not fit for the kingdom of heaven.

Protestant attempts to make such principles of Jesus mere teaching tools to draw out either a *faith alone* theology or a hypothetical principle of law which no one can perform results in a total perversion of the teaching of Jesus and of the gospel itself. The reader is asked to recall our analysis of Paul's teaching which pointed out that many Protestants make the same judgment on the teaching in Romans 2:6-10, where Paul states that those who continue in good works will be given eternal life. That teaching is said to be hypothetical, just like the teaching of Jesus in Matthew 19:17-19 concerning how the Rich Young Man can be granted eternal life. This

[12] Catholic Catechism, Sections 1965-1974; 2052-2074; 2084-2550.

is no coincidence. It is indicative of the unyielding grip that the *faith alone* theology has on its adherents. Anything that infringes on its territory is either summarily dismissed, or, to save exegetical face, made into a hypothesis and called a "teaching tool." Hence, *faith alone* theology becomes the *sine qua non* of the Protestant hermeneutic, and anything that does not conform is reinterpreted to make it fit. *Faith alone* becomes the judge, jury and executioner of any biblical teacher, including Jesus, who would dare cross its threshold uninvited.

Another example of the elevation of *faith alone* theology over the explicit teaching of Jesus is the attempt by some Protestants to erect an impregnable wall between law and grace to the point that Jesus's teachings in the Sermon on the Mount do not apply in our present age, which they understand as the "dispensation of grace." They relegate Jesus's teachings instead to a future millennial kingdom that he will establish on earth.[13] In this way the Evangelicals, rather than make Jesus's teachings hypothetical, summarily dismiss them until a future time.[14] This extreme viewpoint shows us the lengths to which these theologies will go to exalt their understanding of justification by *faith alone*. If one follows their view of

---

13 "This is the hermeneutic espoused by Dispensationalists, a term used to describe a theology that sees God working in seven distinct "dispensations" in the Old and New Testaments. When one dispensation is done, another takes over, and the principles of the preceding one do not carry over to the following one. The present dispensation is one of grace, thus law must be totally eradicated. The champions of this theology are many and varied, but those from Dallas Theological Seminary are among its most prolific and ardent proponents, e.g., Lewis Sperry Chafer, Charles Ryrie, Frank Gabelien, John F. Walvoord, et al. It is no surprise that most of these men are from the "anti-Lordship salvation" contingent of Evangelicalism. The attempt to postpone the principles of the Sermon on the Mount to a future time resembles Martin Luther's attempt to postpone love of God till the eternal state. We will cover these aspects more thoroughly in chapter 9.

14 It is interesting to see the theological friendships that Protestants forge over this issue. Once long time theological enemies, the Dispensational Premillenialists and the Reformed A- or Postmillenialists are now joining ranks against other Protestant theologians, such as John F. MacArthur, who hold to the integral necessity of works in salvation. Ironically, MacArthur admits to being a Dispensationalist. The Reformed group, CURE (Christians United for Reformation), has made scathing critiques concerning MacArthur's emphasis on works and, at the same time, have applauded the efforts of the Dispensationalists in fighting the "Catholic" influence of works in salvation.

the separation of law and grace to its logical conclusion, he will invariably set aside a large portion of the teachings of Jesus as irrelevant in regard to justification.[15]

In this chapter we will revisit the Sermon on the Mount again and show how Jesus upholds not only the law but also obedience to its commands as precisely our gateway into eternal life. We will also see that Paul never objects to Jesus's teaching on works, not only because Paul does not teach a *faith alone* gospel but because he too upholds obedience to the higher law of God as our means of salvation. For now, we will examine Jesus's many other teachings in the gospels. We will see that Jesus never teaches the notion of *faith alone,* nor are any of his teachings "hypothetical." Of all the biblical personages, Jesus has the clearest and most succinct way of teaching the means to eternal life. We can trust his teachings implicitly and need never wonder whether he is speaking hypothetically or whether his teaching is reserved for the distant future.

John 5:24

"Whoever Hears My Word and Believes"

According to Evangelical John MacArthur "...it is easy to demonstrate from Jesus' evangelistic ministry that He taught *sola fide*."[16] One would think after reading this statement that the gospels are just filled with references to *faith alone*. We are surprised to find, however, that this commentator cites only four passages in all of Jesus's teaching to back up his claim that he teaches *sola fide* — and none of them use the phrase "faith alone."[17] Of John 5:24, MacArthur writes, "That verse clearly states that on the basis of faith alone, sinners pass out of death and into eternal life." Let's examine this very closely. John 5:24 reads, "I tell you the truth,

---

15 A good example of this is R. C. Sproul's *Faith Alone*. In the 221 pages of his book, Sproul does not exegete one verse of Jesus's teaching on justification/salvation, except in a passing reference to Luke 18:14 about the tax collector who was justified! Even then, he only quotes Calvin's view on the passage.

16 John MacArthur, *Justification By Faith Alone*, op. cit., p. 15.

17 John 5:24; Luke 23:43; Matthew 9:22 (and its Synoptic parallels in Mark 5:34; 10:52; Luke 8:48; 17:19; 18:42); and Luke 18:9-14 (*Justification By Faith Alone*, op. cit., pp. 15-17).

whoever hears my word and believes him who sent me has eternal life and will not be condemned; he has crossed over from death to life." The attempt to turn these words into a *sola fide* theology is a classic example of the *faith alone* syndrome common among Evangelicals, who impose its ubiquitous imprint upon the most simple of passages. John 5:24 does not even use the word *alone,* yet they attempt to pre-condition the reader to believe it is there. In addition, they attempt to lead the reader to conclude that the absence of the word *works* in John 5:24 is positive proof that Jesus taught *faith alone* justification. Not only is this an argument from silence, it also ignores all Jesus's other teachings that include works as the measure of one's acceptance with God. Not the least of these teachings appears right in the very context under discussion just four verses later in John 5:28-29 where Jesus says, "Do not be amazed at this, for a time is coming when all who are in their graves will hear his voice and come out — those who have *done good* will rise to live, and those who have *done evil* will rise to be condemned." We see that in using such language Jesus is certainly not shy about referring to faith in one breath and works in the next. Apparently he feels it is not a contradiction to say that the one who *believes* has eternal life but that the same person will be evaluated for his *deeds* to determine whether, in the end, he will be saved or not. This is not a novel teaching of Jesus nor of the rest of Scripture.[18] The connection between the faith of John 5:24 and the works of John 5:29 is so pronounced that both verses use a derivation of the Greek word *krisis* ("judgment"), a word that appears seven times in the same context in reference to the final judgment upon men (John 5:23-30). These verses focus on judging men for their deeds, not merely for whether they believe in Jesus.

---

[18] cf., Matthew 16:27; 12:36-39; Rom. 2:6-8; Rev. 20:12; 1 Cor. 3:13-17; 2 Cor. 5:10; Eph. 6:8; et al. In other publications, MacArthur attempts to relegate some of these judgment passages only to the time when Christians receive personal rewards, thus eliminating any possibility of eternal condemnation. Obviously, this does not apply to John 5:28-29, since the phrases "rise to live" and "rise to be condemned" can only refer to eternal life or eternal condemnation (cf., Matthew 25:46; John 6:40;12:48; Acts 24:15; Daniel 12:2). MacArthur's misapplication of the other verses mentioned will be covered in more detail in chapter 8.

Geisler and MacKenzie attempt to create the same impression as MacArthur by the statement, "In the Gospel of John only one condition is laid down for obtaining eternal life: belief (e.g., John 3:16, 36; 5:24; 20:31)."[19] Unfortunately, they make the same mistake that MacArthur made by not reading the rest of the passage. For example, though they are correct in stating that John 3:16 refers to belief, they fail to recognize that this aspect of justification is followed in John 3:21 with the words, "But whoever lives by the truth comes into the light, so that it may be seen plainly that what he has done has been done through God." Here Jesus does not emphasize those who believe but "whoever lives by the truth." In fact, Jesus implies that they come to the light of faith precisely because they have been living in the truth. Jesus is not divorcing faith from works. He is intimately identifying one with the other. Moreover, these are not boastful, self-righteous works done under the system of obligation, but works that have "been done through God."[20] Again, we see the unfortunate tendency of Protestants to interpret Scripture's use of *faith* to be *faith alone*, yet Scripture never uses such terminology; rather, it invariably couples faith with works in the realm of grace for the purposes of justification.

The Good Thief on the Cross

If there is one incident in the New Testament that Protestant commentators have treated as the proverbial rag doll of proof texts, it is the story of the good thief on the cross. They have used his sudden recognition of Jesus's mission and the kingdom of God to deny everything from baptism, to repentance, to works, to holiness as necessary to be saved and enter the kingdom of God. Since few passages in the Gospels can even remotely support *faith alone* theology, we can understand why some Protestants feel so drawn to the thief on the cross. Suffice it to say, this is the lowest form of biblical interpretation. Even if we were to grant that the good thief presents one instance of salvation by faith without works, the exception does not make the rule. In such instances where the normal

[19] *Roman Catholics and Evangelicals*, p. 231.

[20] The Greek reads ποιῶ τήν ἀλήθειαν ("doing the truth") and τὰ ἔργα ὅτι ἐν θεῷ ἐστιν εἰργασμένα ("that they are works wrought in God").

circumstances of life prohibit one from doing what is ordinarily required, God allows exceptions.[21] Such, for example, was the case of David and his men in the Old Testament who, out of hunger, ate the consecrated bread that was only lawful for priests to eat (cf., Lev. 24:5,9; 1 Sam. 21:6; Matt. 12:1-12). Jesus uses this incident to admonish the Pharisees who had accused the disciples of working on the Sabbath as they picked grains to eat. Jesus concludes that the Sabbath was made for man, not man for the Sabbath. Of course, if David had gone in every day and eaten the showbread, making it into the rule of his life rather than the exception, he would have been in sin and condemned by Jesus. But such was not the case. Likewise, neither Jesus nor the thief, with their hands, so to speak, "tied behind their backs," are expected to follow normal procedures. Just as Jesus would not deny salvation to a person unable to do works because he was without arms and legs, so he would not deny it to the man dying on the cross next to him because the man, though contrite, was no longer able to amend his life. A handicapped person can express faith, hope, and love in Jesus and he will be saved, even though someone else must care for him. Such was the case of the good thief. He expressed his faith, hope, and love in Jesus and received salvation in return.

That being said, we can now look more closely at the incident. We notice first that though both thieves reproach Jesus in some measure (Matthew 27:44), eventually the good thief rebukes the unrepentant thief (Luke 23:40). He does this in the face of the others gathered at the cross who are jeering at Jesus and telling him to "save himself" (Luke 23:35-37). Jesus had taught long before: "Whoever acknowledges me before men, I will also acknowledge him before my Father in heaven" (cf., Matt. 10:32; Rom. 10:9). Next, the good thief asks the other, "Don't you fear God?" (Luke

[21] Catholic theology also allows exceptions to its requirements for salvation. For example, as firm as the Church is on the necessity of baptism to be saved (Catholic Catechism, Sections 1214-1284; Council of Trent, Decree on Original Sin), it makes exceptions (e.g., the baptism of desire) for those who cannot possibly be administered this sacrament before death. See also Council of Trent, Session 7, Canon 4; and the Catechism, Section 1257: "God has bound salvation to the sacrament of Baptism, but he himself is not bound by his sacraments." The Church also allows for "deathbed" conversion in conjunction with the Sacrament of the Sick (Catholic Catechism, Sections 1499-1525).

23:40). We must assume that the good thief had an acute and personal fear of God in order to demand it from the other thief. He is like many who the New Testament says fear God and are blessed with salvation (Acts 10:1-4; 17:4,17, 25-26; Rom. 2:6-8). Perhaps this thief had feared God for some time before his sentencing for theft. We are not certain when the good thief committed his crime, nor do we know whether or not he had reconciled with God before his civil punishment on the cross. We cannot just assume he continued wicked and unrepentant up to the very last moment he met Jesus on the cross.

Next, the good thief tells the unrepentant thief that both of them are "punished justly" (Luke 23:41). This shows his inner sense of justice in that he is able to convict himself of sin before God. He also says of Jesus, "this man has done nothing wrong," realizing the goodness of Jesus (Luke 23:41). This implies that he knew something of Jesus prior to their meeting at the cross. He was perhaps familiar with Jesus's life and knew that he had not committed any crimes. Next, he says, "Remember me when you come into your kingdom" (Luke 23:42). We wonder where this man obtained such knowledge if this was the first time he had heard of Jesus. There is no recorded conversation about the kingdom of God during the crucifixion. Jesus was virtually silent during the whole event, speaking only seven short times. The thief might have known about the kingdom prior to the cross. This lowly thief understood Jesus's mission and purpose which even many of the apostles had a hard time understanding (Luke 24:25-26). Hence, everything in this story points to this thief having been prepared for this final moment with Jesus.[22] Finally he hears Jesus say, "Today you will be with me in paradise." Since this statement is an answer to the question about entering the kingdom, we may assume that "paradise" is the kingdom. Taking the man's statement as the thief's admission of guilt, Jesus's invitation into paradise implies the forgiveness that accompanies repentance. The man acts, and Jesus responds. The thief, not Jesus, ini-

[22] Council of Orange, 529 AD, Canon 25: "So very clearly we should believe that the faith — so admirable — both of that famous thief, whom the Lord restored to his native land of paradise, and of Cornelius the centurion, to whom the angel of the Lord was sent, and of Zachaeus, who deserved to receive the Lord Himself, was not from nature, but a gift of God's bounty."

tiates the conversation. As God had blessed Cornelius in Acts 10 for his fear and devotion, so Jesus blesses the thief. All in all, there is no warrant for imposing a *faith alone* theology in this unusual incident. The thief apparently already had faith in God as demonstrated by his "fear of God" that he expressed to the other thief. He now had to put that faith into action by reaching out to Jesus in perfect contrition, however limited he was in doing so. Had he not reached out, he would have been condemned just like the unrepentant thief who remained silent. As we will see in Jesus's remaining encounters with people of faith, they each had to come to him in repentance, seeking to be forgiven; hence, their faith was not alone.[23]

Jesus's Use of the Word "Justification"

Perhaps one of the main difficulties for Protestants attempting to correlate the teachings of Jesus with the teachings of Paul is that Jesus does not often use the verbal form *dikaioo* ("justified") as Paul does. Jesus uses the word only seven times in the gospels, almost half of which are not in contexts dealing with salvation. Paul, on the other hand, uses *dikaioo* twenty- seven times, preponderantly in reference to salvation. Hence, it is tempting for Protestants to make Paul's writings the "dictionary" on the usage of justification. As we have seen earlier in chapter 1, however, Paul emphasizes the specific concept of justification because he must explain in detail to the Jewish mind how the events of Jesus's death and resurrection have changed the face of the world. He must explain that the Jewish nation is no longer the legal custodian of the gospel and that God has transferred this privilege to the Church. He must explain why many Jewish customs and rituals under the ceremonial law are invalid when in Jesus's time they were still valid and practiced widely. He must explain the positive and negative points of the Mosaic law to the Jew who held its ordinances up

23 "To faith must be added: fear of Divine justice, hope in the mercy of God; love of God; hate of sin; cleansing of baptism" (Ott., *Fundamentals of Catholic Dogma*, p. 253; also Council of Trent, Session 6, Chapter 7). The good thief possessed all of these except baptism, which was not formally required until after Pentecost. In chapter 5 we will expose more thoroughly the aversion some Protestant groups have towards combining faith with repentance for justification.

as the only means to approach God. Jesus had started to explain some of these things and had begun to demolish the Jew's dependence on law without grace, but Paul had to put the final nails into the coffin. In order to do this, Paul had to grapple with the technical points of the Mosaic law to satisfy his Jewish critics. He had to begin to use technical terms that were not as frequent in the parlance of Jesus's time. At the same time, Paul had to explain the Christian gospel in such a way that it would answer the intellectual objections of the sophisticated Greeks and Romans who were steeped in philosophy and mythology. In short, Paul had a huge task on his hands. He had to pick up where Jesus left off and face an audience of hostile Jews who were even more hostile now that they realized the Gentiles were superseding them. Paul had to explain that the Mosaic law, which the typical Jew had heretofore taken for granted, now played only a part in the salvation of the individual, and he had to explain what that part was.

In Jesus's use of the word *dikaioo* there is always a clear indication that he is not using it in the Protestant sense of a one-time forensic act of God. For example, in Matthew 12:36-37 Jesus says, "But I tell you that men will have to give an account on the day of judgment for every careless word they have spoken. For by your words you will be *justified* and by your words you will be condemned." Here Jesus mentions the judgment that each man must face at the end of time for the works he did on earth. This in itself is a problem for Protestant theology since a salvation based on *faith alone* should have no room for a final soteriological judgment based on works.[24] To understand this verse completely we must address each of its four components: (1) a judgment for works,

---

[24] Some Protestants are quite candid about this embarrassing contradiction in their theology, e.g., P.T. O'Brien, "Justification in Paul and Some Crucial Issues of the Last Two Decades" in *Right With God*, ed., D.A. Carson, op. cit., p. 70f. John Ellicott admits that if a future judgment of Christians were true it would be as hard to understand on a theological basis as the antinomy between God's sovereignty and human responsibility and other enigmas of the Christian faith (*Commentary on the Whole Bible*, Vol III, p. 380). For similar admissions see also C. K. Barrett, *Commentary on the Second Epistle to the Corinthians*, 1973, p. 161; *The Interpreters Bible*, ed., George Buttrick, Vol X, p. 332; *The Expositor's Bible*, ed., W. Robertson Nicoll, Vol. V, p. 762. Some attempt to dismiss the contradiction, e.g., Charles Hodge, *An Exposition of the Second Epistle to the Corinthians*, p. 125.

(2) the use of the term *dikaioo*, (3) the ultimatum of salvation or condemnation, and, (4) the reference to the final judgment. There is no clearer language from the lips of Jesus other than that of Matthew 12:36-37, which uses the word *justified* in a salvation/damnation context. Surely no one can support an argument that in Matthew 12:36-37 Jesus is using the word *justified* any differently from Paul who also uses the word in similar contexts concerning the final judgment (cf., Rom. 2:13; 1 Cor. 4:4). Although Jesus's words imply the requirement of faith, his focal point is that it is the individual's works that justify or condemn him. Not only that, but no bad work escapes his scrutiny, since the verse specifies that he will judge "*every* careless word." Hence, Jesus, like James, teaches that our works play a primary role in determining our justification.

One of Matthew 12:36-37's most important features is that in it Jesus speaks of the "day of judgment." Whether this is the general judgment when all souls will stand before God, or the particular judgment when individuals will stand for judgment at death, Jesus does not specify.[25] Nevertheless, he does specify that the ultimate justification takes place at the final judgment of that individual. An end-time judgment that alone determines whether the individual is ultimately justified puts the Protestant concept of the one-time, imputed act of justification into an acute contradiction. When a Protestant theologian applies justification, he always speaks of it as a past event never to be repeated. But Jesus is using the word justification far beyond the initial stage of becoming a Christian, making it continue until the end of the person's life at which time it will be determined whether he will be ultimately justified or not. Hence, justification is not a one-time event never to be repeated but is a continual process with its final outcome reserved for judgment day. In addition, the individual's works will be the controlling criterion for the final justification.

The Pharisee and the Tax Collector

In accord with its general use in Scripture, Jesus also uses the word *dikaioo* in reference to the *present* justified state of the individual. In the parable of the Pharisee and the tax collector of Luke

[25] See Catholic Catechism, Section 1021-1023.

18:9-14, Jesus makes this final remark concerning the latter, "I tell you that this man went home *justified* before God. For everyone who exalts himself will be humbled and he who humbles himself will be exalted."

Before Jesus tells the parable, Luke gives the reason for its telling: "To some who were confident of their own righteousness and looked down on everybody else, Jesus told this parable..." Jesus develops the contrast wherein one party thinks he is living in a justified state, yet despises others who do not have the same social or spiritual status he thinks he has attained. Jesus goes on to describe this hypothetical Pharisee as one who prays and thanks God he is not like other sinful people, especially the despised tax collector he is standing next to. Not only does this Pharisee think he is free from sin, but he goes the extra mile, as it were, by fasting and giving tithes. Meanwhile, the tax collector recognizes his sin and pleads to God for mercy. For that repentance, Jesus says he is justified before God.

Jesus makes a similar judgment in Luke 16:15. Speaking of the Pharisees again, he says: "You are the ones who justify yourselves in the eyes of men, but God knows your hearts. What is highly valued among men is detestable in God's sight." It is obvious that Jesus is interested in the heart of the individual, not what he can puff up on the outside to make himself appear righteous before men. Such hypocritical behavior is even more odious to God than other sins. What is significant in this teaching is its remarkable similarity to the teaching of the apostle Paul. Paul was just as concerned about living from the heart as opposed to living merely from a written code of law. We will recall that Paul said in Romans 2:29, "No, a man is a Jew if he is one inwardly; and circumcision is circumcision of the *heart*, by the *Spirit*, not by the *written code*. Such a man's praise is *not from men, but from God*."

It is no surprise that Jesus's and Paul's teaching are identical. Life by the *written code* only breeds pride and arrogance like that displayed by the Pharisee. Instead, God is pleased with one who loves him from his heart, by the Spirit of life, who seeks divine praise, not human praise. It is no coincidence that this principle of Paul's introduces his teaching on justification proper that is followed in Romans 3-4. The Jews thought they could be justified by keeping the outward commands of the law but didn't realize the corruption of their hearts. Paul also spoke about being forgiven of sin within this justification context just as Jesus did of the tax collector (cf. Luke 18:9f; Rom. 3:23-25; 4:5-8; 2:4). The forgiveness of sins is what brings justification. Those who humble themselves before God and admit their sin will be justified. Those who do not admit their sin will not be justified.

One of the assumptions Protestants make when they interpret Luke 18:14 is that the justification of the tax collector is the single point in his life that he was justified. In contemporary understanding, it is as if the tax collector were walking up the aisle after saying the sinner's prayer and finally receives the grace of God into his life and now he is a Christian. Once justified, the tax collector will now go home and lead a life of sanctification. One Evangelical comments on this passage:

> Calvin cites as an example of justification by faith the case of the publican who went to his house "justified" (Luke 18:14):"...it cannot be held that he obtained this justification by any merit of works. All that is said is, that after obtaining the pardon of sins he was regarded in the sight of God as righteous. He was justified, therefore, not by any approval of works, but by gratuitous acquittal on the part of God."...This acquittal rests on the imputation of the righteousness of Christ.[26]

The context of the parable does not support this interpretation, nor is it consistent with the rest of Jesus's teaching. This is confirmed from several vantage points. Granted that, regarding works, the parable does not refer to works specifically, but then neither does it specify the word *faith*. Rather, the emphasis is on *repentance,* which implies both faith and works. The very next chapter in Luke 19:1-9 provides a shining example of how Jesus responds to such repentance in an incident with a real-life tax collector, Zacchaeus. In responding to Jesus's invitation, Zacchaeus says, "Look, Lord! Here and now I give half of my possessions to the poor, and if I have cheated anybody out of anything, I will pay back four times the

[26] R.C. Sproul, *Faith Alone*, op. cit., p. 102

amount." Here is true repentance. Zacchaeus is not just believing that Jesus is his personal Savior, but he is seeking to make a work of restitution for his sins. The very law of Israel required such a work of repentance and Zacchaeus is going above and beyond that law by offering to give as much as *half* his possessions (cf., Exodus 22:1-3; Leviticus 6:4-5; Numbers 5:7; 2 Samuel 12:6). This is just what Jesus had told the Rich Young Man of Luke 18:22 in order to obtain eternal life, "Sell everything you have and give to the poor, and you will have treasure in heaven." Although the account does not state this, we might say that the Rich Young Man stole from the poor indirectly and thus needed to make "restitution."

Notice Jesus's response to this repentant tax collector after he volunteers to pay back the money he stole: "Jesus said to him, 'Today *salvation* has come to this house, because this man, too, is a son of Abraham...'" It is the faith in Jesus coupled with the works of restitution, amounting to a sincere repentance on Zacchaeus' part, which in turn prompts Jesus to grant him salvation. We notice also that Jesus designates Zacchaeus as a "son of Abraham." This does not merely mean that Zacchaeus was a Jew but that he was a "Jew inwardly" who "walked in the footsteps of the faith of Abraham" who was also justified by his "faith" and "works" (cf., Romans 2:29; 4:12,16; James 2:24).

Before we go on to the next point about the parable of the Pharisee and the tax collector, it is significant that within Protestantism there is a long-standing controversy over the nature of repentance. Many in the *faith alone* camp are reluctant to say that repentance is necessary for justification because it could be considered a "work" required before grace is applied.[27] Indeed, if *faith alone* theologians would follow the premise of their teaching to its logical conclusion, they should admit that repentance is a work. In repentance an individual takes an action which in many cases requires a detailed and laborious recounting of one's past sins and seeking ways to rectify the damage caused by those sins, as in the case of Zacchaeus. Moreover, repentance is an ongoing process, a turning away from sin and the continuing performance of acts of

---

[27] E.g., Michael Horton in "Reformation Essentials" produced by CURE, 2034 E. Lincoln Ave #209, Anaheim, CA. Side A: "Christ Alone/Faith Alone," Audio Tape.

obedience. The nature of repentance shows once again how *faith alone* theology begins to crumble under its own weight.[28]

As mentioned above, the Protestant view of the parable of the Pharisee and the tax collector must be that it was the *first* time the tax collector, in Jesus's mind, had come to ask for his sins to be forgiven. Although the opposite view is not crucial to the Catholic apologetic, it is just as likely, in fact even more so, that it was one of *many* times the tax collector came before God to confess his sin. Granted, there would have been an initial time in his life that he came to God to confess his sins as each of us must do. In the non-parabolic story of Zacchaeus cited above, it is apparent that his moment of repentance was the first time he had publically admitted his sin. But nothing in what Jesus says in the parable of the Pharisee and the Tax Collector would make initial justification the exclusive interpretation of the parable. It is just as likely that the tax collector, along with the ever persistent Pharisee, went to the temple on many occasions to confess sin. Just in the way the tax collector talked to God, i.e., "God, have mercy on me a sinner" implies that he already knew God. Moreover, the Jews made a practice of daily confessing their sins as prescribed in the Old Testament (Leviticus 5:1ff). This would be no surprise to the Christian mind since 1 John 1:9-10 teaches us that "If we confess our sins, he is faithful and just and will forgive us our sins and purify us from all unrighteousness. If we claim we have not sinned, we make him out to be a liar and his word has no place in our lives." The tax collector would simply be following this prescription as he may have done many times before. The parable, by pointing out that both the Pharisee and the tax collector "went up to the temple to pray" (Luke 18:10), suggests that in Jesus' mind this scene may have been an ongoing one. The expression "going up to the temple at the time of prayer" used in Acts 3:1 indicates that this was a daily activity in Israel. In Jesus's mind, the Pharisee thought that he had been living a life of righteousness by fasting twice a week for some time prior to this hypothetical incident. The point at issue here is that the Protestant attempt to interpret the parable of the

[28] In chapter 5 we will again analyze and critique the Protestant attempt to separate faith from repentance.

Pharisee and the tax collector in line with the theory of a one-time act of imputation, as noted in the above interpretation by John Calvin, is simply reading into the passage what one's theology dictates, especially since it is only a parable and not a real event.

Though the Protestant polemic claims that the tax collector was "justified, therefore, not by any approval of works, but by gratuitous acquittal on the part of God," is at best a half-truth. Inasmuch as we have already shown that the parallel, non-parabolic, account of Zacchaeus specifically mentions works that brought him salvation, and that repentance itself is a work, Jesus in Luke 18:14 is not dissociating works as an integral part in the justification process. The problem with the Protestant interpretation is that it takes a mere cross-section out of the life of this imaginary character and assumes that just because the parable mentions no specific work, one has license to make the blanket statement that works play no part in justification. This is very short-sighted exegesis. As noted above, the passage simply offers no evidence whether this is an initial justification or an ongoing justification. In any case, God does not demand that a specific work like feeding the hungry or clothing the naked be done on the spot by one seeking forgiveness of sin. This is especially true since the essence of the parable is to reveal the *hearts* of the individuals involved, not to give a dissertation on the so-called "legal imputation of Christ's righteousness" that is forced upon the passage by the Protestant hermeneutic. Again, to conclude such is simply reading one's theology into the text.

Simply put, this parable of Jesus illustrates a proud man and a humble man. The Pharisee is the proud man who, as Paul says, lives by a "written code," not by the "heart" and the "Spirit" (Romans 2:29). He is a man who, because he does certain works, expects and even obligates God to favor him. He is one who wishes to receive justification as something owed for his work. He is operating in the system of law. On the other hand, the tax collector is the humble man who recognizes that God owes him nothing. Unlike the Pharisee, he brings his works before God with sincere faith and love. He repents, and in doing so, comes under God's system of grace rather than law. Under grace, his works are accepted, not because he is obligating God to do so, but because God does so purely from his mercy. Moreover, God expects the tax collector, if he has stolen any money (probably a tax collector's most prominent sin) will cease to do so and give back what he has stolen. Such is the ongoing work of repentance which he initiated in confessing his sin. If he sins again by stealing money, he will have to return to the temple and confess his sin, lest his justification be nullified. Moreover, no one will argue that faith and repentance are the beginning of salvation. Whether the respective tax collectors will continue to be faithful and endure to the end is a matter not addressed by Jesus. All in all, nothing in the passage proves a once-for-all imputed justification by *faith alone*.

The Sermon on the Mount

Jesus frequently uses the person of the Pharisee when he is illustrating the nature of hypocrisy and specifying behavior that will prohibit one from entering the kingdom of heaven. Matthew 23 records Jesus's most famous attack against the Pharisees, commonly known as "the Seven Woes."[29] Each woe begins with the same refrain, "Woe to you, teachers of the law and Pharisees, you hypocrites!" and in each case Jesus points out an action in which the Pharisees and teachers of law give a show of religiosity to men but in their hearts are full of pride and hatred. It is religion based strictly on a written code, without sincere faith and love. Matthew 23 is Jesus's description of those who attempt to be made righteous by law without grace.

In making the Pharisees an example of those who will not enter the kingdom of heaven, Jesus warns others that they must be better than the Pharisees in order to enter the kingdom. In Matthew 5:20, Jesus says, "For I tell you that unless your righteousness *surpasses* that of the Pharisees and the teachers of the law, you will certainly not enter the kingdom of heaven." This saying is included in the Sermon on the Mount. Just prior to this, Jesus had given the nine beatitudes in which he praised the righteous conduct of certain people (Matthew 5:3-12). With each blessing he includes a promise, and each promise points to the final reward of the heav-

[29] According to the Textus Receptus there are eight woes. Some newer translations leave out Matthew 23:14. Luke's version only has six woes (Luke 11:42-52).

enly kingdom, e.g., "Blessed are those who are persecuted because of righteousness, for theirs is the kingdom of heaven."

Following this, Jesus gives six statements beginning with the refrain, "You have heard it was said, but I say unto you..." regarding murder, adultery, divorce, oaths, personal vengeance, and love for enemies (Matthew 5:21-48). In each case, Jesus explains that men must go beyond mere outward obedience to the law and to look at the motives of their actions. For example, Jesus teaches that a man sins not just by physically committing adultery with a woman but also by looking at her lustfully. Jesus wants them to go beyond the rudimentary written code of law that people observe on the outside, (a law in which people do what is basically required and no more) and to embrace a higher law that seeks to examine every thought and action from the perspective of whether it pleases God and truly benefits our neighbor. We must obey, knowing that God judges the heart, not merely the outward actions.[30]

Again, in Matthew 6:1-18, Jesus admonishes us to give to the poor, pray, and fast, in each case telling us not to do these things in front of others in order to be noticed by them but to do them in secret where only the Father sees them. Thus we see that the Sermon on the Mount is basically a sermon on living from one's heart in order to please God, not from mere outward actions in order merely to please men. The Pharisees were of the latter variety, always doing things with an eye toward impressing men while inside they were full of hate for both God and man. Knowing their hearts, Jesus says that our *righteousness* must surpass that of the Pharisees in order to enter the kingdom of heaven (Matthew 5:20).[31] As we have shown above, the whole tenor of the Sermon on the Mount, both before and after this saying, is to teach the inner obedience of the heart, thus it is obvious that the righteousness Jesus wants us to attain is not merely a product of some kind of theological imputation but a personal striving of the individual whose desire is to please God with all of his thoughts and actions. More-

---

30 Catholic Catechism, Sections 1949-1986

31 "Righteousness" is from the Greek word *dikaiosune* (δικαιοσύνη) which is commonly understood in the New Testament as "righteous," "just," or "righteousness." It refers to a quality about the person to whom it is designated. Chapter 5 will analyze this word in more detail.

over, that the attainment of this type of righteousness is directly related to whether one is ultimately saved is clear from Jesus's warning in Matthew 5:20 that if one does not attain such righteousness: "you will certainly not enter the kingdom of heaven." Jesus does not place the challenge of high obedience merely in the realm of *sanctification*, as many Protestants categorize works subsequent to justification; rather, he places these high-order works in the realm of salvation, i.e., as determining whether one will be saved or not.[32]

The theory of imputed righteousness forces those Protestants who believe in it to conclude that the way one surpasses the righteousness of the Pharisees is merely to believe in the alien righteousness of Christ. Supporters view the works of righteousness described before and after the statement in Matthew 5:20 as the fruits of works that inevitably issue forth from true faith. Hence, only the faith, not the works of righteousness, is the criterion for whether we enter the kingdom of heaven. In the Protestant view, the Pharisees are those who do not have faith in Christ and thus do not have works of righteousness.[33] As noted earlier, the problem with such an analysis is that it is at best a half-truth, and as such

[32] It is instructive to note Luther's perspective on Christ's view of works. He wrote, "There's no man living on earth who knows how to distinguish between the law and the gospel...Even the man Jesus Christ was so wanting in understanding when he was in the vineyard that an angel had to console him [John 12:27-29], though he was a doctor from heaven he was strengthened by the angel" (LW 54, 127). It is no wonder that Lutheranism after Luther had a continual problem in solving the relationship between Law and Gospel. It still exists today.

[33] Edmund Clowney's treatment of Matthew 5:20 is a good example of this kind of biased exegesis. Dealing with the issue of how one's righteousness surpasses that of the Pharisees, Clowney writes, "But if the righteousness of the scribes and Pharisees is not adequate for the standards of the kingdom, what hope can there be for harlots, tax-swindlers, and open sinners?...The righteousness of the kingdom cannot be the achievement of proud human beings. It is the fruit of grace for those who know themselves to be sinners...The defrauding tax-collector prays in deep contrition, 'God, be merciful to me, a sinner,' and goes home justified through divine forgiveness and acceptance (Luke 18:9-14)" (*Right With God*, "The Biblical Doctrine of Justification By Faith," op. cit., p. 39). Rather than answering the challenge posed in Matthew 5:20 by addressing the context of Matthew 5-6, Clowney chooses to ignore this information and proceeds right to Luke 18:9-14 which, albeit an important text, concerns only one aspect of righteousness. The context of Matthew 5-6 goes far beyond the initial dimension of forgiveness of sins. It emphasizes the positive dimension of living a holy and obedient life before God as the means to attain righteousness that surpasses that of the Pharisees. Clowney

ends up distorting Jesus's teaching and eliminating its real impact upon the individual. There isn't one word in the Sermon on the Mount about *faith alone* as the measurement for entering the kingdom of heaven. Rather, the Sermon is completely and wholly saturated with admonitions concerning obedience from the heart. Jesus's language is clear. Our righteousness must "surpass" that of the Pharisees. According to the *context*, this can happen only when we make the conscious decision to love God and our neighbor from the heart, performing not as men-pleasers but as God-pleasers. As with Paul's and James's writings, Jesus's focus in the Sermon on the Mount is on pleasing God sufficiently to enter the kingdom. To inject a theory of imputed righteousness into Jesus's words is simply imposing a system of theology onto a text that neither teaches nor has room for such a concept.

Protestants also distort the requirements for forgiveness of sins when they impose the theory of imputation onto the Sermon on the Mount. While in the parable of the tax collector the penitent simply goes to the temple admitting that he is a sinner and is subsequently justified, in the Sermon on the Mount Jesus makes quite an issue about the contingencies surrounding God's forgiveness. Jesus begins by specifying one of the petitions of the Lord's prayer as "Forgive us our trespasses as we forgive those who trespass against us" (Matthew 6:12). The comparative word "as" shows that God's forgiveness of our sins depends on our forgiveness of other's sins. Jesus immediately clarifies that this is indeed his meaning in Matthew 6:14-15, "For if you forgive men when they sin against you, your heavenly Father will also forgive you. But if you do not forgive men their sins, your Father will not forgive your sins."

Jesus also teaches this principle in the parable of the Unmerciful Servant, Matthew 18:21-35, where the master forgives his servant, but the servant does not forgive his subordinate. Jesus concludes in verse 34-35, "In anger his master turned him over to the jailers to be tortured, until he should pay back all he owed. This is

---

33 cont. simply ignores this aspect. We don't have to consider ourselves "proud human beings" if we obey the law to enter heaven, provided we understand that the ability to do such works, and their evaluation, come from the grace of God. That is all Jesus is asking for. Again, we see that if the passage in view does not fit the mold of *faith alone* theology, the Protestant theologian reinterprets the passage to make it fit. No matter what illumination the context provides, the overriding concern is to preserve the tenets of *sola fide*.

how my heavenly Father will treat each of you unless you forgive your brother from your heart."

The message is clear. We obtain forgiveness of our sins not through accepting an alien righteousness of Christ but by the works of forgiving our neighbors who sin against us. By forgiving them, God forgives us and views us as righteous in his sight. The mere fact that Jesus includes the stipulation that God must forgive our sins shows that Jesus is not speaking of an absolutely perfect righteousness that God expects from us. He knows we will sin, perhaps in some cases by not forgiving our brother as we should. But as long as we humbly recognize and confess of our sins from our heart, and as long as we follow through with the works of repentance, we are working in the realm of grace and God is pleased with us and will grant us the kingdom of heaven. This is not a teaching reserved for some "millennial kingdom," nor is it a mere hypothetical means to show us the purpose of the law to reveal sin. Jesus makes his intention clear in Matthew 5:18-19:

> I tell you the truth, until heaven and earth disappear, not the smallest letter, not the least stroke of a pen, will by any means disappear from the Law until everything is accomplished. Anyone who breaks one of the least of these commandments and teaches others to do the same will be called least in the kingdom of heaven, but whoever practices and teaches these commands will be called great in the kingdom of heaven.

Not only is Jesus upholding the precepts of the Law, he is reinforcing them by saying that God will notice our breaking the *least* commandment. The principle of Law will last until "everything is accomplished," or, as Jesus earlier taught, when "heaven and earth disappear." We have already seen this principle in Jesus's use of the word *dikaioo* ("justified") in Matthew 12:36-37 to teach that God will judge "*every* idle word." Although Jesus's death partially fulfills the Law (John 19:30), it did not completely fulfill it. Jesus teaches in Matthew 5:18 that the progressive fulfillment of the Law does not abolish the Law. Those who do not place themselves in God's grace will be subject to the requirements of the Law till the end of time. In addition, those who are in God's grace must obey the Law from their heart to please God as a child seeks to please his father.

The Repentant Woman

In Luke 7:50, Jesus says to the woman who humbly anointed him, "Your faith has saved you, go in peace." One predisposed to a *faith alone* theology would be tempted to seize on this verse and use it to prove his theory. To be sure, faith is one of the main ingredients to salvation, but neither the story surrounding this saying nor anything we have seen thus far in Jesus's teaching will allow it to support a *faith alone* theology.

The setting in Luke 7:36-50 portrays Jesus dining at a Pharisee's house. A woman comes in and, crying, begins wiping Jesus's feet with her hair and pouring perfume on them. The Pharisee is indignant because the woman is a known sinner. He thinks that Jesus should have known better than to associate with her. To explain these impromptu actions, Jesus tells the Pharisee a parable about two men who had their debts forgiven, one a large debt, the other small. At Jesus's prompting, the Pharisee concludes that the one who was forgiven the larger amount would love his master more. Jesus applies this to the sinful woman who is now seeking forgiveness. Jesus further admonishes the Pharisee for not having greeted him with the customary kiss and anointing. These were common customs of greeting and affection for friends and guests in those times. Thus, Jesus is pointing out that Simon did not show Jesus even the least amount of love. The woman, on the other hand, showed her love by doing the very things Simon ought to have done. Perhaps she noticed that Simon had not given the customary greetings and may have felt it her responsibility to do so. Her greeting, however, is filled with emotion, sorrow and love. It is after, not before, this exercise of love by the woman that Jesus remarks about her forgiveness. He then concludes, "Therefore, I tell you, her many sins have been forgiven — for she loved much. But he who has been forgiven little loves little."

Here Jesus is tying in the forgiveness of the woman's sins with the love she showed to Jesus. It is not simply that she believes in Jesus. Faith, of course, prompted her to come. It is what the Council of Trent calls "the beginning of salvation."[34] The real focus, however, is on her humbling herself, coming to a stranger's house in front of many guests and washing Jesus's feet and applying perfume, all in an effort to show her love for him. At the least, the woman's faith is, as Paul says in Galatians 5:6, a "faith working through love," but it is certainly not a faith alone. Jesus would not have specified her love to such a degree if he did not mean to combine her love with her faith as the cause for her forgiveness and salvation. Luke makes it clear that the woman is a known sinner, and thus in sin when she comes to Jesus, by his statement, "who had lived a sinful life" (verse 37). That Luke says these sins are forgiven only *after* she shows the three signs of love to Jesus (verse 48) is confirmation that her love was an integral cause of her forgiveness and justification. For *faith alone* to be the cause of her forgiveness, as the Protestants claim, the story line would have concentrated on her faith as opposed to her love, and Jesus would have forgiven her sins *before* the acts of love. If her faith alone had obtained her forgiveness, Jesus would not have confused the issue by making it appear that her love was the turning point in her spiritual cure. Moreover, if faith had been the only criterion for her forgiveness, Jesus would have said thus before elaborating on Simon's lack of love and the woman's contrasting love. She comes to Jesus doing acts of love because she is seeking forgiveness, not doing acts of love because she has already been forgiven. Jesus never met this woman before, so he could not have forgiven her sins prior to this incident. Luke does not record that the woman says anything to Jesus, that is, she does not verbally ask for forgiveness. Her actions of love alone speak of her desire and need for forgiveness.

If God had forgiven the woman of her sins privately before she ever came to Jesus, there would be cause to say that the love she showed to Jesus was a result of that previous forgiveness. The perfect passive verb in the statement of verse 47, "her many sins have been forgiven" may imply such prior forgiveness. It is more likely, however, that the subsequent statement in verse 48, which uses the same perfect passive tense ("your sins have been forgiven"), and which places the reference point for the past action at the beginning of the time Jesus is speaking to her, acts as a commentary on the verb tense of verse 47 and implies that this was the first time

[34] Council of Trent, Session 6, Chapter 8.

the woman was formally forgiven and the first time she became conscious of her forgiveness.[35] Since nothing else in the context would indicate a forgiveness prior to her meeting of Jesus, we must assume that the woman was not forgiven until after her show of love, as Luke 7:48 suggests. In effect, this scene at the Pharisee's house portrays a woman who is repenting for the first time. She does not do so verbally, but by her tears and sorrow which Jesus understands as an act of love. The repentance and sorrow, as manifestations of her love, are the reasons Jesus forgives her. Hence, the love of the woman is both the cause and the result of the forgiveness. The parable shows that as the woman seeks forgiveness, love simultaneously flows from her. It is the love of the woman which allows Jesus to know she is truly repenting. The Pharisee, on the other hand, doesn't seek forgiveness of sin (because he does not recognize his own sin) and thus he does not express any sorrow or love for Jesus. In fact, he even distrusts Jesus to the point that he secretly accuses him of being a fraud, as verse 39 indicates.

Though love is an integral part of the forgiveness, there still remains some question as to why Jesus tells her in verse 50, "Your *faith* has saved you, go in peace." If love is the key to the passage why didn't Jesus say, "Your love has saved you"? There are several reasons for this. First, as noted above, faith is the beginning of salvation. Without faith it is impossible to please God. Verse 37 tells us that the woman "learned that Jesus was eating at the Pharisee's house," which prompted her to come. Thus, she must have known something about Jesus and had some rudiments of faith in Jesus and a knowledge of her own sinfulness. The text does not tell us if for some time she had already stopped sinning prior to meeting Jesus. It simply calls her "a sinner." But she needed to act on her faith. Jesus was not simply going to read her mind in her house and forgive her of sin. Thus the love that moved her to act brought her faith to fruition, and it was on this basis that the faith saved her.

Second, Jesus is accomplishing two things regarding Simon the Pharisee. The first is to show how little he loves. The key is that Simon does not recognize his own sinfulness but looks down on the woman who is a known sinner, just as in Luke 18:9 of the Pharisee

35 Verse 47 and 48, Greek: ἀφέωνται (have been forgiven).

who looks down on the tax collector who is a known sinner. Jesus, by his parable of the two men who owed money, desires to teach Simon that his capacity to love, whether God or man, can be no greater than his sense of his own sin. The second thing Jesus accomplishes is to show Simon and his guests that *none* of them has any faith in Jesus. Simon first raises doubts about Jesus in verse 39 when he says, "If this man were a prophet he would know who is touching him and what kind of woman she is — that she is a sinner." Thus, Simon not only despises the woman but, more importantly, he even questions the character and veracity of Jesus. This lack of faith in Jesus is also evident among the guests, as verse 49 records: "Who is this man who even forgives sins?" Ingeniously, without remarking directly on their lack of faith, Jesus does so *indirectly* by telling the repentant woman that her faith has saved her. No doubt the guests heard Jesus say this and correctly understood it as an indictment against them for their own lack of faith. Thus we should not take the addition of "your faith has saved you" as a dogmatic statement to promote a *faith alone* theology. Rather, we should understand the statement within the whole context of the passage, a passage that speaks of the great faith and love of the woman, as opposed to the lack of faith and love in Simon and his guests.[36]

---

[36] Though we emphasize the great faith of the woman, we must note that, in contrast to Luther's idea of "cheerful audacity," "bold confidence" or "firm acceptance" of faith for salvation (Hacker, p. 91, n. 26), none of the stories covered thus far, nor any others in the Gospels, exhibits such an unshakable disposition among the penitents. Nothing in the text of the repentant woman of Luke 7 suggests the "certainty" of her forgiveness. We can say the same of the tax collector in Luke 18:9 who cries, "God, be merciful to me a sinner," or even of the centurion in Matthew 8:5-13 who does not consider himself worthy to come to Jesus, sending someone else in his place (Luke 7:7). Similarly, the stories of the man cured of blindness in Matthew 9:28 and the healing of the possessed boy in Mark 9:23-24 are not examples of unequivocal apprehension by a self-asserted act of the conscious mind which could misinterpret itself as faith; rather, they are in fear and trembling in which the seekers, moved by the crisis of the moment, have no choice but to throw themselves upon his mercy without being sure they will obtain it. Fortunately for them, Jesus heals even when he sees only elementary faith. As for forgiveness of sin, these passages [and Scripture in general] offer no evidence that one receives it simply because of his firm belief in being forgiven. (See chapter 9 for more detail on Luther's concept of the "certitude of faith".)

The Woman with an Issue of Blood

Another instance in which faith features prominently is the story of the woman who had an issue of blood for twelve years. Luke's version of this story begins at Luke 8:40 when Jairus, a ruler of the synagogue, came to Jesus begging him to cure his sick daughter. On the way to Jairus's house, the woman with the issue of blood came through the crowd and touched Jesus's clothing, and immediately she was healed. Matthew's version tells us that the woman had thought to herself that touching the garment would bring her healing (Matthew 9:21). As he cures her, Jesus responds with: "Daughter, your faith has healed you." Here is a simple story to illustrate the humble, child-like faith that Jesus wants from us. Among many doubters, the woman stands out as the example par excellence of pure faith in God. She has a faith which recognizes that God is much more powerful than she, a God who has the power to cure a disease that up until this time seemed hopelessly incurable.

Unfortunately, some zealous promoters of the *faith alone* theory of justification try to use this passage to support their view. Seizing on the words of Jesus, "your faith has healed you," they claim that Jesus is giving us an example that all he wants for salvation is faith. Though we must be careful not to minimize the importance of faith, we must also point out a number of factors that militate against extracting a *faith alone* theology out of this simple story. First, it is immediately apparent that the woman *acted* on her faith by reaching out to touch the clothing of Jesus. She did not sit in her home just believing she could be cured. She put her faith into action, and it is the combination of faith and action that cured her. As noted previously, the nature of faith has been a thorn in the side for many Protestant theologians. Since faith is an act of the will, it is something that is performed by the individual. Without exercising the human volition of faith, the individual can neither receive healing or salvation. Second, the passage is not speaking about salvation, per se. The woman may later have become a true child of God, but the story does not say so, nor is it the point of the story. Many people whom Jesus cured of diseases and who saw other miracles of Jesus did not end up believing in him for salvation. The feeding of the five thousand in the next chapter of Luke, or the healing of the ten lepers in Luke 17:11-19 in which only one came back praising God and thanking Jesus are cases in point. John's version of the feeding of the five thousand indicates that after participating in the miracle, most of the people walked away in unbelief when Jesus revealed the true nature of the bread from heaven (John 6:1-65). This is not to say that the woman who was cured of her bleeding did not become a Christian, but only that the story does not mention this dimension and thus cannot be used as an illustration of salvation nor prove a *faith alone* theology.

Mark 2:1-12

The Healing of the Paralytic

The Synoptic gospels record a scene in which the friends of a man with paralysis cut a hole in the roof of a house and lower the man in front of Jesus.[37] As Jesus watches this unusual effort, he acknowledges their faith and subsequently tells the paralytic that his sins are forgiven. The question arises why Jesus did not immediately cure the man, since that seemed to be the concern of his friends. In actuality, the paralytic is not cured until after a confrontation with the Pharisees concerning Jesus's initial act of forgiving the man's sins.

As we compare and contrast this story with the account of the woman with an issue of blood, a question arises concerning the relationship between healing and the forgiveness of sins. In the account of the bleeding woman we concluded that the physical healing of an individual did not necessitate that the sins of the same were forgiven, nor that salvation is necessarily involved at all. This coincides with the many times Jesus performed miraculous works in the midst of various people without any indication that they received salvation.[38] However, in the story of the healing of the paralytic, we have an occasion in which not only is a person healed but is also forgiven of sin because of an act of faith in Jesus. In fact, the paralytic's sins are forgiven first, even though it seems from the story that he came only to be physically healed. This would seem

[37] Luke 5:17-26; Matthew 9:2-8; Mark 2:3-12.

[38] E.g., Matthew 11:20; Luke 17:11-19; John 6:26, 66; 10:31-32.

to contradict our earlier proposition that healing does not necessarily involve the matter of sin and salvation. In order to answer this question, we must examine the context of the passage.

As noted above, alongside the healing of the paralytic is the confrontation between Jesus and the Pharisees. The Pharisees, who consistently challenge the motives and integrity of Jesus, are going to be taught a lesson by Jesus. In fact, Jesus does not cure the paralytic until the discussion with the Pharisees is over, showing that Jesus deliberately refrained from initially healing the man to provoke an objection from the Pharisees. As he usually does in situations like this, Jesus accomplishes his primary task of helping the individual in need, and at the same time, he silences the murmurings of his critics. Colloquially speaking, we could say that Jesus 'kills two birds with one stone.' The Pharisees want to trap Jesus and accuse him of being a fraud. As Jesus forgives the paralytic's sins, the Pharisees immediately accuse him of blasphemy by reminding everyone in the room that only God can forgive sins. Jesus, knowing their thoughts, says, "Which is easier: to say, 'Your sins are forgiven,' or to say, 'Get up and walk'?" Though it is not stated in the text, the answer to this question is that it is easier to say, 'Your sins are forgiven.' Jesus had just begun his ministry and this incident is recorded in only the second chapter of Mark's gospel. For a person, like Jesus, who is attempting to establish his identity and credibility as divine, it is easier to claim to forgive sin. Since they cannot see spiritual things, no one can either prove or disprove whether the sins have been forgiven, or whether Jesus really is God and has the power to forgive. Conversely, it is much harder or riskier to establish one's credibility by attempting to heal someone, since if the person is not healed then that failure would immediately suggest that the healer is a fraud. Assuming that the Pharisees understand his logic, Jesus continues with, "But that you may know that the Son of Man has authority on earth to forgive sins," and then turning to the paralytic, says, "I tell you, get up, take your mat and go home." Here Jesus is coupling the healing of the paralytic with his power to forgive sins. In the people's minds, no one could perform such miraculous feats unless God was with the healer.[39] If God is with the healer to heal, then it is not too much

[39] cf., John 3:2; 9:16, 33.

a stretch of the imagination to reason that he is indeed the Son of God who can forgive sins.

The account of the paralytic has some unique characteristics that are not found in other passages. First, as noted above, the friends expect the paralytic to be cured, but Jesus first forgives his sins. The paralytic did not show any signs that he was in overt sin, nor is there any specific history of him being in sin (as opposed to the sinful woman of Luke 7). Second, by the statement, "When Jesus saw *their* faith, he said, 'Friend, your sins are forgiven'" we see that Jesus recognizes the faith of his four companions, and possibly the faith of the paralytic, but only forgives the sins of the paralytic, rather than the paralytic *and* the four friends. Third, it is because of the faith of the men as a group that Jesus forgives the paralytic's sins, not just the faith of the paralytic. In fact, the faith of the paralytic is not explicit in the passage except for the fact that he is said to "praise God" when he was finally cured some moments later (Luke 5:25). Perhaps the friends thought that the reason the man was paralyzed was that there was some sin in his life. This was a common belief in those times, as suggested by the account in John 9:1-2 of the man born blind who was thought to be in that condition because of his or his parent's sins. The friends of the paralytic may have reasoned that the healing of the paralytic was conditioned on first having Jesus forgive his sins.

The anomalies surrounding the forgiveness of the paralytic's sins, as well as the precise relationship between healing and salvation, are more easily answered when it is noticed in Mark's account that Jesus's main activity prior to the entrance of the paralytic was that he "preached the word to them" that were gathered in the house (Mark 2:2). We can imagine that Jesus had given the same message to this crowd that he had previously given to many others when he preached the word of God. The people were taught to recognize their sins and repent. In Mark 1:15, John the Baptist had introduced the mission of Jesus with the words, "The kingdom of God is near, Repent and believe the good news." After this introduction, Jesus says in Mark 1:38, "Let us go somewhere else — to the nearby villages — so I can preach there also. That is why I have come." Capernaum, where the incident with the paralytic took place, is one of those "nearby villages." In fact, as recorded in Mark 1:21, Jesus had previously been to Capernaum and had preached the word to the people in their synagogue and they were amazed at his authority. He also cast out a demon at that visit. Thus, the mission of Jesus was well known by the people in Capernaum before the curing of the paralytic.

Although much of Jesus's encounters with people involved physical healing, this did not diminish his primary role of preaching the gospel of repentance from sin. Thus when he "preached the word" to these people in the house at Capernaum, we understand that Jesus taught them about sin. Before the arrival of the paralytic, we can assume that Jesus had already told the crowd of his mission from God to bring people to repentance, and possibly, that he himself had the power to forgive their sins, or at the least, he was ready to make his debut that he indeed was God and had power to do such things. In any case, his forgiving of the paralytic's sins was prompted by his teaching to the crowd about sin and the necessity of forgiveness. It is not unlikely that Jesus's preaching of the word was heard and understood by the four friends and the paralytic. This is suggested also by the fact that the four men had first gone to the door before they decided to cut a hole in the roof. No doubt they would have heard Jesus through the door teaching the people about the gospel.

We see in this account that the four men, including the paralytic, had great faith in the person of Jesus. Most likely they knew something about Jesus because already by this time word of his fame had spread abroad (cf., Mark 1:28, 37, 45). This is very similar to the story concerning the woman with an issue of blood. She apparently had heard of Jesus and knew she could be healed by his power. However, whereas the woman with an issue of blood is not said to be forgiven of sin, (from which it can be concluded that faith in Jesus for healing does not necessarily forgive one of sin), the paralytic is specifically forgiven of sin as he is being healed. The difference is explained in that the context of the healing of the paralytic includes the "preaching of the word" by Jesus prior to the healing, whereas the account of the bleeding woman does not.

Because his message would have included the teaching of repentance from sin, it is only then that forgiveness of sin is coupled with physical healing.[40]

Other Teachings of Jesus on Justification

In the gospels, Jesus consistently makes our salvation contingent upon our obedience. There is a marked theme in his teachings regarding people who say they believe, or who believe only for a little while, but whose works are false, missing, or incomplete. It is these who are lost. These teachings warn us that people are damned not merely for lack of faith, per se, but for not following through with their faith, i.e., for not doing works of obedience. But most importantly, not once does Jesus say or teach that someone can be eternally saved by a one-time act of faith. Rather, Jesus's teaching encompasses the whole life of the individual — a life that starts in faith and good works and continues until the end. Only when the individual has reached the end of life in the same fervor with which he started does Jesus consider the individual justified. From the many passages that illustrate this point, let us select a few of the most prominent.

We find Jesus laying the much stress on the requirement of continuing in faith and good works toward the latter end of his public ministry, right before he went to the cross. Most of these teachings concern the judgment he will administer at his Second Coming. No verse better expresses this theme than Matthew 24:13: "...but he who stands firm to the end will be saved." This same saying appears a bit earlier in Matthew 10:22: "All men will hate you because of me, but he who stands firm to the end will be saved." The former verse (24:13) deals specifically with the destruction of Jerusalem and thus is written to a wide audience, i.e., not only to those who would be victims during the destruction of the city, but

[40] For our purposes, the story of the healing of the blind man in John 9:1-41 is especially relevant since the man is cured by Jesus without any initial sign from the man of acknowledging or understanding the identity of Jesus or his own need of faith and repentance. It is not until the end of the story, long after he has been healed, that Jesus comes to him and elicits faith from him for salvation (9:35-41).

also to all future Christians, through the metaphorical telescoping of this event into the Second Coming of Christ in which he will judge the whole world. In the latter verse (10:22) Jesus deals mainly with the ministry of the apostles, warning that as they go to preach the gospel they will be persecuted, but that they must endure to the end, i.e., the end of their life. Hence, these warnings that one must endure to the end to be saved encompass the whole Church age, beginning with the apostles in the first century and ending with the last century at the Second Coming. Each generation of Christians, then, must "endure to the end" in order to be saved.

In these teachings, Jesus constantly reinforces the theme of *enduring to the end* by adding the refrain, "Therefore, keep watch, because you do not know on what day your Lord will come" (Matthew 24:44). He repeats this warning with emphasis in Matthew 24:36, 24:50 and 25:13. In the story of the faithful and unfaithful servants of Matthew 24:45-51, Jesus specifically warns against the kind of thinking exemplified in the unfaithful servant who reasons that his master has stayed away a long time and will not return very soon. The servant then uses this reasoning to engage in evil behavior, thinking that his master will not catch him. But Jesus warns that he will come upon that man at a time that he did not expect and subsequently judge him for his evil deeds. He will be assigned a place in the outer darkness with the hypocrites — people who say one thing but do another.

These teachings of Jesus echo teachings in other Scriptures. Long ago, the prophet Ezekiel wrote a very similar warning in Ezekiel 18:24:

> But if a righteous man turns from his righteousness and commits sin and does the same detestable things the wicked man does, will be live? None of the righteous things he had done will be remembered. Because of the unfaithfulness he is guilty of and because of the sins he has committed, he will die.

Here we see the same teaching, that one must endure to the end in order to be saved. The passage describes a man who has lived righteously for a long time, perhaps all his life, but who then decides to do evil. Naturally, the question would arise: what about all the good that he had done in the past? Will this be taken into account? The answer is a firm no. God will not judge him on how well he lived his life in the beginning but on how his life turns out in the end. This is why Catholic teaching puts such stress on avoiding mortal sin at all costs and preparing one's soul for death. It is the disposition of the soul at the end of one's life that matters. Although the punishment in eternity may be more or less, depending on mitigating factors in the man's earthly life, the point of the teaching is that the unrighteousness he has done at the end of his life will prevent him from entering the bliss of heaven.

The remaining teachings of Jesus in Matthew 25 all illustrate the same point, but from slightly different angles. The parable of the ten virgins in Matthew 25:1-13 is very pointed in its teaching of enduring to the end. The parable opposes the five wise virgins who were ready with oil in their lamps for the coming of the bridegroom to the five foolish virgins who did not have oil. Jesus concludes with the saying, "Therefore, keep watch, because you do not know the day or the hour." The teaching is clear. Salvation is not based merely on an act of faith at the beginning of one's life but on the continual faith and obedience throughout one's life.

The parable of the Talents in Matthew 25:14-30 reaches the same conclusion but from a different angle. Three men receive money to invest for their master. The master goes on a long journey with the proviso that each of the men are to invest his money in order to gain interest. The emphasis on the "long journey" borrows the same theme that was evident in Jesus's earlier teaching in this discourse, i.e., that servants will take advantage of the seemingly extended time that the master will be away so that they can do evil and not get caught. As it turns out, one of the servants does not invest the master's money, and even accuses the master of being a dishonest man. The master senses his deception and banishes him to outer darkness for punishment. Here again the story illustrates the responsibility each of us has to continue in faith and good works while the Lord is away, for he will come at a time we least expect and demand to see the results of his investment in us. If they are not present, he will condemn us.

The last story in this section, the account of the Sheep and Goats in Matthew 25:31-46, is probably the most pertinent for this discussion concerning the significance of works as the determining factor in our salvation. Separating people at the general judgment as a shepherd would divide sheep from goats in his pasture, the Lord will reward the sheep specifically because they, (1) fed the hungry, (2) gave drink to the thirsty, (3) invited the stranger, (4) clothed the naked, (5) took care of the sick, and (6) visited those in prison. These items are not just filler for the story. The whole parable centers around the doing of these virtuous acts in order to gain entrance into heaven. The parable reinforces this point by means of a double exchange. In verses 34-36, Jesus spells out all the virtuous deeds the righteous have done in order to inherit the kingdom of heaven. In verses 37-39, the wicked reiterate each of the virtuous acts and challenge the Lord as to when they ever saw him in such a destitute state that they could feed, clothe, or do any other good work to him. In verse 40, Jesus explains that doing these things to one's neighbor is just like doing them to Jesus. Apparently, the intimate connection between loving a neighbor and loving the Lord is something that they knew intuitively and therefore had no excuse (cf. 1 John 2:7-11). The doubling of this exchange then occurs in verses 41-45 with the same reiteration of each of the six virtuous acts. The only difference between the two sections is from positive to negative, i.e., "whatever you did do" as opposed to "whatever you didn't do." The reiteration of these items shows us the prominence that they hold in the teaching of Jesus.

Many a Protestant exegete would like to relegate this teaching to the category of mere metaphor, concluding that Jesus is not really talking about salvation by good works but only pointing out who among those who follow the Lord really have true faith. Some Protestants have even declared that the six virtuous acts that Jesus mentions are mere symbols for spiritual truths, e.g., the feeding of the hungry is a symbol of preaching the gospel to the unsaved.[41] As with other issues in Protestant theology, their analysis contains some truths, yet because they are incomplete truths, they only end up distorting Jesus's teaching instead of getting to the core of truth he

---

41 As taught by Harold Camping, president of Family Radio, the largest evangelical radio network in the world, headquartered in Oakland, California. Camping has consistently taught this allegorical interpretation of these kinds of passages for over 35 years.

wants us to understand.

We have already seen that Jesus's teaching is permeated with the principle that God will judge us based on our works at the end of time. Jesus makes this clear in Matthew 16:27: "For the Son of Man is going to come in his Father's glory with his angels, and then he will reward each person according to what he has done." The apostle John records the same words of Jesus in Revelation 22:11-12: "Let him who does wrong continue to do wrong...let him who does right continue to do right...Behold, I am coming soon! My reward is with me, and I will give to everyone according to what he has done." And previously in John 5:28-29: "Do not be amazed at this, for a time is coming when all who are in their graves will hear his voice and come out — those who have done good will rise to live, and those who have done evil will rise to be condemned."

These warnings show that Jesus is concerned with the whole life of the individual, not with a mere act of faith he professed a long time ago. Granted, there is certainly an intimate connection between the faith of the sheep and their works in the story of Matthew 25. We must also understand, however, that Jesus specifically uses the doing of good works as the final criterion of the value of the faith and works an individual claims to have. We must take the story at its face value and not force it through the grid of a theology of our liking. If Jesus had a *faith alone* theology in mind, he had ample opportunity to teach it. As it stands in the gospels, however, there is not one specific teaching of Jesus that would lean us in such a direction. The whole tenor of his teaching is just the opposite — works play a most significant part in determining whether we will be saved or not. If this is indeed the theme of the gospels, then there is absolutely no reason to reinterpret the works required in the story of the sheep and goats to be mere symbols or results of faith. We should understand them precisely as they are presented, as the ultimate criterion to determine our final status with God.

Summary Points

1) Because of the nature of Jesus' teaching, if Protestantism sees a problem in reconciling James's teaching with Paul's because

of James's stress on works, there must also be a problem in reconciling Jesus's teaching with Paul because of Jesus's stress on works. Neither Paul nor Jesus, however, say anywhere in Scripture that one can be saved by faith alone.

2) Protestants attempt to deal with Jesus' teaching on works range by saying that Jesus taught obedience to the law merely to show that man could not be justified by keeping the commandments, or that his teachings were merely hypothetical, or that his teachings are not for the present time but are reserved for a future millennial kingdom.

3) In the story of the Rich Man in Matthew 19:16-26 (Mark 10:17-21), Jesus commends the man for his faith and obedience to the commandments and teaches that such is the very means of salvation. Communicating to him in love, Jesus calls him to a higher level of obedience, e.g., giving his riches to the poor, in order to finally attain the kingdom of God. Jesus concludes that if he does not do so he cannot be saved; thus, works pleasing to God must be added to faith for justification.

4) Some Protestants attempt to support *faith alone* theology from Jesus's statement in John 5:24. They do this, however, without admitting that Jesus does not use the word alone, or any other qualifier, in reference to faith, and they also ignore the context which specifies just four verses later that Jesus will judge individuals based on their works.

5) Protestants attempt to support *faith alone* theology by citing the salvation of the thief on the cross. Even if this incident were considered an exception to the necessity of works, such exceptions in Scripture do not make the rule. We should not, however, understand the story of the thief as an exception. In actuality, the thief showed remarkable knowledge of Jesus and his mission, implying that he was familiar with Jesus' teachings prior to the crucifixion. That the thief, though his hands were literally tied, acted on his belief in Jesus, and reached out in defense of Jesus and his mission, shows his willingness to be

obedient to God. He had a sincere desire to do the works of obedience, had it not been too late to do so. This sincere willingness to obey God, and his reaching out to act in the limited capacity still available to him, were sufficient to please God and for Jesus to accept him into heaven.

6) Jesus uses the same word "justified" (Greek: *dikaioo*) that Paul does. As in Paul's usage in Romans 2:13, Jesus, in Matthew 12:36-37, uses the word "justified" in reference to judging the individual's works, showing that God grants or denies justification based on one's works. Jesus indicates the kind of works he has in mind with the words, "every careless word," showing that works as slight as mere words are subject to judgment and can cause loss of justification.

7) Protestants attempt to prove *faith alone* theology from the parable of the Pharisee and the tax collector in Luke 18:9-14. They base their attempt on the theory that justification is a one-time forensic event. First, there is no proof in the context that, in Jesus's mind, this was the first time the tax collector pleaded for forgiveness of his sins, especially since going to the temple to pray was a daily ritual in Judaism. Second, the subsequent account of Zacchaeus, a real-life tax collector, reveals that works of repentance are a necessary requirement in Jesus's mind, since Jesus accepts Zacchaeus' promise to pay back half of his possessions to those he cheated before he grants him salvation.

8) When Jesus teaches that in order to enter the kingdom of heaven our righteousness must exceed that of the scribes and Pharisees, the context will not allow the Protestant concept of the "alien righteousness of Christ" to be imposed on the passage. Rather, the context shows quite clearly that Jesus views works of obedience performed by the individual as the means to righteousness that will allow him to enter heaven.

9) Protestants attempt to support the *faith alone* theory by appealing to the story of the repentant woman in Luke 7:36-50. Although it is true that faith prompted her to come to Jesus, it was

her actual coming to Jesus in a humble act of repentance, coupled with her love of Jesus, that moved Jesus to forgive her sins. This shows that love was added to her faith for justification.

10) The incident of the woman with an issue of blood in Luke 8:43-50 also denies the *faith alone* model. It is clear from the passage that the woman *acted* on her faith by coming to Jesus and touching his garment, and only then was she healed. Moreover, there is no proof that salvation was involved in this, and similar incidents of healing.

11) Various sayings of Jesus are antithetical to a *faith alone* theology. For example, Jesus' statement in Matthew 24:13 ("but he who stands firm to the end will be saved") shows that both faith and works are required up until the very end of a person's life; otherwise he will not be saved.

12) Other teachings of Jesus, e.g., the parables of unfaithful servants, the ten virgins, the talents, and the sheep and the goats, all demonstrate that we must continually add works to faith in order to be saved.

Chapter 4

Is Justification a One-Time Event or an Ongoing Process?

This study has referred to the Protestant theory of justification by forensic imputation. This terminology means that justification is a solitary legal act in which God designates or classifies an individual as righteous — an act which, once performed, is never repeated again. It occurs at the time the individual accepts, by faith alone, Jesus Christ and his work of redemption. More specifically, the theory says that the individual is "credited" with the righteousness of Christ. The theory takes the word *credited* to mean that the person has no righteousness within himself that God is taking into account, but only the righteousness accomplished by the sinless life, death, and resurrection of Christ. God credits the righteousness attained by Christ's righteousness to the account of the individual as when an accountant makes a credit entry into a ledger book. In himself, the individual is still the same being. Nothing but his legal status with God changes in this single moment of justification. It is simply a legal declaration that God makes, designating the person to be in a justified state. The justified state means that God has forgiven his sins because Christ took the guilt and paid the penalty for his sins. Acceptance by faith means that, though undeserving, the individual receives the righteousness of Christ if he simply acknowledges its availability and efficacy by believing that he can receive it. Once this is done, the theological category of justification is complete and secure and the now justified Christian immediately passes into another theological category called *sanctification*. Within the area of sanctification, the Christian begins to live a holy life by refraining from sin, doing good works, praying, etc. The theory stresses that, although related, the area of sanctification is not to be confused with justification. In Protestant theology, justification is a one-time legal act administered by God, while sanctification is the ongoing process of personal holiness.[1]

In Catholic theology, justification is not a one-time act of God. Although for New Testament believers justification begins at a specific point in time, i.e., baptism, justification continues as a process throughout the individual's life. God gives his grace to the individual at baptism, but he also gives grace continually throughout the course of life. A person gains grace as he lives out his Christian life in obedience. As grace increases, justification increases, and the individual becomes more and more righteous in the eyes of God.[2] If God removes justifying grace from the individual, then justification ceases. This occurs when the individual commits serious sin. When God restores grace, he restores justification. He does not give grace in equal measure to everyone. One person can pos-

---

1 From the time of the Reformation to the present, Protestantism has seen many variations on the relationship between justification and sanctification, and just as many variations among today's theologians on precisely what each of the original Reformation theologians taught on this relationship. In chapter 9 we will study these variations in detail. For simplified preliminary analysis, we have tried to reduce the variations to the lowest common denominator.

2 The Council of Trent, Session 6, Chapter 10 states: "Having, therefore, been thus justified and having been made the 'friends of God' and 'his domestics,' 'advancing from virtue to virtue,' 'they are renewed' (as the Apostle says) 'from day to day,' that is, by mortifying the members of their flesh, and by 'presenting them as instruments of justice,' unto sanctification through the observance of the commandments of God and of the Church; in this justice received through the grace of Christ 'faith cooperating with good works,' they increase and are further justified, as it is written: 'He that is just, let him be justified still,' and again: 'Be not afraid to be justified even to death,' and again: 'You see, that by works a man is justified and not by faith only.'" Here the Council uses 2 Cor. 4:16 ("Though outwardly we are wasting away, yet inwardly we are being renewed day by day") to express the increase in justification/sanctification. This coincides with 2 Cor. 3:18 ("And we...are being transformed into his likeness with ever-increasing glory, which comes from the Lord who is the Spirit" in which the NIV translates "glory to glory" as "ever- increasing glory"). The Council also uses Psalm 84:7 (Psalm 83:8 in LXX and Douay-Rheims): "They go from strength [virtue] to strength [virtue] till each appears before God in Zion" which shows the same 'state-to-state' pattern, from the Hebrew חזל. The Council also uses Ecclesiasticus 18:22 ("Let nothing hinder thee from praying always, and be not afraid to be justified even to death; for the reward of God continueth forever" (Douay-Rheims)). Here the LXX contains the verbal form of δικαιόω.

sess more than another depending both on how God wishes to distribute grace, as well as the degree to which the person cooperates with God in obedience. In the final analysis, if the justifying grace begun at baptism is not present at the end of a person's life, then he will remain unjustified and be condemned for eternity.

In regard to sanctification, there is no appreciable difference between it and justification. In fact, the grace received at baptism is called *sanctifying* grace.[3] This is the grace that sets the individual apart for God and makes him holy, and it is because of this "holiness" that he becomes *just* or *justified* in the eyes of God, that is, because he is now intrinsically holy. Paul shows the inseparable and simultaneous application of justification and sanctification very clearly in 1 Corinthians 6:10-11:

> ...nor thieves not the greedy nor drunkards nor slanderers nor swindlers will inherit the kingdom of God. And that is what some of you were. But you were *washed*, you were *sanctified*, you

---

[3] See Ludwig Ott, *Fundamentals of Catholic Dogma*, op. cit., pp. 254-263. Ott explains, by reference to early and medieval theologians, and to the final formulation of the Council of Trent (1563), that the nature of sanctifying grace is: (1) "...a created supernatural gift distinct from God himself." Ott says this to distinguish grace from the God who issues grace. God is present in the soul as the agent of created grace, but he is not the grace. Grace can increase but God does not increase. Pope Leo XIII stated: "By means of grace, God dwells in the just soul as in a temple, in a way profoundly intimate and singular" (DS, 3338). Ott further explicates this concept in the following stipulations: (2) "...a supernatural state of being which is infused by God, and which permanently inheres in the soul." He says this to distinguish sanctifying grace from actual grace — actual grace being the intermittent grace given to prompt to or perform various acts; and also to distinguish mortal sin from venial sin, of which the latter does not destroy the grace that inheres in the soul. (3) "...is not a substance but a real accident which inheres in the soul-substance." He says this to confirm that sanctifying grace does not merely reside in converted man, but actually transforms man into a more divine-like being, yet without changing man's essence as man. (See also Thomas Aquinas, *Summa Theologica*, I-II, Q. 110.) (4) "...a participation in the divine nature"). The *Catholic Catechism* (1994) states: "Sanctifying grace is an habitual gift, a stable and supernatural disposition that perfects the soul itself to enable it to live with God, to act by his love. *Habitual* grace, the permanent disposition to live and act in keeping with God's call, is distinguished from *actual* graces which refer to God's interventions, whether at the beginning of conversion or in the course of the work of sanctification" (CC #2000).

were *justified* in the name of the Lord Jesus Christ and by the Spirit of our God.

Here Paul speaks of a being "sanctified" and "justified" as a simultaneous event, an event that occurred when the person was "washed." The New Testament uses the word "washed" in only one other place. In that passage it refers to the act of baptism.[4] Hence, as noted above, it is baptism that provides the grace of God. Paul treats both "sanctification" and "justification" as a past event that began at baptism.[5] The terms are virtually interchangeable. The context of the passage supports this interchange, since it deals exclusively with the Corinthian's conduct, not the appropriation of an alien righteousness. Moreover, though a Protestant *ordo salutis* would expect "justified" to precede "sanctified," Paul juxtaposes these terms and implies that there is no chronological order to the relationship. In fact, the verbal form "justified" *never*

4 At the baptism of Paul in Acts 22:16, Luke records the event as "Get up, be baptized and wash away your sins." The Greek word for "wash away" is ἀπολούω, appearing only twice in the New Testament. The connection between the "washing" and baptism is reinforced by the fact that it is Paul who is being baptized in Acts 22:16, and is teaching the same "washing" to the Corinthians in 1 Cor. 6:11 as the moment their sins were taken away.

5 Both "sanctified" (ἡγιάσθητε) and "justified" (ἐδικαιώθητε) are aorist verbs, as is "washed" (ἀπελούσασθε). The only difference among them is that "washed" is in the middle voice, while "sanctified" and "justified" are in the active voice. Lutheran commentator R.C.H. Lenski rightly comments on the meaning of the middle voice in this instance: "This middle ἀπελούσασθε does not mean: "you were washed" (passive)...nor "you washed yourselves" (ordinary reflexive middle)...but: "you let yourselves be washed" (causative or permissive middle)...Paul is, of course, speaking about baptism, but when he uses ἀπολούειν he at once names the effect of baptism, the spiritual washing away of sin and guilt, the cleansing by pardon and justification. This causative or permissive middle, which is exactly like the same middle ἐβαπτίσαντο used in 10:2, adds what the passive would omit, namely that with their own hearts the Corinthians themselves desired and accepted this washing and cleansing." In commenting on the passives "sanctified" and "justified," Lenski continues: "This does not mean that the passives are changed and now receive a middle tinge; they remain what they are. But the Corinthians could not also be sanctified and justified by God (passive) if they had not in their own hearts desired and accepted the true cleansing of baptism" (*The Interpretation of I and II Corinthians* (Minneapolis, MN: Augsburg Publishing, 1963) pp. 250-251). See also the *Expositor's Greek Testament*, pp. 817-818. See chapter 5 for further study on the relationship between ἡγιάσθητε and ἐδικαιώθητε in 1 Cor. 6:11.

precedes "sanctified" in the New Testament.[6] In many instances, the New Testament writers use the word "sanctified" or "sanctification" where one would expect, or not be surprised to see, "justified" or "justification."[7]

---

6 The noun form "righteousness" (δικαιοσύνη) precedes the noun form "sanctification" (ἁγιασμός) in two places: Romans 6:19 ("...so now offer them in slavery to righteousness leading to holiness"); and 1 Corinthians 1:30 ("Christ Jesus...that is, our righteousness, holiness [sanctification] and redemption"). In the former case, we understand "righteousness" as the categorical goal, whereas "holiness" is what the individual personally becomes. In the latter case, we attribute all three aspects to Christ as the source of anything we personally attain. Neither passage, however, is attempting to give a chronological order to justification and sanctification. Revelation 22:11 is the only biblical passage where the verb form "justified" precedes the verb form "sanctified" but these forms are in two separate clauses and would not qualify as any type of *ordo salutis*. The Council of Trent uses the verbal form δικαιωθητω with ἔτι ("let him be justified still") to show the progression of justification in Revelation 22:11. (NB: There is a textual variant in this verse. The verbal form δικαιωθητω ("let him be justified") is supported by the historian Eusebius (c. 340); the Clementina Vulgate of 1592; minuscule 2020 from the 1500s, and a few minor minuscules (*Novum Testamentum*, eds. E. Nestle and K. Aland (Germany: Württembergische Bibelanstalt Stuttgart, 1927).This would seem to weigh against the verbal form being the true text except for the fact that only 2 out of 52 papyri contain fragments of the book of Revelation, only 2 uncials out of 46 contain the parts of the book, and 144 minuscules out of 655 contain parts of Revelation (*The Greek New Testament*, eds. Kurt Aland, et al., 3rd ed. (United Bible Society, 1975). We can also point out that the verbal form "let him be justified" would match the verbal forms "let him be sanctified" (ἁγιασθήτω) and "let him be vile" (ῥυπανθήτω) used in the same passage, which have no textual variants. In any case, the addition of "let him do" (ποιησάτω) after the noun form δικαιοσύνη serves to verbalize the noun).

7 e.g., Acts 26:18, in which Jesus connects the turning away from Satan to God, and being forgiven, with *sanctification*, not justification ("so that they may receive forgiveness of sin and a place among those who are sanctified [ἡγιασμένοις] by faith in me"); 1 Peter 1:2, in which Peter connects predestination with *sanctification* ("who have been chosen according to the foreknowledge of God...through the sanctifying work of the Spirit" [ἐν ἁγιασμῷ πνεύματος]); 2 Thessalonians 2:13, in which *sanctification* and faith are connected directly to being chosen for salvation ("...because from the beginning God chose you to be saved through the sanctifying work of the Spirit [ἐν ἁγιασμῷ πνεύματος] and through belief in the truth"); Hebrews 10:29, in which the sacred writer connects blood with *sanctification* ("treated as an unholy thing the blood of the covenant that sanctified him [ἡγιάσθη]"). (NB: This language would be especially troublesome for the Reformed persuasion, since the passage specifies this individual has fallen from *sanctification*. The Reformed view maintains that sanctification cannot take its place in the *ordo salutis* unless justification has already occurred, yet it also maintains that if one falls from faith, he was never justified originally). See also Jude 1 and Ephesians 5:26.

Did Abraham's Justification Require Works?

Since the section above shows that justification is not static but progressive, let us study this matter from other perspectives to get the full picture. In attempting to understand how the book of James fits into their theology, Evangelical theology has claimed that James is only concerned that the faith that saves must be a real faith. In other words, it cannot be like the faith of demons who merely believe that God exists but have no works of obedience to show that they believe unto salvation. Genuine faith is faith that is accompanied by works of love and obedience. Protestants will then make a distinction between faith and works by asserting that in Genesis 15:6 Abraham was justified by faith alone, without any works. He simply believed God. That was the first and only time that Abraham was justified. Protestants claim that the work of Abraham portrayed in Genesis 22, when he offered Isaac as a sacrifice, came after Abraham already believed and was justified in Genesis 15:6. Hence, the chronology of Abraham's faith and works is very important to the Protestant view. This view requires that after Abraham is justified in Genesis 15:6, the justification act is over and complete and Abraham immediately enters into the category of sanctification. We have already made a partial critique of this view in chapters 1 and 2 as we pointed out the Scriptural accounts of the continuing faith and works of Abraham beginning from Genesis 12 and transpiring through Genesis 22. We will now critique the Protestant concept further.

Many Protestants would claim that, if Abraham were to sin and fall away from God after his justification in Genesis 15:6, then one must conclude that he was actually never justified in Genesis 15:6. Since these denominations believe that once the individual is justified he cannot lose the justification for any reason, anyone who appears to have fallen away must never have received it. However, because Scripture treats the justification of Abraham as a true justification, this leaves no possibility of his falling from this state. To reinforce this view, the Reformed persuasion will add that Abraham's justification is secure because Abraham was predestined to be justified and therefore he cannot fall away; Abraham is eternally secure after his act of faith in Genesis 15:6, since Scripture is witness to it and treats it as a past and real event foreordained by God.

As air-tight as the Reformed view tries to make its case, there are leaks in the system that eventually bring it to naught. First, despite the predestination perspective which the Reformed view invariably uses to cover any contingencies in justification,[8] it must still define its categories and use terminology that incorporates the temporal framework in which we live and which the Scripture commonly utilizes. When Paul, for example, is arguing in Romans 4 for the real nature of Abraham's justification, he does not appeal to the predestination perspective to prove his point. Instead, he argues in temporal terms regarding the precise chronology of Abraham's original faith as opposed to his subsequent circumcision.[9] Similarly, James's argument about the "fulfillment of Scripture" in reference to Abraham's justification seeks to make a temporal distinction between one point in Abraham's life (Genesis 15:6) and another point (Genesis 22), the latter being the ultimate test of Abraham's faith. We see, then, that the New Testament writers treat Abraham's justification as one which occurs in the process of temporal events and contingencies. This forces the Reformed view to shape its formula for justification into the temporal and chronological infrastructure that Scripture requires. Beginning with Calvin and continuing today in Reformed circles, the Reformed view has addressed the temporal side of this problem by adopting the formulas "justification is by faith alone but by a faith that is not alone" and "faith for justification must be qualified by works." But this formulation presents a severe theological problem for them. The Reformed view's moment of justification, which Abraham receives by faith, simply leaves no room for works of obedience to qualify faith before the justification takes place. Because Abraham's justification by faith in Genesis 15:6 is a solitary extrinsic event, sealed and impregnable, (i.e., he cannot lose his justification), in reality, Abraham's works cannot penetrate to serve as the qualifier of the kind of faith he had in Genesis 15:6. His works are "after the fact,"

8 Chapter 7 presents a critique of the Lutheran and Calvinistic views of predestination.

9 We are referring to the predestination perspective Paul uses in Romans 8:29-30. For an explanation of this passage see chapters 5 and 7.

as it were. If their theology is followed to its logical conclusion, in the Reformed view, works, whether good or bad, cannot impinge on the theological territory of justification because the works come after justification and are relegated to the area of sanctification. Hence, they must find some other way of measuring Abraham's faith in Genesis 15:6

One way out of this dilemma is to say, as Reformed Evangelical R. C. Sproul suggests, that God does not need to witness Abraham's works in order to know that he is justified:

> Scripture reminds us that we "know" the believer by his fruit, but also that we can see only outward appearances. God has the ability to read the heart. It is not necessary for God to observe outward actions to know if true faith is present in the heart...Such "justification" or vindication is not necessary for God.[10]

In other words, Sproul is postulating that God already knows that Abraham's faith qualifies as "saving faith" because he *knows* Abraham's heart. We assume, of course, that Sproul would also extend this reasoning to each individual who apprehends the alien righteousness of Christ, that is, God knows all their hearts and thus it is not necessary for him to actually view their works. Realizing that if he speaks of works subsequent to the one-time act of justification as "qualifying" the faith, this will force him to go outside the solitary theological category he created, hence, Sproul's appeal to God's omniscience seemingly allows him to confine the quality of justifying faith to the actual moment when someone believes in Christ. In effect, the escape from the dilemma is created by proposing that the alternative way of measuring Abraham's quality of faith is to appeal directly to the omniscience of God. Only in this way can Sproul maintain that the act of justification has all the required ingredients, prior to any works performed, in order to distinguish justifying faith from the faith of demons.

First, we must object that appealing to God's omniscience is not the way the Scripture argues the case for a specific individual's justification. Although it undergirds its handling of justification

---

[10] *Faith Alone*, op. cit., p. 165.

from a general predestinarian perspective (cf., Romans 8:29-30), Scripture argues its case with regard to named individuals, e.g., Abraham, preponderantly and specifically in temporal terms. In other words, Scripture is not in the habit of naming individuals who are *predestined* to justification, let alone attempt to secure that justification by an appeal to what God already knows the individual will do.[11] Second, if we follow Sproul's argumentation to its logical conclusion, it simply proves too much, and ends up nullifying his hypothesis. For example, taking the argument back one step we could say that it was not really necessary for God to draw out even the *faith* of Abraham in Genesis 15:6, since by his omniscience God would have known all along that Abraham was going to have true faith. If Sproul can use divine omniscience to explain why it was not necessary for Abraham to perform works for God, then, to be fair, Sproul should allow the use of divine omniscience to explain why God really doesn't need to draw out the faith from Abraham in Genesis 15:6. In the end, argumentation appealing to God's omniscience is a double-edged sword and does nothing to advance the discussion. If the omniscience argument is used, everything about Abraham, including his act of faith, is superfluous. We all accept that from the very beginning God already foreknows how things will turn out, but that is not the basis from which Paul and James defend their respective doctrines of justification. Neither Paul nor James appeals to divine omniscience to argue his case, rather, they confine themselves to the temporal and chronological account of the Genesis record. Granted, Paul's argument in Romans 4 hinges on Abraham's having true faith prior to his circumcision (Romans 4:10-11). The text, however, is absolutely silent about how we know it was true faith other than its appeal to the spiritual disposition of Abraham himself. It does not appeal to God's omniscience prior to the event. In fact, Scripture often makes a concerted effort to avoid appealing to divine omniscience to explain the actions of God or man.[12]

---

11 We say this while keeping in mind the treatise on predestination that Paul offers in Romans 9:10-13 regarding Jacob and Esau, which we will treat more thoroughly in chapter 7.

12 e.g., Genesis 6:6; Exodus 32:9-14; 33:3-5, Jonah 3:10, et al.

In the end, Sproul's argumentation destroys itself. It not only makes Abraham's *works* superfluous, it also makes his *faith* superfluous since Sproul must admit it was inevitable that Abraham would manifest both faith and works in his life. We must insist that theologians not appeal to the incomprehensible attributes of God in an effort to explain the enigmas of their theology, especially when Scripture chooses to explain them in very ordinary ways. Scripture explains Abraham's faith and works on a purely phenomenological level. Genesis 22:12 makes this clear when it describes Abraham as ready and willing to plunge the knife into his son Isaac. The angel of the Lord, speaking for God, says: "Do not do anything to the child. *Now I know* that you fear God because you have not withheld from me your son, your only son." The angel's temporal analysis of this event is clear and unambiguous. It is only when Abraham actually performs the act of raising the knife that God makes absolute his knowledge of Abraham's intentions. The necessity in Genesis 22:10 of Abraham's raising the knife is just as absolute as the necessity in Genesis 15:6 of Abraham's believing. In fact, Genesis 15:6 comes back to haunt Sproul in another way. For if God sees in Abraham's heart the faith he exhibited in Genesis 15:6, and from this knows that Abraham is a firm believer, why should God have to peer again into Abraham's heart in Genesis 22? Hence we must insist that while God certainly maintains the divine prerogative of foreknowledge, he nevertheless in creating a temporal world has also determined to shape the course of history coincident with the events occurring in the temporal world.[13] Though this is a mystery, we cannot side with one dimension of God's attributes at the expense of others to give ourselves a palatable answer to anomalies in our theology or in Scripture. The point in fact is that James, when speaking of Abraham, uses the same word, *justification*, that Paul uses. Appealing to God's omniscience to allow oneself to change the definition of justification between Paul and James is something Scripture never does and never even remotely teaches us to do. Scripture presents and un-

13 This area of theology touches upon what is known as "secondary" or "contingent" causality in the realm of God's dealing with men. Chapter 7 deals with this aspect of justification.

derstands doctrinal propositions concerning justification at face value, and thus that is the way we should analyze and teach them.

Another problem, and probably the most dangerous one, with appealing to God's omniscience in such cases is that the reciprocal of that appeal leads the individual to think that it may not be necessary for him to do good works because "God knows my heart." If we conclude that Abraham's works were not really necessary because God knew he was already faithful and that he would have done the works in any case, the temptation is very great to view ourselves in the same light. It is exactly this kind of thinking, however, that James warns us against. We cannot "think" we have faith and then ignore a brother or sister in desperate need (James 2:15), claiming that "God already knows my heart." Within that context, James specifies the necessity for Abraham to act on his faith, as well as the necessity for God to be a witness to that act. Nowhere does James entertain the notion that it was not really necessary for Abraham to perform his act in front of God, nor does Abraham, or any other biblical character, ever appeal to God's foreknowledge of his heart in an effort to spare himself the necessity of work. No example of this is more profound than that of the Lord Jesus himself, who prayed at Gethsemane that the cup of God's wrath might pass from him. Jesus did not appeal to God's omniscience of his faithful heart. He understood that he had to accomplish the work of the atonement and without it there would have been no salvation. The Scripture treats the works of Abraham in the same way — without them there could have been no justification. The works have a specific causal and ontological necessity in regard to justification. In fact, God knows that we know that he knows our heart, yet insists that we perform the deed that he desires.

When Was Abraham Justified?

Using the phenomenological perspective of Scripture when speaking in previous chapters of Abraham's faith and justification, we have already seen and understood Abraham's faith as a sequence of events, rather than a one-time act. The commentary on Abraham's life of faith in the book of Hebrews is an invaluable aid in understanding this subject. In Hebrews 11:8 the sacred writer states categorically, in reference to Abraham's faith in Genesis 12, where at God's command he left his homeland in Ur of the Chaldees, that Abraham already possessed the precise kind of justifying faith — the same faith that the Protestant view requires for justification. As we study this passage we see that Paul makes explicit in several ways that Abraham's faith of Genesis 12:1-8 is the same kind of faith as displayed in Genesis 15:1-6. First, he introduces the faith both in Genesis 12 and Genesis 15 under the general heading of faith that "pleases God." This is noted in Hebrews 11:6: "And without faith it is impossible to please God, because anyone who comes to him must believe that he exists and that he rewards those who earnestly seek him." Paul, then, prior to dealing with Abraham, gives three examples of people who had demonstrated such "God-pleasing" faith, i.e., Abel, Enoch, and Noah (Hebrews 11:4-7). The language makes clear in these three examples that they all had faith that justified them before God. Hence when Paul comes to Abraham and speaks in the same glowing terms in reference to his faith in Genesis 12, we can reach no other conclusion than that Abraham had faith that justified him in Genesis 12 long before his next encounter with God in Genesis 15. It would be totally incongruous for Paul to attribute justifying faith to the three personages prior to Abraham but not attribute it to Abraham in Genesis 12.

To reinforce the above facts, the apostle Paul gives another description of Abraham's faith in the Genesis 12 period. He remarks in Hebrews 11:10 that Abraham's faith in leaving his homeland and subsequently sojourning in tents in the promised land was in reality a faith which believed that the earthly land upon which he walked was not what God had in store for him; rather, Abraham believed that God had prepared for him a "city with foundations and whose architect and builder was God." In other words, the faith Abraham possessed in Genesis 12 was already a faith that comprehended the essence of salvation, i.e., living in heaven with God forever. It is not surprising that we see Paul then describing Abraham's faith in the Genesis 15:6 period in precisely the same way. The sacred writer states in Hebrews 11:16, after remarking about Abraham's faith in believing that God would give him a son, that such people show that they are not looking for an earthly city in which to dwell but a "heavenly one," acknowledging that "God has prepared a city for them." Since here he describes Abraham's mental disposition in Genesis 15 the precise way he describes Abraham's faith in Genesis 12, this forces us to conclude again that Abraham was already justified in Genesis 12. It was a faith that "pleased" God, understood that he "existed," was the "rewarder of those that earnestly seek him," and looked for a "heavenly city" built by God.

That Abraham was already justified in Genesis 12 causes insuperable damage to the Protestant view of a "one-time act" of justification which is said to occur only at Genesis 15. This is so because, as stated earlier, the Reformed view, in contrast to Martin Luther's view, holds that regeneration precedes faith. To confirm this, we again quote from R. C. Sproul:

> Reformation theology insists that regeneration that changes the heart of the sinner must *precede* faith. My perception of the value of Christ must change before I will ever embrace him or personally trust him. Without that regenerating change, my response to Christ will mimic Satan's.[14]

Here is where the Reformed concept of justification encounters its ultimate trap. Dancing around the edge of properly defining what "saving faith" really is, Sproul falls headlong into Catholic clutches. Since he affirms that regeneration must precede faith, he must also be willing to admit that Abraham could not have had such faith in Genesis 12 without being regenerated. Abraham could not have had his "perception of the value of Christ...change," as Sproul says, unless God had given him the regenerative powers to do so. Without this regenerative power, Abraham's faith would have been that which, in Sproul's terminology, "mimics Satan's," or, to use James' terminology, it would have been "the faith of demons" (James 2:19). In addition, the Reformed view requires that those who are regenerated — a regeneration upon which they display saving faith — must necessarily be justified. Regeneration and faith cannot be isolated in a theological vacuum; if both are present they

---

[14] *Faith Alone*, op. cit., p. 87.

always result in justification. Hence, by their own definition of terms, it becomes an inevitable corollary that Abraham was already justified in Genesis 12, and that his justification in Genesis 15 merely shows the ongoing nature of the justification process. In turn, this would explain why James refers to Genesis 22 as a "justification." It is just one more instance, in the theological continuum, of Abraham's progressive justification. Accepting Genesis 12 as a justifying faith will, in turn, release the Protestant from having to force a different meaning onto the word *justification* in the epistle of James as opposed to Paul's definition. Once one sees that the justification of Abraham is a process or continuum, he will not be forced to redefine the definition of the terms "justification," "faith," or "works." One first has to open up to the account of Abraham's faith in Genesis 12 and its commentary in Hebrews 11, however, before he can entertain such an understanding of justification. Unfortunately, Sproul does not even make one reference to either Genesis 12 or the related commentary in Hebrews 11:8ff in his entire 221 page book titled *"Faith Alone."*

When Was David Justified?

Not only does a full understanding of the life of Abraham demolish the Protestant position of a one-time act of justification, but Paul's citation of David in Romans 4:5-8 also brings its wrecking ball to the same edifice. The reader will recall from Romans 4 that in giving his principles for justification by faith, Paul quotes from David in Psalm 32:1: "Blessed is he whose transgressions are forgiven, whose sins are covered. Blessed is the man whose sin the Lord does not count against him." David is proclaiming God's forgiveness of his sins of adultery with Bathsheba and the murder of Uriah the Hittite recorded in 2 Samuel 11-12. Obviously, David is rejoicing over the fact that God has forgiven his sins. God sent Nathan the prophet to convict David, forcing him to admit his sin. Nathan's parable of the little ewe lamb brought David to his knees in repentance. This was such a monumental event in the life of David that he remarks again about the same sin and forgiveness in Psalm 51.

The most intriguing aspect of Psalm 32 as regards the discussion on justification is that Paul is using this experience of forgiveness in David's life in order to make David a primary example of a person who is justified before God. Paul's connection between justification and David's own repentance is unmistakable. He says in Romans 4:5-6: "However, to the man who does not work but trusts God who justifies the wicked, his faith is credited as righteousness. David says the same thing when he speaks of the blessedness of the man to whom God credits righteousness apart from works..." By the phrase "David says the same thing..." Paul is indicating that David agrees with Paul's teaching that a wicked man is credited with righteousness by faith without works that attempt to obligate God. Thus, we must conclude that David is saying in Psalm 32 nothing different than Paul is teaching in Romans 4.

The most important aspect of the corresponding doctrine between David and Paul is that David is speaking not only of everyone else's sin, but more specifically of his own. This gives us the reference point we need to understand just what kind of justification Paul has in view, since he and David are, in Paul's words, "*saying the same thing*." Using David as a reference point, we are obliged to look at the circumstances surrounding David which led him to the point of his repentance in Psalm 32. The crucial question is this: Was Psalm 32 the first time David was forgiven his sins? The answer must be an unequivocal no. Yet, according to Paul, the forgiveness David received in Psalm 32 is a "justification" or "crediting with righteousness." Since this was not the first time God forgave David for his sins, we must conclude that neither was it the first time God justified or credited David with righteousness. Moreover, since Paul, in the same context, treats Abraham as a real personage who was justified, then it is only natural to conclude that Paul understands David as a real personage who was justified. Although David's experience may also represent how others after him are justified, our starting point for interpretation should be this passage's "face value" fact that Paul is speaking of David himself as the one who is justified at the precise moment in time that Nathan confronted him and David repented.

Reinforcing this interpretation is Scripture's clearly expressed view of David's life prior to the incident with Bathsheba as a very intimate relationship with God. In his youth David called on the Lord to defeat the mighty Goliath (1 Samuel 17). David is so close to God that 1 Samuel 13:14 and Acts 13:22 call David a "man after God's own heart," a distinction given to no one else in the Bible, which shows how close was the relationship David had developed with God long before he committed his heinous sin with Bathsheba. The Psalms, and the corresponding historical accounts in the books of 1 and 2 Samuel, prior to his incident with Bathsheba are filled with the most beautiful tributes of one who was utterly dependent upon and in love with the Lord. By all respectable standards, we must conclude that David was a true child of God many years prior to his sin with Bathsheba. Thus we would have to conclude as well that David was justified in God's sight many years prior to his sin with Bathsheba. If he was not justified, then he was not a man of God, and he had lived his life prior to Psalm 32, and had written earlier Psalms before his encounter with Bathsheba, as a pagan, one who spoke intimately about God but really had no personal relationship with him.

We cannot escape the fact that Paul, in using the example of David in the context of justification, is saying not merely that David's sins were forgiven, but also that David was actually justified at this point. Paul, in Romans 4:5, underscores this fact both by speaking of "crediting righteousness" to David when he confessed his sin in Psalm 32, and by calling him a "wicked" person whom God must justify in order to return him to righteousness. We must understand, then, that a "crediting of righteousness" occurs at each point that one confesses his sins. Since this was not the first time David confessed sin before the Lord (which other Psalms verify, cf., Psalms 25:7,18; 51:5), he must have been "credited with righteousness" on each occasion of repentance. Since he was credited with righteousness upon repentance in Psalm 32, and since it is an established fact that he was a man of God prior to his sin with Bathsheba, we must therefore consider all previous acts of repentance a "crediting of righteousness."[15]

---

[15] The reader should recall from chapter 1 the established fact that it is not even necessary for Scripture to use the phrase "credited with righteousness" when it is describing the justification or salvation of an individual. This is true of most Old Testament saints, e.g., Enoch, Noah, Moses, Samuel, Job, et al, who never had the words "credited with righteousness" specifically applied to them, yet Scripture is clear that they were justified in the same way that Abraham was justified.

As Paul speaks in Romans 4:5 of "God justifying the *wicked,*"[16] and then follows with David's experience of being justified upon his repentance in Psalm 32, we must also conclude that David was considered a "wicked" man once he committed his heinous sin with Bathsheba. This is precisely the reason why David needed to be credited with righteousness, for he had lost his righteousness before God and had become a vile, wicked person in God's sight. Adultery and murder are despicable sins, sins that Paul elsewhere speaks of as sufficient to relinquish one's inheritance in the kingdom of heaven (Gal. 5:21; 1 Cor. 6:9). In Catholic theology, David, after his sexual escapade with Bathsheba and murder of Uriah, was in a state of "mortal" sin, i.e., sin that leads to eternal death. Mortal sin is that state of wickedness in which one loses the grace of salvation. At *that* point one is "ungodly" and "wicked." Unless God forgives the sin and restores the grace, such a sinner is under eternal damnation.

We should also add, as Catholic theology teaches, that in confessing his sin, David must still do penance and undergo the temporal punishment for that sin.[17] The subsequent account in the second book of Samuel records very severe punishments given to David for his mortal sin. The first was to witness God taking the life of the child born to Bathsheba, a punishment of which David was extremely sorrowful (2 Samuel 12:15-23). The second was to witness the rape and pillage of his other wives (2 Samuel 12:11-12). Although God forgave his sin, afterwards David's life was never quite the same.

---

[16] Some Protestant theologians try to accuse Catholicism of denying the *justificatio impii* ("justification of the ungodly"). John Gerstner, for example, claims that Thomas Aquinas was the first and one of the only Catholics who held to *justificatio impii* and thus claims Aquinas for Protestantism (*Justification By Faith Alone*, op. cit., p. 111). One wonders how Gerstner has the audacity to make such a claim since it was Aquinas who systematized "meritum de condigno" for the Catholic Church. Moreover, the Catholic Church taught the *justificatio impii* long before Aquinas. The Council of Orange in 529, Canon 5, declared: "by which we believe in Him who *justifies the impious*...reforming our will from infidelity to faith, from impiety to piety..." The Council of Trent, Session 6, Chapter 7, declared: "For although no one can be just but he to whom the merits of the passion of our Lord Jesus Christ are communicated, yet this does take place in this *justification of the ungodly*..."

[17] Catholic Catechism, Sections 1472-1473

Catholic theology also teaches that even though one in mortal sin has lost the grace of salvation, he does not necessarily lose his faith.[18] This was the case with David. When Nathan approached him, David still believed in God. It was this belief in God that led him to acknowledge he had sinned against God. As he says in Psalm 51:5, "Against you, you only, have I sinned and done what is evil in your sight." Hence, his sin did not destroy his belief, although it did destroy his works of obedience that had previously justified him. Only the work of repentance, through the faith he retained, would restore the grace of God to his soul. Here we see another reason why Catholicism teaches that faith alone cannot save. David still had faith after he sinned with Bathsheba, but that faith by itself could not save him. The faith could bring him only to acknowledge his sin and then allow him to know that if he repented and sought God's forgiveness it would be granted to him. How could this happen? Because God had replaced the system of law with the system of grace, in anticipation of Christ's atonement and resurrection, which allowed him to look with mercy at David's repentance. If David had been under the system of law, then no work could have brought him God's forgiveness, let alone restore David to a right relationship with God. Any work done in an attempt to appease God before grace was restored would have been repugnant in the eyes of God. Repentance is a work under the system of grace, not law, and thus Paul could say in Romans 4:6 that David was justified "apart from works." This is why Paul includes David in the New Testament teaching of justification, since as we learned previously in Romans 3:25, God had "left the sins committed beforehand unpunished," in anticipation of Christ who set aside the power of the law to condemn the sinner for those who repent.

Protestants may object at this point that to use David's life as an example of the justification Paul speaks of in Romans 4:5-6 is beyond the scope of Paul's intentions. One could argue that Paul is simply referring to the forgiveness of David's sins after he had already been justified, once-for-all, many years earlier. But this cannot be the case, for several reasons: (1) Romans 4:6, as noted above, specifically says that David was "credited with righteous-

[18] Council of Trent, Session 6, Chapters 14-15; Canons 27, 29.

ness" in the event described in Psalm 32. Paul writes, "David says the same thing when he speaks of the blessedness of the man to whom God credits righteousness apart from works." Paul does not only say that Abraham was credited with righteousness (Romans 4:5); he also speaks of "the man" to whom God "credits righteousness," which man, in this case, happens to be David. (2) To say that David was justified "once-for-all" prior to the incident in Psalm 32 is simply begging the question. The historical books give no indication that David had a single, point-in-time act of declarative justification such as Protestants are so apt to attribute to Abraham in Genesis 15:6. The historical books, and many word pictures in the Psalms, present David's life of righteousness as a collage of continuing, intermingled faith and works. (3) To say that Paul would extract a few verses out of Psalm 32 without reference to either the context of Psalm 32 or the entire life of David would be to accuse Paul of the grossest form of contextual distortion that a reputable commentator ever perpetrated on Scripture. Who would dare to say that Paul would take a quote out of context to prove his own theological point, all the while knowing that the quote, if read in context, would never support that point? No doubt, the Bereans of Acts 17, faced with that kind of shoddy exegesis, would have totally rejected Paul's teaching. (4) One cannot use a chronological basis to reject our analysis of David's justification, an attempt Protestants often make with the chronology of Abraham's justification. Scripture simply offers no specific chronological framework to David's faith, works, and justification in Scripture. We have seen earlier in chapter 2 that the Epistle of James analyzes the justification of Rahab in a similar fashion. Unlike James's accounting of the life of Abraham which he separates into Genesis 15 and Genesis 22, he does not do so with Rahab. Instead, he highlights her works as the pivotal point of her justification, making no chronological distinction between her faith in God and her works in hiding the spies. James introduces the account of Rahab in James 2:25 with the important phrase, "In the same way," showing that Rahab's justification was "the same" as Abraham's justification. If Rahab's works were the crucial point in her justification, it follows that Abraham's works were the crucial point in his justification; otherwise, they would not be "the same." Similarly, Paul uses the same language as James by introducing David's crediting with righteousness in Romans 4:6 when he says, "David says the same thing," showing that David's justification was the same as Abraham's. Since the respective stories of David and Rahab show no chronological distinction between faith and works, Protestants cannot make chronology a factor in supporting their belief in a single point-in-time forensic justification.

As we proved with an exhaustive study of the life of Abraham as recorded in the books of Romans, Galatians, Hebrews and James, so we have proved with the life of David. The Scripture shows that each person's justification is an *ongoing* one. To be sure, justification begins at a certain point in one's life, but it can be lost, restored or reinforced depending on one's response to God's prompting grace. In the accounts of Abraham, David, and Rahab, there is simply nothing to dissuade us of the truth that justification is not merely a single point-in-time event but a progressive, on-going process.

The "Blessing" of Genesis 12

Some Evangelicals argue that since God, in Genesis 22:17, said to Abraham "I will surely bless you," instead of "I will credit you with righteousness," one cannot consider this incident as a salvific justification.[19] Clearly this argumentation assumes that when the Old or New Testament uses the word "bless," it is never referring to justification. This assumption is false. In Galatians 3:8, Paul says, "The Scripture foresaw that God would justify the Gentiles by faith, and announced the gospel in advance to Abraham: 'All nations will be blessed through you.'" In Galatians 3:9 he adds, "So those who have faith are blessed along with Abraham, the man of faith." In the first verse, Paul juxtaposes *justify* with *blessed.* More specifically, the justification of the Gentiles fulfills the Old Testament prophecy that through Abraham the nations would be "blessed." Hence, we can only conclude that their "blessing" is their justification. Reinforcing this correspondence, in the next verse the word *blessed* stands for the word *justify:* "So those who have faith are blessed along with Abraham..." If Paul had said, "So those

[19] McCarthy, *The Gospel According to Rome*, op. cit., p. 48.

who have faith are justified along with Abraham" it would have meant exactly the same.

Even more significant about the above verses from Galatians 3 is that they are quoted from Genesis 12:3 — the passage that records Abraham's encounter with God many years before he is said to be "credited with righteousness" in Genesis 15:6. The phrase "along with Abraham" in Galatians 3:9, which correlates the *justification* of the Gentiles with the *blessing* of Abraham, shows that Paul considers the blessing given to Abraham in Genesis 12:3 and Genesis 22:17 as his justification. Hence, not only do these verses obliterate the Evangelical argument, but in Galatians 3:8-9 we have one of Scripture's clearest proofs that precisely because the word *blessed* appears in both Genesis 12 and Genesis 22 we must consider those two events as *justifications* precisely the same as we do the event in Genesis 15.

Galatians 3:8-9 becomes even more significant when we realize that this passage appears right after Paul's reference to Genesis 15:6 in Galatians 3:6-7. He writes, "Consider Abraham: 'He believed God, and it was credited to him as righteousness.' Understand, then, that those who believe are children of Abraham." Coupling verses 6-7 with 8-9, we see that Paul is showing us that Abraham's belief and his being credited with righteousness in Genesis 15:6 represent the same justification process as when God blessed Abraham in Genesis 12:2, and then promised in Genesis 12:3 likewise to bless and justify the Gentiles as he had just blessed and justified Abraham. Clearly then, Paul sees no line of demarcation between the "faiths," "blessings" or "justifications" of Genesis 12 and Genesis 15.

In Galatians 3:14 Paul reinforces this truth: "He redeemed us in order that the *blessing* given to Abraham might come to the Gentiles through Jesus Christ, so that by faith we might receive the promise of the Spirit." Here again, Paul couples the *blessing* given to Abraham with justification, this time, however, using different words for justification, namely, "the promise of the Spirit" which also comes by "faith." Thus, as noted above, Paul considers the blessing given to Abraham in Genesis 12 as representing the time of both Abraham's justification and his reception of the Spirit. Abraham received this "blessing" and "justification" by faith in

Genesis 12, the same faith that provides the Gentiles with justification, and the same faith that the sacred author referenced in Hebrews 11:8: "By faith Abraham when called to go to a place he would later receive as his inheritance, obeyed and went, even though he did not know where he was going."

Paul's other treatise on justification, Romans 4:6, also couples "blessing" and "justification." Paul writes, "David says the same thing when he speaks of the *blessedness* of the man to whom God credits righteousness apart from works." Here Paul uses Genesis 15:6's phrase "crediting of righteousness" and refers to it as the "blessedness of the man." None other than God bestows this blessing. Thus, as God blesses, he also justifies. Paul reinforces his intended meaning of the word *blessedness* in verse 9: "Is this *blessedness* only for the circumcised, or also for the uncircumcised? We have been saying that Abraham's faith was credited to him as righteousness." Here again, Paul treats the *blessedness* as the justification itself. Paul could just as easily have said "Is this *justification* only for the circumcised" and meant the same thing. The word "blessedness" refers to none other than the "crediting with righteousness" that Paul keeps repeating in the context. Again, Scriptural evidence forces us to conclude that Abraham was justified in Genesis 12, 15, 22, and throughout his life. Justification, as both Scripture and Catholic doctrine teach, is a continuing process.

More Evidence of Progressive Justification

Let us now respond to the claim of some Evangelicals that the Galatian heresy about which Paul is concerned refers to the Galatians, being already justified, seeking to be *sanctified* by works.[20] This view would necessitate that the justification to which Paul refers is (1) a one-time imputation, and (2) that Paul also taught that sanctification, like justification, is by faith alone. The first is a common Protestant belief which we deal with thoroughly in chapter 5. The second is a recent and novel explanation of sanctification from Protestant theology. Neither, however, represents what Paul is teaching in Galatians. As for the postulation that Paul is

[20] N. Geisler and R. MacKenzie, *Roman Catholics and Evangelicals*, pp. 236-237.

teaching "sanctification by faith alone," we must point out that Paul does not even mention the word *sanctification* or its cognates in the entire Galatian epistle. Equally significant, Paul does use the word *sanctification* and its cognates in *every other* New Testament epistle he wrote.[21] In Galatians, Paul only uses the word *justification* and its cognates.

Evangelicals Geisler and MacKenzie argue that in Galatians Paul is concerned only with initial justification and not progressive justification:

> In short, he did not want them to replace grace with works as the means of sanctification. This is evident from his pivotal plea: "Having *begun* in the Spirit, are you *now* being made perfect in the flesh?" (Gal. 3:13, NKJV, emphasis added).[22]

Let us start by pointing out that if Geisler and MacKenzie are implying that "having begun in the Spirit" equates with justification, they have failed to add that the New Testament uses "Spirit" preponderantly in conjunction with the intrinsic, transformational changes in the individual. Paul already notes the concept of transformation in the context by asking in Galatians 3:5, "Does God give you his Spirit and work miracles among you?" Elsewhere in his epistles, Paul understands this particular ministry of the Spirit as applying to spiritual gifts, not forensic imputation.[23] We also see the interchange between the Spirit and justification in Galatians 3:14 where Paul says "so that by faith we might receive the prom-

---

[21] The verbal form "sanctified" is the Greek ἁγιάζω, appearing 28 times in the New Testament. The noun form is ἁγιασμός which appears 10 times. The adjectival form ἅγιος appears 132 times, as well as the noun cognates ἁγιότης appearing 1 time, and ἁγιωσύνη appearing 3 times. None of these forms are ever used in the Galatian epistle.

[22] Geisler and MacKenzie, op. cit., p. 236-237.

[23] 1 Corinthians 12:4-11. This is precisely why the Council of Trent coalesces the Spirit in justification with the Spirit in the distribution of gifts. This is evident in Session 6, Chapter 7: "But we are truly called and are just, receiving justice within us, each one according to his own measure, which the Holy Spirit distributes to everyone as he wills [1 Cor. 12:11], and according to each one's own disposition and cooperation." Likewise Paul's use of the "Spirit" in the context of justification in Galatians 3:1ff. vindicates the Catholic position, which joins justification and sanctification.

ise of the Spirit." Paul could easily have replaced "promise of the Spirit" with "justification" and meant the same thing, especially in view of his exclusive attention to justification in the verses immediately preceding, i.e., Galatians 3:6-13.

Commentators generally agree that in Galatians 5:1-6 Paul sets up a context that considers Christians free, i.e., initially justified. He says in Galatians 5:1, "It is for freedom that Christ has set us free. Stand firm, then and do not let yourselves be burdened by a yoke of slavery." How were they assuming a yoke of slavery? By requiring circumcision. In 5:2 Paul says, "if you let yourselves be circumcised, Christ will be of no value to you at all." Following this in 5:4, however, Paul makes a very "Catholic" statement: "You who are trying to be justified by law have been alienated from Christ; you have fallen away from grace." Since the premise of Geisler and MacKenzie is that the Galatians were already so completely justified that Paul is now teaching "sanctification by faith alone," from their perspective Paul should have said, "You who are trying to be *sanctified* by law have been alienated from Christ." That Paul uses *justified* instead of *sanctified* shows not only that "Protestant sanctification" is not his concern, but also that he is fearful they will lose their present justification. The words "fallen from grace," then, must not mean "fallen from sanctification" but "fallen from justification." In other words, they should be seeking to maintain and increase their justification by the Spirit, not by the law.[24]

Proving that Paul's concern is falling from justification, not Protestant "sanctification," are his choice of topic and the ominous tone into which he digresses in the remaining context. Picking up the same theme of "freedom" with which he began in Galatians 5:1, and thus showing that he is connecting the two contexts, Paul says in 5:13-16:

> You, my brothers, were called to be free. But do not use your freedom to indulge the sinful nature; rather, serve one another in love. The entire law is summed up in a single command:

[24] Reinforcing this idea, "justified" (δικαιοῦσθε) in Galatians 5:4 is a Greek present tense verb (indicative, passive) which denotes an ongoing concern with justification.

> Love your neighbor as yourself. If you keep on biting and devouring each other, watch out or you will be destroyed by each other. So I say, live by the Spirit and you will not gratify the desires of the sinful nature.

Hence, he condemns not only a retreat to the ceremonial law, but a neglect of the moral law. Perhaps they were doing moral evil by treating those who were not circumcised with contempt and slander. If they find themselves continuing in these sins, he gives them the ominous ultimatum in 5:21 and 6:8: "I warn you, as I did before, that those who live like this will not inherit the kingdom of God...The one who sows to please his sinful nature, from that nature will reap destruction, the one who sows to please the Spirit, from the Spirit will reap eternal life." Paul sets "eternal life" in opposition to "destruction," showing that the latter term refers to eternal damnation. This is the second time he has warned them of this, as noted in the phrase "as I did before," indicating that he is seriously concerned that they are putting their justification, not merely their sanctification, in jeopardy.

The Case of Phinehas

In light of Paul's teachings on works of obedience as necessary for justification, Protestant exegesis has invariably chosen to overemphasize Paul's negative teaching about works while deemphasizing his positive teaching about works. Not only do many deny that Paul taught that works are necessary for justification, they also maintain he specifically avoids Old Testament teachings that teach justification by works. One of Reformed Protestantism's most honored theologians, John Murray, provides an example of this kind of interpretation.[25] Psalm 106:30-31 records, "But Phinehas stood up and intervened, and the plague was checked. This was *credited to him as righteousness* for endless generations to come."[26] Exegeting this passage, Murray writes:

---

[25] Late Professor of Systematic Theology at Westminster Theological Seminary, Philadelphia, PA.

[26] See also Ecclesiasticus 45:23-26 for a description of Phinehas's deed and subsequent reward. Malachi 2:5-6 may also allude to Phinehas.

> For if he [Paul] had appealed to Psalm 106:31 in the matter of justification, the justification of the ungodly, then the case of Phinehas would have provided an inherent contradiction and would have demonstrated justification by a righteous and zealous act...Genesis 15:6 is dealing with justification, as Paul shows. Psalm 106:31 is dealing with the good works which were the fruit of faith.[27]

Psalm 106:30-31 is referring to the incident recorded in Numbers 25 in which some of the men of Israel engaged in cultic sexual intercourse with Moabite and Midianite women. For this sin, the Lord ordered Moses to kill them. In defiance, an Israelite man brought a Midianite woman into his tent, most likely to engage in sexual intercourse. Phinehas, the priest, saw this happen, grabbed a spear, and went into the tent and killed both the man and the woman. For this act, God praises Phinehas very highly and stops the plague he had inflicted on the people, which had by this time already killed 24,000. God tells Moses that Phinehas was zealous for God's honor, and that as a result of his act Phinehas had turned God's wrath away from killing even more people. God makes a "covenant of peace" and a "lasting priesthood" with Phinehas and his descendants. It is obvious that Phinehas's act of vengeance was of extreme importance to God.

In the Psalmist's evaluation of Phinehas's deed, he uses language that those of a Protestant mindset find quite puzzling. The Psalmist uses the identical phrase for Phinehas that Genesis 15:6 used for Abraham, i.e., "was credited to him as righteousness."[28] Protestants are trained to think of the word *credited* as something that one is *considered* as having but not something inherent within the person. Thus, they say that Abraham is credited with Christ's righteousness by the "non working" instrument of faith, and that Abraham has no intrinsic righteousness worthy of God's acceptance for justification. A severe problem arises in this formulation, however, since Psalm 106:31 attributes the "crediting of righteous-

---

27 John Murray, *Commentary on Romans*, Vol. 1, p. 131.

28 Hebrew: (ויּתשׁבה לו צדקה) *chashab lo tsadaqah.* The only difference between the two is that Genesis 15:6 uses the Qal form of the verb, as opposed to the Niphal form in Psalm 106:31, with no significant change in meaning. The Septuagint renders Genesis as καὶ ἐλγίσθη αὐτῷ εἰς δικαιοσύνν which is identical in Psalm 106:31 (LXX =Psalm 105:31).

ness" to a work. The Psalm presupposes Phinehas's faith in God, and its stress on Phinehas's work becomes all the more significant when we realize that in all of Scripture only Abraham and Phinehas are individually assigned the designation "credited with righteousness." Because it is applied to a concrete act, one cannot understand the "crediting" as a mere *considering* of righteousness that does not in reality exist, but only as a recognition of an inherent quality of the individual. In other words, one must *consider* him righteous because he ***is*** righteous.[29]

Murray's claim that Paul's quoting of Psalm 106:31 would have "created a contradiction" is only true if one's theology predisposes one to view Abraham's crediting of righteousness as a forensic imputation — a mere *considering* of righteousness that is not inherent — rather than as a manifestation of infused righteousness inherent within the individual and appearing at a specified time. Murray's theological presupposition forces him to put Paul in the dubious position of having purposely to ignore the only other time the phrase "credited with righteousness" is used of an individual in Scripture (Psalm 106:31) just to prove a point and avoid a contradiction in his own theology. In fact, the only thing, according to Murray, that saves Paul from contradiction is Paul's deliberate refusal to bring Psalm 106:31 into the discussion. Though Murray makes a valiant attempt to salvage his own theology, he inadvertently puts Paul at odds with Scripture. This is a highly untenable situation in biblical hermeneutics since it has long been accepted by responsible theologians that Scripture is one cohesive whole which does not contradict itself. It also puts Paul at odds with himself, since it was he, inspired by the Holy Spirit, who quoted incessantly from obscure Old Testament passages — for example, Paul's quote from the obscure passage of Habakkuk 2:4 in Romans 1:17 — to prove to his audience what was not immediately obvious about the gospel and its relationship to the old covenant. Moreover, it was Paul himself who said that "*All* Scripture was inspired and profitable for teaching..." (2 Timothy 3:16), Psalm 106:31 presumably included. Murray's words, "For if he had appealed to Psalm 106:31...then the case of Phinehas would have provided an inherent contradiction..." show the desperate lengths faith alone theolo-

[29] See the discussion of the Greek word *logizomai* (λογίζομαι) and the Hebrew word *chashab* (חשׁב) in chapter 5 for a more thorough analysis.

gians will go to protect their presupposition. Can we imagine Paul ever teaching someone not to appeal to a certain Scripture — a Scripture that is so intimately related to the topic at hand — because it would contradict one's interpretation of a another Scripture? In the annals of biblical revelation, there is no such suggestion ever made by any of the sacred writers.

Moreover, Murray's claim that the work of Phinehas was merely the "fruit of faith," does not offer him an escape from the clear language of Psalm 106:31. If he can claim that Paul could not have used Psalm 106:31 to prove his point about justification in Romans 4, then he must also admit that the Psalmist chose the wrong terminology to describe Phinehas's righteousness, since under Murray's hypothesis the specific words "credited with righteousness" may only refer to *imputed* righteousness. Murray cannot have it both ways, that is, he cannot, on the one hand, say that the language of Psalm 106:31 is so strong toward teaching justification by works that Paul was forced to ignore the verse to avoid a contradiction, and, on the other hand, say that Psalm 106:31 refers only to the fruit of faith but not justification proper. In the first suggestion he attempts to make the verse very strong, in the latter suggestion he attempts to make it very weak. Both cannot be true.

Hence, someone is wrong, either the Psalmist or Murray. The evidence is against Murray, since his position argues from silence whereas the language of Psalm 106:31, like the language of Genesis 15:6, is clear and unambiguous. The Holy Spirit, through inspiration, assigns the work of Phinehas the same justifying nomenclature that is given to Abraham, i.e., "credited with righteousness." Granted, Paul has a major point to make in Romans 4 concerning the crediting of righteousness to Abraham, but Paul sets the context of Romans 4 in opposition to the concept of legal obligation and the incessant boasting of the wayward Jews, not in opposition to God-glorifying and grace-prompted works such as those done by Phinehas. In effect, Murray's error exposes the false notion in Protestant thought which understands work only as the *qualifier* of faith, rather than as an independent virtue which when added to faith has power to justify under the grace of God. Hence, the "inherent contradiction" Murray predicted is merely a contradiction in his own theology.

The Case of Cornelius

Scripture often portrays God's drawing, calling, and justification of the individual as very fluid, a quality in justification which again speaks of an ongoing process, not a static imputation. At the enlightenment of Peter in Acts 10:34-35 on learning that God will accept all men for salvation, he says, "I realize how true it is that God does not show favoritism but accepts men from every nation who fear him and do what is right."[30] The Acts 10 account opens up a whole new dimension in our discussion of the righteousness God seeks in men. At the time Luke wrote Acts, specifically the incident with Cornelius he recorded in Acts 10, the gospel had not spread far beyond the borders of Judea. Cornelius was one of the first Gentiles to hear the Christian gospel formally proclaimed. Peter's understanding is that God is coming to Cornelius with the gospel because Cornelius had shown that he "feared" God and was "doing what was right" (Acts 10:2, 35). Since God does not play favorites, he will bless anyone from any nation who fears him and does good.

This portrayal of God's nature is quite different from that which Protestants often force upon us by their narrow interpretations of Romans 3:11 ("there is no one who understands; no one seeks for God"). Apparently, many outside the orb of the formalized gospel *do* seek God and in turn God seeks them as well. How can this be if Romans 3:11 seems so adamant that none seek God? We can answer in two ways. First, in Romans 3:10, Paul is speaking from the perspective of the system of law. We know this is true because Paul concludes this section in Romans 3:19 with the words, "Now we know that whatever the law says, it says to those who are under the law, so that every mouth may be silenced and the whole world held accountable to God." From the perspective of the system of law there is no one who does good or seeks after God. God is perfect and not one can measure up to his perfect standards. Paul, in the context of Romans 2-4, applied this principle especially to those Jews who "boasted" in God's face with their legalistic works. Sec-

---

[30] The NIV phrase "do what is right" is translated from the Greek ἐργαζόμενος δικαιοσύνη, literally "working righteousness." Acts 10:35 is also used at Vatican Council II in *Lumen Gentium 9*.

ond, as a logical corollary, Paul paints a picture describing the condition of the whole human race without the grace of God. Without the grace of God to prompt them, no one would ever seek God on his own. God must make the first move. Once he sheds his grace upon men, then men have the responsibility to respond to God. Some do, as the case of Cornelius proves.[31]

The psalm that Paul quotes in Romans 3:11 shows that some do respond. To begin, Paul quotes from the first three verses of Psalm 14. These verses make it clear that no one does good or seeks God. As noted above, no one who bases his actions on the system of law, can please God or seek him. Again, Paul specifies this perspective in Romans 3:19, "Now we know that whatever the law says, it says to those who are under the law..." Being "under the law" is being in the system of law — the system from which God previously viewed the human race. But in the system of grace are some who seek God and do his will. Like Cornelius, they "do what is right" — a righteousness that God can and does accept. The latter part of Psalm 14, which Paul does not quote in

[31] Council of Orange, 529 AD, Canon 25: "So very clearly we should believe that the faith — so admirable — both of that famous thief, whom the Lord restored to his native land of paradise, and of Cornelius the centurion, to whom the angel of the Lord was sent, and of Zachaeus, who deserved to receive the Lord himself, was not from nature, but a gift of God's bounty." Council of Orange, Canon 4: "If anyone contends that in order that we may be cleansed from sin, God waits for our good will, but does not acknowledge that even the wish to be purged is produced in us through the infusion and operation of the Holy Spirit, he opposes the Holy Spirit himself, who says through Solomon: 'Good will is prepared by the Lord' [Prov. 8:35, LXX], and the Apostle who beneficially says: 'It is God, who works in us both to will and to accomplish according to his good will' [Phil 2:13]." Council of Trent, Session 6, Chapter 5: "It [the Council] furthermore declares that in adults the beginning of that justification must be derived from the predisposing grace of God through Jesus Christ, that is, from his vocation, whereby without any existing merits on their part they are called, so that they who by sin were turned away from God, through his stimulating and assisting grace are disposed to convert themselves to their own justification, by freely assenting to and cooperating with the same grace..." Vatican Council I, Chapter 3: "Moreover, although the assent of faith is by no means a blind movement of the intellect, nevertheless, no one can 'assent to the preaching of the Gospel,' as he must to attain salvation, 'without the illumination and inspiration of the Holy Spirit, who gives to all a sweetness in consenting to and believing the truth. Wherefore, 'faith' itself in itself, even if it 'works not by charity,' is a gift of God, and its act is a work pertaining to salvation, by which man offers a free obedience to God Himself by agreeing to, and cooperating with His grace, which he could resist."

Romans 3, speaks of those who do respond under God's grace. The Psalmist writes in Psalm 14:4-6:

> Will evildoers never learn, those who devour *my people* as men eat bread and *who do not call on the Lord?* There they are overwhelmed with dread, for God is present in the *company of the righteous*. You evildoers frustrate the plans of the *poor* but the Lord is their refuge.

Here the Psalmist contrasts "my people" with those "who do not call on the Lord." Hence, Scripture testifies to a clear distinction between those who do seek God and those who do not. These evil people that "do not call on the Lord" *remain* the ones of whom Paul speaks in Romans 3:11 as "no one who understands, no one who seeks God." Typical of this description are the Jews to whom Paul is primarily directing his message in Romans 3. God has offered them the grace to respond but they have spurned God's advances. Yet Psalm 14:5 is clear that there is a "company of the righteous," in contradistinction to "there is none righteous" in Romans 3:10. Under law there is none righteous; under grace as many as desire can be righteous before God. As Paul says in Romans 3:19, "Whatever the law says it says to those who are under the law..." If one comes out from under the system of law, the law cannot condemn him. So it is with those who seek God. They are no longer under law but are now under grace.

God expects men to seek after him within the grace he has spread abroad to the whole world. Scripture states this no better than in Acts 17:26-27:

> From one man he made every nation of men, that they should inhabit the whole earth; and he determined the times set for them and the exact places where they should live. God did this *so that men would seek him* and perhaps reach out for him and find him, though he is not far from each one of us.

We notice here that when Paul is specifying that God desired men to seek him he starts by referring to "one man," namely Adam. It is not surprising, then, to find in proximity to Adam in one of the earliest chapters of the Bible that "men began to call on the name of the Lord" (Genesis 4:26). This "calling on the Lord" occurs thousands of years before the Jews existed. It was occurring long before the flood of Noah's day. Paul states that God subsequently made all the nations (i.e., the table of nations in Genesis 10) with their specific "times and locations" for the express purpose that these men would *"seek him and find him."* As history records, some found him; some did not. But the point is clear that God created a dynamic relationship for himself and man right from the beginning. God has been seeking faithful and obedient men since the dawn of time.[32] Although he formalized this relationship at various points, (e.g., Noah, Abraham, Israel, the Church), God was always and everywhere looking for anyone who would "do what is right" as Cornelius had done. As the prophet Zechariah records (Zechariah 1:3), "This is what the Lord Almighty says: 'Return to me,' declares the Lord Almighty, 'and I will return to you,' says the Lord Almighty." God found one such seeker in Cornelius.

What exactly did God see in Cornelius? Acts 10 gives us a vivid description. Acts 10:2 says that Cornelius and his whole family are "devout and God-fearing." Several references in Acts address non-Jews who seek God as "God-fearers," "God-fearing Greeks" or "God-fearing Gentiles."[33] Cornelius is a centurion of the "Italian regiment," most likely, not a Greek but a Roman. There is no evidence that he is a Jewish convert; on the contrary, he is "uncir-

---

[32] "The desire for God is written in the human heart, because man is created by God and for God; and God never ceases to draw man to himself...this invitation to converse with God is addressed to man as soon as he comes into being..." (Catholic Catechism, Section 27; Vatican Council II, *Gaudium et spes*, 19 § 1). "Man's faculties make him capable of coming to a knowledge of the existence of a personal God. But for man to be able to enter into real intimacy with him, God willed both to reveal himself to man and to give him the grace of being able to welcome this revelation in faith. The proofs of God's existence, however, can predispose one to faith and help one to see that faith is not opposed to reason" (CC, Section 35). "By natural reason man can know God with certainty, on the basis of his works. But there is another order of knowledge, which man cannot possibly arrive at by his own powers: the order of divine Revelation" (CC, Section 50). "By revealing himself God wishes to make them capable of responding to him, and of knowing him, and loving him far beyond their own natural capacity" (CC, Section 52). "The Spirit prepares men and goes out to them with his grace, in order to draw them to Christ" (CC, Section 737). "Through his grace, the Holy Spirit is the first to awaken faith in us and to communicate to us the new life..." (CC, Section 684).

[33] Acts 13:16, 26; 16:14; 17:4, 17.

cumcised" (Acts 10:45), a Gentile, according to Peter's previous thought, with whom a Jew could not associate or even visit (Acts 10:28), whereas a Jewish convert would enjoy fellowship with Jews. Cornelius is simply a God-fearing Gentile such as Romans 2:14-15 describes, one who seeks God based on the law written on the heart. Moreover, Cornelius's entire household is "devout" and "God-fearing;" clearly he understands and acknowledges God to an extent that has filtered down to all those with whom he is intimately associated. In Acts 10:2 Luke begins to describe Cornelius's good works: "He gave generously to those in need and prayed to God regularly." Here we have a man of faith who loves and communicates with God, and who loves his neighbor as himself. Although we know that Cornelius is responding to the grace that God has given him, Acts 10:4 shows us the perspective from which God views Cornelius: he is one who has pleased God by working righteousness. It records: "Cornelius stared at him in fear. 'What is it Lord?' he asked. The angel answered, 'Your prayers and gifts to the poor have come up as a memorial offering before God.'"

This incident makes it clear that God is responding to the faith and good works of Cornelius. According to Acts 10:35, he is one who "fears God and does what is right." It is Cornelius's righteousness upon which God looks, not an alien righteousness. In the language of Acts 17:25-26 already cited, Cornelius is one whom God places in a certain 'time and location' so that he will seek God and find him, and find him he does. Cornelius seeks God through the grace God gives him and God, in turn, blesses Cornelius with the full gospel.[34] At Peter's direction, Cornelius is baptized and received as a member of the Church. The full blessings of the Christian life now flow to him and his family, and they will be witnesses to others of God's tremendous grace. Granted, Cornelius's sins are formally forgiven at his baptism, and thus the righteous work of Christ is applied to him. But one cannot miss the point of the story: clearly Cornelius is a recipient of this formal grace as a result of God's response to his works of righteousness done under the aus-

[34] Catholic Catechism, Sections 1996-2004; "For he wishes to give eternal life to all those who seek salvation by patience in well-doing" (CC, Section 55). "At all times and in every race, anyone who fears God and does what is right has been acceptable to him" (CC, Sections, 761, 781). "...and you overlook people's sins, so that they may repent" (Wisdom 11:23).

pices of grace. Before Peter comes to visit, Cornelius is one whom God has been graciously viewing, thus allowing Cornelius to please God with his "prayer and gifts to the poor." Thus one does not have to be a formal member of the Church in order to be viewed or included in the grace of God. As Peter says, "God is no respecter of persons; he accepts anyone who fears him and does what is right." Unlike so many of the Jews of his day, Cornelius is a humble man who does not demand that God pay him for his good works. As Paul says in Romans 4:3-4, God is not obligated to reward anyone with anything because all are sinners, and so is Cornelius. But from the perspective of the system of grace which stems from the atonement of Christ, God can view Cornelius, and any man from any nation who fears him and does what is right, as righteous and a candidate for God's salvation.

The case of Cornelius also shows us the reality of the Catholic concept of *gracious* merit. Cornelius is a man like that of Acts 17:25-27 who is placed by God in a certain time and place for the precise reason that he should seek God. Prompted by the grace and knowledge of God, he acts upon this grace by prayer and good works, e.g., giving to the poor.[35] On a strict basis, Cornelius is a sinner like everyone else in the human race and from that perspective he does not deserve God's favor. On the basis of gracious merit, however, Cornelius can acknowledge God with the power God has placed in him, and God in turn can bless him for his efforts. In Cornelius's case God blesses him with salvation. The reward of salvation is much greater in value than the devotion and work that Cornelius performs. This is precisely how the concept of merit works in Catholic theology. God's reward of salvation far outweighs our gracious merit of it.

Given God's substantial preparation in Cornelius's soul prior to his baptism, let us underscore these points in light of various criticisms levied against the Catholic Church. Some Evangelicals criticize the Catholic practice of preparing candidates for baptism. Evangelical James McCarthy claims, for example, that the teach-

---

[35] As noted in chapter 1, God prompts to salvation by *actual* grace. Once one responds to actual grace, God provides the *sanctifying* grace of salvation. Council of Trent, Session 6, Canon 7: "If anyone says that all works performed before justification, no matter how they were performed, are truly sins or deserve God's hatred; or that the more earnestly one tries to dispose oneself for grace, the more grievously one sins, anathema sit" (JD 1557).

ing of the Catholic introductory rite, RCIA (Rite of Christian Initiation for Adults), prior to baptism is unbiblical because it makes the candidate "work" prior to receiving baptism and thus contradicts Paul's statements in Romans that salvation is not by works.[36] As McCarthy notes, RCIA teaches adult candidates for baptism to "love and worship God, pray, fast, love their neighbor, practice self-renunciation, obey the commandments, bear witness to the Catholic faith, follow supernatural inspiration in deeds, and confess the major doctrines of the Church." First, these preparations are not against Paul's teaching of works, which, as we have seen repeatedly, refer to obligating God to reward us with eternal life for our own efforts outside of his grace. Second, the rudiments of this Catholic teaching are already evident in the baptism of Cornelius noted above. God himself recognizes Cornelius's "love of God and neighbor, prayer, self-renunciation, obedience, witness, and deeds" prior to his baptism. As for "witness" and "confession" of the faith, Cornelius is filled with the Spirit and speaks in tongues prior to his baptism (Acts 10:44-48). He also teaches his family about God (Acts 10:2). The New Testament directives for the preparation of Baptism are similar elsewhere. John the Baptist, for example, sets the precedent for baptismal preparation. In Luke 3:7, John accuses the crowd coming to be baptized of being a "brood of vipers" who need to repent before receiving baptism. The people ask John what to do and John replies that they should: (1) share food and clothing with their neighbor (Luke 3:11); (2) to the tax-collectors: do not steal (Luke 3:13); (3) to the soldiers: do not steal, lie or complain (Luke 3:14). Thus it would be hard to argue that these people do not require substantial preparation prior to baptism. Finally, Luke 3:18 states, "And with many other words John exhorted the people and preached the good news to them." With John's "many other words" we can imagine that he made the most concerted effort to prepare his baptismal candidates. Would we accuse John of a "works gospel" for telling the people to stop doing their evil deeds and do good works prior to baptism? Of course not.

One may object, however, that in some instances the New Testament treats baptism as an event without much prior preparation. This seems clear in Acts 16:31-34 at the baptism of the jailer and his household in the middle of the night. This passage, however, is

---

[36] *The Gospel According to Rome*, p. 46.

not teaching that there should be no preparation. The circumstances surrounding the baptism of the jailer are highly unusual. An earthquake releases Paul and Silas from the jail. Since the jailer will be held responsible for their escape, he attempts to kill himself. Paul pleads with him to stop. The jailer agrees to listen to Paul. Paul, however, is still a fugitive and the jailer still must answer to his superiors. Thus there is little time for preparation outside of providing the jailer with an early morning lesson on the rudiments of the Christian faith, at which time he and his family are promptly baptized. Knowing that he was a fugitive, thinking that he may never see the jailer again, and knowing baptism to be essential to his salvation, Paul quickly administers the sacrament in the middle of the night. Even in this haste, however, we can be sure that Paul requires of the jailer knowledge and love of God, as well as a confession of sin, before he is baptized. Acts 16:32 suggests this very thing: "Then they spoke the word of the Lord to him and to all the others in his house."[37]

The Case of Paul

Another case of the interplay between God's grace and the concept of gracious merit appears in how Paul speaks of his own conversion to Christianity. In 1 Timothy 1:13-16, Paul writes:

> Even though I was once a blasphemer and a persecutor and a violent man, I was shown mercy *because I acted in ignorance and unbelief*. The grace of our Lord was poured out on me abundantly, along with the faith and love that are in Christ Jesus. Here is a trustworthy saying that deserves full acceptance: Christ Jesus came into the world to save sinners — of whom I am the worst. *But for that very reason I was shown mercy so that in me*, the worst of sinners, Christ Jesus might display his unlimited

[37] Catholic Catechism, Section 1229: "From the time of the apostles, becoming a Christian has been accomplished by a journey and initiation in several stages. This journey can be covered rapidly or slowly, but certain essential elements will always have to be present: proclamation of the Word, acceptance of the Gospel entailing conversion, profession of faith, Baptism itself, the outpouring of the Holy Spirit, and admission to Eucharistic communion." (See sections 1230-1233 for more on RCIA).

patience as an example for those who would believe on him and receive eternal life.

Here we see a connection between the mercy that God showed Paul for his sins and Paul's ignorance and unbelief in committing such things. Although he calls himself "the worst of sinners," mainly because of his utter hatred and persecution of the first Christians, Paul also tells us that it was in his zeal for the faith of his Judaistic fathers that he blasphemed and persecuted, because he simply did not know Jesus and his mission. In the accounts of Paul's conversion in the book of Acts 9:1-19; 22:1-16; 26:9-23, we find that Paul was not the worst of sinners in the sense of living a malicious life of reckless abandon or having totally disregarded the commandments of God. He says of himself in Philippians 3:6 that he was "faultless" in the righteousness of the law. Let us make clear that this is not to say that Paul gained any merit with God because of his law-keeping. Surely if Paul had died in this unconverted state he would have come under God's judgment. Jesus, however, appearing to Paul on the Damascus road, is coming not as the vengeful God who wants to destroy Paul for his sins but as a gentle inquisitor asking, "Saul, Saul, why do you persecute me?" Jesus speaks to Paul almost as if he had known him previously. Paul answers, "Who are you, Lord?" As soon as Paul hears Jesus's answer, "I am Jesus whom you are persecuting...now get up and go into the city and you will be told what you must do," Paul obeys. He has finally found the answer he was looking for and responds immediately. We must notice, however, that there is something about Paul that Jesus seeks. Paul has misdirected his godly energies out of ignorance. Paul's zeal and honesty for what he believes can now be pressed into service by Jesus for Christianity. While Paul was persecuting the Church in his zeal for God, Jesus had "patience" with him because Paul was acting in ignorance. All he needed was a push in the right direction and he would become the greatest missionary for Christianity the world had ever known. As God led Cornelius to Christianity, he likewise led Paul to Christianity — by a direct communication. As Cornelius was baptized, so Paul was baptized, that God's grace could wash away his past sins. Acts

22:16 records God's command to Paul: "Get up, be baptized and wash your sins away, calling on his name."[38]

The Verb Tenses of "To be Justified"

Protestants attempt to combat the idea of *ongoing* justification by claiming that the many references to justification in Paul's writings are in the past tense, e.g., "having been justified" or "we have been justified" as recorded in Romans 5:1[39] They conclude from such passages that justification is an act done in the past and thus is complete and unalterable. Then they use this conclusion, in turn, to support the Protestant conception of a one-time, forensic imputation of justification given to the individual at the moment of an act of faith. Arguments of this nature are quite naive. No one would dispute that justification occurs at a point in life which one can look back upon after a few years and understand as a past event. Even though the Catholic view holds that the justification is a process and can be repeated, as one moves on in his Christian life he still remembers and understands the initial point of justification as a past event. Baptism, in Catholic theology and some Protestant denominations, is just such an occurrence. It is the beginning of our salvation, the point in the past to which we can look back to confirm our initial justification. Thus, we can affirm that we "have been justified." It is simply false and unprovable, however, to conclude that because an event occurred in the past, that a present or future event cannot subsequently alter, eliminate, or repeat it. In Romans 5:1, Paul is making the point that the audience he is addressing has received the grace of God and is no longer in the bondage of the law and sin. Whether these people will remain in that state he does not address. They are in the state of justification for the time being only, this being intimated as Paul says, "There is *now* no condemnation for those who are in Christ Jesus" (Romans

[38] The concept of gracious merit — in which God does something good to the individual based either on the goodness God sees in the individual's intentions or on his actual obedience — permeates Scripture, especially the Old Testament (cf., 1 Kings 14:13; 2 Kings 20:1-6; 2 Chronicles 12:12; 19:3; 24:16; 30:18-20; Psalm 37:4-9; 84:11; Proverbs 12:2; 13:21; Ecclesiastes 2:26; Jeremiah 5:25; 18:10; Ezekiel 18:21; 33:14-16; Luke 8:15; Romans 2:10).

[39] MacArthur, *Justification by Faith Alone*, p. 13.

8:1). The word "now" is the operative word. It speaks of a present state but not necessarily a future state. There is nothing in Paul's context in Romans 5 that suggests the justification cannot be nullified or repeated. To assert the contrary simply begs the question.

We can also prove this point grammatically. In Romans 5:1 Paul begins by declaring, "Therefore, since we have been justified through faith..." As noted above, this statement treats the justification as a past event. In fact, the Greek verb in the phrase, "having been justified" is a *perfect passive* Greek verb which denotes a *completed* past event.[40] Evangelical James White claims that such usage of the past tense precludes entertaining the Catholic teaching that one must fulfill "all conditions which are necessary for achieving justification" as quoted from Catholic theologian Ludwig Ott.[41] What White fails to tell his readers is that the same verbal tense appears in reference to *love* when Paul says in verse 5, "God *has poured out* his love into our hearts by the Holy Spirit." The perfect passive tense of "has poured out" indicates that the "pouring out of love into our hearts" also occurred as a *completed* event in the past.[42] Not only does this imply that God infused love into the individual at the same time he was justified (a thoroughly Catholic doctrine), but we can also conclude that since the Holy Spirit

40 The form δικαιωθέντες ("having been justified") in Romans 5:1 is in the perfect tense, passive voice which in Greek denotes an action in the past that is complete, anticipating future results.

41 *The Roman Catholic Controversy*, pp. 137, 145

42 This tense is the same Romans 5:5 uses in the word ἐκκέχυται ("having poured out"), from the Greek root, ἐκχέω (in which Titus 3:6 uses the aorist indicative ἐξέχεεν. This identical usage shows that both events, i.e., the justification and the Holy Spirit's pouring out of love in Romans 5:1-5 occur in the past and both are considered completed actions. This is why Catholic doctrine insists that in justification love is added to faith. The Council of Trent states: "For although no one can be just but he to whom the merits of the passion of our Lord Jesus Christ are communicated, yet this does take place in this justification of the ungodly when by the merit of that same most holy passion 'the charity of God is poured forth by the Holy Spirit in the hearts of those justified,' and inheres in them. Hence man through Jesus Christ, into whom he is ingrafted, receives in the said justification together with the remission of sins all these [gifts] infused at the same time: faith, hope, and charity. For unless hope and charity be added to it, neither unites one perfectly with Christ, nor makes him a living member of his body. For this reason it is most truly said that 'faith without works is dead...and is of no profit...but faith, which works by charity'" (Session 6, Chapter 7).

has not ceased pouring love into our hearts, the perfect tense as used here does not preclude God's continuing to infuse love into the individual. The Holy Spirit continues to pour love into our hearts during our whole Christian life. The perfect passive tense used by Paul merely shows us *when this process started.* Hence, just as God can perform an independent act of pouring love into our hearts in the past, and then do so again in the future, so God can begin our justification at a specific time in the past but continue to manifest and increase it throughout our Christian lives.[43]

We can also prove that justification is a process by noting that Paul uses the word *justification* in reference to the future. Romans 2:13 states, "But the doers of the law *will be* justified."[44] The context of this passage points to the final judgment when "God will render to each man according to what he has done" (Romans 2:6). Hence, it is not a future tense which merely anticipates when someone will repent of his sins on earth, but a future tense which is not fulfilled until the judgment of God comes upon each man at the end of time.

Jesus used the same future tense of the word *justified* in Matthew 12:36-37: "But I tell you that men will have to give account on the day of judgment for every careless word they have spoken. For by your words you will be justified[45] and by your words you will be condemned." Clearly, God holds our future justification in abeyance until the final judgment. This does not, however, dis-

---

[43] Council of Trent, Session 6, Chapter 7: "Justification...the instrumental cause is the sacrament of baptism, which is the "sacrament of faith," without which no one is ever justified." Chapter 9: "...in this justice received through the grace of Christ "faith cooperating with good works," they increase and are further justified, as it is written: "he that is just, let him be justified still" (Rev. 22:11), and again: "Be not afraid to be justified even to death" (Ecclesiasticus 18:22), and again: "you see, that by works a man is justified and not by faith only (James 2:24). And this increase of justice the Holy Church begs for, when she prays: "Give unto us, O Lord, an increase of faith, hope, and charity" [13th Sunday after Pentecost]. In light of this prayer, it is significant that in Romans 5:1-10 Paul speaks of faith, hope, and love all in the context of *justification.*

[44] δικαιωθήσονται: third person, future, passive, indicative.

[45] δικαιωθήσῃ: second person, future, passive, indicative.

count a past justification; it only reinforces the idea that justification is a process with beginning and end.[46]

We should also point out that in certain instances the New Testament uses the word *sanctified* in the past tense. In 1 Corinthians 6:11 Paul says, "But you were washed, you were sanctified,[47] you were justified." Protestants believe that sanctification is an ongoing process. Would we conclude, then, that because sanctification is used in the past tense in 1 Corinthians 6:11 that this limits its meaning to the past? Certainly not. Paul reinforces this interpretation by using the word *justification* in the past tense in the same verse. We must reason, then, that if sanctification cannot be confined to the past, even though it is used in the past tense, then neither can justification be confined to the past though used in the past tense.[48]

1 John 2:19

"None of Them Belonged to Us"

In Chapters 1-3, we saw how the Protestant views the relationship between faith and works in justification. The Protestant understands works merely as the "qualifier" of faith, rather than as a separate category of action that must be consciously and consistently added to faith in order to be justified. By keeping works merely as the qualifier of what kind of faith is present, the Protestant maintains that *faith alone* justifies, albeit it must be a "saving faith." If, perchance, one either repudiates his faith in this life or discovers at the final judgment that he is under condemnation for

46 Some have suggested that Romans 3:20 ("because through the works of the law no flesh shall be justified") also refers to a future justification because of the presence of the future indicative δικαιωθήσεται. Although this is possible, it is also possible that Paul is referring to those in his time who will eventually be justified under the parameters he is outlining. In other words, the future may serve to stand for the present. The context of Romans 3 would suggest as much. Only when the final judgment is included in the context is it safe to say that the future tense of δικαιόω refers to a future justification.

47 1 Corinthians 6:11 uses the aorist of "sanctified" as it also does for "justified" in the same sentence.

48 Chapter 5 addresses more fully the context and verbal tenses of Romans 5:1-5.

his unrepentant sins on earth, many Evangelicals claim that from the beginning such a person never had "saving faith" and thus was *never* justified. Hence, he did not lose his justification; he never had it originally. This notion has become a handy little polemic in the Evangelical arsenal both to support the concept of a one-time, forensic imputation and to give some rationale for why many people who once seemed very enthusiastic eventually leave the Christian faith. The Reformed persuasion has also developed this idea into a plausible explanation of the stress on works in the epistle of James. They maintain that James cares only about the individual's quality of faith, not works for justification. This false notion has misled Protestants into viewing justification not as an ongoing process waiting for its completion at the end of time, but a one-time past event that is either genuine or not genuine. Ironically, Evangelicals often chide their Catholic opponents for believing that a Christian cannot know whether he will go to heaven.[49] Yet, according to the Evangelical's own belief, any Christian who finds himself in unrepentant sin may, after waiting until judgment day, find that he was never justified originally. This theory not only presents just as much uncertainty about one's final salvation as the Catholic view does, but it also gives many who will eventually fall away in the future a false sense of security in the present by leading them to think their salvation is assured merely because they believe it to be so.[50]

In order to support the notion that Christians do not actually fall from salvation but were never justified originally, Protestants invariably use a particular passage, 1 John 2:19, as a proof text: "They went out from us but they did not really belong to us. For if they had belonged to us, they would have remained with us; but their going showed that none of them belonged to us." They claim that the apostle John is teaching in this passage that if one leaves Christianity it must be concluded that one never belonged to Chris-

---

[49] Council of Trent, Session 6, Chapters 12-14. In proselytizing, one of Evangelicalism's most popular introductions is to inquire, "If you died tonight are you sure you will go to heaven?"

[50] The Council of Trent fought vigorously against this idea. Canon 14 states: "If anyone shall say that a man is absolved from his sins and justified, because he believes for certain that he is absolved and justified, or that no one is truly justified but he who believes himself justified, and that by this faith alone absolution and justification are perfected, let him be anathema."

tianity. From this understanding, they postulate as a corollary that *any* individual who falls away from the Christian faith does so because he was never a true Christian.

The main problem with this kind of interpretation is that it takes a specific truth concerning *some* who fall away and makes it into a general truth applicable to *everyone* who falls away. Certainly a large contingent of people who leave the church never genuinely embraced the Christian faith. Jesus teaches very clearly in Matthew 7:22-23, "Many will say to me on that day, 'Lord, Lord, did we not prophesy in your name, and in your name drive out demons, and perform many miracles?' Then I will tell them plainly, 'I never knew you. Away from me, you evildoers!'" The phrase, "I never knew you" implies that they were never true Christians but only appear to be through manifesting various miracles. This condition of hypocrisy was perhaps true of many of the Jews in Jesus's day. The parables Jesus tells both before and after this teaching, (e.g., concerning trees that bear good or bad fruit and those who build on either rock or sand), confirm Jesus's intent to point out their false faith and works. Passages like this, however, do not prove that a true Christian cannot fall from his Christian faith and lose a salvation that he once possessed. They only prove that *some* people who leave the faith were never true believers. John already implies this condition within the context of his epistle when he writes in 1 John 2:18: "Dear children, this is the last hour; and as you have heard that the Antichrist is coming, even now many antichrists have come. This is how we know it is the last hour." Since verse 18 precedes the verse in question (verse 19), we understand that the people to whom John refers in verse 19 are the "antichrists" of verse 18. We know that John, in using the word "antichrists," is not referring to the run-of-the-mill Christian believer but to treacherous *antichrists* whose sole purpose in life is to thwart the cause of Christianity and upset the faith of the average church-going Christian. John does not hesitate to equate them with the supreme Antichrist, Satan, for after referring to him in the words, "*the* Antichrist is coming," John adds, "*even now* many antichrists have come," showing that they are of the same breed as Satan.

In 2 Corinthians 11:13-15 Paul spoke about these same "antichrists" as present within the Corinthian church: "For such men are false apostles, deceitful workmen, masquerading as apostles of Christ. And no wonder, for Satan himself masquerades as an angel of light. It is not surprising, then, if his servants masquerade as servants of righteousness..." Paul's reference to both Satan and the false apostles "masquerading" as angels of light shows that their intent is to deceive.[51] They come into the church by stealth for the sole purpose of upsetting the faith of sincere believers. Paul also expresses this concern in verse 3 of the same chapter: "But I am afraid that just as Eve was deceived by the serpents's cunning, your minds may somehow be led astray from your sincere and pure devotion to Christ." It is these whom Paul considers as sincere believers in Christ, not the false apostles and antichrists masquerading as angels of light.

We can conclude that though 1 John 2:19 certainly makes clear that some will leave the church who were never sincere believers originally, in context this principle applies primarily to the antichrists whose purpose is to destroy Christianity. Satan, the supreme Antichrist, was never a Christian, and it follows that the antichrists who follow in his footsteps were never Christians either. Thus, 1 John 2:19 proves that *some* groups of people who were never true Christians may defect but it by no means proves that *all* people who lose their faith were never true Christians.

Not only does 1 John 2:19 fail to support the contention of Evangelicals that all those who fall away were not justified originally, the verse also leaves them without an explanation as to how someone could practice the Christian faith his whole life and suddenly find at judgment day that he was never saved. This is so because 1 John 2:19 is the *only* verse in the whole New Testament that even *remotely* suggests such a possibility. The New Testament contains no other verse that either explicitly or implicitly implies that a practicing Christian who falls from faith was never saved from the beginning. Every other passage that addresses the issue of departing from the faith speaks of those in the Church who are following the gospel as true believers but in a moment or continuation of serious sin or infidelity fall from the grace of God. Thus, with no evidence for support, either within the verse or any-

51 "Masquerade" is from the Greek word μετασχηματίζω and refers to a total transformation (Phil. 3:21).

where else in the New Testament, the all-or-nothing Evangelical view of 1 John 2:19 is at best unprovable, but more likely unbiblical and heretical.[52]

Hebrews 11:29

The Faith of Israel

In this book we have frequently cited the heroes of faith in Hebrews 11 as some of the best examples of those who lived a life of faith, walked with God, and pleased him continually. People like Abel, Enoch, Noah, Abraham, Sarah, Moses, showed how one presses on in his life of faith despite the daily temptation to doubt and complain. Especially in the life of Abraham, we have seen clear evidence that his faith and justification were not confined to one event in his life but were the product of a whole life of faith and obedience that finally allowed God to bless him with final justification.

Since most of the examples mentioned in Hebrews 11 are of individual people who we know led exemplary lives of faith and obedience, we might assume that all the instances mentioned in Hebrews 11 fall in the same category. This is not the case. There is at least one instance of faith in Hebrews 11:29 regarding a group of people who as we know from later Old Testament accounts and New Testament commentaries, did not continue in faith. The verse reads, "By faith, the people passed through the Red Sea as on dry land; but

52 Evangelical R. C. Sproul, for example, although he should realize that the answer to this profound question is pivotal to the whole Reformed understanding of the gospel, offers only 1 John 2:19 as a support for the Reformed view. He does so without any exegesis of the verse or analysis of the context to back up his claim (*Chosen By God*, pp. 180-181). Sproul and other Evangelicals, wittingly or unwittingly, place themselves in opposition to the whole weight of traditional Christian understanding of this issue, as well as to most other Protestant denominations. In contrast, the Council of Trent, Session 6, Canon 23 states: "If anyone shall say that a man once justified can sin no more, nor lose grace, and that therefore he who falls and sins was never truly justified...let him be anathema." Augustine, in *Admonition and Grace*, contradicts the Reformed view: "But if someone already regenerate and justified should, of his own will, relapse into his evil life, certainly that man cannot say: 'I have not received'; because he lost the grace he received from God and by his own free choice went to evil" (PL 6, 9; JR 1944).

when the Egyptians tried to do so, they were drowned." Here it is clear that "the people," not just Moses, had faith in God and thus were able to cross the Red Sea. Accounts in Exodus and Numbers tell us that close to or over a million Jews crossed the Red sea.[53]

Although Paul, by picking a particular cross section of the entire forty years that Israel was in the wilderness, can speak in glowing terms about one incident of faith on a mass scale, Paul gives a further commentary on these same Israelites that is not so flattering. In 1 Corinthians 10:1-5 Paul writes:

> For I do not want you to be ignorant of the fact, brothers, that our forefathers were all under the cloud and that *they all passed through the sea*. They were all baptized into Moses in the cloud and *in the sea*. They all ate the same spiritual food and drank the same spiritual drink; for they drank from the spiritual rock that accompanied them, and that rock was Christ. Nevertheless, God was not pleased with *most of them*; their bodies were scattered over the desert.

We understand that Paul, by specifying, "they all passed through the sea," is beginning his analysis from the crossing of the Red Sea. Once in the desert, however, the Jews began to rebel. Forty years later, virtually none of the original one million people who crossed the Red Sea entered the promise land. Only two of the one million, Joshua and Caleb, along with all the children twenty years old and younger, were worthy enough in God's eyes to enter.[54] Hence Paul, when he says above "God was not pleased with *most* of them," refers to everyone except two people out of a million or more. It is significant, then, that Paul uses this account to warn the Corinthians that though they have started out well in the faith, this does not mean that they will continue in the faith. Their good start does not mean a battle already won. Paul specifies this in verses 11-12: "These things happened to them [the Old Testament Jews]

---

53 Numbers 1:46 gives the total amount of men at 603,550. This does not include women and children, who would bring the total population well over one million.

54 cf., Numbers 14:20-45; Hebrews 3:18.

as examples and were written down as warnings for us...So, if you think you are standing firm, be careful that you don't fall."

In other places also Paul shows us most of the people who crossed the Red Sea ended up in unbelief and judgment. In Hebrews 3:16-18 he writes:

> Who were they who heard and rebelled? Were they not *all those Moses led out of Egypt?* And with whom was he angry for forty years? Was it not with those who sinned, whose bodies fell in the desert? And to whom did God swear that they would never enter his rest if not to those who *disobeyed*? So we see that they were not able to enter, *because of unbelief.*

The importance for the present discussion of this apparent anomaly between Hebrews 11:29 and Hebrews 3:16-18 is to show that an individual or group can at one moment have a very genuine faith and be pleasing to God, yet at the next moment can fall from faith and end up unjustified. Since Paul is assuring us that the faith of all the people and groups he mentions was faith that "pleased God" (Hebrews 11:6), it is clear that the subsequent unbelief of the same people does not mean that they never had genuine faith from the beginning. It can only mean that they lost the sincere faith they once enjoyed and subsequently lost their justification. This again is clear evidence that *faith alone* cannot save. Through disobedience, and despite their sincere faith, the Hebrews of the Exodus lost their salvation. Moreover, this example shows that the faith that justifies comes not in a moment of imputation but in a process that must be as strong at the end as it was at the beginning.

Are We Eternally Secure?

An Analysis of Romans 8:38-39 and John 10:28-29

In light of the foregoing passages which indicate that some people who were once justified could fall from that state, we must now investigate other passages that various Protestant denominations use to teach that the Christian cannot fall from salvation once he is justified. Afterward, we will analyze other New Testament passages that indeed teach that a Christian can fall from justification.

Romans 8:38-39

In Romans 8:38-39, Paul writes:

> For I am convinced that neither death nor life, neither angels nor demons, neither the present nor the future, nor any powers, neither height nor depth, nor anything else in all creation, will be able to separate us from the love of God that is in Christ Jesus our Lord.

In interpreting this passage, many Evangelical theologians assert that Paul teaches that the individual who has been justified cannot fall from his salvation. He is said to be "eternally secure." Nothing can take away his salvation once he has been imputed with the righteousness of Christ, whether the cause is sin, loss of faith, apostasy, or anything else. Since Paul in Romans 8:38-39 appears to argue so strongly and pervasively against any infringement upon salvation, many Evangelicals use this passage frequently to support the notion of eternal security. Several facets of the passage preclude such a teaching, however.

First, of the ten items Paul says cannot separate us from the love of God, all of them, without exception, are forces external to the individual. Death and life, angels and demons, present and future, powers, height and depth, nor any creature,[55] are things that God has created and over which the individual has no control. He

[55] The NIV translation "nor anything else in all creation" in Romans 8:39 is more literally rendered as "nor any other creature" or "nor any other created thing." The word "creature" or "creation" is from the Greek κτίσις which is also used by Paul in Romans 8:19, 20, 21, 22; 2 Cor. 5:17; Gal. 6:16; Col. 1:15, 23 to refer either to the created world or to a created being. Some supporters of "eternal security" attempt to make κτίσις refer to the individual Christian, even though the other nine items in Romans 8:38-39 are all external to the individual (e.g., John MacArthur, "Grace to You" radio broadcast, May 3, 1996). This interpretation fails to see both the universal context that Paul uses in Romans 8:38-39, and the global significance of the word κτίσις. It also fails to consider the many times Paul states unequivocally that the individual Christian can fall from his salvation.

cannot control whether he is born or whether he will die; he cannot control the acts of angels or demons; he cannot control time nor the cosmos; he cannot control any other created thing or being external to himself. In Romans 8:35 Paul adds seven other items: trouble, hardship, persecution, famine, nakedness, danger, and sword. These also are external forces, and since Paul suffered most of them himself, thus he can testify that none of them stopped Christ from loving him. In other words, God has made the process of salvation so secure that he will allow no external force to disrupt its progress and completion. The individual has the guarantee, speaking colloquially, that God will not "pull the rug out from under him" by failing to provide the grace of salvation. God is not a capricious tyrant who offers salvation one day, but decides the next day to withdraw his offer, nor will he allow anything in the universe to curtail his plan. The God of the Old and New Testament is not like the gods of Roman or Greek mythology who are fickle and fight amongst themselves. He is a solid rock that cannot be moved.

Yet Paul, while portraying God as immovable, does not include *internal* forces — forces within the individual — among those things that cannot separate the individual from the love of God. Nowhere does Paul teach that the individual cannot choose to take himself out of the salvation plan of God. Moreover, Paul does not include things such as fornication, adultery, idolatry, and stealing, in the list of Romans 8:38-39 (i.e., Paul does not say, "Neither fornication, nor adultery, neither idolatry nor stealing...can separate us from the love of God") simply because he has stated previously in passages like 1 Corinthians 6:9-10, Galatians 5:21, and Ephesians 5:5 that these sins are the very reason one could lose their salvation. God is faithful and will let no external force disrupt the salvation process, but whether the individual who claims to follow God will himself continue to be faithful is not a question Paul addresses in Romans 8:38-39.

It is clear from surrounding passages that Paul does not believe that the individual is immune from falling away. For example, two chapters earlier, addressing baptized Christians in Romans 6:12-13 he says, "Therefore, brothers, we have an obligation — but it is not to the sinful nature, to live according to it. For if you live according to the sinful nature, you will *die*; but if by the Spirit you put to death the misdeeds of the body, you will live." The *dying* Paul has in view here is the same as that in Romans 6:23: "for the wages of sin is death." Later, in Romans 11:22, Paul writes to the Gentile Christians: "Consider, therefore, the kindness and sternness of God: sternness to those who fell, but kindness to you, provided that you continue in his kindness. Otherwise, you also will be cut off."

Second, Paul's choice of language in Romans 8:31-39 de-emphasizes the individual and emphasizes the community of believers. We see this in his use of "we," "us," and "ours" throughout the text. For example, in Romans 8:31 Paul says, "What, then, shall *we* say in response to this? If God is for *us*, who can be against *us*." Similarly, in verse 32 he says, "...but gave him up for *us* all...graciously give us all things"; and in verse 34, "...and is also interceding for *us*. Who shall separate *us* from the love of Christ"; and in verse 37, "...*we* are more than conquerors through him who loved *us*." This is typical of New Testament language that categorizes the security of salvation within the confines of the universal community of Christians, e.g., the Church, which is conscious of both its relationship with the Lord and that the Lord will not disown his Church. God does not, however, guarantee salvation to groups and individuals within the ecclesial community should they fall into serious and unrepentant sin.[56]

Third, in Romans 8:38-39 Paul does not speak specifically of individual salvation, rather, he specifies the "love of God." We also see this in verse 35 where Paul says, "Who shall separate us from the *love of Christ*." The focus is on the "love of God" or "love of Christ" as that which issues forth from the Godhead to the community of believers. In other words, since God will fulfill his eternal plan dependably and with integrity, we can always depend on having the love of God. God does not love us one day and then

---

[56] In light of this ever present possibility of our falling away, we should also remark that Luther's translation of Romans 8:31, "If God is for *me*, who is against *me*" distorts the universal perspective from which Paul makes his comments. See chapter 9 for further details on Luther's translation of this text. This critique of Luther's translation is not to say that predestination does not include the individual along with community, but only that Luther's translation, which was an attempt to give the individual certainty of his salvation, reads too much into the passage.

hate us the next day. As Paul says succinctly in 2 Timothy 2:13, "If we are faithless, he will remain faithful, for he cannot disown himself." God is always faithful to his plan of salvation. He always continues to love us, so much so that he gave his only begotten Son that whoever believes in him should not perish but have eternal life (John 3:16). Wisdom 1:24 records, "For you love all things that exist, and detest none of the things that you have made, for you would not have made anything if you had hated it." By the same token, however, Paul warns us in 2 Timothy 2:12, "If we disown him, he will also disown us." Paul clearly puts the onus on the individual, whom God has left free to take himself out of God's grace and love, yet Paul makes it equally clear that God will never capriciously withhold his love and grace from those who seek it.

John 10:28-29

In John 10:28-29 Jesus says, "I give them eternal life, and they shall never perish; no one can snatch them out of my hand. My Father, who has given them to me, is greater than all, no one can snatch them out of my Father's hand. I and the Father are one." Protestants who believe in eternal security feel that this passage teaches that once a Christian has received eternal life he cannot lose it. In the words of one author:

> The simplest, shortest description of the perseverance of the saints is: Once saved, always saved. It is one of the grandest thoughts in the Bible: Once you believe, you can never be lost, you can never go to hell. Christ will always be your Savior. It is to get your eternal destiny settled once and for all so that you never have to worry about it.[57]

If true, what wonderful comfort these words offer the individual. No need to worry about his eternal destiny. He may question the salvation of others, but he has no need to question his own. If false, however, this teaching represents one of the most deceptive strategies of the devil, since it gives a false sense of security to

---

57 Edwin H. Palmer. *The Five Points of Calvinism*, 1972, p. 68.

the individual and a license to fall into whatever sin may come his way, all the while thinking neither that God will judge him nor that his eternal destiny hangs in the balance.

In reference to Jesus giving eternal life to the sheep in John 10:28-29, advocates of eternal security also commonly say that "if eternal life can be lost, then it is not eternal." This kind of argumentation is quite naïve. It confuses the possessor with what he possesses. One can possess eternal life at one time and lose it at another without changing the quality or nature of eternal life. For example, one can possess a license to drive a car. If he drives recklessly, the state that issued the license can take it away. However, the revocation of licenses does not change the quality or nature of a driver's license. Anyone else who possesses a driver's license will be able legally to drive on the road, provided of course that he, too, obeys the rules. Similarly, if one's name is included in a will, we can safely say that he "possesses" the inheritance. It is just a matter of time until he will reap the full benefit of the inheritance. This does not mean, however, that it is impossible to disinherit him if the benefactor judges his behavior to warrant such action. Likewise, if God disinherits us from eternal life — a possibility, as we have seen earlier, which Paul does not hesitate to warn us if we sin and do not repent (cf., Gal. 5:21; 1 Cor. 6:9-10) — this does not change the meaning of eternal life but merely defines how one can lose it. Peter tells us in 1 Peter 1:4 that the inheritance itself is incorruptible, and he also tells us in 1:5 that our possession of it is through "faith." But the individual, Peter tells us in 2 Peter 1:5-10, must cultivate this faith with good works; if he does not, he is "blind" and cannot "make his calling and election sure." According to Peter, we can possess the inheritance through faith but then lose the inheritance through faithlessness. In 2 Peter 2:20-22 he writes:

> If they have escaped the corruption of the world by knowing our Lord and Savior Jesus Christ and are again entangled in it and overcome, they are worse off at the end than they were at the beginning. It would have been better for them not to have known the way of righteousness, than to have known it and then to turn their backs on the sacred command that was passed on to them. Of them the proverbs are true: 'A dog returns to its vomit,' and, 'a sow that is washed goes back to her wallowing in the mud.'

The belief in eternal security began with John Calvin (1509-1564).[58] Calvin writes of John 10:28-29: "This is a remarkable passage, teaching us that the salvation of all the elect is as certain as God's power is invincible...Therefore we infer that Christ's saying indicates that the elect are firmly certain of their salvation."[59] Calvin, as he often does, takes a passage that teaches the general security of the elect and transposes it into a passage that teaches that he and those who believe they are saved possess the *certainty* of salvation. He translates mere belief that they are saved into the absolute decree of God that they are predestined.[60] The passage, however, does not teach that the individual himself can know absolutely that he is one of the elect. Even if the passage were teaching predestination, all we could extract from it is that no one can thwart God's decree of election. John 10:28-29 does not discuss how the election is worked out, or who among those on earth are elected.

---

58 The early Fathers of the Church, as well as the medieval theologians, never taught the concept of eternal security. Augustine, for example, taught that God could regenerate an individual without causing him to persevere (*City of God*, PL 41, 10, 8). We cover Augustine's and Aquinas's views of predestination, perseverance, and free will more thoroughly in chapter 7.

59 *Commentary on John*, op. cit., p. 273.

60 The Council of Trent rejected this correlation in Canon 15 of Session 6: "If anyone shall say that a man who is born again and justified is bound by faith to believe that he is assuredly in the number of the predestined: let him be anathema." In the Reformed apologetic, various tactics are attempted to support its doctrine of eternal security. For example, in refutation to the Protestant Arminian doctrine which believes that Christians can fall from salvation by their own free will, Sproul argues that since the saints in heaven, incapable of sinning even though they have a free will, cannot fall from salvation, then the same dynamic between eternal security and free will could also be compatible on earth, and thus the Arminian position proves too much and has nothing left to distinguish its belief (*Chosen By God*, p. 177). This is a faulty comparison. It goes without saying that God can sustain man's free will in heaven or on earth. By the same token, however, we can pose the question as to why God himself cannot sin even though he has a free will. The reason he cannot sin is that it is not in his nature to do so. Similarly, when men are glorified they also "participate in the divine nature" which reaches full fruition in heaven (cf., 2 Peter 1:4; 1 John 3:2; Hebrews 8:10-13). It is because they are thus divinized that they cannot sin, not because there is any difficulty or discrepancy in the notion of free will, or that man cannot fall from salvation. "Created in a state of holiness, man was destined to be fully "divinized" by God in glory" (CC, Section 398).

Calvinistic and Lutheran perspectives on this verse diverge, as we can show by this quote from renowned Lutheran commentator, R. C. H. Lenski: "However weak the sheep are, under Jesus they are perfectly safe. Yet a believer may after all be lost (15:6). Our certainty of eternal salvation is not absolute. While no foe of ours is able to snatch us from our Shepherd's hand, we ourselves may turn from him and may perish willfully of our own accord."[61] Rather than reading into the verse one's elective theology and concluding that one's own salvation is certain, this author is careful to read the passage in its context and does not allow himself to say more that what the passage actually teaches. Since Jesus opened the context by speaking in John 10:1-10 of the robber who enters the sheepgate by stealth to steal away the sheep, and in John 10:14-16 of the hired hand who does not protect the sheep when the wolf appears, it is obvious that Jesus is emphasizing *his* faithfulness to the sheep in contrast to the evil intent and carelessness of others. He is not attempting to teach that the individual sheep know absolutely that they themselves will remain in the fold. As Paul taught in Romans 8:38-39, John teaches in John 10:1-16 that Jesus will allow no outside force to snatch these sheep out of his hand.[62] This passage, however, does not deny the possibility of internal forces within the sheep themselves that could eventually turn them away. As Lenski has pointed out above, however, many other passages in the teaching of Jesus *do* entertain the question of internal forces that draw one away from God and make it quite clear that such a falling away is a real possibility.

We must also realize that Jesus is speaking to Jews who consistently showed their stubbornness and hardness of heart. Other passages make it clear that Jesus experiencing repeated rejection of God's message to Jews, knew that God had blinded them so that

---

[61] *Commentary on John*, op. cit. p. 756.

[62] Other like passages are Hebrews 13:5-6, "Keep your lives free from the love of money and be content with what you have, because God has said, 'Never will I leave you; never will I forsake you.' So we say with confidence, 'The Lord is my helper; I will not be afraid. What can man do to me?'" and Jude 24, "To him who is able to keep you from falling and to present you before his glorious presence without fault and with great joy..." These verses teach only that God will faithfully help us to the end to reach salvation; they certainly leave open the possibility, as do the contexts in which they are contained, that the individual himself may refuse God's help.

they could not understand the gospel (Matthew 13:11-17). Hence, they were not sheep of his "fold" and could not understand his voice. Jesus remarks about the inability of certain sheep to understand him and the ability of others to understand (John 10:1-5, 16, 26). Though some Jews did understand and follow Jesus (Matthew 13:11), the nation as a whole had rejected Jesus, and Jesus in turn is rejecting the Jewish nation. He will turn to "other sheep that are not of this sheep pen" and "bring them also." Jesus is referring, of course, to the Gentile nations (Matthew 8:11-12). Hence, we see that in John 10 Jesus is speaking in very general categories. He is not teaching that any one individual can be certain that he will be saved. The individual can be certain of God's plan of salvation, and that if he is faithful to God that God will allow no one to snatch him out of it, but he cannot be certain that he himself will remain faithful. If he could be certain, then Paul's warning in 2 Timothy 2:12-13, and many other passages, simply have no relevant meaning.

Scripture's Testimony:

We Can Fall From Salvation

Though some tout eternal security as one of the "grandest thoughts in the Bible," careful exegetical scrutiny reveals surprisingly very little scriptural evidence for such a teaching. Passages that are construed to teach eternal security are invariably those that speak to God's general plan of predestination,[63] or passages like Romans 8:38-39 and John 10:28-29 studied above. Other than that, the Bible has precious little suggesting a doctrine of eternal security. In reality, next to the person of Christ, Scripture attends to no topic more than the warning to Christians not to fall away from the faith and lose their salvation. In fact, every book in the New Testament, with the possible exception of Philemon, in some way or other suspends the outcome of our eternal destiny based on the duration and degree of our faith and obedience. Scripture offers absolutely overwhelming evidence that a believer can fall from the salvation he once possessed.

[63] All the relevant passages concerning predestination will be studied in chapter 7.

The Scriptural passages which teach that a Christian can fall from the salvation he once possessed are so clear they hardly need explanation. Their impact is greatest when we see them amassed together. To prove the point made above, i.e., that our salvation is not certain until our last breath, we will now demonstrate this teaching with a representative sample from each book of the New Testament so that the reader can see this consistent and overwhelming message in Scripture. (This is not to say, however, that the Old Testament does not contain just as much or more evidence on the same topic). Along the way, we will analyze certain passages that need more elaboration. Other chapters of this book also reference and discuss some of these passages.

Matthew

7:21-23 — "Not everyone who says to me, 'Lord, Lord,' will enter the kingdom of heaven, but only he who does the will of my Father who is in heaven. Many will say to me on that day, 'Lord, Lord, did we not prophesy in your name, and in your name drive our demons and perform many miracles? Then I will tell them plainly, I never knew you. Away from me, you evildoers."

10:22, 28, 33 — "All men will hate you because of me, but he who stands firm to the end will be saved...Do not be afraid of those who kill the body but cannot kill the soul. Rather, be afraid of the one who can destroy both soul and body in hell...But whoever disowns me before men I will disown him before my Father in heaven."

24:12-13 — "Because of the increase of wickedness, the love of most will grow cold, but he who stands firm to the end will be saved."[64]

---

[64] The phrase literally reads, "But the one who endured to the end, this one will be saved." This translation emphasizes both the focus on the *individual* who must persevere and the aorist of the substantivized participle which refers to a completed action of endurance that can provide salvation.

Mark

9:43 — "If your hand causes you to sin, cut it off. It is better for you to enter life maimed than with two hands to go into hell, where the fire never goes out."

10:21-23 — "'One thing you lack,' he said. 'Go, sell everything you have and give to the poor, and you will have treasure in heaven. Then come, follow me.' At this the man's face fell. He went away sad because he had great wealth. Jesus looked around and said to his disciples, 'How hard it is for the rich to enter the kingdom of God!'"

13:22 — "For false Christs and false prophets will appear and perform signs and miracles to deceive the elect — if that were possible."[65]

---

[65] The phrase "if possible" (εἰ δυνατόν) is often interpreted to teach that the "elect," in this context, could not be deceived and therefore cannot lose salvation. However, we do not know from the text whether to understand "elect" in the general or in the specific sense. The general sense would allow for deception among them. Similar usages of the word "elect" are 2 Timothy 2:10 in which Paul says, "I endure everything for the sake of the elect, that they too may obtain the salvation that is in Christ Jesus...," or, 2 Peter 1:10, "be all the more eager to make your calling and election sure," both leaving an open-endedness to the election. Second, to understand an elect that could not be deceived would not correlate with Jesus's statement in the same context (Matthew 24:13) that "he who endures to the end will be saved." If it is a foregone conclusion in this context that the elect will be saved, Jesus would not restrict salvation to those who "endure to the end" which would subsequently nullify the conditionality and impact of his solemn warning. Third, we must understand the statement in verse 25, "See, I have told you ahead of time" as a forewarning to the elect not to be deceived by the false prophets. Thus, the elect will not be deceived, not because it is impossible to deceive them, but because they have been given adequate warning which gives them knowledge on how to spot the false prophet. Hence, the phrase "if possible" should not be misconstrued to teach eternal security; rather, it simply shows how strong a challenge the faithful will face in the magnitude and pervasiveness of the false prophet's attempt to deceive — such a challenge that, according to Matthew 24:22, "If those days had not been cut short, no one would be saved..."

Luke

8:13 — "Those on the rock are the ones who receive the word with joy when they hear it, but they have no root. They believe for a while, but in time of testing they fall away."

12:43-46 — "It will be good for that servant to whom the master finds doing so...But suppose the servant says to him, My master is taking a long time in coming and he begins to beat the men servants and maid servants, and eat and drink and get drunk. The master of that servant will come on a day when he does not expect him and an hour he is not aware. He will cut him to pieces and assign him a place with the unbelievers."

John

12:47-48 — "As for the person who hears my words but does not keep them...there is a judge for the one who rejects me and does not accept my words; the very word I spoke will condemn him at the last day."

15:6 — "If anyone does not remain in me, he is like a branch that is thrown away and withers; such branches are picked up, thrown into the fire and burned."[66]

Acts

13:43, 46 — "...Paul and Barnabas, who talked with them and urged them to continue in the grace of God...Since you reject it and do not consider yourselves worthy of eternal life, we now turn to the Gentiles."

---

[66] This passage assumes that the person who falls away was already "in" Christ, that is, as a genuine branch of the vine, not a pseudo-branch or branch that was never connected to the vine. Rather, Jesus pictures a branch, once a healthy part of the vine, that subsequently withered. Once withered, it falls off the vine and is thrown in the fire.

20:29-30 — "I know that after I leave, savage wolves will come in among you and will not spare the flock. Even from your own number men will arise and distort the truth in order to draw away disciples after them. So be on your guard. Remember that for three years I never stopped warning each of you night and day with tears."

Romans

2:6 — "God will give to each person according to what he has done. To those who by persistence in doing good seek glory, honor and immortality, he will give eternal life. But for those who are self-seeking and who reject the truth and follow evil, there will be wrath and indignation."

8:12-13 — "Therefore, brothers, we have an obligation — but it is not to the sinful nature, to live according to it. For if you live according to the sinful nature, you will die..."[67]

11:20-22 — "But they were broken off because of unbelief, and you stand by faith. Do not be arrogant but be afraid. For if God did not spare the natural branches, he will not spare you either. Consider therefore the kindness and sternness of God; sternness to those who fell, but kindness to you, provided that you continue in his kindness. Otherwise you also will be cut off."[68]

---

[67] Although Paul may have physical death in view, as noted in the death of Christians for abusing the Lord's Body and Blood (1 Corinthians 11:30), his general usage of death includes both physical and spiritual aspects, and the two aspects are often interchangeable (e.g., Romans 1:32; 5:12-21; 6:21-23; 7:5-24; 8:2-6; 2 Cor. 2:16; 7:10 (cf., James 1:15; 5:20; 1 John 5:16-17).

[68] Some advance the argument that Paul is speaking only of cutting off the Gentiles as a group rather than individuals within the Gentile group. We submit that although the context certainly addresses the distinction between Jews and Gentiles as respective representatives of God's blessings, it is not limited to such a theme. Paul, for example, makes this clear in Romans 11:17 by revealing that only "some" of the Jews, out of the nation of Jews, were cut off for unbelief (*viz.*, "But if some [Greek: τινες] of the branches were broken off..."). The word "some" distinguishes those in Israel who were unfaithful from those who remained faithful. Paul says as much in Romans 11:4 by specifying that even in Israel there were 7,000 individuals who did not fall away.

1 Corinthians

3:17 — "If anyone destroys God's temple, God will destroy him."[69]

4:5 — "My conscience is clear, but that does not make me innocent. It is the Lord who judges me. Therefore, judge nothing before the appointed time; wait till the Lord comes. He will bring to light what is hidden in darkness and will expose the motives of men's hearts."[70]

6:8-9 — "You yourselves cheat and do wrong, and you do this to your brothers. Do you not know that the wicked will not inherit the kingdom of God?"[71]

---

[69] Paul uses a play on words here. The Greek word for "destroy" is φθείρει which appears seven times in the New Testament. The common meaning is "corrupt" (e.g., 1 Cor. 15:33; 2 Cor. 7:2; 11:3; Eph. 4:22; Jude 10; Rev. 19:2). Lexically, φθείρε refers to "destroy, ruin, corrupt, spoil" in which the meaning of "destroy" or "to be doomed to destruction" is reserved to 1 Cor. 3:17 (Walter Bauer, *A Greek English Lexicon of the New Testament and Other Early Christian Literature*, eds. Gingrich and Danker, p. 857). The cognate φθορά, appearing ten times in the New Testament, also shows the interconnection between "corruption" and "destruction" (e.g., Rom. 8:21; Gal. 6:8; Col. 2:22; 2 Peter 2:12). The preponderant usage in the LXX is "destruction" (e.g., Ex. 10:15; Lev. 19:27; Deut. 34:7; 2 Sam. 20:20; 1 Chr. 20:1; Job 15:32; Isa. 24:3-4; 54:16; Jer. 3:19). Ultimately, Paul has eternal destruction in view in 1 Cor. 3:17.

[70] Some attempt to limit Paul's self-imposed warning to how God will evaluate Paul's behavior in his apostolic ministry. In other words, it is postulated that Paul may be judged by God for unseen faults in his ministry, but Paul's salvation is totally secure. We would maintain that although Paul's ministry is certainly in view, this does not mean that Paul is excluded from eternal judgment if his ministerial behavior is sinful. If not, this would contradict his own dictum in 1 Cor. 3:17 that ministers who destroy the temple will be destroyed by God, or the inclusion of himself in 1 Cor. 9:27-10:13 of the warning concerning falling away from the faith. The "praise" received in 1 Cor. 4:5 would apply only to those whose "motives" are judged righteous by God. See also Hebrews 4:11-13.

[71] Since Paul says in verse 11 that they "were" like the sinners of the world but they are now cleansed, some have attempted to make Paul mean that only unbelievers will not inherit the kingdom, but that believers are totally secure. This is a distortion of the text since Paul is clearly directing the warning of "not inheriting the kingdom" to those Christians who "cheat" and "do wrong" to their brothers.

9:27-10:6 — "No, I beat my body and make it my slave so that after I have preached to others, I myself will not be disqualified. For I do not want you to be ignorant of the fact, brothers, that our forefathers were all under the cloud and that they all passed through the sea. They were all baptized into Moses in the cloud and in the sea. They all ate the same spiritual food and drank the same spiritual drink; for they drank from the spiritual rock that accompanied them, and that rock was Christ. Nevertheless, God was not pleased with most of them; their bodies were scattered over the desert. Now these things occurred as examples to keep us from setting our hearts on evil things as they did."

10:11-12 — "These things happened to them as examples and were written down as warnings for us, on whom the fulfillment of the ages has come. So, if you think you are standing firm, be careful that you don't fall!"[72]

15:1-2 — "Now, brothers, I want to remind you of the gospel I preached to you, which you received and on which you have taken your stand. By this gospel you are saved, if you hold firmly to the word I preached to you. Otherwise, you have believed in vain."[73]

---

[72] As noted above, Paul includes himself in the warning of falling away as he begins the section in 1 Cor. 9:27 by saying he could become "disqualified for the prize" in the context of the warning in 10:12 about falling away. Some claim that the "disqualification" in 9:27 refers only to Paul being barred from ministerial work if and when he fell into sin or became unfaithful to the Christian cause. Not only does the context not support such a conclusion, the New Testament's use of the Greek word ἀδόκιμος (NIV: "disqualified for the prize"), in almost every case, is in contexts of apostasy from the faith (cf., 2 Cor. 13:5-7; 2 Tim. 3:8; Heb. 6:8; Tit. 1:16; Rom. 1:28).

[73] This is a Greek conditional sentence in which the protasis εἰ κατέχετε ("if you hold fast") conditions the apodosis δι᾽ οὗ καὶ σῴζεσθε ("through which also you are saved") showing that the salvation is dependent upon holding firm the gospel. This condition is reinforced by a second condition ἐκτος εἰ μὴ εἰκῆ ἐπιστεύσατε ("except unless in vain you believed"), with an implied apodosis.

2 Corinthians

5:20- 6:2 — "...We implore you on Christ's behalf: Be reconciled to God...As God's fellow workers we urge you not to receive God's grace in vain. For he says, 'In the time of my favor I heard you, and in the day of salvation I helped you.' I tell you, now is the time of God's favor, now is the day of salvation."[74]

11:3 — "But I am afraid that just as Eve was deceived by the serpent's cunning, your minds may somehow be led astray from your sincere and pure devotion to Christ."

12:21-13:5 — "I am afraid that when I come again my God will humble me before you, and I will be grieved over many who have sinned earlier and have not repented of the impurity, sexual sin and debauchery in which they have indulged...Examine yourselves to see whether you are in the faith; test yourselves. Do you not realize that Christ Jesus is in you — unless of course, you fail the test?"[75]

Galatians

5:19-21 — "The acts of the sinful nature are obvious...I warn you, as I did before, that those who live like this will not inherit the kingdom of God."

6:7-9 — "Do not be deceived: God cannot be mocked. A man reaps what he sows. The one who sows to please his sinful nature, from that nature will reap destruction; the one who sows to please the Spirit, from the Spirit will reap eternal life."[76]

---

[74] See chapter 5 for a detailed explanation of this passage.

[75] The NIV phrase "fail the test" is from the Greek ἀδόκιμος, noted above in f. 72 to refer to apostasy. Since 2 Cor. 12:20-21 includes this warning in the context of "quarreling, jealousy, anger, factions...disorder,"..."impurity, sexual sin and debauchery," and the reiteration of the warning against sin in 13:2, "failing the test," then, must be in reference to the possibility of falling from salvation due to sin.

[76] See chapter 5 for a detailed explanation of both these passages.

Ephesians

5:5-6 — "For of this you can be sure: No immoral, impure or greedy person — such a man is an idolator — has any inheritance in the kingdom of Christ and of God. Let no one deceive you with empty words, for because of such things God's wrath comes on those who are disobedient. Therefore do not be partners with them."

Philippians

3:10-16 — "I want to know Christ and the power of his resurrection...and so, somehow, to attain to the resurrection from the dead. Not that I have already obtained all this, or have already been made perfect, but I press on to take hold of that for which Christ Jesus took hold of me. Brothers, I do not consider myself yet to have taken hold of it...all of us who are mature should take such a view of things...Only let us live up to what we have already attained."[77]

Colossians

1:21-23 — "Once you were alienated from God and were enemies in your minds because of your evil behavior. But now he has reconciled you by Christ's physical body through death to present you holy in his sight, without blemish and free from accusation — if you continue in your faith, established and firm, not moved from the hope held out in the gospel."[78]

---

[77] Paul uses two conditional statements: (1) εἴ πως καταντήσω (literally: "if somehow I may attain to"); and (2) εἰ και καταλάβω (literally: "if indeed I may lay hold of"), followed by a series of statements which emphasize that he has not yet attained to his goal.

[78] This is one of the strongest and clearest conditional statements written by Paul. The conditional clause εἴ λε ἐπιμένετε τῇ πίστει ("if indeed ye continue in the faith") is intensified by the addition of "λε" and made to be a permanent condition by the inclusion of two participles, τεθεμελιωμένοι (literally: "having been established") and μὴ μετακινούμενοι (literally: "not being moved away"). "Faith" is understood as objective, i.e., 'the Christian faith,' rather than subjective.

1 Thessalonians

4:1-8 — "Finally, brothers, we instructed you how to live in order to please God, as in fact you are living...it is God's will that you should be sanctified: that you should avoid sexual immorality...the Lord will punish men for all such sins, as we have already told you and warned you...Therefore, he who rejects this instruction does not reject man but God, who gives you his Holy Spirit."

2 Thessalonians

2:13-15 — "...because from the beginning God chose you to be saved through the sanctifying work of the Spirit and through belief in the truth...So then, brothers, stand firm and hold to the teachings we passed on to you, whether by word of mouth or by letter."

3:6,14 — "In the name of the Lord Jesus Christ, we command you, brothers, to keep away from every brother who is idle and does not live according to the teaching you received from us...If anyone does not obey our instruction in this letter, take special note of him. Do not associate with him in order that he may feel ashamed."

1 Timothy

4:1 — "The Spirit clearly says that in later times some will abandon the faith and follow deceiving spirits and things taught by demons."

5:15 — "Some have in fact already turned away to follow Satan."

6:10-19 — "For the love of money is the root of all kinds of evil. Some people, eager for money, have wandered from the faith and pierced themselves with many griefs....Take hold of the eternal life to which you were called when you made your good confession...command those who are rich in this present world not to be arrogant nor to put their hope in wealth, which is so uncertain, but to put their hope in God...in this way they will lay up treasure for themselves as a firm foundation for the coming age, so that they may take hold of the life that is truly life."

6:20-21 — "Turn away from godless chatter and the opposing ideas of what is falsely called knowledge, which some have professed and in so doing have wandered from the faith."

2 Timothy

1:15 — "You know that everyone in the province of Asia has deserted me, including Phygelus and Hermogenes."

2:12 — "If we endure we will also reign with him. If we disown him he will also disown us."

2:17 — "Their teaching will spread like gangrene. Among them are Hymenaeus and Philetus, who have wandered away from the truth. They say that the resurrection has already taken place and destroy the faith of some."[79]

4:10 — "for Demas, because he loved this present world, has deserted me and has gone to Thessalonica...Alexander the metal worker did me a great deal of harm. The Lord will repay him for what he has done."

4:16 — "At my first defense, no one came to my support, but everyone deserted me."

Titus

1:16 — "They claim to know God, but by their actions they deny him."

3:10 — "Warn a divisive person once, and then warn him a second time. After that, have nothing to do with him. You may be sure that such a man is warped and sinful; he is self-condemned."

[79] These passages in the letter to Timothy are some of the only times that Paul mentions by name those who have fallen away. This specificity reinforces to the reader that apostasy really does happen — and to people that they did not suspect previously.

Hebrews

2:1 — "We must pay more careful attention, therefore, to what we have heard, so that we do not drift away.[80] For if the message spoken by angels was binding, and every violation and disobedience received its just punishment, how shall we escape if we ignore such a great salvation."[81]

3:1, 6 — "Therefore, holy brothers, who share in the heavenly calling, fix your thoughts on Jesus, the apostle and high priest whom we confess...And we are his house, if we hold on to our courage and the hope of which we boast."[82]

3:12-14 — "See to it, brothers, that none of you has a sinful, unbelieving heart that turns away from the living God. But encourage one another daily, as long as it is called Today so that none of you

---

80 The phrase, "so that" is from the Greek μήποτε which carries the meaning of "lest," i.e., "lest you drift away;" 3:12 — "lest anyone has a sinful, unbelieving heart that turns away from the living God;" 4:1 — "lest the promise of entering...you fall short of it." The usage of such "lest" clauses is common in the book of Hebrews. Other usages include ἵνα μή (e.g., Heb. 3:13 — "lest any of you be hardened"; 4:11 — "lest any man fall after the same;" 6:12 — "lest you become lazy"; 12:3 — "lest you grow weary"; 12:13 — "lest the lame be turned aside"). There are also many uses of μή (e.g., 3:8, 15; 4:7 — "harden not your hearts"; 4:2 — "not combined with faith"; 10:35 — "do not throw away your confidence"; 12:15 — "that no one misses the grace of God"; 12:25 — "do not refuse him who speaks").

81 Paul uses the third person plural "we" throughout his warnings against falling away. In this passage he uses it four times. This shows that he includes himself in the warnings. Hence, the audience to whom he is writing is all Christians, not just those who have made a profession of faith.

82 Here, the address is to "holy brothers," not people of quasi-Christian sentiment. The word "if" introduces a Greek fifth class conditional sentence in a present general supposition. The apodosis contains the present indicative ("whose house we are") and the protasis contains ἐὰν with the subjunctive verb κατάσχωμεν ("if...we hold on to"). Of the six classes of Greek conditionals, this is one of the strongest. In both classical and koine Greek, it specifies, without any contingencies, that the apodosis cannot be or come true unless the protasis is satisfied. (See Smyth, Herbert W. *Greek Grammar* (Cambridge, MA: Harvard University Press, 1920, 1980), p. 528).

may be hardened by sin's deceitfulness. We have come to share in Christ if we hold firmly till the end the confidence we had at first.[83]

4:1 — "Therefore, since the promise of entering his rest still stands, let us be careful that none of you be found to have fallen short of it."

4:11-13 — "Let us, therefore, make every effort to enter that rest, so that no one will fall by following their example of disobedience...Nothing in all creation is hidden from God's sight. Everything is uncovered and laid bare before the eyes of him to whom we must give account."

4:14 — "Therefore...let us hold firmly to the faith we profess."

6:4-6 — "It is impossible for those who have once been enlightened, who have tasted the heavenly gift, who have shared in the Holy Spirit, who have tasted the goodness of the word of God and the powers of the coming age,[84] if they fall away, to be brought back to repentance, because to their loss they are crucifying the Son of God all over again and subjecting him to public disgrace."[85]

---

[83] The same conditional ἐὰν...κατάσχωμεν is used here as in 3:6, except that the condition is more intensive with the addition of ἐάνπερ ("if indeed").

[84] Here we see that Paul uses the word "taste" twice in this verse. It is from the Greek γεύομαι, appearing also in Hebrews 2:9 of Jesus who "might taste death for everyone," showing that Paul understands "tasting" as an actual partaking, not a superficial one. See also Matthew 16:28; Mark 9:1; Luke 9:27. Γεύομαι is sometimes used of "eating" (e.g., Acts 10:10; 20:11; 23:14).

[85] The reference to "impossibility" (Greek: ἀδύνατον, used also in Matt. 19:26; Rom. 8:3; Heb. 6:18; 10:4: 11:6; the latter verses showing Paul's understanding of the word), explicit here and implied in other parts of Hebrews, is very similar to the stipulation in Deuteronomy 29:19-20: "When such a person hears the words of this oath, he invokes a blessing on himself and therefore thinks, 'I will be safe, even though I persist in going my own way.' This will bring disaster on the watered land as well as the dry. The Lord will never be willing to forgive him; his wrath and zeal will burn against that man. All the curses written in this book will fall upon him, and the Lord will blot out his name from under heaven." The description in Hebrews 4:6 is very similar to that in Hebrews 10:26-27; 12:17 (see below).

6:11-12 — "We want each of you to show this same diligence to the very end, in order to make your hope sure. We do not want you to become lazy, but to imitate those who through faith and patience inherit what has been promised."

10:26-27 — "If we deliberately[86] keep on sinning after we have received the knowledge[87] of the truth, no sacrifice for sins is left, but only a fearful expectation of judgment and of raging fire that will consume the enemies of God."

10:35-38 — "So do not throw away your confidence; it will be richly rewarded. You need to persevere so that when you have done the will of God, you will receive what he has promised...And if he shrinks back, I will not be pleased with him."[88]

[86] From the Greek ἑκουσίως, appearing also in 1 Peter 5:2. Ecclesiasticus 5:4-7 states: "Do not say, 'I sinned, yet what has happened to me?' for the Lord is slow to anger. Do not be so confident of forgiveness that you add sin to sin. Do not say, 'His mercy is great, he will forgive the multitude of my sins,' and his anger will rest on sinners. Do not delay to turn back to the Lord, and do not postpone it from day to day; for suddenly the wrath of the Lord will come upon you, and at the time of punishment you will perish."

[87] See remarks on 2 Peter 2:20-22, f. 93, for more information on the meaning of "knowledge" in Hebrews and other New Testament passages.

[88] It is important to note that the verses preceding this warning (10:32-34) do not speak of superficial Christians who, as Jesus says in Luke 8:13, believe for awhile and then fall away at the first provocation. Paul describes them as "those who have received the light (Greek: φωτισθέντες, used also in Hebrews 6:4 as "enlightened"); who "stood your ground in a great contest in the face of suffering"; "publicly exposed to insult and persecution"; "sympathized with those in prison"; and "joyfully accepted the confiscation of your property." These are seasoned believers, nevertheless believers that receive the same warnings as new Christians. The remaining verse of the chapter, Hebrews 10:39, "But we are not of those who shrink back and are destroyed, but of those who believe and are saved" cannot be used to support the concept of eternal security. This would make no sense in light of what Paul has just said about the possibility of "shrinking back" in verse 38, "throwing away your confidence" in verse 35, and the "punishment" for deserting the truth in verse 27-29. Hebrews 10:39 is simply a challenge to his readers to remain a part of those who do not shrink back. It is similar to his challenge in Hebrews 6:9 issued after he had warned them of the possibility of falling away from the faith. He writes: "...we are confident of better things in your case — things that accompany salvation." Again, the challenge is to remain steadfast in the faith and perform the works associated with salvation, not that one is immune from falling away.

12:1, 3 — "Therefore, since we are surrounded by such a great cloud of witnesses, let us throw off everything that hinders and the sin that so easily entangles,[89] and let us run with perseverance the race marked out for us...Consider him who endured such opposition from sinful men, so that you will not grow weary and lose heart."

12:14-17 — "Make every effort to live in peace with all men and to be holy; without holiness no one will see the Lord. See to it that no one misses the grace of God and that no bitter root grows up to cause trouble and defile many.[90] See that no one is sexually immoral, or is godless like Esau, who for a single meal sold his inheritance rights as the oldest son. Afterward, as you know, when he wanted to inherit this blessing, he was rejected. He could bring about no change of mind, though he sought the blessing with tears."

12:25, 29 — "See to it that you do not refuse him who speaks. If they did not escape when they refused him who warned them on earth, how much less will we, if we turn away from him who warns us from heaven?...for our God is a consuming fire."[91]

James

1:14-16 — "But each one is tempted when, by his own evil desire, he is dragged away and enticed. Then, after desire has conceived, it gives birth to sin; and sin, when it is full-grown, gives birth to death. Don't be deceived my dear brothers."

---

[89] From the Greek word εὐπερίστατον, whose cognate παραπεσόντας ("fall away") is used in Heb. 6:6, i.e., "sins that make one fall away"; as also used in classical Greek (cf., Bauer, op. cit., p. 324). This would suggest that the sin which so easily entangles, or the most besetting sin, is the sin of apostasy.

[90] Cf., Deuteronomy 29:18 "...make sure there is no root among you that produces such bitter poison." This is said in a context of worshiping other gods and upon which God offers no more forgiveness (Deuteronomy 29:19-21).

[91] Paul quotes many passages which issue these kinds of warning from Deuteronomy. This one appears in Deuteronomy 4:24. As Hebrews 4:2, 6 makes clear, the same gospel of salvation and judgment is true in the New Testament as it was in the Old.

1:21-22 — "Therefore, get rid of all moral filth and the evil that is so prevalent, and humbly accept the word planted in you, which can save you. Do not merely listen to the word, and so deceive yourselves. Do what it says."

2:13-14 — "Because judgment without mercy will be shown to anyone who has not been merciful...What good is it, my brothers, if a man claims to have faith but has no deeds? Can such faith save him?

4:4 — "You adulterous people, don't you know that friendship with the world is hatred toward God? Anyone who chooses to be a friend of the world becomes an enemy of God."

5:9 — "Don't grumble against each other, brothers, or you will be judged. The Judge is standing at the door."

1 Peter

4:17-18 — "For it is time for judgment to begin with the family of God; and if it begins with us, what will the outcome be for those who do not obey the gospel of God? And, if it is hard[92] for the righteous to be saved, what will become of the ungodly and the sinner?"

5:8 — "Your enemy the devil prowls around like a roaring lion looking for someone to devour. Resist him, standing firm in the faith..."

2 Peter

1:9 — "But if anyone does not have them, he is nearsighted and blind, and has forgotten that he has been cleansed from his past sins.

[92] From the Greek μόλις, understood more commonly as "scarcely" (cf., Acts 14:18; 27:7-8,16; Rom. 5:7). This verse is explicit that salvation is not easy to attain. It takes hard effort, and there is a high potential of falling away and eventually coming under judgment (cf., Matthew 7:13-14; Luke 13:24; 16:16-17; Prov. 11:31 (Hebrew)).

Therefore, my brothers, be all the more eager to make your calling and election sure. For if you do these things you will never fall."

2:20-22 — "If they have escaped the corruption of the world by knowing our Lord and Savior Jesus Christ and are again entangled in it and overcome, they are worse off at the end than they were at the beginning. It would have been better for them not to have known the way of righteousness, than to have known it and then to turn their backs on the sacred command that was passed on to them. Of them the proverbs are true: 'A dog returns to its vomit,' and, 'a sow that is washed goes back to her wallowing in the mud.'"[93]

3:14-17 — "So then, dear friends, since you are looking forward to this, make every effort to be found spotless, blameless and at peace with him...Therefore, dear friends, since you already know this, be on your guard so that you may not be carried away by the error of lawless men and fall from your secure position."

1 John

2:24-26 — "See that what you have heard from the beginning remains in you. If it does, you also will remain in the Son and in the Father. And this is what he promised us — even eternal life. I am writing these things to you about those who are trying to lead you astray."[94]

2:28 — "And now, dear children, continue in him, so that when he appears we may be confident and unashamed before him at his coming."

---

[93] The words "knowing" and "known" are from the Greek words ἐπιγνώσει and ἐπεγνωκέναι, respectively, which are more accurately translated as "full knowledge" and "fully known," due to the presence of the prefix ἐπι. This again shows that such apostates did not have a mere superficial knowledge of the faith, but a deep and convicting knowledge, which they forthrightly rejected. They fully know what the Christian faith is, but they do not want it. Ἐπιγνώσει is also used in Hebrews 10:26 — "if we deliberately sin after receiving the *[full] knowledge* of the truth..."

[94] See chapter 8 for an explanation of John's saying in 1 John 5:13, "we know that we have eternal life."

2 John

8 — "Watch out that you do not lose what you have worked for, but that you may be rewarded fully. Anyone who runs ahead and does not continue in the teaching of Christ does not have God; whoever continues in the teaching has both the Father and the Son."

3 John

9-11 — "I wrote to the church, but Diotrephes, who loves to be first, will have nothing to do with us. So if I come, I will call attention to what he is doing, gossiping maliciously about us. Not satisfied with that, he refuses to welcome the brothers. He also stops those who want to do so and puts them out of the church. Dear friend, do not imitate what is evil but what is good. Anyone who does what is good is from God. Anyone who does what is evil has not seen God."

Jude

5 — "Though you already know all this, I want to remind you that the Lord delivered his people out of Egypt, but later destroyed those who did not believe."

Revelation

2:5 — "You have forsaken your first love. Remember the height from which you have fallen! Repent and do the things you did at first. If you do not repent, I will come to you and remove your lampstand from its place."

2:10 — "Be faithful, even to the point of death, and I will give you the crown of life."

2:16 — "Repent therefore! Otherwise, I will soon come to you and will fight against them with the sword of my mouth."

2:23 — "Then all the churches will know that I am he who searches hearts and minds, and I will repay each of you according to your deeds."

2:26 — "To him who overcomes and does my will to the end, I will give authority over the nations."

3:3 — "Remember, therefore, what you have received and heard; obey it, and repent. But if you do not wake up, I will come like a thief, and you will not know at what time I will come to you."

3:11 — "I am coming soon. Hold on to what you have, so that no one will take your crown."

3:16 — "So, because you are lukewarm — neither hot nor cold — I am about to spit you out of my mouth."

3:21 — "To him who overcomes, I will give the right to sit with me on my throne..."

16:15 — "Behold, I come like a thief! Blessed is he who stays awake and keeps his clothes with him, so that he may not go naked and be shamefully exposed."

22:12 — "Behold, I am coming soon! My reward is with me, and I will give to everyone according to what he has done."

22:19 — "And if anyone takes words away from this book of prophecy, God will take away from him his share in the tree of life and in the holy city, which are described in this book."

Summary Points

1) It is a fact that Protestant denominations have differing, and sometimes diametrically opposed views, of the relationship between justification and sanctification. Chapter 9 will detail these differences.

2) Protestants view justification as a one-time, unrepeatable event, yet at the same time hold that works of obedience must qualify the faith required for justification. This view presents a very difficult theological problem because it leaves no room for works to qualify the condition of the faith before justification.

   a) Some Protestants attempt to deal with this dilemma by claiming that although works are required in order to qualify the faith of justification, because God will read the individual's heart it is not necessary for him actually to see the works. In response, we insist that Scripture argues the case for personal justification not by appealing to God's omniscience, but from a temporal vantage point, as noted, for example, in Paul's contention in Romans 4 that Abraham was justified *chronologically* prior to his circumcision.

   b) In the Genesis 22 account of Abraham's sacrifice of Isaac, God acknowledges Abraham's faith and works only at the precise time that Abraham raises the knife to slay Isaac. To prove Abraham's faith and obedience, God insists on being an actual witness to this event. Nothing in this text suggests that God can or will view this test from his omniscience.

3) As regards the Catholic teaching that justification is not a one-time event but an ongoing process, the following points are in order:

   a) New Testament writers interpret Abraham's justification as a sequence of events or a progressive justification, culminating in his willingness in Genesis 22 to sacrifice Isaac. Expressing his view, Paul equates the faith of Abraham in Genesis 12 (when he left his homeland at God's command) with the faith of Genesis 15 (when he believed that God would give him a son). Both of these instances of faith fall under the Hebrews 11:6 rubric of faith that "pleases God" for salvation, and therefore both must be salvific, as is the faith of Abel, Enoch, and Noah mentioned in the same context.

b) Paul reinforces his view that the faith of Abraham in Genesis 12 is the same salvific faith in Genesis 15 by describing the former as Abraham "looking forward to the city and foundations, whose architect and builder is God" and the latter in precisely the same terms as "...instead, they were longing for a better country — a heavenly one. Therefore God...has prepared a city for them." Since the faith described in both passages share the same vision of the future, Abraham's faith in Genesis 12 was therefore salvific, and he was thus also justified at that time. This presents a particular problem for the Reformed persuasion since they insist that regeneration must precede faith. If faith can only be the product of regeneration, yet regeneration necessitates that the individual is justified, then Abraham's faith which Hebrews 11 speaks of in glowing terms, must be justifying faith.

c) Paul, extending his understanding of Abraham's justification as ongoing process, follows the same pattern in his description of David. Paul quotes David's gratitude to God in Psalm 32 for forgiving his sin of adultery with Bathsheba and murder of Uriah. Paul includes this incident within his description of justification in Romans 4. Since the earlier Psalms, as well as the historical record in 1 and 2 Samuel, record that David was a man of God long before the forgiveness he received in Psalm 32, the forgiveness recorded in Psalm 32 is not the only time David was justified in his life. This agrees with Catholic theology that one who commits adultery and murder is in *mortal sin* — a sin that removes sanctifying grace from the soul and puts one in an unjustified state before God. When sanctifying grace is restored, the individual is again justified in the sight of God, as Paul claims of David in Romans 4:5-8.

d) Countering the Protestant argument that the Galatian epistle is concerned with progressing in sanctification rather than establishing and progressing in justification, Paul does not use the word "sanctification" at all in the epistle. Moreover, Paul speaks of the Galatians "falling from grace" in reference to "justification," which shows that he considers it an event that can be reversed in the future. It is true that the Galatians had a problem with the ceremonial law of Israel, but they also had a moral problem. We see this in Paul's stern warning that they will lose their inheritance in the kingdom of God for moral disobedience (Galatians 5:14-21).

e) The case of Phinehas in which Psalm 106:31 uses "crediting of righteousness" (the exact phrase used to describe Abraham in Genesis 15:6, and the only other time it is used in the Old Testament) to describe God's response to Phinehas's act in executing the apostates of Israel, shows that the Old Testament writers understand works as that which produce salvific justification, the same understanding James expresses in his New Testament epistle.

f) The case of Cornelius, whom Acts 10 describes as a man who knows and seeks for God, and whom God blesses with salvation in recognition of Cornelius's faith and works, shows the Catholic concept of the individual responding to grace and God's rewarding the individual by bestowing gracious merit for his response.

g) The case of Paul — who in 1 Timothy 1:13-16 states that God had mercy on him, a mercy in which Paul receives forgiveness of sins, because of Paul's prior ignorance of the gospel, and in order to save others by this example of Christ's patience — shows again that God is waiting for men to respond to his impulses of grace and views their response accordingly.

h) Protestant attempts to limit justification to a one-time event by citing the Greek past tenses of the verb *dikaioo* ("justified") in, for example, Romans 5:1 ("having been justified by faith"), fail because (1) Paul makes use of the same past tense form of other virtues, such as love, normally associated with the concept of Protestant sanctification. This is done by Paul in the very same context that speaks of the same event of justification as he says in Romans 5:5 "God has poured out his love into our hearts"; (2) Paul also uses the word "sanctified" in 1 Corinthians 6:11 in the past tense at the same time he uses the word "justified" in the past tense, making both refer to salvation and thus making neither a temporal nor a substantive distinction between the two.

i) Protestant usage of 1 John 2:19 to support the idea that all people who fall away from the faith were never justified originally, is not legitimate. Though the New Testament can be used to support the possibility that some people who fall away were never justified originally, it does not apply this to every case. In fact, the New Testament describes most individuals falling away as those who truly embraced the gospel and were justified. New Testament writers usually confine instances in which people are said to fall away who were never justified originally to false prophets and antichrists who come into the Church to draw true believers away from the faith.

j) Hebrews 11:29's account of the Israelites falling away shows that a person or group can have the same faith that in others (for example, the "heroes of faith" recorded in the entire chapter of Hebrews 11) is true salvific faith, but later fall away from that faith and lose their salvation.

4) Romans 8:38-39 and John 10:28-29 do not support the concept of eternal security since, (1) the passages, read in context, refer only to external forces that God will prohibit from disrupting the salvation plan, not to sinful forces within the individual himself that can make him turn away from God; and (2) these passages, and others like them, speak only in general terms of the plan of predestination, and do not cite any specific individuals who belong in this category.

5) Next to the person of Christ, Scripture attends to no topic more than the warning to Christians not to fall away from the faith and lose their salvation. In fact, every book in the New Testament, with the possible exception of Philemon, in some way or other suspends the outcome of our eternal destiny based on the duration and degree of our faith and obedience. Scripture offers absolutely overwhelming evidence that a believer can fall from the salvation he once possessed.

Chapter 5

Is Justification an Imputed or Infused Righteousness?

Between Catholics and Protestants lies a great divide concerning whether the Christian has imputed or infused righteousness. Indeed, this difference is probably the most crucial in the ongoing debate, because it encompasses the most theological territory. In fact, the original motivation of the Reformation was to distance itself from the medieval concept of infused righteousness formulated largely by the theology of Augustine.

Before we begin, let us once again review the terms of this debate. Imputed righteousness, as Protestant proponents usually defend it, refers to that righteousness which derives solely from the merits of Christ's active and passive obedience, which, in turn, is applied to the sinner's account. The sinner can perform absolutely no work in order to obtain that righteousness. It is a righteousness that is "alien" but which the sinner can have credited to himself by simply believing in Christ and his work. Probably the best analogy to explain the concept of imputed righteousness is that of an accountant's ledger book. Into his ledger book the accountant adds a credit entry representing a sum of money obtained as a gift which puts the total account in the black; similarly, under imputed righteousness God credits the "alien" righteousness of Christ to the sinner in order to make his standing with God positive. Since the wages of sin is death, then without a righteousness from another source to countermand the negative entries, the sinner could not be justified. Moreover, since God demands perfect righteousness, the man, being sinful and imperfect, is unable to make his own "credit entry" through his own righteous acts. Therefore, the righteousness must come from a perfect source outside of the sinner and be applied to him by a free act of God. The righteousness is "imputed" to him but it is not his own.[1]

The Catholic concept of infused righteousness refers to that righteousness which also comes from God, but which God gives to the sinner not as a mere "credit" but as an infusion of actual righteous quality into the person. Using the analogy above, rather than say he receives a "credit entry," we could say that he becomes "credit worthy." As God infuses his divine righteousness into the individual, he instills the virtues of faith, hope and love. As the individual, through God's helping grace, maintains this personal righteousness, he becomes increasingly justified and sanctified in the eyes of God, leading to his final justification and glorification in heaven. One of the best analogies to explain the concept of infused righteousness is that of pouring a sufficient quantity of white liquid into a beaker full of black liquid so that the final solution turns from dark to light. The white liquid is analogous to the grace of God which is "infused" into the sinner, changing the whole person and sufficiently overcoming the blackness of sin. The infused righteousness restructures or renovates the sinner to the point that he becomes acceptable in the eyes of God and may enter heaven. Developing the analogy to show that the justification process is an ongoing one, we can picture God continually pouring white liquid into the dark liquid to make it whiter and whiter. At the same time, however, sin may combat this process and once again make the

---

1 Protestant historian Philip Schaff supports this view, but with an interesting admission in favor of the Catholic view. He states: "Modern exegesis has justified this view of δικαιόω and δικαίωσις, according to Hellenistic usage, although etymologically the verb may mean *to make just*, i.e., to sanctify, in accordance with verbs in όω (e.g., δηλόω, φανερόω, τυφόω, *to make* manifest, etc)." (Schaff, *History of the Christian Church*, Vol. VII, f. 2, p. 123). A study of the New Testament's usage of these three words confirms Schaff's admission. The word, δηλόω appears 7 times in the epistles, all of which denote a recognition of an *actual* manifestation (e.g., 1 Cor. 3:13, Col. 1:8); φανερόω appears 50 times, denoting the same (e.g., 1 Cor. 4:5; 1 Tim. 3:16); τυφόω is used 3 times, referring to an *actual* blindness (John 12:40). Similarly, M. J. Lagrange states: "First, we should note that verbs in όω mean to make whatever the root indicates. Thus δικαιόω should properly mean "make just." (*La Justification selon saint Paul*, RB 1914, 121, cited by C. Spicq, *Theological Lexicon of the New Testament*, trans. J.D. Ernest. 3 vols. (Peabody, MA: Hendrickson Publishers, 1995), 1:341. See also Joseph Fitzmeyer in the *Jerome Biblical Commentary*, op. cit., pp. 295ff.

liquid dark or darker. It is the condition of the soul, e.g., the whiteness of the liquid, at the end of the person's life that is the criterion for final justification.[2]

Protestant Objections

At this point in the discussion many Protestants recoil.[3] If God is perfect and demands perfection, how can one expect to be "restructured" or "renovated" to the point of satisfying God's standard of perfection? Does it not seem that the only possible way to meet God's perfect standard is to have a perfect righteousness given to the individual since he cannot attain it on his own? The problem

---

2 The Council of Trent, Session 6, Chapter 7: "Justification itself follows this disposition or preparation, which is not merely remission of sins, but also the sanctification and renewal of the interior man through the voluntary reception of the grace and gifts, whereby an unjust man becomes a just man, and from being an enemy becomes a friend..." The Council also speaks of the grace of justification as that which "*inheres in them*" (Session 6, Chapter 7; Canon 11); "*infuses* His virtue into the said justified...because we are justified through its inherence in us" (Chapter 16; Canon 2,10,11). The Roman Catechism authorized at the Council of Trent stated of grace: "a divine quality *inhering* in the soul." Cyril of Alexandria wrote: "grace is a quality...a certain Divine form" (Hom. pasch. 10,2). Pius V in the 1567 Bull *Ex Omnibus Afflictionibus*, condemned the proposition of Michael De Bay that: "The justice by which the sinner is justified...does not consist in any sort of grace infused in the soul by which one becomes God's adopted child, is internally renewed and is made a sharer in the divine nature so that, renewed in this way through the Holy Spirit, one many henceforward lead a good life and obey the commandments of God" (JD 1942).

3 Evangelical R. C. Sproul objects to infusion on the basis that "the atonement involves the judicial imputation of our sins to Christ. If our sins were infused into Him rather than imputed, He would become inherently evil and therefore unable to offer an atonement for Himself, let alone us" (*Justification By Faith Alone*, ed. D. Kistler, p. 37). This objection lacks merit because it is unscriptural to say that our sins were "imputed" to Christ. Scripture never uses the Greek word *logizomai* (λογίζομαι = "credited," "accounted," "reckoned") in reference to Christ; only to man. The only balanced equation the Scripture offers is that found in Romans 5:19 where upon the disobedience of Adam man was made a sinner and upon the obedience of Christ many will be made righteous. We can understand both sides of the equation in the infused sense, as we will show later in this chapter. In addition, Sproul himself believes that in regeneration and sanctification God infuses his grace into the individual. Would we then conclude that, in reciprocal fashion, God is infused with the individual's sin while the latter is being sanctified? Of course not. There is no one-to-one correspondence between the two that Sproul is trying to force into the issue.

with these questions, as we have noted earlier in this study, is that they assume a premise that is not true. Granted, before the atonement of Christ, the sinner can do nothing on his own to become acceptable in God's eyes. That is why the Council of Trent insisted that neither faith nor works can merit the grace of justification.[4] No one can do anything to appease God without the atonement of Christ, let alone strive to attain a perfect righteousness to meet God's standards. But once the atonement was accomplished, the grace of God was made available to the whole world. For those who wish to avail themselves of this grace, God will no longer look at them through the eyes of the uncompromising and exacting system of law that was put in place as their judge after Adam's sin.[5] God will now look at them as a father looks upon his children, not as a judge looks upon a criminal. As a father does not exact, without compromise and forgiveness, a perfect and faultless obedience from his children, neither does God demand such from his children. Within the system of grace, God will extend his mercy and love to those who genuinely seek him, even though they are not perfect. The perfect righteousness of Christ which satisfied God's wrath, in turn, set aside the system of law and opened the door for a gracious relationship between God and man. The change in status the sinner undergoes is one which transfers him from the system of law to the system of grace. Once in the system of grace, he must now abide by the conditions of that system. The system of

---

4 Council of Trent, Session 6, Chapter 8: "...because faith is the beginning of human salvation, the foundation and root of all justification, without which it is impossible to please God and to come to the fellowship of his sons; and are, therefore, said to be justified gratuitously, because none of those things which precede justification, whether faith or works merit the grace itself of justification; for if it is a grace, it is not now by reason of works; otherwise (as the Apostle says) grace is no more grace."

5 Another important aspect of this principle relates to the terms *actual grace* and *sanctifying grace* in Catholic theology. *Actual grace* is the grace that God distributes as he wishes to each individual. This grace prompts man to seek for God and to do acts worthy of God's notice. Prior to his conversion and baptism, however, man is still under the condemnation of the law for his sins. It is not until he cooperates and responds to God's *actual grace*, that the judgment of the law is removed. The correct response to *actual grace* provides *sanctifying grace* and it is at this time that he is formally removed from the system of law and becomes a child of God. See the *Catholic Catechism*, sections 1996-2005; Ludwig Ott, *Fundamentals of Catholic Dogma*, pp. 225-267.

grace requires that the cleansed person maintain the righteousness that was infused into him. If he does so, then God will reciprocate and grant him heaven as his eternal dwelling. He maintains this righteousness by continuing in faith, hope and love. If he falters, God can forgive and restore him, but he must seek God's forgiveness and the continual infusion of His righteousness. In short, God does not demand perfect righteousness as seen through the uncompromising edicts of the law, but perfect righteousness that is in accord with his viewing of man from his grace and mercy.

Protestants often misunderstand another aspect of infused grace, believing that the doctrine assumes the person himself is producing the righteousness, and concluding that such a system bespeaks a salvation based on human works. The typical Protestant adage, "nothing do I bring, simply to the cross I cling," which appears so God-glorifying and totally selfless, reinforces these views. Catholic theology teaches, however, that though God demands human effort, and often severe human effort as recorded in the story of Abraham detailed earlier in this study, only the power given to us by the grace of God can provide and maintain that righteousness. Without God's grace to view the work and his grace to help in actually performing the work, the person would not be righteous. The good works we do are a result of the cooperation of our wills with the divine will.[6] Paul says in Philippians 2:12-13:

> Therefore, my beloved, just as you have always obeyed me, not only in my presence, but much more now in my absence, work out your own salvation with fear and trembling; for it is God who is at work in you, enabling you both to will and to work for his good pleasure.

This passage clearly shows the participation of both parties, God and man. Paul states that they have "obeyed" and then asks that they "work out their salvation with fear and trembling." This means that the fear of and reverence for God's scrutiny and ultimate judgments must always guide obedience. When Paul says

[6] Council of Trent, Session 6, Chapter 5: "...freely assenting to and cooperating with the same grace...nor on the other hand can he of his own free will without the grace of God move himself to justice before Him."

they have "always" obeyed, he is indicating that they have maintained the obedience, or righteousness, that they originally received. Maintaining the obedience is the means by which they "work out" their salvation. They will continue to obey because they fear God and tremble before him, knowing that disobedience leads to damnation.[7] Yet Paul does not want them to think that they are totally on their own. That notion would plunge them into abject fear with no hope of persevering.[8] Paul reassures them that God is there to

---

7 Council of Trent, Session 6, Chapter 13: "For God, unless men be wanting in his grace, as He has begun a good work, so will He perfect it, working to will and to accomplish [Phil. 2:13]. Nevertheless, let those who think themselves to stand, take heed lest they fall [1 Cor. 10:12], and with fear and trembling work out their salvation [Phil. 2:12] in labors, in watchings, in almsdeeds, in prayers and oblations, in fastings and charity [2 Cor. 6:3]. For they ought to fear, knowing that they are born again unto the hope of glory, and not as yet unto glory in the combat that yet remains with the flesh, with the world, with the devil, in which they cannot be victors, unless with God's grace they obey the Apostle saying, 'We are debtors, not to the flesh, to live according to the flesh. For if you live according to the flesh, you shall die. But if by the spirit you mortify the deeds of the flesh, you shall live [Rom. 8:12]." Session 6, Chapter 16: "And whereas in many things we all offend, each one should have before his eyes the severity and judgment as well as mercy and goodness; neither ought anyone to judge himself, even though he be not conscious to himself of anything, since the whole life of man must be judged and examined not by the judgment of men, but of God, who will bring to light the hidden things of darkness, and will make manifest the counsels of the heart, and then shall every man have praise from God, who, as it is written, 'will render to every man according to his works.'"

8 Evangelical James McCarthy opposes the Catholic view of Philippians 2:12-13 by saying that the verses do not teach "that Christians must work for their eternal salvation." McCarthy goes on to say that Paul was addressing the main problem he was dealing with in the context, namely, the internal rivalries in the Philippian church, and thus Paul was merely exhorting them to be "of the same mind, to maintain the 'same love,' to be 'united in spirit, intent on one purpose...not to act from selfishness or empty conceit." McCarthy concludes that "Paul was exhorting the Christians in Philippi to work out the *consequences* of their salvation [not their actual salvation]. Christ had...given them eternal life...More specifically, the Philippians needed to work out their salvation or deliverance from the disputes within the Church" (*The Gospel According to Rome*, p. 67). In this way, McCarthy empties the passage of its eternal dimensions and attempts to limit the discussion to "working out their disputes." The verse that McCarthy fails to quote is Phil. 2:16: "as you hold out the word of life — in order that I may boast on the day of Christ that I did not run or labor for nothing." Here Paul speaks of the final judgment, the "day of Christ." Hence, all the fear and trembling that the Philippians are encouraged to work out is for the purpose of passing the judgment of that final day. If Paul finds that he has

help them in their obedience.[9] He provides sufficient grace for each act of faith, hope, and love.

The Catholic Concept of Grace

In order to have a complete understanding of the synergism between God's grace and man's responsive action it is necessary to comprehend thoroughly the Catholic concept of grace, as well as the biblical evidence that supports this teaching. As noted above, when we speak of grace being infused into a person, we have to imagine it as something that can be quantified and stored. As a spirit or soul is real yet unseen and untestable, so grace has real existence.[10] Though it comes in many forms, (e.g., sanctifying grace, actual grace, efficacious grace), it is not just a mere concept or attribute of God. Grace is a spiritual power that God gives us, not merely favor through which

---

8 cont. "labored in vain," we know from other passages that the salvation of his hearers is either in jeopardy or has yet to be determined (cf., Gal. 2:2; 2 Cor. 6:1; 1 Thess. 3:5). Even Paul does not think of himself as eternally secure, for in the same context he speaks of himself as "not having already obtained all this...but I press on to take hold...Brothers, I do not consider myself yet to have taken hold of it...I press on toward the goal to win the prize" (Phil. 3:12-14). Elsewhere when Paul speaks of "winning the prize," it is in the context of either attaining or forfeiting salvation (cf., 1 Cor. 9:27-10:13).

9 Council of Trent, Session 6, Chapter 16: "For since Jesus Christ Himself...continually infuses His virtue into the said justified, a virtue which always precedes their good works, and which accompanies and follows them, and without which they could in no wise be pleasing and meritorious before God...Thus neither is our own justice established as our own from ourselves, nor is the justice of God ignored or repudiated; for that justice which is called ours, because we are justified through its inherence in us, that same is (the justice) of God, because it is infused into us by God through the merit of Christ." The grace given to the faithful for the purpose of performing some special task or overcoming a certain obstacle is called "actual" grace (*Catholic Catechism*, Sections 1084, 1127-31, 1392-1395, et al.). One obtains it through the sacraments and prayer (CC, Section 1966, 2003, 2558-2865).

10 The concept of grace was taught throughout the medieval period but developed more fully by St. Thomas Aquinas who put it in a metaphysical framework. Grace has ontological existence, or what we may call "ontic" grace. See essay by William Marshner in Reasons For Hope: Catholic Apologetics, *Justification By Faith* (Front Royal, VA: Christendom College Press, 1978), p. 222. The Council of Trent described grace as that which "*inheres in them*" (Session 6, Chapter 7) or "through its *inherence in us*" (Chapter 16). See also Ludwig Ott, *Fundamentals of Catholic Dogma*, p. 255.

he observes us.[11] The more of this grace we obtain from God, the higher our spirituality can be. Although Scripture often speaks of grace as the relationship we now enjoy with God, (i.e., the state or system of grace in which God views us differently than through the system of law), Scripture also speaks of grace as coming in various measures, e.g., Acts 4:23, "*great* grace was upon them"; James 4:6, "He gives us more grace"; 1 Peter 4:10, "the *manifold* grace of God"; 2 Peter 1:2, "Grace and peace be *multiplied* to you." Scripture also speaks of grace given in proportion to the need at hand or the specific service to be performed, e.g., Romans 12:6, "We have different gifts according to the grace given to us"; Romans 15:15, "because of the grace that God gave me to be a minister to the Gentiles"; Galatians 2:9, "they recognized the grace given to me"; Ephesians 4:7, "but to each one of us grace has been given as Christ apportioned it"; Hebrews 4:16, "Let us then approach the throne of grace with confidence so that we may find mercy and find grace to help us in the time of need." Paul says in 1 Corinthians 15:10: "But by the grace of God I am what I am, and his grace to me was not without effect. No, I worked harder than all of them — yet not I, but the *grace of God* that was with me." In Hebrews 13:9 it states: "It is good for our hearts to be *strengthened by grace*, not by ceremonial foods, which are of no value to those who eat them." And in 2 Corinthians 1:12: "We have conducted ourselves...in holiness...according to God's grace." And in 2 Corinthians 9:8: "And God is able to make *all grace abound* to you, so that in all things at all times, having all that you need you will abound in every good work."

These passages represent grace not merely as an attribute of God but as a spiritual power that God gives to the individual. When God gives his grace, a *strengthening* occurs. When Paul says in 1 Corinthians 15:10, "by the grace of God that was with me," the impression we receive is that of a power resident in Paul which allows him to do his work. Paul repeats this theme again in Philippians 4:13, "I can do all things through Christ who strengthens me."[12]

---

[11] Council of Trent, Session 6, Chapter 7: "...but we are truly called and are just, receiving justice within us, each one according to his own measure, which the Holy Spirit distributes to everyone as he wills [1 Cor. 12:11], and according to each one's own disposition and cooperation."

[12] The Old Testament also speaks of such action of God, cf., Exodus 31:2-3; Psalm 84:11; Numbers 6:25.

From these passages we learn two lessons: (1) Grace is not merely a way God views us but it is also a power emanating from God given to help the individual lead a Christian life; (2) The individual's works incorporate both his free will to do the work and the grace of God that prompts him and provides the power to do the work. The Christian cannot take strict credit for his work since it was God who enabled him to do the work. God does, however, graciously reward him for cooperating with him, for example, in Hebrews 6:10 it says, "God is not unjust; he will not forget the work and the love you have shown him..."

Revelation 21:27: "Nothing Impure Will Enter"

One of the passages often cited to support the Catholic view of infused righteousness, (i.e., righteousness which is sufficient to enter heaven) is Revelation 21:27: "Nothing impure will ever enter it, nor will anyone who does what is shameful or deceitful, but only those whose names are written in the Lamb's book of life." Catholic theology argues that if we are only legally righteous (as in the Protestant view), not intrinsically righteous, then we will not fulfill the requirement of Revelation 21:27 to be "pure" as we enter heaven. Protestants invariably interpret such a verse to mean that only Christ's righteousness imputed to the individual can make him pure in God's sight and able to enter heaven. Though in the Protestant view the Christian may attain a certain degree of sanctification and holiness as he leads his life, this is not what gets him into heaven. In the Protestant scenario, when the individual stands before God to be judged for his sins, he is said to "plead the blood of Christ," and God responds not by looking at the individual's sinful life but upon the perfect righteousness of Christ. Since Christ was his substitute at his initial justification, he will also be his substitute when he stands before God at the final judgment seat. The Christian's works will determine not whether he enters heaven, but rather what kind of reward, if any, he will receive in heaven. We will cover the aspect of reward for works more fully in chapter 8. For now, we must analyze the Protestant concept of imputed righteousness more thoroughly.

To many, the Protestant concept of imputation seems to be the most appropriate theory. After all, looking at ourselves in a moment of sin we wonder if we will ever be worthy enough in God's eyes to enter heaven. If Catholics claim to be infused with righteousness in justification yet also know that God examines and judges every motive and action, then how, one may ask, can we ever expect to please God sufficiently to enter heaven? Does not the Protestant view sound so much easier and simpler? Doesn't it give us more certitude to claim that Christ is our righteousness and then let God figure out what kind of personal reward we will receive once we enter heaven? Certainly one could create many plausible scenarios of salvation. Protestant denominations have given us many of them, e.g., Lutheranism, Calvinism, Arminianism, Methodism, Dispensationalism, Lordship Salvation, etc. All of these seem to be plausible, reasonable systems, at least to some degree. However, one obvious problem with such a variety of plausible systems is precisely the disagreements among them. At best, only one could possibly have the truth. Moreover, each claims to use Scripture alone to arrive at its particular soteriological system. In reality, each denomination tends to stress a particular set of Scriptures while downplaying others. The set of Scriptures stressed by one denomination inadvertently overrules another set that provides a rival denomination with a differing view of a particular doctrine. We have seen many examples of this tendency thus far. Apparently, something is missing in each of these "plausible" salvation scenarios. Perhaps, as we suggested in this book's Introduction, it is right to conclude that understanding how one is saved is not as easy and simple as one would like it to be. Theology is often complex. Whenever the infinite and the finite commingle, as they did when God created the world, we should not be surprised to see long and complicated explanations in each category where the two intersect.

Although the Protestant explanation of Revelation 21:27 is plausible, one immediate problem with such a view is that it does not do justice to the literal or "face value" language John chooses. John does not speak in terms of "imputed righteousness" in Revelation 21:27. He speaks only of what is observable as the person attempts to gain entrance into heaven. Those who are "impure" are also those who do what is "shameful" or "deceitful." It is not a matter of whether they have accepted the alien righteousness of

Christ; it is a matter of whether they have been obedient.[13] The remaining context provides corroboration that the internal righteousness which qualifies them for heaven is John's intended meaning. He points to the obedience or disobedience of each individual as the distinguishing mark between them. In Revelation 22:11 he writes, "Let him who does wrong continue to do wrong; let him who is vile continue to be vile; let him who does right continue to do right; and let him who is holy continue to be holy." Again, in Revelation 22:15 he writes, "Outside are the dogs, those who practice magic arts, the sexually immoral, the murderers, the idolaters, and everyone who loves and practices falsehood." The focus is on the good or evil actions of the individual, not the reception of an alien righteousness.

We see, then, that while the Protestant system may seem easy and plausible, it often misses the simple language of Scripture. Rather than taking each verse as it stands and allowing the differing "face-value" facts of Scripture to create as many theological categories as necessary to explain its complete message,[14] the Protestant hermeneutic invariably elevates "faith alone," and its counterpart "imputed righteousness," as all-encompassing theological categories into which the rest of the Scripture's language must fit. If the "face value" information that a passage provides does not conform to the *faith alone* theory, the Protestant hermeneutic nevertheless imposes it on the text. The theological category of *faith alone* becomes the overriding criterion — the *sine qua non* of bib-

---

[13] Calvinists may lay claim to the remaining portion of Revelation 21:27 which states, "but only those whose names are written in the Lamb's book of life." The proposed interpretation suggests that their names were written in the book of life by predestination and therefore they are now "pure" because it was predestined. Taking Scripture at "face-value," however, this is simply a half-truth. For example, Scripture's face-value language makes it clear that one can have his name "blotted" out of the book whose name was originally present (cf., Exodus 32:33; Psalm 69:28; Revelation 3:5).

[14] The Council of Trent, as well as the recent *Catholic Catechism* (1994), displayed a remarkable ability to hold in tension the aspects of grace and freedom. These documents create as many categories of theological thought that are necessary to accommodate these differing aspects. For a more detailed analysis on this feature of Tridentine hermeneutics see Michael Schmaus's *Dogma: Justification and the Last Things*, 1977), pp. 3-48.

lical hermeneutics — by which to judge or interpret any other Scripture. Passages like Revelation 21:27; 22:11, 15, and many others, instead of simply being taken at their own face-value, become the victim of a theological system.[15]

New Testament Terminology

Justification and Righteousness

The Greek verb for "justification" (δικαιόω) is transliterated *dikaioo*. The Greek noun for "righteousness" (δικαιοσύνη) is transliterated *dikaiosune*. In certain contexts these words are distinguished. *Dikaioo* normally refers to the act of justifying the individual, whether at the beginning, middle, or end of his life. *Dikaiosune* normally describes the state or disposition of the individual who has been justified. Hence, if he has been "justified," he is "righteous" or possesses "righteousness." These terms refer both to how God views us and to what God gives us. Simply put, if a person is "justified" or "righteous" this means that from God's perspective he is worthy to enter heaven. The main difference between the Catholic and Protestant interpretations of these terms, as stated earlier in the chapter, is that the Catholic view holds that the individual is worthy for heaven only after God has sufficiently prepared him. It is the Holy Spirit who prepares him by "restructuring" or "renovating" his once sinful soul. All the trials, suffering, prayers, and good works a Christian experiences on earth serve for the express purpose of preparing his person to be worthy of heavenly citizenship. As Hebrews 11:6 requires faith that "pleases" God, this faith must (1) believe that God exists, and (2) believe that "God

---

[15] It was this mind-set that led Luther to determine the biblical canon based on the notion of "justification by faith alone." Since Luther could not bring himself to accept the "face value" information that the epistle of James and other New Testament books gave him, i.e., that one is justified by works and not by faith alone, Luther chose instead to reject the veracity of James. Other Protestants following Luther, who felt they had no prerogative to question the veracity of an accepted book of the New Testament, were then forced to change James's "face value" teaching and superimpose the theory of "forensic imputation" and its counterpart "demonstrated justification" onto James's epistle.

is the rewarder of those who diligently seek him." As the Christian increases in holiness by the infusion of God's grace, he is showing that he is "diligently seeking" the God who will reward him.[16]

Another word that needs to be investigated is the Greek word *dikaios* (δίκαιος), ordinarily translated as "just" or "righteous."[17] Normally, *justified* is used to describe the act of justification, *righteousness* the state of being just or justified, whereas *just* refers to the person or entity which is just or justified. Which word is used depends on the shade of meaning required in the context of the passage.[18]

In using the words "just" or "righteous," the Scripture often refers to specific men as being such. Joseph is a "righteous man" (Matt. 1:19). John the Baptist is a "righteous and holy man" (Mark 6:20). Simeon is "righteous and devout" (Luke 2:22). Lot is "righteous Lot" (2 Peter 2:7-8). A passage of this kind that especially stands out is Luke 1:5-6: "...there was a priest named Zechariah...his wife Elizabeth was also a descendant of Aaron. They were both *righteous* before God, walking in all the commandments and ordinances of the Lord, blamelessly." The key facet of this passage is that *God* is the reference point in determining the righteousness of Zechariah and Elizabeth. It is not men, who see only the outside, doing the evaluating. God, who peers into the hearts of this couple, sees them as righteous. This would certainly lead us to reevaluate the meaning and extent of the statement by Paul in Romans 3:10 that there are "none righteous, no not one." How can God view the

---

[16] Citing the work of Alister McGrath, R. C. Sproul attempts to make a case that the Catholic concept of *infused righteousness* is attributable to a mistake made by Augustine who used the word *iustificare*, which in Latin means "to make righteous," to translate the Greek word δικαιοσύμη and the Hebrew צדקה. For a detailed critique of McGrath's thesis see **Appendix 2**.

[17] Other cognates of δικαιόω include δικαίωμα, translated as "ordinances" (Luke 1:6; Heb. 9:1,10) or "righteousness" (Rom. 2:26; 5:18; 8:4); δικαίως, translated as "righteousness" or "righteously" (1 Cor.15:34; Tit. 2:12); δικαίωσις, translated as "justification" (Rom. 4:25; 5:18).

[18] A ten-verse pericope which uses almost all the cognates of δικαιόω is Romans 5:9-19 [(5:9) "...being justified (δικαιόω) by his blood"; (5:17) "the gift of righteousness" (δικαιοσύνη); (5:18) "by the righteousness (δικαίωμα) of one"; (5:18) "upon all men unto justification" (δικαίωσις); (5:19) "shall many be made righteous" (δικαιός)].

whole human race as unrighteous sinners in Romans 3:10 and yet speak of Zechariah and Elizabeth as "righteous before God"? The answer, as we have been arguing thus far, is to take Luke 1:6 at "face-value" and conclude that they were seen as righteous because they actually "walked in all the commandments and ordinances of the Lord blamelessly." The second and more general answer, as noted throughout this study, is that prior to God's grace and the repentance that grace prompts from man, Paul is absolutely correct that all men are sinners and unrighteous. Moreover, there is nothing they can do in themselves to rectify that situation. God must make the first move. God provides the grace, through the atonement of Christ, which allows him to forgive men's sins and look upon them much differently than he was required to do through the uncompromising system of law. Thus, within the system of grace, Zechariah and Elizabeth pleased God sufficiently that God could look upon them as "righteous." They fit the category of Paul who said that faith which "pleases" God is that which acknowledges his existence and believes that he rewards those who diligently [by obedience] seek him" (Hebrews 11:6). This means not that they were sinless but that they understood their sinful nature and used God's grace to subdue it. The subduing of sin allowed them to "walk in the commandments and ordinances of the Lord, blamelessly." This is the same language used of Noah, for example, who is said to be "a righteous man, *blameless* among the people" (Genesis 6:9); of Job who is said to be "*blameless and righteous*; he feared God and shunned evil" (Job 1:1), or of Abel who is called "*righteous* Abel" (Matt. 23:35). Scripture also speaks of individuals or groups of men as righteous without specifying a name, e.g., "the righteous and the unrighteous" (Matt. 5:45), "he that receives a righteous man" (Matt. 10:41), "prophets and righteous men" (Matt. 13:17), "you garnish the tombs of the righteous" (Matt. 23:29), "the resurrection of the righteous" (Luke 14:14; Acts 24:15), "the eyes of the Lord are over the righteous" (1 Peter 3:12), "the prayer of a righteous man" (James 5:16); "her parents were righteous" (Susanna 1:3).

An interesting parallel between Christ and righteous men, and one that Scripture is not in the least ashamed of making, regards the righteousness of Christ and the righteousness of godly men. To set up this parallel, Scripture first refers to Christ as a "righteous man" (Acts 3:14; 7:52; 22:14; 1 John 2:1); then 1 John 3:7 makes the parallel: "He who does what is right is righteous, just as he is righteous."[19] In very simple language that does not mince words, John tells us that one acquires the state of being righteous by doing righteousness. In fact, the measure of the righteous state is such that it is equal to the righteous state of Christ. This is quite a statement. God says we are righteous not merely to placate our sensibilities and make us feel good, but because, as God views us within the system of grace, we are as righteous as Christ. The degree of our sins and faults is not in view here. It is understood from John's earlier writing that if one sins he can confess that sin and God will forgive him (1 John 1:8-10). The sins being set aside, John then goes on to tell us that we are as righteous as Christ is righteous.

The Greek word *dikaiosune* similarly conveys recognition of individual righteousness. For example, Jesus requires that our righteousness "must exceed the righteousness of the scribes and Pharisees" or we shall "not enter into the kingdom of heaven" (Matt. 5:20). There is no thought here of entering heaven merely because we have obtained an "alien righteousness." The responsibility is on the individual to make sure his righteousness is true righteousness. Jesus goes on to explain exactly how one can measure his own righteousness. In the remaining context of Matthew 5, Jesus refers to the "sayings" or code of ethics that the Old Testament formerly required but that he is now going to enhance in the New Testament. Thus, in Matthew 5:21, it is no longer sufficient to refrain only from physically killing someone; rather, Jesus says that even being angry with one's brother puts one in danger of judgment, i.e., judgment that results in not being able to "enter the kingdom of heaven" as he has just stated in Matthew 5:20. Hence, the way our righteousness "exceeds" the righteousness of the Pharisees is by refraining from anger, whereas the Pharisees, though

---

[19] The literal rendering is "the one doing righteousness (δικαιοσύνη) is righteous (δίκαιος) as *that one* is righteous (δίκαιος)." The demonstrative adjective ἐκεῖνος (translated as "that one" or "he") refers to Christ. This same grammatical usage of John is also noted in 1 John 2:6 and John 2:21.

they did not murder their brother, hated him and reviled him in their heart. Again, by interpreting the biblical language for its "face value" meaning within its own context rather than superimposing a theological system upon it, we learn that we do not exceed such Pharisaical righteousness by laying claim to someone else's [i.e., Christ's] righteousness but by exercising our own righteousness unto the God whom we can please under his grace. In the remaining context, Jesus tells us many ways that our righteousness must exceed that of the Pharisees, e.g., not looking with lust on a woman (verse 28), not divorcing illegitimately (verse 32), not swearing (verse 34), not seeking vengeance (verse 39), loving one's enemy (verse 44). We must do these things, according to verse 45, "that you may be[20] the children of your Father which is in heaven," not merely because we "are" his children.

The word "righteousness" (*dikaiosune*) is also used in Luke 1:75 where Zachariah, the same person who is said to be "righteous before God" in Luke 1:6, upon the birth of Christ, says, "that we might serve him without fear, in holiness and righteousness before him." This again shows the reason why Zachariah was recognized as "righteous before God" — he was one who sought to live that way.

"The Righteousness of God"

Scattered throughout the New Testament are references to "the righteousness of God" (Greek: δικαιοσύμνη θεοῦ, transliterated as *dikaiosune theou*). A total of ten passages use this phrase.[21] The phrase "the righteousness of God" is important to study because Martin Luther claimed that it was the watershed that gave him clear insight into the nature of justification. Before his new understanding, Luther was under the impression that the phrase referred to the vindictive nature of God who, if the individual did not measure up to the highest form of spirituality, would come down with his

[20] Aorist, subjunctive of γίνομαι.

[21] Matt. 6:33; Rom. 1:17; 3:5,21,22; 10:3; 2 Cor. 5:21; Phil. 3:9; James 1:20; 2 Pet. 1:20.

righteous vengeance.[22] Luther's notion of such a God fits in well with his extremely scrupulous nature. It is said that Luther whipped himself with chains as a self-imposed chastisement in order to show God sorrow for sin and receive his favor. According to Luther's own account, one day he awoke from his dogmatic slumber and saw the "righteousness of God" in a whole new light. In reading Romans 1:17, Luther reasoned that the clause "For in the gospel a righteousness from God is revealed..." was referring to the status of righteousness into which the judicial verdict of God places the believer.[23] Having attained the "status" of righteousness, one could be considered righteous by God without actually being righteous. One acquired the status of righteousness by faith — faith alone. This "discovery" became the hallmark of Luther's theology. Indeed, if it is possible to point to one verse that spawned a reformation, Romans 1:17 may be the most likely candidate.

From Luther's interpretation of Romans 1:17 came the beginnings of the Protestant concept of *imputation*. A righteousness which God's verdict establishes, the argument goes, is a righteousness beyond dispute and one that will hold up even in God's strict court of justice. Though a man may bring many versions of his own righteousness to God, no man could claim his own righteousness

---

[22] Catholic historian Heinrich Denifle, in his critique of Luther, pointed out that after examining sixty-six commentaries on Romans written in the Latin Church from the fourth to sixteenth century, from Ambrosiaster to Augustine to Denis the Carthusian, he had found no commentator who understood the meaning of *iustitia puniens* ("righteous punishment") for δικαιοσύνη ("the righteousness of God") in Romans 1:17 (Stauffer, *Luther as Seen by Catholics*, p. 14). Hence, Luther's apparent escape from an incorrect interpretation of Romans 1:17 was perhaps a figment of his own imagination. Opposing this view, Evangelical Alister McGrath claims that Denifle's research is "clearly unjustified" because "Luther made no global reference to the tradition of the western church upon the matter, but referred specifically to the doctors who taught him" (*Iustitia Dei*, II, p. 4). This explanation, however, does not excuse Luther. As the patristic and medieval scholar he was thought to be, Luther should have realized that the doctors who allegedly gave him such information were simply mistaken, especially with a doctrine upon which the church stands or falls. Ironically, Luther later said of Romans 1:17, "I have preached for twenty-five years and still do not understand this text" (LW, 54, 442; 54, 287).

[23] Luther takes the genitive θεοῦ as a type of objective genitive. His German phrase, "die Gerechtigkeit, die vor Gott gilt" ("the righteousness that avails before God") shows this more clearly.

in God's court. The righteousness must be credited to the man's account, even though the man was not righteous in himself. Indeed, Luther believed that the person, at the moment of imputation, was, figuratively speaking, simply a pile of dung. The righteousness of God that was given to him was analogous to a covering of snow over the dung in such a way that when viewed from the surface only the white snow would be observable. Luther obtained this imagery from his own culture and economy. The farmers in his area used to show off their economic status by mounting a pile of dung in their front yards, which they eventually used as fertilizer for their crops. When winter came, snow would fall on the dung and thus change its appearance and mask its odor. To Luther, this served as a perfect example of his new interpretation of Romans 1:17.

The problems with Luther's interpretation of Romans 1:17 are manifold. First, no theologian prior to him had understood the "righteousness of God" as an imputation. We will recall from this book's Introduction that Evangelical theologian Alister McGrath has argued quite correctly that Luther's concept of the nature of justification was a "theological novum" that made its first entrance into Christendom in the 16th century.[24] Naturally, then, the burden of proof lay upon Luther, and what a great burden it was. The same men of previous centuries who had defined such esoteric and enigmatic doctrines such as the Trinity, the Deity of Christ, the Inspiration and Canonicity of Scripture, Heaven and Hell, and many other doctrines, had, Luther said, missed the boat, as it were, when it came to the very nature of salvation. Second, Luther's proof texts for the concept of imputation simply begged the question. Since the very verses he offered as proof could logically and consistently be understood in a totally different way than he was presenting,

[24] On the other hand, McGrath attempts to make a case that the concept of legal imputation possibly stems from the concept in Roman private law called *acceptiliation* which refers to the dissolution of an obligation (such as a debt) by a verbal decree on the part of the one to whom the debt was due, without any form of payment having taken place or necessarily being envisaged as taking place in the future (*Iustitia Dei*, II, p. 45). This ancient practice, however, does not fit the Protestant concept of imputation since the theory claims that Christ *actually paid the debt*, not merely let the culprit go free without anyone making a payment to the one owed.

extracting a theory of imputation out of such passages really had no substantive and irrefutable proof. Imputation became simply a plausible theory without historic precedent and without unambiguous Scriptural proof. The many and varied interpretations of "the righteousness of God" that followed in Protestantism after Luther bear this out.[25]

The early fathers and medieval theologians before Luther had, to be sure, understood "the righteousness of God" as a quality of God. But they had gone a step further. They taught that God could give this righteous quality to men, not through an imputation, but as a qualitative sharing of God's righteousness. In other words, God put his righteous qualities into man — in a word, he *infused* it into them. This made them righteous internally, not merely externally. When God looked at them he saw a righteous individual, not someone who just appeared to be righteous on the outside because God gave him a label of "righteous." We have already noted the use of "righteous" (δίκαιος) in Scripture which referred to several men and women as "righteous before God," e.g., Noah, Job, Zachariah, Elizabeth, et al. These texts make it clear that it was for their particular faith and obedience that the term "righteous" was attributed to them, not because God had merely labeled them with his righteousness. Granted, the only way God could recognize their internal righteousness was through the grace provided by Christ's atonement to forgive their sins. Nevertheless, the resulting righteousness that men actually possess through faith is what Paul and the other New Testament writers are speaking of when they refer to the righteousness which justifies.

How can we better understand the "righteousness of God" as used in Scripture? If the phrase is subjective, then the righteousness would be a quality of God, i.e., his righteous character. If the phrase is objective it would refer to the righteousness that God expects to view in others or gives to others. Scripture uses both senses. In Romans 3:5, for example, the subjective sense is evident: "But if our unrighteousness brings out the *righteousness of God* what shall we say? That God is unrighteous for bringing his

[25] These variations concern whether to take δικαιοσύνη θεοῦ as a objective genitive (a righteousness before God), a subjective genitive (the righteous quality of God), or somewhere in between the two.

wrath on us?" This passage establishes God's righteousness by contrasting it with the unrighteousness of men. Both by verse 3, which refers to the "faith of God" or "God's faithfulness" in contrast to the unbelief of the Jews, and verse 7, which refers to the "truth of God" in contrast to the "lies" of men," clearly refers to the righteous quality of God. Since these phrases are subjective, the "righteousness of God" is also subjective.

On the other hand, a passage in which "the righteousness of God" is used objectively in reference to the kind of righteousness God instills into and expects from man is James 1:19-20: "...Let every man be quick to hear, slow to speak, slow to anger. For the anger of man does not produce the righteousness of God." Here it is clear that the "righteousness of God" is a quality that God desires to see in man. Being slow to anger is how one produces the righteousness that is pleasing to God. Since God infuses his own righteousness into the individual, then it is only logical to understand that as God "reveals" his righteousness to man, as taught in Romans 1:17, he disseminates it not by mere gospel proclamation but by the actual implantation of that righteousness into the hearers and believers of that gospel. In essence, God "reveals" himself *to man* (in the gospel) and *in man* (infusing his righteousness).[26]

In Romans 1:17 and subsequent passages in the epistle, Paul faults the Jews for trying to manufacture their own righteousness rather than seeking the righteousness that appeals to God. Paul notes this contrast clearly in Romans 10:3: "For not knowing the righteousness of God, and seeking to establish their own, they did not submit to the righteousness of God." Here Paul describes the "righteousness of God" as a quality of God to which they did not submit. Similarly, Romans 1:17, says in two ways that the righteous quality of God is "revealed," and it is up to man to access it and live by it. First, the phrase "from faith to faith" implies a continuity of faith in the life of the individual. Second, the quote taken from the book of Habakkuk, "the just by faith shall live," also im-

[26] Council of Trent, Session 6, Chapter 16: "Thus neither is our own justice established as our own from ourselves, nor is the justice of God ignored or repudiated; for that justice which is called ours, because we are justified through its inherence in us, that same is (the justice) of God, because it is infused into us by God through the merit of Christ."

plies such a continuity by specifying that one "lives" by faith. The section immediately following, Romans 1:18, speaks of the "unrighteousness of men," thus contrasting the righteousness that comes from faith with a merely human quality of righteousness which in God's eyes is so unsatisfactory as to be unrighteous.

The Habakkuk passage has several additional facets: (1) Nowhere does Habakkuk suggest that faith has anything to do with imputed righteousness. Chapter 1 of this book pointed out Habakkuk's complaint that God was ignoring the plight of the righteous by not bringing swift judgment upon the evildoers of Israel. In answer God tells Habakkuk that he will bring the Babylonians to punish Israel at the appointed time. Habakkuk then complains that God would be punishing Israel by using an unrighteous heathen nation, that itself is worthy of punishment. God retorts that in due course he will also bring judgment upon the Babylonians. Habakkuk must wait patiently for God's complete vengeance, and not lose heart. He must believe that God will do what he says he will do even when it seems he is never going to do it. In the midst of this trial, Habakkuk wrote those famous words concerning the Lord's judgment on Israel and Babylon: "For the revelation awaits an appointed time; it speaks of the end and will not prove false. Though it linger, wait for it; it will certainly come and will not delay" (Habakkuk 2:3). He then describes the wicked disposition of the Babylonians: "he is puffed up, his desires are not upright." He contrasts this with the disposition of the righteous person, namely Habakkuk himself: "but the righteous will live by his faith." Habakkuk, already a righteous man, must now continue to live out his faith by believing that God is doing everything in the best and swiftest way possible, even though it doesn't seem that way. Later, Habakkuk reassures himself of God's integrity by reminiscing about God's ancient fame and wonderful deeds (Habakkuk 3). Hence, nowhere do we find in the book of Habakkuk Luther's concept of the "righteousness of God" as a judicial verdict of righteousness. Habakkuk is merely demonstrating that a righteous man will continue to live by faith in the face of circumstantial evidence that tempts him not to believe in God. The issue is continuity of faith. That is the kind of faith God desires to see in man. That is the faith that pleases God and which will allow man to enter heaven.

The last usage of the Habakkuk quote in the New Testament also opposes Luther's concept of a judicial imputation of righteousness. Hebrews 10:36-38 states: "You need to persevere...He who is coming will come and not delay. But my righteous one will live by faith. And if he shrinks back I will not be pleased with him." Paul displays the same theme that was evident in Habakkuk, that is, persevering in faith while one waits on the Lord to act. The object of the waiting is the "eternal promise" and thus the faith must continue for their entire lives. The continuity of the faith is crucial since those who "shrink back" from it will not "please" God. Just a few verses later, we see Paul describing the kind of faith that does "please" God. It is faith that believes both that God exists and that he is the rewarder of those who diligently seek him (Hebrews 11:6). This demonstrates again why justification cannot be by a one-time juridical act sparked by faith alone. Since one's faith must be measured in order to have value, and since the measurement of that faith cannot be determined until the end of one's life, therefore one cannot be justified "once-for-all" in a legalistic framework.

We see another facet of the principle that the righteous will live by faith when we understand that, as Paul speaks in Romans 1:17 of the righteousness of God being revealed in the "gospel," the gospel about which he speaks is not confined to the New Testament. In fact, Paul's quote from the Old Testament book of Habakkuk already contains the very gospel message Paul is preaching![27] In turn, the reference in Romans 1:18 to those who "suppress the truth by their wickedness" must refer to those who suppress the gospel — a gospel that requires men to live by faith. It does not merely refer to the world of pre-New Testament Gentiles who did not have the written word. In fact, the Jews committed many of the sins that Paul enumerates in Romans 1:21-32 just as much, if not more, than the Gentiles. We see, then, that not only

[27] Compare the following: Romans 1:2, "the gospel of God — the gospel he promised beforehand through his prophets in the Holy Scriptures regarding his Son..."; Romans 3:2, "But now a righteousness from God, apart from the law, has been made known, to which the Law and the Prophets testify"; Hebrews 4:2, "For we also have had the gospel preached to us, just as they did..."; Hebrews 4:6, "...and those who formerly had the gospel preached to them did not go in, because of their disobedience."

disbelieving the gospel, but also "wickedness," suppresses the truth of the gospel. Those who act wickedly show that they are not living by faith in God. This is why Paul stresses *obedience* in relation to the kind of faith he seeks when he says in Romans 1:5: "...we received grace and apostleship to call people from among the Gentiles to the *obedience that comes from faith.*" Paul is not calling them to a *faith alone* but to *obedience*. Paul says the same in Romans 16:26: "the gospel...which was made known to all the nations for the *obedience of faith.*"[28] Here again Paul equates the gospel of salvation not with *faith alone* but with the obedience God requires of those who claim faith. Not only is obedience coupled with faith but the mere act of faith in response to the command of God is itself an act of obedience.

The next instance of "righteousness of God" appears in Romans 3:21- 22: "But now a righteousness of God, apart from law, has been made known...this righteousness of God comes through faith in Jesus Christ to all who believe." As stated above, the use of "righteousness of God" refers both to God's personal righteousness and the righteousness God instills in man for justification. The phrase "but now" develops a contrast with the previous verses, i.e., verses 19-20, which speak about the system of law under which the whole world is held accountable in sin. These verses further state that no one can be justified by law, rather, the law makes us aware of how sinful we are. Paul further develops the contrast in verse 24 in speaking of being "justified freely by his grace through the redemption that came by Jesus Christ." In other words, the opponents are the law on the one hand and grace on the other — two competing systems, one of which cannot save, while the other can. We understand the system of grace which does save as "the righteousness of God." The passage describes the kind of righteousness that God has revealed and requires. It is not a legal righteousness but a godly righteousness. As Paul proceeds to explain further in Romans 4:3-4, we see that the righteousness that God accepts from man is not a righteousness whereby man seeks strict payment from God for his righteous acts. Under the system of law,

28 The Greek phrase is ὑπακοὴ πίστεως ("obedience of faith") and is identical in Romans 1:5 and 16:26. The genitive case of πίστεως indicates that obedience is an integral part of faith.

nothing man does can be viewed as righteous since the law will always expose the sinful side of man. Rather, the righteousness of God that he imparts and wants reciprocated comes first when the individual admits his sinful condition by acknowledging the law's case against him. He then seeks to be included in the system of God's grace, apart from law, so that God can now view his faith and works as righteousness. It is the atonement of Christ that makes all this possible. All men need do at this point is to obey the command of God to believe it and act upon it.

Another important usage of "the righteousness of God" appears in 2 Corinthians 5:21: "He made the one not knowing sin to be sin on our behalf in order that we might become the righteousness of God in him." Taking this verse in isolation from its context, many Protestant exegetes have concluded that 2 Cor. 5:21 teaches an imputed righteousness since Paul speaks of righteousness that resides "in him," i.e., in Christ. Thus they say that the Christian, being "in him," is one and the same with Christ. They then stipulate that God is not looking at the righteousness in the Christian but at the righteousness of Christ. Hence, the righteousness of Christ is imputed to the Christian and thus we, in Christ, become the righteousness of God. The problem with this interpretation, as with most Protestant interpretations of the atonement and justification, is that although there is some truth to their view, it is at best a half-truth and as a result distorts the full meaning and intent of the passage. We can see this in two ways. First, the grammatical construction of 2 Cor. 5:21 does not necessarily treat the subordinate clause ("in order that we might become the righteousness of God in him") as an actual or definite result of the main clause ("He made the one not knowing sins to be sin on our behalf").[29] The English correctly

[29] The subordinate clause in 2 Cor. 5:21 is a Greek ἵνα clause, with the verb in the aorist subjunctive, middle deponent. The ἵνα clause has seen a wide range of usage in Koine Greek. Probably the only biblical usage of the actual result intended in a ἵνα clause is Revelation 13:13. Some might argue that the main verb of the ἵνα clause is aorist and thus indicative of a precise moment in time, e.g., an event of imputation. The aorist, however, is always used with a subjunctive clause and the clause in question is correctly translated in English as "might become," denoting both a potentiality and a process. Without the subjunctive aorist, the only other way to say the same thing in Greek would be to use the future indicative, which would also denote the potential in the future of an intended result.

translates the main verb in the subordinate clause as "might become" showing a *potential* result in process rather than a punctiliar event. Second, the context of 2 Corinthians 5-6 specifies the *impediments* to the realization of the subordinate clause of 2 Corinthians 5:21. We first note this in verses 19-20 in which Paul states that he is an ambassador for Christ with the message of reconciliation. He then says in verse 20: "We implore you on Christ's behalf: Be reconciled to God." The command to "be reconciled" is a present imperative. Hence, if becoming the righteousness of God was a punctiliar event in the past no longer to be questioned, we must ask why Paul is appealing ("begging" in Greek) for them to be reconciled? The audience to whom he is speaking consists of recognized Christians. This is the second letter he has written to them and thus their Christian faith has long been established. What is the problem? It is the same problem the Corinthian church has had from the beginning. The faith of many in the church is lax and on the verge of disappearing. Paul had consistently warned them of this fact in his first letter. In almost every chapter of 1 Corinthians he brings an indictment against them for their sin and lack of faith. He carries this over into his second letter which concludes in 2 Corinthians 13:5 with, "Examine yourselves to see if you are in the faith; test yourselves. Do you not realize that Christ Jesus is in you — unless of course you fail the test."

We see other indications of their slipping away from the faith in the context under discussion. In 2 Corinthians 6:1-2 Paul says: "As God's fellow workers we urge you not to receive the grace of God in vain. For he says, 'In the time of my favor I heard you, and in the day of salvation I helped you.' I tell you, now is the time of God's grace, now is the day of salvation." This is quite a stinging indictment and warning to the wretched Corinthians. Paul is so worried about whether they will remain in the faith that he warns them not to receive God's grace "in vain." He further reinforces what he means by pleading for them to recognize "the day of salvation." In other words, if they receive the grace of God in vain they will lose their chance for salvation. Paul is not playing around with them. If they continue on the path they are on, they will not "become the righteousness of God." We also note that Paul sandwiches 2 Corinthians 5:21, which speaks of Christ becoming sin for them so that they might become the righteousness of God, between verse 20 in which Paul pleads for them to be "reconciled" to God, and verse 6:1 which warns them not to receive the grace of God in vain. Verse 21, then, is a reminder to them of the potential result of Christ becoming sin for them, a potential result that in many of the Corinthians has thus far not been thoroughly realized. Though they started out with the "righteousness of God," the remaining question for the Corinthians is whether they will continue to possess and cultivate that righteousness to the end.

"And it Was Credited Unto Him as Righteousness"

We must now investigate one of the most popular Protestant arguments for the concept of imputed righteousness. This matter concerns the use of the Greek word *logizomai* translated as, "reckoned," "credited," "accepted," "counted," "considered."[30] The lexical definition carries several meanings as well: reckon, calculate, take into account, put on someone's account, estimate, evaluate, look upon as, consider, think, dwell on, believe, be of the opinion of.[31] Protestant exegesis, especially that of Romans 4 where the Greek word *logizomai* appears twelve times, has consistently understood the word in the sense of "credited." As noted earlier, the analogy drawn to describe the righteousness credited to Abraham in Romans 4 is that of an accountant giving a "credit" to Abraham's ledger book, a credit that was secured completely by the work of Christ in the atonement. Abraham is understood as one who has "something to his credit" so that when God looks at his ledger book, as it were, he sees that, in accounting terms, Abraham is in the black. Evangelical Joel Beeke comments on this verb:

> This verb most often indicates "what a person, considered by himself, is not, or does not have, but is reckoned, held or regarded to be, or to have. It is clear then that when Abraham was justified by his faith, the righteousness which was reckoned or "charged to his account" was a righteousness not his own but that of another, namely, the righteousness of Christ.[32]

---

30 The Greek word λογίζομαι transliterated as "logizomai."

31 Lexicons by Walter Bauer, p. 475-476; Liddell and Scott, p. 416.

32 Beeke, *Justification by Faith Alone*, op. cit., p. 56.

Unfortunately, Beeke presents a false premise which leads him to make a false conclusion. First, the Greek verb *logizomai* does not "most often indicate" what someone or something is merely "considered" to be but is not so in reality. The New Testament uses *logizomai* 41 times. Most of these refer to what someone is thinking as a mental representation of the *reality* they are witnessing.[33] Contrary to Beeke's proposition, in only a few instances is *logizomai* used as a mental representation of something that does *not exist* in reality.[34] Hence, the preponderant evidence shows that *logizomai* denotes more of what is *recognized* or *understood* intrinsically of a person or thing than a mere crediting to the person or thing something that is not intrinsic to it. In the case of Abraham, for example, we can understand the phrase "his faith is reckoned as righteousness" in Romans 4:5 such that God is recognizing or viewing Abraham's faith as righteousness, or that God interptreted the faith Abraham demonstrated as righteousness, or both. This is very different from saying, as Beeke claims, that God "credited" Abraham with righteousness as if to say that Abraham was not really showing any righteous qualities when he demonstrated his faith but that God, because of the alien righteousness of Christ, merely gave him the label of righteousness.

The Protestant failure to understand the word "credited" as including a recognition of the inherent righteousness of the individual has led to some fallacious criticisms of Catholic theology. Protestant theologians have given such a limited spectrum to the Catholic view of justification that they have erroneously divorced certain elements from the definition that are vital to its complete understanding. This attempt is evident in the "proof texts" that Protestant theologians amass to show that "to justify" does not mean "to make righteous." We have already seen an example of this in the writings of one major Protestant theologian who claimed that Augustine misinterpreted the Hebrew and Greek works for "to justify" by using the Latin word *justificare* to translate them.[35]

---

[33] cf., Luke 22:37; Rom. 3:28; 6:11; 9:8; 1 Cor. 4:1; 13:5,11; Phil, 3:13; 4:8; Heb. 11:19, et al.

[34] cf., Rom. 2:26; 2 Cor. 12:6

[35] Alister McGrath in *Iustitia Dei*, see **Appendix 2**.

Other attempts have used similar etymological and linguistic arguments. The effort is to divorce any *declaratory* dimension from the Catholic concept of justification in an attempt to reserve such language for the Protestant viewpoint. This tends to put the Catholic concept of justification in a theological vacuum, isolating it so that it can be attacked. For example, in his 1841 work on the Protestant concept of justification, Charles Hodge gathered twelve passages of Scripture that he felt provided the definitive proof that "justified" and its cognates did not mean "to *make* righteous," rather, "to declare or pronounce righteous." Hodge's thesis attempts to create a false dichotomy in the reader's mind between something that God declares and something that he recognizes within the individual.

To prove his case, Hodge points out the following passages: Deuteronomy 25:1 ("If there be a controversy between men, and they come into judgment, that the judges may judge them, then they shall justify the righteous, and condemn the wicked"); Exodus 23:7 ("I shall not justify the wicked"); Job 32:2 ("because he justified himself rather than God"); Psalm 51:4 ("that you might be justified when you speak"); Proverbs 17:15 ("He that justifies the wicked is an abomination to the Lord"); Isaiah 5:23 ("which justify the wicked for reward"); Matthew 11:19 ("Wisdom is justified of her children"); Luke 7:29 ("All the people that heard him, and the publicans, justified God"); 10:29 ("He wishing to justify himself"); 16:15 ("You are they which justify yourselves before men"); Galatians 2:16 ("A man is not justified by works of the law"); 5:4 ("Whosoever of you are justified by the law you have fallen from grace"). In reference to these passages, Hodge concludes:

> The word expresses a judgment, whether of the mind, as when one man justifies another for his conduct, or officially of a judge. If such be the established meaning of the word, it ought to settle all controversy as to the nature of justification. We are bound to take the words of Scripture in their true and established sense. And, therefore, when the Bible says, "God justifies the believer," we are not at liberty to say that it means that he pardons, or that

> he sanctifies him. It means, and can mean only, that he pronounces him just.[36]

Here Hodge makes the same mistake that Beeke had made in the understanding of the Greek word *logizomai* ("credited"), yet in the reverse direction. Hodge admits that "to justify" can refer to the occasion when "one man justifies another for his conduct," which shows that he is aware that to call one "justified" means that the designator recognizes rightful "conduct" in the individual. This understanding is precisely what we found in critiquing Beeke's use of *logizomai*. As noted above, Beeke failed to see that *logizomai* referred not only to considering something as existent that was not really so but considering it as existent because one recognizes that the quality which one has "considered" actually exists within the object observed. Using Hodge's words, we can say that man pronounces the other man "just" because he observes that the other man possesses and has demonstrated just behavior. In many of the "proof texts" that Hodge cites to show that "to justify" means "pronounce," upon critical examination the passages reveal that what is "pronounced" is what is actually *existent*. For example, in Deuteronomy 25:1, the man who has actually *exhibited* justice is only then justified by the judges. Hence, it is not valid for Hodge to use such a verse to support the Protestant concept that one is "pronounced" just who is not righteous intrinsically. The Protestant view fails to see that God can "pronounce" someone justified because God sees that the person has exhibited good "conduct." If anything, the Scripture's use of "to justify" supports the Catholic view since Scripture does not ascribe the word to an individual who has not shown righteous qualities.

Hodge's other "proof texts" exhibit the same problem. Most of the passages Hodge picks are negative in character, i.e., they portray the attempt of one party to falsely justify himself or another party, e.g., Job 32:2; Isaiah 5:23; Proverbs 17:15; Luke 10:29; 16:15. These do not prove his point, however. They merely show that it is invalid to apply the term "justified" or "righteous" to someone who is inherently evil or who has performed evil actions. If anything,

---

[36] Hodge, *Justification By Faith Alone*, p. 48.

the use of the term "justified" in these passages proves that the word can only be used when a righteous quality is recognizable in the individual observed. The remaining passages he cites speak of *God* being justified, e.g., Psalm 51:4; Job 32:2; Luke 7:29. But again, the same principle is evident: God is justified because he has the quality of justice within him, or because he is the subsisting source of all goodness and thus of all justice. This use of *justified* is in direct opposition to the Protestant conception. If anything, recognizing that God is justified in what he is and does proves the Catholic view of justification, not the Protestant view.

Evangelical James White uses the same argument as Hodge. He adds that there is a "legal" context in view when the word "justify" appears. After quoting Deuteronomy 25:1 ("If there is a dispute between men and they go to court, and the judges decide their case, and they justify the righteous and condemn the wicked..."), White states, "Note the context: a law court. To justify the righteous obviously means to give a legal, forensic declaration regarding a person's proper standing before the law."[37] First, it is very misleading to support the notion of forensic imputation by appealing to the "courtroom" context of Deuteronomy 25:1 for the simple fact that the Old Testament also uses the word "justify" in many *non-courtroom* situations. Thus it is not its use in the courtroom that makes the word legal. In reality, because of the general meaning of the word "justify" it can be used in many different contexts, most having nothing to do with the courtroom or anything of a legal nature.

Following this, White makes a further remark on Deuteronomy 25:1:

> This is clearly seen here by the term that is paralleled with the act of justifying: to condemn. Neither involves a subjective change of the individual; the righteous man was righteous inwardly even before the declaration of his righteousness, just as the guilty man was guilty before the proclamation of his guilt and condemnation. This is the source of Paul's understanding of justification in the New Testament. Paul's use of the terms *de-*

[37] *The Roman Catholic Controversy*, p. 154.

> *mands* that this be so. The conjunction of the two terms "impute" and "to justify" in Paul's teachings clearly show that the Protestant understanding of God's declaration of the righteousness of the believer is the biblical one.

Here White tries to turn the tables but in the end he traps himself. It is granted that there is no "subjective change" of the individual in this courtroom scene. White's diagnosis of the verse is correct when he says, "the righteous man was righteous inwardly even before the declaration of his righteousness." But White fails to see two things in this admission: (1) there is no need for a "subjective change" specifically because the individual was already subjectively righteous; (2) that the term "justify" is being used to recognize this subjective righteousness. In other words, the term "justify" is not being assigned to an individual who lacks inwardly righteous qualities. He is being given the term "just" precisely because that word best describes his inward condition. No one, especially not judges, should designate as "just" someone who is not intrinsically just in the matter at hand. This is a real problem for the Protestant position for it holds that in the imputation of righteousness there is neither a subjective change *nor* a recognition of inward righteousness in the individual. To the Protestant, it is necessary to give the individual the label "righteous" precisely because there is *nothing* righteous about him. We know White agrees with this position because in the following pages (pp. 156-158) he supports Luther's analogy of the dunghill covered with snow. But if Deuteronomy 25:1 is, as White says, "the source of Paul's understanding of justification," then Paul should be using the term "justify" not as a label for someone who is still unrighteous but for one in whom he recognizes righteous qualities. Hence, for White, Deuteronomy 25:1 simply proves too much. For Catholicism, there is no problem with Deuteronomy 25:1 because in assigning the word "justified" to an individual she sees either the making righteous or the recognition of that inward righteousness. This is possible because justification is not solitary and static but is a fluid continuum.

White then attempts to support his theory by referencing a usage of the Greek *logizomai* in Leviticus 17:4 of the LXX. White quotes a portion of the verse with the words,

> Any man who did not bring an animal he had slaughtered to the door of the tabernacle as an offering to the Lord, as the Scripture says, "bloodguiltiness is to be *reckoned* to that man." Surely this guilt is not infused into the man, but he is legally declared guilty of blood.

Here White reveals a fatal flaw in his analysis. First, in failing to quote the remainder of the verse he hides from the reader the very reason the man was *reckoned* as "bloodguilty." The verse actually reads, "...the man shall be considered guilty of bloodshed; he has shed blood and must be cut off from his people."[38] We notice here that the man is "considered guilty of bloodshed" precisely because "he has shed blood." In other words, he contemplated shedding blood in his heart, it was an intrinsic part of his thought and his nature, and he finally committed the very act he is accused of doing. He is not being legally labeled for something he did not do, or that was not in his nature, but for precisely for what he did do from his nature. This use of *logizomai* presents a fundamental problem for the Protestant theory of imputation since such a theory proposes that a man can be forensically declared righteous who has neither done a righteous act nor is righteous in his own nature. White then tries to support his theory by citing the use of the Hebrew equivalent of *logizomai,* the word חשׁב (*chashab*) used in Genesis 31:15. White states:

> In Genesis 31:14-15, Rachel and Leah, Jacob's wives, speak of their father and the treatment they have received at his hand. They say, "Do we still have any portion or inheritance in our father's house? Are we not *reckoned* (*hasav*) [sic] by him as foreigners?" Of course, Rachel and Leah were not foreigners, but they were *reckoned* as such by their father.

White's analysis is faulty on several counts. First, he again fails to quote the remainder of the passage in question. It reads,

---

[38] This is a literal translation from the Hebrew.

"Does he not regard us as foreigners? Not only has he sold us, but he has used up what was paid for us." Rachel and Leah are speaking of their father Laban who took payment from Jacob as dowry for the right to have both Rachel and Leah as wives. Rachel and Leah recognize that Laban had actually "sold" them to Jacob and subsequently squandered all the wealth leaving nothing for his daughters. It is to these actions that Rachel and Leah view themselves as "foreigners" in Laban's eyes — precisely because Laban was treating them as one would treat a foreigner who had no rights and was subsequently cheated out of money. Practically speaking, they were foreigners in Laban's eyes. He treated them the same as foreigners, upon which they decided to take back what they determined he stole from them. After taking Laban's possessions, they left with their husband Jacob for another land (Genesis 31:16-21). We can apply the same principle to other issues of life. For example, if a wife commits adultery against her husband and he subsequently calls her a "whore," it is not because she necessarily has caroused in the streets enticing men to her rented apartment. The wife is a "whore" because she has acted, at least in one instance, as a whore would act — she fornicated with another man. She has not only acted like a whore but has exhibited, to whatever degree, the intrinsic qualities of a whore. Similarly, Rachel and Leah were treated as "foreigners" by their father because of the financial position in which he put them, where upon they disowned him and terminated the familial bonds. Although they were still connected by blood ties, they cut themselves off from Laban and made themselves "foreigners" to him and even went to live in a *foreign* land. Again, they considered themselves foreigners because of the reality of being treated as foreigners, not because they thought Laban was just calling them names.

In addition to the above analysis we might also point out that White does not address the preponderance of instances in the LXX in which *logizomai* refers to the actual reality and existence of the thing or matter in view.[39] In fact, of the over one hundred times *logizomai* is used in the LXX it is rarely, if ever, used other than to actualize the reality of the matter or object it has in view.

[39] cf., Lev. 27:23; Deut. 2:11,20; 3:13; 2 Sam. 4:2; 14:13,14; 19:19,43; 1 Kings 10:21; 2 Chr. 5:6; 9:20; Job 31:28; 34:37; Ps. 34:4, et al).

In regards to imputation versus infusion, after citing Paul's reference to David in Romans 4:6-8, White inquires:

> Note the parallels that Paul presents: the imputation (reckoning) of righteousness and the non-imputation ("will not take into account") of sin are likened to forgiveness of those sins, and to their "covering." Where is the subjective change taught by Roman Catholic theology? It does not find support in the Scriptures because it doesn't exist there.[40]

We hope that the information already supplied in this chapter will help in seeing where Scripture teaches justification by infusion. But in respect of White's specific reference to David, let us investigate more thoroughly how Scripture explicitly portrays the concept of infusion. First, we can begin by citing the entire verse of Psalm 32:1. David declares: "Blessed is he whose transgressions are forgiven, whose sins are covered. Blessed is the man whose sin the Lord does not count against him and in whose spirit is no deceit." Notice that in connection to being "forgiven," "covered," and "sin...not counted against him," David speaks of one "in whose spirit is no deceit." This statement is speaking of the inner quality — the spiritual essence — of the person as he is being forgiven. His spirit has no deceit. It is not merely a legal covering given to David but a restoration or recognition of his inner nature. Lest we be confused about this additional dimension to David's justification, he reiterates these same terms even more vividly in the companion passage of Psalm 51, a passage which is concerned with the same sin of David. In Psalm 51:9-12, David writes of himself:

> Hide your face from my sins and blot out all my iniquity. Create in me a pure heart, O God, and renew a steadfast spirit within me. Do not cast me from your presence or take your Holy Spirit from me. Restore to me the joy of your salvation and grant me a willing spirit to sustain me.

---

40 *The Roman Catholic Controversy*, p. 154-155.

As we learned in chapter 4, Paul is using David's experience in Psalm 32 and its companion passage of Psalm 51 as the reference point and definition for justification. In other words, what happened to David in Psalms 32 and 51 is what happens when one is justified. His sins are blotted out, but in addition, David speaks of his inner nature being changed. He wants God to create a "pure heart" and "renew a steadfast spirit" within him. He asks that God not take his "Holy Spirit" from him and desires that God will grant a "willing spirit" to sustain him. What clearer language could there be to describe the subjective change of the one whose sins are blotted out and covered? Similarly, statements such as "Wash away all my iniquity and cleanse me from my sin" in 51:2 and "Surely you desire truth in the inward parts; you teach me wisdom in the innermost place" in 51:6 show the convergence of God's mindful forgiving of sin at the same time that he changes the inner essence of the person he forgives. The two events are simultaneous and it is Paul who is combining the simultaneity under the exclusive term *justification* in Romans 4:5-8, not the Protestant notion of sanctification.

As we learned in chapter 4, justification is a process. The process comprises both the infusion of righteousness into the individual and God's recognition of that righteousness. These two facets of justification are like two strands of a rope, intertwining and interweaving with each other. It is the action of God's grace that initiates and accomplishes the process. God makes the first move in the life of the individual through "prevenient" grace, i.e., "that which comes before."[41] As the individual responds to this grace both by faith and works, he attains a specific righteous quality in the eyes of God by merely responding to God's call and continuing to respond in faith, hope, and love. As we learned in previous

[41] Council of Trent: "It furthermore declares that in adults the beginning of that justification must be derived from the predisposing grace of God through Jesus Christ, that is, from his vocation, whereby without any existing merits on their part they are called, so that they who by sin were turned away from God, through His stimulating and assisting grace are disposed to convert themselves to their own justification, by freely assenting to and cooperating with the same grace..." Session 6, Chapter 5, (cf., Lamentations 5:21; Jeremiah 3:22; Zechariah 1:3).

chapters, God can look upon man's faith and works as meritorious and with the potential to gain righteousness because God is not viewing them from the system of uncompromising law but through the eyes of grace.[42] It is the atonement of Christ that has made this new view of man possible. Thus, grace is both the lens through which God views us and the infused quality we receive from God to help us maintain his gracious view. At each point that God gives the individual his grace and he responds to that grace, one can say that he is "justified" in God's eyes. God gives both a justifying quality (infused grace) and continually recognizes and pronounces the individual "just" because he has the quality of righteousness within him. Hence, "to justify" refers both to the making righ-

---

42 Geisler and MacKenzie raise the counter-argument that "Scripture teaches that grace and meritorious works are mutually exclusive" or that the Catholic problem "stems from a fallacious inference that simply because something is prompted by grace it is not obtained by merit." Hence they conclude, "When one is rewarded for works, the reward is not a matter of grace, since the payment is *owed* (at least in part) for work done...Romans 11:6" (op. cit., p. 230). This is precisely where the Protestant polemic has created a strawman and made a false characterization of Catholic theology. Catholicism would heartily agree that grace and meritorious works are mutually exclusive. That is why the Council of Trent used the same verse, Romans 11:6, in reference to grace and works: "because none of those things which precede justification, whether faith or works, merit the grace of justification; for, if it is a grace, it is not now by reason of works, otherwise (as the same Apostle says) grace is no more grace [Romans 11:6]." However, the mutual exclusivity of grace and works is only true under the system of law, which legally, strictly, and absolutely requires the one for whom work is done to pay what is *owed* to the worker. In this sense, and in this sense only, it is appropriate to use the word "*owed*" in reference to works. The system of law does not save individuals and it is therefore totally invalid for Geisler and MacKenzie to use the word "owed" to describe the Catholic concept of works. Geisler and MacKenzie hint that they are aware of this distinction by inserting the parenthetical expression "at least in part," but they were not willing to follow this distinction to its logical conclusion, i.e., that one can view works from two entirely different systems of evaluation, law or grace. As we "please" God in the latter system, he rewards us for our work because he is kind and benevolent, not because he "owes" us something. Even Geisler and MacKenzie state themselves that we are unable "to please God unless enabled by grace" (op. cit., p. 246). What they need to see, however, is that not only does God prompt works through grace, he also evaluates them through the same grace.

teous of the individual and the recognition of that same righteousness in God's eyes.[43]

---

[43] Geisler and MacKenzie, in reference to Hans Küng's attempt to coalesce the forensic and transformational aspects of Protestant and Catholic theology, respectively, suggest: "It would be proper to say that Trent allows for but does not teach forensic justification as one element in the overall process of justification" (f. 16, p. 224). The authors, appealing to the analysis by Alister McGrath (*Iustitia Dei*, Vol. II, p. 72), stress the clause, "and not only are we reputed" used by the Council of Trent in reference to justification. The following are the Council's actual words: "...and not only are we reputed, but we are truly called and are just, receiving justice within us..." (Session 6, Chapter 7). Contrary to Geisler and MacKenzie's claim, Trent did not by this language "allow for" the view of forensic justification. Trent does not entertain the notion of forensic justification anywhere in the Sixth Session or anywhere else in the Council. Let us make clear that Trent rejected the Protestant concept of forensic justification. Trent's purpose in using "and not only are we reputed," as understood and defined by subsequent Councils and official ecclesial documents (e.g., the *Catholic Catechism*, 1994), was that God does not "repute" man as "just" if he is not "just" intrinsically. Thus, the clause serves not to open up a future possibility to accept the Protestant concept of forensic justification in Catholic soteriology, but it does precisely the opposite — it defines "reputed" *only* in terms of intrinsic transformation. As St. Robert Bellarmine said: "When God justifies the sinner by declaring him just, He also makes him just, for God's judgment is according to truth" (*De iustificatione*, II, 3). Louis Bouyer cites modern scholarship in support of Bellermine. He writes: "...Nevertheless, modern scientific exegesis unanimously acknowledges that the word [δικαιόω] can only mean 'to declare officially just someone who is so in reality.' (*Spirit and Forms of Protestantism*, p. 148). Citing the writings of Lutheran Karl Holl [*The Cultural Significance of the Reformation* (New York: Meridian Book, 1959); *The Reconstruction of Morality* (Philadelphia: Fortress Press, 1979); *What Did Luther Understand by Religion?* (Philadelphia: Fortress Press, 1977)], Lutheran Carl Braaten states: "...Holl distinguished between analytic and synthetic justification. Synthetic justification was defined as a declarative judgment of God whereby the sinner was justified solely on the basis of the work of Christ. Holl maintained that Luther rejected this view of justification, as did Holl himself. It was Melanchthon who made the great mistake of narrowing justification down to the declaration that sinners are righteous on account of the external merits of Christ, whereas Luther allegedly understood justification as a real transformation of persons from the state of sinfulness to that of righteousness. For Holl God does not only declare a person righteous, he literally makes a person righteous. If God were to declare a person righteous who is in fact unrighteous, God would be a liar, trading on a legal fiction. God would be dealing with sinners as though they were perfectly righteous. Holl called this the fatal 'as though.'" (Braaten, *Justification*, pp. 13-14). Braaten goes on to explain how Holl's view was pitted against that of Theodosius Harnack [*Luthers Theologie mit besonderer Beziehung auf seine Versohnungs-und Erlosungslehre*, I, 1862, 1865, reissued 1927] at the 1963 Lutheran World Federation meeting in Helsinki with no resolution to this day.

Hodge makes another attempt to support his Protestant definition of "to justify" by appealing to the language of Romans 8:33:

> Who, he asks, 'shall lay anything to the charge of God's elect? It is God who justifies. Who is he that condemns?'...Against the elect in Christ no ground of condemnation can be presented. God pronounces them just, and therefore no one can pronounce them guilty. This passage is certainly decisive against the doctrine of subjective justification in any form.[44]

Romans 8:33 is one of the more popular verses of Scripture for theorists of imputed righteousness, and Hodge's usage is no exception. Analyzing this verse in its context, however, shows that it not only denies the theory of imputation, but it resolutely confirms justification by infusion.

The first thing we need to address is Hodge's underlying premise. In the same paragraph cited above, Hodge writes:

> Condemnation is not the opposite either of pardon or of reformation. To condemn is to pronounce guilty or worthy of punishment. To justify is to declare not guilty, or that justice does not demand punishment, or that the person concerned cannot justly be condemned.

As we have pointed out previously, although some of what Hodge claims is true, it is at best a half-truth, and as a result, distorts the picture of justification presented in the New Testament. Granted, the opposite of "condemnation" is "justification." But a person is not condemned who does not have qualities about him that can be condemned — qualities that by his "conduct" (to use Hodge's word) he has exhibited to the world. He does not receive a sentence of condemnation for something he is not or that he has not done or with which he has not been identified. That would be a "legal fiction." Similarly, in a court of law, the judge does not justify a person he knows is guilty of the crime in question. He cannot pronounce him just if he is unjust. Moreover, if he is condemned

[44] Hodge, op. cit., p. 49. White also uses the same argument (op. cit., p. 155).

for what he *is* or *has done*, by the same token, it is only equitable that he is justified for what he *is not* or the crime he *has not done*.

These elementary principles of equity hold as regards the *justification* and *condemnation* in Romans 8:33. For example, in Romans 8:30, Paul lays out the *ordo salutis* of salvation, that is, predestined, called, justified, glorified: "And those he predestined, he also called; those he called, he also justified; those he justified, he also glorified." This *ordo salutis* is connected to the previous verse which adds "foreknowledge" to the order: "For those God foreknew he also predestined to be conformed to the likeness of his Son, that he might be the firstborn among many brothers." Here we see that the purpose of predestination is to conform one to the likeness of Christ. This verse uses two concepts: "conformed to the likeness" and "firstborn among many brothers," which have their end result in the final resurrection of the body, or what Romans 8:33 terms "glorification." The same usage of these phrases in other parts of the New Testament supports this interpretation.[45]

Immediately noticeable by its absence from the *ordo salutis* of Romans 8:33, however, is the aspect of *sanctification*. This is no accident. It shows us that Paul is subsuming sanctification within the realm of justification. In Paul's view, justification occurs after the "call" and continues until the "glorification." Protestant theology holds that sanctification occurs between justification and glorification and is distinct from both. As we have noted previously, this is not the way Paul or other New Testament writers portray justification. Though justification is used in reference to the past, it is also used in reference to the present and future.[46]

---

[45] The word "conformed" is from the Greek σύμμορφος which appears only one other time, i.e., Philippians 3:21, where it speaks of our glorification in the final resurrection. The verbal cognate, συμμορφόομαι, appears one time in Philippians 3:10 referring to being "conformable" to Christ's death in anticipation of the final resurrection. This would seem to encompass the latter two terms of the *ordo salutis* in Romans 8:30, viz., "justification and glorification." The New Testament uses the word "firstborn" nine times: six times to identify Christ as God's firstborn son; once in reference to the firstborn children in Egypt; and twice in reference to Christ being the first to experience the resurrection (Colossians 1:18, Revelation 1:5).

[46] *Past*: Romans 5:1; 1 Cor. 6:11; Titus 3:7. *Present*: Romans 8:33; Acts 13:39; Gal. 2:17; James 2:24. *Future*: 1 Cor. 4:4-5; Matt. 12:37; Romans 2:13.

To demonstrate the transformational aspect of justification, even though the primary reference to being *conformed to the image of the Son* is to the future glorification, the New Testament also uses such terminology in reference to the process of justification/sanctification. We note this in the verbal cognate of the word "conformed" used in Philippians 3:10-12:

> That I may know him and the power of his resurrection and the fellowship of his sufferings, *being conformed* to his death, if somehow I may attain to the resurrection from the dead. Not as though I had already received it or been made perfect, but I follow after if indeed I may lay hold of that for which I was laid hold of by Christ Jesus.

Here Paul speaks of presently "being conformed to his death" in expectation of attaining to the resurrection, hence, the *conforming* that is taking place here is prior to the resurrection. Within the present *conforming*, Paul includes "the fellowship of his sufferings" and that he has "not already...been made perfect." His final goal is to be totally conformed to the image of Christ in the resurrection, but prior to that he is "being conformed to his death" through his suffering and his striving for perfection on earth. In other words, he must be conformed to his death before he can be conformed to his resurrection. Because Christ's death entailed suffering, Paul must also go through similar suffering so that he may finally attain to the resurrection. As Paul goes through this suffering, he is justified and sanctified.

Paul speaks similarly of the justification/sanctification process in other passages. For example, in 2 Corinthians 3:18 he writes: "And we, who with unveiled faces all reflect the Lord's glory, *are being transformed into his likeness*, with ever-increasing glory..." Here Paul speaks of the ongoing "transforming[47] into

---

[47] The word "transforming" is from the Greek word μεταμορφόομαι, from which we get the English word "metamorphosis." The New Testament uses this word four times, twice in reference to the sanctification process (2 Cor. 3:18; Rom. 12:2), and twice in reference to Christ's transfiguration (Matt. 17:2; Mark 9:2). Christ's transfigured body points to his glorified body.

the likeness"[48] of Christ. This is occurring presently in the life of each Christian as his will is conformed to Christ's. As Paul said above in Philippians 3:10, this transformation into Christ's likeness occurs through the sufferings he sustains and his striving for perfection. According to Colossians 3:10, it is also accomplished through knowledge: "And having put on the new self which is being renewed[49] in *knowledge* in the image [likeness] of his Creator." Paul also speaks of the "transformation" and "renewal" in Romans 12:2: "Do not conform any longer to the pattern of this world, but be *transformed* by the *renewing* of your mind."

We can see from all these interconnecting passages that Romans 8:29's teaching that we are conformed into the image of Christ involves both our present life and our future life at the resurrection. Under the terms of Paul's *ordo salutis* in Romans 8:30, the present "conforming," "transforming," and "renewing" into the likeness of Christ falls under the rubric of "justification." It is in this justification that we are conformed to the image of Christ presently, awaiting our final conforming at the glorification as we receive our resurrection bodies.

Paul also makes clear that our conforming to the likeness of Christ involves our justification by the way he uses the word "justified" in connection with sanctification. We note this in 1 Corinthians 6:11 where Paul writes:

> ...nor thieves nor the greedy nor drunkards nor slanderers nor swindlers will inherit the kingdom of God. And that is what some of you were. But you were washed, you were sanctified, you

48 The word "likeness" is from the Greek word εἰκών, from which we get "icon." It is the same word used in Romans 8:29 ("conformed to the *likeness* of his Son") and Colossians 3:10 ("and having put on the new self which is being renewed in knowledge in the *likeness* of its Creator").

49 The word "renewed" is from the Greek word ἀνακαινόω or its noun cognate ἀνακαίνωσις which are used only three times in the New Testament: 2 Cor. 4:16 ("inwardly we are being *renewed* day by day"); in Romans 12:2 ("Be transformed by the *renewing* of your mind") and in Titus 3:5 ("regeneration and *renewing* of the Holy Spirit").

were justified[50] in the name of the Lord Jesus Christ and by the Spirit of our God.

The context of this passage concerns the present life of the Corinthians. The reference to "washed" probably refers to their baptism (cf., 1 Cor. 1:14-17; 12:13; Acts 22:16). It is at this "washing" that they are "sanctified" and "justified." Clearly, by the context in which these words are placed in 1 Corinthians 6:10-11, this tripartite event in the past refers exclusively to the time they were *intrinsically* made righteous.[51] They were once despicable sinners engaging in many and varied sins but at their washing, sanctification, and justification, these sins were removed and they became righteous — new creations (cf. 2 Cor. 5:17; Gal 6:16). Thus, 1 Corinthians 6:11 associates the term "justification" with the transformational change in the individual that we have seen above in Romans 12:2; 2 Corinthians 3:18; Philippians 3:10; and Colossians

[50] Both "sanctified" (ἡγιάσθητε) and "justified" (ἐδικαιώθητε) are in the Greek aorist tense (past tense). It is highly significant that "sanctified" precedes "justified" since this is the only place in the whole New Testament where the two verbs are coupled together, except for, perhaps, Revelation 22:11, but there each word is in a separate clause. There are only three places in the New Testament where the noun δικαισύνη even appears in the same context with the verb ἁγιασμός or the noun ἁγιάζω (Romans 6:19; 1 Corinthians 1:30; 2 Timothy 2:21-21) but there is no suggestion in the text that the former takes chronological precedence over the latter. Of the four remaining δικαιόω cognates, none of them ever appear with the ἁγιάζω cognates. Hence, it cannot be overstated that the only place "sanctified" and "justified" are ever coupled together in the New Testament, is a place where the former precedes the latter, and both are in a context of intrinsic and causative righteousness, not forensic or imputational righteousness.

[51] Protestant lexicons, who would normally be predisposed to interpret δικαιόω as forensic, do not hesitate to call its usage in 1 Corinthians 6:11 as "causative," i.e., to make one pure or righteous as opposed to declaring one forensically righteous (See: *A Greek-English Lexicon of the New Testament*, 4th ed. of Walter Bauer's Griechisch-Deutsches Worterbuch zu den Schriften, by William F. Arndt and F. Wilbur Gingrich (Chicago: University of Chicago Press, 1957,1979) p. 197. Bauer also adds that "in the mystery religions (Rtzst. Mysterienrel. 258ff.) *dikaiousthai* refers to a radical inner change which the initiate experiences (Herm. Wr. 13,9)...and approaches the sense of becoming deified. Some are inclined to find in 1 Tim. 3:16 a similar use."

3:10.[52] Paul reinforces this concept in 1 Corinthians 6:11 by referring to the action of "the Spirit of our God" which is normally associated with the transformational aspects of the Christian life, especially in the extended context of the verses in question, i.e., Romans 8:1-27. That Paul is subsuming sanctification under justification (or vice-versa) is also evident by his listing sanctification *before* justification in 1 Corinthians 6:11 as if to break down any notion that the two are separate, distinct or follow any particular order. This agrees with the evidence in Romans 8:30, which leaves sanctification out and subsumes it under the title of "justified."

We see the Spirit's action in justification as well in Titus 3:5-7:

> ...he saved us not because of righteous things we had done but because of his mercy. He saved us through the *washing of rebirth and renewal by the Holy Spirit* whom he poured out on us generously through Jesus Christ our Savior, so that, *being justified by his grace...*[53]

Here we notice that in the same breath that Paul speaks of "being saved through the washing[54] of *regeneration and renewal* by the Holy Spirit," he pinpoints the time this was done for us as "being justified by his grace." Justification occurs when we were "saved," "rebirthed," and "renewed." The New Testament uses the word "renewed" in only one other passage, Romans 12:2, cited

[52] To this we can add Scripture's numerous metaphors which illustrate the soul's transformation by the removal of sin. Sin is said to be: (1) washed or cleansed away: Psalm 51:2,7; Isaiah 1:16; Ezek. 36:25; Acts 22:16; Hebrews 1:3; 1 John 1:7; (2) blotted out: Isaiah 43:25; (3) swept away: Isaiah 44:23; (4) wiped out: Acts 3:19; (5) taken away: 2 Sam. 12:13; 1 Chr. 21:8; John 1:29; (6) removed: Psalm 103:12; (7) leaving no deceit: Psalm 32:2.

[53] The NIV translation "having been justified" is not warranted here. The word δικαιωθέντες is an aorist participle, not a perfect passive indicative, thus it should read "being justified." This matches the other aorists in the preceding verses, e.g., ἔσωσεν ("he saved")," and ἐξέχεεν ("he poured out").

[54] Many evangelical theologians have admitted that the "washing" of Titus 3:5 most likely refers to baptism. See: Gaffin, Richard. *Resurrection and Redemption*, op. cit., p. 141.

above.[55] In that verse Paul refers to the "renewing of your mind" in the context of the holiness expected in Christian life. The word "rebirth" is used only one other place in the New Testament, Matthew 19:28, in which Jesus speaks of the final glorification as the "regeneration"[56] As we have seen, other New Testament passages use similar terms for justification, sanctification and glorification.The terminology is fluid such that one aspect can stand for another or overlap into another's territory. Justification is a "rebirth" and "renewal" as much as sanctification and glorification. Hence, one cannot escape observing that justification is spoken of in *transformational* terms by Paul.

In the description of justification in Titus 3:5-7, the phrase in verse 6 accentuates the Holy Spirit's life-changing action: "by the Holy Spirit whom he ["God our Savior," from verse 4] poured out on us...so that being justified..." Here we see that Paul uses the term "pouring out" of the Holy Spirit to describe the "justification," "rebirth" and "renewal."

Paul uses the words "pouring out" in another passage that speaks of justification — Romans 5:1-5. He begins in verse 1 by declaring, "Therefore, since we have been justified through faith..." This statement treats the justification as a past event. In fact, in Greek it is a completed past event.[57] Yet the same past tense is used

---

[55] From the Greek noun: ἀνακαίνωσις. The verbal cognate, ἀνακαινόω is used in Colossians 3:10 "renewed in knowledge" and 2 Cor. 4:16 "the inward man is renewed day by day." Evangelicals Geisler and MacKenzie comment on the use of "renewal" in Titus 3:5: "This cannot apply only to initial justification as Catholics claim, since the present tense ("renewing") is used in this text." (op. cit., p. 232). This is very misleading analysis since ἀνακαινόω, as used in Titus 3:5, does not have a tense because it is a *noun*, not a verb. As such, it merely describes the specific ministry of the Holy Spirit in salvation. Moreover, the Holy Spirit initiates his ministry of "washing" and "renewal" when, as it says in Titus 3:5, "he saved us," which according to verse 7, is the time we were "being justified." Thus, the Catholic claim stands.

[56] From the Greek noun, παλιγγενεσίᾳ. It has no New Testament verbal cognates.

[57] The form δικαιωθέντες ("having been justified") in Romans 5:1 is a perfect passive verb in Greek denoting an action in the past that is complete, anticipating future results. This is the same tense Romans 5:5 uses of the word ἐκκέχυται ("having poured out") from the Greek root ἐκχέω (the aorist indicative of ἐκχέω appears in Titus 3:6). This shows that both events in Romans 5:1-5, i.e., the justification and the pouring out of love by the

of *love* when Paul says in verse 5, "God has *poured out* his love into our hearts by the Holy Spirit." This shows us that both the justification by faith and the pouring out of love into our hearts occurred in the completed past, with future results anticipated. The past reception of faith and love is coupled with "hope" as Paul says in verse 3, "we rejoice in the hope," and in verse 5, "hope does not disappoint us." Hence, we understand that at the justification introduced in Romans 5:1, the individual received an infusion of faith, hope and love.

Romans 6:6-7 also uses the term justification in reference to sanctification: "For we know that our old self was crucified with him so that the body of sin might be done away with, that we should no longer be slaves to sin — because anyone who has died has been *justified*[58] from sin." As in 1 Corinthians 6:11 cited above, the context of Romans 6 concerns the Christian life. In fact, Paul, just as he reminded the Corinthians, reminds the Romans of their baptism. Paul mentions baptism specifically in verses 1-4:

> What shall we say, then? Shall we go on sinning so that grace may increase? By no means! We died to sin; how can we live in it any longer? Or don't you know that all of us who were bap-

---

[57 cont.] Holy Spirit, occur in the *past* and are both considered *completed* actions with future results anticipated. This is why Catholic doctrine insists that love is added to faith in initial justification. The Council of Trent states: "For although no one can be just but he to whom the merits of the passion of our Lord Jesus Christ are communicated, yet this does take place in this justification of the ungodly when by the merit of that same most holy passion the charity of God is poured forth by the Holy Spirit in the hearts of those justified, and inheres in them. Hence man through Jesus Christ, into whom he is ingrafted, receives in the said justification together with the remission of sins all these [gifts] infused at the same time: faith, hope, and charity. For unless hope and charity be added to it, neither unites one perfectly with Christ, nor makes him a living member of his body. For this reason it is most truly said that 'faith without works is dead...and is of no profit...but faith, which works by charity'" (Session 6, Chapter 7).

[58] Most translations render the word δικαιόω in Romans 6:7 as "freed" (KJV, RSV, NASB, NIV, TEV). Some retain the word "justified," e.g., ASV (1901) and the Douay-Rheims. Some of the same versions which translate δικαιόω as "freed" in Romans 6:7, however, use the word "justified" in Acts 13:39 where it would be just as appropriate for them to use "freed" (KJV, NIV, Moffatt); others, however, use "freed" as well (RSV, NASB, TEV).

> tized into Christ Jesus were baptized into his death. We were therefore buried with him through baptism into death in order that, just as Christ was raised from the dead through the glory of the Father, we too may live a new life.

As Paul pointed to the "washing" in 1 Corinthians 6:11 and Titus 3:5, so he points to "baptism" in Romans 6:1-4. As it was for the Corinthians, baptism is the beginning of justification and sanctification also for the Romans. In being baptized, they become partakers in Christ's death and thus become "dead" to sin. Paul tells them that they must live a new life — a life free from sin. Paul concludes in Romans 6:7 that one who has "died" [died with Christ in baptism] has been *justified* from sin. One of the more curious aspects of this verse is that Paul could have used two other words in place of *justified* that would have given the same meaning he intended. He uses them elsewhere in this context. One appears in Romans 6:18, where Paul says, "you have been set *free*[59] from sin and become slaves to God." Romans 6:20, 22 uses the same phrasing. In all three cases Paul is using the "free/slave" metaphors for illustration. The other word Paul could have used is "sanctified" (i.e., "anyone who has died has been sanctified from sin"). Since "sanctified" carries the meaning of "set apart from" or "separated from" it would have been an appropriate term to show the Christian's separation from sin. In fact, "sanctified" may have been a better word to use since it specifically denotes cleansing and holiness. Its noun cognate is used in Romans 6:19 ("leading to holiness") and 6:22 ("leads to holiness").[60] Yet Paul chose to use the word "justified" in Romans 6:7, the same word he used singularly in reference to God "justifying the ungodly" in Romans 4:5, for example. In other words, in Romans 6:7 Paul understands and is using the term "justification" as a synonym for sanctification. Now we can understand even more why the latter usage does not refer to a forensic justification but can and must refer to a transformational justification. The justification involves a separation or cleansing

[59] The word "freed" in Romans 6:18,20,22 is from the Greek word ἐλευθερωθέντες meaning literally "to be free."

[60] The noun cognates are usually translated as *sanctification* (e.g., 1 Cor. 1:30; 1 Thess. 4:3,4,7; 2 Thess. 2:13; 1 Pet. 1:2).

from sin. The ungodly become justified because sin has been washed from their soul and they have become renewed.

Further evidence regarding the transformational aspect of justification in Romans 6:7 is the emphasis beginning in 6:5-6 in which Paul states: "If we have been united with him in the likeness of his death, we will certainly also be united with him in his resurrection. For we know that our old self was crucified with him so that the body of sin might be done away with..." We will recall that Paul spoke of the same occurrence in Philippians 3:10: "I want to know the power of his resurrection and the fellowship of sharing in his sufferings, becoming like [conformed to] him in his death..." In the former verse, Romans 6:5, Paul is connecting "being united with Christ in his death through baptism" with the death of the old self and renunciation of the sinful life. In the latter verse, Paul speaks of becoming like Christ in his death by going through the "fellowship of his sufferings." Both are speaking about the sanctified Christian life and both anticipate its completion in the resurrection of the body.

We will also recall that Paul used a particular word in Philippians 3:10 that was used in Romans 8:29 — the word *conformed*.[61] In Philippians 3:10, Paul indicates that he is "conformed to the death of Christ" in anticipation of the resurrection, whereas in Romans 8:29 he is "being conformed to the image of the Son" in anticipation of his glorification, i.e., the resurrection. In Romans 6:1-6 it is baptism that initiates the conforming to the Son in his death. According to 1 Corinthians 6:11, it is the "washing," i.e., baptism, that initiates the justification and sanctification to make one righteous and pure, conformed to the image of Christ. What all of this points to is that when Paul says in Romans 8:33, "It is God who justifies, who is he that condemns," the justification to which he is referring encompasses the entire life of the Christian. The sanctification of the Christian is subsumed under the term justification in Romans 8:33 just as it is in Romans 8:30. It is the process by which sin is eradicated from the life of the individual so that he may be conformed to the image of Christ presently in his soul and finally in his body at the physical resurrection of the last day.

---

61 From the Greek word συμμορφόμαι or its noun cognate σύμμορφος, one or the other which is used in Romans 8:29; Philippians 3:10 and 3:21.

More on the "Crediting of Righteousness"

The difference between God viewing Abraham's faith as a measure of righteousness (the Catholic view) and God merely crediting Abraham with an alien righteousness (the Protestant view), hearkens back to the distinction made earlier in chapters 1-2 concerning the kind of faith that Abraham was required to give to God. Abraham's faith was not merely believing that God was his Savior. He did not merely accept God into his heart and then go on his way never having to be concerned about his salvation again. Rather, from the beginning to the very end in Abraham's life, God required great faith and love from Abraham. God placed Abraham in situations that seemed to question the very integrity of God, e.g., calling him from his home to go to a promised land that he never received (Gen. 12; Heb. 11); promising a child to parents who were a century old (Gen. 15; Rom. 4:16f); telling him to slay his own son (Gen. 22). In putting Abraham through these tests, God was attempting to draw out something deep within the heart of Abraham. In other words, God was looking for something intrinsic to Abraham — an uncompromising, undaunted faith and love in God that accepted Him regardless of the circumstantial evidence. When God determines, from the capacity given, that a person such as Abraham has developed this kind of deep and seasoned character, he in turn views that faith and love as *righteousness*. In short, it is faith, hope and love, that ***is*** the righteousness of Christ, not faith that forensically apprehends the righteousness of Christ.[62]

In commenting on the possibility that faith ***is*** the righteousness that leads to justification, Reformed theologian Charles Hodge candidly admits that Scripture's choice of language does

[62] As Catholic theologian Joseph Fitzmeyer writes: "It would be false to Paul's whole theology to understand his use of Gn 15:6 to mean a mere legal fiction, that uprightness was imputed to Abraham, although he was not really upright. Theoretically, the words could mean no more than this. But there is not the slightest hint either in the Gn story or in Paul's treatment that Abraham was not previously upright. Again, Paul's ideas about faith and uprightness otherwise indicate that in the sight of God, who sees things as they are, Abraham's faith counted as uprightness; it was formally recognized to be just what it was. The manifestation of his faith was *de se* justifying" (*The Jerome Biblical Commentary*, op. cit., p. 303.).

suggest such an understanding. In reaction to the Arminian doctrine, which believes that faith is the ground of justification, Hodge said the following:

> There is one passage in the Bible, or rather one form of expression that occurs in several places, which seems to favor this view on the subject. In Romans 4:3 it is said that Abraham believed God, and it was counted unto him for righteousness; and again in verse 22 of that chapter and in Galatians 3:6. If this phrase be interpreted according to the analogy of such passages as Romans 2:26, "Shall not his uncircumcision be counted for circumcision?" it does mean that faith is taken as accepted for righteousness.[63]

Hodge goes on to say that though the language in these passages implies that faith itself is the reason one is credited with righteousness, this would be "inconsistent" with other Scriptures. Hodge appeals to the "analogy of Scripture" for support. To counterbalance the force of the language used in Romans 4:3, 22 and Galatians 3:6, Hodge takes our focus off these clear passages and brings Galatians 3:16 into the picture. He then claims that the object of Abraham's faith was the singular seed of Christ and the redemption promised in that seed:

> What, therefore, Abraham believed was that the seed of the woman, the Shiloh, the promised Redeemer of the world, was to be born of him. He believed in Christ as his Savior, as his righteousness and deliverer; and therefore it was that he was accepted as righteous — not for the merit of his faith and not on the ground of faith, or by taking faith in lieu of righteousness — but because he received and rested on Christ alone for his salvation.[64]

---

[63] Hodge, op. cit., p. 115. Evangelical Alister McGrath defends Luther at this point, stating: "In no way can Luther be said to teach that we are justified *on account of faith*, as some of his more unperceptive critics have suggested" (*ARCIC II and Justification*, op. cit., p. 12). McGrath directs his footnote on this point against Catholic convert John Henry Newman's work in 1837 titled "Lectures on Justification." McGrath seems to have a particular animosity towards Newman, accusing him of "gross misunderstanding, verging on a deliberate misrepresentation, of Luther" (Ibid., p. 53).

[64] Ibid., p. 116.

Although this is an admirable attempt to support his theology, in reality Hodge misdirects us. On a grammatical basis, Hodge realizes that he is not able to silence the clear and unambiguous language of Romans 4:3, 22 stating that Abraham's personal faith was the very reason he was credited with righteousness. This points back to our earlier criticism of the Protestant hermeneutic which tends to avoid the "face value" information in Scripture in lieu of the overarching theory of *faith alone*. In light of this perhaps unconscious motive, Hodge's only recourse is to appeal to a Scripture that seems to modify such face value language, i.e., Galatians 3:16. In effect, Hodge puts Paul in the dubious position of saying one thing but meaning another.[65]

Be that as it may, Hodge's attempt to explain the language of Romans 4:3, 22 by making the object of the faith to be exclusively a belief in Christ as Savior, in reality, makes a false dichotomy between faith in God and faith in Christ's atoning sacrifice. Though Galatians 3:16 specifies *God's ultimate intent* in providing the promised seed, this was neither the exclusive nor the explicit message to Abraham as recorded in the Genesis accounts. The object of Abraham's faith in Genesis 12-22 is God Himself, in *all* his plans, works, and majesty. The preponderant message in Genesis is that Abraham must believe not only that God is his Savior, but also that *God is all that he says he is*, despite the circumstantial evidence suggesting otherwise. The descriptions of faith in the Genesis accounts, and in Hebrews 11, state clearly that it is not merely that he acknowledge the promised seed, but that he fully make God his Lord — that he believe and obey without question everything that God tells him no matter how difficult it may be to accept. Paul,

[65] Evangelical theologian George Eldon Ladd arrives at the same conclusion as Hodge. He writes: "In classical Reformed theology, a corollary of justification is the doctrine of the imputation of Christ's righteousness to the believer. However, Paul never expressly states that the righteousness of Christ is imputed to believers. His words are, "And to one who does not work but trusts him who justifies the ungodly, his faith is reckoned as righteousness" (Rom. 4:3). These words could be taken to mean that God regarded faith as the most meritorious human achievement, and therefore God accounts faith as the equivalent to full righteousness. *This, however, would ignore the context of Pauline thought"* (*A Theology of the New Testament* (Grand Rapids: Eerdmans, 1974), p. 437, (emphasis mine).

likewise, makes this very clear in Romans 4:17-21 where he takes great pains to describe the tremendous inner quality of Abraham's faith by such phrases as "against all hope," "without weakening," "not wavering," and finally "was fully persuaded that God had power to do what he promised." These words would be superfluous if all Abraham had to do was accept God as his Savior. And Paul quotes these very words of undying faith right before Romans 4:22, the very verse Hodge said had nothing to do with faith being the reason for God counting Abraham righteous!

In fact, Romans 4:18 explains that precisely because of Abraham's undying faith in God, it *then* becomes possible for him to become the father of many nations and produce the promised seed of Galatians 3:16. Paul writes in Romans 4:18, "Against all hope, Abraham in hope believed and so became[66] the father of many nations, just as it had been said to him, 'So shall your offspring [seed] be.'" The very salvation of Abraham, and the salvation of the nations coming from him, rides on the deep and sustained faith of Abraham. Paul insists that it was *this* faith — the faith that believed God had power to do what he said despite the circumstances — that was "credited to him as righteousness," as Paul says in Romans 4:22: "*This is why*[67] it was credited to him as righteousness."

Paul reinforces this meaning by the next two verses which speak of the faith that those coming after Abraham must also have to be credited with righteousness: "The words, 'it was credited to him,' were written not for him alone, but also for us, to whom God will credit righteousness — for us who believe ***in him*** who raised Jesus our Lord from the dead." Here we see that it is not merely believing in the atonement, but believing ***in him*** [God] — the God who calls things that are not as if they were — behind the atonement. Just as Abraham believed that God had the power to raise Isaac from the dead, so we who believe God had the power to raise Jesus

---

66 The phrase "so became" is from the Greek εἰς το γενέσθαι in which the preposition εἰς governs the infinitive γενέσθαι with the article το. It expresses "purpose" and Paul uses it frequently in his writings, e.g., Romans 1:11; 3:26; 7:4; Eph. 1:12; Phil. 1:10. See Burton's Grammar, op. cit., p. 161.

67 The phrase "this is why" is from the Greek word διὸ which means, "therefore," "wherefore," or "for which cause," cf., Romans 1:24; 2:1; 15:22. It specifies the reason behind the action.

from the dead will be credited with righteousness for that belief. This faith, combined with a continuing life of love and hope, even as Abraham exhibited, will procure our salvation. God can graciously accept our faith, hope, and love because Christ provided such gracious acceptance of us in the atonement and resurrection. Through grace, God infuses these qualities into the individual, making him righteous in God's eyes and worthy of salvation.

Evangelical Joel Beeke attempts to negate the language of Romans 4:22 by appealing to nuances in the Greek language:

> But the objection is raised: Does not the preposition *eis* as used in Romans 4:5, 9, 22 ("Abraham's faith is counted *for* righteousness...faith was reckoned to Abraham *for* righteousness...it was imputed to him *for* righteousness") imply that the act of believing is imputed to the believer for righteousness? In these verses the Greek preposition *eis* does not signify "in the stead of," but always means "with a view to" or "in order to." It could be translated "towards" or "unto." Its meaning is clear from Romans 10:10, "with the heart man believeth *unto* [*eis*] righteousness" — i.e. faith moves toward and lays hold of Christ Himself.[68]

As he did earlier with his analysis of the Greek word *logizomai*, Beeke makes a false premise and then inserts a false conclusion. The Greek word *eis* (εις) is used over 1700 times in the New Testament and translated a half dozen different ways according to the context in which it appears. Many times, *eis* refers to the intended goal or result of a particular action or circumstance, hence the translations "toward," "in order to," "for," "for the purpose of," etc. However, to conclude, as Beeke does, that *eis* does not refer to "in the stead of" but *always* means "with a view to" not only sets up an incomplete understanding of the word, but even the use of *eis* that Beeke proposes, which grammatically denotes the goal or result of the faith in Romans 4:3, 5, 9, 22, expresses the righteousness of the *person* who exhibited the faith. In other words, we understand the faith of Abraham as that which *results* in *his* righteousness.

[68] Beeke, op. cit., p. 56.

There is nothing in the grammatical structure of the sentences which points to a righteousness other than Abraham's, that is, there is no "alien" righteousness specifically mentioned in the verse. As noted previously, Charles Hodge has admitted that the verses express such a stipulation but couldn't bring himself to accept it. Clearly, then, to claim that the righteousness referred to in the verse is the "alien righteousness of Christ" is simply reading one's theology into the text. We see the same truth in the very verse Beeke attempts to use as a counterpoint, Romans 10:10. That the man believes with the *result* of righteousness is confirmed by the next statement in the same verse, "and with the mouth one confesses unto [*eis*] salvation," i.e., with the mouth one confesses with the *intended result* of salvation to that individual.[69]

Reformed theologian John Murray recognized this problem in the Protestant interpretation but by his own admission did not have an adequate answer for it. He writes:

> ...in New Testament teaching the righteousness contemplated in justification is not faith itself but something that comes into our possession by faith. The question remains why, in the formula of Genesis 15:6 as quoted by Paul, is faith represented as reckoned for righteousness? It may not be possible to answer this question with any decisiveness.[70]

Rather than twist the meaning of *eis* ("for") to point to Christ as Beeke did, Murray realizes that grammatically he must some-

---

[69] Beeke again attempts to prove his point by claiming that the New Testament writers never used the Greek words διὰ πίστεως ("through faith") in the accusative form, only in the genitive. This is not a new argument; Charles Hodge presented it 150 years ago (*Justification by Faith Alone*, op. cit., p. 117). Since διὰ in the accusative would denote causality, i.e., "because of faith" or "on account of faith," Beeke concludes that the Holy Spirit prohibited the New Testament writers from using the accusative form of *dia* so as not to teach that one's righteousness is "because of" or "on account of" one's faith. To Beeke, the accusative διὰ τὴν πίστιν would convey the notion of 'on the ground of' or 'on account of faith,' thereby making faith the meritorious reason for the believer's acceptance with God" (See Beeke, *Justification By Faith Alone*, p. 59-60). See **Appendix 12** for a thorough refutation of Beeke's claim.

[70] Murray, John. *Redemption Accomplished and Applied* (Grand Rapids: Eerdmans, 1965), p. 358

how join the faith to the righteousness without bringing in an alien source to make the connection complete. Since the Reformed system does not allow one to view the faith of the individual as representative of or leading to his righteousness before God, it invariably retreats to the forensic model of imputed righteousness and either leaves the precise relationship between faith and righteousness an open question or inserts another element of their theology to join the two as Hodge does.

Regarding the difference between the Protestant view of "declared righteousness" and the Catholic view of "infused righteousness," Evangelical Roger Wagner writes:

> It has been pointed out repeatedly that even if one grants that justification is based on the inherent righteousness (or on the "infused-grace"- produced righteousness) of the person justified, the act of justification can, nevertheless, be nothing other than declarative. Just as "condemn" cannot mean "to make sinful or criminal" so "justify" (its consistent biblical antithesis) cannot mean "to make just or righteous." The categories are inescapably ethical and legal, not metaphysical.[71]

The problem with Wagner's reasoning is that he does not take it to the next logical step. It is much more reasonable to understand that one is declared righteous because *he is* intrinsically righteous rather than to say he is declared to be righteous but not righteous in reality. In everyday law courts, a judge or jury never declares a defendant righteous or not guilty when they know that he is unjust or guilty. Why would God be expected to do anything less? The New Testament, except when it is specifying the source or basis of justification (e.g., "blood" — Romans 5:9; "grace" — Titus 3:7), contains no passage which grants justification unless it is recognizing some intrinsic quality in the individual, whether it be faith or works. God forgives the individual's sin because of the individual's intrinsic faith in God (e.g., Romans 5:8), a faith that is tested many times (e.g., Romans 4:18-21). If God "considers" the

71 Wagner, Roger. "New Confusions for Old: Rome and Justification," *Antithesis,* Vol. 1, No. 5, September/October, 1990 p. 30.

individual righteous, it is not because he merely thinks of him as righteous while really knowing that he is unjust. In the same way, God "declares" one condemned not because he has no criminal or condemnable qualities, but precisely because he does.

As Protestant theologians attempt to confine the object of faith to "faith in the alien righteousness of Christ,"[72] in effect, faith becomes merely a "code word" for "Christ's righteousness" so as to confine faith to the soteriological area of legal imputation. *It is a fact, however, that the New Testament never uses such language.* Although no one would dispute that faith certainly includes the righteousness of Christ as its object, it is never limited to that dimension. The New Testament uses the phrase "faith in Jesus Christ" several times but never in a one-to-one correspondence with the atonement; rather, it refers to faith in the whole person of Christ as creator, sustainer, provider, redeemer, helper, healer, etc. In other words, it is belief in *Him,* as a personal being, that is the substance and object of faith. As noted in chapter 1, Romans 4:24 specifies belief "in *Him* (God) who raised Jesus our Lord from the dead," not just a belief that Jesus was raised. Hence, we are not "appropriating" Christ's righteousness, we are believing in God, the Trinity, in all his splendor and magnificence, though we cannot see Him physically. It is the belief in Him, personally, and in all that he stands for and has done that is recognized as righteousness in the eyes of God precisely because we cannot see him.

One might ask that if God is viewing Abraham's faith as the righteousness itself, then what part does the righteousness of God or the atonement of Christ have in the righteousness of Abraham? The answer is very simple. God and Abraham are working together. God has provided the means by which he can place Abraham in the way of grace. The means is the atonement of Christ. As we learned from Romans 3:25, "God presented him as a sacrifice of atonement...and in his forbearance he had left the sins committed beforehand unpunished..." Abraham's sins, like those of everyone else who receives the grace of God, are atoned for and forgiven in anticipation and on the basis of the death and resurrection of Christ. Through the power of the atonement, God puts Abraham in a gra-

[72] Sproul, *Justification By Faith Alone*, op. cit., p.107.

tuitous relationship. Within this relationship, Abraham is expected to continue in faith, love, and obedience in order to please God and develop an intimate relationship. To do this, God tests him, at times very severely, to cultivate and draw out faith, hope, and love. Through the grace that God has infused into Abraham, Abraham is able to act in faith. It is not just Abraham who is involved in the act of faith. God also is intimately at work in Abraham's heart. Though God is at work in Abraham, Abraham must respond and cooperate with the grace of God to procure the faith that God requires. God will not test Abraham above what he can bear but Abraham must act on the measure of grace that God gives him.[73]

We are not any different from Abraham. Paul states that we must also "walk in the footsteps of faith that our father Abraham had..." (Romans 4:12). As Abraham did, we must believe in a God who "calls things that are not as though they were" (Romans 4:18); we must "not weaken in faith" or "waver in unbelief regarding the promise of God" (Romans 4:19-20); we must be "strengthened in faith" and "give glory to God" being "fully persuaded that he has the power to do what he promised" (Romans 4:20-21). In short, God will view us as righteous if we "believe ***in him*** who raised Jesus our Lord from the dead." It is not just a belief in the resurrection, per se, but a belief in "him" (that is, God) who we believe has the power to raise Jesus even though it seems impossible.[74] We must believe he has done what he promised and will do what he promises, even though we face many temptations to believe otherwise (cf. 1 Cor 15:1-18; Hebrews 3:12-14; 2 Peter 3:3-9). As God tested Abraham's faith, so he will test our faith, over and over for our entire lifetime. At each point God will attempt to draw out of us the faith that "pleases" him — a faith, as Paul says, "believes that he exists *and* is the rewarder of those who diligently seek him" (Hebrews 11:6). We work out our salvation in faith and obedience and we have the confidence that God, through his grace infused in us, is enabling us to please him.

---

[73] cf., 1 Cor. 10:13; 1 Peter 1:6-7; 2 Peter 2:9.

[74] In light of this difficult requirement, it is no surprise that the very first thing liberal theologians who have departed from orthodox faith attack is the resurrection of Christ. Though they will accept the existence of Christ, to them resurrection is impossible.

Why is Faith Necessary?

One of the main problems with the theory of imputed righteousness is that it ends up proving too much. If we carry the theory of imputation to its logical conclusion, then there should be no reason why the individual must exhibit faith as a prerequisite for the imputation. If the process is all God's, then he would just impute righteousness to the individual and the matter would be over. Any faith or works that came from that imputation would merely be the result of God's action but not a prerequisite for God's action. This presents a huge problem for the imputation theory for the theory holds that those who do not exhibit faith cannot receive the imputed righteousness. To compound the problem, the Protestant understanding requires a high quality of faith in order to appropriate the alien righteousness of Christ. For the Protestant theory to be compatible with the teaching of James, the individual's faith must be of such a measurable quality that it is then, and only then, able to be the instrument to receive the alien righteousness of Christ.

Let us investigate these problems more thoroughly as they apply to Abraham. Besides the works that James's epistle specifies, even in Paul's view the kind of faith required of Abraham to receive justification is of extraordinary quality. Abraham is not merely believing that God is his Savior, he must believe that God can do something that is impossible, i.e., produce a son from two people who are a century old. If faith is a mere instrument to attain alien righteousness, why is it necessary for Abraham to have such an extremely high quality of faith, a faith that is tested again even more severely in Genesis 22?

Lutheran Carl Braaten pinpoints the dilemma for Protestants:

> A tension could arise between the role of God and the human role which then must be systematically balanced in an *ordo salutis*. Salvation might become conceived of as a synthesis of two factors, one divine and one human, with the priority always, of course, reserved for the former, but the all-decisive finality conceded to the latter. Theology, then, becomes a matter of calculating the proportionate contributions of divine grace and human free will in the total event of salvation...In any case, faith is

> a work. It is an act. But how is it related to justification — as a means to an end or as the effect of a cause?[75]

In light of the need of high-quality faith, Dispensationalist Zane Hodges, the major spokesman for an opposing tangent of Evangelical thought, has declared that the faith which appropriates the righteousness of Christ cannot be qualified in any manner without falling into a salvation by works. Hodges is at least being true to the implications of a *faith alone* theology, in that if one makes faith to be the sole instrument of justification then it must truly be alone, without works to qualify it. But even Hodges has not followed the implications of imputed righteousness to its logical conclusion, for faith, even in his purist notion, is still a *condition* to receive the alien righteousness of Christ. Perhaps Hodges finds it easier to maintain such a position since in the Dispensational theology behind his reasoning there is the element of the individual's free will to come to God which is not present in the Reformed theology of Sproul, Gerstner, Beeke, Armstrong, et al.[76] Some in the Reformed persuasion attempt to answer this dilemma by attributing the reception of faith totally to the predestination plan of God without any recourse to man's free will to generate, accept or maintain that faith. But the Reformed position ends up in the untenable position of not adequately addressing Scripture's "face value" language that

---

75 Braaten, op. cit., p. 25. What is Braaten's solution to this problem? He writes: "Therefore, it may be said that faith justifies in the sense that it is becoming aware of that forgiving love by which it was first engendered. Justification precedes faith, whereas faith is the corresponding acknowledgment of itself as gift and of God as gracious giver of that gift through creative forgiving love. Faith is by all means not a cause of forgiveness and not a prior condition of justification which can possibly be fulfilled by a human will in bondage. It would only be possible to say that Luther reversed the relation between justification and faith, making justification dependent upon a contingent human act, if one regarded the repudiation of free will *in spiritualibus* as a heterogeneous element in Luther's mind. This itself is most implausible when we recall that Luther expressed the desire in his later life to swallow, like another Saturn, all his literary children, listing *The Bondage of the Will* among the very few exceptions" (ibid., p. 26). Thus, Braaten's solution is to discount any human volition to faith, attempting to make Luther, and his extreme predestinarian views, his confidant. For a thorough critique of Luther's predestinarian views, see chapter 7: "Predestination, Free Will and Justification."

76 See chapter 9 for a more detailed analysis of Zane Hodges' view of justification.

emphatically treats faith as a volitional prerequisite on the part of the individual to receive justification. Historically, Reformed theologians have struggled desperately with this anomaly in their theology, as we will see momentarily.

Evangelicals are very confused on whether or not Scripture's "face value" language makes faith a *condition* for justification. Evangelical co- authors are taking somewhat contradictory positions on the subject. Joel Beeke writes:

> Second, is it accurate to call faith "a condition of justification" as frequently has been done? Given the meaning of "by faith" in the original Greek, it is more accurate to speak of faith as an instrument rather than as a condition of justification and salvation, for a condition generally denotes a meritorious quality for the sake of which a benefit is conferred. We are justified not merely by faith, but by faith in Christ; not because of what faith is, but because of what faith lays hold of and receives.[77]

Conversely, his colleague, R. C. Sproul says:

> The three elements of saving faith — *notitia, assensus, and fiducia* — separately and individually lack the force of a sufficient condition. When added together they compose the essence of saving faith and then achieve the level of sufficiency. When these three necessary conditions of saving faith are met, then the faith that is present is a sufficient condition for justification...We will recall that the formula "justification is by faith alone" means that faith (as noted above) is the *instrumental cause* of our justification. This instrumental cause is sufficient for justification and in effect works *ex opere operato*.[78]

Here we have one (Beeke) saying faith *is not* a condition for justification and the other (Sproul) saying that faith *is* a condi-

---

[77] Beeke, op. cit., p. 62. Donald Bloesch uses the same language: "The decision of faith is a sign that grace is working for us and in us; it is not the condition for receiving grace" (*Roman Catholicism*, op. cit., p. 155).

[78] Sproul, *Faith Alone*, op. cit., p. 88.

tion. The one says faith is an instrument, not a condition; the other says faith can only be an instrument if it meets three conditions. Though in the final analysis both may agree that faith "apprehends Christ's righteousness," it is obvious that the emphasis in one or both authors is to require a definitive quality to faith. In a word, faith is not just an instrument, it is an instrument that must be "tuned" properly, as it were, in order to function as intended. In the end, then, justification depends on the intrinsic quality of faith in the individual. How does the Christian know if he has met the three conditions of making faith an instrument for justification? If he cannot be justified until his faith meets these three conditions, then it is imperative that he have some way to measure whether he has met them. But how can he know? Does he examine himself each day? Is it dependent on the subjective judgment of himself? In addition, if it is true, as it is commonly held among evangelicals, that his works will show whether he has saving faith, must he then wait till he has accumulated a sufficient amount of works to know whether his faith has met the three conditions? If he must wait to see his works, then what if he falls into serious sin and finds that his works are not what he wants them to be or what they used to be? Has he still met the three conditions? Or, as some Evangelicals may propose, are the three conditions part of the one-time event of justification that once exhibited to God the individual need not be concerned with any longer? We must insist that if the faith that is used as an instrument is a one-time event without works, then there is nothing objective to qualify the faith to determine if it has met the three conditions. As we have argued before, if the justification is a one-time act dependent solely on faith, then there is no theological room for works to enter into a description of the moment of faith. In reality, the man could spend his whole life wondering if his faith had met the three conditions. If he sins and falls away from faith then he will be told that he never was a Christian originally because he never had "saving faith." What a terrible predicament. In a system that boasts of giving the individual assurance that he is saved, he really has no assurance at all, for he can never be certain if he has exhibited the "proper" faith.

In an effort to support his assertion that faith is not a condition, Beeke states: "The very act of faith by which we receive Christ is an act of utter renunciation of all our own works and righteousness as a condition or ground of salvation."[79] Here Beeke takes the argument back one step, but he does not solve the problem of faith being a condition. In fact, he makes faith even more of a condition by adding to it the element of "renunciation." The act of renouncing his own righteousness is something Beeke insists the candidate for salvation must do — a condition he must meet in order to be saved by God's grace. In short, renouncing his own works means that he recognizes his own sin, that he must rely on the grace of God, and that he must now stop sinning and be obedient to the Lord. In a word, he must *repent.* Unfortunately, however, Evangelicals have a tendency to separate faith from repentance, as we shall see shortly. Granted, renunciation involves a repudiation of a salvation on my own terms and conditions, but it does not relieve me of God's terms and conditions.

Regarding works, Sproul says: "For the Reformers the good works that flow out of justification are not good enough to meet the perfect demands of the law of God. Our best works remain tainted or soiled by the vestigial remnant of sin."[80] Regarding faith, Beeke says: "Moreover, since we cannot be accepted by God with less than a perfect righteousness, our faith would have to be perfect. No one's faith, however, is perfect. All our faith is impaired by sin. Nothing in us, including our faith, could possibly succeed as a condition."[81] As regards Sproul's comment, Catholic theology would agree that works, if God were to judge them on the strict basis of law, could not even begin to satisfy his perfect standards. But as Beeke admits, the same is true of faith. Without the grace of God as the basis for judging, God cannot accept *anything* we have to offer him, whether faith or works. We have already noted this fact in chapter 1 when we delineated the distinction between the system of grace and the system of law. If God were to view us from the system of law, nothing we do could please him. Our faith,

---

79 Ibid., p. 65

80 *Faith Alone*, op. cit., p. 157.

81 Beeke, op. cit., pp. 63-64.

just as much as our works, is tainted with sin. It is inescapable that the same sinful person performs both faith and works. So how is faith any better an instrument than works, especially since, as Sproul admits, faith must meet certain conditions to be an instrument worthy of accepting justification? Clearly, *faith alone* theology has painted itself into a corner out of which there is no escape.

Evangelical Michael Horton offers another explanation how faith fits into justification:

> And the reason it is faith, is because faith is the only instrument that is properly suited to receiving something without giving something. Sure, in repentance we give ourselves, our souls and bodies, over to Christ, but in justification its justified by faith alone, by relying and trusting in someone outside of us. Notice that faith becomes a work when we see it as the one thing we did in salvation. Faith is the gift of God, Paul says elsewhere.[82]

Here, Horton reveals another contradiction in the Protestant view of faith. In order to define faith as that which is "without giving something," Horton attempts to separate faith from repentance in justification. Apparently, Horton feels that in repentance one is "giving" something to God. Scripture will not allow such a separation. Paul makes this clear in Acts 20:21: "I have declared to both Jews and Greeks that they must turn to God in repentance and have faith in our Lord Jesus Christ." Similarly, Mark 1:5 states: "Confessing their sins, they were baptized by him in the Jordan River."[83]

Horton also attempts to separate faith from other virtues by referring to faith exclusively as the "gift of God." He does this in order to support his thesis that faith is "without giving something." He alludes to Ephesians 2:8 as a reference when he says, "Paul

---

82 "Reformation Essentials" produced by CURE, 2034 E. Lincoln Ave #209, Anaheim, CA. Side A: "Christ Alone/Faith Alone," Audio Tape.

83 See also the following Scriptural examples where in each case repentance is coupled with initial faith: Mark 6:12; Luke 24:47; Acts 2:38; Acts 3:16-19; Acts 19:4; Acts 26:20 (in this instance we find Paul telling the people to "prove their repentance by their deeds." He would normally be saying this in relation to faith), cf., Acts 5:31; 11:18; 17:30. Accordingly, the Council of Trent states: "...by that repentance, which must be performed before baptism..." (Session 6, Chapter 6).

says elsewhere." We need to point out two things here. First, the Catholic Church has always maintained that faith is a gift of God.[84] She has never taught that man gives something to God on his own without God's grace leading him to do it. The point of difference, however, is that man needs to cooperate with the grace of God, as all the Councils throughout Christian history have made clear.[85] In this sense, faith does "give back something" to God. It gives back one of the most important qualities of man that God is looking for — an acknowledgment and use of the grace God has given him. Second, it is incorrect to use Ephesians 2:8 to say that faith is a gift, that is, to the exclusion of the other virtues in the verse. The grammar of the verse points to the whole panorama of salvation, not just faith, as the gift of God.[86] Faith, good works, holiness, and love are all gifts of God's grace. Since all these virtues are from God's grace, man cannot claim any legal right to God's blessing or salvation. Man is sinful and thus can never obligate God to reward him with salvation. To attempt such would be a salvation by works. Paul assures us in Ephesians 2:8 that salvation is "not of works, so that no one can boast." "Boasting" implies that the man is claiming to have done something totally on his own that necessitates that God "pay" him for his work. This is the same principle that Paul uses in Romans 4:2,4 as he says of Abraham: "If, in fact, Abraham was justified by works, he had something to *boast* about — but not before God...Now when a man works, his wages are not credited to him as a gift, but as an obligation." As we have outlined in chapter 1, here Paul reveals his chief concern. He is not against

---

84 Council of Orange, 529, Canon 5: "If anyone says, that just as the increase of faith so also the beginning of faith and the very desire of credulity, by which we arrive at the regeneration of holy baptism is not through the gift of grace, that is, through the inspiration of the Holy Spirit reforming our will from infidelity to faith, from impiety to piety, but is naturally in us, he is proved to be antagonistic to the doctrine of the Apostles..." Council of Trent, Chapters 5, 6: "...nor on the other hand can he of his own free will without the grace of God move himself to justice before Him...Now they are disposed to that justice when, aroused and assisted by divine grace, receiving faith "by hearing," they are freely moved toward God..."

85 Chapter 7 covers this aspect of faith more thoroughly.

86 The word "this" (Greek: τοῦτο) in the clause "and *this* is not of yourselves it is a gift of God" is a neuter demonstrative pronoun which does not refer to the feminine noun "grace" (Greek: χάριτί) or the feminine noun "faith" (Greek: πίστεως).

doing work for God, but doing work that *obligates* God to pay the man with salvation — a work in which a sinful man can *boast* that he has done something on his own, without God's help. It is in this sense, and this sense only, that Paul opposes works to faith.

Evangelical John Gerstner offers yet another explanation of the faith of justification:

> Faith is an act but not a work. Faith means to trust in Jesus Christ...No text of Holy Scripture tells it quite as well as Romans 4:5, "To the man who does not work, but trusts God who justifies the wicked, his faith is credited as righteousness." Notice how many different ways (7) this Scripture teaches justification by faith alone in one verse:[87]

Besides the fact that Gerstner attempts to pass by the reader an unsupported distinction between an "act" and a "work," he goes on to list the "7" things he sees in this verse that teach justification by faith alone. He makes "7," points, of course, without considering that the verse does not use the word "alone." More importantly, however, Gerstner misses the real message of Romans 4:5 and sets up his own Catholic strawman to oppose. Paul's only point is that the man should trust *God* to justify him rather than attempting to justify *himself.* As Paul noted in the previous verses, if the man works with a view to obligating God for eternal "pay;" boasting of his own goodness outside of God's grace; attempting to make himself appear just on his own terms; not recognizing his own sin, then he is not justified in God's eyes but he may be justified in his own eyes. As we noted earlier in chapter 3 in the teaching of Jesus, it is precisely the attempt of man to *justify himself* that Jesus condemns. As he said to the Pharisees in Luke 16:15, "you are the ones who *justify yourselves* in the eyes of men, but God knows your hearts." It is the "heart" of man into which God is looking.

In the end, though the theory of imputed righteousness attempts to make justification so extrinsic and other-worldly, ironically, it begins to crumble as soon as the element of intrinsic faith is introduced. Since faith must issue forth from the individual and be of a

---

[87] *Justification By Faith Alone*, op. cit., p. 107.

certain quality before the righteousness can be imputed, this introduces an uncertain variable into the imputation formula. Since the imputation depends on the quality and persistence of this variable, then justification cannot be reduced to the "alien righteousness of Christ." Christ's atonement does not automatically impute righteousness to sinners *en masse* but is only appropriated by the faith-disposition of the individual; thus it is baseless to claim that justification by imputation has any ethical superiority over justification by infusion. In the end, only justification by infused righteousness is consistent with and allows for the variable of qualified faith (i.e., faith that works in love) to receive the grace of God.

The "Ground" of Justification

Current argumentation in Evangelical circles has begun to emphasize the "ground" of justification as the distinguishing feature between Reformation thought and Catholicism.[88] Since, they admit, both theologies recognize the "necessity" of works,[89] it is concluded that it is fruitless to base differences in justification on "necessity." Hence, some Evangelicals have shifted the argument to the *ground* of justification so as to have a basis from a higher theological category to assert, as Roger Wagner puts it, "that any human quality or action could be added to the righteousness and satisfaction of Jesus Christ..."[90] This kind of argumentation only brings the discussion back one step but it does not resolve the issue at hand, i.e., how, when, where, and why is the righteous work of Christ *applied* to the sinner. We have already pointed out the difficulties Protestantism

---

88 In reference to the "ground" of justification Sproul says: "James nowhere says that the *ground* of Abraham's justification before God was his works" (*Faith Alone*, p. 167). Although this is true, neither does Paul use the word "ground" in relation to faith. Hence, Sproul's comment is superfluous.

89 Although Evangelicals use the word "necessity" today in reference to works, this was not a term used commonly in the Reformation period.

90 Wagner, op. cit., p. 30. Charles Hodge also popularized the term "ground": "The righteousness, therefore — on the ground of which the sentence of justification is passed upon the believing sinner — is not his own, but that of Jesus Christ...If he believes the ground of his acceptance is in himself, or even wishes it were so, he is not prepared to join in those grateful songs of acknowledgment to him who has saved us and called us with an holy calling, not according to works, but according to his own purpose and grace" (Hodge, op. cit., p. 29, 31).

has in applying the righteousness of Christ to the individual since it requires that conditions be met for a "saving faith."

In regard to the *ground* of justification, unless one is Pelagian (a doctrine which the Catholic Church condemned in early centuries), only the work of Christ can be the *ground* of justification.[91] Although Catholics and Protestants dispute the means by which the work of Christ is applied to the individual, Catholicism has made it very clear in their historic documents that the *meritorious cause* ("ground," if you will) of justification is solely the atonement of Christ.[92]

In stressing the *ground* of justification as the distinctive feature of Reformation thought, R. C. Sproul, in reaction to Canon 11 of the Council of Trent, also sees the need to include the event of regeneration in the *complex* of justification. He writes:

> The Reformers did not exclude the infusion of grace from the justified sinner. Indeed, grace is poured into the soul via regeneration and the indwelling of the Holy Spirit. The issue was the ground of our justification. For the Reformers the ground of our justification is the imputed righteousness of Christ, not the infused righteousness of Christ that inheres in the believer.[93]

Here Sproul attempts to answer the Council of Trent's charge that the Reformers excluded regeneration from the realm of justification. Sproul maintains the Protestant distinction by saying that justification is imputed and therefore is the "ground," but he also says that regeneration is infused and therefore not the ground. This

---

[91] The word "ground" in itself is still weak and incomplete to express the full implications of Christ's atoning work. We are using it here as an accommodation to the Evangelicals who have coined the expression to advance their theory of forensic justification.

[92] Council of Trent, Session 6, Chapter 7: "...the meritorious cause is His most beloved only-begotten Son, our Lord Jesus Christ, "who when we were enemies," "for the exceeding charity wherewith he loved us," merited justification for us by his most holy passion on the wood of the cross, and made satisfaction for us to God the Father..." In fact, the Council goes a step further in denying the individual any strict merit in his justification. It says: "...none of those things which precede justification, whether faith or works, merit the grace itself of justification" (Session 6, Chapter 8).

[93] *Faith Alone*, op. cit., p. 128.

form of argumentation begs the question. To show this, we might ask what the "ground" of the *regeneration* is if not the righteousness of Christ? Certainly regeneration does not exist in a vacuum nor does God apply it arbitrarily, especially since it comes before justification in Sproul's view. He can regenerate us only because of the merits of Christ. Any attempt to regenerate us without a proper basis for doing so would violate God's own principles. Hence, no distinction can be made between justification and regeneration since both begin and end under the grace of God supplied by the merits of Christ. Thus, Trent is correct in insisting that neither faith nor works merit the grace of justification, and also correct in negating any detailed or extended *ordo salutis* between infusion, regeneration, faith, justification, and sanctification. This is why Scripture's *ordo salutis* is limited to "predestined, called, justified and glorified" (Romans 8:30).[94]

At this point, the Evangelical may shift the argumentation to the necessity of alien righteousness in order to obtain an *absolute* justification. For example, Reformed theologian John Murray writes, "Only a perfect righteousness can provide the basis for a complete, perfect and irreversible justification. Furthermore, justification gives a title to and secures eternal life (Romans 5:17, 18, 21)."[95] Although the Catholic would certainly agree that Christ's atoning work was perfect, complete, and irreversible, Murray admits the *real* reason why he must push for using the phrase "ground of justification." His agenda is to have an "irreversible justification" and one that "secures eternal life." In other words, he assumes that, once justified, the individual cannot lose his justification. The only way to have an "irreversible justification" is to take the matter of justification totally away from the individual and place it on the shoulders of God alone. As we noted above, this only takes the discussion of justification back one step, but it does not solve the problem of how the justification is applied to the individual, i.e., how you make God solely respon-

---

94 In light of the absence of any detailed *ordo salutis*, Scripture often juxtaposes the order and tenses of justification, sanctification and other terms of redemptive significance, or substitutes one for the other, e.g., 1 Cor. 6:11; 1 Cor. 1:30; Acts 26:18; Rom. 15:16; 2 Thess. 2:13; 1 Pt. 1:2.

95 John Murray, *Redemption Accomplished and Applied*, 1955, p. 156.

sible for justification, if it can only be applied when the individual has met the conditions of making faith an instrument worthy of receiving the divine justification. To safeguard this formula, the Reformed mind will then postulate that if the individual sins without repentance, falls from faith, or does not exhibit the works that are required to accompany "saving faith," he is classified as one who "was never justified originally." Ironically, this solution preserves the doctrine of "irreversible justification," but not the individual's salvation.

We have earlier critiqued the concept of "irreversible justification" or "eternal security" in chapter 4. We will recall that the very person from whom Paul quotes in Romans 4:5-8 when he is giving his dissertation on justification is one who was justified before God but then lost his justification and became an ungodly man when he committed adultery and murder. That person was David, a man after God's own heart. His justification was restored when he repented. Second, we have already noted that the Scripture speaks of holding the final stage of justification until the future judgment (cf., Matt. 12:36-37; Rom. 2:6-13; 1 Cor. 4:4, 3:13-17, et al.). Third, a plethora of Scriptures, many of which we covered in chapter 4, directly contradict the notion of "eternal security." Fourth, one of the only verses that is used to support the notion that one who falls away was never justified originally is 1 John 2:19. We have addressed that verse also in chapter 4. Finally, the very verses that Murray cites to support an "irreversible justification" and a "securing of eternal life" (viz., Rom. 5:17, 18, 21) do not prove the notion at all. Paul is simply making a statement of fact, that because of the principle of *representation* which God established long ago, Christ can serve to bring God's grace and justification to men even as Adam brought sin, death and condemnation to men. In that sense, the work of Christ is "irreversible," but the context of Romans 5 does not address at all the question of for whom specifically the work will be applied and completed.

Charles Hodge makes an interesting admission about the Calvinist doctrine of "irreversible justification" The reader will recall some of Hodge's quote from chapter 1 regarding how God views us through the system of grace. Hodge writes:

> The sins which are pardoned in justification include all sins past, present, and future. It does indeed seem to be a solecism that sins should be forgiven before they are committed. Forgiveness involves remission of penalty. But how can a penalty be remitted before it is incurred? This is only an apparent difficulty arising out of the inadequacy of human language. The righteousness of Christ is a perpetual donation. It is a robe which hides, or as the Bible expresses it, covers from the eye of justice the sins of the believer. They are sins; they deserve the wrath and curse of God, but the necessity for the infliction of that curse no longer exists. The believer feels the constant necessity for confession and prayer for pardon, but the ground of pardon is ever present for him to offer and plead. So that it would be a more correct statement to say that in justification the believer receives the promise that God will not deal with him according to his transgressions, rather than to say that sins are forgiven before they are committed.[96]

Hodge has candidly revealed an inconsistency in his theology but has done his best to lessen its impact. Since an "irreversible justification" would necessitate that no future sins, no matter how horrible, could put the individual's salvation in jeopardy, Hodge must explain how sins not yet committed can have their penalty remitted. Hodge's answer: It is not so much that God forgives sins before they are committed but that God will not deal with the individual as his transgressions require. His sins "deserve the wrath and curse of God" but Hodge says that God will not employ this wrath, that "he covers the eye of [his] justice" when observing and dealing with the Christian's sins. Even more revealing is Hodge's admission that the individual "receives this promise," i.e., that God will not deal with his sins the way the law requires, "in *justification*."

Before we comment further, let us hear Hodge's further explanation of the problem of the remission of future sins:

> This subject is thus presented by the Apostle: Believers "are not under the law but under grace" (Romans 6:14). They are not

[96] Hodge, op. cit., p. 108.

> under a legal system administered according to the principles of retributive justice, a system which requires perfect obedience as the condition of acceptance with God, and which says, "Cursed is every one that continues not in all things which are written in the book of the law to do them." They are under grace, that is, under a system in which believers are not dealt with on the principles of justice, but on the principles of undeserved mercy in which God does not impute "their trespasses unto them" (2 Corinthians 5:19). There is therefore to them no condemnation. They are not condemned for their sins, not because they are not sins and do not deserve condemnation, but because Christ has already made expiation for their guilt and makes continual intercession for them.[97]

Anyone who has been following this study closely will recognize a familiar theme in what Hodge has proposed. In chapter 1 of this book we proposed precisely the same perspective to understand the writings of the apostle Paul in regards to grace and works. We spoke of the system of law as opposed to the system of grace, the latter which God can now use to view and evaluate us because Christ's atonement has provided that grace. Given this common ground, we might venture to say that the only difference between Hodge's view and the Catholic view is the point at which the "covering of the eyes of justice" is applied. That Hodge may realize this fact seems evident in a previous statement in which he denies Catholic theology's distinction between the system of grace and the system of law. Hodge earlier wrote:

> ...or for their inherent righteousness and subsequent good works as the Romanists say, there would have been no room for this formidable objection. Or, if through any misapprehension of his teaching the objection had been urged, how easy it would have been for the Apostle to set it aside. How obvious would have been the answer, "I [Paul] do not deny that really good works

97 Ibid., p. 109. Hodge says as much in his *Systematic Theology*: "[God] Having graciously promised for Christ's sake to overlook the imperfection of their best services..." (Vol. III (London: James Clark and Co.), p. 244).

> are the ground of our acceptance with God. I only say that ritual works have no worth in his sight, that he looks on the heart"; or, that "works done before regeneration have no real excellence or merit"; or, that "God is more lenient now than in his dealing with Adam"; that "he does not demand perfect obedience, but accepts our imperfect, well-meant endeavors to keep his holy commandments." How reasonable and satisfactory would such answers have been. Paul, however, does not make them. He adheres to his doctrine that our own personal moral excellence has nothing to do with our justification; that God justifies the ungodly; that he receives the chief of sinners.[98]

Here we see that Hodge giveth and Hodge taketh away. He allows himself to use the system which allows God to be "more lenient now," "not demanding perfect obedience," and "accepting of our well-meant endeavors" to solve his theological problem with "irreversible justification" in relation to the remission of sins "not yet committed," but he does not allow other theological positions, namely, Roman Catholicism, to use the same system to explain the nature of justification. It is hard to understand how Hodge can deny such a system to Catholicism when he has stated above that "in *justification* [emphasis mine] the believer receives the promise that God will not deal with him according to his transgressions" for this is precisely the point at which Catholicism says we receive that promise! The difference between Hodge and Catholicism, however, is that for the latter the promise is conditional based on how seriously the individual transgressed and whether he repented of that sin before death. God's grace does not give us license to commit any sin we desire and remain unrepentant in that sin. If we abuse God's grace, he can put us right back under the system of law which will forthrightly condemn us. It appears that Hodge recognizes these implications by the topic of the next paragraph immediately following Hodge's first quote above. He writes:

> The second consequence attributed to the imputation of Christ's righteousness is a title to eternal life. This in the older writers is

[98] Ibid., p. 75.

> often expressed by the words "adoption and heirship." Being made the children of God by faith in Christ Jesus (Galatians 2:36 [sic]), they are heirs of God and joint heirs with Jesus Christ of a heavenly inheritance (Romans 8:17).[99]

Having "title to eternal life" means the same thing as Murray's "irreversible justification." The Reformed presuppositions will not allow anything to terminate the justification. God will always look upon the Christian with "leniency" and thus he has nothing to fear at judgment day. His "adoption" and "heirship" are sealed and cannot be altered. Unfortunately, Hodge and most Reformed writers fail to mention the passages that speak of forfeiting the adoption and heirship upon the presence of serious, unrepentant sin. Paul is very clear about this. In Galatians 4:7 he writes, "So you are no longer a slave, but a son, and since you are a son, God has made you an heir." But then in 4:9-11 he writes: "how is it that you are turning back to those weak and miserable principles? Do you wish to be enslaved by them all over again...I fear for you, that somehow I have wasted my efforts on you." In 5:4 he says: "you have fallen away from grace." In 5:13-15 he says: "do not use your freedom to indulge in the sinful nature...if you keep on biting and devouring each other, watch out or you will be destroyed by each other." Finally, he delivers the ultimatum in 5:19-21:

> The acts of the sinful nature are obvious: sexual immorality, impurity, and debauchery; idolatry and witchcraft; hatred, discord, jealousy, fits of rage, selfish ambition, dissensions, factions and envy, drunkenness, orgies, and the like. I warn you, as I did before, that those who live like this will not *inherit* the kingdom of God.

Could it be any plainer that it is possible for them to lose their inheritance through sin? Paul speaks specifically of denying the "inheritance" to those engaged in these gross sins. One of the key phrases in this statement is, "I warn you, *as I did before...*" Apparently, this is the second time he has warned these Christians of the

---

99 Ibid., p. 109.

eternal punishment awaiting those who sin in such manner. Obviously, some of them had not repented of these serious sins and thus, in Paul's view, they had already forfeited their inheritance.

To show that Paul's use of the word "inheritance" is not generic but applies to the specific inheritance that Christians receive, Paul issues a similar warning to the Christians in Ephesus. In Ephesians 5:3-5 he states, "But among you there must not be even a hint of sexual immorality...For of this you can be sure: No immoral, impure or greedy person — such a man is an idolater — has any *inheritance* in the kingdom of Christ and of God." Earlier in Ephesians 1:14 and 18 Paul indicated that they had received the inheritance: "who is a deposit guaranteeing our inheritance...the riches of his glorious inheritance in the saints." This is the same truth discovered in Romans 8:37-39. God absolutely "guarantees" his plan of salvation. He even gives us a "deposit" of this inheritance by giving us his Spirit.[100] No force anywhere in the universe can thwart God's plan of salvation, except the very one that Romans 8:37-39 does not mention, that is, a person in unrepentant disobedience. Paul says as much in Ephesians 1:14 and 5:5. God guarantees the plan and we must be obedient to that plan, otherwise he will be exclude us from the plan. Colloquially speaking, God can refund to himself the deposit. Finally, Paul mentions forfeiting the inheritance in 1 Corinthians 6:8-9. "Instead, you yourselves cheat and do wrong, and you do this to your brothers. Do you not know that the wicked will not *inherit* the kingdom of God? Do not be deceived: Neither the sexually immoral...nor thieves, nor greedy...nor swindlers will *inherit* the kingdom of God." Other evidence that the Corinthians were engaging in illicit behavior is noted in the admonition of Paul's second letter. In 2 Corinthians 12:21 he says, "...when I come again...I will be grieved over many who have sinned earlier and have not repented of the impurity, sexual sin and debauchery in which they have indulged."

We must probe one more aspect to Hodge's view of the "leniency of God." In the above quote, he references the statement of Paul in 2 Corinthians 5:19, "God does not impute 'their trespasses

[100] From the Greek ἀρραβὼν, used also in 2 Corinthians 1:22; 5:5 ("...put his Spirit in our hearts as a deposit, guaranteeing what is to come.").

unto them,'" as well as Paul's teaching in Romans 8:34 which Hodge paraphrases as, "but because Christ has already made expiation for their guilt and makes continual intercession for them."[101] In using these two quotes, Hodge is attempting to commandeer them into the area of Protestant *sanctification* so as to have support for his assertion that God will not look with the "eyes of justice" toward the future sins of the Christian. God will be "lenient" with them and thus they will not receive what their sins deserve. Though it is legitimate for Hodge to use 2 Corinthians 5:19 to support this concept, he fails to notice that this passage, its surrounding context, and the New Testament's usage of identical words refer just as much to *justification* as to sanctification.[102] First, we find Paul in Romans 4:8 using a phrase almost identical to 2 Corinthians 5:19 in the statement "Blessed is the man to whom God will not impute sin" (KJV). Yet the context of Romans 4 is dealing only with what Protestants refer to as *justification*. Such dual usage by Paul supports the Catholic view that holds both justification and sanctification as simultaneous and continuing. Second, the context of 2 Corinthians 5-6 is one in which Paul expresses great concern for the very salvation of the Corinthians, that is, whether they will end up being saved or not. We see this indicated first in 2 Cor. 5:20 where Paul says, "We implore you on Christ's behalf: Be reconciled to God."[103] Knowing the many sins of the Corinthians, some of which Paul detailed above in 1 Corinthians 6:8-10 and 2 Corinthians 12:20-21, we can understand why Paul desires that the Corinthians be forgiven of sin and, in turn, be "reconciled" to God. Again, this supports Catholic theology since an individual in *mortal* sin has lost his justification and indeed needs to be "reconciled" to God so that God does not "count his sins against him."[104] We note further proof that Paul is concerned with the very salvation of

---

[101] Ibid., p. 109.

[102] Calvin used the same passage against Osiander to support imputed justification (*Institutes* 3:11:11). See chapter 9 for more details.

[103] Paul uses the Greek imperative form καταλλάγητε. Except for 1 Corinthians 7:11, which deals with marriage, Paul uses this word, and its verbal cognate, exclusively in justification contexts, e.g., Romans 5:10,11; 11:15.

[104] It is for this reason that Catholic theology uses 2 Corinthians 5:19-21, in conjunction with John 20:23; Matthew 16:18-19 and James 5:14-16 as supportive of auricular confession and absolution.

the Corinthians is noted in 2 Corinthians 6:1-2: "As God's fellow workers we urge you not to receive God's *grace in vain.* For he says, 'In the time of my favor I heard you, and in the day of salvation I helped you.' I tell you, now is the time of God's favor, *now is the day of salvation.*"

Similarly, Paul told the Corinthians in 1 Corinthians 15:2, "By this gospel you are saved, if you hold firmly to the word I preached to you. Otherwise, you have believed in vain." And his parting words to them in 2 Corinthians 13:2-5:

> I already gave you a warning when I was with you the second time. I now repeat it while absent: On my return I will not spare those who sinned earlier or any of the others...Examine yourselves to see whether you are in the faith; test yourselves. Do you not realize that Christ Jesus is in you — unless, of course, you fail the test?[105]

We see, then, that Paul has deep concern for the very salvation of the Corinthians. Through their sins they have put their salvation in jeopardy. Hence, it is highly inappropriate for Hodge to use these verses to support the notion that the salvation of the Corinthians is totally secure, or that God will not hold them eternally accountable for their sins. God will not be "lenient" with them if their sins are serious and continuous. Neither the context nor Paul's usage of the same words and themes elsewhere support such a notion.[106]

---

105 The last phrase of 2 Corinthians 13:5 is better translated, "unless you are counterfeits" or "unless you are reprobates." The Greek word is ἀδόκιμοί which is used 8 times in the New Testament exclusively in reference to sin, apostasy, and losing faith, e.g., Rom. 1:28; 1 Cor. 9:27; 2 Tim. 3:8; Titus 1:16; Hebrews 6:8. The NIV turns the noun into a verb and also weakens the force of the word by referring to it merely as the failing of a test. The word has much more ominous overtones, especially in the context.

106 Hodge also tries to support his view by interpreting the "judgment seat of Christ" mentioned in 2 Corinthians 5:10 to say that the "good deeds" of Christians will be evaluated and be given various degrees of reward, but the "bad deeds" of the unsaved will be evaluated and damned with degrees of punishment. The "bad deeds" of Christians and the "good deeds" of non-Christians do not come under judgment, so says Hodge (*An Exposition to the Second Epistle to the Corinthians*, 1973), pp. 125- 126. We will deal more with this view and other such views in chapter 8.

To conclude this section, we must also comment on Hodge's use of Romans 8:34 — the "intercession of Christ." Since Hodge uses this phrase in reference to the sins of Christians, the main question that arises in this case, is why Christians need an "intercessor" for their sins if indeed, as Protestant theology teaches, that Christ has 'once-for-all paid for their past, present or future sins'? The whole notion of Christ being an "intercessor" for sin to appease God's wrath should be superfluous in Protestant theology. We grant, as Protestants teach, that a sinning Christian can be "out of fellowship" with God and thus needs to be restored, but as we have already seen in 2 Corinthians 5-6,13, the "intercession of Christ" and the "reconciliation of the Christian" are not limited to "fellowship" but include the very salvation of the Christian. In light of this, there are two important points concerning the "intercession" of Christ. First, as used in Romans 8:33-34, Christ's intercession is in the context of *justification*. In Romans 8:33 Paul says, "It is God who *justifies*" and then says in the next sentence that "Christ Jesus who died...is at the right hand of God *interceding* for us." This is why Paul can say in the next verse, "Who can separate us from the love of Christ?" Because Christ is continually *interceding* for us and *justifying* us before the Father, nothing can separate us from God, unless, of course, Christ stops interceding and the justification is taken away. This occurs when we sin mortally.

Second, when the Scripture speaks elsewhere of Christ's intercession it is in the context of final salvation. Hebrews 7:25 states: "Therefore he is able to save completely those who come to God through him, because he always lives to intercede for them." According to the grammar, Paul is explaining to us that because of Christ's continual intercession to God, he is able to complete the salvation of those who come to God.[107] Simply put, the reason they can have their salvation completed is that Christ makes con-

[107] The word "completely" is from the Greek εἰς τὸ παντελὲς which is used again only in Luke 13:11. There it refers to a woman not being able to lift herself up completely. The lexical definition can vary between "complete, perfect, fully" and "forever, for all time." The phrase "because he always lives to intercede" is εἰς τὸ ἐντυγχάνειν, in which the preposition governs the infinitive with the article to denote purpose. The word "come" is the Greek present participle προσερχομένους which refers to those presently approaching.

tinual intercession for them. For Hodge, this presents a dilemma. On the one hand, he says the propitiatory sacrifice of Christ is sufficient to remit all past, present, and future sins of the Christian. Yet Hodge admits above that it is illogical to remit the punishment for sins that have not yet been committed. We will recall that his solution to this problem was to say that God did "not to deal with the Christian according to his transgressions" rather than to say the sins are forgiven ahead of time. Thus, we would have to conclude concerning Hodge's view that the continual intercession of Christ is for the very purpose of maintaining this promise of God not to deal with the sins of the Christian as he normally would have, i.e., with death. But we ask, why must the intercession be performed? Why is the forensic, once-for-all imputation of justification insufficient to maintain that promise of God itself? If the single act of imputation put in place the "irreversible justification, does this not make the intercession of Christ, in the context of sin, superfluous? Other Protestants cannot help Hodge by saying that the intercession of Christ is only for the purpose of "fellowship with God." The context of Hebrews 7:25 and Romans 8:33-34 will not allow such a dimension. These contexts deal with *justification* and *final salvation*, not "fellowship," per se. Once again, Hodges' dilemma vindicates the Catholic position. Christ's continual intercession is necessary because we continually need God's grace to forgive our sin, especially if we fall into mortal sin. Hodge was right in one sense — we do appease an angry God against sin through the intercession of Christ, but it happens every day of our lives. Christ "begins" our salvation at baptism, but he "completes" it in his role as intercessor. As some translations say, "he saves us to the uttermost."

The Charge of "Legal Fiction"

During the Reformation, the Catholic Church charged that the Protestant conception of justification was a "legal fiction." The Church maintained that if justification is only a legal category into which God places a man without being truly just in his own person, then the justification is not real. A "declared" justification (which is another term for a forensic justification) without a just object in view is merely a legal label, hence a "legal fiction."[108] Seeing the merit of the Catholic rejoinder, John Murray attempted

[108] R. C. Sproul misses the point when he says: "The forensic declaration of justification is not a legal fiction. It is real and authentic because the imputation upon which it is based is no fiction. It is a real imputation of real righteousness of a real Christ" (*Justification By Faith Alone*, op. cit., p. 39). Geisler and MacKenzie attempt the same argument with a little more subtlety: "Our status is not merely legal (as in forensic justification) but also ontological (real) for we become the actual children of God at the initial moment of salvation... (op. cit., f. 67, p. 239). Catholic theologians have no contention with Protestants if they desire to think of their imputation as "real." The Counter-Reformation charge of "legal fiction" referred rather to the forensic justification's theory that the individual was still said to be *unjust,* though *justified.* This infringed on the integrity of God, who was put in the position of calling something *just* that was not really *just.* Analogously, a gold-plated coin is *real* but that does not mean that the metal underneath is *real gold.* Thus, for someone to call the coin a genuine gold coin would be a lie. George Eldon Ladd refutes the charge by saying that the justification is *relational* as opposed to ethical. He writes: "The forensic righteousness of justification is a *real righteousness*, because a man's relationship to God is just as real as his subjective ethical condition. A man's relationship to God is no fiction" (Ladd, op. cit., pp. 439-40). Though Catholic theology would not deny that there is a definitive relational change between God and man in justification, limiting the exchange to relationship is neither biblical nor logical. It would be analogous to a bachelor who marries claiming only that his marital status (i.e., his relationship with the woman) has changed but who ignores the fact that he desired to marry her because he loved and admired her for who she was as a person (i.e., her ethical and other virtuous qualities). The formal moment of marriage is analogous to baptism, which defines the relational change. However, just as a man marries only because he loves his fiance for who she is before the wedding ceremony, so God seeks and begins an ethical change in the individual prior to his baptism. That pre-baptismal ethical change, initiated by the grace of God, is called "repentance" (cf., Matthew 3:6-8; 4:17; Mark 1:5; 6:12; Luke 3:3-8; 5:32; 24:47; Acts 2:38; 3:19; 10:1-4; 17:30; 20:21; 22:16; 26:20; 2 Peter 3:9). From another vantage point, Douglas Jones attempts to escape the charge of legal fiction by first asserting that "...God justifies those who have the real, ontological property of corporate righteousness. No legal fiction. No imperfect individual righteousness." Although *corporate* righteousness is certainly part of the righteousness God gives to the Church at large, yet God still requires the individual to have and obtain his personal righteousness from the corporate entity. This is precisely why Catholicism insists that individuals obtain justification and infused righteousness from the graces given to the Church, e.g., sacraments, communion of saints, etc. Justification is both corporate and individual and it is therefore erroneous to elevate the former at the expense of the latter. Jones also claims that Catholicism by not attributing man's guilt of sin to Christ engages in a "legal atrocity" which, he claims, makes God a slayer of the innocent, i.e., Christ ("Non Est" in *Credenda Agenda*, Vol. 8, No. 3, p. 23,

to resolve this anomaly in Reformed thought by introducing the word "constitutive" into the imputation formula. Speaking for Murray, Roger Wagner writes:

> John Murray was concerned to point out that there was a potential danger in the Protestant emphasis on justification as a *declarative* act. The danger he saw was that the church would overlook the fact that justification is also revealed in Scripture as a *constitutive* act. "For as through the disobedience of the one man the many were constituted sinners, even so through the obedience of the one the many will be constituted righteous" (Rom. 5:19)...Therefore, what God does in this case is that he constitutes the new and righteous judicial relation as well as declares this new relation to be...[109]

After introducing this new dimension to Reformed thought in three short paragraphs, Wagner concludes:

> Such an understanding of the biblical doctrine should have silenced the charges of "mere legalities" long ago, but as we have seen, it has not. The same accusations are being made against the forensic character of justification today as in the sixteenth century. Rome is still not listening to Scripture.[110]

[108 cont.] emphasis mine). First, Catholicism does not speak of the death of Christ in "legal" terms. It is a personal decision by a loving Son to obey his Father in order to provide grace to mankind. Second, Jones ignores the appeasement motif throughout Scripture, wherein Christ offers himself in death to appease God's personal anger against sin. God is not "slaying the innocent," rather, it is Christ who *voluntarily* offers himself up to the Father as an act of love for mankind. There is quite a difference between shedding the innocent blood of an involuntary victim (e.g., Deut. 19:1-10; 1 Sam. 19:5; Psalm 106:38) and offering oneself up voluntarily in love for others (John 10:18; Hebrews 7:27; Philippians 2:6-8).

[109] Wagner, op. cit., p. 32. Andrew Sandlin attempts the same kind of argumentation in his critique of Norman Shepherd's semi-Catholic view: "To imply as does Shepherd, however, that condemnation cannot be used in an exclusively forensic sense is to do injustice to Paul's usage in Romans 5:16,18. Hence, the condemnation to which Paul refers is the forensic declaration of guilt of Adam's posterity which corresponds to the forensic declaration of righteousness of Christ's posterity" (Sandlin, op. cit. p. 22).

[110] Ibid., p. 32.

We wonder who is not listening to Scripture. Besides Wagner's failure to define just what "constituted" means in this context, which clouds his hypothesis, if there is one verse of Scripture which supports the concept of infused righteousness, it is the very verse that Wagner (and Murray) cite, namely, Romans 5:19. This verse uses the phrases "made sinners" and "made righteous" in reference to Adam and Christ, respectively.[111] The first part of the verse indicates that by Adam's disobedience many were "made sinners." The significant point to note here is that being "made sinners" does not mean merely placing them in a legal category of sin, but that Adam's fall, in essence, transfused (or "constituted") them with sin, and with a nature bent towards sin that was transmitted from Adam, and later all his progeny, the moment they were conceived (cf., Psalm 51:5; 58:3-4). The Church has always understood this transmission of sin as *original sin* — a real, ontological, sinful state of the soul.[112] Not only is the death that Adam's sin transferred to all men *real* in that all men die, but in the same way the stain of sin, and the inclination to sin, is also *real* in each person. This being the case, the second part of Romans 5:19 must then convey the same understanding. Thus, those who were "made righteous" by the obedience of Christ were not just placed into a *category* of righteousness, but were actually *infused* with the substance of righteousness. If we were transfused with Adam's sin we must also be in-

[111] The word "made" or "constituted" in Romans 5:19 is from the Greek κατεστάθησαν, which can refer to an "appointing" or a "making or causing" (Walter Bauer, *A Greek-English Lexicon of the New Testament and Other Early Christian Literature*, 1957, 1979, p. 390). The New Testament uses both meanings, e.g., Acts 6:3; 2 Peter 1:8. The word "righteous" in the phrase "made righteous" is the Greek word δίκαιος, which is frequently applied to inherently righteous men in the New Testament.

[112] Council of Trent, Session 5, Number 2: "If anyone asserts that the transgression of Adam has harmed him alone and not his posterity. . .or that he having been defiled by the sin of disobedience has *transfused* only death and the punishments of the body into the whole human race, but not sin also, which is the death of the soul, let him be anathema." We highlight the word "transfused" to show Trent's understanding that sin is transmitted or generated from Adam and propagated to all individuals at birth.

fused with Christ's righteousness, otherwise, the equation of Romans 5:19 is not in equilibrium. The stain of original sin was removed from the soul and replaced with God's sanctifying grace. This is why the very next topic that Paul discusses in Romans 6:1-3 after the transfusion of sin is baptism — the very means God has ordained to remove original sin from the soul and infuse it with righteousness.[113] Though the residual effects of original sin remain in the body until Christ redeems it at the last day, this only serves to remind us in this life how *real* was the original sin when it was placed in us at conception.

Summary Points

1) The Protestant concept of justification teaches that by an act of faith man is credited or imputed with the alien righteousness of Christ. Although there are many views of justification among Protestant denominations, generally speaking, Protestants understand justification as an extrinsic legal act of God which does not involve any transformation of the individual's inner nature. They reserve the inner change of the individual for the area of sanctification. The Catholic concept of justification teaches that by the same act of faith God infuses man with sanctifying grace which justifies the individual before God by transforming his inner nature. The individual increases in sanctifying grace and thus his justification increases and progresses throughout his life.

---

[113] As Aquinas has written: "The being freed from sin is prior to the obtaining of justifying grace" (*Summa Theologica*, I-II, 113,8, ad 1). It is the cleansing action of Baptism that removes sin and fills the individual with grace. As Ananias said to Paul in Acts 22:16:,"Stand up, be baptized, and wash away your sins." (See also the Catholic Catechism, Section 1213-1284, on Baptism.) In the New Testament, the sacrament of Baptism confers justification on the individual. Numerous passages either explicitly or implicitly refer to baptism and its resulting work of regeneration, justification, and sanctification. Some of the more prominent are Matt. 28:19; Mark 16:16; John 3:5; Acts 2:38-39; Acts 22:16; Rom. 6:1-3; Gal. 3:26-27; Eph. 4:5; 5:26; Col. 2:12; Tit. 3:5; 1 Pet. 3:21.

2) Catholic theology teaches that God prompts the individual to seek for justification through the action of *actual* grace. God requires that man respond to and cooperate with his grace in order to receive salvation. Once justified, man continues to cooperate with God within the realm of grace.

3) Scripture consistently uses the Greek words *dikaioo* (δικαιόω), *dikaios*une (δικαιοσύνη), and *dikaios* (δίκαιος) to refer to the righteousness of the individual, thus affirming the Catholic view.

4) The phrase "righteousness of God" refers to the righteous quality of God but also to the righteousness that God infuses into the individual.

5) Habakkuk 2:4 ("the just shall live by faith"), which Paul quotes in Romans 1:17, is not concerned with righteousness by imputation; rather, it refers to an intrinsic quality of faith God expects of Habakkuk while he waits for God's providence to work things out. Similarly, Paul's use of Habakkuk 2:4 has precisely the same meaning, extending, however, the intrinsic quality of faith till his final judgment from God.

6) The use of 2 Corinthians 5:21 ("in order that we might become the righteousness of God in him") to prove the Protestant concept of imputation is illegitimate since it distorts the grammar of the text.

7) The Protestant claim that the word "credited" or "reckoned" (Greek: *logizomai* or λογίζομαι) refers not to what actually exists within the person, but only what God designates or classifies him to be, is incorrect. The preponderant usage of *logizomai* in the Scripture refers to what actually exists within the individual.

8) The New Testament is replete with evidence connecting the inner renewal or transformation of the individual with justification.

9) Attempts by Protestants to alter the language of Romans 4:3, 22 and Galatians 3:6 to say that Abraham's belief is *not* what God counts for righteousness, are incorrect. God recognizes Abraham as righteous precisely for his faith.

10) The Catholic view understands that what God declares is in accord with what he views in the object he is addressing. In other words, God declares man righteous in justification because he has made him intrinsically righteous.

11) The Protestant theory of legal imputation neither offers no adequate answer as to why God requires faith from the individual in order to attain justification, nor does it adequately explain why God requires a certain quality of faith. Some Protestants understand faith as a condition for justification, others do not.

12) Protestants also falsely separate faith from repentance in order to maintain the stance that no works are required for justification.

13) In order to maintain the exclusivity of the theory of imputation over against infusion, some Protestants shift the argument to one of "ground" as opposed to what is "necessary" for justification. This is a fallacious argument since Catholicism holds that the meritorious cause for justification is the work of Christ.

14) In order to account for the theory of imputation's requirement that God forgive sins that have not yet been committed, Protestants postulate that Christ continually makes intercession for sinners, that God does not demand perfect obedience, and that he looks upon those in grace with a more lenient view. These aspects, however, correspond precisely to the way Catholicism views justification. Thus, what Protestantism must apply to future sins in the area of sanctification, Catholicism applies to all sins under the grace of justification.

15) The use of Romans 5:19 to support the Protestant concept of imputation by saying that God "constitutes a judicial relationship" is fallacious. In actuality, the verse compares the transfusion of sin into man from the sin of Adam with the infusion of righteousness from Christ to the Christian. The Council of Trent rightly characterized the Protestant view as a "legal fiction."

Chapter 6

Is Justification a Courtroom Decree or a Familial Restoration?

In this chapter we enter into the third technical phase of the presentation of justification. In the first phase covered in Chapter 4 we addressed the progressive nature of justification. In the second phase covered in Chapter 5 we addressed justification in terms of infused grace. In the third phase covered in this chapter, we will gather the evidence from Scripture to support the idea that the correct model to understand the nature of justification is a familial restoration to our Father in heaven.

The Protestant view of justification begins with the idea that God is a Judge who must bring the accused sinner before the bar of justice to be condemned for his crimes. In God's courtroom, the law stands as the prosecuting attorney exposing the utter imperfection and multitude of sins of the defendant. Having no defense against these charges, the sinner is convicted as a criminal and sentenced to condemnation. But there is a way of escape. God has provided a substitute who will stand in place of the accused criminal. The substitute is Christ. Christ stands before the bar of God's justice in place of the sinner and takes the full wrath of God for the latter's crimes. Prior to Christ taking the punishment for the sinner, he shows the judge by his perfect obedience to the law that he himself is not a criminal. Thus, Christ's active obedience (living a sinless life) and his passive obedience (suffering condemnation) constitute the "righteousness of Christ." In turn, this righteousness of Christ is "imputed" to the sinner, that is, the righteousness is transferred or credited to the sinner so that God's scrutiny as judge is directed towards the transferred righteousness, not the sinner himself. Having the perfect righteousness of Christ given to him, the accused criminal, though still a sinner within his nature, can be set free from the court of law. Once freed, the justification process is over. He is granted all the rights and privileges of the pardon that stems from his release. In his freedom, he must now imitate Christ and be obedient to his new Father, God Almighty. There is one requirement in this gracious provision, however. In order for it to be appropriated by him, the convicted sinner must *believe* all this is possible. Even though he does not have to show that he himself is righteous to the Judge, he must exercise the proper faith in order for the Judge to allow Christ to serve as his substitute. If he does not believe, then he must stand before the Judge on his own and with the certainty that he will be convicted and sentenced.

Catholicism's view of justification, although it may have its legal facets, is not defined nor dependent on western society's notion of courtroom legality. The first fact we must recognize is that Scripture does not use courtroom imagery to describe our initial justification. If the courtroom model were being portrayed, we would expect Scripture to create vivid scenes of a criminal standing before a judge, perhaps with an attorney present to defend his case. We would expect, in reference to justification, to see terminology associated with a courtroom scene, e.g., court, judge, jury, verdict, books, defendant, witness, attorney, acquitted, etc. Although Scripture employs scenes and descriptions of this nature, it does so only in reference to the Final Judgment.[1] Instead, we invariably see Scripture using *familial* imagery to describe our initial justification. For example, Romans 8:15-33; Galatians 3:24-4:5 and Ephesians 1:5 describe justification in terms of filial *adoption*.[2] To illustrate related topics, Paul uses

---

1 The Final Judgment will be addressed in Chapter 8.

2 The Council of Trent described justification in terms of filial restoration and divine sonship. It states: "In these words a description of the justification of the sinner is given as being a translation from that state in which man is born a child of the first Adam to the state of grace and of the "adoption of the sons" of God through the second Adam, Jesus Christ, our Savior" (Chapter 4); "...that all men might receive the adoption of sons [Gal. 4:5]" (Chapter 2); "...and come to the fellowship of his sons; and are therefore said to be justified gratuitously..." (Chapter 8). The Council of Trent did not use forensic or courtroom terminology to describe initial justification. Trent referred only to the "tribunal" of the future judgment: "...they are commanded immediately on being reborn, to preserve it pure and spotless as the first robe...so that they may bear it before the tribunal of our Lord Jesus Christ and have life eternal" (Chapter 7). See **Appendix 21** for study on adoption.

the imagery of the marriage and its dissolution through death in Romans 7:1-4 as a prelude to his discussion on the relationship between law and grace in Romans 7:5-25. Similarly, he uses the allegorical account of the two wives of Abraham, Sarah and Hagar, in Galatians 4:21-31 to illustrate the difference between the promise and law. These, and other passages, suggest that there is much more to the understanding of justification which is beyond the courtroom. As we have learned from chapters 4 and 5, justification is a process whereby God continually infuses his grace into the individual, substantially changing him to be pleasing to God and acceptable for citizenship in his kingdom. The present chapter will show us that it is the familial model, not the courtroom model, that effectively incorporates these two elements into justification.[3]

The following is a brief sketch of how this takes place. God calls the sinner, estranged from his heavenly Father because of the sin of Adam,[4] back to join again the heavenly family. A judge does not acquit him; rather, his father forgives him (as in the parable of Luke 15 when the Prodigal son came home to his father and received forgiveness).[5] In reuniting with his spiritual family, he must resume the qualities of a son, and to receive divine sonship, he must be divine-like. Through his grace, God infuses these divine-like qualities into him, and he is now ready to become the

---

3 "They [faith, hope, and love] are infused by God into the souls of the faithful to make them capable of acting as his children and of meriting eternal life. They are the pledge of the presence and action of the Holy Spirit in the faculties of the human being" (Catholic Catechism, Section 1813).

4 John Paul II, *Dominum et vivificantem*, 27-48: "For in spite of all the witness of creation and of the salvific economy inherent in it, the spirit of darkness is capable of showing God as an enemy of his own creature, and in the first place as an enemy of man, as a source of danger and threat to man. In this way Satan manages to sow in man's soul the seed of opposition to the one who "from the beginning" would be considered as man's enemy — and not as Father..."

5 The Council of Trent uses the imagery from the parable of the Prodigal Son in reference to justification: "Therefore, when receiving true and Christian justice, they are commanded immediately on being reborn, to preserve it pure and spotless as the 'first robe' [Luke 15:22] given to them through Christ Jesus in place of that which Adam by his disobedience lost for himself and for us..." (Session 6, Chapter 7).

adopted son of God. The adopted son now in line for the inheritance, must show himself faithful and obedient to his Father, after which he, in turn, will receive a reign in the heavenly kingdom and live with the family of God forever. The process whereby he, under the tutelage of his Father, shows himself faithful and obedient, is justification. He continually pleases the Father and in turn shows himself to be a worthy son, justly deserving of the Father's blessing and inheritance.

To understand the familial model better one can simply look to the basic structure of family relationships. The relationships between the members of the family are primarily based on the mutual love and concern generated from emotional attachment. Within this framework, the family members show spontaneous and continual care and affection for each other. The parents love, protect, teach, and discipline their children, giving top priority to their spiritual, physical, emotional, and social well-being. The parents themselves show mutual love and respect to one another. When friction occurs among the family members, the offender is expected to seek forgiveness from the one harmed, and, of course, the one harmed is expected to forgive. Then, except in very serious confrontations, the concerns evaporate without thought of revenge. A family member does not, for example, seek "compensatory damages" from a court of law if one family member happens to get into a minor altercation with another. The emotional bond usually supersedes any recourse to legal action outside the family. Families usually settle altercations "in-house," as it were, as each family member, stimulated by the bonds of love, strives to work out any differences by mutual respect and forgiveness. If spouses are at odds with one another we expect them to reconcile in due time and make up for any harm by resuming acts of love and affection. If children disobey certain household rules, we expect the parent to deal with the infraction, discipline the child, and put things back to normal so that the household runs smoothly.

Yet while the familial model is for the most part based on the personal and emotional relationship between the members that supersedes recourse to law, there is a degree of overlap between the familial and legal dimensions of life.[6] For example, before they are married, the bride and the groom must secure legal documentation stating that each partner is legally free to marry, e.g., that he or she has not previously created another family with someone else. Once married, the husband and wife are expected to treat each other with mutual respect and love. Even in these emotional family bonds, each spouse is expected to obey certain household "rules" for the benefit of the entire family. If, for example, the husband abuses the wife, it may become so serious (e.g., her life is threatened) as to force the wife to avail herself of the legal authorities outside the home to put a restraining order on her husband. If one of the spouses engages in sexual intimacy with another person, the other spouse may eventually see no option except to seek a legal divorce to terminate the spousal relationship. Similarly, parent and child are expected to have a reciprocal relationship. The parent is expected to love, protect, and provide for the child, and, the child, in turn, is expected to honor and obey the parent. If, however, the parent begins abusing the child, the legal authorities are brought in to separate the family member, punish the abuser, or both. Likewise, if the child shows himself to be unduly insubordinate (e.g., threatening the family with bodily harm or destruction), the civil authorities can become involved and put the child in juvenile detention. Hence, though the family is based on the mutual love and concern of each member for the other, a breakdown of that love and concern leaves only the law to deal with the deteriorated relationship. Relationships within the family can only supersede recourse to law if the family members maintain the dimensions of relationship that law does not have, i.e., love and forgiveness.

In contrast to family relationships, the relationship between a member of western society and his government, or other legal entity, is quite different. Each sector of society has a specific code of

[6] Catholic theologian Joseph Fitzmeyer's thoughts are appropriate here. In his commentary on Romans he writes: "...What happens to man in this new manifestation of God's uprightness is not without its forensic, judicial aspects. But to maintain that Paul means that man is only "declared upright," though still a sinner, would imply a watering down of the "New Creation" and the whole Christian reality that he is proclaiming. For in this "New Creation" man actually becomes the "uprightness of God" (*Jerome Biblical Commentary*, op. cit., p. 301).

law by which it regulates and judges the conduct of its citizens. The government expects each member of society to obey all the rules and regulations stipulated. Whereas the family's laws are usually unwritten, the society's laws are written in fine detail. Specific laws prohibit every offense from jaywalking to murder. For example, if the speed limit is 55 mph and one travels 56 mph, technically, he has broken the law. In that sense, the law is exacting and uncompromising, showing no mercy to the offender and exacting a specific punishment or fine for every infraction.

Yet strict though the law may be, it often overlaps with elements of personality and emotion seen in family relations. In other words, it contains aspects of forgiveness and leniency. For example, a police officer does not always issue a ticket for a person who goes over the 55 mph speed limit. He may show mercy to someone who travels 56 mph. The police officer also has certain limitations in enforcing the law. He cannot physically stop everyone at the same time. Thus, there is a certain amount of involuntary forgiveness associated with law, as well as a certain amount of voluntary forgiveness depending on the disposition of the judge who is evaluating a particular infraction against the law. The judge may decide to give someone the "full extent of the law" for a particularly heinous crime or because of a defendant's belligerent attitude. Within the bounds set by the law, he may be more lenient to one person or another depending on the circumstances. Whereas the law itself is a rigid and uncompromising code that requires unconditional compliance, the judge is a thinking personality who can evaluate one contingency against another and make a final balanced decision that will serve the best interests of the law, the individual and the society as a whole. Because life and the situations it presents are frequently complex, judgments cannot always be made simply on the strict basis of law in computer-like fashion. Nevertheless, there is one thing about the law to which even the judge must submit. Once a person is brought before the law for an alleged crime, the law requires that the accused person receive a verdict of guilty or not guilty. The judge may determine the degree of punishment for a convicted criminal, or he may even decide that the case has no merit and thus throw it out of court. In any case, however, he must decide whether the accused has broken the law or not. He must convict him with a certain degree of punishment or he must set him free. Moreover, he cannot do this arbitrarily. If the accused is guilty of the crime, the judge, in his striving to be just, must punish the criminal; otherwise, law and justice have no meaning. As we move on in this study we will see more clearly the relationship between love and law, or mercy and justice.[7]

God, The Family and The Law

From all eternity God has existed. He had no beginning and will have no end. As He said to Moses when the latter inquired who God is, He simply yet profoundly replied, "I am who I am" (Exodus 3:14). In relation to our discussion comparing and contrasting family and law, God's identity is defined within himself, specifically in his Trinity. The Church has best defined the Trinity as "three persons in one God" or "three persons in one nature," that "nature" being Divinity. Within the Trinity, the position of each person defines his role; thus there is a Father, a Son, and a Holy Spirit. These are three distinct persons yet all are one God — a mystery indeed. For our purposes, however, as God identifies himself as Father, this forms the basis of our understanding of his relationship with the other members of the Godhead and with his creation. From all eternity God is a Father. He is not *like* a father nor does he merely have fatherly qualities. He is a real Father and he has a real Son, who one day became flesh.[8] There was love and

7 See also the Catholic Catechism's remarks on "The Person and Society," Sections 1877-1948.

8 The Church teaches that the Son was begotten or generated by the Father, and the Holy Spirit "proceeds" from the Father and the Son. This last relation termed *filioque*, following an ancient Latin and Alexandrian tradition, was held as dogma by Pope St. Leo I in 447, and at the Council of Chalcedon in 451 (CC, Sec. 247); and inserted into the Nicene Creed at the Council of Toledo in 589 AD but became a source of contention between the Western and Eastern churches. Finally the latter broke off in schism in 1054, maintaining that the Holy Spirit "proceeded" from the Father only, not from the Son. The Council of Florence in 1438 reinforced the teaching of *filioque*.

communication within the Trinity before the creation, during the creation, and there will be forevermore.[9]

Being a Father to his eternal Son, God was also a father to his newly created son, Adam. This is where the Catholic understanding of God's paternal relationship to man begins. Though not identical to Christ who is the natural Son of God, Adam was the "adopted" son of God. In Luke 3:23-38, Scripture even provides the genealogical record showing that the relationship between God and Adam is as father and son: "He was the son...of Enosh, the son of Seth, the son of Adam, the son of God."[10]

For Adam, God the Father provided everything necessary to sustain life, both spiritually and physically. God gave Adam a garden that could produce various kinds of nourishment, and he protected Adam and Eve from all harm. In turn, God established certain "family" rules. He gave Adam and his wife, Eve, a "household rule" that they were to take care of the garden God created, to be

9 "No other formal relationship allows a human being to reveal God as Trinity so perfectly. The family allows us an insight into the very heart of God: we are never so much ourselves as when we are most for the other in mutual love, sharing, and concern" (F. J. Parrella, "Towards a Spirituality of the Family," *Communio* 9 (1982), p. 137; cited in Hahn, *Kinship by Covenant*, op. cit., p. 662).

10 The Greek of Luke 3:38 does not specify the word "son," leaving open the possibility of an ancestral relationship for any of the names listed in the genealogy of Luke 3:23-38. There are several names missing from Luke's genealogy. The same is true of the genealogy in Matthew 1. The Greek genealogical formula is "X of Y" implying that "Y" is the son or ancestor of "X." Rather than using the word "son" with any of the names in the genealogy, Luke simply uses the genitive article τοῦ meaning "of." Hence, Seth is said to be "of Adam," Enos is said to be "of Seth," Cainan is said to be "of Enos," etc. However, we know that the immediate "son" is certainly to be understood with most of the names since Luke 3:23 begins the formula with "being the son [Greek: ὢν υἱός] ... of Eli ... of Matthat ... of Levi..." Hence, we can understand Adam as "the son of God" because God immediately generated him, and because God is the Father of the whole human race. This also ties in with the Hebrew concept of the father-son relationship, as well as with the Hebrew use of "son" in reference to nonhuman entities. Generally speaking, "son" can mean anything that issues forth from a progenitor or primary source, for example, "sons of Israel," "son of man" (Num. 23:19; Psalm 8:4), "sons of Elohim (God)" (Gen. 6:4; Ps. 82:6; Job 1:6) "sons of Yahweh" (Deut. 14:1; 32:19). God calls us his "sons" (Psalm 2:7), and "sons of the living God" (Hosea 1:10). Adopted children are "sons" (Exodus 2:10). In Genesis 17:12 a newborn ready for circumcision is literally a "son of eight days."

its protector and cultivator. One specific rule God gave to Adam and Eve was not to eat of the tree of the knowledge of good and evil. This was to test their faithfulness and obedience. If Adam passed the test, he and all his sons would enjoy the position of remaining the sons of God forever. As one author notes:

> The eating of proper food was a sign that Adam was remaining in the covenant established by God. The teaching is sealed by "food sacrament," the sign of continuity and faithfulness to the covenant. Adam was a faithful son of God as long as he was being "fed" by God in every aspect of the Word of God. To eat God's food is to be in communion with Him. . .Adam exchanges fathers in his eating of the forbidden fruit. He refuses the revelation and food of God and comes to be fed from the hand of Satan himself. Adam and Eve believed the doctrine of Satan instead of the teaching of God. Then, to seal their belief, they partook of an unholy communion. The ate the food provided for them by their new father, the devil.[11]

Failing the test, Adam plunged himself and the whole human race into sin and death. In place of the intimate relationship of sonship, the Father convicted him and all his future sons of sin and they became outcasts in the eyes of God under sentence of death. Adam became a rebellious son, who was disinherited by his Father. Fortunately for Adam and the rest of the human race, God, in his mercy as Father, did not carry out the punishment of death immediately. God threw Adam out of his "house" and made him struggle for his sustenance in pain and sweat. Eventually, it would be necessary for something to be done concerning the impending sentence of death. If not, it would be carried out and condemn Adam and the human race to eternal banishment from sonship with God.

God, as Father, is gracious, merciful, and ready to forgive. He seeks to restore the familial relation that was severed with his adopted son. Fathers do not want to see their sons become victims of the unmerciful law which will utterly condemn them. God the Father is merciful with the human race. He is not willing that any should

[11] Mark J. Kelly in "The Fatherhood of God" in Our Sunday Visitor's *The Catholic Answer*, Vol. 10, No. 4, Sept./Oct., 1996, pp. 36-37.

perish but that all should come to repentance (2 Peter 3:9). Or, as in the parable of the Prodigal son, the father wishes for the son to come to his senses and make his way back home to the family in repentance. As Peter says, "we call on a Father who judges each man's work impartially (1 Peter 1:17). After Adam's sin, God's first sign of fatherly mercy was Genesis 3:15's promise of a redeemer. In anticipation of this redeemer, God offered Adam and his progeny a way back. Although God had put Adam under the curse of sin and death, through his grace as Father, he did not totally forsake Adam nor leave him totally incapable of responding to God's invitation to be restored to the full rights of the family. Rather than execute him immediately for his crime as a Judge and Jury would do, God allowed Adam to exist, produce children, and subdue the earth, yet all the while facing the residual punishment for his disobedience if he did not make his way back to be a full-fledged membership in the family.[12] If God did not make provisions for him to rise from the dead, he would remain in a condemned state for eternity — unable to rise to eternal fellowship with his Father, forever abandoned to the abyss of the second death, eternal disinheritance.

The Covenant

Scripture also speaks of the agreement between God and Adam as a covenant — a covenant that was broken. Hosea 6:7 states: "Like Adam, they have broken the covenant — they were unfaithful to me there."[13] Here Hosea compares Israel's breaking of the covenant

---

12 Other instances of this merciful principle in the character of God include his reaction to the sin of Israel when they worshiped the golden calf in the desert. Exodus 32:9f reveals that, in his anger, God seeks to destroy Israel. Moses pleads with God to relent, citing the shame God would feel in the face of Egyptian ridicule, as well as the covenant God had made with Abraham to bless Israel. Through his grace, God changes his mind and does not destroy them. Instead, God establishes another covenant with them by adding to the previous covenant (cf., Deut. 29:1; 5:1ff).

13 The Hebrew word used for "covenant" in Hosea 6:7 is *berith* (בּרית), the same word used throughout the Old Testament in which God establishes various covenants with his people, e.g., Genesis 6:18; 15:18; 17:2ff; Exodus 2:24; 24:8; 34:27; Psalm 78:10; Jeremiah 31:31, Ecclesiasticus 17:11-12; et al. The word "Adam" in Hosea 6:7 is a transliteration of the Hebrew אדם which is used over 500 times in the Old Testament to refer to man, e.g., Gen. 1:26,27; 2:5,7,8; 6:1-7. Other words referring to man are: *ish* (אִישׁ Gen. 2:23,24; 6:9); *enosh* (אנשׁי Gen. 6:4); *gebar* (גבר Deut. 22:5; Dan. 2:25).

God established with them to the covenant Adam broke with God. Through his grace,[14] God made the covenant with Adam which stated that he and all his progeny would be blessed if he would be faithful to the commands that God gave him. On the other hand, the covenant required that if Adam did not abide by its stipulations then he would have to suffer its penal sanctions. The penal sanctions of the covenant between God and Adam required that Adam, the one who sinned against the covenant, be put to death for his violation. Similarly, in Israel, those who broke the covenant, either of the nuclear family, the extended family or the remainder of society, were punished. Those of a serious nature were punished with death.

Pre-western cultures, like that of Israel (and upon which the Old Testament is based), exhibit a higher degree of convergence between the family and the society. The family was the basis of society and kinship among its members was very strong. The Old Testament describes families and extended families in very intimate language, e.g., one member was the "flesh and bone" of another.[15] It would not be an exaggeration to say that Israel was originally one big family, which then filtered down into and made up the society on all levels. It was through the family unit that one understood reality and comprehended his standing with God and his place in the world. Within the family, each member learned the rules of life and was expected to carry this knowledge and commitment to the relationships within his extended family of grandparents, uncles, aunts, cousins, and other generic groups such as tribes and clans (e.g., Joshua 7:16-18).The father was the head of his family, yet he was only one of a long line of fathers that could be traced back to the beginning of Israel's history. To be a true Israelite, one had to know his genealogy. This is one reason why the Chronicler, after the Jews returned from 70 years in captivity in Babylon, records the history of Israel by first listing the genealogy of Israel in minute detail (1 Chronicles 1-10). The time after the Babylonian captivity began a new era and in doing so each

---

[14] The establishment of the relationship between God and Adam through grace will be addressed more thoroughly in Chapter 7.

[15] cf., Genesis 29:14; 37:27; Judges 9:2; 2 Samuel 5:1; 19:12-13; 1 Chronicles 11:1. Even husband and wife share this language; first with Adam and Eve (Gen. 2:23) which then serves as the basis for spouses becoming "one flesh" (Genesis 2:24; Matthew 19:4-6; Ephesians 5:31).

family had to know whence it came and all the families preceding it. Israelite society knew and defined families by the father's family name and reputation. These fathers were kings, priests, elders, prophets, soldiers, etc. The father of one family had intimate ties with the father of another family. Even in death, one was said to "go to his fathers" (Gen. 15:15). In the father and son relationship, the son inherited everything that the father was, e.g., his character, his aspirations, his accomplishments, his possessions, his learning, his trade. The son was so identified with the father that he was known as "the son of" his father's name.[16] If a son became disobedient, he disgraced his father, and, particularly, his father's name. Honor then had to be restored to the father. Sometimes, as is the case of the rebellious son in Deuteronomy 21:18-21, the father publicly repudiated and punished his son for his sins. This restored the honor of the father in the eyes of his fellow fathers.

The glue that held the nuclear family together, and connected it with all the extended families of Israel, was the concept of "covenant."[17] Basically, covenant was an agreement between two or more consenting parties to show mutual love and concern and to abide by certain rules agreed upon by both parties for the benefit of each. The covenant's purpose was to perpetuate the relationship between the parties and thus avoid its disintegration and destruction. Hence, while personal interest motivated those within a covenant, rules of legality also prohibited one party from taking ad-

[16] E.g., "In the fifth year of Joram son of Ahab king of Israel, when Jehoshaphat was king of Judah, Jehoram son of Jehoshaphat began his reign as king of Judah" (2 Kings 8:16).

[17] According to Catholic theologian, Scott Hahn: "The covenant serves as the transcendent principle that reveals the moral and theological frame of reference for the family. As such, it discloses the real meaning of kinship relations and obligations, and why the family is not reducible to mere biology, or socio-political convention. Indeed, the family is divinely sanctioned by covenant. The family thus represents the immanent principle of the covenant. As such, the family provides the covenant with its concrete historical and social forms in salvation history. The practical reality of the family prevents the covenant principle from becoming a mere theological abstraction or utopian ideal. Moreover, the family has a certain transcultural continuity and permanence, even allowing for a wide diversity of family types and values. This applies to the father-son relationship...which has a certain ubiquitous quality that renders it particularly apt to convey the meaning and reality of covenant to a wide variety of people of different periods and cultures" (*Kinship by Covenant*, op. cit., pp. 656-657).

vantage of the other. Such covenantal relationships permeated Israelite society.[18] If one of the parties broke the covenant, the guilty party incurred specific penalties.[19]

---

[18] The major areas of life protected by covenant relationships were: personhood (Ex. 20:13; 21:16-21, 26-31; Lev. 19:14; Deut. 24:7; 27:18); truth (Ex. 20:16; 23:1-3; Lev. 19:16; Deut. 19:15-21); women (Ex. 21:7-11,20,26-32; 22:16-17; Deut. 21:10-14; 22:13-30; 24:1-5; punishment (Deut. 25:1-5); dignity (Ex. 21:2, 5-6; Lev. 25; Deut. 15:12-18); inheritance (Lev. 25; Num. 27:5-7; 36:1-9; Deut. 25:5-10); property (Ex. 20:15: 21:33-36; 22:1-15; 23:4-5; Lev. 19:35-36; Deut. 22:1-4; 25:13-15); labor (Lev. 19:13; Deut 24:14; 25:4); produce (Ex. 23:10-11; Lev. 19:9-10; 23:22; 25:3-55; Deut. 14:28-29; 24:19-21); rest (Ex. 20:8-11; 23:12); marriage (Ex. 20:14; Lev. 18:6-23; 20:10-21; Deut. 22:13-30; the disabled (Ex. 22:21-27; Lev. 19:14, 33-34; 25:35-36; Deut. 23:19; 24:6,12-15; 27:18); trial (Ex. 23:6,8; Lev. 19:15; Deut. 1:17; 10: 17-18; 16:18-20; 17:8-13; 19:15-21); social order (Ex. 20:12; 21:15,17; 22:28; Lev. 19:3,32; 20:9; Deut. 17:8-13; 21:15-21; 27:16); law (Deut. 17:18-20); animals (Ex. 23:5,11; Lev. 25:7; Deut. 22:4,6-7; 25:4).

[19] Genesis 15:7-21 describes a dramatic example of "cutting a covenant" between God and Abraham. Here God tells Abraham to bring various kinds of animals to a place of meeting. Abraham cut the animals in two. This halving of the animals signifies that the one who breaks the covenant, either God or Abraham, will likewise be cut in half. Genesis 15:18 refers to this as, "On that day the Lord made a covenant with Abram..." God promised that Abram's descendants would inherit all the land from the "river of Egypt to the great river Euphrates." God kept his promise of the covenant as recorded in Deuteronomy 1:7; Joshua 21:43-45; Nehemiah 9:7-8. Here we see that God *obligates* himself to keep his half of the covenant. In regard to the principle of obligation investigated in chapter 1, it was established that man could not put God in a position of obligation for the purposes of justification. We see the inverse of that principle in Genesis 22. God swears an oath to Abraham to keep the covenant of blessing to Abraham and his progeny (cf., Hebrews 6:13-15 — "For in making the promises to Abraham, since there was no one greater to swear by, God swore by himself, saying, 'In blessing I will bless you, and in multiplying I will multiply you.' And so, being patient, he received the promise"). The difference is that God is obligating himself; man is not forcing God into a position of obligation. In light of this, we must also recognize several qualifications to God's obligation. First, the decision to obligate himself is made from God's grace, not because he is forced by some law to obligate himself. This is noted in the words, "...since there was no one greater to swear by, God swore by himself..."). Although God recognizes Abraham's faith and obedience, God is not required to offer Abraham a covenant promise of blessing for such acts. He does so only out of his gracious nature. Though God obligates himself, Scripture does not interpret such self-imposed obligation as an infringement on the principles of grace (cf., Romans 4:16-17; Galatians 3:18). Second, the obligation of God within the covenant is still conditioned by the faith of the individual. Thus, God is not obligated to justify anyone unless that person fulfills his portion of the conditions of the covenant. If the covenant conditions are fulfilled, then God, stemming from his benevolence, obligates himself to justify the person.

As an agreement between two parties that involves penal sanctions for violations, the concept of covenant incorporates a certain degree of legality into the various relationships it encompasses. In effect, no matter how personal and emotional the relationship between two parties, a legal dimension is always present. In other words, as we have noted earlier in this chapter, to one degree or another, personal relationships and legal relationships overlap and converge. This is especially true in a sinful world in which there is a high likelihood that one party will violate the established personal relationship and thereby force the other party to take legal action to rectify the damage caused by the breach of trust and receive punitive compensation. This relationship between the personal and the legal is also true of God's relationship to man. In fact, the personal and the legal meet in the concept of *covenant*. As understood in the Old Testament, a covenant implied a very personal relationship between two parties, yet a relationship which also bound both by law to be faithful to the covenant. When Adam sinned against God, for example, Adam broke trust with the personal relationship God had established with him. As a result, Adam had to suffer the legal consequences of his breach with God, as did his progeny. They are all covenant breakers, having spurned the personal relationship God desired with them, and thus they suffer the penal sanctions of the covenant, e.g., the curse of sin and death.

The same relationship between the personal and the legal exists in the human family. The members of the family have a very personal relationship with one another, but a severe violation of the personal relationship may require the guilty party to incur legal sanctions. Israelite society furnishes a dramatic example of this in the civil actions taken against a rebellious son. Deuteronomy 21:18-21 records:

> If a man has a stubborn and rebellious son who does not obey his father and mother and will not listen to them when they discipline him, his father and mother shall take hold of him and bring him to the elders at the gate of his town. They shall say to the elders, 'This son of ours is stubborn and rebellious. He will not obey us. He is a profligate and a drunkard.' Then all the men

of his town shall stone him to death. You must purge the evil from among you. All Israel will hear of it and be afraid.

Here we see that if the son does not obey the rules of the family, his parents hand him over to the legal authorities to be put to death. Prior to this, parents could tolerate their son's minor infractions. Through their grace, love and mercy, their child was not expected to be absolutely perfect. Yet when the son crosses the line of propriety and continually engages in insubordinate behavior, they disown and condemn him.[20]

Focusing on his divine person as Father, we can understand his relationship with mankind in much the same way as in the above example. As a Father, God created Adam to be his son. He wanted to develop a strong, intimate relationship with Adam. The Father established a covenant with Adam obligating Adam to subdue the earth, increase and multiply, and rule the earth. But Adam did not subdue the earth. Instead, he let it subdue him. In doing so, Adam broke the covenant with his Father and lost the trust of their personal relationship. Though he was still a son, he was now an estranged son, stripped of his previous rights and privileges. God brought the legal sanctions of the covenant against him and made him suffer for his sin. In order to restore the blessings of the covenant, Adam had to regain the rights and privileges of divine sonship; otherwise, the Father would banish him forever.

The Father, The Covenant, and Justification

Viewing God's relationship with man from the perspective of God as Father helps us understand how the legal dimensions of justification integrate with the personal dimensions. Once we see that the legal dimensions stem from the familial model of God as

[20] John Paul II, *Domimum et vivificantem*, 27-48: "...but in the 'depths of God' there is a Father's love that, faced with man's sin, in the language of the Bible reacts so deeply as to say: 'I am sorry that I have made him.'...But more often the Sacred Book speaks to us of a Father who feels compassion for man, as though sharing his pain. In a word, this inscrutable and indescribable fatherly 'pain' will bring about all the wonderful economy of redemptive love in Jesus Christ..."

Father who can take legal action against his sons who break the covenant, we have the proper framework to understand the personal and legal aspects of justification. Viewing God only as a Judge who brings sinners to the bar of justice as in a court of law severely distorts the concept of justification. The separation between the personal and the legal in western society, has caused a strong tendency in Protestant thought to represent justification purely in legal terms which view the individual strictly as a courtroom defendant who is to be acquitted of crimes.[21]

As noted earlier, Scripture does not use courtroom imagery to describe the justification of man before God. This is so because God is a Father with qualities of justice, not a courtroom judge with fatherly qualities. As 1 Peter 1:17 puts it: "...a Father who judges each man's work impartially..." One proof of this is that God, in his relationship with the individual, requires personal faith in him. Conversely, a framework based on the courtroom model leaves no room for faith simply because in any system of law or practice of jurisprudence, the defendant's faith is not a criterion for acquittal or condemnation. If he is guilty he is sentenced, regardless of whether or not he believes in the judge or the judicial system. Or, if one tells a defendant convicted of crimes that another individual has accepted his punishment so as to let the defendant go free, (assuming that the court would allow for such substitution), the defendant's faith, either in the system which provides the substitution or in the individual substituting for him, would not affect the outcome. If the judge allowed another to accept the punishment, then the law would be satisfied and the judge would be forced to release the defendant, whether or not the defendant *believed* in the substitution or wanted to be released. In fact, if the defendant, not believing that the substitute would pay for his crime, insisted on receiving his own sentence, the judge would be forced to call the bailiff to remove him from the courtroom, since the judge could not issue two sentences for the same crime.

As Father, God can love his sons whether they are with him or estranged from him. As Paul says in Romans 5:8, "But God

---

[21] Martin Luther was the first to formulate the rudiments of a "forensic" view of justification. His protégé, Philip Melanchthon, was the first to see justification as *purely* forensic. See chapter 9 for further discussion.

demonstrates his own love for us in this: While we were still sinners, Christ died for us." God does not love us only after we have gone through the bar of justice. As Jesus said of his Father in John 3:16: "For God so loved the world that he gave his only begotten Son, that whosoever believes in him will not perish but have everlasting life." As Father, "God causes his sun to rise on the evil and the good" (Matthew 5:45), and places men in specific times and locations so that they would "seek him and find him, though he is not far from each one of us" (Acts 17:27). Likewise, God tells us to "love our enemies" and "pray for those who persecute you" for the express purpose that "we may be sons of your *Father* in heaven" who shows love to good and bad alike. We are to imitate God's love to such an extent that we "be perfect, therefore, as your heavenly Father is perfect" (Matthew 5:44, 48). But judges cannot show love and forgiveness. They do not love the criminals who appear before them. Only the code of law directs their actions.

We understand, then, that although faith is not at all involved in the courtroom, it is intimately involved with personal relationships outside of jurisprudence. Within the family, for example, the faithfulness between husband and wife, in the face of temptations to be unfaithful, establishes, strengthens, and solidifies the relationship. Not only their faith in each other, but also their mutual love, sustain them as each looks after the other's needs and desires. They hope in a bright future as their relationship produces offspring and the ultimate blessing of eternal life. Similarly, children are faithful to their parents, obeying the law of respect and honor for the guardians God has placed over them. And friends, too, are also faithful to one another. The whole relationship of friendship is built on trust. Without trust, friendship dies. No "code of law" can make them trust and sacrifice for each other. Rather, in each of these relationships — as spouse, child, or friend — one individual seeks to *please* the other by his faith, hope and love. In essence, our human relationships mirror our relationship to God in his grace.

Considering the above principles, we insist that if justification were only a forensic matter, then God could have saved the whole human race by one extrinsic legal action. As God condemned the human race in its solitary representative, Adam, he could easily have saved the whole human race by a solitary legal act. This, however, is not the way the salvation of man occurs. To receive the power of the atonement, man must have faith in God; otherwise, he will remain condemned. This is one of the reasons why the Protestant concept of imputed righteousness is unbiblical. As we have stressed previously, the issue is not a contest between the "alien righteousness of Christ" and the righteousness of man, but how the individual can appropriate and maintain any righteousness, whether of Christ or of himself. As even Protestant sources have stipulated, to receive the benefits of Christ's righteousness, the individual must appropriate and maintain it through faith, and furthermore, through a faith characterized by a firm resolve and outward obedience. The real crux of justification, then, is the individual's *personal response* to his heavenly Father's pleading, not merely an external, legal restitution. As noted above, faith has nothing to do with jurisprudence, since faith denotes the *personal* relationship required between God and his creature that law simply does not provide or have any room to include. Legal adjudication does not depend on whether the defendant believes in the system but only on whether the system has determined him innocent or guilty.

There is another stark contrast between the courtroom model and the familial model. From the courtroom model, Protestants understand justification as a one-time event in which God the Judge sets the accused sinner free. As a result, once the defendant is imputed with another's righteousness, he acquires a kind of "judicial immunity," that is, he will never have to appear in the courtroom again. Thus, belief in the courtroom model inevitably gives rise to the teaching of the individual's "eternal security." As detailed in chapter 4, however, the teaching of eternal security contradicts overwhelming biblical evidence that the individual can fall from his justified state, either by loss of faith or by overt sin, or both. The familial model of justification, on the other hand, readily allows for such a contingency. In the familial model, the son who is no longer faithful and seriously disobeys the Father, can be disowned by the family, lose his inheritance, and face the condemnation of the law. The Father hands the disowned son over to the legal magistrate and he is punished for his crimes. In effect, the courtroom is reserved until the very end when all personal attempts to bring the son back to the family have failed.[22]

Scripture's Use of the Father/Son Relationship

Scripture contains numerous statements and allusions to the father/son relationship. For example, in Psalm 89:26 the Psalmist writes, "He will call out to me, 'You are my Father, my God, the Rock my Savior." In Isaiah 63:16 the people plead, "But you are our Father, though Abraham does not know us or Israel acknowledge us; you, O Lord, are our Father, our Redeemer from of old is your name." In Isaiah 64:8 they repeat, "Yet, O Lord, you are our Father. We are the clay, you are the potter." In Jeremiah 3:4,19 the prophet writes, "Have you not just called to me: 'My Father, my friend from my youth, will you always be angry? Will your wrath continue forever?...I myself said, 'How gladly would I treat you like sons and give you a desirable land the most beautiful inheritance of any nation.' I thought you would call me 'Father' and not turn away from following me." In Deuteronomy 1:31, Moses writes of God, "...in the desert. There you saw how the Lord your God carried you, as a father carries his son, all the way you went..." In Wisdom 2:16 the wicked complain that the righteous "boasts that

---

22 Evangelical John Gerstner argues against Catholic theologian Scott Hahn: "We have no opposition whatever to Scott's reference to the covenant as involving family. We only oppose him when he represents family as if that were opposed to the forensic. It rests on the forensic and is the corollary and outgrowth and inseparable association of the removal of guilt and the bestowal of righteousness that occurs in the courtroom act of God in justification by faith alone" (*Justification by Faith Alone*, op. cit., p. 180); Dr. Hahn responds: "The results of our study show how the covenant, which is the basis for God's law and judgments, is ultimately a familial reality. This means that God's 'forensic' decree of justification must be understood primarily as the covenantal/familial act of the divine Father. The 'right standing' which this 'forensic' decree effects is nothing less than divine sonship, just as Paul argues in Gal. 3:6-4:7, and Trent defines it (Session VI, ch. 4). The classical Protestant doctrine of justification wrongly defines it as an exclusively judicial act (i.e., mere legal imputation of Christ's righteousness). As a consequence, its primary meaning (divine sonship) is overlooked or suppressed. Thus, the forensic character of justification ultimately rests on a covenantal-familial basis — the denial of which leads to a nominalistic view that opposes the forensic to the familial (i.e., imputation versus adoption), as Gerstner would have it" (*Kinship by Covenant*, op. cit., p. 664).

God is his father" and in 14:3 that it is "your providence O Father that steers its course." Ecclesiasticus 23:4 records: "O Lord, Father and God of my life" and in 51:10 "I cried out, 'Lord, you are my Father.'" We see in these passages God's yearning for the most intimate relationship possible with his people — as a father who wants to care for their every need, expecting only obedience in return.

To explain why the son must be faithful to his heavenly Father, Paul uses the model of familial relations to show Christians that they are indeed God's sons and daughters. In 2 Corinthians 6:18, quoting from Isaiah 43:6, Paul says, "I will be a Father to you and you will be my sons and daughters, says the Lord Almighty." On the other hand, he tells the same people that if they sin seriously and are unrepentant, that is, if they become like the "profligate and drunkard" son of Deuteronomy 21:18-21, God will disown them from his family and sentence them to death. In 1 Corinthians 6:8-9 Paul writes:

> ...you yourselves cheat and do wrong, and you do this to your brothers. Do you not know that the wicked will not inherit the kingdom of God? Do not be deceived: Neither the sexually immoral nor idolaters nor adulterers nor male prostitutes nor homosexual offenders nor thieves nor the greedy nor drunkards nor slanderers nor swindlers will inherit the kingdom of God.

Scripture speaks of such judgment as "the second death." Revelation 21:7-8 states:

> He who overcomes will *inherit* all this, and I will be his God and he will be *my son*. But the cowardly, the unbelieving, the vile, the murderers, the sexually immoral, those who practice magic arts, the idolaters and all liars — their place will be in the fiery lake of burning sulfur. This is the *second death*.

Here we see all the elements of the previous verses converge. The apostle John speaks first of those who "overcome" as being "sons" of God who will "inherit" the eternal kingdom. Next, he specifies the kinds of sins, as Paul did in 1 Corinthians 6:8-9, that would disinherit individuals from the kingdom. For these sins John says that they will die the "second death."

John uses similar language in Revelation 20:14-15: "Then death and Hades were thrown into the lake of fire. The lake of fire is the *second death.* If anyone's name was not found written in the book of life, he was thrown into the lake of fire." Here John connects the "second death" with those whose "names were not found in the book of life." The "book of life" is mentioned earlier in John's writing in Revelation 3:5: "He who overcomes will, like them, be dressed in white. I will never blot out his name from the *book of life*, but will acknowledge his name before my Father and his angels." John shows us the potential of having one's name "blotted" out of the book of life if he does not overcome. He also says he will not have his name brought before the "Father," a familial recognition of God. This is identical to Revelation 21:7-8's statement that he who "overcomes" will receive the inheritance and will be called a "son." The Old Testament speaks similarly of being "blotted out of the book of life." Psalm 69:27-28 states, "...do not let them share in your salvation. May they be blotted out of the book of life and not listed with the righteous." Exodus 32:33 states, "The Lord replied to Moses, 'Whoever has sinned against me I will blot out of my book.'" Deuteronomy 29:19-20 states:

> When such a person hears the words of this oath, he invokes a blessing on himself and therefore thinks, 'I will be safe, even though I persist in going my own way.'...The Lord will never be willing to forgive him; his wrath and zeal will burn against that man. All the curses written in this book will fall upon him, and the Lord will blot out his name from under heaven.

Paul uses similar language in Ephesians to describe the *inheritance.* In Ephesians 1:14, he speaks of Christians as receiving the Spirit as a "deposit guaranteeing our inheritance." In Ephesians 5:5-6, however, he speaks of them having to forfeit the inheritance because of disobedience:

> For of this you can be sure: No immoral, impure or greedy person — such a man is an idolater — has any inheritance in

> the kingdom of Christ and of God. Let no one deceive you with empty words, for because of such things God's wrath comes on those who are disobedient. Therefore, do not be partners with them.

Again, we see the same theme — the sins that will prohibit one from receiving the inheritance — and an inheritance that belongs to a *son*, a member of God's family. Paul's use of, "Of this you can be sure" and "let no one deceive you" shows his concern that none of the Ephesians fall into these sins and so subject themselves to the "wrath" of God that others will receive for their sins. Instead, Paul exhorts them in verse 10 to "find out what pleases the Lord." Again, as we have seen over and over again in our study, we, as sons, are to *please* our Father and he in turn will reward us with the inheritance. If we do not please him he will disown us.

We also see the filial imagery in connection with the concept of *propitiation*. The apostle John states it this way in 1 John 2:1-2

> My dear children, I write this to you so that you do not sin. And if anyone sins, we have an Advocate with the Father, Jesus Christ the righteous. He is the propitiation for our sins, and not ours only but also for the whole world.

Here John uses filial terminology (e.g., "dear children," "the Father") in the context of Christ being the "propitiation" for our sins. As noted in chapter 1, Christ is able to intercede to the Father on behalf of the sinner because he is "righteous." The Father is appeased because a righteous person pleads for mercy and satisfies his wrath. In other places, Paul speaks of Christ being the propitiation for those who are not yet Christians (e.g., Romans 3:25: "Whom God purposed to be a propitiation, through faith in his blood, to demonstrate his righteousness"). In 1 John 2:1-2 above, however, the important point is that John is addressing people who have already become Christians, yet people who are still in need of a propitiator for their sins. Thus we understand that the propitiation is not just a one-time event of justification but to an individual's ongoing need of a continuing propitiation for his present and future sins.[23] The "Father" provided the propitiation to bring him to salvation and continues to provide the propitiation to keep him in salvation.[24]

These passages have helped to familiarize us with the all-pervasive familial model that Scripture so often employs to describe our relationship with God. One persistent theme in this familial model is the right of the Father not only to bestow the blessing of sonship upon the faithful, but also to terminate that sonship for the

---

[23] Note the use of the verbal form ἱλάσκομαι in Luke 18:13 in the parable of the Pharisee and the tax collector. We can translate the tax collector's words as "God, be a propitiation for me, a sinner." As we learned in chapter 3, the tax collector's pleading with God cannot be confined to his initial contact with God but must also include his continual seeking of God through his daily repentance. This parable provides further support for the concept of propitiation as an ongoing process.

[24] Since these Scripture passages clearly show that propitiation is necessary for sins both before and after conversion, they support the Catholic concept of progressive justification as opposed to the Protestant concept of a one-time forensic event. Christ the propitiator propitiates both past and future sins. This process implies that the sinner must continually seek to have his sins propitiated in order to receive the continuing mercy of the Father. To promote a purely forensic notion of the propitiation, some Protestants have seized upon the word "Advocate," claiming that it portrays a legal representative pleading a case before a judge (e.g., Michael Horton in: "*What Still Divides Us: A Protestant and Roman Catholic Debate*," Produced by: Christians United For Reformation, March, 1995, audio tape series). The problem with this view is twofold. First, as we have already noted, John is addressing people who are already Christians — Christians who may fall into sin from time to time. From the Protestant perspective, this would encompass the area of sanctification, not justification. The Protestant claim that only justification is forensic, and not sanctification, leaves no room to include forensic categories in 1 John 2:1-2. Second, the word "Advocate" is from the Greek παράκλητος, and appears elsewhere in the New Testament only in reference to the ministry of the Holy Spirit (cf., John 14:16, 26; 15:26; 16:7). Since in Protestant theology the ministry of the Holy Spirit is not forensic, it must be conceded that "Advocate" is not necessarily a forensic term. Third, the context of John's epistle, identical to that of the verse in question, portrays God as "Father," not as legal magistrate (e.g., 1 John 1:2, 3; 2:13, 15, 16, 23; 3:1). In an effort to support the forensic view, Lutheran commentator Lenski points to the usage in 1 John 1:9 of the Greek noun δίκαιος ("just") to describe the Father as "just," that is, judicially disposed to forgive our sins (*Commentary on the First Epistle of John*, p. 398). We must insist, however, that the usage of "just" refers in the first place to the character of God, not merely the model through which he relates to us. Similar usages of "just" to describe God's character appear in Hebrews 6:10, "For God is not unjust to forget your work," and in 1 Peter 1:17, "Since you call on a Father who judges each man's work impartially." God is just to his children, as a father should be, treating them fairly as they respond to his mercy.

unfaithful. This again is one of the main reasons why the courtroom model for justification is not appropriate. Since the forensic model requires that the person acquitted must leave the courtroom never to return again to face judgment for his sins, it cannot fit the biblical evidence that speaks directly contrary to such a possibility.

Baptism and Sonship

One of Paul's more elaborate descriptions of the filial relationship between God the Father and his Christian sons is in the third and fourth chapters of Galatians. In Galatians 3:26-27 Paul states, "You are all *sons of God* through faith in Christ Jesus, for all of you who were baptized into Christ have clothed yourselves with Christ." This passage indicates that there was a definite time in which we became the sons of God. It was at baptism. Baptism was the time when our sins were washed away and we became new creations in Christ (Acts 22:16). As noted earlier in the chapter, for us to become adopted sons of the Father, we must become divine-like. The Father cannot adopt a son who is not like him. Hence, baptism was the point-in-time when we were changed — when Christ enveloped our body and soul. Paul's use of "clothing" imagery to convey the idea of total envelopment also appears in Ephesians 4:24, "and *put on* the new self created to be like God in true righteousness and holiness," and in Colossians 3:10, "and have *put on* the new self which is being renewed in knowledge in the image of its Creator."[25]

Paul also expresses a similar theme of sonship in Romans 8:13-17:

> For if you live according to the sinful nature, you will die; but if by the Spirit you put to death the misdeeds of the body, you will live, because those who are led by the Spirit of God are *sons of God*. For you did not receive a spirit that makes you a slave again to fear, but you received the Spirit of *sonship*. And by him we cry, Abba, Father. The Spirit himself testifies with our spirit that we are God's *children*. Now if we are *children*, then we are

[25] cf., John 1:13; 3:3-8; 1 John 2:29; 3:9; 4:7; 5:14,18.

> heirs — heirs of God and co-heirs with Christ, if indeed we share in his sufferings in order that we may also share in his glory.

Paul represents baptism in Galatians 3:27 as the time when sin is washed away, and he has a similar theme in mind in Romans 8:13-17 as the Christian *son* continues to refrain from sins after the baptism Paul required of him in Romans 6:1-3. The sonship with God continues as long as he remains free of serious sin. To reinforce this idea, Paul in Romans 8:15 contrasts the imagery of sonship over against slavery. One who has succumbed to the sinful nature has made himself a slave of the father's house and relinquished his privilege as a son and the right to the inheritance.

Paul continues the contrast between sonship and slavery in Galatians 4:1-7:

> What I am saying is that as long as the heir is a child, he is no different from a slave, although he owns the whole estate. He is subject to guardians and trustees until the time set by his father. So also, when we were children, we were in slavery under the basic principles of the world. But when the time had fully come, God sent his Son, born of a woman, born under the law, that we might receive the full rights of sons. Because you are sons, God sent the Spirit of his Son into our hearts, the Spirit who calls out, 'Abba, Father.' So you are no longer a slave, but a son, God has made you also an heir.

Here is an interesting twist to the sonship model. Paul equates being under the law with being a young child who has not received his full rights of sonship and inheritance. As a young child whose father has died and left him an inheritance, but designates caretakers for the child until he comes of age and may legally assume his father's wealth, so the law was a tutor and governor of the people of God until they were ready to assume the inheritance of God's kingdom through faith in Christ. By the use of "we" in Galatians 4:3, Paul is including himself in this category. Although "we" refers primarily to the Jews since they were considered the "children of God" in the Old Testament, by extension it applies secondarily to the Gentiles, since Paul uses the same "we" in reference to the global extent of the law in Galatians 3:22-23, "But the Scripture declares that the whole world is a prisoner of sin...before this faith came we were held prisoners by the law, locked up until faith should be revealed." In principle, the child was in a different class than the slave; the child expected an inheritance, the slave did not.[26] Similarly, God had promised a redeemer for those under the law in expectation of their future inheritance of the kingdom of God. Practically speaking, however, the child was just like the slave since he had no control over his estate. The child was under the jurisdiction of the guardians and had to obey them in order to abide by the terms of the inheritance. Finding himself in the situation of many in Israel whose sons forsook their inheritance by faithlessness and disobedience to the law, the father puts a provision in the will stating that the son cannot receive the inheritance unless he shows himself faithful to the father's wishes. If the child is disobedient and renounces his sonship and inheritance, he reverts to the status of a slave and is out of the father's will. This is why Paul in Galatians stresses the necessity of faith in such phrases as "to those who believe" in 3:22, "justified by faith" in 3:24, "through faith in Christ Jesus" in 3:26, yet also warns them in 4:9-10:

> But now that you know God — how is it that you are turning back to those weak and miserable principles?[27] Do you wish to be enslaved by them all over again? You are observing special days and months and seasons and years! I fear for you that somehow I have wasted my efforts on you.

Paul's stress in this section of Galatians is on the ceremonial dimensions of the Mosaic law. As we have learned in previous chapters, God gave many of these ceremonies to Israel specifically as a burden for their continual sin and rejection of God (e.g., "be-

---

26 Jesus also uses this theme in John 8:34-35.

27 The word "principles," also used in Galatians 4:3, is from the Greek word στοιχεῖον. Although Colossians 2:8,20; Hebrews 5:12; 2 Peter 3:10,12 also use στοιχεῖον, these references do not have precisely the same meaning as Paul has in mind when he uses the word in Galatians. The context of Galatians is perhaps the only judge of this particular application of στοιχεῖον.

cause they had not obeyed my laws...I also gave them over to statutes that were not good and laws they could not live by..." — Ezekiel 20:24-25). The Jews, by their unnecessary elevation of the ceremonial law as the *sine qua non* of religious experience, showed that they were relying on the law for salvation. Paul's warning, as in Galatians 3:10, is that anyone who bases his relationship with God on law, any part of the law, is obligated to comply perfectly with the whole law or else be condemned by it, and his warning not to go back to the "weak and miserable principles" is for this sole purpose. This warning applies equally to the Gentiles. Although they have no ceremonial law as the primary expression of reliance on law, they also must come to understand that law cannot save them. For them, too, the law is a tutor to bring them to the grace of God in Christ. Hence, what is *specific* to the Jews in regards to law (i.e., the ceremonial law as the primary example of their reliance on law), applies in *general* to the Gentiles (i.e., the utter futility of the law as the basis for salvation).

The Consequences for Unfaithful Sons

Before we proceed to the next passage concerning the Christian's sonship with God, we must understand the extended application of both sonship and slavery under law. As we have shown many times in this study, those in the Old Testament were saved by faith and obedience just as were those in the New Testament. Hebrews 11 gives us a running account of many Old Testament figures who "pleased God by their faith" and as a result gained the inheritance of the kingdom. Abraham was particularly prominent in this regard. In fact, Paul reinforces our connection with Abraham through faith in Galatians 3:29 as, "If you belong to Christ, then you are Abraham's seed, and heirs according to the promise." Hence, though *formally* established "when the time had fully come" according to Galatians 4:4, nevertheless, grace was *informally* active in the Old Testament just as much as it was in the New. Now the same understanding is also true of the law. Though *formally* established in the Old Testament as the "tutor" and "guardian" to bring us to Christ, law is *informally* active in the New Testament to bring us to Christ and keep us close to him.[28] Analogously, as the general society has its laws, so the family also has laws. Although society generally uses "written" laws, whereas the family uses "unwritten" laws, nevertheless the law and its influence are still evident in both. We see Paul speak of the "unwritten" law in Hebrews 10:15-16:

> The Holy Spirit also testifies to us about this. First he says: 'This is the covenant I will make with them after that time, says the Lord. I will put my laws in their hearts and I will write them on their minds.' Then he adds: 'Their sins and lawless acts I will remember no more.

This passage instructs God's family members — his sons and daughters — to obey the unwritten laws of familial comradery in their heart. As we discovered earlier in this chapter, if the son does not adequately obey the laws of the family, the family casts him out and hands him over to the legal authorities who will punish him with death (cf., Deut. 21:18-21). Not surprisingly, Paul alludes to this theme immediately after he speaks of these unwritten laws and the forgiveness of sins in Hebrews 10:26-31:

> If we deliberately keep on sinning after we have received the knowledge of the truth, no sacrifice for sins is left, but only a fearful expectation of judgment and of raging fire that will consume the enemies of God. Anyone who rejected the law of Moses died without mercy on the testimony of two or three witnesses. How much more severely do you think a man deserves to be punished who has trampled the Son of God underfoot, who has treated as an unholy thing the blood of the covenant that sancti-

[28] "God, the inspirer and author of the books of both Testaments, in his wisdom has so brought it about that the New should be hidden in the Old and that the Old should be made manifest in the New ... For although Christ founded the New Covenant in his blood, still the books of the Old Testament, all of them caught up into the Gospel message, attain and show forth their full meaning in the New Testament (Mt. 5:17; Luke. 24:27; Rom. 16:25-26; 2 Cor. 2:14-16) and, in their turn, shed light on it and explain it" (Vatican Council II, *Dei Verbum* 16). "...for the Old Covenant has never been revoked" (CC, Section 121).

fied him, and who has insulted the Spirit of grace. For we know him who said, 'It is mine to avenge; I will repay,' and again, 'The Lord will judge his people.' It is a dreadful thing to fall into the hands of the living God.

Completing this thought, Paul continues in Hebrews 10:35, 38, "So do not throw away your confidence; it will be richly rewarded...my righteous one will live by faith, and if he shrinks back, I will not be pleased with him." In the former passage, Hebrews 10:28 shows us the *informal* application of the law in the New Testament. Paul compares those who rejected the "law of Moses" in the Old Testament and who were subsequently punished with death to those in the New Testament who disobey the "knowledge of the truth," i.e., the law of Moses written on their hearts. In addition, as the Old Testament required "two or three witnesses" in order to convict, in the New Testament the two or three witnesses that convict are (1) the "Son of God" and (2) the "Spirit," both mentioned in Hebrews 10:29, and perhaps (3) "God" mentioned in 10:27. In this respect, God is no longer the kind father; rather, Hebrews 10:30 calls him "judge." With witnesses against them, they have left the family of the Father, who hands them over to the law to be judged.

Hebrews 12 furnishes another application of the sonship theme. In encouraging his readers to resist the temptation to sin, the apostle Paul explains how the discipline of the Lord helps in this process. Beginning in Hebrews 12:6 he writes, "My son, do not make light of the Lord's discipline and do not lose heart when he rebukes you, because the Lord disciplines those he loves and he punishes everyone he accepts as a son." Again, we see the familiar New Testament familial model. The next verse explains the kind of discipline they are undergoing: "Endure hardship as discipline; God is treating you as sons. For what son is not disciplined by his father." Apparently, the "hardships" they were undergoing refer to the harsh events they were encountering in their own personal lives, yet we see Paul balance these conditions with verse 12:4's statement that they, "have not yet resisted to the point of shedding your blood." Hebrews 11:35 had referred to those who did shed their blood as the ones who were "tortured," "jeered," "flogged," "put in prison," "stoned," "sawed in two," "destitute," "persecuted," and "mistreated."

Paul then continues to develop the familial model in the following verses of Hebrew 12:8:

> If you are not disciplined (and everyone undergoes discipline), then you are illegitimate children and not true sons. Moreover, we have all had human fathers who disciplined us and we respected them for it. How much more should we submit to the Father of our spirits and live!

Here the writer contrasts sonship with not being a son. If one claims to be in the family of God, then he can expect God to discipline him for sin, just as his earthly father disciplined him. This does not mean that God stands over him with a whip for every little infraction. Earthly fathers do not do that either. God determines when it is proper to discipline his children. The more serious the sin, the more serious the discipline.

Hebrews 12 continues in keeping with the ultimatum the sacred writer had stressed in earlier chapters — eternal judgment for those who had rejected their faith and fallen into unrepentant sin. Immediately after the section dealing with the Lord's discipline of his sons, Paul begins a series of warnings about falling away from the faith. In 12:14 he begins: "Make every effort...to be holy; without holiness no one will see the Lord." In 12:15 he continues: "See to it that no one misses the grace of God and that no bitter root grows up to cause trouble and defile many." Here the writer speaks about "missing the grace of God." He reinforces these warnings by referring again to the filial imagery as he speaks of the "godless Esau" who sold his inheritance and could not get it back though he sought it with tears. This implies that those in the Church who sin like Esau, turning their back on the inheritance to which they are entitled as sons of God, will lose the inheritance forever. In Hebrews 12:25 he reiterates the same warning: "See to it that you do not refuse him who speaks. If they [the Old Testament Jews] did not escape when they refused him who warned them on earth, how much less will we, if we turn away from him who warns us from heaven?"

Again, the warning is unmistakable. The Israelites were "children of God" and had the law as their tutor to bring them to faith, but many with whom God was not pleased because of their disobedience were then led to their eternal judgment. The same is true in the New Testament. Though one is a son of God by faith, he must maintain his faithfulness, otherwise he too will be judged, only to become an "illegitimate son" who has no father.

Summary Points

1) The Protestant view of forensic imputation uses the model of the courtroom in which God is the Judge convicting the sinner of crimes. As his substitute, Christ takes on the guilt and punishment of the accused, thereby freeing him from condemnation.

2) The Catholic view uses the family model in which God is understood as a Father who either blesses and saves his children or punishes and condemns them. Christ does not take on the guilt and punishment of the individual; rather, he appeases the Father so that the latter will not bring his judgment upon his disobedient children. The children must, in turn, show faithfulness and love to the Father in order to acquire and maintain his paternal blessing.

3) The familial model includes the possibility that the individual may become disobedient and thus lose his inheritance from the Father, i.e., lose his salvation. On the other hand, the forensic model, since the act of adjudication in a court of law is singular and final, has no room within its system to allow for the individual's falling away from his justified state.

4) In the same way, the forensic model has no room to require *faith* from the individual simply because faith is not a dimension of law. In the courtroom, the individual is not required to believe in the judicial system in order to be acquitted or condemned. The familial model, on the other hand, does require faith; faith and trust are integral parts of familial relationships,

and so important that in the familial model it is the loss of these virtues that severs the relationship.

5) Adam was the first adopted son of God. Through his disobedience he became an outcast from the Father's family. God gave him a suspended sentence of death for his insubordination; but in his mercy as a Father still paved a way for Adam to repair his relationship by faith and obedience. Only if Adam failed to become faithful wold God finally execute the suspended sentence and finally hand him over to the law for his condemnation.

6) Christ, in being our propitiation, serves to appease the wrath of God against his disobedient sons, and to open the avenue of the Father's gracious mercy upon his children. They must now respond in faith and obedience to their Father in order to attain the inheritance with which he wishes to bless them. If the sons disobey the Father, they are subject to his chastisements and his condemnation.

Chapter 7

Predestination, Free Will, and Justification

Any study of justification invariably leads back to the very beginnings of God's program and ultimately back to God himself and how we understand him. Since God is infinite and we are finite, our understanding of God is limited and to that extent so is our understanding of salvation. Posing a few simple questions will illustrate the great complexity of the subject we are undertaking. For example, how can God foreknow all events before they occur and yet still give Adam a free will to obey or disobey in the Garden of Eden? If God knew Adam was going to sin and that people would be sent to hell because of that sin, why did he bother creating the world? Is God himself a determined being or does he also have free will to change a decision he had previously thought otherwise?[1] Whence did evil come? Did God predestine it? What did God do before he created the world? Since he foreknew from all eternity that his Son would become a man and remain in that state forevermore, does this mean that manhood, though coming at a point-in-time, is somehow part of God's nature? We can multiply such questions countless times. Many of them will never be answered until, perhaps, we see God face to face.

Despite these enigmas about God, Scripture does not hesitate to take us back to the very beginning of God's salvation plan. In so many words, it tells us the "thinking process" that went on in God's mind as he planned the creation and the salvation of man. Being

---

1 One of the more remarkable Scriptural passages in this regard is Genesis 6:6, "The Lord was sorry that he had made man on the earth, and his heart was filled with pain." Here we see regret in God. In addition, the Hebrew uses the hitpa'el verb form which denotes intense pain.

infinite in knowledge, certainly God knew that Adam was going to sin before he sinned. It follows that God, if he wanted to save mankind, had to have an eternal plan to deal with that sin. Moreover, God's plan could have no flaws. Everything had to work out in accord with God's calculations and determinations. Nothing could exist outside God's plan and purview. Something that did escape his knowledge and calculations could totally disrupt his and our existence. Hence, it should comfort us that God knows about and controls everything that happens. Though we might not understand how all the pieces fit together, we can rest assured that God has calculated all things out ahead of time.[2]

Predestination

The doctrine of predestination is an integral part of the predeterminations and calculations of God. However, because the concept of predestination is intimately dependent on the nature of God in his unfathomable infiniteness, many conflicting ideas of predestination have been proposed by various theologians in Christian history, both Catholic and Protestant. Suffice it to say, however, that the doctrine of predestination is not a "Calvinistic" idea. The early fathers of the Church taught predestination and incorporated it into the official statements of the Catholic Church early in its history. After having dealt with the issues of the Trinity, the Incarnation of Christ, the Canon of Scripture and many other topics, the Church at the Councils of Carthage (416 AD), Arles (475 AD), Orange (529 AD), Quiersy (853 AD) Valence (855 AD), Langres (859 AD) and Trullo (860 AD) investigated and formed precise understandings of the doctrine of predestination. Prompted by the writings of Augustine in which he had denounced the anti-predestina-

2 "The witness of Scripture is unanimous that the solicitude of divine providence is concrete and immediate; God cares for all, from the least things to the great events of the world and its history. The sacred books powerfully affirm God's absolute sovereignty over the course of events" (CC, Section 303). "From the beginning to the end of time he can see everything... For the Most High knows all that may be known; he sees from of old the things that are to come... No thought escapes him, and nothing is hidden from him... We could say more but could never say enough; let the final word be: He is the all" (Ecclesiasticus 39:20; 42:18-20; 43:27).

tion theology of Pelagius, these Church Councils formulated very strong statements in favor of predestination, which despite challenges to the contrary, continue today as official statements in the Catholic Church.[3] Realizing from the beginning that predestination is an enigmatic subject and that men on both sides of the issue would invariably set forth opposing ideas that could not easily be proved or disproved, the Church, though not explaining all the intricate details concerning the nature of God and predestination, told its people what they *could* say about predestination and what they *could not* say. As we continue in this study, we will discover the "official parameters" which the Church has formulated to help us understand this very important yet puzzling doctrine.

As noted above, Scripture does not hesitate to bring us right to the "thinking process" of the mind of God as he determined the predestination plan. Ephesians 1:4, 5, 11 offer some examples:

> For he chose us in him before the creation of the world to be holy and blameless in his sight. In love he predestined us to be adopted as his sons through Jesus Christ, in accordance with his pleasure and will... In him we were also chosen, having been predestinated according to the plan of him who works out everything in conformity with the purpose of his will.

Paul states clearly in this passage that God has worked out everything ahead of time. God does not guess. Paul specifies that God formulated the predestination plan from his "pleasure and will" showing that God did what pleased himself and what he had determined to do by his own will. Paul also tells us that God has calculated

[3] Although the Catholic catechism (1994) does not have any index references to the topics of predestination or election, the doctrine nevertheless permeates the catechism's teaching, many times very explicitly (Sections 600, 602, 769, 969, 1037, 1045, 1308). Prior to the catechism, Vatican Council II, in *Lumen Gentium* 2, stated: "All the elect, before time began, the Father, 'foreknew and also predestined to become conformed to the image of his Son, that he should be the firstborn among many brethren' (Rom. 8:29). He determined to call together in a holy Church those who should believe in Christ." *Lumen Gentium* 3 states: "The Son, accordingly, came, sent by the Father who, before the foundation of the world, chose us and predestined us in him for adoptive sonship. For it is in him that it pleased the Father to restore all things (Eph. 1:4-5 and 10)."

"everything"[4] to be in conformity to his will — nothing escapes his notice or plan. Since God is perfect, we must conclude that everything in and about his creation is the best it could possibly be.

Other Scriptures give the same information. For instance, 1 Peter 1:1-2 states:

> To God's elect, strangers in the world, scattered throughout Pontus, Galatia, Cappadocia, Asia, and Bithynia, who have been chosen according to the foreknowledge of God the Father, through the sanctifying work of the Spirit, for obedience to Jesus Christ and sprinkling by his blood.

Here Peter introduces us to the words "elect" and "foreknowledge," both of which become very important in understanding predestination. Scripture uses the term "foreknowledge" to describe the means by which God provided salvation to man. In Acts 2:22-23, Luke writes, "Jesus of Nazareth was a man accredited by God to you by miracles...This man was handed over to you by God's *set purpose and foreknowledge*; and you with the help of wicked men, put him to death by nailing him to the cross."[5]

Luke 22:22 presents the same conception, that God had predestined the death of Christ: "The Son of Man will go as it has been *decreed*, but woe to that man who betrays him."[6] In this passage, Luke specifies Judas — "that man" — as the main culprit among those whom Peter accuses in Acts 2:23. Here we see that even though God had pre-determined the crucifixion of Christ, nevertheless the man who precipitated that event, namely, Judas Iscariot, was fully culpable for his devilish actions. Acts 4:27-28 presents the same understanding, "...against your holy servant Jesus whom you

[4] Greek: πάντα.

[5] The words "set purpose and foreknowledge" are from the Greek words, ὡρισμένῃ which, in the Greek perfect, passive, participle, literally reads, "having been determined by counsel and foreknowledge."

[6] The word "decreed" is from the Greek word ὡρισμένον, the same word appearing in Acts 2:23 as "set" in the phrase "set purpose." Luther, as we shall see shortly, held that this word, when used in such passages, meant *absolute necessity*: "we answer that after the time had been predetermined by God, it infallibly had to happen that Judas should willingly betray Christ" (WA 18, 721, 2f: "disputamus..an tempore praedefinito a Deo infallibiliter fieri oportuerit, ut Iudas volendo proderet Christum").

anointed. They did what your power and will had *decided beforehand* should happen."[7] Is Scripture telling us that God pre-determined the sin of Judas to betray Jesus and yet still holds him guilty and damnable for his action? Later in this chapter we will investigate how these seemingly opposing ideas can be reconciled.

Romans 8:28-30 ties predestination to our justification in even more detail:

> And we know that in all things God works for the good of those who love him, who have been called according to his purpose. For those God foreknew [8] he also predestined to be conformed to the likeness of his Son, that he might be the firstborn among many brothers. And those he predestinated, he also called; those he called, he also justified; those he justified, he also glorified.

Here Paul identifies the stages of our Christian life which comprise God's plan of predestination. We can know that everything that happens works out for our good because in God's foreknowledge and predestination he desired that we would become like his Son, both in our present life and in our future life when we are resurrected. It is very clear that those who are justified and glorified were predestined by God. What a comforting doctrine — a doctrine that teaches us not to worry about how everything fits

---

7 The words, "decided beforehand" are from the Greek word, προώρισεν which is the same word translated as "predestined" in other New Testament passages, cf., Romans 8:29-30; Eph. 1:5,11, or as "destined" in 1 Cor. 2:7.

8 The word "foreknew" is from the Greek word προγινώσκω a cognate of the word πρόγνωσις that appears in Acts 2:23 and 1 Peter 1:2. Προγινώσκω appears five time in the New Testament (Acts 26:5; Rom. 8:29; 11:2; 1 Pet. 1:20; 2 Pet. 3:17). It means literally "a knowing beforehand of events that will occur in the future." Some have attempted to dilute this meaning by confining "foreknowledge" to God's "foreloving" of his people (e.g., Rom. 11:2), thus removing the chronological dimension out of the term. This, however, is not the preponderant denotation in Scripture. In addition, the terms, "predestined," "called," "justified," and "glorified" are in the past tense; that is, Paul does not say, "those whom God predestined he *will* also call...*will* justify...*will* glorify." Paul, in using the past tense throughout the passage, may intend either to eliminate the time element completely so as to rest the plan purely in the mind of God who is by nature timeless, or, to specify those believers who have already lived and died and thus whose predestination, calling, justification and glorification Paul considers completed, thus assuring present believers on earth that if they are faithful, God can and will do the same for them.

together or whether God has somehow forgotten us in the masses of people on the earth. As Jesus said to the apostles in Matthew 10:30, "And even the very hairs of your head are all numbered."

Continuing in the same context Paul elaborates in detail in Romans 9-11 how God brings his plan of predestination to bear on individual groups and people. For example, in Romans 9:10-13 Paul writes:

> Not only that, but Rebekah's children had one and the same father, our father Isaac. Yet, before the twins were born or had done anything good or bad — in order that God's purpose in election might stand: not by works but by him who calls — she was told, "The older will serve the younger." Just as it is written: "Jacob I loved, but Esau I hated."

Paul stresses that even before Jacob and Esau had done any good or evil, God chose one over the other. In fact, he chose Jacob over Esau precisely to show that one is not justified by works but because of God's election. God goes so far as to say that he actually "hated" Esau — before he was even born. How can God say such a thing? God reserves such language for the wicked people of the world, as recorded in Psalm 5:5, "The arrogant cannot stand in your presence, you hate all who do wrong,"; Psalm 11:5, "the Lord examines the righteous, but the wicked and those who love violence his soul hates" and Ecclesiasticus 12:6 "For the Most High also hates sinners." Was Esau counted among these whom God hates for their iniquity? Hebrews 12:16-17 leans us in this direction by specifying Esau's wickedness with details that do not appear in the Old Testament:

> See that no one is *sexually immoral* or is *godless* like Esau, who for a single meal sold his inheritance rights as the oldest son. Afterward, as you know, when he wanted to inherit this blessing, he was rejected. He could bring about no change of mind, though he sought the blessing with tears.

Since the context of this passage speaks of those who fall away from the faith, the apostle Paul seems to be using Esau as an example of someone who was not ultimately saved.[9] Thus there is evidence to explain the "hate" of God toward Esau as that which finalized his damnation.

Paul realizes that when we first hear these truths of predestination, they immediately raise a question in our minds as to God's fairness. Does God just arbitrarily decide to hate someone, even before they are born, holding them culpable for sin and then damn them to hell? Paul elaborates on this dilemma in Romans 9:14-18:

> What then shall we say? Is God unjust? Not at all! For he says to Moses, "I will have mercy on whom I have mercy, and I will have compassion on whom I have compassion." It does not, therefore, depend on man's desire or effort, but on God's mercy. For the Scripture says to Pharaoh: "I raised you up for this very purpose, that I might display my power in you and that my name might be proclaimed in all the earth." Therefore God has mercy on whom he wants to have mercy, and he hardens whom he wants to harden.

Although Paul answers the objection, he does not do so, at least in this passage, in a way that some may have expected or even like. Rather than revealing detailed criteria within the mind of God by which he chooses one over the other, Paul's argument is that God simply does as he wishes, and also makes clear that such determinations do not "depend on man's desire or effort..."

Paul continues his role as the hypothetical objector in the next series of verses (Romans 9:19-21). Here he introduces the example of the potter and his clay:

> One of you will say to me: "Then why does God still blame us? For who resists his will?" But who are you, O man, to talk back to God? "Shall what is formed say to him who formed it, 'Why did you make me like this?' Does not the potter have the right to make out of the same lump of clay some pottery for noble purposes and some for common use?[10]

---

9 Judgments of this type, however, are reserved to God, not to the Church or any individual.

10 "Some he blessed and exalted, and some he made holy and brought near to himself; but some he cursed and brought low, and turned them out of their place. Like clay in the hand of the potter, to be molded as he pleases, so all are in the hand of their Maker, to be given whatever he decides" (Ecclesiasticus 33:12-14).

Now the question of blame or culpability comes to the fore. In other words, the objector might accept the fact that God does as he wishes but if that is the case, why does God, who seems to be controlling me, blame me for the way I am? Again, Paul does not answer this question in the way that the objector would find especially pleasing. In so many words he says that we do not have the right to bring up the subject, let alone require an answer from God. Is Paul playing games with us? Why doesn't he just come right out and give us the real reason for what seem to be God's "arbitrary" decisions?

Perhaps purposely, Paul continues the same line of argumentation in the next verses (Romans 9:22-24):

> What if God, choosing to show his wrath and make his power known, bore with great patience the objects of his wrath — prepared for destruction? What if he did this to make the riches of his glories known to the objects of his mercy, whom he prepared in advance for glory — even us whom he also called, not only from the Jews but also from the Gentiles?

Here Paul speaks of those "prepared for destruction," which suggests that God had preordained these people for destruction. We also notice a shift in those to whom he applies this dynamic of God's dealings with men. In verses 10-11 he applied God's election to individuals, e.g., Jacob as opposed to Esau. In verses 24ff. he is applying predestination to groups, e.g., Gentiles as opposed to Jews. Hence we cannot dilute God's plan of predestination by claiming that he only predestines particular ethnic groups or communities, and not individuals within those groups. No, God's predestination is all pervasive; encompassing both the community and the individual. Whether it is communal or individual, however, we still do not know the criterion God uses, in his own mind, for choosing one over the other. Before we complete this study of predestination, we will see elsewhere how Paul explains this haunting question. For now, we must develop and illuminate the other side of this issue — the free will of man.[11]

[11] Other passages that explicitly or implicitly teach predestination are Matthew 25:34; John 6:65; 10:28; 15:16; 17:12; 18:9; Gal. 1:4; 1 Thess. 1:4; 2 Thess 2:13-14; 2 Tim. 1:9-10.

Free Will

Theologians and philosophers have given various descriptions to the term "free will." Basically, it refers to the capability and freedom of man to choose, from among two or more alternatives, his future course of action. Free will, in order to be free, necessitates the absence of force and coercion. Although the individual may be inclined to one degree or another to make a certain choice, the basic requirement of free will is that he is not programmed to make a choice nor does an entity with greater power force a choice upon him. If one does not define free will in this or a similar way, then there is no use in speaking about a "free will" since in that case it would not be free.[12]

Scripture, complementing its teaching on predestination, also teaches that man's will is presently free to accept or reject God. The first test of man's free will occurred in the Garden of Eden when Adam and Eve were tempted by Satan. God had told Adam

[12] "To be human, 'man's response to God by faith must be free, and...therefore nobody is to be forced to embrace the faith against his will. The act of faith is of its very nature a free act.' 'God calls men to serve him in spirit and in truth. Consequently they are bound to him in conscience, but not coerced...' Indeed, Christ invited people to faith and conversion, but never coerced them. 'For he bore witness to the truth but refused to use force to impose it on those who spoke against it" (Catholic Catechism, Section 160; see also Sections 1730-1742). Close to free will is the concept of freedom, usually understood in three senses: (1) *natural freedom*, which refers to the decision making power in man; (2) *circumstantial freedom*, which refers to decisions man makes based on or despite the circumstances within which he finds himself; and (3) *acquired freedom*, which refers to the release from spiritual bondage through salvation. From a circumstantial perspective, Pope John Paul II states: "Sin, in the proper sense, is always a personal act, since it is an act of freedom on the part of an individual person, and not properly of a group or community. This individual may be conditioned, incited and influenced by numerous and powerful external forces. He may also be subjected to tendencies, defects and habits linked with his personal condition. In not a few cases such external and internal factors may attenuate, to a greater or lesser degree, the person's freedom and therefore his responsibility and guilt. But it is a truth of faith, also confirmed by our experience and reason, that the human person is free. This truth cannot be disregarded, in order to place the blame for individuals' sins on external factors such as structures, systems or other people. Above all, this would be to deny the person's dignity and freedom, which are manifested — even in a negative and disastrous way — also in this responsibility for sin committed." *Reconcilatio et paentitentia*, 16.

and Eve that they could eat of any tree of the Garden except the tree of the knowledge of good and evil. God warned Adam that in the day he ate of the tree, he would die. Adam was a man unencumbered by the effects of sin and physical deterioration that have plagued man ever since. Nevertheless, being a mere man and created out of nothing, Adam still needed God's power for his existence and for his capabilities. In light of this, God did not leave Adam on his own to confront the Devil. He gave him sufficient grace so that he would be able to resist the temptations to sin.[13] In time, Adam confronted the Devil through his wife Eve. Eve had been enticed to think that God was holding something back from the new human couple, that he was not the best caretaker of his own creation, and in essence, was deceiving Adam and Eve.[14] Once she ate of the fruit, Eve told Adam of her decision and convinced him to eat so that he, too, could "be like God." At this point, Adam should have told Eve that she had sinned against God and to ask for His forgiveness. Since Eve was not the head of the human race, the world could still be saved from the curse of sin and death if

---

13 The Council of Trent stated: "...although free will was not extinguished in them, however weakened and debased in its powers..." (Session 6, Chapter 1); "If anyone shall say that man's free will moved and aroused by God does not cooperate by assenting to God who rouses and calls, whereby it disposes and prepares itself to obtain the grace of justification, and that it cannot dissent, if it wishes, but that like something inanimate it does nothing at all and is merely in a passive state; let him be anathema" (Session 6, Canon 4); "If anyone shall say that after the sin of Adam man's free will was lost or destroyed, or that it is a thing in name only, indeed a title without a reality, a fiction, moreover, brought into the Church by Satan; let him be anathema" (Canon 5); "If anyone shall say that it is not in the power of man to make his ways evil, but that God produces the evil as well as the good works, not only by permission, but also properly and of Himself, so that the betrayal of Judas is no less His own proper work than the vocation of Paul: let him be anathema" (Canon 6); "If anyone shall say that all the works that are done before justification, in whatever manner they have been done, are truly sins or deserving of the hatred of God, or that the more earnestly anyone strives to dispose himself of grace, so much the more grievously does he sin: let him be anathema" (Canon 7). Augustine wrote: "The first man did not have that grace by which he would never will to be evil; but surely he had that in which, if he willed to remain, he would never be evil, and without which, even by free choice, he could not be good, but which, nevertheless, by free choice, he could forsake. Neither, then, did God will him to be without His grace, which He left within that man's free choice..." (*Admonition and Grace*, 426 AD; PL 11, 31; JR 1954).

14 See John Paul II's encyclical: *Dominum et vivificantem*, 27-48.

Adam had obeyed God. When confronted with Eve's decision to eat the fruit, Adam was faced with a cataclysmic decision. He could either bring Eve to God for retribution or he could partake with her in the sin. As we know all too well, Adam chose the latter course. He did so by his own free will. God did not coerce him in any manner. God simply gave Adam a test of faithfulness and he failed. By grace, God gave him the ability to choose the right path. If he had obeyed, the test would have been over and God would have allowed Adam to live on the earth and produce his children in anticipation of a final consummation in which man would be divinized for eternity. Shunning God's grace and his offer of being made like God, Adam sought to become like God on his own terms.[15]

Throughout the course of human history, man has been confronted with situations similar to that of Adam where he must make a choice to serve himself and his own interests or to serve God and His interests. The story of Cain and Abel is the next incident involving man's free will. Cain and Abel had both offered sacrifices to God. According to Hebrews 11:4, Abel's was pleasing to God because of his faithfulness. Cain's was not for the opposite reason. Enraged with jealousy, Cain murdered his brother Abel. Because of the inheritance of original sin from his father Adam, the proclivity to sin was great. Man would be influenced by the working of sin in his body and would find it easier to disobey God and follow in his own way. Yet in keeping with his promise to help man by the power of his grace — a grace that could legitimately be given due to the anticipated atonement of Christ — man had sufficient power from God to refrain from sin. Abel had apparently succeeded in

[15] The Reformed concept puts the prelapsarian Adam in a "Covenant of Works" to be obeyed or disobeyed by his own free will, without the help of infused grace. Once Adam failed, man no longer possessed free will but was totally depraved. Catholic theology understands that Adam was infused with grace for the purpose of helping his free will to make the right decision. If Adam obeyed God it would not be a result of his works but a result of God's grace that helped Adam overcome the temptation of the Devil. Once Adam sinned, man would inherit the curse of sin and death, and though not totally depraved, he would be severely hampered in his desire and search for God unless God provided grace equal to the power of sin. God provided this grace by means of the atonement of Christ which restored the possibility that man, through his free will in cooperating with grace, could once again obey God and be blessed, even as Adam was originally intended to be blessed for his obedience under grace.

this endeavor. He used the grace that God had given him and thus was made "pleasing" to God by his faith and works. Cain shunned this grace and decided to take matters into his own hands — to alleviate the problem, so he thought, more quickly than reliance on God's grace would afford.

Since Cain and Abel, all the men of the earth have been in similar situations. Under the curse of sin and death, they find themselves with a desire to sin yet a desire that God commands them to overcome. Scripture does not even remotely question man's ability and responsibility to avoid sin by the power of his own decision, aided, of course, by grace. As Paul said in Acts 17:26-27 to all those who came after the sin of Adam:

> From one man he made every nation of men, that they should inhabit the whole earth and he determined the times set for them and the exact places where they should live. God did this so that men would seek him and perhaps reach out for him and find him, though he is not far from each one of us.[16]

Here we have the first indication of a tension between God's predeterminations and man's free will to choose for God. On the one hand, God "determines" the times and places men inhabit. On the other hand, God does this precisely so that men will have ample opportunity to seek for him. Does God offer himself for men to

---

[16] Paul uses three different words to describe man's quest for God: The first word, ζητεῖν ("to seek"), is the ordinary word the New Testament uses for seeking God (e.g., Matthew 6:33; 7:7-8; Luke 12:31; 17:33; Romans 2:7; Colossians 3:1), and is used here as an infinitive of purpose, i.e., it is the purpose of God for men to seek him. The second word, ψηλαφήσειαν ("reach out for him"), appears three other times in the New Testament in reference to feeling or touching God or Jesus (e.g., Luke 24:39; Hebrews 12:18; 1 John 1:1). The third word, εὕροιεν is the ordinary word for "find." Both ψηλαφήσειαν and εὕροιεν are optative verb forms through which Paul is expressing a clear and distinct expectation from men. Paul reinforces this expectation by καὶγε οὐ μακρὰν ἀπὸ ἑνὸς ἑκάστου ἡμῶν ὑπάρχοντα ("though he is not far from each one of us") preceded by the strong conditional εἰ ἄρα γε ("so that" or more emphatically "if then" or "if therefore" (as ἄρα γε is used in Matthew 7:20; 17:26), and by the strengthened καί with the addition of γε to read "*even* being not far from each one of us"). Also, the expectation of the *each individual* to seek God, not merely men as a group seeking God, is made emphatic by Paul's addition of "each one of us."

seek him but not really mean it? To answer "yes" to such a question would be an affront and contradiction to the integrity and character of God. God does not lie or give us the pretense of truth.[17] If he states that he provides man with the environment specifically so that man can choose for him, then we can be assured that God truly desires man to be saved and has given him the ability to respond to the times and places in which God has put him. In short, we must assign as much force to these kinds of Scripture verses as we have done with the verses which speak of predestination.[18]

Further tension between God's plan of predestination and the free will of man is evident in Acts 13:46-48. Luke writes:

> Then Paul and Barnabas answered them boldly: "We had to speak the word of God to you first. Since you reject it and do not con-

---

[17] Luther and Calvin, as we shall see shortly, answered this question in the affirmative and virtually stood alone among all Christian exegetes of their time. Most Reformed theologians today take the same stance. R. C. Sproul, for example, states: "The Calvinist view of predestination teaches that God actively intervenes in the lives of the elect to make absolutely sure that they are saved. Of course, the rest are invited to Christ and given an "opportunity" to be saved *if they want to*. But Calvinism assumes that without the intervention of God no one will ever want Christ...The question that remains is this: Does God give the ability to come to Jesus to all men? The Reformed view of predestination says no" (*Chosen By God*, pp. 34, 68). Patristic evidence that addresses this issue held that God did not ask men to do impossible things, e.g., Chrysostom, *On Hebrews*, PG 63, 16, 4; Jerome, *Against Jovinian* PL 23, 2, 3; Augustine, *Forgiveness of Sin*, PL 44, 2, 3, 3; 2, 6, 7; *Nature and Grace* PL 43, 50. Pius V in *Ex Omnibus Afflictionibus* (1567), condemned the proposition of Michael De Bay which stated: "The proposition that God has not commanded the human person to do the impossible is falsely attributed to Augustine, since it belongs to Pelagius" (JD 1954).

[18] In light of this balance, we should also note that the same words used of God's free choice or good pleasure are used of man's free choice, e.g., the Greek verb εὐδοκέω ("well pleased" or "willing") is used of God in Matthew 3:17; 12:18; 17:5; Luke 12:32; 1 Cor. 1:21; 10:5; Gal. 1:15; Col. 1;19 and of man in Rom. 15:26; 2 Cor. 5:8; 12:10; 1 Thess. 2:8; 3:1. The noun form εὐδοκία is used of God in Matt. 11:26; Eph. 1:5,9 (referring to election); Phil. 2:13; and of man in Rom. 10:1. The verb αἱρέομαι is used of God in 2 Thess. 2:13 (referring to election) and with man who must choose between two possibilities in Phil. 1:22; Heb. 11:25. The verb ἐκλέγομαι is used of God in Mark 13:20; John 15:16; Eph. 1:4 (referring to election); Acts 1:24; 15:7; 1 Cor. 1:27-28; James 2:5 (in which more than one choice is available); and of man in Luke 10:42; 14:7; Acts 6:5; 15:22, 25. The Hebrew בחר is used of God choosing (Deut. 7:6) and man choosing (Deut. 30:19).

> sider yourselves worthy of eternal life, we now turn to the Gentiles...When the Gentiles heard this, they were glad and honored the word of the Lord; and all who were appointed for eternal life believed.[19]

On the one hand, the Jews to whom Paul and Barnabas spoke had both "rejected" the word and "considered themselves unworthy of eternal life." This speaks plainly of their free will to reject God. On the other hand, the Gentiles believed because they were "appointed to eternal life."

The same tension between the plan of God and the free will of man is evident in John 1:12-13. John writes, "Yet to all who received him, to those who believed in his name, he gave the right to become the children of God — children born not of natural descent, nor of human decision or a husband's will, but born of God." As used in the Greek, both "received" and "believed" denote one who is acting on his own volition to accept God.[20] Yet John is also indicating that those who do receive and believe in his name do so because they are born from God's spiritual power, not by man's earthly means.

John's gospel states again the tension between God's predestination and man's free will as Jesus confronts the Jews. In John 6:39-40 Jesus says:

> And this is the will of him who sent me, that I shall lose none of all that he has given me, but raise them up at the last day. For my Father's will is that everyone who looks to the Son and believes in him shall have eternal life, and I will raise him up at the last day.

---

[19] The word, "appointed" is from the Greek word τάσσω which appears nine times in the New Testament, referring to an "appointment" or an "ordaining" (cf., Matt 28:16; Acts 15:2; 22:10; 28:23; Rom. 13:1). In Acts 13:38 it is used in the perfect tense, passive voice, denoting that an outside entity had done the appointing. The word "believed," however, is in the aorist tense, active voice, denoting the personal decision of the Gentiles to believe.

[20] Both ἔλαβον ("received") and πιστεύουσιν ("believed") in John 1:12 are in the Greek active voice denoting the personal decision of the individual, as opposed to the passive voice which would mean that they were made to receive and believe.

Here John reiterates the same theme noted in Romans 8:28-30. God has calculated his whole plan with such care that he knows the very number of those whom he will give to Jesus to be saved.[21] In John 17:12 Jesus adds, "While I was with them, I protected them and kept them safe by that name you gave me. None has been lost except the one doomed to destruction so that Scripture would be fulfilled." Here Jesus tells us that Judas's betrayal and perdition were foreknown by God and recorded in Scripture. This does not mean, however, that Judas or anyone else who does not come to God did not have a free will to choose for God or that God did not give them the power to respond positively to God. As Jesus says, it is the Father's will that all who believe [choose to believe] will be raised on the last day.

Jesus reiterates these themes in John 6:37,44-45:

> All that the Father gives to me will come to me, and whoever comes to me I will never drive away...No one can come to me unless the Father who sent me draws him, and I will raise him up at the last day. It is written in the Prophets: 'They will all be taught by God.' Everyone who listens to the Father and learns from him comes to me.

Again, Jesus states clearly that it is the Father who initiates the salvation process. The Father must draw to Jesus those whom he desires to save. At the same time, however, Jesus specifies that each person has the choice to "listen" to the "teaching of God." When they "listen" and "learn" they will come to Jesus.[22] Yet Jesus is clear in John 5:40 that it is man who decides not to come to God: "These are Scriptures that testify about me, yet *you refuse to come to me* to have life."

Paul teaches the same two dimensions of salvation. On the one hand, Paul's strong predestinarian teaching is very clear in Ro-

[21] Augustine wrote: "I speak thus of those who are predestined to the kingdom of God, whose number is so certain that one can neither be added to them nor taken from them" (*On Rebuke and Grace*, NPNF, Vol. V, 8, 39, p. 487).

[22] Reformed theologians attempt to absolutize the meaning of ἑλκύσῃ ("draw") in John 6:44 so as to make the passage refer exclusively to an irresistible force upon the individual in conjunction with their belief in "irresistible grace." See **Appendix 13** for a refutation of the Reformed view of John 6:44.

mans 8:28-30 and Romans 9-11. On the other hand, right in the same context, Paul continually urges people to choose for God. For example, in Romans 10:9-13 he says:

> That if you confess with your mouth, "Jesus is Lord," and believe in your heart that God raised him from the dead, you will be saved. For it is with your heart that you believe and are justified, and it is with your mouth that you confess and are saved. As the Scripture says, "Anyone who trusts in him will never be put to shame." For there is no difference between Jew and Gentile — the same Lord is Lord of all and richly blesses all who call on him, for "Everyone who calls on the name of the Lord will be saved."

Here is very clear language that puts the responsibility on the individual to believe in his heart and articulate his conviction in order to be saved. If one is going to respect the face value language of this passage, one can only conclude that the reason a person would not be saved is precisely because *he* did not choose to call on the name of the Lord.

In the above passage, Paul is using both the communal and individual aspects of God's call to the individual as we have seen earlier with his discussion of predestination in Romans 9:10-29. The call of salvation is for groups, both Jew and Gentile, yet God finally directs the call to each individual within that group. Paul indicates this in Romans 10:9-13 by his use of the singular "you confess" and "everyone who calls."

Later in the same context, Paul gives us at least some answer as to why some people whom God draws do not respond. After explaining in Romans 9:30-10:3 and again in 10:16-21 that though the gospel came to Israel, yet they had rejected it, Paul adds that God is directly involved in the rejection. Recording a conversation that the prophet Elijah had with God, Paul writes in Romans 11:3-8:

> "Lord, they have killed your prophets and torn down your altars; I am the only one left, and they are trying to kill me"? And what was God's answer to him? "I have reserved for myself seven thousand who have not bowed the knee to Baal." So too, at the

present time there is a remnant chosen by grace. And if by grace, then it is no longer by works, if it were, grace would no longer be grace. What then? What Israel sought so earnestly it did not obtain, but the elect did. The others were hardened, as it is written: 'God gave them a spirit of stupor, eyes so that they could not see and ears so that they could not hear, to this very day.'

This is quite a passage. Now we can see why Paul had to raise the objections against God's determinative will in Romans 9:14-24 and then answer those queries before he came to Romans 11:3-8 by telling us "not to talk back to God."[23] Here we find that the unbelief of the Jews is actually included within God's plan of predestination. God is the one who "gave them a spirit of stupor" so they could not believe. Moreover, he elected only a mere seven thousand people out of a nation of millions of people.[24] What kind of God are we dealing with here? The "hardening" of the Jews is the same hardening to which Paul in Romans 9:16-21 attributes Pharoah's decision not to let Israel leave Egypt. This also explains why Jesus must stress several times to the Jews in John 6 that in order for them to be saved God must "draw" them (John 6:44). In their hearts the Jews are hardened, not believing what Jesus has said about himself and God, and Jesus concludes that they do not

---

[23] When Paul uses the command "don't talk back to God" as his final argument in the inquiry, he is not suggesting that God has acted improperly or that he cannot provide a satisfactory answer, as when a child asks an exasperated parent why he must do a certain task and the parent simply says, "Because I said so." Paul uses the "don't talk back to God" form of argumentation because it is not possible to explain to the human intellect the inner workings of the divine mind and its dynamic relationship with the human mind. It is simply beyond our comprehension. We have no better example of this incomprehensible dynamism between God and man than the last four chapters of the book of Job, in which God explains his workings to Job not by giving a point-by-point response of why he does what he does but by simply reminding him of the incomprehensibility of His nature in the midst of finite creatures such as Job (Job 38-42).

[24] According to Numbers 1-2; Ecclesiasticus 46:8, over 600,000 Israelite men left Egypt during the exodus. Assigning one wife and one child to each, this would bring the total to 1.8 million people. The exodus took place in the 15th century BC. Elijah is a prophet in the 9th century BC. We can estimate that the population of Israel during these six centuries grew to several million. A conservative estimate of 5 million would then make the 7,000 who did not bow to Baal a mere .14% of the total population.

believe because the Father has not drawn them but actually blinded them. This look behind the scenes is further detailed in Matthew 13:13-17, indicating that Jesus spoke to the people in parables in order to hide the truth from them:

> This is why I speak to them in parables: "Though seeing, they do not see; though hearing, they do not hear or understand. In them is fulfilled the prophecy of Isaiah: "'You will be ever hearing but never understanding... For this people's heart has become calloused; they hardly hear with their ears, and they have closed their eyes. Otherwise, they might see with their eyes, hear with their ears, understand with their hearts and turn, and I would heal them.

This passage displays the same dynamic we have seen in the other passages. On the one hand, we see that God is not neutral when it concerns belief in Him. If the individual does not accept God from the knowledge and grace that God has given him, God may blind him to the truth so that he cannot understand it.[25] On the other hand, this desperate situation is induced by the individual's free choice, a choice to turn from God which has made his own heart calloused.

Paul alludes to the same dynamic relationship between God and man in discussing God's dealing with Pharaoh in Romans 9:16-18, when he speaks of the hardening of Pharoah's heart. The account in Exodus 9:34-10:1 reads:

> When Pharaoh saw that the rain and hail and thunder had stopped, he sinned again: *He and his officials hardened their hearts*. So

---

[25] Other passages which indicate similar blinding are: Isaiah 6:9-10; 44:18; Jeremiah 6:21; Matthew 11:25; John 12:40; Romans 1:28; 11:8; 2 Thess. 2:11. Other passages show God controlling or influencing the thoughts of men, e.g., Lev. 26:36; Deut. 28:28, 65-67; 1 Sam. 16:14; 26:12; Prov. 21:1; Job 12:24; Is. 29:10, 14; Ezk. 7:26; 14:9; Zech. 12:4. The early Fathers taught that God hardened men due to their sin, e.g., Augustine, *Homilies on John*, PL 53,6; *Against Julian* PL 44, 5, 3, 12; but that to whatever degree they were hardened, sufficient grace was given to them to repent and be converted, e.g., Chrysostom, *On Hebrews*, PL 63, 16, 4; Jerome, *Dialogue Against the Pelagians* PL 23, 3, 6; Cyril of Alexandria, *Commentary on the Psalms* PL 70, 4, 2.

> Pharaoh's heart was hard and he would not let the Israelites go, just as the Lord had said through Moses. Then the Lord said to Moses, "Go to Pharaoh, for *I have hardened his heart and the hearts of his officials* so that I may perform these miraculous signs of mine among them...

Again, we are somewhat stunned at the "behind the scenes" information revealed to us. The passage clearly states that Pharaoh and his officials "sinned again" by "hardening their hearts." Apparently, they chose of their own free will to harden their hearts. Yet in the same breath we learn that God specifically tells Moses that HE was the one who did the hardening. What is going on here? Is God making Pharaoh sin?[26] Some would like to conclude such a thing. Yet Scripture makes it clear that God does not make, coerce, or program man to sin. Man sins of his own free will. In James 1:12-15 the apostle writes:

> When tempted, no one should say, "God is tempting me." For God cannot be tempted by evil, nor does he tempt anyone; but each one is tempted when, by his own evil desire, he is dragged

---

[26] Many Reformed commentaries simply ignore the stipulation in Exodus 9:34 that Pharoah and his officials hardened their own hearts. If an explanation is attempted, Reformed theologians claim that Pharoah's sin is attributed to the removal of God's restraint of sin in men so that, in the words of one author, "God gives them enough rope to hang themselves" (Sproul, *Chosen By God*, p. 145). Rather than attributing Pharoah's actions to his own free will, or at least saying that God hardened Pharoah's heart because of or in conjunction with Pharoah's free decision to harden his own heart, the Reformed view persists, perhaps inadvertently, to make God responsible for Pharoah's sin. For if God removes "restraint" arbitrarily from one individual but not another — a removal that is not contingent on the individual's free choice or some other indication that he is moving away from God, then the Reformed view has not escaped the clutches of a determinism that makes God into a tyrant who arbitrarily imposes his will on his creatures. Conversely, we should not understand Paul's statement in Romans 9:18-20 ("...he hardens whom he wants to harden...Shall what is formed say to him who formed it, 'Why did you make me like this?'") as referring to an arbitrary imposition of God's will on men irrespective of their free will, but precisely an imposition that takes into account or is the result of their free decisions. In this way, one cannot complain to God (i.e., "Then why does God still blame us? For who resists his will?") because as men make decisions, God makes decisions, for he is not neutral with respect to the free acts of men.

> away and enticed. Then, after desire has conceived, it gives birth to sin; and sin, when it is full-grown, gives birth to death.

James tells us that when one sins it is because of "his own evil desire." He contemplates his sin for a period of time and then suddenly sin is born. James assures us that God does not have any role in this process because "God cannot be tempted by evil;" that is, since it is evil to tempt someone to sin, God, being all good, cannot be tempted to tempt anyone to sin. Although God has a role in the hardening or spiritual plight of the individual after he sins, God has no role in the individual's sinful thoughts or actual sin. But how does man's free will to sin balance with God's foreknowledge and predestination? Are we not still a product of God's predetermined plan and therefore can we still not plead that we only do what we were made to do? We will attempt to answer that question momentarily. First, we need to see other aspects of God's nature and program.

Sometimes the teaching of free will is implicit in Scripture. For example, in Matthew 11:21-24 Jesus states:

> Woe to you, Korazin! Woe to you, Bethsaida! If the miracles that were performed in you had been performed in Tyre and Sidon, they would have repented long ago in sackcloth and ashes. But I tell you, it will be more bearable on the day of judgment for Tyre and Sidon on the day of judgment than for you. And you, Capernaum, will you be lifted up to the skies? No, you will go down to the depths. If the miracles that were performed in you had been performed in Sodom, it would have remained to this day. But I tell you that it will be more bearable for Sodom on the day of judgment than for you.

Here Jesus teaches a profound truth. Korazin, Bethsaida, and Capernaum were Jewish cities which had witnessed many of Jesus' miracles, yet they remained hardened in their unbelief. One of the purposes of the miracles was to convince the people of Jesus's divinity. Using this premise, Jesus puts forth an alternate scenario for the Gentile cities of Tyre, Sidon, and Sodom other than the destruction they experienced for their unrepentant sin. Jesus asserts that if the same miracles had been done in those cities as was done in the Jewish cities, they would have repented of their sin.[27] This is quite a remarkable statement, since we are very aware of the utter debauchery that was present in the city of Sodom (cf., Genesis 18-20). Since their destruction is a past event, sealed, as it were, in time and space, it should strike us as either odd or illogical that Jesus would make such a bold declaration to the opposite extreme concerning their possible repentance. In respect of Jesus' divinity and integrity, it is unlikely that he is using this possible scenario as a mere hyperbolic teaching tool without any reality to the Sodomite's possible repentance upon seeing the miracles. Moreover, if the Sodomites were "predestined" to reprobation without consideration of their free will, this would contradict the reliance on their free will that Jesus is using to indict the Jews of his day. Of course, the question could be raised why God did not provide miracles for the Sodomites if he knew they would repent upon witnessing them. Could one not make a claim that since miracles were not given to them, then in that sense the Sodomites were predestined to reprobation? The answer is that God has his own reasons for not providing miraculous events to everyone, most of which are tied up with the redemptive/historical nature of miracles; not because God wishes not to see men repent of their sin.[28] In any case, if we give full force to Jesus's assertion that the Sodomites would have repented given the right set of circumstances, we see again the tension Scripture creates between what God has determined and what man has freely chosen.

One of Scripture's most beautiful passages detailing the free will with which God has blessed man and the fact that God does not lead men to sin is found in Ecclesiasticus 15:11-20:

---

[27] This is similar to the account in Luke 4:24-30 in which Jesus reminds the Jews that the miracle worker, Elijah, was not sent to any of the widows of Israel but was sent to the Gentile woman of Zarephath in Sidon, and that his successor, Elisha, was not sent to cure any of the lepers in Israel but was sent to the Gentile, Naaman from Syria.

[28] "Redemptive/historical" is a term used to show that miracles were usually performed by God only to inaugurate or authenticate a change or development in his redemptive program, e.g., the miracle of the Flood, the ten plagues of the Exodus, the conquest of Caanan, the birth of Christ, Pentecost, the end of the world, etc.

> Do not say, 'It was the Lord's doing that I fell away'; for he does not do what he hates. Do not say, 'It was he who led me astray'; for he has no need of the sinful. The Lord hates all abominations; such things are not loved by those who fear him. It was he who created mankind in the beginning, and he left them in the power of their own free choice. If you choose, you can keep the commandments, and to act faithfully is a matter of your own choice. He has placed before you fire and water; stretch out your hand for whichever you choose. Before each person are life and death, and whichever one chooses will be given. For great is the wisdom of the Lord; he is mighty in power and sees everything; his eyes are on those who fear him and he knows every human action. He has not commanded anyone to be wicked, and he has not given anyone permission to sin.

God Desires All Men To Be Saved

As Scripture is clear about God's plan of predestination and his blinding of people who turn away from him, Scripture is also clear about God's desire to see all men saved. He has no desire to see men remain in eternal condemnation for their sins. He gives them every opportunity to repent and even blesses them while he waits for them. Ezekiel said as much long ago in Ezekiel 18:21-23,32:

> But if a wicked man turns away from all the sins he has committed and keeps all my decrees and does what is just and right, he will surely live; he will not die. None of the offenses he has committed will be remembered against him. Because of the righteous things he has done he will live. Do I take any pleasure in the death of the wicked? declares the Lord. Rather, am I not pleased when they turn from their ways and live?...For I take no pleasure in the death of anyone, declares the Sovereign Lord. Repent and live!

Speaking for himself, God lets us know quite clearly that he is waiting for man to use his free will and repent of his sins. If he does so, then God in turn will allow him to live. Moreover, in anticipating objections that God enjoys casting judgment upon sinners, God solemnly declares that no such disposition is to be found in him. If we do not repent and live, God takes no pleasure in our death.

Jesus echoed this same sentiment in Matthew 23:37-38 as he contemplated the Jews of Jerusalem:

> O Jerusalem, Jerusalem, you who kill the prophets and stone those sent to you, how often I have longed to gather your children together, as a hen gathers her chicks under her wings, but you were not willing. Look, your house is left to you desolate.

Jesus is certainly not playacting here. He really means it when he says that God sent them prophets in hopes that they would repent of their sins, just as Ezekiel had stated in the previous passage. Jesus also means it when he says that he "longed to gather" them but that "they were not willing." It wasn't because God predestined them to refuse. They refused Jesus of their own free will. They rejected his call and the prompting of God's grace.[29]

Paul expresses the same teaching about God's desire in 1 Timothy 2:1,4:

> I urge, then, first of all, that requests, prayers, intercession and thanksgiving be made for *everyone*...This is good, and pleases God our Savior, who wants *all men* to be saved and to come to a knowledge of the truth. For there is one God and one mediator between God and man, the man Christ Jesus, who gave himself as a ransom for *all men*...

This is exactly what we would expect of a kind, benevolent God — one who shows no respect of persons but desires all men to come to salvation. We see Paul's universal perspective of God's desire for the salvation of all men first by his urging that "prayers"

[29] The early Fathers taught that God gives sufficient grace to everyone for faith and salvation: Clement, *Letter to the Corinthians*, PL 1, 7, 4; Arnobius, *Against the Pagans*, PL 5, 2, 64; Chrysostom, *On John*, PG 59, 8, 1; Ambrose, *On Psalms*, PL 15, 8, 57; Augustine, *Psalms*, PL 36, 18, 1, 7; *Genesis Defended*, 34, 1 ,3, 6; *Nature and Grace*, 44, 4, 4; *Corrections*, 32, 1, 9, 2; *Predestination of the Saints*, 42, 10, 19; Prosper of Aquitane, *The Call of All Nations*, 51, 2, 17.

and "intercessions" be made on behalf of "*everyone,*" because such prayers are "pleasing" to God who uses the prayers of the faithful to provide salvation for "*all men.*" Paul reinforces the inclusion of *everyone* in God's desire to save as he concludes that Christ was given "as a ransom for *all men,*" not just a certain few. This echoes the teaching in 1 John 2:2 which states, "He is the atoning sacrifice for our sins, and not only for ours but also for the sins of the *whole world.*"[30]

Peter indicates God's sincere desire to save all men in 2 Peter 3:8-9:

> But do not forget this one thing, dear friends: With the Lord a day is like a thousand years, and a thousand years are like a day. The Lord is not slow in keeping his promise, as some understand slowness. He is patient with you, not wanting anyone to perish, but everyone to come to repentance.

This passage is in the context of the end of the world. Scoffers, on hearing the prediction that the world will end, ridicule the truth that God is coming back because the world has gone on for thousands of years without so much as a hint of his return. It is typical of man to turn God's care and concern for the world into an indictment against God — that he doesn't really care about man but has left him on his own. However, it is precisely because God loves mankind that he delays his return, allowing them as much opportu-

[30] Some Calvinists interpret this verse as saying that God has a desire to save only various ethnic groups in the world, not each and every individual within those groups; or that God's desire to see men saved can refer only to the "elect" since they are the only ones eventually saved. Both interpretations take liberties with the context that are simply not justified. The inspired author's stress on individuals through the use of "everyone" and "anyone" in 1 Timothy 2:1 and 2 Peter 3:9 clearly indicates that God is interested in saving individuals and suggests nothing about ethnic groups. Moreover, to say that God's desire to save applies only to the elect contradicts other passages, e.g., Ezekiel 18:21-32; 33:11; Acts 17:25-26, in which God sincerely pleads with all the wicked to turn from their evil ways. That such misinterpretations could persist in light of these contrary Scripture passages shows how important it is to give each Scripture its full weight and meaning, without dilution or misrepresentation, in understanding the subject of predestination and free will. It is much too tempting to "read into" each passage one's particular bias or presupposed theology.

nity as possible to examine their ways and turn back to God. Peter, as Paul did, emphasizes the *individual* in this call to repentance with words such as "you," "anyone," and "everyone." As Jesus said in John 3:16, "For God so loved the world that *whoever* believes in him shall not perish but have eternal life." This promise applies to every human being, past, present, and future.[31]

How Does Predestination Work With Man's Free Will?

Augustine, Aquinas, and the Church

The evidence for God's plan of predestination, man's endowment with free will both before and after Adam's fall, and God's desire to see all men come to salvation, compel us to investigate how these three components work together without contradicting each other. The answer to this question is crucial for a proper understanding of God, man, and the topic at hand, namely, justification. Indeed, as we have noted previously, the issue of God's predestination plan and man's free will was one of the Reformation period's two major concerns. The other concern, addressed in chap-

[31] Council of Trent, Session 6, Canon 17: "If anyone shall say that the grace of justification is attained by those only who are predestined unto life, but that all others who are called, are called indeed, but do not receive grace, as if they are by divine power predestined to evil: let him be anathema." Reformed evangelicals often dilute the meaning of the call to each and every individual. Michael Horton, for example, under the title "The Whosoever Will," asserts that there are only two reasons why God uses the language of invitation: (1) it is the means by which God gets the message of salvation to the elect, and (2) it is the means by which God will hold unbelievers without excuse at judgment day (*Putting Amazing Back Into Grace,* 1991, 1994, pp. 160-161). Although this is a logical deduction within Horton's system of theology, it characterizes God as someone who really doesn't mean what he says, that is, he invites everyone but he really doesn't mean it. The distortion Horton creates is evident by his partial quotation of Ezekiel 33:11, in which he limits God to saying, "I take no pleasure in the death of the wicked..." (p. 162). The remainder of the verse (which Horton does not quote) says: "...but rather that they turn from their ways and live. Turn! Turn from your evil ways! Why will you die, O house of Israel?" It is clear from this exclamatory language that God really wants them to repent. God does not plead with crocodile tears. It is an affront to his very character to say that he issues the invitation without the possibility of every person invited being able to fulfill it. Nothing less than the integrity of God is on the line.

ter 5, was whether to understand justification as an imputed or infused righteousness.

Historically, one common theme united those who formulated some opinion on predestination and free will — for the most part, they recognized the errors of Pelagius[32] while maintaining to represent the authentic views of St. Augustine.[33] To many since his time, Augustine is the consummate theologian, highly esteemed among Catholic and Protestant alike.[34] Augustine certainly was a great theologian, perhaps the best the Church has ever produced. Yet one thing about Augustine has tended to confuse those who appeal to his works: Augustine, as one of the most prolific writers

---

[32] Pelagius (d. 420) denied original sin and man's common guilt inherited from Adam. He believed that physical death, whether of Adam or of his descendants, is not the result of sin, but is a necessity of nature. Spiritual death is not the inherited consequence of Adam's sin but comes to each individual who misuses the power of free choice by choosing to sin. All men by virtue of their reason and free will have the power to avoid making this unrighteous choice. If man so chooses in the exercise of his free and morally responsible will, he may grasp the eternal aid of divine grace which is bestowed according to man's merit. The unassisted human will takes the determining initiative in the matter of salvation. Writing on Pelagius, Augustine says: "he parries their question when they ask him, 'Why do you affirm that man without the help of God's grace is able to avoid sin?' Here the opinion is expressed which all along was kept in the background...The reason why he attributes to the grace of God the capacity of not sinning is, that God is the Author of nature, in which, he declares, this capacity of avoiding sin is inseparably implanted." *(On Nature and Grace*, NPNF, Vol. 5, p. 141). At the Councils of Jerusalem and Diospolis in 415, Pelagius had agreed that a man could do nothing without God's help. As Tavard remarks, however, Pelagius "establishes a double system of justification. Initial justification is due solely to grace through faith; continuing justice derives from ascetical efforts and achievements" *(Justification: An Ecumenical Study* (New York: Paulist Press, 1990) p. 21).

[33] This is not to say that the Fathers before Augustine did not believe in predestination, grace and freedom of the will. For an extensive bibliography of patristic witness to this issue see McSorley, op. cit., *Luther: Right or Wrong?* p. 59. For a more general analysis on the understanding of justification among the Fathers, see George H. Tavard, *Justification: An Ecumenical Study,* pp. 17-48. Tavard sees a tendency among some of the Fathers to claim that the individual can put himself in the way of grace prior to grace, e.g., Hilary of Poitiers, Ambrose, Gregory of Nyssa, Chrysostom, et al.

[34] Augustine's complete authority on the issue of predestination was slightly modified, however, in the Jansenist controversy in 1653 which led Pope Pius XI in *Ad salutem* (April, 1930) to say that Augustine's authority was not to be set above the teaching authority of the Church. Augustine himself said that he was not to be followed on all points (*The Gift of Perseverance*, PL 45, 21, 55).

in Christian history, says, or seems to say, different things in different contexts. Since theology, especially in the area of predestination, is rather difficult to comprehend, one theologian or historian may think Augustine is saying one thing but another may think he is saying something quite different.[35] Augustine himself is aware of his own shortcomings and shifts in thinking in his theological career.[36] Though he and his followers all condemned Pelagianism, the degree of condemnation became a topic of debate from the medieval period up to the Reformation and beyond.

Although the various interpretations of Augustine's writings by Catholic and Protestant alike tend to cloud his views on the subject of predestination and free will, the Church Councils provided valuable guidelines and parameters to the issue.[37] On the one

[35] The following conclusions on Augustine's writings provide an example of these differing interpretations: "We suggested that the passage about grace acting might possibly mean that God enabled man to choose the right if he wished. We must now conclude, however, that such an interpretation is almost certainly incorrect and that in *De Correptione*, as in all other of Augustine's later works, man is not even able to accept or reject whatever graces may or may not be offered to him." (John Rist, "Augustine on Free Will and Predestination," in *Journal of Theological Studies* 20 (October, 1969), n.4, p. 438). An opposing view states: "Admittedly, as far as salvation is concerned, God takes the first initiative but He does not undertake this against mankind's free consent. Augustine himself said that to claim otherwise would be an absurdity...No matter how much God took the initiative in people's conversion, it was obvious to Augustine that this conversion was the work of both God and the individual. The person who believed in God truly chose to believe in Him" (Mathijs Lamberigts, "Augustine, Julian of Aeclanum and E. Pagels' *Adam, Eve, and the Serpent*," in *Augustiniana* 39 (1989), n.3, pp. 401-402; cited in an unpublished paper by David Liberto, "Augustine, Calvin and Free Choice").

[36] Augustine wrote of changes in his doctrinal views in the work *Retractationes*. Although because of the Pelagian controversy he had shifted more to a predestinarian stance in the later years of his life, Augustine never relinquished the dialectic between predestination and free will. See **Appendix 9** for more details.

[37] The Fathers taught that grace/predestination does not destroy free will: Irenaeus, *Against Heresies*, PG 7, 4, 37, 1; Clement of Alexandria, *The Rich Man*, PG 9, 21, 1; Gregory of Nyssa, *The Great Catechism*, PG 5, 31; Chrysostom, *Homilies on Genesis*, PG 54, 22, 1; *On John,* 59, 8, 1; 10, 1; 46, 1; *On Romans*, 60, 18, 5; *On Ephesians*, 64, 4, 2; *On Hebrews*, 12, 3; Jerome, *Against Jovinian*, PL 60, 2, 3; *Commentaries on Jonah*, PL 25, 3, 6; Augustine, *Letters*, JR, 1417; *Sermons*, 46, 156, 11; *Questions to Simplican*, 40, 1, 2, 10; 1, 2, 12, 13; *Debate with Felix*, 42, 2, 4; *Forgiveness of Sins*, 44, 2, 17, 26; 2, 18, 28; *The Spirit and The Letter*, 44, 33, 58; 34, 60; *Homilies on John*, 35, 25, 12; 26, 7; *Homilies on the Epistle of John*, 35, 4, 7; *Grace and Original Sin*, 44, 1, 25, 26; 1, 29, 30; *Against the Pelagians*, 44, 1, 19, 37; *Admonition and Grace*, 44, 11, 31, 32; 14, 43; John Damascene, *The Source of Knowledge*, 94, 3, 2, 30.

hand, they left room for future discussion and refinement; on the other hand, they did not hesitate to condemn as heretical any theory which deviated from its parameters. As with most Council decrees, these parameters were issued following the controversy surrounding the issue. The first controversy, as mentioned above, arose between Augustine and Pelagius. The extreme "free will" ideas of Pelagius were condemned at the local Councils of Carthage[38] and Mileum in 416 AD (confirmed by Pope Innocent I and Pope Zosimus), and condemned again at the ecumenical council of Ephesus in 431 AD and the *Indiculus de gratia* by Pope Celestine I. The second controversy, in an opposite direction, occurred in the late 5th century as the extreme "predestinarian" views of a priest from Gaul named Lucidus arose. The Council of Arles in 475 AD condemned his ideas.[39] The third controversy arose in the early 6th century over a milder form of Pelagianism called "Semi-Pelagianism." This doctrine, introduced by Faustus of Riez (c. 408-490), claimed (1) God provided equal grace to everyone and thus any differences among people comes solely from their own disposition; and (2) God provided grace for the later stages of salvation but left man to initiate his coming to God.[40] In this instance, the Second Council of Orange in 529 AD came to the rescue. Prompted by the teachings of Caesarius of Arles and Prosper of Aquitaine, the Council issued 25 canons on the subject of Original Sin, Grace,

---

[38] The fifth canon of the Council of Carthage (416) stated: "It has likewise been decided that whoever says that the grace of justification is given to us for this reason: that what we are ordered to do through free will, we may be able to accomplish more easily through grace, just as if, even if grace were not given, we could nevertheless fulfill the divine commands without it, though not indeed easily, let him be anathema..."

[39] The Council recorded the repentance of Lucidus as follows: "I condemn with you that view which states that the work of human obedience does not have to be united with divine grace; which says that, after the fall of the first man the free choice of the will was totally destroyed; which states that Christ our Lord and Savior did not incur death for the salvation of all; which states that the foreknowledge of God violently impels man to death, or that they who perish, perish by the will of God..." DS, 160a.

[40] Faustus wrote: "This alone is ours, that, being incapacitated by our frailty, at best we may placate [God] through the importunity of our searching and knocking" (*De gratia Dei et libero arbitrio*, PL 58, 832).

and Predestination. The first 24 canons dealt with the issue under the terms of "grace" and "free will" rather than "predestination" and "free will." In summary, these canons state clearly that Adam possessed a free will; and that his sin left man's free will impaired yet not obliterated. Because of this impairment, man now required a stronger movement of God's grace in order for him to respond, a grace that must continue throughout his life. The Council, however, did not address the finer points of predestination. On predestination, the Council reserved its comments to denying that God predestined men to do evil.[41] Augustine's views on predestination dominated the thinking of the Latin Church, and served to steer most away from Pelagianism, and even from its modified form, Semi-Pelagianism. The Council of Orange chose to allow room for Augustine's predestinarian views without making a formal statement to that effect, but did define dogma that was based mostly on Augustine's views of sin and grace.

The fourth controversy regarding the doctrine of free will and predestination arose about three hundred years later. A Saxon monk named Gottschalk (c. 805-868) had advanced the idea of "double-predestination" which necessitated that God predestine the wicked irrespective of their free will of which they had none.[42] This was a view in which God is said to have elected some individuals to eternal life but condemned the rest to eternal death, without any distinction between God's foreknowledge of all events and his foreordaining of events. Like Lucidus in the 5th century, Gottschalk also believed that Christ died only for those elected to eternal life. Gottschalk's views were condemned by the archbishop of Mainz, Rabanus Maurus, who countered that God's foreknowledge and

---

41 The Council of Orange stated in Canon 25: "We not only do not believe that some have been truly predestined to evil by divine power, but also with every execration we pronounce anathema upon those, if there are [any such], who wish to believe so great an evil." This Council was confirmed by Pope Boniface II in 531.

42 This was in opposition to the concept of "single predestination" in which God is said to have only elected some individuals to eternal life but merely "passed by" the others, leaving them to suffer the just consequences of their sin, otherwise known as "preterition."

foreordination are distinct in such a way that the former conditions the latter. Hence, Rabanus could say that God foreknows sin but does not foreordain it. Finally, in 849, Hincmar of Reims (845-882) brought Gottschalk before the Council of Quiersy where his views were condemned.[43] Notwithstanding, some milder elements of Gottschalk's ideas as well as those of Rabanus were coalesced in the Council of Valence in 855. Though Rabanus accused Gottschalk of teaching that God predestined man to sin, some think that Gottschalk did not hold to such an extreme view.[44]

The Council of Valence in 855 added to the chapters of the Council of Quiersy, refining and defining quite a bit more the nature and extent of predestination. The Council stated that God foreknows the good and evil deeds of man. Good men know that they do good by the grace of God while evil men know they do evil by

[43] In 853, the Council of Quiersy formulated the following: Chap. 1: "Man using his free will badly sinned and fell, and became the 'mass of perdition' of the entire human race. The just and good God, however, chose from this same mass of perdition according to His foreknowledge those whom through grace He predestined to life, and He predestined for these eternal life; the others, whom by the judgment of justice he left in the mass of perdition, however, He knew would perish, but He did not predestine that they would perish, because He is just; however, He predestined eternal punishment for them. And on account of this we speak of only one predestination of God, which pertains either to the gift of grace or to the retribution of justice;" Chap. 2: "...we have free will for good preceded and aided by grace, and we have free will for evil, abandoned by grace;" Chap. 3: "Omnipotent God wishes all men without exception to be saved although not all will be saved. However, that certain ones are saved, is the gift of the one who saves; that certain ones perish, however, is the deserved punishment of those who perish;" Chap. 4: "Christ Jesus our Lord...so there is...no man for whom he has not suffered; although not all will be saved by the mystery of His passion."

[44] Schaff notes the following from Gottschalk's shorter Confession which he wrote after being condemned: "I believe and confess that God foreknew and foreordained the holy angels and elect men to unmerited eternal life, but that he equally foreordained the devil with his host and with all reprobate men, on account of their foreseen future evil deeds, but a just judgment, to merited eternal death." In the larger Confession he states: "Those, O God, of whom thou didst foreknow that they would persist by their own misery in their damnable sins, thou didst, as a righteous judge, predestinate to perdition" (Schaff, Vol. 4, p. 531). Although Ratramnus, Lupus, and Magister Florus held similar views, each was careful not to say that God predestined man to sin, thereby avoiding the error of making God the author of sin.

their own malice. God's foreknowledge, however, does not necessitate man to sin, as if the man could not do anything differently. It stated that God does not arbitrarily condemn men but does so based only on the sin of the man himself. More specifically, the Council stated that God predestines the elect to life and predestines the wicked to death. God predestines them to death because he foreknows their sin and unrepentance. God can do this because all things are timeless to him in his infinity.[45] Once again, the Councils preserved the dialectic between grace and free will. Pope Leo IX confirmed the dialectic in 1053. Although Peter Abelard (1079-1142) resurrected the teaching of an independent free will apart from grace, the Council of Sens condemned his views, and debate on the issue remained relatively quiet for a few years. Anselm of Canterbury (1033-1109) had further refined the understanding of free will and was faithful to the Augustinian dialectic between grace and free will.[46] Bernard of Clairvaux (1039-1153) added that grace and free will do not work together as mere percentages of a total but each as a total cause with its own properties.[47] Peter Lombard (1095-1160) and Bonaventure (1217-1274) also followed in line with the grace/free will dialectic, sometimes siding more with one than the other. The complex and prolific Thomas Aquinas also upheld the grace/free will dialectic by showing that free will must be deduced from

[45] See **Appendix 7** for excerpts from the Council of Valence. The Council of Langres in Lyons, France in 859, and the Council of Trullo (some read "Douzy") in 860, confirmed the decisions of the Council of Valence, the latter going a little further in asserting the free will of the baptized and the capacity to do good, as well as the fact that God "wants no one to perish" and that "after the fall of the first man God does not want to take away violently the free choice of his will (suae voluntatis liberum arbitrium);" and that to all men God "is prepared to give what is just" (cited in Tavard, p. 28).

[46] Anselm wrote: "neither grace alone nor free will alone accomplishes the salvation of man" (Latin: "nec sola gratia nec solum liberum arbitrium salutem hominis operetur" (*De Concordia* III, 5, — PL 158, 526)). According to Tavard, however, Anselm's "quantitative" or "measured" understanding of grace opened the door to a legalistic assessment of both justice and injustice, which led to the mathematical dispensing of grace in the form of indulgences in later centuries.

[47] DTC, 2, 746-785.

the fact that man is a rational creature.[48] Using Augustine's argumentation, Aquinas agrees that unless man has a free will, all commands, exhortations and prohibitions would be in vain. If man acts of necessity, then all basis for reward and punishment and all principles of moral philosophy are overthrown.[49] If necessity is that which is unable to be or that which is immutably determined to one end only (Thomas' definition), then a will moved by necessity is a heretical theology.[50] This being the case, (i.e., that free will is a fact), according to Thomas, God knows some things contingently.[51]

---

[48] *Summa Theologica* I-II, Q. 6, A. 2c; *De Veritate*, Q. 24, A. 1,2. Thomas gives a succinct formulation of this dialectic in the following: "God does not justify us without ourselves, because while we are being justified we consent to God's justification by a movement of our free-will. Nevertheless this movement is not the cause of grace, but the effect; hence the whole operation pertains to grace" (*Summa Theologica*, I-II, 111.2, ad 2.). Modern Protestant theologians sometimes accuse Aquinas of siding too much with nature in the nature/grace relationship. His Aristotelian method of analysis is probably the most evident reason for this opinion. This is a short-sighted view of Aquinas, however. By the same token, it was Luther and Calvin who put too much emphasis on the grace side of the nature/grace relationship. This resulted in many extreme and esoteric beliefs in their theology. From a philosophical perspective, the Catholic Church was careful throughout history to keep nature and grace in balance, maintaining the same dialectic as she did with predestination and free will, grace and the sacraments, primary and secondary causes, etc. Without the proper dialectic between nature and grace, a one-sided emphasis on grace, though appearing to be God-glorifying, actually distorts and degrades the grace side of the equation.

[49] *De Potentia*, Q. 3, A. 7.

[50] *De Veritate*, Q. 24, A. 1c; *De Malo*, Q. 6, q.un.c.

[51] *De Veritate*, Q. 2, A. 12c. "Contingency" is the theological term used to distinguish between God's sole predeterminations as opposed to determinations based on man's free will decisions or the natural working out of events. In other words, "contingency" means that some or all of God's predeterminations are made based on what man will decide to do or the natural outworking of events. Scripture gives us some interesting examples of contingency. In one instance, David inquires of the Lord if a certain event will take place in the future if David stays at the place where the event would have happened. God tells him that the event will occur if David stays there. David decides not to go to that place and the foreseen event never occurs (1 Samuel 23:1-14). Although this is a rudimentary example of contingency, it nevertheless gives us a glimpse into the dynamic relationship between what God sees as real possibilities in the future and the free decisions of man. "God is the first cause who operates in and through secondary causes" (CC, Section 308).

Luther's Views of Predestination

The fifth controversy over the doctrine of predestination occurred in the time of Martin Luther. Although much of the doctrine of absolute predestination coming out of the Reformation is attributed to John Calvin, in actuality, it was Luther who first taught this doctrine. Prior to 1515, however, Luther believed in a free will unaided by grace and that the natural man could will for good and receive gracious merit.[52] Something happened between 1510 and 1515 to make Luther go to the other extreme. Some suggest that it was Luther's "tower experience" in reinterpreting Romans 1:17. Little known among Protestants is that Luther's view of predestination was more extreme than Calvin's. It was the doctrine that Luther considered the most important, even more so than justification by faith alone since the latter depends on the former. Many scholars feel it was Luther's complete denial of free will that was his main reason for proceeding with the Reformation.[53] Luther's protégé, Philip Melancthon, understood that almost all of Luther's theological views were essentially related to the question of free will. Though a close colleague of Luther, Melancthon eventually rejected Luther's view of predestination and become an ardent supporter of free will.[54]

---

52 WA 9, 31f; 79, 10, 35.

53 K. Zickendraht, "Der Streit zwischen Erasmus und Luther uber die Willensfreinhiet" (Leipzig, 1909), p. 8. Schweibert concludes: "Luther's whole doctrinal system would crumble if the thesis of *De Servo Arbitrio* were invalid." Hans J. Iwand concludes, "...evangelical theology stands or falls with this doctrine of the unfree will." Cited in McSorley, op. cit., p. 9, 11.

54 In his Galatian commentary Luther states: "...and that the flesh cannot think, say, or do anything except what is diabolical and opposed to God...For the Law says: 'You are an evil tree.' Therefore everything you think, speak, or do is opposed to God. Hence you cannot deserve grace by your works. But if you try to do so, you make the bad even worse; for since you are an evil tree, you cannot produce anything except evil fruits, that is, sins" (LW 54, 125-126). The Lutheran *Formula of Concord* records that a great debate occurred in the Lutheran community over this issue. It states: "The chief issue is solely and alone what the unregenerated man's intellect and will can do in his conversion and regeneration, by those powers of his own that have remained after the Fall, when the Word of God is preached and the grace of God is offered to him. Can man prepare himself for such grace, accept it and give his assent to it? This is the issue which has been argued by some of the theologians of the

After reading the anti-Pelagian writings of Augustine, Luther formulated his predestinarian views. However, Luther far exceeded the teaching of Augustine. The key areas of Luther's departure from Augustine were: (1) Luther's insistence that all things occurring in the world happen by *absolute necessity*, including the sin of man, and (2) Luther's total denial of free will.[55] Hence, in Luther's view, God was the first cause for the sin of man as well as the one who predestined some of these men to eternal perdition. Luther states this idea in his *Assertio omnium articulorum* of 1520 directed against the excommunication issued by Pope Leo X:

> Do you have anything to growl at here, you miserable Pope? It is necessary to revoke this article. For I have incorrectly said that free will before grace exists in name only. I should have said candidly: "free will is a fiction, a name without substance." Because no one indeed has the free power to think good or evil, but (as the article of Viglephi [Wycliffe] condemned at [the Council of] Constance correctly teaches) all things happen by *abso-*

54 cont. churches of the Augsburg Confession for quite some years." Philip Melanchthon held the view that although weak and in need of the Holy Spirit, "nevertheless, man still has so much of his natural powers prior to his conversion that he can to some extent prepare himself for grace and give his assent to it" (FC, p. 520). The *Formula of Concord* dismissed Melanchthon's view stating: "We believe that in spiritual and divine things the intellect, heart, and will of unregenerated man cannot by any native or natural powers in any way understand, believe, accept, imagine, will, begin, accomplish, do, effect, or cooperate, but that man is entirely and completely dead and corrupted as far as anything good is concerned. Accordingly, we believe that after the Fall and prior to his conversion not a spark of spiritual powers has remained or exists in man by which he could make himself ready for the grace of God or to accept the proffered grace...either altogether or half-way or in the tiniest or smallest degree..." FC, p. 521. To answer this, the Council of Trent issued two statements. On the one hand, Session 6, Canon 1 affirmed that man can do nothing apart from the grace of God; while, on the other hand, Canons 4, 5, 6, 7 affirmed that man possessed the power of free will, could cooperate with God's grace, and could do works prior to conversion that were not sinful, and that through these actions could put himself in the way of grace.

55 Luther believed man had a will (*voluntas*) but not a free will (*liberum arbitrium*).

> *lute necessity.*[56] This is what the Poet [Virgil] meant when he said: "all things are determined by a fixed law." And Christ says in Matthew 10: The leaf of a tree does not fall to the ground without the will of your Father in heaven, and even the hairs of your head are all numbered. And in Isaiah 41 he insults them saying, "Do good or evil if you can."[57] (emphasis mine)

In *Table Talk*, Luther writes on his understanding of Free Will:

> One ought properly call it a changeable, mutable will because God works in us and we are passive; like a potter, from the same material he can make a vessel either for honor or dishonor. Accordingly our free will is passive, not active, because it doesn't lie in our power.[58]

Contrary to Augustine, Luther held that using passages as James 4:8; Luke 11:9; Jeremiah 3:22; 29:13; and Zechariah 1:3 to prove

---

[56] John Wycliffe (1320-1384) was condemned at the Council of Constance (1418) in 45 theological censures: #27 was Wycliffe's view of "*omnia de necessitate absoluta eveniunt*" (that is, "all things happen from absolute necessity"); #44 was Wycliffe's view of religious communities which stated: "Augustine, Benedict and Bernard have been damned, unless they repented about this...and thus from the pope to the last religious, all are heretics" (DS, 607, 624, pp. 210-211). A similar argument from "necessity" was proposed by Michael De Bay who was condemned by Pius V in 1567 for stating, "One sins and even merits damnation in that which one does of necessity" (JD 1967).

[57] WA 7, 146, 3-12: Latin: "Habes, miserande Papa, quid hic oggannias? Unde et hunc articulum necesse est revocare. Male enim dixi, quod liberum arbitrium ante gratiam sit res de sole titulo, sed simpliciter debui dicere 'liberum arbitrium est figmentum in rebus seu titulus sine re.' Quia nulli est in manu sua quippiam cogitare mali aut boni, sed omnia (ut Viglephi articulus Constantiae damnatus recte docet) de necessitate absoluta eveniunt. Quod et Poeta voluit, quando dixit 'certa stant omnia lege,' Et Christus Matth. x. 'Folium arboris non cadit in terram sine voluntate patris vestri qui in coelis est et capilli capitis vestri omnes numerati sunt.' Et Esa. xli. eis insultat dicens 'Bene quoque aut male si potestis facite.'"

[58] LW 54, 260. The remaining line of the section records of the conversation: "Therefore he instructed him [the student] to read the Bible and Philip's [Melanchthon's] *Loci Communes*." This is somewhat ironic since it was Melanchthon who in his early career followed Luther in holding *absolute necessity*, but later denied such views and replaced them with a stress on the power of free will even apart from grace — a view so extreme, echoing the very doctrines of Pelagius, that the Lutheran *Formula of Concord* in 1577 totally rejected it.

grace working *with* free will is Pelagian.[59] As noted previously, Augustine had used these verses to show that such biblical imperatives were proof of free will. In the end, it is precisely this kind of hermeneutic which totally ignores Scripture's explicit assertion of free will that makes Luther stand alone against the history of Christian exegetes.

Luther stated again in the *Assertio omnium articulorum*:

> A man's way is that which we speak of as his natural power to do what is in him. But this very thing is not in the free will of man, so then, what is this so-called free will but a matter of *empty words*? How can a man prepare himself for good? It is not even in his power to make his ways wicked. *For God works even the evil works in the wicked*, as it says in Prov. 16, "He has made all things for himself, even the wicked for the day of evil," and Rom. 1, "God handed them over to a reprobate mind so that they should do things not fitting," likewise, Rom. 9, "whom he will he hardens and whom he wills he pities," and in Exodus 9, "for this very reason I raised you up that I might show my power in you." So then, God is terrible in his judgments and in his works.[60] (emphasis mine)

To say that free will is a matter of "empty words" and that "God works even the evil works in the wicked" was not a traditional or Scriptural teaching. One can speak of God permitting or using the sin of evildoers for a greater good, but not that God works or causes evil. Such a position, if taken literally, is blasphemous. Indeed, Canons 5 and 6 of the Council of Trent condemned both of these ideas.[61]

---

[59] Other passages, e.g., Tobit 13:6, display the same principle.

[60] WA 7, 144, 30-36; 145, 1-4. Latin: "Via enim hominis est ea, quam ipsi vocant naturalem virtutem faciendi, quod est in se. Ecce haec non est in arbitrio hominis seu liberi arbitrii: quod ergo liberum arbitrium est nisi res de solo titulo. Quomodo potest sese ad bonum praeparare, cum nec in potestate sit suas vias malas facere? Nam et mala opera in impiis deus operatur...ideo enim est terribilis deus in iudiciis et operibus suis."

[61] Session 6, Canon 5: "If anyone shall say that after the sin of Adam man's free will was lost and destroyed, or that it is a thing in name only, indeed a title without reality, a fiction, moreover, brought into the Church by Satan, let him be anathema." Canon 6: "If anyone shall say that it is not in the power of man to make his ways evil, but that God produces the evil as well as the good works, not only by permission, but also properly and of Himself, so that the betrayal of Judas is no less His own proper work than the vocation of Paul: let him be anathema."

Luther believed that God works in the will of man to such an extent that God is the cause of everything that occurs, including sin, and in such a way that God has no recourse to foreknowledge of contingencies or secondary causes. This concept is more evident in his 1525 work *De Servo Arbitrio*[62] which was his answer to Erasmus' *De Libero Arbitrio:*

> This too, then, is first off necessary and salutary for Christians to know, namely, that God does not foreknow anything contingently[63] but that he foreknows, proposes and does all things with an unchangeable, eternal and infallible will. By this thunderclap, free will is utterly cast down and overthrown so that those who wish to assert free will must either negate this, hide it or in some way dispose of it...Wasn't it you, my dear Erasmus, who asserted just a little while back, that God is by nature just and by nature most merciful? If this is true, doesn't it follow that he is unchangeably just and merciful?[64]

Luther held that God damned those undeserving of damnation:

> But when God condemns the undeserving, the human heart finds this intolerable, argues back, murmurs, and blasphemes because this is inconvenient to the human heart....But if God crowning the unworthy pleases you, his condemning the unworthy should not at the same time displease you. If he is just in the one case why is he not just in the other. Here he bestows grace and mercy upon the unworthy. Here, on the other side, he confers wrath

62 Sometimes translated as "Bondage of the Will" but the literal meaning is "On the Enslaved Will." The German translation of Luther, "eyn gefangenen Willen" is closer to the former. Catholic theology does not use such terminology, instead referring to the bondage of man to sin.

63 Luther did not distinguish between an absolute and contingent necessity as Aquinas and Augustine had. This was the major cause of his extreme views. Luther claimed that such a distinction was "empty words."

64 WA 18, 615, 12-17. Latin: Est itaque et hoc imprimis necessarium et salutare Christiano, nosse, quod Deus nihil praescit contingenter, sed quod omnia incommutabili et aeterna infallibilique voluntate et praevidet et proponit et facit. Hoc fulmine sternitur et conteritur penitus liberum arbitrium, ideo qui liberum arbitrium volunt assertum debent hoc fulmen vel negare vel dissimulare aut alia ratione a se abigere."

> and severity upon the unworthy, both wrong from a human point of view but just and true from God's point of view.[65]

Another paragraph from the same work suggests why Pope Leo X could accuse Luther not only of denying free will but of verging on or actually making God the author of sin:

> Hence you see that when God works in the wicked and through the wicked, evil things are indeed done, and yet God himself cannot do evil, though he does evil things through the wicked. He himself being good, cannot do evil, but he uses evil instruments which cannot escape the capture and motion of his power. The vice, therefore, is in the instruments which God does not permit to be idle, the vice out of which evils are done by God's own acting. It is as if a worker chopped badly with a dented hatchet, hence it comes about that the wicked man cannot fail to always err and sin because he is not permitted to be idle by the capture of the motion of divine power, but wills and desires as he himself is.[66]

---

65 WA 18,730, 26-28: "At cum immeritos damnat, quia incommodum sibi est, hoc iniquum, hoc intolerabile est, hic expostulatur, hic murmuratur, hic blasphematur. WA 18, 731, 6-13: "At si placet tibi Deus indignos coronans, non debet etiam displicere immeritos damnans. Si illic iustus est, cur non hic iustus erit? Illic gratiam et misericordiam spargit in indignos, hic iram et severitatem spargit in immeritos, utrobique nimius et iniquus apud homines, sed iustus et verax apud seipsum.

66 WA 18, 709, 28-36. Latin: "Hic vides Deum, cum in malis et per malos operatur, mala quidem fieri, Deum tamen non posse male facere, licet mala per malos faciat, quia ipse bonus male facere non potest, malis tamen instrumentis utitur, quae raptum et motum potentiae suae non possunt evadere. Vitium ergo est in instrumentis, quae ociosa Deus esse non sinit, quod mala fiunt, movente ipso Deo. Non aliter quam si faber securi serrata et dentata male secaret. Hinc fit, quod impius non possit non semper errare et peccare, quod raptu divinae potentiae motus ociari non sinitur, sed velit, cupiat, faciat taliter, qualis ipse est." The editor adds a footnote: "Dazu, wie Luther hier doch Gott in eine gewisse Entfernung von der Sunde ruckt, trotz der spateren Stelle uber die Verursachung des Sundenfalls Adam durch Gott, vgl. Kattenbusch a.a. O.S. 22f," translated: "On this, Luther here puts God at a certain distance from sin despite a later passage dealing with the causation of Adam's fall by God..." which indicates that the editor, who directs the reader to the work of the German theologian Kattenbusch, thinks that Luther's particular view of how God brought about the fall of Adam makes God more the author of sin than even

In order to understand the possible reasons for Luther's extreme views, we need to peer into some of the major schools of thought prior to Luther. On the one hand, Luther was fighting the Nominalist[67] school of thought propagated by William of Ockham

---

66 cont. the above passage (See WA 614, 27-616). Luther allowed free will in the natural world or "the things beneath us" as suggested in WA 18, 672, 7f, "Igitur ab hoc loco: Si volueris, incipit quaestio de libero arbitrio, ut per Ecclesiasticum intelligamus hominem in duo regna distribi. Uno, quo fertur suo arbitrio et concilio, absque praeceptis et mandatis Dei, puta in rebus sese inferioribus. His regnat et est dominus, ut in manu consilii sui relictus" (Translation: "Therefore from this passage he begins the question about free will that by Ecclesiasticus we should understand man to be divided into two kingdoms, in the one where he is born by his own will and counsel apart from the precepts and commandments of God, say, in matters inferior to us. Here man reigns and is lord and is in the hand of his own counsel. Not that God deserts him thus so as not to be cooperating with him in all things, but that the use of lower things shall have been conceded to man through choice and God did not inhibit him with any laws or commandments"); and WA 18, 752, 7f: "Scimus liberum arbitrium natura aliquid facere, ut comedere, bibere, gignere, regere, ne nos delirio illo velut argutulo rideat, quod nec peccare quidem liceret sine Christo, si vocem illam, nihil, urgeamus, cum tamen Lutherus donarit liberum arbitrium valere nihil nisi ad peccandum, adeo libuit sapienti Diatribe ineptire etiam in re seria" (Translation: "We know that free will by nature does something, such as to eat, to drink, to beget, to rule, lest he mock us with holding the madness that one can't even commit sin without Christ, if we press this word 'nothing' since, nevertheless, Luther granted that it avails for nothing except sin"). In light of this information, we would not agree with Michael Schmaus' assessment of Luther: "If he speaks of the enslaved will, this does not mean a formal denial of man's power of choice" (*Dogma: Justification and the Last Things*, p. 17).

67 Nominalism is the view in philosophy that Universals, i.e., abstract ideas, are mere words and have no basis in reality nor an objective counterpart. From this we get the word "nominal," meaning "in name only." It should be emphasized, however, that the Ockham-Biel school was only one of several schools of thought in the Scholastic period, among them Thomist, Scotist, Augustinian, Abelardian, and Mystical. Contrary to popular opinion among Evangelicals that nominalism was a distinct theological school of thought, Alister McGrath makes quite a convincing case that nominalism was purely a philosophical movement in the medieval period. McGrath chooses to use the term *via moderna* rather than "nominalism" to describe this pervasive thought. McGrath further postulates that the tendency among Protestants to equate nominalism with Pelagian theology is misleading. Of the *via moderna* McGrath writes: "[it] is to be interpreted in a sense which allows a man to play a positive role in his own justification, without elevating that role to Pelagian proportions. In this way, the theologians of the *via moderna* were able to maintain the teaching of both the early and later Franciscan schools concerning man's meritorious disposition towards justification, while establishing a conceptual framework within which this teaching could be safeguarded from the charge of Pelegianism..." *Iustitia Dei*, II, pp. 170-171.

(1280-1349), the popular Tübingen theologian Gabriel Biel (d. 1495), along with Robert Holcot (d. 1349), Peter d'Ailly (1350-1420) and Jean Gerson (1363-1429). Luther had first been introduced to theological study by Biel but later thought that there was a strong "Pelagian" influence in this particular school. Luther concluded that when Ockham and Biel claimed that man could make some movement toward God unaided by grace from which God would respond congruently by giving grace, they were attributing too much power to man's free will. Luther's diatribe expanded as he confronted the writings of Desiderius Erasmus (1466-1536). Erasmus had engaged Luther in a debate on one particular point of Pope Leo's 41 disputations with Luther — proposition 36 — which represented Luther's view as, "Free will after sin is a matter of title only; and as long as one does what is in him, one sins mortally."[68] Luther is pleased that Erasmus understands the real issue at stake[69] but he disagrees vehemently with Erasmus's defense of free will. Many believe that it was Luther's overreaction at this point that produced his retort to Pope Leo X, quoted above, opting for "free will as a fiction" in which "no one has the power to think good or evil" but that "all things happen of necessity." Besides insulting Pope Leo, Luther further enraged the Catholic hierarchy by supporting his thesis with a quote from the pagan poet Virgil, showing a peculiar affinity to the pagan notion of fatalism.[70] Luther compounded the problem by offering no Scriptural basis for his concept of *absolute necessity,* arriving at the notion by speculative theological reasoning. Moreover, Luther began to say that man's

---

68 DS, p. 242. Latin: "Liberum arbitrium post peccatum est res de solo titulo, et dum facit quod in se est, peccat mortaliter." Perhaps if Luther had simply said that free will or freedom was not the same after the fall, his view would have been more acceptable; but to deny the existence of free will after the fall put him in conflict with St. Augustine and all of Christian tradition.

69 Luther calls the issue of free will the "res ipsa summa causae" ("the most important aspect of the matter") and the "cardo rerum" ("the hinge on which all turns").

70 In light of this, it is interesting to note that Cicero (106-43 B.C.) posed the query of "either God's foreknowledge or man's free will." Augustine promptly answered: "we are, therefore, in no way compelled, if we retain the foreknowledge of God, to discard our choice of will...we embrace both..." (*City of God*, PL 41, 5, 10, 2).

creatureliness excluded his free will, thus implying that God was the author of sin. What the Catholic hierarchy saw in Luther's new concept was a resurrection of the old Manichean heresy denying free will, a view which had even influenced the early Augustine in the 4th century though he later repudiated it. Luther's extreme view made him appear as a fatalist or determinist, a doctrine found in rudimentary form in the writings of John Wycliffe (1320-1384).[71] Though he correctly attacked Luther's view of *absolute necessity* in *De Libero Arbitrio*, Erasmus apparently did a poor job in defending the Church's official stand on free will, which would only come at the Council of Trent almost fifty years later. Trent reaffirmed the Scriptural and anti-semi-Pelagian doctrine molded by Augustine and the Council of Orange. Though Erasmus mentioned God's grace, he failed, at least in some of his writings, to speak of grace undergirding free will as an aid to salvation, thus opening the door for Luther to accuse him of Pelagianism.[72] The proposition that the will could act apart from grace in pursuit of God had been condemned by the Catholic Church at the Council of Orange in 529 AD[73] yet Erasmus seemed to be unaware that Anselm of Canterbury (1033-1109), Bernard of Clairvaux (1090-1153), Thomas Aquinas (1224-1274), and Gregory of Rimini (d. 1358), all of whom recognized Augustine and his anti-Pelagian theology as the norm for the Church, had upheld the Church's stance. All these theologians recognized that man could do nothing except by the grace of God, a grace properly called "prevenient." This is why Luther is often accused of not really knowing, or perhaps not be-

---

71 Historian Philip Schaff says of Luther: "The Reformer held the most extreme view on divine predestination, and in his book on the Slavery of the Human Will, against Erasmus, he went further than Augustin before him and Calvin after him" (Schaff, op. cit., Vol. 4, p. 524).

72 Without mentioning grace, Erasmus wrote: "By free will we mean the power of the human will by which man can apply himself toward or turn himself away from the things which lead to eternal salvation." Unfortunately for Erasmus, most of the estimations of his debate with Luther do not take into account his great work titled *Hyperaspistes*, which critics say is much more to the point and in line with Catholic teaching.

73 The Councils of Trent, Vatican I and Vatican II also affirmed the absolute necessity of the grace of God prior to man's free will.

ing fair, to the Scholastic theology he repudiated.[74] Ockham, Biel, and Erasmus were certainly not the most informed spokesman for Catholicism.[75] However, once Luther overreacted to Erasmus by denying a dialectic between grace and free will, speaking rather of man's will moved by "absolute necessity," Catholics never again gave him a hearing, thus, proposition 36, among others, sealed his fate and his excommunication. Although in a few places Luther seems to suggest a belief in contingent necessity,[76] in toeing the fine line required to maintain the proper balance between grace and free will, Luther, in language or intent, simply fell off the edge in an overreaction to perceived Pelagian influences in his time. Neither Augustine, Aquinas, Anselm nor any Council taught the "either-or" theology of Luther.[77] Luther's teachings almost force

---

74 See the work by Dominican scholar Stephanus Pfürtner, *Luther and Aquinas — a Conversation*, pp. 35-45. See also Harry McSorley's Excursus in *Luther: Right or Wrong*, op. cit., pp. 139-141. There is today a renewed appreciation for the theology of Aquinas among many Evangelicals (Arvin Vos, *Calvin, Aquinas, and Contemporary Protestant Thought*, 1985; Norman Geisler, *Thomas Aquinas: An Evangelical Appraisal*, 1991, et al.). Aquinas, in fact, had already specifically answered Luther's "necessity" argument in *De Veritate*, Q. 24, A. 1, ad 13 by saying, "It cannot be concluded from God's foreknowledge that our acts are performed out of absolute necessity." Aquinas speaks instead of "conditional necessity" that does not take away free will (*De Veritate*, I, Q. 23, A. 3, ad 3, ad 6).

75 Ockham was eventually excommunicated from the Church for his unorthodox and extreme views. Ockham was noted for proposing that God could have made mortal sin, or anything else, the condition for entering heaven, as well as asserting that God could have crucified a donkey to procure the atonement.

76 Luther wrote: "For God first gives operating grace; he lets it be used and he lets it co-operate..." (Latin: Quia gratiam dat primo operantem, qua sinit uti et cooperari usque dum aliam incipit infundere" — WA 56, 379) and "it is impossible that willing be coerced and not free, therefore, it is necessarily free and necessarily wills freely" (Latin: "impossible est, quod velle sit coactivum et non liberum ergo necessario est liberum et necessario libere vult" — WA 1, 366).

77 Despite the evidence against him, Luther insists to Erasmus: "Augustine, whom you do not refer to, agrees with me completely" (Rix, *Martin Luther: The Man and the Image*, p. 212, n. 7). Erasmus had referred to Augustine, but only sparingly. He failed to refer to Augustine's works such as *Grace and Free Will*, *On the Free Will* and *The City of God* which are three of the strongest works supporting free will. Luther had studied *The City of God* in his earlier years, but seems not to remember its contents. When he discusses the issue of foreknowledge and free will with Erasmus, he fails to refer to Augustine who states clearly that one does not cancel out the other. All in all, Luther is either oblivious to or takes great pains to conceal the divergence between himself and Augustine on this point. In effect, Erasmus became Luther's scapegoat. It seems that Luther

us to see him as a fatalist or determinist, especially in light of his response to Pope Leo's bull, which seemed to expose the core error of his theology. Curiously, many who do not wish to see Luther as a determinist, conspicuously avoid references to Luther's reply to Pope Leo. Luther's possible rescue from the charge of determinism is his belief that man has free will "in the world beneath"[78] or his increasing uneasiness about his extreme view as suggested in his *Lectures on Genesis*, completed in 1545, a year before his death. Despite Luther's attack on the popes, no pope ever taught the error that fallen man can prepare himself for justification by his own free will apart from grace. Unfortunately, to his dying day, Luther never admitted this.

Calvin's Views on Predestination

Calvin's understanding of Christianity is multifaceted and comprehensive. He seems to have a much more balanced approach than his predecessor Martin Luther. Whether or not it is fair to him, however, Calvin has become most widely known in today's Protestantism for his strong, or what some would call his "extreme," views on predestination.[79] Searching for the most logically consistent theology, Calvin attributed all that occurred to the foreordination of God.[80] To Calvin, what God foreknew he foreor-

---

[77 cont.] concealed his deterministic beliefs, for he included them only in Latin writings for the academicians, while ignoring them in his German works for the ordinary citizen. Even in the works of Augustine that he did address, clearly he was skirting the issue. For example, in remarking on *The Spirit and the Letter,* Luther achieved a dramatic effect by quoting Augustine as, "A man's free will awaits for nothing except to sin..." What he didn't divulge to his readers was the rest of the sentence: "...unless he knows the way of truth" (Ibid., p. 223).

[78] Luther wrote: "in rebus sese inferioribus." WA 18, 672, 9-10.

[79] Alexander Schweitzer, *Die protestantishen Centraldogmen* (Zurich: Orell, Fussli, 1854). Others emphasize Calvin's central theme to be "union with Christ," (e.g., Brian Gerrish, *Grace and Gratitude* (Minneapolis: Fortress, 1993)); and attribute the extreme views of predestination to such figures as Theodore Beza, (e.g., John S. Bray, *Theodore Beza's Doctrine of Predestination* (Nieuwkoop: B. de Graaf, 1975)).

[80] While we do not know for certain how much it influenced him, Calvin was a great admirer of the Stoic philosopher Seneca, whose logic led to a fatalistic view of the world and Stoicism's "stiff upper lip" attitude. Calvin claims, however, that his strong view of God's foreordination is not influenced by Stoic philosophy (*Institutes* 1:16:8).

dained to happen.[81] For example, Calvin believed, in opposition to Augustine, that God had predestined the fall of Adam, and thus, before sin had ever entered the world, had predestined the elect to eternal life and the rest to eternal damnation. Calvin spells this out very clearly in his *Institutes of the Christian Religion*.[82] Calvin

---

[81] Calvin writes: "We, indeed, place both doctrines in God, but we say that subjecting one to the other is absurd...Therefore, as any man has been created to one or the other of these ends, we speak of him as predestined to life or to death" (*Insititutes* 3:21:5). Alister McGrath remarks: "Predestination, for Augustine, refers only to the divine decision to redeem, not to the act of abandoning the remainder of fallen humanity. For Calvin, logical rigour demands that God actively chooses to redeem or to damn. God cannot be thought of as doing something by default: he is active and sovereign in his actions. Therefore God actively wills the salvation of those who will be saved and the damnation of those who will not...Salvation thus lies outside the control of the individual, who is powerless to alter the situation" (*Reformation Thought*, 2nd edition, 1993, p. 125, 127). Francois Wendel concurs with McGrath: "...on this particular point Calvin diverges from St. Augustine, for whom the elect alone are the object of a special decision which withdraws them from the 'massa perditionis' while the reprobate are simply abandoned by God to the ruin they have incurred by their sins (*De correptione et gratia*, 7, 12, M. L. xliv, 923)."

[82] Calvin writes: "The Father has chosen us in Christ before the foundation of the world...Here, surely, the fall of Adam is not presupposed as preceding God's decree in time; but it is what God determined before all ages that is shown, when he willed to heal the misery of mankind" (*Institutes*: 2:12:5). Elsewhere he writes: "And it ought not to seem absurd for me to say that God not only foresaw the fall of the first man, and in him the ruin of his descendants, but also meted it out in accordance with his own decision" (*Institutes* 3:23:7; see also 3:24:12). On double predestination, Calvin concludes: "For all are not created in equal condition; rather, eternal life is foreordained for some, eternal damnation for others. Therefore, as any man has been created to one of the other of these ends, we speak of him as predestined to life or death" (*Institutes* 3:21:5). "As Scripture, then, clearly shows, we say that God once established by his eternal and unchangeable plan those whom he long before determined once for all to receive into salvation, and those whom on the other hand, he would devote to destruction. We assert that, with respect to the elect, this plan was founded upon his freely given mercy, without regard to human worth; but by his just and irreprehensible but incomprehensible judgment he has barred the door of life to those whom he has given over to damnation" (*Insitiues* 3:21:7). Commenting on Calvin's "double predestination," Jaroslav Pelikan writes: "Reprobation to damnation by the eternal will of God was an ineluctable corollary of election to salvation by the same eternal will of God; it was not based on God's foreknowledge of human conduct any more than salvation was...Calvin argued that the only possible doctrine of predestination was a doctrine of double predestination" *(The Christian Tradition*, Vol. 4: *Reformation of Church and Dogma* (1300-1700), 1984, pp. 222, 224).

believed so firmly in his view of "double- predestination" that it became to him, as Luther's *sola fide*, the article upon which the church stands or falls.[83] Sensing how his doctrine would be viewed by others Calvin writes: "It is a horrible decree, I confess, but no one can deny that God foreknew the future, final fate of man be-

[83] Schaff., op. cit., VIII, p. 546. Despite this firm belief, however, Calvin, strangely, did not include predestination within his own Genevan catechism, and address the topic in the third section of his *Institutes* rather than the first. Some from the Reformed position hold that Calvin was not a supralapsarian; others hold that he was. Calvinist, Charles Hodge, defines supralapsarianism as follows: "According to this view, God, in order to manifest His grace and justice, selected from 'creatable' men (i.e., from merely possible men whom He had not yet purposed to create) a certain number to be vessels of mercy and certain others to be vessels of wrath. In order of thought, election and reprobation precede the purposes to create and to permit the fall. Creation is the means to the end of redemption. God creates some to be saved and others to be lost...This scheme is called supralapsarianism because it supposes that men before the fall were the objects of election to eternal life and foreordination to eternal death" (*Systematic Theology*, 1988, p. 326). The confessions of the Reformed faith appear to view Calvin as supralapsarian and thus create a distance from his views; e.g., the Belgic Confession and the Synod of Dort (1618) profess a clear infralapsarian view, while the Heildelberg Catechism gives no statement on reprobation. Many subsequent Reformed theologians, after the influence of the extreme views of Theodore Beza had subsided, did not side with the views of Calvin but understood themselves as infralapsarians, e.g., Charles Hodge, W.G.T. Shedd, Henry B. Smith. The revised Westminster Confession also qualified Calvin's views and steered away from Luther's view of non-contingency, stating: "God, from all eternity, did by the most wise and holy counsel of His own will, freely, and unchangeably ordain whatsoever comes to pass: yet so, as thereby neither is God the author of sin, nor is violence offered to the will of the creatures; nor is the liberty or contingency of second causes taken away, but rather established" (WC, chapter 3). Subsequent understanding of predestination among the Reformed congregations ultimately came to side more with the Catholic understanding of predestination than with Calvin's. Some contemporary evangelicals seem to soften Calvin's supralapsarianism by claiming a distinction between "Calvinism" and what is called "hyper-Calvinism," as well as disguising Calvin's views by shifting the reference from "Calvin" to "Calvinism," the latter, today at least, being a much diluted form of the former (e.g., R. C. Sproul, *Chosen By God*, pp. 96-97).

fore he created him, and that he did foreknow it, because it was appointed by his own decree."[84]

Calvin makes his extreme view of predestination very clear in his interpretation of the phrase "vessels of wrath prepared for destruction" in Romans 9:22. He writes in his commentary:

> There are vessels prepared for destruction, i.e., appointed and destined for destruction. There are also vessels of wrath, i.e., made and formed for the purpose of being proofs of the vengeance and displeasure of God....The reprobate, however, are the vessels of wrath, since they serve to display the judgment of God...there is no doubt that the preparation of both is dependent

[84] Schaff comments on the "decretum horrible" of Calvin with the words: "Our best feelings, which God himself has placed in our hearts, instinctively revolts against the thought that a God of infinite love and justice should create millions of immortal beings in his own image — probably more than half of the human race — in order to hurry them from the womb to the tomb, and from the tomb to everlasting doom! And this not for any actual sin of their own, but simply for the transgression of Adam of which they never heard, and which God himself not only permitted, but somehow foreordained. This, if true, would indeed be a 'decretum horrible'" (VIII, p. 559). The *Oxford Dictionary of the Christian Church* concurs with Schaff: "According to him [Calvin], before the fall and even before creation, God, in his eternal counsels, predestined some of His creatures to salvation and others to damnation. This entails that God wills not only the reprobation of the damned but also the sin which leads to it, as he who wills the end must will the means" (1983, p. 224). Calvinist Erwin Lutzer agrees: "Did God predestinate the Fall? The answer is yes; Calvin called this the dreadful decree" (*All One Body — Why Do We Disagree*, p. 178). In an attempt to lessen the force of Calvin's words, Calvinist evangelical Douglas Jones states: "Calvin's *decretum horribile* translates as "awesome," or "terrible" in the older sense, not as "horrible, in our usage. And in this sense, yes, the Reformed understanding *does* inspire a passion for the lost. How could it not?" ("An Exchange of Ideas: Election" in *Credenda Agenda*, Vol. 8, No. 3, p. 31). It is hard to see much difference between "terrible" and "horrible, given Calvin's purpose in creating this title is to call attention to the difficulty, from our perspective, in conceiving of a God who, as Schaff notes above, and as explained in Calvin's position, arbitrarily picks whom he will save and whom he will damn before the sin of man ever becomes an issue. It is "awesome," "terrible," or "horrible" precisely because it is repudiating to the human mind, even as Calvin himself intimates by the words, "I confess..."

on the secret counsel of God. Otherwise Paul would have said that the reprobate yield or cast themselves into destruction. Now, however, he means that their lot is already assigned to them before their birth.[85]

Here Calvin leaves no room for the possibility of men *making themselves* vessels of wrath by their decision to sin; rather, he attributes it to the "secret counsel of God." Once this is said, Calvin discourages us from any further inquiry.[86] It almost appears as if Calvin understands man as a playtoy in the hands of God, a God who must have a human vehicle to demonstrate His divine attributes. He infers that it was absolutely necessary for God to display his glory in this

---

85 *Calvin's New Testament Commentaries*, The Epistle of Paul to the Romans, trans. David and Thomas Torrance, 1960) pp. 211-212. This view of Calvin's is continued with current Reformed evangelicals such as Michael Horton who writes: "If the Father places some — indeed, many — in Christ to 'be holy and blameless in his sight' (Eph. 1:4), then we must agree that the rest are not chosen and not placed in Christ to be holy and blameless in his sight. In fact, Scripture identifies these as 'the objects of wrath — prepared for destruction' (Rom. 9:22)" (*Putting Amazing Back Into Grace*, op. cit., p. 131).

86 The words, "prepared for destruction" are from the Greek words, κατηρτισμένα εἰς ἀπώλειαν using the perfect, passive, participle of καταρτίζω which is normally understood as "perfected" (Matt. 21:16; Luke 6:40; 1 Cor. 1:10; 1 Pet. 5:10); "mended" (Matt. 4:21);"formed" (Heb. 11:3). The perfect tense can be translated "having been formed" or "having been made." This verb could also be in the middle voice which would be translated, "having made themselves for destruction." Whether middle or passive, this word is in contrast to the words "prepared in advance" (Greek: προητοίμασεν) in Romans 9:23 which is in the Greek *active* voice, denoting that God initiated the preparation for glory but did not necessarily take part in those who were "prepared for destruction." Calvin ignores the distinction in the Greek voice, instead, attributing to God an *active* role in preparing the vessels of wrath for destruction. 1 Peter 2:8 uses the phrase, "which is also what they were destined for" from the Greek aorist, passive ἐτέθησαν which normally refers to placement or appointment. Calvin likens this passage to his view of Romans 9 in which "Pharaoh is said to have been put into the position of resisting God, and all unbelievers are destined for the same purpose" (*Calvin's Commentary*, op. cit., 1 Peter, p. 264). In like fashion, some have attempted to use Jude 4 to teach supralapsarianism by the KJV translation, "who were before of old ordained to this condemnation." However, the Greek verb translated "ordained" by the KJV is the word, προγεγραμμένοι which should be translated "having been written before."

way, having no better way to do it.[87] Some have said that if Calvin's view is taken to its logical conclusion, it would end up making God the "author of sin." Many Reformed apologists claim that Calvin avoided this position and that it is wrong to force it upon him. Whether he intended it or not, in some of his writings it appears that Calvin either supported or came very close to this position:

> Here they [Calvin's opponents] have recourse to the distinction between will and permission. By this they would maintain that the wicked perish because God permits it, not because he so wills.[88] But why shall we say "permission" unless it is because God so wills? Still, it is not in itself likely that man brought destruction upon himself through himself, by God's mere permission and without any ordaining? As if God did not establish the condition in which he wills the chief of his creatures to be![89]

Calvin's lack of distinction between God's will and God's permission is one point at which his critics find his doctrine hard to

---

[87] Calvin, writing against his opponents, states: "We admit the common guilt, but we say that God's mercy succors some. Let it succor all, they say. But we reply that it is right for him to show himself a fair judge also in punishing. When they do not allow this, what do they do but either try to deprive God of his capacity to show mercy or at least allow it to him on the condition that he give up his judgment completely?" (*Institites* 3:23:11). "For the first man fell because the Lord had judged it to be expedient; why he so judged is hidden from us. Yet it is certain that he so judged because he saw that thereby the glory of his name is duly revealed" (*Institutes* 3:23:8). Commenting on Calvin's view, Fred Klooster writes: "Calvin emphatically contended that sinful works are not the cause or basis for God's eternal decree of reprobation...What is the cause of God's decree of reprobation? Calvin's answer is, the sovereign good pleasure of God. No cause other than His sovereign will can be adduced...For Calvin, then, God's sovereign will is the ultimate cause of Adam's fall and of reprobation, while human sin is the proximate cause" (*Calvin's Doctrine of Predestination*, 2nd edition, 1977, pp. 61, 63, 70).

[88] Here Calvin is referring to Erasmus' work "*De Libero Arbitrio*," ed. von Walter, p. 53.

[89] *Insititutes* 3:23:8. Editor John McNeil heads this section with the title, "God willed, not only permitted, Adam's fall and the rejection of the reprobate, but with justice." Some from the Reformed persuasion attempt to explain, rather weakly, Calvin's non- distinction between "will" and "permission" by saying that God "willed" his "permission."

accept.[90] The fact that some of his contemporaries and followers found in Calvin's language the license to push the envelope toward making God the "author of sin" (e.g., Heinrich Zwingli, Theodore Beza)[91] makes us wonder what Calvin's true intent was and if he himself was fearful of taking his own theory to its logical conclusion. That Calvin's extreme views could be interpreted as implying that God was the author of sin, is strongly suggested in a letter to Calvin from his contemporary Philip Melanchthon:

> As regards the question treated in your book, the question of predestination...I maintain that God is not the author of sin, and therefore cannot will it. David was by his own will carried into transgression. He might have retained the Holy Spirit...Let us accuse our own will if we fall, and not find cause in God. He will help and aid those who fight in earnest...God promises and gives help to those who are willing to receive it. So says the Word of God, and in this let us abide..."[92]

Unlike Luther, however, Calvin seems to have held to some acceptance of contingent causes within the providence of God. Commenting on the bones of Christ that God prohibited from being broken, Calvin writes: "Whence again we see that distinction concerning relative necessity and absolute necessity, likewise of consequent and consequence..."[93] On the other hand, Calvin did not hesitate to emphasize the *necessity* side of this relationship. He

---

[90] "God is in no way, directly or indirectly, the cause of moral evil. He permits it, however, because he respects the freedom of his creatures and, mysteriously, knows how to derive good from it" (CC, Section 311).

[91] Similar to Theodore Beza, Heinrich Zwingli's extreme views allowed him to make God the "sinless author of sin" (Schaff, VIII, p. 547). McGrath writes of Zwingli: "Whether an individual is saved or condemned is totally a matter for God, who freely makes his decision from eternity" (*Reformation Thought*, p. 121). In answer to this, the Council of Trent added Canon 17 to its Sixth Session: "If anyone shall say that the grace of justification is attained by those only who are predestined unto life, but that all others, who are called, are called indeed, but do not receive grace, as if they are by divine power predestined to evil: let him be anathema."

[92] Schaff, VIII, pp. 391-392

[93] *Institutes* 1:16:9. Editor John McNeil, in an attempt to support Calvin, comments that, in this respect, Calvin's view is similar to Aquinas and Melanchthon.

did so often by appealing, as Luther did, to the writings of Augustine. Calvin writes: "I shall not hesitate, then, simply to confess with Augustine that 'the will of God is the necessity of things,' and that what he has willed will of necessity come to pass, as those things which he has foreseen will truly come to pass."[94] In another place Calvin writes: "Augustine everywhere speaks of this necessity; and...did not hesitate to affirm it in these words: 'Through freedom man came to be in sin, but the corruption which followed as punishment turned freedom into necessity.'" Calvin concludes this section with: "But if this is true, then it is clearly expressed that man is surely subject to the necessity of sinning."[95] It is hard for one to read these words and not conclude that a dimension of fatalism exists in the theology of Calvin. Although it is true that Augustine speaks of necessity it is for a completely different reason, and even then, these kinds of statements are almost always balanced with inverse truths, the kind that are often missing in Calvin's writings.[96]

While Calvin admits that despite God's providence through which he foreordains all events men are neither "absolved from responsibility," "seeking prudence" in all areas of life, nor "exculpated from wickedness,"[97] nevertheless he refuses to mention these aspects under the rubric of "free will." For Calvin, Adam was the only man who possessed a free will in regard to salvation.[98] This is where Trent and Calvin parted ways, as did Calvin with Augustine

---

94 *Institutes* 3:23:8. The editor references Augustine's work *On the Literal Interpretation of Genesis*, PL 34, 350, as the source. We show that Calvin took Augustine's quote completely out of context and failed to give the reason Augustine spoke in such a manner. See **Appendix 19** for further development.

95 *Institutes* 2:3:5

96 On the issue of necessity, Augustine balances his views by such statements as the following reply to Pelagius: "God, therefore, does not command what is impossible, but in commanding He also admonishes you to do what you are able, and to ask His help for what you are unable to do" (*On Nature and Grace*, PL 43, 50; JR 1795). Augustine's statement is very similar to the reply, noted above, that Melanchthon gave to Calvin regarding Calvin's attempt to place the cause of sin in God.

97 *Institutes* 1:17:3-5.

98 *Institutes* 1:15:8.

and Aquinas.[99] For those after Adam, Calvin wrote: "But I hold that because it [free will] cannot be retained without great peril, it will, on the contrary, be a great boon for the church if it be abolished. I prefer not to use it myself, and I should like others, if they seek my advice, to avoid it."[100]

From another perspective, however, we must point out that if Calvin was not claiming that God is the author of sin (in opposition to his followers Zwingli and Beza), then his logical system, a system which leads directly to "God's will," not "God's permission," as the ultimate cause for man's predicament, suddenly becomes *illogical.* The moral absolute that God is good and does not cause or predetermine sin must eventually override Calvin's view of predestination. Rather than try to explain this dichotomy, Calvin resorted to saying that to question the issue any further would be to delve into areas where the human mind dare not enter.[101] Though Calvin claims that the perdition of the reprobate "depends upon the predestination of God in such a way that the cause and occasion of it are found in themselves,"[102] he never explains how this is possible, without contradiction, within his own system. Calvin creates a dilemma for his followers. They are now left with the proposition that God chooses people arbitrarily without regard to sin and free will, yet requires the same people not to make arbitrary or amoral decisions in life but to judge things rightly. How can it be that Calvinist theology places God, who clearly states in Scripture that he abhors partiality and unequal measures, in the very position of being partial? Is not God the one who judges fairly, is no respecter of persons and who justly rewards those who diligently seek for Him, yet man who arbitrarily chooses his favorites many times based on partiality? (cf., Col. 3:23-4:1; 1 Peter 1:17). Calvin's only answer to this is that, in regards to salvation, God does not

---

99 Council of Trent, Session 6, Canons 4, 5, 9, 17 (See Appendix 20).
100 *Institutes* 2:2:8.
101 *Institutes* 3:23:5.
102 *Institutes* 3:23:8.

show partiality toward "persons," but does show partiality between one individual as opposed to another.[103]

In another seeming inconsistency in Calvin's view, he attributes to Adam a genuine "free will" before his sin — a free will, he believes, that man no longer possesses once Adam sinned — but at the same time maintains that God willed, not merely permitted, Adam's sin. Calvin writes:

> In this integrity man by free will had the power, if he so willed, to attain eternal life. Here it would be out of place to raise the question of God's secret predestination because our present subject is not what can happen or not, but what man's nature was like. Therefore Adam could have stood if he wished, seeing that he fell solely by his own will. But it was because his will was capable of being bent to one side or the other, and was not given the constancy to persevere, that he fell so easily.[104]

Here Calvin senses immediately an opponent's likely rejoinder: "if God has willed, not merely permitted, Adam's fall, how could Adam have had a genuine free will?" Calvin attempts to dif-

---

[103] To his critics, Calvin writes: "First, Scripture denies that God shows partiality toward persons in another sense than that in which they judge. For it [Scripture] means by the word "person" not a man but those things in a man which, conspicuous to the eye, customarily either produce favor, grace, and dignity, or arouse hatred, contempt, and disgrace...Thus, Peter and Paul teach that "the Lord shows no partiality toward persons" [Acts 10:34; cf. Rom. 2:11; Gal. 2:6], for he does not distinguish between Jew and Greek [Gal. 3:28] so as to reject one but embrace the other on grounds of race alone." For Calvin, then, it seems that it is not right for God to be partial when judging one group against another, but it is perfectly right to be partial when judging one individual against another. God is portrayed as one who has two opposing standards of partiality. We must also point out that Calvin fails to see the emphasis Paul puts on the *individual* within the larger ethnic groups, e.g., Rom. 2:11: "but glory, honor and peace for *everyone* who does good: first for the Jew, then for the Gentile. For God does not show favoritism" (cf., Rom. 2:6: "God will give to *each person* according to what he has done;" 2:9: "for *every human being* who does evil;" 1 Pet. 1:17: "a Father who judges *each man's* work impartially;" Col. 3:25: "*Anyone* who does wrong will be repaid for his wrong, and there is no favoritism.")

[104] *Institutes* 1:15:8.

fuse this objection by appealing to "God's secret predestination." This explanation is consistent with Calvin's distinction between "the revealed will of God" and the "secret will of God,"[105] or his distinction between God's "general calling" to salvation as opposed to his "special calling."[106] However, it is ironic that Calvin will not allow a distinction in the mind of God between his "will" and his "permission," yet insists on a distinction between "revealed will" and "secret will." Using Calvin's criterion that one must make no artificial distinctions of God to accommodate the finite mind of man, he does not seem to see that a distinction between "revealed" and "secret" wills is just as artificial, leading both to a dualism and contradiction in the divine will.

In Calvin's attempt to support his views of predestination, it becomes quite obvious to those who are familiar with the writings of Aquinas and Augustine that Calvin engages in a most selective citing of their writings. This is noted first in Calvin's consistent quotes from Augustine which are strung together to make it appear that Augustine denied the free will of post-Adamic man in regard to salvation. In actuality, Augustine denied free will only when it was made a strength of man outside the grace of God, the very notion of free will for which Augustine had condemned Pelagius. Unlike Augustine, Calvin did not see intrinsic grace cooperating with Adam to help him resist the fall; rather, he understood Adam to have external or "general grace" which allowed him to "excell in these pre-eminent endowments [mind, conscience and will], so that his reason, understanding, prudence, and judgment not only sufficed for the direction of his earthly life, but by them mounted

---

[105] *Institutes* 3:21:1. Calvin used the same explanation in his interpretation of 1 Timothy 2:4 ("God our Savior, who wants all men to be saved and come to the knowledge of the truth..."). In other places, Calvin holds that God's will, at least in the mind of God, is one: "But even though his will is one and simple in him, it appears manifold to us because, on account of our mental incapacity, we do not grasp how in divers ways it wills and does not will something to take place" (*Institutes* 1:18:3).

[106] "There is the general call, by which God invites all equally to himself through the outward preaching of the word...The other kind of call is special, which he deigns, for the most part, to give to the believers alone, while by the inward illumination of his Spirit he causes the preached Word to dwell in their hearts" (*Institutes* 3:24:8).

up even to God and eternal life."[107] Without internal grace, Calvin's Adam is on his own. For Augustine, man is never at a point that he has free will apart from the intrinsic grace of God, either before or after Adam's fall.[108] God constantly surrounds man with grace as a help to bend his will toward God. Although Augustine's views on predestination were strong, he never relinquished man's free will to accept or reject God's grace — a grace given for the purpose of leading him to salvation. As noted previously, all the Councils of the Church that addressed the issue of grace, maintained the dialectic between grace and free will for post-Adamic man. Moreover, in man's decision to accept God, Augustine maintained that man could never take strict credit for his actions, since it was God's grace which prompted him to do the good, and without which he could not decide in favor of God. Thus, as Augustine says, when God rewards us he rewards his own work.[109] On the other hand,

---

[107] Calvin writes: "Man in his first condition excelled in these pre-eminent endowments, so that his reason, understanding, prudence, and judgment not only sufficed for the direction of his earthly life, but by them men mounted up even to God and eternal bliss...In this integrity man by free will had the power, if he so willed, to attain eternal life...Therefore Adam could have stood if he wished, seeing that he fell solely by his own will...his choice of good and evil was free, and not that alone, but the highest rectitude was in his mind and will, and all the organic parts were rightly composed to obedience..." (*Institutes* 1:15:8). Although Calvin speaks of "grace by external symbols" (*Commentary on Genesis* 2:9), or that God "lavished upon the universe all manner of good things" (*Institutes* 1:14:2), or "general grace" (Ibid., 2:2:17), he does not speak of grace which God posited in Adam to assist him that he not sin.

[108] Augustine writes: "The first man did not have that grace by which he would never will to be evil; but surely he had that in which, if he willed to remain, he would never be evil, and without which, even by free choice, he could not be good, but which, nevertheless, by free choice, he could forsake. Neither then did God will him to be without His grace, which he left within that man's free choice. Free choice, therefore, suffices for evil, but is too little for good, unless it be assisted by good that is almighty. If man had not forsaken that assistance by his free choice, he would have been good always; but he did forsake it and he was forsaken. For such was the nature of this assistance that he could forsake it if he so willed and he could remain in it if he so willed; but it was not such that it would bring it about that he would so will" (*De correptione et gratia* PL 44, 11, 31; *Admonition and Grace*, JR 1954). Pius V, in the 1567 Bull *Ex Omnibus Afflictionibus*, condemned the proposition of Michael De Bay which stated: "It is absurd to hold that from the beginning the human being was raised above the natural human condition through a certain supernatural and gratuitous gift so as to worship God supernaturally with faith, hope and charity" (JD 1923).

[109] *Letter to Sixtus*, AD 418; JR 1452.

Calvin's inability to reconcile how grace and merit could work together in post-Adamic man, forced him to find a means by which man would be totally outside the realm of merit.[110] He found that solution in absolute predestination without free will. Then, by quoting selectively from Augustine's writings, Calvin tried to make Augustine his mentor.[111]

Calvin's reluctance to posit intrinsic grace as the prompting element within Adam's pre-lapsarian condition may be because of at least two facets of his theology. First, it is necessary in Calvin's post-lapsarian theology to avoid the position that suggests, in regard to salvation, that God's grace can be resisted. For Calvin, man is 'totally depraved' after the fall and when God finally moves him to salvation, the grace that does so is 'irresistible.' Consequently, if Adam sins, even though prompted by grace not to sin, it would show that Adam could resist God's grace. Since one of the major tenets of Calvin's doctrine of absolute predestination is that grace cannot be resisted, this would exclude grace in the pre-lapsarian state of Adam. The absence of grace for the pre-lapsarian Adam will then allow Calvin to formulate the notion of "irresistible grace"

---

110 This is a common understanding of Calvin's thought. Williston Walker, for example, writes: "...Calvin's severe logic, insistent that all salvation is independent of merit, led him to assert that damnation is equally antecedent to and independent of demerit...The sole cause of salvation or of loss is the divine choice" (*John Calvin*, 1969, p. 417).

111 In some places, however, Calvin seems to admit the principle of merit and man's ability to respond to God. In a sermon on Deuteronomy 7:11-15, Calvin writes: "...yet God makes this condition, that we will be blessed if we have served and honored him. At first glance there seems to be some contradiction here. If God loves us without regarding our merits, then He should not say: "If..."! Then there should be no condition. Well, he makes a condition, as we see in this passage. And even the whole Scripture is full of this doctrine: that God renders to each one according to what he deserves" (Corpus Reformatorum XXVI: 532). Though Calvin admits a conditionality in regard to merit, he fails to explain how it fits into his system. Moreover, we agree that the "whole Scripture is full of this doctrine" for this is precisely why the Council of Trent preserved the free will and gracious merit of post-Adamic man, since otherwise, passages like Deuteronomy 7:11-15 would be mere words without meaning — a position in which God appears to be saying one thing but meaning something entirely different.

and an external forensic imputation of righteousness for post-lapsarian man, since the grace given must be effectual and it becomes so because it is totally extrinsic to man, unimpeded by man's will to accept or reject it. Calvin's concept of "total depravity" after the fall of Adam also fits into this scheme. For if Adam is without intrinsic grace before the fall, then the ability to accept or reject God comes purely from his own being, however strong that being was made by Calvin's built in "endowments" or external "general graces" of his environment. Hence, once that "being" is destroyed by sin, it is a total destruction, a total alienation from God with no internal residual grace. For Augustine, the rejection of God's grace to avoid sin alienates Adam from God, but to a lesser degree than for Calvin, since Augustine's Adam still retains the internal grace of God — a grace that both sustains his physical life (e.g., by the mere fact that God did not destroy him immediately for his sin), and which prompts and leads him spiritually back to God, a grace that was maintained due to the promise in Genesis 3:15 of a future redeemer. The Council of Trent highlighted this teaching of Augustine and declared that man's free will was not destroyed by the fall, however weakened and debased it became, and that men after Adam are continually assisted and aroused by divine grace, a grace that can be resisted.[112]

Second, Calvin's theology cannot accommodate internal grace in the pre-lapsarian Adam since if Adam obeyed under the prompting of God's grace and thus attained eternal life by such obedience, this would mean that Adam would have graciously "merited" eternal life in the same way that Catholicism speaks of the gracious merit of men after Adam, and thus, to Calvin's consternation, grace and merit would then be compatible. But for Calvin, grace can never share any existence with merit. This is made evident in his critique of Aquinas' proposition that God's foreknowledge of man's merits is due to the predestination of grace to man

[112] Session 6, Chapters 1, 5, 6.

that made such merits possible.[113] Calvin retorts that there is no difference between the predestination of men and the predestination of grace, because God uses the latter to accomplish the justification of his elect. Moreover, he says of the order of election that God chose us that we should be holy, not because he foresaw that we would be so.[114] As to Calvin's first objection, though the Scripture does speak of grace and predestination working together, it also distinguishes grace from predestination by specifically indicating that an individual can fall from grace.[115] Moreover, the grace of God is made available to all men so that Christ becomes a pro-

[113] *Summa Theologica* I. 23. 5. Strong statements are made by Aquinas, such as: "God's intention cannot fail...Hence if God intends, while moving it, that the one whose heart he moves should attain to grace, he will infallibly attain to it..." (Ibid., I-II. 112. 3). Aquinas made such statements, however, always with a view accommodating the free will of man, as noted previously. God's "infallible intention" is mysteriously predicated and contingent upon man's free will, and thus the dialectic between the two is preserved.

[114] *Institutes* 3:22:3. Calvin also writes: "But what if I should raise the objection that predestination to grace is subordinate to election to life, and is like a handmaiden to it? that grace is predestined for those to whom the possession of glory has long since been assigned because it pleases the Lord to bring his children from election to justification?" (*Institutes* 3:22:9).

[115] 2 Cor. 6:1f; Gal. 5:4; Heb. 10:29; 12:15f. Calvin does hold, however, that even the "special calling" can be resisted. After speaking of special grace, Calvin completes his statement with: "Yet sometimes he also causes those who he illumines only for a time to partake of it; then he justly forsakes them on account of their ungratefulness..." (*Institutes* 3:24:8). We wonder, then, how Calvin can deny a salvific free will in man if his salvation is made contingent upon whether the individual shows "ungratefulness" to God for the illumination God has given him? To answer this, Calvin creates a distinction between "general election" and "special election." In his commentary on Romans 11:22 Calvin writes: "Those who have been enlightened by the Lord must always turn their minds to perseverance, for those who...by no means continue in the goodness of God, and thus by their ingratitude deserve to be blinded again. Paul does not address each of the godly separately (as we have said before), but compares the Gentiles and the Jews" (*Commentary on Romans*, op. cit., p. 252). When Calvin says, "(as we have said before)," he is referring to the same principle we noted previously in which Calvin asserts that God can show no partiality to "persons" (e.g., between Jews and Gentiles as respective groups), but can do so with individuals. To Calvin, then, elect "persons" can resist God's grace, but elect individuals cannot. Hence, in the final analysis, we see again that Calvin's view of predestination overrides the free will of the *individual*, a view that Trent did not accept.

pitiation for the whole world.[116] After God gives the grace, the question then becomes, from Adam onward, who among men will utilize this grace to reap God's blessing (e.g., John 3:16; Acts 17:26-27). As to Calvin's second objection, it goes without saying that God did not predestine the elect because he saw them as holy. If they were holy prior to predestination there would be no reason to predestine them. Thus the question is not whether predestination makes them holy, but to what degree does man's free will cooperate with God in this process — a dialectic Scripture itself teaches, as Paul says in Philippians 2:12-13:

> Therefore, my dear friends, as you have always obeyed — not only in my presence, but now much more in my absence — continue to work out your salvation with fear and trembling. For it is God who works in you to will and to act according to his good pleasure.[117]

Conclusion

Although we have tried to give a fair treatment in this short exposé, the discussion of predestination and free will can hardly be exhausted. If we are faithful to Scripture, however, we must

[116] John 3:16; 1 John 2:1-2; 4:10; 1 Timothy 2:4; 4:10; 2 Peter 3:9. Calvin arbitrarily dismisses 1 John 2:1-2 on the grounds that the "world" really refers to the "whole Church" and thus the propitiation is limited to all those who would eventually believe (Calvin's Commentaries, op. cit., p. 244). He dismisses 1 Timothy 2:4 on the grounds that Paul is addressing "classes of men" not "individuals" (ibid., p. 209), yet we insist that the context does not specify or base God's desire on such a distinction. Regarding 2 Peter 3:9, Calvin does not use the "class of men" argument since the wording "anyone" and "everyone" will not allow it. Instead, he appeals to the "secret decree of God by which the wicked are doomed to their own ruin" and that though "God stretches out his hand to all alike, but He only grasps those whom He has chosen before the foundation of the world" (ibid., p. 364). Of John 3:16, while Calvin finally admits that "God..shows He is favorable to the whole world when He calls all without exception to the faith of Christ," he nevertheless concludes, "But God opens the eyes only of the elect that they may seek Him by faith" (ibid., pp. 74-75).

[117] "God is the first cause who operates in and through secondary causes: 'For God is at work in you, both to will and to work for his good pleasure.' Far from diminishing the creature's dignity, this truth enhances it" (Catholic Catechism, Section 308).

conclude that it teaches both predestination and free will.[118] Sometimes Scripture speaks as if man does everything and at other times as if God does everything. However, rather than simply viewing grace and free will in total tension, let us take the discussion to a higher level: Without the grace of God, man would have no free will. In other words, without the imprint of God, man would be an empty vessel with no God-like quality to make free decisions. When he made man in his image, God imparted himself in man, and with that impartation came man's character and abilities. Since God, in his nature, is a being who both knows and determines all things before time (including those of himself), and yet we must also insist that he is equally free to make choices as he wishes, then man, being made in God's image, should also have these two distinguishing facets to his being. If both determination and free will can coexist in God without contradiction, then it is not difficult to understand that because God imparts himself into man then man also is, without contradiction, both "predestined" and "free," This, indeed, is a profound mystery.[119]

Unfortunately, with our finite minds, we will probably never understand how these seemingly opposing truths can be reconciled. Since Scripture does not seek to reconcile predestination and free will, we should use much caution when we make such attempts. It is as enigmatic as trying to understand the Trinity in which Scripture presents God as Three yet as One, or the Incarnation in which Jesus is presented as fully God yet fully man. There

---

[118] After two thousand years of discussion on the issue, the Catholic Catechism (1994) may have summed it up best: "To God, all moments of time are present in their immediacy. When therefore he establishes his eternal plan of "predestination," he includes in it each person's free response to his grace." (CC, Section 600). Catholic Michael Schmaus has correctly observed that the Catholic Church has the uncanny ability to hold in absolute tension concepts that are seemingly irreconcilable (Ibid., pp. 13-15). Evangelical Sinclair Ferguson expresses similar sentiments: "...the genius of Rome, unlike that of Wittenberg and Geneva, has always been its ability to hold opposite tendencies together" (*Sola Scriptura: The Protestant Position on the Bible*, p. 191).

[119] Catholic Catechism, Section 1705: "By virtue of his soul and his spiritual powers of intellect and will, man is endowed with freedom, an 'outstanding manifestation of the divine image' (f. 8: GS 17.)" "Man is rational and therefore like God; he is created with free will and is master over his acts" (CC, Section 1730; Gaudium et spes 17). "For God...made us in the image of his own nature" (Wisdom 2:23).

is a great degree of mystery to the Christian faith that we will not be able to understand in this life. As 1 Corinthians 13:12 teaches, "Now we see but a poor reflection as in a mirror; then we shall see face to face. Now I know in part; then I shall know fully, even as I am fully known." Or, as Ecclesiasticus 39:16-17 teaches, "All the works of the Lord are very good, and whatever he commands will be done at the appointed time. No one can say, 'What is this?' or 'Why is that?' — for at the appointed time all such questions will be answered."[120]

These conclusions, however, should not be taken to mean that we should cease all intellectual discussion of the issue. In order not to go to one extreme or the other, we must be aware of the intrinsic polarity of this topic as well as the balance needed to keep the poles in perspective. In actuality, to deny that man has free will simply because one cannot understand how to reconcile it with God's sovereignty or foreknowledge of events inadvertently infringes on God's sovereignty. Such argumentation necessitates that God can create creatures with dignity and intelligence but does not have the power to create and uphold their free will.[121] Though Luther and Calvin both decided not to entertain the notion of free will for fear that the masses would be "pitifully deceived and led astray" or "proud" to think that they could take credit for their own salvation,[122] they simply did not take into ac-

[120] St. Augustine recounts that as he walked along the beach one day contemplating the Trinity, trying desperately to understand how Three are in One and One in Three, he suddenly heard an inner voice telling him to put the whole ocean in the sea shell he had just picked up. Augustine replies, "How can I put such a vast amount of water in such a little shell." The voice replied, "In the same way that you cannot understand that, neither can you understand the Trinity." As Michael Schmaus says, "The fact of the matter is that the process involved eludes any concise formulation which will not be subject to misunderstanding" and "How the will preserves its freedom under the influence of a divine premotion is something which we cannot understand" (*Dogma: Justification and the Last Things*, pp. 22, 40).

[121] "God is the sovereign master of his plan. But to carry it out he also makes use of his creatures' cooperation. This use is not a sign of weakness, but rather a token of almighty God's greatness and goodness" (Catholic Catechism, Section 306).

[122] WA 18, 637.

count that it is equally as dangerous to deny free will. A denial of free will inevitably force the masses to put the onus on God as the author of sin and subsequently question the very integrity of God. It is exactly at this point that both Luther and Calvin failed to give adequate answers to their extreme views and thereby ignored the most important theological argument for free will. Instead of keeping the dialectic between predestination and free will an unfathomable mystery, Luther and Calvin chose to use their own human logic and side with the former over the latter. Though attempting to make their theology divinely centered, it became centered on human reason and logic. Earlier we pointed out Luther's concept of "firm" faith for justification. Now we understand more clearly why he thought in these terms. Luther himself stated, "It takes the highest degree of faith to believe that he is merciful, though he saves so few and damns so many; to believe that he is just, *though of his own will he makes us by necessity proper subjects for damnation*"[123] (emphasis mine). We will grant to Luther that anyone who subscribes to such an extreme theology certainly needs a lot of faith to believe in the God behind it.

Although there is much about predestination and free will that we cannot understand, certain aspects of the relationship we do know. We must keep these aspects in mind in order to avoid going to one extreme or the other. In the course of Christian history, putting too much stress on either predestination or free will caused many heresies, in one form or another. We have already seen ample evidence of this in this chapter's descriptions of so many varied theological positions and the personalities behind them. Hence, let us conclude the chapter by stating ten things — ten "facts" — about predestination and free will that we do know because the Church has defined them:

1. As opposed to the views of Luther, Calvin, Zwingli, and Beza, God did not predestine the sin of Adam, nor does he predestine the sin of man following Adam. God foreknew

[123] WA 18, 633, 15ff (Latin: "Hic est fidei summus gradus, credere illum esse...iustum; qui sua voluntate nos necessario damnabiles facit").

their malice but did not predestine it because it is not from him. Man sins of his own free will, uncoerced and undirected by God.[124]

2. God permitted the fall of Adam but he is not the cause.[125]

3. God abandons no one without having been abandoned by them.[126]

4. God does not permit temptation beyond our powers to resist.[127]

5. God predestined the punishment of the wicked.[128]

6. Grace, for the ability of conversion, is given to all sinners. God does not command impossibilities. In commanding

[124] This doctrine was affirmed first at the Council of Arles in 475 against the Catholic priest, Lucidus. It was again affirmed by the Councils of Quiersy in 853, of Valence in 855, of Langres in 859, of Trullo in 860 and of Trent in 1563. See **Appendix 7** for excerpts from these Councils. In the writings of Cornelius Jansen, bishop of Ypres in 1636-1638, the Catholic Church fought its own version of this heresy. Jansen's views were condemned by Pope Innocent X (1644-1655) who listed 5 major errors of Jansenism (DS, p. 316) and Pope Alexander VIII (1689-1691) who listed 31 errors of Jansenism (DS, pp. 339-341). The Church also condemned a related view called Baianism. Baius held that Adam was endowed with the Holy Spirit before the fall in such a way that it was his natural state of being. Hence the natural man endowed with the Spirit has certain rights before God, and thus the divine assistance he requires arises from an obligation on God's part because the assistance is an integral part of his natural state. (Augustine held that God's assistance came gratuitously, not by obligation). Adam's sin has put man into an unnatural state. The stain of original sin is a habitual concupiscience which causes man to sin; thus there being no difference between concupiscience and sin, all works prior to justification are sinful, an idea propagated by Martin Luther. Baius understood justification as a restoration of the state of innocence and the natural faculties of Adam that allowed him to lead a moral existence. This view was condemned by Pope Pius V in 1567 in the Bull *Ex omnis afflictionibus*.

[125] Council of Trent, 816,827; Pius IX, (DS, 1677).

[126] Council of Trent, 804,806; Pius IX (DS, 1794).

[127] Council of Trent, Session 6, Canon 9.

[128] Council of Valence, Canon 3.

all men to repent, God gives all men the power to repent. God desires all men to be saved and gives them the ability to be saved.[129]

7. God does not predestine the elect based on the foreknowledge of their own good works. That is the Pelagian teaching and heretical.

8. God did not predestine the elect only for the initial or latter stages of salvation, leaving them on their own, at some point, to persevere in the faith. That is the Semi-Pelagian teaching and heretical.[130]

9. Man cannot do good in the eyes of God without the aid of grace.[131]

10. The predestination of the elect is infallible. It will come to pass.[132]

[129] Council of Trent, Session 6, 804, 807.

[130] The Council of Orange in 529 condemned both Pelagianism and Semi-Pelagianism. See **Appendix 7** for excerpts from this Council.

[131] The Council of Orange in 529 and the Council of Trent in 1563 affirmed this doctrine. The remaining question to be answered is: Did God predestine the elect with a view toward the positive response they would give to the grace he provided for them to lead them to respond. Or, did they respond because God, without any view toward how they would respond to grace, elected some because of his own unqualified predeterminations? See **Appendix 14** for further discussion of these opposing views.

[132] Pope Clement XI (1700-1721) in the Bull "Unigenitus," Sept. 8 1713. DS 1380.

Chapter 8

The Final Justification

The Final Judgment

Since justification is a process that begins when God infuses his Spirit into the individual, continuing as the individual cooperates with that same Spirit to increase in grace, so must justification come to an end as the individual finally attains his heavenly inheritance. As the name implies, *final justification* is the time when God makes his ultimate evaluation of the individual's life. If one has been a faithful son, he will indeed be completely justified and receive the inheritance. If he has been unfaithful and finds himself without the grace that was infused into him at his initial justification, he will be eternally condemned. In regard to condemnation, the picture of God as "Judge" is especially prominent in contexts of Christians on the verge of sin. This appears often in the epistle of James. James 4:11-12 states: "Brothers, do not slander one another...There is only one Lawgiver and Judge, the one who is able to save and destroy. But you — who are you to judge your neighbor?" Again, in James 5:9: "You too, be patient and stand firm, because the Lord's coming is near. Don't grumble against each other, brothers, or you will be judged. The Judge is standing at the door." These passages remind us of Jesus' admonition in John 10:28: "Do not be afraid of those who kill the body but cannot kill the soul. Rather, be afraid of the One who can destroy both soul and body in hell." Peter also tells us about the judgments of the Father: "Since you call on a Father who judges each man's work impartially, live your lives as strangers here in reverent fear" (1 Peter 1:17).

These passages remove all doubt that while God is a kind Father to his Christian sons, he can turn into a wrathful Father and

Judge very quickly when serious sin is present. Other passages such as Acts 10:42 ("he is the one that God appointed as judge of the living and the dead") or Hebrews 12:23 ("you have come to God the judge of all men") show us that God is King over all creation and holds men accountable for his righteous laws.[1] For those who have not received the grace of God, or who have rejected that grace after once having it, God will be the ultimate Judge — "a consuming fire," as Paul says, who will eternally destroy his enemies and all those who have been unfaithful. There is no worse punishment than to be banished by one's Father for eternity. For those who have remained in the state of grace, however, God will continue forever to be their kind heavenly Father.

Indeed, the New Testament's description of God's judgment upon the wicked and unfaithful is awesome and frightening, yet for the faithful, unspeakably comforting. In 2 Thessalonians 1:5-10 Paul writes:

> All this is evidence that God's judgement is right, and as a result you will be counted worthy of the kingdom of God, for which you are suffering. God is just: He will pay back trouble to those who trouble you and give relief to you who are troubled, and to us as well. This will happen when the Lord Jesus is revealed from heaven in blazing fire with his powerful angels. He will punish those who do not know God and do not obey the gospel of our Lord Jesus. They will be punished with everlasting destruction[2] and shut out from the presence of the Lord and from the majesty of his power on the day he comes to be glorified in his holy people and to be marveled at among all those who have believed. This includes you, because you believe our testimony to you.

---

1 Council of Trent, Session 6, Canon 21: "Christ...as legislator whom they should obey." Pope Pius X: "Christ is king with legislative, judicial, coactive and administrative jurisdiction over all men." DS, 2194, 2196. "After the era of the patriarchs, he taught this nation, by Moses and the prophets, to recognize him as the only living and true God, as a provident Father and just judge" (Vatican Council II, *Dei Verbum* 3). See also Pope Pius XI's encyclical *Quas Primas*, (1925).

2 Recently, some Evangelicals have advanced the idea that the punishment of Hell is not eternal, i.e., without end. They propose instead that each condemned person will sustain the degree of punishment appropriate for their sin and then be annihilated. For a comprehensive treatment of this theory consult: Edward Fudge, *The Fire That Consumes: A Biblical and Historical Study of the Doctrine of Final Punishment,* Foreword by F. F. Bruce, (Texas: Providential Press, 1982, 4th printing 1989). See **Appendix 6** for further details and critique of this view.

Revelation 20:11-15 records another ominous scene:

> Then I saw a great white throne and him who was seated on it. Earth and sky fled from his presence, and there was no place for them. And I saw the dead, great and small, standing before the throne, and books were opened. Another book was opened, which is the book of life. The dead were judged according to what they had done as recorded in the books. The sea gave up the dead that were in it, and death and Hades gave up the dead that were in them, and each person was judged according to what he had done. Then death and Hades were thrown into the lake of fire. The lake of fire is the second death. If anyone's name was not found written in the book of life, he was thrown into the lake of fire.

In this passage, the apostle John refers twice to being "judged according to what they had done," the first time indicating that the deeds of each person were written in "the books." Here the plural "books" is used to indicate the massive volumes, as it were, which are needed to record all the deeds of each person, thus leaving the reader with the impression that nothing escapes the scrutiny of God. Every thought, word and deed has been documented. This closely resembles the prophecy Jesus gave in Matthew 12:36-37, "But I tell you that men will have to give an account on the day of judgment for *every careless word* they have spoken. For by your words you will be justified and by your words you will be condemned." As Ecclesiasticus 28:1 states, "...for he keeps a strict account of their sins."

Most importantly, the above passage speaks of the "day of judgment." Whether this is the general judgment when all souls will stand before God, or the particular judgment when individuals will stand for judgment at death, is not specified.[3] Neverthe-

---

[3] The judgment in which all men must take part is called the general judgment (cf., John 5:28-29; 6:40, 44; 12:48; Acts 24:15; Romans 14:10-12; 1 Cor. 3:13-17; 2 Cor. 5:10; 2 Tim. 4:8; Rev. 20:11-15, Eccles. 16:12-14, 2 Macc. 7:14; et al). Catholic theology also teaches a "particular" judgment which determines the destiny of each man upon his death (Hebrews 9:27; Luke 16:22; 23:43;2 Cor. 5:8; Council of Trent, Ch. 7; Catholic Catechism, Sections 1021-1022). The judgment for sin at the particular judgment is analogous to the temporary detaining of a criminal in jail without bail prior to his formal trial date and conviction. He is put in temporary detention since the evidence against him is very great.

less, it is specified that the *justification* takes place at the judgment of that individual.

In regard to the final justification about which Jesus speaks in Matthew 12:37, such an end-time judgment that alone determines whether the individual is ultimately justified forces the Protestant concept of the one-time imputed act of justification into an acute contradiction. Protestant theology understands justification, once applied, as a past event never to be repeated. In Matthew 12:37, however, Jesus is using *justification* as continuing far beyond the initial stage of becoming a Christian, making it last, in fact, until the end of the person's life, at which time it will determined whether that person will be justified or not. Hence, justification cannot be a one-time event never to be repeated again, but must be understood as a continual process with its final outcome reserved for judgment day. The above passage also makes it clear that the criterion for the final justification is the individual's *works*.[4]

Paul used a similar context to explain the final justification in Romans 2:5-8,13:

> But because of your stubbornness and your unrepentant heart, you are storing up wrath against yourself for the day of God's wrath, when his righteous judgment will be revealed. *God will give to each person according to what he has done*. To those

[4] Scripture consistently judges a man's standing with God by the good or evil deeds he has done, not by his faith alone. Scripture, for example, in its evaluation of the kings of Israel and Judah, begins its record of each king's reign by stating whether he did good or evil, i.e., the king is judged on the basis of his works, whereas his belief in God is presupposed, e.g., "In the eighteenth year of the reign of Nebat, Abijah became king of Judah...He committed all the sins his father had done before him; his heart was not fully devoted to the Lord, as the heart of David his forefather had been" (1 Kings 15:1-3); "In the twentieth year of Jeroboam king of Israel, Asa became king of Judah, and he reigned in Jerusalem forty-one years...Asa did what was right in the eyes of the Lord, as his father David had done" (1 Kings 15:9-11); "This is what Hezekiah did throughout Judah, doing what was good and right and faithful before the Lord his God. In everything that he undertook in the service of God's temple and in obedience to the law and the commands, he sought his God and worked wholeheartedly. And so he prospered."

> who by persistence in doing good seek glory, honor and immortality, he will give eternal life. But for those who are self-seeking and who reject the truth and follow evil, there will be wrath and anger...For it is not the hearers of the law who *are just* with God, but the *doers of the law will be justified*.[5]

Here Paul connects God's positive evaluation of an individual's good deeds with the fact that they are presently "just," adding that they will also be "justified" in the future. Although a present justification is implicit in the phrase "will be justified,"[6] it cannot be confined only to the present given the unmistakable reference to the future judgment in the context of Romans 2:5-13. Paul couples the justification with "the day of God's wrath," which can only refer to the final judgment. Hence we see again that Scripture uses the term justification as a past, present and future event. This agrees with what we have learned in Chapter 4 that justification is a process with a beginning, middle, and end.[7]

As noted in chapter 1, some Protestant interpreters have serious difficulty with a passage like Romans 2:5-13. In fact, some see so much difficulty in reconciling a *faith alone* theology with Romans 2:5-13's teaching that one's justification is based on the evaluation of his deeds that they have deemed the passage a "hypotheti-

---

5 The NIV translation of Romans 2:13 shows a bias toward forensic, declaratory justification by translating the Greek future passive δικαιωθήσονται as "will be declared righteous" rather than the literal "will be justified," thus, the correction in the above verse.

6 I.e., it refers to the continuing stream of persons who come into existence on earth and will be justified during their lifetime.

7 It is granted that as Romans 2:13 applies to both the present and future, the future application has what Catholic theologian Joseph Fitzmeyer calls "the eschatological forensic nuance of justification" (*Jerome Biblical Commentary*, op. cit., p. 298). In this study, we have understood that God, as Father, deals with his children justly. For those who have been obedient sons, the Father will justly reward them with eternal life. For all those who have not been obedient to the Father, he will justly exhibit his divine wrath to the covenant breakers.

cal" teaching of Paul's.[8] In effect, they say Paul is giving a plausible means of salvation *only if* one could keep the law perfectly. Since no one can keep the law, then this way must be rejected in favor of "the way of faith" which Paul proceeds to explain in Romans 3-6. Even if a Protestant exegete is not predisposed to interpret Romans 2:5-13 as hypothetical, he still faces great difficulty in dealing with the many other passages in the New Testament which also teach that a person's eternal destiny is dependent on God's final evaluation of the person's deeds. Theoretically, if salvation is by *faith alone* there should be no room for a judgment based on works to determine that salvation.[9]

---

8 See chapter 1. Alister McGrath attempts to deal with Romans 2:13 by admitting that "justification has future as well as past reference (Rom. 2:13) and appears to relate to both the beginning of the Christian life and its final consummation." McGrath can say this because he views the future justification as a mere formality of a justification that was eternally guaranteed in the past. This is noted in his subsequent statement: "It [justification] is a complex and all-embracing notion which anticipates the verdict of the final judgment...declaring in advance the verdict of the ultimate acquittal." (*Christian Theology: An Introduction,* Oxford, UK: Blackwell Publishers, 1994, pp. 340-341). McGrath's failure to deal with the possibility of someone not being justified at judgment day who was previously justified on earth simply does not do justice to the context of Romans 2:5-13, or of Matthew 12:36-39. The Calvinistic framework within which McGrath is dealing forces him to exclude any such eventuality, yet Scripture is replete with references to this contingency. Other Protestant commentators attempt to deal with this anomaly by using the "already..not yet" approach to justification. Ralph P. Martin states: "There is an open-ended aspect of justification that keeps the final day of acquittal in view (1 Cor. 4:5). The continual tension 'already justified...not yet saved' was throughout Paul's correspondence and provides a basis for his paraenetic (hortatory) counsel to the churches" (*Reconciliation: A Study in Paul's Theology,* 1981, p. 109). As we critiqued McGrath's attempt to deal with this issue, we must similarly critique Martin. The 'already justified...not yet saved' formula only has meaning if the 'not yet saved' end of the equation includes the possibility of losing the initial justification and ending up 'not saved,' otherwise, Paul's injunctions and indictments are innocuous.

9 Some Protestants are quite candid about this embarrassing contradiction in their theology, e.g., P.T. O'Brien,"Justification in Paul and Some Crucial Issues of the Last Two Decades" in *Right With God*, ed., D.A. Carson, op. cit., pp. 70f. John Ellicott admits that if a future judgment of Christians were true it would be as hard to understand on a theological basis as the antinomy between God's sovereignty and human responsibility and other enigmas of the Christian faith (*Commentary on the Whole Bible*, Vol III (Grand Rapids: Zondervan) p. 380; For similar admissions see also C. K. Barrett, *Commentary on the Second Epistle to the Corinthians* (Harper and Row Publishers,

In chapter 5 of our study we showed the nature of justification to be one in which God infuses grace into the individual to transform him into a righteous person. When God justifies the individual and recognizes him as justified, it is because the individual possesses righteous qualities in his own person, instilled in him by God. This principle agrees precisely with Paul's statement in Romans 2:13 that justification is based on the good works of the individual. As God gives the final justification, he is recognizing the previous justification which transformed the individual into a righteous person and prompted him to do good works pleasing to the Father. A system that defines justification in terms of the moral quality of the individual has precedent for understanding passages like Romans 2:13 in this way. A system that does not view justification in terms of moral quality, such as the Protestant system of forensic imputation, has no basis for resolving how justification is determined by works in Romans 2:13.

Protestant Interpretations: Bad Works or Sins?

One of the ways Protestant interpreters deal with Scripture's emphasis on a future judgment of works is to relegate such evaluation exclusively to the area of Christian rewards. This theory, while apparently salvaging justification by *faith alone* since it accomplishes its primary purpose of securing the salvation of the Christian, also guarantees, in accord with Romans 2:13 and the like, that he can be evaluated for his works for the sole purpose, however, of determining what his status in heaven will be or what kind of personal reward, if any, he will receive.[10] Since the evaluation of works

[9 cont.] 1973), p. 161; *The Interpreters Bible*, ed., George Buttrick, Vol X (Abingdon Press), p. 332; *The Expositor's Bibl*e, ed., W. Robertson Nicoll, Vol. V (Southern Baptist Convention), p. 762. Some attempt to dismiss the contradiction, e.g., Charles Hodge, *An Exposition of the Second Epistle to the Corinthians* (Grand Rapids: Eerdmans, 1973), p. 125.

[10] e.g., John MacArthur, F. F. Bruce, Philip Hughes, Norman Geisler, Ralph MacKenzie, and most Dispensationalist and popular Evangelical thinkers. Some in the Reformed and Lutheran persuasions, e.g., Alford, Barnes, Hendriksen, Lenski, et al. have seen the same verses as representative of a universal judgment for salvation. Others, e.g., Calvin, C. Hodge, L. Berkhof, et al., refer to these judgments as issuing rewards to Christians but giving various degrees of punishment to the wicked.

does not determine his actual salvation, only his rewards after salvation, then salvation, according to this theory, is by *faith alone*. Hence, salvation is determined by faith; rewards are determined by works. The remaining Protestants who do not associate the judgment of works to personal rewards are satisfied to categorize the evaluation of works for salvation as enigmatic but not devastating to the *faith alone* theory.

Although Scripture teaches that God will reward Christians personally in heaven according to the degree of their faith and obedience on earth, it teaches neither that this event occurs in a separate judgment apart from that of final justification nor that God judges works merely to determine reward. In *all* the passages that specify a judgment for deeds, the primary purpose of the judgment is to determine the eternal destiny of the individual and only secondarily to determine the degree of reward or punishment. We cannot escape the New Testament's explicit teaching that God evaluates the works of the individual to determine his eternal destiny. In fact, no New Testament passage concerning the final judgment even mentions, let alone incorporates, *faith alone* as the criterion for entering heaven.

In previous chapters we have already cited many New Testament judgment passages. Some we will mention again, others we will look at in more detail to gain a more precise picture of the future judgment.

Jesus' teaching contains several references to judgment based on works as determining one's eternal destiny. John 5:28-29 states: "Do not be amazed at this, for a time is coming when all who are in their graves will hear his voice and come out — *those who have done good* will rise to live, and *those who have done evil* will rise to be condemned." In John 6:40 Jesus adds faith to works: "For my Father's will is that everyone who looks to the Son and believes in him shall have eternal life, and I will raise him up at the last day." Similarly, in John 12:48 Jesus states: "There is a judge for the one who rejects me and does not accept my words; that very word which I spoke will condemn him at the last day." Jesus says in Matthew 16:27: "For the Son of Man is going to come in his Father's glory with his angels, and then he will reward each person *according to what he had done*."

In Matthew 25:41-46, Jesus vividly describes the final judgment:

> Then he will say to those on his left, 'Depart from me, you who are cursed into the eternal fire prepared for the devil and his angels. For I was hungry and you gave me nothing to eat, I was thirsty and you gave me nothing to drink'...They also will answer, 'Lord, when did we see you hungry or thirsty'...He will reply, 'I tell you the truth, *whatever you did not do for one of the least of these*, you did not do for me.' Then they will go away to eternal punishment, but the righteous to eternal life.

We have also noted that Paul clearly teaches a judgment based on works that determines one's eternal destiny. First, in Romans 2:6-8:

> *God will give to each person according to what he has done*. To those who by persistence in doing good seek glory, honor, and immortality, he will give eternal life. But for those who are self-seeking and who reject the truth and follow evil, there will be wrath and anger.[11]

Though Romans 2 is more a general description of judgment, Paul in Romans 14 orients the same message specifically to his Christian audience. In Romans 14:10-12 he states:

> You, then, why do you judge your brother? Or why do you look down on your brother? For we will all stand before God's judgment seat. It is written, "'As surely as I live,' says the Lord, 'every knee will bow before me; every tongue will confess to God.'" So then, *each of us will give an account of himself to God.*

Similarly in 2 Corinthians 5:10: "For we must all appear before the judgment seat of Christ, that each one may receive what is

[11] This passage may be taken from Psalm 62:12, "...Surely you will reward each person according to what he has done" (cf., Job 34:11, Jeremiah 17:10, Daniel 12:1-2; Ecclesiasticus 35:24).

due him for the *things done while in the body, whether good or bad.*" 1 Corinthians 3:12-15 also uses similar language:

> If any man builds on this foundation using gold, silver, costly stones, wood hay or straw, his work will be shown for what it is, because the Day will bring it to light. It will be revealed with fire, and the *fire will test the quality of each man's work.* If what he has built survives, he will receive his reward. If it is burned up, he will suffer loss; he himself will be saved, but only as one escaping through the flames.

As noted above, in interpreting Romans 14:10-12, 2 Corinthians 5:10, and 1 Corinthians 3:12-15, most Protestants have attempted to confine these passages to a judgment for Christians in which their works are judged to determine the degree of personal reward they will receive in heaven.[12] In order to arrive at this interpretation, these commentators must make certain assumptions. First and foremost, they must assume that these passages which speak of judging an individual's bad works are not referring to sin. Therefore they must assume a distinction between "sin" and "bad works," since the Christian, who they say has already been justified and forgiven of sin by *faith alone* in Christ, cannot be judged for sin without creating a severe contradiction in *faith alone* theology.[13]

---

[12] Such commentators add the stipulation "if any" to specify that mediocre or lackluster Christians will not receive a personal reward. Thus, the judgment for their bad deeds does not result in any punishment but merely the loss of a personal reward.

[13] As representative of the majority of Evangelical thought on this notion, Evangelical James White states in reference to 1 Corinthians 3:12-15: "...What is judged is the sort or kind of works the Christian has done. Sins, and their punishments, are not even mentioned...The believer has already been judged with reference to sin in Christ Jesus, and has passed out of death into life, never to come into judgment for sin again (John 5:24). The believer's sins were judged in Christ Jesus. The remaining judgment is not about salvation, but it is about reward" (James White, *The Fatal Flaw*, 1990, pp. 179-180). Similarly, in reference to 1 Cor. 3:10-14 and 2 Cor. 5:10, Geisler and MacKenzie claim that "these works, however, have nothing to do with *whether* we will be in heaven, but only with *what status* we will have there" (*Roman Catholics and Evangelicals*, p. 237) and in reference to 1 Cor. 3:14, "The question here is not *sin* and its punishments but *service* and its rewards" (Ibid., p. 336). In reference to 2 Cor. 5:10, Philip Hughes states: "The apostle is not suggesting

There is a fatal flaw in this theory — Scripture *never* makes a distinction between bad deeds and sins. Each time bad deeds are mentioned they are in the context of sin. In light of this, it is no coincidence that proponents of the distinction between sins and bad deeds do not offer any definition of what constitutes a "bad deed" as opposed to what constitutes "sin," nor do they offer any Scriptural evidence for the distinction. They deliberately leave the categories of distinction ambiguous, because, as becomes apparent, they are making the distinction on purely arbitrary grounds. Since Protestant theology demands that a Christian not be judged for his sins, the only possible means to avoid the eventuality of his judgment for sin is to categorize his bad deeds as something other than sin. Such literature forces the reader to come away with a mental distinction that sounds theologically plausible, yet the authors offer not the slightest lexical or biblical analysis to prove their point.

In this total absence of lexical or biblical analysis, Protestant authors attempt to buttress their distinction between sin and bad deeds by appealing to the internal thought processes of the individual, otherwise known as one's "motives." In this scenario, there are no "bad deeds," per se, but only good deeds made bad by the doer's im-

[13 cont.] here the punishment of sin...The declaration of Christ's judgment seat is not the ultimate sentence of salvation or damnation; for it is the redeemed alone who stand before it..." (The New International Commentary on the New Testament: *Second Corinthians*, 1962, p. 182). More than anything else, the vehicle that has popularized the notion of a distinction between sin and bad works are the notes that appear in many Protestant Bibles, e.g., "The judgment of the believer's works, not sins, is under discussion here. His sins have been atoned for and are remembered no more forever...but every work must come into judgment...The result is reward or loss of reward, 'but he himself (the Christian) shall be saved'" *The New Scofield Reference Bible* (Oxford University Press, 1967), p. 1255. Geisler and MacKenzie also side-step the implications of reward and merit by stating, "While Protestants sometimes speak of the 'reward' of eternal life in the sense of something graciously given by God, they do not believe this reward is based on our works but only on God's grace received through our faith alone" (Ibid., p. 227, n. 3). This assessment ignores the clear language in numerous New Testament passages that reward is given specifically for one's works; not faith, or faith alone.

proper attitude. This views turns "bad deeds" into "bad motives," thus conveniently diminishing any ostensible impropriety.[14]

Such analysis contains numerous problems and unbiblical assumptions. First, Scripture never classifies "motives" as sinless occurrences. In fact, motives are potentially some of the worst kinds of sins. Scripture condemns anyone who does a "good deed" in front of others while harboring bad intentions or motives, and treats it as one of the highest forms of hypocrisy. Scripture admonishes us that motives and intentions must be as pure as the act itself. We must not be men-pleasers but God-pleasers. We must not show outward pleasantries and yet secretly despise the person for whom it is done or hope that by such external performance others will recognize us as holy. In fact, the entire Sermon on the Mount deals with the very issue of personal motives, showing that sin resides deep within the intentions of the heart, whether or not they reach fruition. For example, Jesus says it is not good enough to refrain from physical adultery, rather, one must also refrain from lust in the heart (Matthew 5:27-28). Both are sins. When we give alms, the motivation can never be to gain the accolades of men; rather, we are to give in secret for our heavenly Father who sees in secret (Matthew 6:2-4). In short, whether an action is sinful or not depends on the individual's motivation in doing that action.[15] Moreover, in defining sin, Scripture provides very wide parameters. On the one hand, Paul states in Romans 14:23 that "everything that does not come from faith is sin." Again, we see that unless the proper mental attitude is present, the action performed is sinful. On the other hand, James expands the boundaries of sin even further when he says in James 4:17, "Anyone, then, who knows the good he ought to do and doesn't do it, sins." Here again, the attitude of the individual is at the forefront. He "knows" what is good and what he ought to do but refuses to put his thoughts into action. Thereby he sins in his own thoughts — without ever lifting a fin-

---

[14] Thus, evangelical James White continues: "For the Christian, the idea of not being able to present to his Lord works that were done for the proper motivation, works that were built with gold, silver, and precious stones, is a terrifying one indeed. It is no light matter to stand before the judgment bar of Christ" (Ibid., pp. 179-180).

[15] See Catholic Catechism, Sections 1752-1753.

ger to harm someone.[16] Hence, Scripture certainly does not give any room for a distinction between "bad deeds" and sins, or between "bad motivations" and sins. Such distinctions arise purely because a *faith alone* theology demands them.

1 Corinthians 1-4

Be Careful How You Build The Temple of God

Not only does the general information in Scripture fail to support a distinction between "bad deeds" and sins, neither do the contexts of the verses in question. Paul introduces his teaching on the judgment of works in 1 Corinthians 3:12-17, and begins the chapter in 1 Corinthians 3:3 by pointing out the sins of "jealousy and quarreling" among the Corinthians: "You are still worldly. For since there is *jealousy and quarreling* among you, are you not worldly? Are you not acting like mere men? For when one says, 'I follow Paul,' and another, 'I follow Apollos,' are you not mere men?" Such is the context that begins his pericope concerning building on the foundation with gold, silver and costly stones or wood, hay and straw in 3:12 and leads into his description of the passing of that work through the fire in 3:13-15. Clearly the "fire tested works" are directly related to their "jealousy and quarreling" over Paul and Apollos, since Paul continues with the same theme of quarreling with one another over certain men in the church immediately following the passing through fire in 3:21-22: "So then, no more boasting about men! All things are yours, whether Paul or Apollos or Cephas or the world..."

In fact, the first four chapters of 1 Corinthians deal specifically with the sinful factions occurring in the Corinthian church. Already in 1:11-12, Paul mentions the "quarrels" created over the allegiances they are giving to certain men: "My brothers, some from Chloe's household have informed me that there are *quarrels* among you. What I mean is this: One of you says, 'I follow Paul,' another, 'I follow Apollos,' another, 'I follow Cephas,' another, 'I follow Christ.'" Three chapters later, Paul concludes on the same

16 "But all mortal sins, even those of thought, make men children of wrath and enemies of God..." (Council of Trent, DS 1680).

theme in 1 Corinthians 4:6: "Now, brothers, I have applied these things to myself and Apollos for your benefit so that...you will not take pride in one man over against another."[17] All in all, the first four chapters of the epistle contain four interspersed references to these false allegiances. In the midst of these is Paul's specific warning that their works will be tested by fire. It is apparent, then, that his warning of a judgment for works has something to do with the divisive disturbances going on in the church. In any case, he understands *jealousy* and *quarreling* as sins, as Scripture plainly teaches.[18] In fact, Paul mentions the same sins of jealousy and quarreling in 2 Corinthians 12:20 in addition to other sins in the Corinthian church that greatly concerned him: "I fear that there may be *quarreling, jealousy*, outbursts of anger, factions, slander, gossip, arrogance, and disorder." To these Paul adds in verse 21 the sins of a sexual nature that were prevalent in the church: "I am afraid that when I come again my God will humble me before you, and I will be grieved over many who have sinned earlier and have not repented of the impurity, sexual sin, and debauchery in which they have indulged."

It is also obvious that Paul was competing against ideas and teachings of worldly philosophy and wisdom. He notes this in a momentary discussion in Corinthians 1:18-2:16. Here Paul emphasizes the apparent "foolishness of the cross of Christ" over against the wisdom of the world or the quests of miracle seekers (1:18-24). Paul says that God chose the things that appear weak, (e.g., the cross and the gospel), to frustrate the wise of the world.

---

17 In reference to "applying these things to myself and Apollos" in 1 Corinthians 4:6, Paul may be suggesting that it was not necessarily to Paul and Apollos that the Corinthians were giving allegiance but to certain men in the Corinthian congregation who seemed to be wise and eloquent or who had created dissension by appealing to the teachings of one apostle over the other. The Greek word for "applied" is μετεσχημάτισα. The New Testament uses it 5 times referring to a "transformation" (cf., 2 Cor. 11:13, 14, 16; Phil. 3:21). Paul is saying, "I have figuratively transferred these things to myself and Apollos..." It is highly probable that Paul mentions Apollos as an example of eloquent speech (Acts 18:18-28). In any case, the Corinthians had a serious problems with "in-house" quarrels.

18 The word "jealousy" is from the Greek ζῆλος, frequently referring to "envy" in the context of serious sin, e.g., Rom. 13:13; 2 Cor. 12:20; Gal. 5:20; James 3:14,16. The word "quarreling" is from the Greek ἔπις and is also used in the context of serious sin, e.g., Rom. 1:29; 13:13; 2 Cor. 12:20; Gal. 5:20; 1 Tim. 6:4.

Such apparent "weakness" is the Lord's strength and wisdom. Paul's conclusion: rather than boast in men as they were so prone to do (1 Cor. 3:21), he exhorts them: "Therefore, as it is written: 'Let him who boasts boast in the Lord'" (1 Cor. 2:31). Paul continues to reiterate the same theme in 1 Cor. 2:1-16, making a sharp contrast between how the world thinks and how God thinks. The world simply does not understand God's ways.

Since Paul's digression to the discussion of worldly wisdom appears in the context of his warnings against the in-house quarreling of the Corinthians regarding their human allegiances, we can safely assume that some of these prominent and eloquent teachers in Corinth were either mixing the gospel of Christ with the philosophies and wisdom of the world, or, emasculating the gospel altogether. Since the gospel seemed weak and unattractive to the sensibilities of the cosmopolitan city of Corinth — a center of various Greek and Roman mythologies and cults — the Corinthian teachers may well have been tempted to placate their larger audience by integrating ideas from these false religions into Christianity. Different views of the Christian gospel led to different messages. Combined with the divisive personalities of the various teachers, the potential for factions and quarreling within the church was very great. It is no wonder, then, that Paul warns them, using himself as an example, that a teacher must only do God's bidding. They can't make the church grow by artificial means because only "God gives the increase" (1 Cor. 3:6-8). Not only is it futile to preach any other gospel than the one that God gives, God also exacts a stiff penalty for those who pervert the gospel. After warning them to build on the foundation of Christ alone, he charges them to examine their own work of building the temple of God. In so many words, 1 Corinthians 3:12 asks: Have they been building with gold, silver and costly stones, or have they been building with wood, hay, and straw? Paul implies that the jealousy and quarreling that resulted in the esteeming of men and the creation of factions and division, and the incorporation of worldly wisdom into the gospel of Christ crucified, are building the temple with wood, hay, and straw. Paul warns the Corinthians that they will be judged for such false building. On the one hand, he says that some will be judged and yet still be saved (1 Cor. 3:15). On the other hand, he warns that some will receive

God's ultimate punishment of destruction. In 1 Cor. 3:17 he writes, "If anyone destroys God's temple, *God will destroy him*; for God's temple is sacred; and you are that temple."[19]

In the next verses (1 Corinthians 3:18-21), Paul reiterates that both the worldly wisdom that has crept into the gospel and the factions created by esteeming men, are the two main reasons for God's destructive wrath. He writes: "Do not deceive yourselves. If any one of you thinks he is wise by the standards of this age, he should become a fool that he may be wise. For the wisdom of this world is foolishness in God's sight...So then, no more boasting about men."

To return to our main point, the context of 1 Corinthians 1-4 makes it abundantly clear that Paul considers the Corinthian's behavior as anything but non-sinful. It is precisely because of the Corinthian's sins that God could ultimately "destroy" them for destroying his church.

Romans 14

Romans 14 conveys the same message regarding sin in the midst of the church. This passage is significant since, as noted previously, verses 10-12 describe the final judgment of both those in the church and those in the world. As they do with 1 Corinthians 3:12-17, many Protestants view the *judgment seat of God* as one set aside exclusively for Christians in which the personal reward is allocated to each deserving recipient. Again, they accomplish this by claiming that God is not including the Christian's sins in the judgment, only his "good and bad deeds." As in 1 Corinthians 3 just analyzed, however, the context of Romans 14 does not support a distinction between sins and bad deeds that this view requires.

First, in the context of Romans 13:13-15:4, Paul takes great pains to list his grievances against the Romans, much having to do with the despising and mistreatment of the weaker brother. Paul begins in 13:13-14 by referring directly to their potential of sin:

---

[19] "...and in another those who at one time freed from the servitude of sin and the devil, and on receiving the gift of the Holy Spirit, did not fear to 'violate the temple of God knowingly' (Council of Trent, DS, 1690).

> Let us behave decently, as in the daytime, not in orgies and drunkenness, not in sexual immorality and debauchery, not in *dissension and jealousy*. Rather, clothe yourselves with the Lord Jesus Christ, and do not think about how to gratify the desires of the *sinful nature*.

Here we see the same sins that Paul mentioned in the Corinthian church, "dissension and jealousy." Paul calls these the "desires of the sinful nature." He then leads into his discussion of the weaker brother in Romans 14:1: "Accept him whose faith is weak, without passing judgment on disputable matters...The man who eats everything must not look down on him who does not, and the man who does not eat everything must not condemn the man who does." Apparently, the one who did not have a strict diet was "looking down on him" who did, and those with strict religious diets were "condemning" those who did not refrain from certain foods. This seriously divided the church, with each side hurling epithets at the other. Paul reiterates this in Romans 14:13 telling them to "stop passing judgment on one another"or "not to put a stumbling block or obstacle in your brother's way." In 14:15 he tells those who persist in this behavior that they are "no longer acting in love" and are "destroy[ing] your brother for whom Christ died." In 14:20 he warns them, "Do not destroy the work of God for the sake of food" and "it is wrong[20] for a man to eat anything that causes someone else to stumble."

With all these descriptions of sinful activity, especially under the heading of "dissension and jealousy" which are termed "sinful desires," we can only conclude that what is being evaluated at the judgment seat of Christ in Romans 14:10-12 is sin, and serious sin at that. Judging, destroying, not acting in love, putting stumbling blocks in the way, and condemning are all sinful attitudes and actions that will receive harsh judgment from God. The Roman Christians have exhibited just as much potential of "destroying the temple of God" as the Corinthians, and they too will "be destroyed" if they persist in such activity.

---

[20] The word "wrong" is from the Greek: κακόν which is normally understood as "evil" in the New Testament, e.g., Romans 2:9; 7:19-21; 1 Cor. 10:6; 1 Pet. 3:12.

We must also point out that in Romans 14:10-12 Paul has in view a judgment not for Christians but for the whole world. The context of Romans 14 refers mainly to Christians only because that is Paul's major concern — keeping Christians faithful to their commitments so that they don't fall away. He has, however, a global concern which he notes in Isaiah 45:23 in Romans 14:11 by quoting: "It is written: As surely as I live, says the Lord, every knee will bow before me; every tongue will confess to God." Paul's emphasis on "every knee" and "every tongue" carries an ominous tone for it implies that whether willingly or unwillingly, sinful or not sinful, everyone will appear in this judgment to be evaluated and to confess to God. Just prior to this warning in Isaiah 45:23, Isaiah warns Israel to turn from her idols and speaks of God as the Savior for them and the whole world, pleading with all men to turn to him and be saved:

> I am the Lord and there is no other. I have not spoken in secret, from somewhere in a land of darkness; I have not said to Jacob's descendants, 'Seek me in vain.'...a righteous God and a Savior; there is none but me. Turn to me and be saved, all you ends of the earth...by myself I have sworn, my mouth has uttered in all integrity, a word that will not be revoked; Before me every knee will bow; by me every tongue will swear. (Isaiah 45:18-23).

Isaiah 45:24 describes two outcomes to God's judgment in Isaiah 45:23: First: "They will say of me, 'In the Lord alone are righteousness and strength...But in the Lord all the descendants of Israel will be found righteous and will exult." Second, "All who have raged against him will come to him and be put to shame." The context makes clear that those who will be "put to shame" are the Egyptians, Cushites and Sabeans of verse 45:14 and who will be "put to shame and disgraced" in verse 45:16. Conversely, the hand of Cyrus in 45:1, a type of Christ, saves those in Israel.

We see from the universal context in Isaiah 45, which describes the two opposing outcomes of the judgment of God, i.e., salvation and damnation, that the context of the judgment seat of God in Romans 14:10-12 is more than one in which God merely issues rewards for good Christians. Rather it is a judgment in which God determines who is saved and who is not. If there are rewards to be given for the saved God will determine at that time, but inescapable is the fact that one must first pass the judgment of salvation before God gives him any further rewards.

2 Corinthians 5:10

Paul writes: "For we must all appear before the judgment seat of Christ that each one may receive what is due him for the things done while in the body, whether good or bad."[21] This is the second time Paul refers to the "judgment seat of Christ."[22] It is sometimes referred to as the *beema seat* since it comes from the same Greek word.[23] Unlike Romans 14:10, 2 Corinthians 5:10 specifies the "good or bad things done in the body." Thus, there is a definite polarity in the judgment. Paul assumes that some people will have good deeds and others bad, or that each person will have a mixture of good and bad deeds. Since, as noted in the study of 1 Corinthians 3:12-17, there is no distinction between "bad deeds" and sin, Paul's reference to "things done in the body" that are "bad" must refer to sin.

Paul introduces the concept of judgment in 2 Corinthians 5:9 when he says: "So we make it our goal to *please* him, whether we

---

21 "...the souls of those who depart in actual mortal sin immediately after their death descend to hell where they are tortured by infernal punishments, and that nevertheless on the day of judgment all men with their bodies will make themselves ready to render an account of their own deeds before the tribunal of Christ, 'so that everyone may receive the proper things of the body according as he has done whether it be good or evil' [II Cor. 5:10]" (*Benedictus Deus*, Benedict XII, DS 1002).

22 The reading "judgment seat of Christ" in 2 Corinthians 5:10 and "judgment seat of God" in Romans 14:10 both use the Greek word βῆμα The reading, "of God" in Romans 14:10 is supported by Codices ℵ,A,B,C,D,G, a 10th and 14th century minuscule. Manuscripts that contain "of Christ" are corrected version of ℵ and a questionable reading of C, along with codices P, Ψ, with 22 minuscules and a majority of early patristic witnesses.

23 The word βῆμα is used 12 times in the New Testament, referring twice to Jesus standing before Pilate (Mt. 27:19; John 19:13); the throne of Herod (Acts 12:21); the court of Gallio where Paul was taken (Acts 18:12,16,17); the court of Festus where Paul was taken (Acts 25:6,10,17); and a "foot of ground" in Acts 7:5. This latter reference is similar to the usage of βῆμα in the LXX in Deut. 2:5. The other two references to βῆμα in the LXX are Nehemiah 8:4 as Ezra stood on a wooden platform to speak to the people, and 2 Maccabees 13:26 which uses it in the same way.

are at home in the body or away from it." As we have learned previously in this study, the New Testament strongly emphasizes "pleasing" the Lord. Paul uses the same word in Romans 14:18 ("because anyone who serves Christ in this way is pleasing to God and approved by men"), referring to the "judgment seat of God" in Romans 14:10. Those who did not mistreat their brother did not anticipate being condemned at the judgment seat of God, and thus God considered them "pleasing." This shows us that "pleasing God" is more than just making God feel good; it entails our committed obedience to him, which, in turn, means that disobedience carries the ominous potential of condemnation. As Paul stated, "without faith it is impossible to *please* God." Faith is the beginning of our quest to please God. After faith we continue to obey him even as Paul says of Abraham, "by faith he obeyed." The same is true in 2 Corinthians 5:9-10. Paul says we must "please" God (by faith and obedience) while in the body because someday we must all stand before his judgment seat. If we are not pleasing to him, then we will be like the Israelites Paul mentions in 1 Corinthians 10:5: "God *was not pleased* with most of them; their bodies were scattered over the desert."

Since "pleasing" God implies we can also "displease" him, Paul continues in 2 Corinthians 5:11 with, "Since, then, we know what it is to fear the Lord, we try to persuade men." Although there may be some question whether Paul, as suggested by verses 12-13, is trying to persuade the members of the Corinthian church of his apostolic commission or perform his evangelical duty to warn the ungodly of God's future judgment, the latter seems the more likely since Paul uses the general reference "we persuade men" as opposed to the more specific "we persuade you."[24] Reinforcing this evangelical perspective, other New Testament references to judging good and bad deeds include *all* men.[25] The "fear" that is instilled in Paul because of this judgment is what motivates him to complete his task as an apostle. Similarly, he writes of himself in 1 Corinthians 4:4-5:

---

[24] The word "persuade" is used frequently in situations of witnessing to the ungodly, e.g., Acts 17:4; 18:4; 19:26; 26:28; 28:23.

[25] Romans 2:5-13; Matthew 16:27; John 5:28-29; Revelation 22:11-12.

> My conscience is clear, but that does not make me innocent. It is the Lord who judges me. Therefore judge nothing before the appointed time; wait till the Lord comes. He will bring to light what is hidden in darkness and will expose the motives of men's hearts. At that time each will receive his praise from God.

Here Paul states that "the Lord...judges me" but he further stipulates that that judgment is at "the appointed time...when the Lord comes." In other words, this future judgment takes place at the same time as the "judgment seat of Christ" in 2 Corinthians 5:10 which Paul says he "fears." The "bringing to light what is hidden in darkness" in 1 Corinthians 4:4 is the same as the judgment of the "bad deeds done in the body" in 2 Corinthians 5:10. Similarly, the "receiving his praise from God" is the same as being rewarded for "good deeds done in the body."

That Paul is concerned not only about fulfilling his evangelical duty to the world of men but also about keeping the Corinthians on the straight and narrow road to Christ is evident in how he speaks to the Corinthians in the remaining context. First, in 2 Corinthians 5:15, he suggests that there are some who have come to "live" in Christ but who must learn not to "live for themselves but for him who died for them..." He follows this in 5:20 with the plea, "We implore you on Christ's behalf: Be reconciled to God." One does not say this to a group of Christians unless he is worried about their spiritual disposition.[26] In the next verses, 2 Corinthians 6:1-2,

---

[26] Conversely, some commentators have pointed out that the word "you" in "implore you" is not in the original Greek (Philip Hughes, *2 Corinthians*, p. 217, et al.), therefore concluding that Paul is only showing his desire to evangelize the world using "we implore" as the action of ministry and "be reconciled" as the imperative for the world to repent. If Paul were merely defending his purpose in ministry, this reasoning would perhaps be appropriate. In this case, however, the Greek imperative "be reconciled" would be unnecessarily awkward when Paul could more easily have said, "we implore on Christ's behalf for men to be reconciled to God," in which the indicative "for men to be reconciled" would fit more naturally with the indicative "we implore." It is more likely that Paul is directing the Greek imperative "be reconciled" to close and expected hearers, i.e., he is commanding the Corinthians to be reconciled. Supporting this conclusion, in 2 Cor. 6:1, where Paul says, "we urge you not to receive God's grace in vain," the "you" appears emphatically in the Greek and refers exclusively to the Corinthians. The matter, then, of whom Paul is specifically addressing in 5:20 becomes academic.

confirm this concern; Paul does nothing short of warning them to be saved: "...we urge you not to receive God's grace in vain...I tell you, now is the time of God's favor, now is the day of salvation."

This is not the first time Paul issued such an ultimatum to the Corinthians. In 1 Corinthians 15:2 he writes: "By this gospel you are saved, if you hold firmly to the word I preached to you. Otherwise, you have believed in vain." In 2 Corinthians 13:2,5 his warning is even more direct:

> On my return I will not spare those who sinned earlier or any of the others...Examine yourselves to see whether you are in the faith; test yourselves. Do you not realize that Christ Jesus is in you — unless, of course, you fail the test.[27]

One of the more important questions arising from the above passage, as regards the present discussion, is what sins Paul has in view. Elsewhere, in 2 Corinthians 12:20, Paul lists the sins:

> I fear that there may be *quarreling, jealousy*, outbursts of anger, factions, slander, gossip, arrogance and disorder. I am afraid that when I come again my God will humble me before you, and I will be grieved over many who have sinned earlier and have not repented of the impurity, sexual sin and debauchery in which they have indulged.

This admonition has two significant dimensions. First, Paul specifies that "many" in the Corinthian congregation have sinned in these ways. Second, the admonition comes at the end of Paul's second letter, indicating that after a year's passage of time the Corinthians have not heeded the warnings of Paul from his first letter.[28]

We see, then, that from (1) the context of 2 Corinthians 5-6, (2) the general warnings in the Corinthian epistles; and (3) the reference to the *beema seat* the New Testament uses exclusively to de-

---

27 The phrase, "fail the test" is from the Greek ἀδόκιμος which is used 8 times in the New Testament in reference to extreme evil or apostasy (Rom. 1:28; 2 Tim. 3:8; Tit. 1:16; Heb. 6:8, 1 Cor. 9:27; 2 Cor. 13:5-7).

28 Guthrie, *New Testament Introduction*, op. cit., p. 441-442.

termine the guilt or innocence of the party in question rather than to issue rewards, that none of these references treat the judgment seat of Christ as a time or place in which God ignores the sins of Christians in favor of giving rewards for their good works. God will certainly reward good works, with the inheritance of heaven, with the beatific vision, and with the personal honor God will bestow individually on his faithful. However, there is no escaping the fact that God judges bad works as sins. If the sins are serious enough, the Scriptures stipulating a judgment for bad works specify that eternal damnation awaits him. In order to enter heaven, the Christian must show that he, in the state of grace, has "pleased" his Father by his faith and obedience. If he has not, he will be condemned with the wicked. He will be like the rebellious son of Deuteronomy 21:18-21, discussed earlier in chapter 6, who was disowned and handed over to the executioners for insubordination.

Confidence in the Day of Judgment

Although Paul makes it clear from 2 Corinthians 5:9-11 and other passages that we must both *please* God and *fear* his judgment at the same time, nevertheless the faithful and obedient Christian need not stand in abject terror of the future judgment. As we have learned throughout this study, God is a loving Father who does not evaluate us by the strict and uncompromising standards of law. Under his grace, God tolerates many of our sins and faults just as a father would do for his children. As we saw in Hebrews 12, God disciplines his sons. Though we fear his discipline, we also treasure it for it shows our Father's cares for us, otherwise, we would be like illegitimate orphans.

Scripture instructs us to be both confident and cautious as we anticipate the final judgment. In 1 John 4:16-17 the apostle writes:

> And so we know and rely on the love God has for us. God is love. Whoever lives in love lives in God, and God in him. In this way, love is made complete among us so that we will have confidence on the day of judgment, because in this world we are like him.

Here John establishes the same truth found in Hebrews 12. God loves us dearly. In fact, he *is* Love. As his children, we strive to imitate his love. As we show more and more love to God and our neighbor we are perfecting our love. The more we love the more we become like God. We have already noted that God shows his love for all mankind in both giving his Son for a redeemer and by causing his sun to shine on the good and bad alike. So too, we reflect the Son in our lives both by expressing our faith to others and by helping them in their needs. We must do this to friend and foe alike. The more we perfect this love, John says, the more we can then have "confidence in the day of judgment." The people in Corinth who had committed sins of jealousy and quarreling were not loving each other. Similarly, the people in Rome who were looking down upon and condemning their brothers for the kind of food they ate were not loving each other. It was precisely because of those unloving actions that Paul warned them about the judgment seat of Christ and how the fire will test their works. Simply put, "those who do not love will not see the kingdom of God."[29] John says we can have "confidence" in judgment only if we see ourselves imitating our heavenly Father's love.[30]

John speaks of the same confidence in 1 John 2:28: "And now dear children, continue in him so that when he appears we may be *confident* and unashamed before him at his coming," and in 1 John 3:21: "Dear friends, if our hearts do not condemn us, we have *confi-*

[29] Or, as St John of the Cross said, "At the evening of life, we shall be judged on our love" (*Dichos* 64). Catholic Catechism, Section 678: "Our attitude about our neighbor will disclose acceptance or refusal of grace and divine love. On the last day Jesus will say: 'Truly I say to you, as you did it to one of the least of these my brethren, you did it to me.'"

[30] As noted previously, faith has a communal aspect suggested by the pronoun "we." It is through the community of believers that the individual's confidence is expressed. 1 John 3:2 expresses the same communal confidence, "Dear friends, now we are children of God, and what we will be has not yet been made known." John warns in 1 John 3:3-10, however, that it is the individual who is the cause of the separation between himself and God. This is evident in his consistent references to "everyone who..." or "he who..." or "anyone who..."

dence before God."[31] Most such passages focus on the *feeling* a Christian can have toward his salvation and relationship with God. The opposite, according to 1 John 2:28, is feeling "ashamed" — a feeling our first parents had when they sinned against God (Gen. 3:8-10). John also speaks of "knowing" our salvation. In 1 John 5:13 he says, "I write these things to you who believe in the name of the Son of God; so that you may *know* that you will have eternal life, and that you may believe on the name of the Son of God."[32]

Paul, speaking of one of his friends who showed great love to him, hopes this friend, too, can be confident on the day of judgment. In 2 Timothy 1:16-18 Paul writes:

---

31 The word "confident" is from the Greek παῤῥησία, which appears 31 times in the New Testament. It is often used in contexts of "boldness" or "openness of speech," e.g., Matt. 8:32; Acts 2:29. A similar usage appears in its cognate παῤῥησιάζομαι (Acts 9:27-29; 13:46; 14:3). Παῤῥησία is used often in contexts which teach the Christian how he is expected to approach God, e.g., Eph. 3:12 — "in whom we have *boldness* and access with confidence by the faith of him"; Heb. 4:16 — "let us therefore come *boldly* before the throne of grace, that we may obtain mercy, and find grace to help in time of need"; Heb. 10:19 — "Let us draw near with a true heart in *full assurance* of faith..."; Heb. 10:35 — "do not throw away your *confidence;* it will be richly rewarded..." Another word Paul uses for such confidence is πεποίθησις, appearing in the above passage in Eph. 3:12 as "*confidence* by the faith of him." Paul often uses this word in relationships with people, e.g., 2 Cor. 1:15; 3:4; 8:22; 10:2.

32 "Know" is the Greek 2nd person, plural, subjuctive mood of εἰδῆτε from the second perfect tense system, of which the indicative οἶδα is commonly translated in classical and Koine Greek as "I know" or "you know." All the other Greek moods take their conjugations from the irregular verb εἴδω, which means "to see," and as such, οἶδα and εἴδω are used interchangeably in the New Testament. John does so in many cases (c.f., 1 John 2:20, 21, 29). These words appear over 600 times in the New Testament. In each case, the kind of "knowing" is conditioned by the entity doing the knowing and the thing known. John frequently speaks of factual knowledge about the Christian faith that can be known absolutely (e.g., 1 John 3:15 — "we know that no murderer has eternal life"; 1 John 5:20 — "we know also that the Son of God has come"), yet knowledge that is also conditioned on how God wishes to reveal it to us (e.g., 1 John 5:15 — "And if we know that he hears us, whatever we ask, we know we have what we have asked of him."). In any case, except for one instance, John invariably uses "know" in the plural verb form, denoting that it is the *community of believers* who possess the factual knowledge of the aspects of the Christian faith, not the individual possessing factual certainty of his own salvation without contingencies (cf., 1 John 2:20, 21, 29; 3:2, 5, 14, 15; 5:13, 15, 16, 18, 19, 20; 3 John 12, 14). John's use of "know" in the singular appears in 1 John 2:11. Here, however, he is speaking of an individual in sin who does not know where he is going.

> May the Lord show mercy to the household of Onesiphorus, because he often refreshed me and was not ashamed of my chains. On the contrary, when he was in Rome, he searched hard for me until he found me. *May the Lord grant that he will find mercy from the Lord on that day!* You know very well in how many ways he helped me in Ephesus.

Apparently, Onesiphorus was a man of great love. In two cities, Rome and Ephesus, he was right by Paul's side. It is Paul's desire that Onesiphorus find mercy from the Lord on "that day," i.e., judgment day. Even then, notice the reserve that Paul uses in his statement, "*May*[33] the Lord grant..." He is not stating absolutely that Onesiphorus will find mercy. Mercy entails pardon of sin and overlooking of faults. Only the Lord who sees into every dark corner of our lives can judge whether we deserve his mercy. In all probability Onesiphorus did find mercy from the Lord and entered the kingdom. But our point in fact is that he had to wait till that final day for the complete mercy of God to be applied to him.

As we have noted on 1 Corinthians 4:4-5, Paul also spoke in a guarded manner about himself. He reflected on the fact that while his own conscience was clear, God was the final judge of whether he was faithful to his ministry, because it is God alone who "exposes the motives of men's hearts." In 1 Corinthians 9:27, Paul admonishes himself to "beat his body and make it his slave" so that he does not become a "reprobate."[34] This passage is especially significant because the following context in 1 Corinthians 10:1-13 deals entirely with those Israelites who did fall away from their faith. Paul, who does not want to be like one of them, "beats his body" into submission so that it won't sin. He wants the wayward Corinthians to do the same.

Yet, despite this caution, Paul later shows a robust confidence about his life and what he expects God to do for him. In 2 Timothy 4:8 he writes:

---

33 From the Greek δῴη, the aorist, optative of δίδωμι.

34 As noted previously, the word translated by the NIV as "disqualified for the prize" is the Greek ἀδόκιμος which is used preponderantly in the New Testament in reference to apostasy.

> I have fought the good fight, I have finished the race, I have kept the faith. Now there is in store for me the crown of righteousness, which the Lord, the righteous Judge, will award to me on that day — and not only to me, but to all who have loved for his appearing.

Here Paul uses the same imagery of the boxer and runner in a race that he used in 1 Corinthians 9:27. There is a definite air of confidence here. Paul, as he writes the pastoral epistle of Timothy from prison in Rome, has come to the end of his life. He says as much in 2 Timothy 4:6: "...the time has come for my departure." Apparently, Paul knew of his impending martyrdom at the hands of the Roman officials. He could look back on his life now and know with confidence that he had been faithful and obedient to the Lord. Though God was his final judge, Paul's conscience was clear and his expectations were high. As far as he knew, he had not sinned grievously against the Lord. He knew that he loved the Lord with every fiber of his being and he knew that God loved him even more. With that confidence he was ready to meet his maker. Paul wants each of us to have the same confidence. However, we must note that it is not by faith *alone* that Paul has this confidence. Although Paul refers to "keeping the faith," this is accompanied by "fighting the good fight" and "loving his appearing." His confidence is based on the fulfillment of his work and on his continual love, not on faith alone.

A Merciful Father

Disciplining, Purging, and Saving His Sons

While the apostle John speaks of "confidence in the day of judgment," he says this in an epistle that consistently emphasizes understanding, avoidance and confession of sin.[35] No matter how high our confidence, no matter how high our aspirations, sin is constantly with us in this life. Though we fight mightily against it, what happens when sin enters our life? How does it affect our relationship with God and what are its consequences? We have already answered

[35] 1 John 1:7-10; 2:1-2; 3:4-9; 4:10; 5:16-18.

these questions to a large degree in the preceding chapters. We have discovered that for those who make shipwreck of their faith or sin grievously against God, God will judge them with eternal condemnation. God will no longer be a loving Father, but a wrathful Father, one who finally and completely disinherits his wayward children.

God also deals with the sins of his sons on earth by disciplining them, as Hebrews 12 teaches. The father's discipline of his children has a twofold purpose. On the one hand, discipline shows the child what he has done wrong and sets him on the path of obedience. It strengthens and purifies him. It makes him ready for the next event in life. On the other hand, discipline also punishes the child for his disobedience. While fathers are kind and merciful, they are also just. Their sense of justice demands that the child undergo a certain degree of payment for his infraction, however minor the infraction may have been. The father may spank the child, confine him to his room, or take away his allowance. Whatever the choice of punishment, it is for the good both of the child and the father. In order to make a proper entrance into the society and be a fine upstanding citizen, the child must be self-disciplined. It is the parent's job, by instilling this self-discipline, to prepare the child for the future.

God works in exactly the same way with his Christian children, except that he needs to prepare them for citizenship in the kingdom of heaven. Everything that God does prior to heaven he does to prepare us for heaven. Through the infusion of the grace of his Spirit at baptism, God renovates the inner essence of his children, extending it throughout their whole lives in preparation for the kingdom. For many, physical suffering plays a great part in that preparation. It refines the soul. For others, the everyday trials of life play a greater part in their preparation. Whatever the mode, God uses each event of life to mold us to be conformed to the image of his Son in preparation for his kingdom. Wisdom 12:2 states, "Therefore you correct little by little those who trespass, and you remind and warn them of the things through which they sin..." God cannot allow anyone into heaven who is not prepared for it. As the apostle John said in Revelation 21:27, "Nothing impure will ever enter it..."

In order to be a fine upstanding citizen in the kingdom of heaven, the child of God must be disciplined, with punishment, for his infractions against the rules of the Father's house. This is for his own good and the good of all the people with whom he will interact for eternity. Part of this discipline is accomplished on earth. Frequently, the Scripture speaks of this discipline and punishment as purging fire. In 1 Peter 1:7 the apostle writes:

> ...until the coming of the salvation that is ready to be revealed in the last time. In this you greatly rejoice, though now for a little while you may have had to suffer grief in all kinds of trials. These have come so that your faith — of greater worth than gold, which perishes even though *refined by fire* — may be proved genuine and may result in praise, glory and honor when Jesus Christ is revealed.

Peter uses the same imagery in 1 Peter 4:12: "Dear friends, do not be surprised at the fiery trial[36] you are suffering, as though something strange were happening to you."

God's fire can be used in two ways: for purification or for destruction. Scripture often refers to the latter as the "unquenchable fire" of eternal destruction.[37] The former is used by Peter in both of the above passages as he describes the trials, and thus the discipline, from the Lord as equivalent to being passed through fire like gold. Just as one removes impurities of gold by passing it through fire so that the dross will melt away, so God passes us through fire to dissipate our sinful impurities.[38] This fire is "quenchable" because when the impurities are dissipated the fire is removed.

Scripture also speaks of a purging fire after death. It is a fire similar to the purging fires we sustain on earth, for this fire also prepares us to take our place in the heavenly kingdom.[39] Paul alludes to these postmortem fires in 1 Corinthians 3:13, 15:

---

36 The NIV translation "painful trial" is replaced here by "fiery trial." The Greek word behind this phrase is πυρώσις which is a derivative of the word πυρ ("fire"); πυρώσις is used two other times, e.g., Revelation 18:9,18 in the context of burning fire.

37 cf., Mark 9:43-49; Luke 3:17; Matt. 18:8-9; 25:41.

38 The Old Testament uses the same imagery of "purging fire," e.g., Zechariah 13:9; Malachi 3:2; Daniel 12:10; Isaiah 48:10; Wisdom 3:5-9.

39 "...but after death they undergo purification, so as to achieve the holiness necessary to enter the joy of heaven" (Catholic Catechism, Section 1030). "The Church gives the name *Purgatory* to this final purification of the elect, which is entirely different from the punishment of the damned" (CC, Section 1031).

> The work of each person will become manifest, for the Day will declare it because it will be revealed by fire and the fire will test each person's work of what sort it is. If anyone's work remains which he built on, he will receive a reward. If anyone's work is consumed, he will suffer a penalty,[40] but he will be saved in the same way as through fire.[41]

Various modern translators, not understanding the intent of 1 Corinthians 3:15, and trying to fit it into a *faith alone* theology, have had much difficulty in giving an accurate picture of what Paul is saying. The major difficulty Protestant translators face is always the

40 Liberty has been taken to include the words "suffer a penalty" in place of the traditional "suffer loss" and the words "in the same way" in place of the traditional "yet so." This alternate translation will help others not familiar with this concept to see more clearly the reasons for this particular belief in Catholic theology. Though "suffer loss" and "yet so" are legitimate translations, the exclusive use of this translation tends to limit the possibilities for a fuller meaning that becomes apparent when one investigates and applies the alternative definitions for these Greek words. The word ordinarily translated "suffer loss" derives from the Greek verb zhmi'w and appears 6 times in the New Testament in contexts of "loss," "harm" or "damage" (cf., Matt. 16:26; Mark 8:36; Luke 9:25; Phil. 3:8; 2 Cor. 7:9). The noun cognate zhmàa appears 4 times in the New Testament in much the same way (Acts 27:10, 21; Phil. 3:7, 8). Although the "suffering loss" or "damage" for the laborer could certainly be in view in 1 Cor. 3:15 due to the fact that the work is destroyed by fire, penalty for the laborer can also be in view due to the alternate meaning of zhmi'w in reference to punishment. The Septuagint uses the alternate meaning of zhmi'w more frequently. The LXX uses the verbal form zhmi'w 6 times. 5 of these usages refer exclusively to the concept of punishment or punishment by fine (i.e., Exodus 21:22 — "the offender must be fined"; Deut. 22:19 — "they shall fine him"; Prov. 17:26 — "to punish" (coupled with "flogging officers"); Prov. 19:19 — "a hot tempered man must pay the penalty"; Prov. 21:11 — "when a mocker is punished"). The last reference, Prov. 22:3 — "the simple keep going and suffer for it" could mean either that stupidity has natural consequences or that one will eventually face civil punishment for his folly. Various translations render zhmi'w in Prov. 22:3 as "punishment" (eg., KJV, NASB, NEB), or as "suffer" (e.g., ASV, RSV, NIV, Douay-Rheims). In any case, the variances in these translations show the semantic range or interplay of the word zhmi'w. Either zhmi'w can refer to suffering loss or punishment, or to suffering as a form of punishment. The LXX uses the noun cognate zhmàa 3 times: once in 2 Kings 23:33 in reference to the imposition of tribute money; another in Prov. 22:3 in reference to the suffering of the simpleminded; the last in Ezra 7:26, in a more revealing translation of zhmàa as "confiscation of property" or "fining of property." More significant is the context of *punishment* within which zhmàa is contained. The entire verse reads, "And whosoever shall not do the law of God, and the law of

explicit reference to a judgment of the individual's works. As noted earlier in this chapter, many resolve this anomaly by relegating the judgment of works to the arena of personal rewards for Christians, claiming that the bad works implied in the passage do not refer to sin. In dealing with these difficulties, some Protestant translators have attempted to picture the fire of 1 Corinthians 3:15 as one which singes the coattails, as it were, of one escaping from a burning building. This is evident in the New International Version's rendering, "he himself shall be saved, but only as one escaping through the flames"; the New English Bible's "and yet he will escape with his life, as one might from a fire" and the Today's English Version's "as

[40 cont.] the king readily, judgment shall be taken upon him, whether for death or for chastisement, or for a fine of his property, or casting into prison." Here we see clearly that zhmi'w can mean corporal punishment for sins against God and crimes against the society. Greek lexicons also recognize this distinction as Walter Bauer lists "punishment" as the alternate meaning. Significantly, Bauer references 1 Cor. 3:15 as the New Testament support for the alternate meaning. He also references Lysias 31, 26 al.; the Orientis Graeci Inscription 669, 40; the Tebtunis Papyri 5,92; the Theologiesches Worterbuch, II, 890, edited by Gerhard Kittel; the lexicon by Moulton and Milligan; Josephus's Antiquities, 15, 16; and Proverbs 19:19; all of which support the alternate meaning (Bauer, op. cit., p. 338).

[41] The translation "in the same way" is used in place of the traditional "yet so," in order to bring out the grammatical nuance of the Greek adverb οὕτως as it modifies the verb ζημιωθήσεται ("shall be saved"). The New Testament uses the adverb οὕτως over 150 times. It can be translated as "even so" (Matt. 24:33; Luke 21:31); "in the same way" (Matt. 17:12; Luke 15:7,10; 17:10; Rom. 6:11; 1 Cor. 2:11), or simply "so" (John 3:16). It is pointing out in what manner the person is saved, e.g., "he is saved thusly." The adverb must get the complete direction of its modification from the remaining noun phrase δὲ ὡς διὰ πυρός ("as through fire"). When accompanied by the subordinate phrase, the adverb οὕτως seeks to direct the action of the verb ζημιωθήσεται. The total connection between the subordinate phrase ("as through fire") and its preceding verb ("shall be saved") is understood by the usage of "fire" in the previous verse, i.e., 1 Cor. 3:13. There the fire tests or refines the *work* of the individual. Consequently, the fire of 3:15 is also proving or refining but with its object of consumption now in the individual himself. Hence, the thrust of the passage can be stated thus: as the *work* of the individual is brought through the fire to be tested, "in the same way," the *individual* is brought through the fire in order to be saved. The time reference for bringing the individual through the fire is limited to "the day" (in this case, the particular judgment) and prior to his entrance into heaven.

if he had escaped through the fire."[42] The impression is that the individual was saved, but just barely. The flames, though perhaps singeing him, did not harm or change him in any way. The major problem with this conception, especially with the connotation that the salvation was "just barely attained," is that it tends to contradict the major dictum of *faith alone* theology, i.e., that works do not serve as a criterion for one's salvation. There is no room in forensic *faith alone* theology for salvation to come by degrees.

The contradiction in Protestant interpretations and translations of 1 Corinthians 3:15 becomes even more noticeable when we analyze God's warning in 1 Corinthians 3:17 of his destruction of the individual for destroying the temple.[43] In this case, the individual is not saved by fire but is destroyed. This shows that God does not judge the improprieties of the individual in 3:15 in the same way as for the individual in 3:17, since he still saves the former but not the latter. Ironically, the Protestant conception of "just barely being saved" in 3:15 is forced to accommodate the suggestion in 3:17 that the same individual could actually lose his salvation for worse deeds.[44] Yet Protestant theology simply has no theological rationale for determining one's salvation by the degree of good or bad works. We can understand why Protestant theology has had an extremely difficult time translating and interpreting 1 Corinthians 3:13-17. It just does not fit into the mold of Paul's thinking as Protestants normally understand it.

---

[42] Other translations have not taken such liberties: KJV: "yet so as by fire"; RSV: "but only as through fire"; NASB: "yet so as through fire"; Douay-Rheims: "yet so as by fire."

[43] Paul uses a play on words in 1 Corinthians 3:17. The Greek word for "destroy" is φθείρει which appears seven times in the New Testament. The common meaning is "corrupt" (e.g., 1 Cor. 15:33; 2 Cor. 7:2; 11:3; Eph. 4:22; Jude 10; Rev. 19:2). Lexically, it can refer to "destroy, ruin, corrupt, spoil" in which the meaning of "destroy" or "to be doomed to destruction" is reserved to 1 Cor. 3:17 (Walter Bauer, *A Greek English Lexicon of the New Testament and Other Early Christian Literature*, eds. Gingrich and Danker, p. 857). The cognate φθορά, appearing ten times in the New Testament, also shows the interplay between "corruption" and "destruction" (e.g., Rom. 8:21; Gal. 6:8; Col. 2:22; 2 Peter 2:12). The preponderant usage in the LXX is "destruction" (e.g., Ex. 10:15; Lev. 19:27; Deut. 34:7; 2 Sam. 20:20; 1 Chr. 20:1; Job 15:32; Isa. 24:3-4; 54:16; Jer. 3:19). Ultimately, Paul would have eternal destruction in view in 1 Cor. 3:17.

[44] Protestant literature is virtually silent regarding the connection between the salvation offered in 1 Cor. 3:15 and the condemnation stipulated in 1 Cor. 3:17.

Relating the connection between 1 Cor. 3:15 and 1 Cor. 3:17, which speak of testing and destruction by fire, to the general context, we see that 1 Corinthians 1-4 emphasizes the false allegiances in the church, the jealousy and quarreling among them, and the dabbling in worldly wisdom. Instead of working together, the Corinthians were competing against one another, vying for leadership in the church at the expense and subjugation of their brothers. Using planting-and-watering imagery, Paul explains that there should be no such competition; rather, each should realize that it is God's field and God's building and only he can make things grow. In verses 5-9 Paul writes:

> What, after all, is Apollos? And what is Paul? Only servants through whom you came to believe — as the Lord has assigned to each his task. I planted the seed, Apollos watered it, but God made it grow. So neither he who plants nor he who waters is anything, but only God, who makes things grow. The man who plants and the man who waters have one purpose, and each will be rewarded according to his own labor. For we are God's fellow workers; you are God's field, God's building.

Clearly Paul's concern is people. He calls them "God's building" in 3:9, reinforces it in 3:16 by the question, "Don't you know that *you yourselves are God's temple...*" and reiterates it again in 3:17 in the phrase, "and *you are that temple*." Since the temple is God's, they must be extremely careful how they help construct that building. In 1 Corinthians 3:10-11, Paul warns each one to "be careful how he builds" on the "foundation of Jesus Christ." If they perpetuate a gospel of quarreling rather than love, a gospel of division rather than unity, or a gospel of worldly wisdom rather than the message of Christ crucified, then either they have "laid another foundation" or they have begun to build on the present foundation with wood, hay, and straw instead of gold, silver, and costly stones. Ezekiel had used similar imagery in his address to Israel. In Ezekiel 13:10-16 the prophet writes:

> ...and one builds a boundary wall, and they plaster it with untempered mortar — say to those who plaster it with untempered

> mortar, that it will fall...Surely, when the wall has fallen, will it not be said of you, 'Where is the mortar with which you plastered it...So I will break down the wall you have plastered with untempered mortar and bring it to the ground, so that its foundation will be uncovered; it will fall, and you shall be consumed in the midst of it. Then you shall know that I am the Lord. (NKJV.)

Ezekiel 28:28-30 uses similar language:

> Her prophets plastered them with untempered mortar, seeing false visions and divining lies for them, saying, 'Thus says the Lord God,' when the Lord had not spoken...Therefore I have poured out My indignation on them; I have consumed them with the fire of My wrath; and I have recompensed their deeds on their own heads, says the Lord. (NKJV.)

Here we see an uncanny resemblance to the language of Paul in 1 Corinthians 3:10-17. Building with "untempered mortar" is the same as building the temple of God with "wood, hay and straw." The "false visions" and the pseudo-prophets who say, 'Thus saith the Lord' in Ezekiel's time resemble those in Corinth who come with a gospel of worldly wisdom instead of "Christ crucified." The "uncovering of the foundation" is similar to Paul telling the Corinthians to be certain they are building on the "foundation of Jesus Christ." The "fire of his wrath that will consume them" resembles the warning of Paul in 1 Cor. 3:17 that God will "destroy those who destroy his temple." The same problems and the same warnings exist — just at different times. It comes as no surprise that Paul takes great pains to compare the plight of Israel to that of the Corinthians, in 1 Corinthians 10:1-13, and in particular in verses 5-6,11:

> Nevertheless, God was not pleased with *most* of them; their bodies were scattered over the desert...We should not commit *sexual immorality*, as some of them did — and in one day twenty-three thousand of them died...Now these things occurred as examples to keep us from setting our hearts on evil things as they did...These things happened to them as examples and were written down as warnings for us, on whom the fulfillment of the ages has come.

We have already noted that these were not just idle warnings from Paul. The Corinthians were already engaging in sexual immorality, as 2 Corinthians 12:21 makes clear: "I am afraid when I come again...I will be grieved over *many* who have sinned earlier and have not repented of the impurity, *sexual sin,* and debauchery in which they have indulged." Obviously, the Corinthians had already fallen into the same sexual sins as Israel. A remarkable feature in this comparison is Paul's statement in 1 Corinthians 10:5 that God was not pleased with "most" of the Israelites, and then his reference in 2 Corinthians 12:21 to "many" in the Corinthian church who have likewise sinned. Further, those in Corinth were refusing to repent of their sin, just as the people in Israel who were eventually destroyed.

In all these warnings Paul is trying to show the Corinthians that they cannot just "play church." To be a custodian of the gospel is serious business. The eternal destiny of every individual who comes in contact with the gospel hangs in the balance. That being the case, the custodian must be absolutely faithful in the propagation of that gospel as God gave it, as well as obedient to it himself. If not, then he will face destruction by God for destroying the temple, as 1 Corinthians 3:17 makes clear.

God, as a merciful Father who looks at his people through the eyes of grace, does not penalize every single infraction with eternal damnation. Such punishment is reserved for continual or very serious offenses against his temple.[45] For offenses within the category

---

[45] This precedent was established in Old Testament civil law that required death for capital crimes. Deuteronomy 21:22, "If a man guilty of a capital offense is put to death...," e.g., for adultery (Deuteronomy 22:22); for murder (Numbers 35:30), kidnaping (Deuteronomy 24:7), insubordination (Deuteronomy 21:18-21; Leviticus 20:9), blasphemy and idolatry (Numbers 4:14; Deuteronomy 13:10; 17:5), contempt for judge or priest (Deuteronomy 17:12), false prophecy (Deuteronomy 18:20), false accusation (Deuteronomy 19:16-21), sacrificing children (Leviticus 20:1-5), sexual intercourse with the same sex or relative (Leviticus 20:11-13); marrying a woman and her mother (Leviticus 20:14); bestiality (Leviticus 20:16), sexual intercourse during menstruation (Leviticus 20:18), sorcery and spiritism (Leviticus 20:27). Death could be given only when there were two or three witnesses to the offense (cf. Deuteronomy 17:6; 19:15; 22:22; 24:1-4; Numbers 5:13; 35:30; Deuteronomy 21:1-9; John 8:17). For noncapital crimes, punishment was given in accord with the offense (Deuteronomy 25:1-5). Greater punishment for more serious offenses is evident in the New Testament, e.g., Matthew 23:14 (TR), Mark 12:40; Luke 20:47; 12:47; 10:12; Heb. 10:26; 2 Pet. 2:20; John 19:11; 1 Thess. 2:16; James 3:1.

of eternal damnation, however, it is just a matter of measuring the extent of the damage done and meting out its appropriate punishment. The more one destroys God's temple, the harsher will be his eternal punishment. In 1 Corinthians 3:13-15, however, the person has sinned and produced some bad works that are burned in the fire, yet his improprieties are not so great as to incur the "destruction" in 1 Corinthians 3:17. Naturally the question arises: if a man suffers penalty for his bad works, will God still allow him to be saved? The answer is "yes," but it is a *qualified* yes. He can only be saved through the same fire that burned away his bad works. The bad works were his, not another's and thus responsibility is his. He is the source of the works; therefore the source must also be tested and purified of evil. Hence, he, as well as his works, must pass through the fire. If all he is is evil, then the fire will consume him in eternal destruction. If his constitution is only partly evil, then the fire will purge him of any remaining evil in order to prepare him to be a member and builder of God's eternal temple — a man of pure gold, silver, and costly stones who produces the same. This is why Jesus says in John 5:29, "those who have *done good* will rise to live, and those who have *done evil* will rise to be condemned."

This understanding of the context also shows why the notion conveyed by the translation "suffer loss" in 1 Corinthians 3:15 is somewhat inadequate. One could suffer loss of work without the question being raised whether he would still be saved. When penalty is introduced into the picture, however, one would then have to know the degree of penalty to be suffered, which, according to the context of the passage, depends on the degree of offense. We must know whether the individual will be given a temporary sentence and eventually be set free or be sentenced to eternal imprisonment. If the focus of the passage were only on whether the individual will receive a personal reward, then the matter of salvation would not be an issue, and certainly the eternal destruction of 3:17 would be a totally foreign element in the discussion. However, it is precisely the reference to the gain or loss of salvation (i.e., "he will still be *saved*" in 1 Cor. 3:15) that puts this passage into a totally different dimension than one merely concerning the degree of personal reward. Moreover, because 3:17 requires a penalty for sin, then it is only logical that 3:15 would also require a penalty, albeit, less severe. Though reward is certainly a facet of the passage, it is only secondary. The main question is whether the individual being judged will, in the end, be at the place where rewards will finally be issued. If he is "destroyed" as verse 3:17 stipulates, he certainly will not be there. As the false prophets in Ezekiel's time were destroyed by God for building with defective material, Paul tells the Corinthians in 1 Corinthians 10:6,11 that those incidents were written down precisely to warn those in the new age that they too, will be destroyed if they build with defective material and thereby destroy God's temple.

In conclusion, we see that 1 Corinthians 3:10-17 specifies the three destinations which will be the ultimate outcomes of judgment day for each individual. Those in 3:14 whose work survives the fire receive their reward immediately. Although part of the reward may be the eternal companionship of the very people that we persuaded to seek the kingdom of God,[46] the ultimate reward is the kingdom of God itself. Second, those in 3:15 who see some of their works burned and yet have not committed capital sins against God, must first pass through the purging fires both as a penalty for their sins and as a preparation for the eternal kingdom, for, as the apostle John said, "nothing impure will enter." Finally, those in 3:17 who have deliberately and maliciously destroyed the temple of God without repentance will themselves be destroyed in the eternal and unquenchable fire of God, never to escape.[47]

Summary Points

1) Justification is a process with beginning, middle, and end. The end of justification takes place at the final judgment. It is here that the entire life of faith and obedience is judged by God. The Scripture often speaks of God judging our works at the end time judgment to determine our eternal destiny. If the individual is in serious, unrepentant sin when he meets the judgment he will be

---

[46] In certain passages, e.g., 1 Corinthians 9:18-23; Philippians 4:1, Paul speaks of the people who were converted and remained faithful as his "reward."

[47] Regarding the Catholic teaching of Purgatory and its Patristic evidence, see **Appendix 8**.

eternally condemned. If the individual has "pleased" God by his faith and works, he will receive the eternal inheritance.

2) Attempts by Protestants to minimize the judgment of the individual's works to the receiving of personal rewards are thoroughly unbiblical. Often such attempts are made by positing a distinction between sin and bad works in an effort to dismiss sins from being judged at the final judgment. Scripture does not support a distinction between sin and bad works. The evaluation of bad works is for the primary purpose of determining the eternal destiny of the individual, and secondarily to determine his personal reward.

3) If he is living a good Christian life, loving God and his neighbor as he should, the Christian can have confidence that God will justify him. He cannot, however, have absolute assurance that he will be saved precisely because he may fall into sin, depart from the faith, and remain unrepentant until death.

4) God is a merciful Father who desires to prepare his sons and daughters for citizenship in the kingdom of heaven. In order to prepare us, God sends us firey trials and sufferings in this life so that we may grow in his grace. God will also purge any remaining corruption from us in post-mortem purgatorial fires.

Chapter 9

Will "Faith Alone" Be All Alone?

To close this study we will now analyze *faith alone* theology from a historical perspective, addressing and critiquing the Reformation personalities that began the movement as well as those up to the present day who maintain a defense of the classical Protestant position on justification. This chapter is designed to reveal the extremely diverse and often very confusing notions of justification prevalent in historic Protestant theology, including current Evangelical and Fundamentalist thought. It is our hope that as the contradictions and inadequacies of faith alone theologies are revealed, the reader will be more disposed to reevaluate Protestant theologies, and to develop a new and healthy respect for Catholic theology.

Martin Luther (1483 - 1546)

Studying the history of a particular person and time always presents a problem. The reason: we weren't there. We are at the mercy of the perceptions and opinions of those who went before us. Studying the literature on the life and beliefs of Martin Luther is no exception. Depending on the author's slant, Luther can be viewed with everything from total disgust, to sympathy, to unqualified admiration.[1] Especially today, 475 years removed from the

---

1 Joseph Ratzinger, presently Cardinal and head of the Sacred Congregation for the Doctrine of the Faith at the Vatican, wrote in 1970: "The fact is that today both sides of the two faiths (Catholic and Lutheran) to a great extent regard it as necessary to speak of Luther only in terms of praise. But does the effort to understand one another exclude a critical study if the cause of truth is served in this way? Is it not true that, besides the known differences in the tenets of the Catholic and Lutheran religions, there is a basis of differences even in the writings of Luther himself?" (Preface to Paul Hacker's *The Ego in Faith: Martin Luther and the Origin of Anthropocentric Religion* (Chicago:

storm of the Reformation, opinions vary widely as to precisely what Luther believed as well as how his Reformation peers and his opponents in the Catholic Church understood his beliefs.[2] Not surprisingly, some of Luther's writings conflict with or modify other writings.[3] This is no surprise, since Luther wrote over a period of many years and was one of the most prolific writers in the history

[1 cont.] Franciscan Herald Press, 1970), p. v). In the same work, Hacker writes: "There is no one today who denies that there are genuinely Christian values in Luther's teaching...But with the emergence of a new idea of the nature of faith, a thorough mutation of Luther's theology and spirituality set in...This concept was a seed whose germinative power has remained unimpaired throughout four and a half centuries. It is the inchoate form of anthropocentric theology...There are elements in Luther's thought that are consistent with the gospel and, accordingly, with Christian unity, and there are others that are not so. Only if we succeed in eventually isolating the negative elements can we properly take up the positive suggestion" (p. xiii).

[2] Even Catholic scholars do not agree in their assessment of Luther. Starting with the work of John Cochlaus' *Commentaria de actis et scriptis Martini Lutheri* in 1549, various biographies and evaluations of Luther have appeared and continue down to the present day. Those written in the 1900s include Denifle (1904), Grisar (1911), Ganss (The Catholic Encyclopedia), O'Hare (1916), Kiefl (1917), Fisher (1929), Jedin (1931), Clayton (1937), Lortz (1939), Herte (1943), Hessen (1946), Adam (1947), Richter (1954), Sartory (1961), Rix (1983), et al. These works offer widely differing assessments of Luther and his contribution to Christendom. Recently, American psychologist Erik Erikson analyzed Luther and gave him a very unfavorable evaluation (*Young Man Luther* (New York: Norton, 1958). Herbert David Rix in his 1983 book: *Luther: The Man and the Image*, uses modern psychological terms to describe Luther and his actions. For more detailed information, see **Appendix 1**.

[3] Catholic theologian Paul Hacker points out, for example, that in 1520 Luther's notion of "fides apprehensiva," in which the individual is taught to "seize" salvation by "stating with certitude" God's favor toward himself, was said to be comparatively easy to attain. But in some of his later works of the late 1520s and early 1530s, especially in the commentaries on Isaiah and Galatians, Luther described the attainment of "certitude" as very difficult, and he emphasized that the believer must continually struggle in his mind to reach the consoling conviction of being in God's favor (*Catholic Scholars Dialogue with Luther*, ed. Jared Wicks, S.J. (Chicago: Loyola University Press, 1970), p. 87). Of his own writings Luther says, "My book ought by no means to be placed in the library, especially not the earliest books which I wrote at the beginning, for they are offensive not only to my adversaries but also to me" (in *Table Talk*, 1536, LW 54, 213). Luther esteemed his works *De Servo Arbitrio* ("The Bondage of the Will"), and his Catechism, as his best works.

of Christendom.[4] Add to this the polemical atmosphere in which Luther wrote and it is easy to see why his views might be open to variation and misinterpretation.

Although the issue of indulgences could be considered the spark that ignited a reformation, the material which it burned had laid on the refuse pile for quite some time. Contrary to popular opinion, Luther did not reject the basic doctrine of Indulgences when he posted his 95 theses on the church door in Wittenberg, Germany. It was the abuse of the doctrine, characterized by what Luther called the "selling of salvation," that was the main objection. Luther did not feel compelled to reject the doctrine of Indulgences until some years later after he had been excommunicated over other important issues, e.g., free will, imputed justification, the sacrament of penance, and the authority of the Pope. In reality, the 95 theses "did not all represent his personal views, some of them indeed contrary to his views, and others dealt with topics about which he was of uncertain opinion."[5]

Certain facts about Luther, however, clearly set him apart from the Christian history before him. Though he allegedly started from a desire to reform abuses occurring in the Church of his day, Luther ended up rejecting almost the entire soteriological system of his predecessors. Reacting against what he perceived as a proliferation of a works-oriented theology, Luther spoke in the most vile manner against the popes and bishops of the 16th century, equat-

---

4 The Weimar edition of Luther's works, for example, contains scores of volumes, most of which exceed 500 pages in length.

5 Rix, *Luther: The Man and the Image*, p. 42. Rix continues: "The little treatise setting forth Luther's actual views is one of the most thoroughly suppressed items in the entire catalog of topics that Luther-cult biographers have not seen fit to disclose to their public. While the text of the 95 Indulgences Theses appeared in Vol. 1 of the Weimar edition in 1883, the "Treatise on Indulgences," so embarrassing to Luther partisans, was delayed until 1967 (WABr 12, 2-9) with the editorial comment 'hitherto little noticed.'" (See also Jared Wick's, *Man's Yearning for Grace*, p. 241f).

ing them with the devil and the Antichrist.[6] The popes did not take this lightly. In 1520, Pope Leo X issued the bull *Exsurge Domine*, excommunicating Luther from the Catholic Church. In a show of defiance, Luther promptly incinerated the bull. At the end of forty-one censures of Luther's views, the Pope wrote:

> All and each of the above-mentioned articles or errors, so to speak, as set before you, we condemn, disapprove, and entirely reject as respectively heretical, or scandalous, or false, or offensive to pious ears, or seductive of simple minds, and in opposition to Catholic truth.[7]

Before Luther, the Church had met hundreds of dissenters. Yet Luther's case was markedly different. In the opinion of his opponents, Luther was attacking the very heart and soul of the gospel. His indictment against the Church was audacious and serious. In essence, Luther claimed that the medieval Church no longer conveyed the true gospel, and that the Catholic Church may never have

---

6 Luther wrote: "I believe the pope is the masked and incarnate devil because he is the Antichrist...The kingdom of the pope really signifies the terrible wrath of God, namely, the abomination of desolation standing in the holy place" (LW 54, 259); "...the papists, the monks, nuns, and priests. They are creatures of the devil and of the Antichrist, who do not serve God at all but see the kingdom of heaven and the service of God purely in the traditions of men" (LW 23, 26). At Schmalkalden in 1537, he prayed that God might fill all Protestants with hatred of the Pope. One of his last and most violent books is directed *Against the Papacy at Rome, Founded by the Devil*, Wittenberg, 1545. He calls Paul III the "Most hellish Father," addressing him as "Your Hellishness" instead of "Your Holiness." He promises at the close to do still better in another book, and prays that in case of his death, "God may raise another one a thousand-fold more severe; for the devilish papacy is the last evil on earth, and the worst which all the devils with all their power could contrive. God help us. Amen" (Schaff, Philip. *History of the Christian Church*, Vol. VII, pp. 251-252. In the work, *Table Talk* (1539), Luther writes: "I'm done, except for tweaking of the pope's nose a little now and then...There's no name by which the pope could be called that is as odious as he deserves. Even if he is called greedy, impious, idolatrous, these ascriptions do not come up to his barbarity" (LW 54, 343). According to Rix, the practice of applying the term "antichrist" to the Pope as a supreme insult did not originate with Luther, but rather in antipapal circles during the latter middle ages (op. cit., p. 51).

7 *Sources of Catholic Dogma*, 13th edition of Henry Denzinger's *Enchiridion Symbolorum*, trans. Roy J. Deferrari, p. 243.

possessed it until she was privileged to receive it in full-flower from his teachings.[8] Perhaps Luther's battle cry against the Church could be best summarized in the phrase *faith alone.*[9] Although there are many conflicting opinions as to just what Luther meant by this phrase, it is clear he was using it against what he thought the Church of his

---

[8] Luther wrote: "Under the papacy no one knew what the Gospel was as distinguished from Law or what Law was as distinguished from the Gospel: for they have faith that refers to Law only" (WA 36, 10, 2-5 — Latin: "Si hoc, tum alterum amittitur vel ambo, ut in papatu nemo novit, quid Euangelium [unterfchiedlich a lege vel gfez unterfchiedlich gegen das] Euangelion, quia eorum fides est, quae tantum credit de lege, diligit deum, proximum non occidie quando...").

[9] Luther writes: "Hence, faith alone justifies when it takes hold of this [Christ]...Here we are perfectly willing to have ourselves called 'solafideists' by our opponents" (LW 26, 138). Not finding the teaching of *sola fide* among Augustine's teachings, Luther concluded of him: "Augustine has sometimes erred and is not to be trusted. Although good and holy, he was yet lacking in the true faith, as well as the other fathers...But when the door was opened for me in Paul, so that I understood what justification by faith is, it was all over with Augustine" (LW 54, 49). Elsewhere Luther writes: "It was Augustine's view that the law...if the Holy Spirit assists, the works of the law do justify...I reply by saying 'No'" (LW 54, 10). Against such convictions, many Evangelicals still attempt to maintain the bridge between Augustine and Luther. Alister McGrath, for example, states: "The origins of the Lutheran Reformation at Wittenberg are almost totally due to the conviction that the recovery of Augustine's authentic insights into how sinners are justified *coram Deo* was essential to both the *esse* and the *bene esse* of the church" (*ARCIC II and Justification*, op. cit., p. 8). Of his views on Jerome (347-420), Luther stated: "I know no doctor whom I hate so much, although I once loved him ardently and read him voraciously. Surely there's more learning in Aesop than in all of Jerome" (LW 54, 72). Of some other early Fathers of the Church, he writes: "I have no use for Chrysostom either, for he is only a gossip. Basil doesn't amount to anything; he was a monk after all, and I wouldn't give a penny for him. Philip's [Melanchthon] apology is superior to all the doctors of the church, even to Augustine himself. Hilary and Theophylact are good, and so is Ambrose" (LW 54, 33). Luther's attacks, however, were more concentrated on the Scholastic theologians, beginning with Duns Scotus (1266?-1308) and William of Ockham (1280-1349) but also with high scholasticians such as Thomas Aquinas (1224?-1274). Scottish Protestant James Buchanan (1804-1870), who was addressing the Protestant liberals of his day, in *The Doctrine of Justification*, claimed, contrary to Luther's view, that Augustine implicitly believed in *faith alone* and forensic justification, and in believing such, laid the groundwork for Luther. He adds: "...extending from Apostolic times down to Bernard, the last of the Fathers, abundantly sufficient to prove that the doctrine of Justification by grace through faith alone had some faithful witnesses in every succeeding age of the Church." He cites Faber *(The Primitive Doctrine of Justification)* and the Anglican Archbishop Usher (*Answers to a Jesuit*

day believed concerning the doctrine of justification, i.e., how sinners are justified before a holy God.[10] Luther was quite confident as he condemned the Pope and the rest of the Catholic hierarchy. He wrote: "Because I am certain of my teaching, with it I will be judge over the angels, so that whoever does not accept my teaching cannot attain heaven, because it is God's, not mine."[11] He also said: "In matters of faith each Christian is for himself Pope and Church, and nothing may be decreed or kept that could issue in a threat to faith."[12]

Perhaps Luther's intention regarding the use of the slogan *sola fide* for the Reformation can be introduced for study by observing his view of the book of James. James 2:24 contained a most troublesome phrase for Luther. It simply reads "not by faith alone." Even more troubling, James adds a clear affirmation to the same verse, "You see that a person is justified by works." Both the negation and the affirmation are clear and unambiguous declarations about the nature of justification. In the Catholic view, the epistle of James

---

9 cont. *Challenge*) as giving various patristic testimony to forensic, reciprocal imputation, and the *faith alone* formula among the Fathers, citing Basil, Ambrose, and Jerome for the latter dimension ((Carlisle, PA: Banner of Truth Trust, 1867, 1961, 1984, 1991), pp. 92-93, — of which the latest reprint contains a Foreword by evangelical J. I. Packer. Buchanan's citations of Basil, Ambrose, and Jerome using the formula *faith alone* are isolated cases, and at the least, did not mean anything near what Luther contrived it to be. Aquinas also used 'faith alone' once in his writings: "Therefore there is no hope of justification in these [the law] but in faith alone" (1 Tim. 1. III, 21, on 1 Tim. 1:8); but nowhere near the same sense as Luther's. Buchanan fails to address the contexts in which the formula is used in Basil, et al., all of which are attempting to make a sharp distinction between justification by faith and the Jewish ceremonial law, not between faith and works of moral obedience. In addition, Buchanan fails to mention the Fathers who explicitly state that faith and [moral] works are necessary for justification, as well as failing to cite the preponderance of patristic evidence which equates justification with sanctification and regeneration. (For a refutation of Buchanan's claims by qualified Protestant Evangelicals, see Alister McGrath, *Iustitia Dei*, Vol. 1, pp. 183-187; and Norman Geisler and Ralph MacKenzie, *Roman Catholics and Evangelicals*, p. 85. See also John Henry Newman's *Lectures on Justification*, pp. 440f).

10 Luther writes: "Once this has been established, namely, that God alone justifies us solely by the grace through Christ, we are willing not only to bear the pope always on our hands but also to kiss his feet. But since we cannot obtain this concession, we, in turn, become immensely proud in God" (LW 26, 99).

11 WA 10II, 107, 9 (German).

12 WA 5, 407, 35 (Latin: In his enim, quae sunt fidei, quilibet Christianus est sibi Papa et Ecclesia, nec potest statui aut statutum tenere aliquid quod in fidei periculum cedere quoquomodo possit").

is an excellent commentary for anyone struggling with the sometimes "hard to understand" language of the apostle Paul.[13] For Luther, and Protestantism following him, the epistle of James has become one of the greatest stumbling blocks in all of Scripture. In fact, much of Protestant theology after Luther is a series of attempts, in one form or another, to put the teachings of James back into a total and Scriptural understanding of justification, and yet preserve the theology of *faith alone*.

Luther saw the epistle of James as a formidable foe that had to be vanquished rather than explained. He writes of James in a most derogatory manner:

> Therefore James concludes falsely that now at last Abraham was justified after that obedience; for faith and righteousness are known by works as by the fruits. But it does not follow, as James raves: 'Hence the fruits justify,' just as it does not follow: 'I know a tree by its fruit; therefore the tree becomes good as a result of its fruit. Therefore let our opponents be done with their James, whom they throw up to us so often.[14]

> Therefore St. James' epistle is really an epistle of straw, compared to these others, for it has nothing of the nature of the gospel about it.[15]

> The epistle of James gives us much trouble, for the papists embrace it alone and leave out all the rest...Accordingly, if they will not admit my interpretations, then I shall make rubble also of it. I almost feel like throwing Jimmy into the stove, as the priest in Kalenberg did.[16]

---

13 Peter writes of Paul: "Even as our beloved brother Paul wrote to you according to the wisdom given to him, as he does in all his epistles, speaking in them concerning these things, of which some things are hard to understand, which the unlearned and unstable twist to their own destruction as they do with the remaining Scriptures" (2 Peter 3:16).

14 LW 4, 26.

15 LW 35, 362.

16 LW 34, 317. The "priest in Kalenberg" refers to an instance in which a priest had used wooden statues of the apostles as kindling to start a stove fire, saying, "Now bend over, Jimmy, you must go into the stove; no matter if you were the pope or all the bishops, the room must become warm" (WA 39II, 199, n. 2).

> Besides, he [James] throws things together so chaotically that it seems to me he must have been some good, pious man, who took a few sayings from the disciples of the apostles and thus tossed them off on paper...In a word, he wanted to guard against those who relied on faith without works, but was unequal to the task. He tries to accomplish this by harping on the law what the apostles accomplish by stimulating people to love. Therefore I cannot include him among the chief books, though I would not thereby prevent anyone from including or extolling him as he pleases, for there are otherwise many good sayings in him.[17]

Four years before his death, Luther still viewed James with contempt. In his *Table Talk* lectures of 1542 he wrote:

> We should throw the epistle of James out of this school [Wittenberg], for it doesn't amount to much. It contains not a syllable about Christ. Not once does it mention Christ, except at the beginning. I maintain that some Jew wrote it who probably heard about Christian people but never encountered any. Since he heard that Christians place great weight on faith in Christ, he thought, 'Wait a moment! I'll oppose them and urge works alone.' This he did. He wrote not a word about the suffering and resurrection of Christ, although this is what all the apostles preached about. Besides, there is no order or method in the epistle. Now he discusses clothing and then he writes about wrath and is constantly shifting from one to the other. He presents a comparison: 'As the body apart from the spirit is dead, so faith apart from works is dead.' O Mary, mother of God! What a terrible comparison that is![18]

The following comments well illustrate Luther's resolve on this issue:

---

17 LW 35, 397. Luther's suspicions that James was a spurious book are confirmed in that it is one of the only books of the Bible from which he did not produce a commentary.

18 LW 54, 424-425.

> 'Faith justifies' [Rom. 3:28] stands in flat contradiction to 'faith does not justify' [James 2:24]. If anyone can harmonize these sayings, I'll put my doctor's cap on him and let him call me a fool.[19]

> ...yet I would rather have the honor of believing in Christ alone than of being persuaded by all the passages that they could produce against me in support of the righteousness of works...I am not put off at all by passages of Scripture, even if you were to produce six hundred in support of the righteousness of works and against the righteousness of faith, and if you were to scream that Scripture contradicts itself.[20]

Of his favorite book of the New Testament he said: "The Epistle to the Galatians is my dear epistle. I have put my confidence in it. It is my Katy von Bora."[21]

For Luther, *faith alone* became the quintessential theological truth. It was elevated to such a height in his thinking that it also became the sole criterion for determining the canon of Scripture. If

---

19 Cited in *The New Testament: The History of its Investigation and Problems* by W.G. Kümmel, pp. 23, 26, 411, n. 15. Concerning *sola fide*, Luther is said to have coined the saying: "articula stantis et cadentis ecclesiae" (i.e., "the article upon which the church stands or falls") [cited in *What Luther Says: An Anthology*, ed., Edward Plass, 2:704, n. 5]. Others say this exact wording has not been documented to have come from Luther but from the Lutheran tradition. The minor variation, "If this article stands the church stands; if it falls the church falls" is said to have come from Luther. In the *Smalcald Articles* Luther wrote concerning justification: "Nothing in this article can be given up or compromised, even if heaven and earth and things temporal should be destroyed...On this article rests all that we teach and practice against the pope, the devil, and the world" (*Book of Concord*, ed. Theodore Tappert, p. 292).

20 LW 26, 294f.

21 LW 54, 20. Katy von Bora was Luther's wife. Luther's colleague Philip Melanchthon hoped his marriage to von Bora would curb the excessive "drinking, carousing, and unseemly jesting" in which Luther was known to indulge (Rix, op. cit., p. 80). In a letter to Staupitz, Luther says of himself: "I am a man exposed to and involved with socializing, drunkenness, carnal temptations, neglect of duty and other troubles in addition to the cares my profession burdens me with" (WABr, 1, 156, ID 344-345). Luther reveals much of his sordid habitual problems in his tract "The Assassin of Dresden" directed against Duke George in the early 1530s.

a book, such as the Epistle of James, did not teach *faith alone*, Luther held it in high suspicion or rejected it altogether.[22]

Besides excising the Epistle of James from Scripture, Luther, at the other extreme, made quite an audacious move in biblical translation by adding words to Paul's epistles. In his German translation of Romans 3:28, Luther added the word *allein* [*alone* in English]. In Luther's version, Romans 3:28 read: "allein durch den Glauben" (viz., "we maintain that a man is *justified by faith alone* without works of law"). Luther claimed that the word *alone* was required by the German idiom for the sake of clarity.[23] When the Catholic hierarchy accused him of a deliberate attempt to add to and change the meaning of Paul's words, Luther had this to say:

> If your Papist makes much useless fuss about the word *sola, allein*, tell him at once: 'Dr. Martin Luther will have it so,' and says, 'Papist and donkey are one thing...For we do not want to be pupils and followers of the Papist, but their masters and judges.[24]

Mimicking the style of Paul to his Judaizing opponents in 2 Corinthians 11, Luther continues:

> Are they doctors? So am I. Are they learned? so am I. Are they preachers? so am I. Are they theologians? so am I. Are they

---

22 The idea of justification by faith serving as the criterion of canonicity continued in the Lutheran tradition. Reformed theologian Richard Gaffin remarks: "...Reformed theology has not been guilty of the one-sided Paulinism of Lutheran theology. It has not, for instance, made the proclamation of justification by faith a virtual criterion of canonicity" (*Resurrection and Redemption: A Study in Paul's Soteriology*, p. 12, n. 2).

23 Evangelical R. C. Sproul, quoting from Charles Hodge's commentary on Romans [London: Banner of Truth Trust, 1909, 1972, pp. 156-157] gives the impression that Catholics of the 16th century had accepted the addition of *alone* to Romans 3:28. Sproul writes: "Hodge also notes that, though modern Roman Catholics protest Luther's insertion of the word *allein*, Catholic translators before Luther had done the same: 'So in the Nuremberg Bible (1483), 'Nur durch den glauben.' And the Italian Bibles of Geneva (1476) and of Venice (1538), 'per sola fede'" (*Faith Alone*, op. cit., p. 168). See **Appendix 5** for a refutation of Sproul's claim.

24 Schaff, Philip. *History of the Christian Church*, Vol. VII, p. 362. Luther often appealed to his doctor's degree as the grounds for his authority to instruct and reform the Church (LW 13, 66; 54, 74).

disputators? so am I. Are they philosophers? so am I. Are they writers of books? so am I. And I shall further boast: I can expound Psalms and Prophets; which they cannot. I can translate; which they cannot...Therefore the word *allein* shall remain in my New Testament, and though all the pope-donkeys should get furious and foolish, they shall not take it out.[25]

Luther's Concept of Faith and Justification

One can perhaps summarize Luther's concept of faith as the individual's firm subjective conviction in the objective work of Christ. More specifically, it is the believer's certitude that God has saved him.[26] As proof texts, Luther uses such passages as Romans

25 Schaff, p. 363. Schaff notes that though Luther claimed to add *allein* for the sake of clarity, he did not do so in Galatians 2:16 where it might just as well be added by the same rationale. Moreover, Schaff, along with Meyer and Weiss whom he references among 19th century Protestant exegetes, affirms that *allein* has "no business in the text as a translation." Of Coverdale's 19 New Testament notes in his 1535 edition of the Bible, he writes concerning Luther's addition of *allein*: "Rom. 3:28, Some reade [sic], 'By faith onely' [sic] — Luther; text: 'through faith' — Tyndale" (John Eadie. *The English Bible*, p. 292.

26 Luther's piece, *Acta Augustana* (1518), an elaboration of the 95 theses, which also included his defense against Cardinal Cajetan, the central issue was Luther's view that faith justified only if a man believed with certitude that he was justified, without doubting about his receiving grace. In *Table Talk*, Lauterbach records the following conversation with Luther: "On June 16, [1539], there was an examination of candidates for ordination at which the proposition put for debate was, 'Faith justifies; faith is a work; therefore works justify.' He [Martin Luther] responded, 'Faith justifies not as a work, or as a quality, or as knowledge, but as assent of the will and firm confidence in the mercy of God" (LW 54, 359-360). In another place: "Faith that takes hold of Christ is the faith that justifies...For if faith is to be sure and firm, it must take hold of nothing but Christ alone" (LW 26, 89); and "But if it is true faith, it is a sure trust and firm acceptance in the heart" (LW 26, 129). Luther sometimes speaks of the certitude of faith without reference to Christ: "Faith is the substance of things hoped for, and the evidence of things not seen. This is the firm and constant opinion of justice and salvation" (WA 8, 323, 12-13 — Latin: "Est autem fides substantia rerum sperandarum, argumentum non apparentium. Hoc est, firma opinio constansque conscientia iustitiae et salutis"). Kittel has argued, however, that "in the translation of ὑπόστασις here [Hebrews 11:1] and 3:14, Melanchthon advised Luther to use the rendering 'sure confidence.' Whereas all patristic and medieval exegesis presupposed that ὑπόστασις was to be translated *substantia* and understood in the sense of *ousia*, Luther's translation introduced a wholly new element into the understanding of Hb. 11:1. Faith was now viewed

1:17 ("The just shall live by faith") and Romans 4:3 ("Abraham believed God, and it was credited to him as righteousness").[27] Before his official break with Rome, Luther had already investigated the notion of certitude, claiming that in the sacrament of Penance the penitent received grace through the *firm belief* that he was forgiven, not necessarily through the power of the sacrament itself. In a move that immediately brought his exegetical capability into question, Luther used Matthew 16:19 ("Whatever you loose on earth shall be loosed in heaven") as support for the certitude of faith. He states: "Therefore, if you come to the sacrament of Penance and do not firmly believe that you will be absolved in heaven, you come to your judgment and damnation."[28] This shows Luther's

---

26 cont. as a personal, subjective conviction. This interpretation has governed Protestant exposition of the passage almost completely, and it has strongly influenced Roman Catholic exegesis. It has also had a broader effect. Yet there can be no question but that this classical Protestant understanding is untenable. The starting point of exposition must be that ὑπόστασις in Hb. 11:1 has to have not only a meaning like that in Greek usage elsewhere but also a sense similar to that it bears in the other HB references" *(Kittel's Theological Dictionary of the New Tesament*, Vol. VIII, p. 586). For more on this analysis see **Appendix 15.** It is no surprise that Protestant existential theologians such as Søren Kierkegaard point to Luther as the first to see faith itself as justification — a 'faith in faith' theology in which the object of faith is not as important as the faith itself. In contrast to Luther, the Reformed/Calvinistic view holds that God gives only objective justification but the realization of it — the feeling — grows and is different for each Christian. Luther did not make this distinction; thus, faith had to be made firm initially. Later 19th and 20th century Protestant liberal theology concludes that everyone in the world is saved (i.e., universalism) but that only the Christians know it or believe it.

27 We must point out from our study in previous chapters that Abraham's faith is not the same as Luther's understanding of faith. Scripture describes Abraham's faith as a belief in God, his integrity, and his promises, viz., that God was who he claimed to be. Luther's view of firm faith was primarily the certitude in one's personal salvation. Scripture, however, provides no indication that Abraham had certitude of his own salvation. Abraham understood the nature of salvation, and that salvation was his goal (cf., Heb. 11:10, 16), but it is never specified that he had certitude he would receive it. If anything, Abraham's seasoned relationship with God taught him not to be presumptuous about anything until all was completed.

28 LW 31, 271. In answer to this the Council of Trent stated: "For this reason, therefore, do some falsely accuse Catholic writers, as if they taught that the sacrament of penance confers grace without any pious endeavor on the part of those who receive it, a thing which the Church of God has never taught or pronounced. Moreover, they also falsely teach that contrition is extorted and forced and that it is not free and voluntary" (DS 1678).

emphasis on the subjective or reflexive nature of justification, since Matthew 16:19, though it presupposes faith, does not refer to faith as the instrument of forgiveness, nor to the individual Christian, but to the institution of the Church through the apostles who had been granted this objective power.[29] Hence, we can understand why Luther, in later exegesis, would see no need for the clerical priesthood, since an overemphasis on the disposition of the penitent had made the role of the priest virtually insignificant.[30]

The unprecedented burden placed on the certitude of faith as the criterion for justification was clearly a deviation from the Church's previous understanding. Indeed, Luther's most persistent critic, Cardinal Cajetan, pinpointed this aspect of Luther's thought as "a new and erroneous theology."[31] Canons 12, 13, and 14 of the Council of Trent also recognized Luther's overemphasis on certitude and likewise rejected it.[32] In establishing his concept of certitude, Luther put a tremendous stress on the mental faculties of the individual and of modern man in general. One's salvation was now dependent on the success or failure of one's self-assessment and the ability to reflect on one's own faith in God. By rejecting the Catholic concept which taught the individual to "co-operate with grace" within the confines of the Church, Luther now

---

29 Specifically, the words "you" (σοι), "you bind" (δήσῃς), and "you loose" (λύσῃς) in Matthew 16:19 are all Greek singulars referring to one person, namely, Peter.

30 Catholic theologian Paul Hacker points out that Luther's "theology of the cross," which was the center of his theological thinking prior to 1518, had allowed for *incertitude* of faith. Luther equated incertitude with the spiritual desolation required to abandon oneself totally to the will of God. This concept appears in the 1518 work *Resolutiones*, which contained the proofs of his 95 theses on Indulgences. By 1520, however, Luther had abandoned the idea of incertitude and desolation, replacing them with a theology of *certitude* to the point that *incertitude* now equated with damnation (*The Ego in Faith*, op. cit., pp. 35-36).

31 As recorded by Luther in *Acta Augustana*: "Hanc theologiam novam videri putant et erroneam" (WA 2, 13, 6-10.

32 See **Appendix 20** for the wording of these canons. Despite opinions both then and now that Trent did not deal with the Reformers' objections, evangelical Alister McGrath confirms that "The evangelical may rest assured that the theologians assembled at Trent really did wrestle with the crucial issues at stake. The competence and quality of the Tridentine proceedings on Justification allow us to conclude that the desire for theological integrity and competence far outweigh any temptation merely to indulge in ecclesiastical diplomacy..." (*ARCIC II and Justification*, p. 15).

had to find an ulterior means of access to God and a tangible means of measuring that access. To resolve this dilemma, he turned to man's psychological faculties. He replaced the traditional "waiting on God to move the soul" with the individual's sheer force of will in affirming his salvation and standing with God. In one of his more revealing comments, Luther writes: "if boasting ceases then grace also ceases."[33]

Luther not only created a tremendous strain by forcing the individual to tap into his psyche for certitude, he also forced the individual to decide the content of his certitude. No longer having an authoritative Church and Tradition to sort out and decide upon the subtleties and complexities of theology, the individual faced the additional hardship of having to reinvent the wheel, as it were, of theology and his relationship with God. If he wondered why he was impelled to believe something different than his neighbor believed, he could resolve the dilemma by holding on, with certitude, to his own beliefs while viewing those of others as misguided or even heretical. This divisive kind of mentality, of course, became the blueprint in the centuries following the Reformation of the advancement of individual belief, and the proliferation of the denominational structures needed to formally distinguish one belief from another. As noted previously, Luther maintained that "in matters of faith, each Christian is for himself Pope and Church."

Emphasizing certitude of faith also put a tremendous burden on Luther's own theology. As noted above, Luther insisted that the individual must mentally assert his faith and generate a firm belief. On the other hand, he held that man "cannot by his own powers believe in Christ," since faith is "a divine work in us"[34] and a "gift of the Holy Spirit."[35] These two poles created an unbearable tension in Luther's thought — a tension exacerbated by his failure to offer a reconciliation between the power of personal affirmation and the bestowing of the divine gift. This was especially troublesome for Lutheranism in the centuries after the Reformation which found it difficult to reconcile Luther's total denial of free will in

33 WA 10I, 337, 17 (German).

34 WA 12, 422, 32. (German).

35 WA 39I, 44, 1. (Latin: "Fides hic verat et donum illud spiritus Sancti intelligi debet").

pre-regenerate man with the ability and requirement of the same man to exhibit faith for justification.[36]

Luther developed his emphasis on the subjective nature of faith by introducing the "special" or "particular" moment of conviction. Drawing from such passages in the Gospels as Matthew 15:28 ("Woman, you have great faith! Your request is granted") or Matthew 9:29 ("According to your faith will it be done to you"),[37] Luther asserted that the penitent need not prepare for justification, and thus concluded that faith alone brings grace.[38] In seeing that the passages Luther chose referred to physical healing but not necessarily salvation, Cardinal Cajetan rightly commented on Luther's

---

[36] We should also remark here that assessments of Luther's theology such as that of Alister McGrath: "Luther does not understand 'justification by faith' to mean that man puts his trust in God, and is justified on that account...rather, it means that God bestows upon that man faith and grace, without his cooperation, effecting within him a real and redeeming presence of Christ as the 'righteousness of God' withing him, and justifying him on this account" (*Iustitia Dei*, II, p. 123) are highly simplistic; virtually ignoring the unending struggle Luther exhibited in his writings between faith as a divine gift and faith as a volitional act of the human will.

[37] Other passages Luther used were Matthew 8:8; 17:20; Mark 11:24; John 4:50; James 1:5-7.

[38] Following in the steps of Luther, Philip Melanchthon wrote in the Apology of the Augsburg Confession: "The faith that justifies, however, is no mere historical knowledge but the firm acceptance of God's offer promising forgiveness of sins and justification. To avoid the impression that it is merely knowledge, we add that to have faith means to want and to accept the promised offer of forgiveness of sins and justification" (*Book of Concord*, op. cit., p. 114). We notice here that Melanchthon studiously avoids the Calvinist position by specifying that faith must be a "firm acceptance" and a disposition "to want." In Melanchthon's mind, the real difference is between "mere historical knowledge" and the "firmness" or "wanting" to be forgiven. Of love, Melanchthon writes: "And because it receives the forgiveness of sins and reconciles to God, we must be accounted righteous by this faith for Christ's sake before we love and keep the law, although love must necessarily follow" (Ibid., p. 123). On the other hand, Luther also made room for a "weak" faith which could assent to three main beliefs which would allow the individual to be justified. He writes: "Indeed, all three truths must be believed: that Christ is God, that He is man, and that He became man for us, as the Apostles' Creed teaches: conceived by the Holy Spirit...If one item of this creed is lacking, all items must fall. Faith must be complete and embrace everything. Although it may be weak and subject to trial, it must in any case be complete and not false. To be weak in the faith does not do the damage, but to be wrong — that is eternal death" (*What Luther Says*, Edward Plass, ed., vol. 1, pp. 487-88).

interpretations of these gospel passages: "They were not to the point and were misunderstood."[39]

Regarding the certitude of faith, the side of Luther's teaching that much of Protestantism desires Christendom to accept is, of course, the certainty of salvation. According to his own writings, Luther went through a long period as an Augustinian monk in which he was constantly fearful of the wrath of God against his sins. This, in turn, put him in perpetual doubt concerning his status with God and whether he would be saved. He found that the remedy was to assert continually and forcefully his faith in Christ in order to suppress his sin and doubt. The stronger the faith the more sin was emasculated. Thus, in his commentary on Philippians 3:12, Luther wrote, "I have sinned and yet not sinned."[40] To Luther, a man could be the most despicable sinner, yet appear before God as if he had never sinned. It was this contradictory language that Rome found impossible to accept.[41] It is precisely because of the possibility of

---

39 WA 1, 234, 47 ("...de fide sacramentorum implet papyrum locis sacrae scripturae omnino impertinentibus et perperam intellectis") from Cardinal Cajetan's letter of October 25, 1518 to Prince Frederick the Wise. Cited in Hacker, pp. 88, 196, n. 30.

40 This strongly resembles Luther's more popular phrase, "at the same time, just and sinner" (Latin: "simul iustus et peccator"). Hacker points out that Luther's interpretation of Philippians 3:12 — a passage from which Luther assumes that Paul was "weak in faith" and that he is to be overcome this weakness by the assertion of certitude — ignores the context. The context says nothing of self-assertion or suppressing of sin but of "pressing on" in his apostolic work. In fact, Paul says quite emphatically, in opposition to Luther's thesis, "I count not myself to have apprehended." From another perspective, we must point out that Catholicism denied the "simul iustus et peccator" on the basis that the residual effects of original sin, e.g., the inclination to sin, must be understood not as sin but as *concupiscence*. Concupiscence turned into sin only when the individual made a deliberate attempt to act on his sinful inclinations (See Catholic Catechism, Section 405). Conversely, Luther and Lutheran theology viewed such sinful inclinations only as *peccatum regnatum*, that is, "controlled sin," yet still sin. Thus, to Luther, the individual always carried with him a controlled yet existing sinful state. The sinful state remained internally even though the individual was justified externally.

41 Luther prides himself on such contradictory language, as noted in his view of his own 95 theses (LW 31, 39). It is precisely here, however, that Luther lost much of his audience. Theological formulations, especially of dogma, allow very little poetic license. Luther's never ending exaggerations, contradictions, and caricatures, only ended up distorting and degrading the message of reform.

serious, unrepentant sin that, according to Catholic teaching, God holds the individual's complete justification in abeyance until the final judgment, thus preventing absolute certainty of his salvation in the present. Catholicism allows the individual to have *confidence* but not certainty. Certainty implies presumption and audacity, the very opposite sentiments from that found in the virtues of patience and humility displayed in the New Testament, which also includes a preponderance of passages that forbid absolute certainty.[42] All in all, it seems Luther was impatient with having to wait for salvation, and subsequently formed his theology to give him the assurance he so desperately wanted. He writes: "The remission of sin, the justice, the life and the freedom which we have through Christ is certain, ratified and eternal as soon as we believe so."[43] Here, and consistently in his writing, we see Luther misinterpreting the New Testament's teaching on faith, making it out to be a mere assertion of one's conscious convictions. Rather than seeing faith as the beginning or prerequisite for salvation, Luther mistakenly made the assertion of faith equal to salvation. One was saved simply because one said so.[44]

To emphasize the sufficiency of the individual's personal affirmation of faith, Luther consistently changed plural pronouns (we, us) into singular pronouns (I, me) in both Scriptural passages and Confessional statements. This phenomenon appears especially in

---

42 These passages were enumerated in chapter 4 of this book.

43 WA 40I, 6, 20. Modern Lutheran theologians confirm this conception of Luther. For example, German existentialist theologian Gerhard Ebeling states: "Faith is not a precondition of salvation but the certainty of it; and as such it is itself the event of salvation" (Das Wesen des Christiloichen Glaubens, p. 173, cited in Hacker, op. cit., n. 24).

44 Evangelical Alister McGrath seems to dilute Luther's real intent in this regard by claiming: "The particular importance of this insight concerns the assurance of salvation, a leading feature of both Lutheran and Reformed spirituality. The believer needs assurance that he really is justified, that he really has begun the Christian life" *(ARCIC II and Justification*, op. cit., p. 12). Hardly any Catholic theologian would disagree with the intent of McGrath's statement. It is precisely the Tridentine doctrine that "baptism, the sacrament of faith" (Session 6, Chapter 7), coupled with the fact that "faith is the beginning of salvation" (Session 6, Chapter 8) from which the individual Catholic can be assured that he is objectively justified, or, in McGrath's language, "has begun the Christian life." The question remains, however, as to whether the individual will continue in the grace of God and complete what he has begun.

his *Summary of the Apostles Creed* and the *Small Catechism* of 1529. Where the Apostles' Creed contained "We believe..." Luther changed this to "I believe..." One cannot help but see the emphasis on the *self* become more and more predominate in Luther's thinking as he was distancing himself from the Church's catholicity.[45] In Scripture, Luther makes the same plural-to-singular pronoun substitutions in, for example, Romans 8:38, which he changes to read, "If God is for *me*, who can be against *me*?"[46] instead of the literal reading, "If God is for *us*, who can be against *us*?" To support his pronoun shift, Luther tries to set a precedent from the wording of Galatians 2:20 ("Christ gave himself for *me*"). Luther infers from this: "Therefore read these words 'me' and 'for me' with great emphasis and accustom yourself to accepting this 'me' with a sure faith and applying it to yourself. Do not doubt that you belong to the number of those who speak this 'me.'"[47] Again, it seems that Luther misses the point of the passage. First, since Galatians 2:20 is the only occurrence in the New Testament in which Paul speaks of salvation acquired from Christ in the singular, this makes Luther's emphasis highly suspect. The preponderant New Testament language is plural, e.g., "for us," "for you," "for all," "for many," for the Church," etc. One of the most remarkable uses of the plural pronoun to signify the communal aspect of faith, even though it is often prayed in solitude, is the Lord's Prayer, which begins with "*Ou*r Father" instead of "*My* Father," and ends up with "deliver *us* from evil," not "deliver *me* from evil." The stress of the New Testament is often away from the individual and towards the community of believers. Second, the context of Galatians 2:15-17 indicates that Paul already established the plural "we" (i.e., "So *we*, too, have put *our* faith in Christ Jesus...*we* seek to be justified in Christ..."), showing that the use of the singular in 2:18-21 is used to represent the community of Christ in his crucifixion (viz., "I have been crucified with Christ"), not the assertion of one's in-

---

45 Hacker points out that a significant omission in the *Small Catechism* is Luther's neglect to mention anything about the Last Judgment, showing that he doesn't want to subject the "I" to the possibility of being found guilty and subsequently being damned.

46 WA 6, 528, 34 ("Si Deus pro me, quis contra me?").

47 LW 26, 179.

dividual salvation. The words "for me" denote union with Christ and his Church of which Paul is only a part, not Paul's assertion of individual salvation in spite of the Church.[48]

Regarding the faith of the individual, another area in which Luther departed from Augustine concerned how one should view faith itself. Luther understood the Catholic concept of faith merely as the cognitive assent to matters of doctrine, morals, God, and Church. In one sense, Luther was correct. The individual was not easily separated from the community of faith. He believed what the Church believed. Although the individual progressed in various degrees of faith, which resulted in a sharp contrast between the average Catholic and the Catholic saint, nevertheless the beginnings of faith among the masses tended to be more cognitive. Most Catholics were children who grew up in the faith; some made their learning very personal, others fell away. Except for the necessity of the Church to provide a true doctrinal basis for the faith, a necessity Luther did not acknowledge, Catholic teaching concurs with Luther's view of adult conversion.[49] However, Luther insisted that

---

48 Hacker, *The Ego in Faith*, op. cit., pp. 61-62. Hacker also notes that Luther misinterprets the affirmation of the "calling and election" in 2 Peter 1:10. Luther categorizes what one has "forgotten" as "ingratitude toward the baptism received" or "to the sin of infidelity." The context, however, says nothing of either. In 2 Peter 1:1 the apostle Peter presupposes faith in these immediate hearers. Rather, Peter says one must "add to your faith" works of "goodness...self-control...godliness, brotherly kindness...and...love" to make one's calling and election sure, not merely assert one's personal convictions. Hacker concludes: "So whenever Luther tried to demonstrate his theory of faith from Scripture, he could not but twist the texts. That the doctrine of reflexive faith is contrary to Scripture is shown by the strained nature of Luther's arguments" (Ibid., p. 67). Of Luther's earlier commentary in 1518 on the Lord's Prayer, Herbert Rix notes that Luther interprets "Thy kingdom come" as "we are still rejected," and "Hallowed by thy name" with the comment "we defile, blaspheme, dishonor, profane and desecrate God's name. In all of Scripture, I don't know any text that more powerfully and shamefully destroys us than this petition" (Rix, op. cit., p. 53).

49 Note these words from John Paul II: "From the outset, conversion is expressed in faith which is total and radical, and which neither limits nor hinders God's gift. At the same time, it gives rise to a dynamic and lifelong process which demands a continual turning away from 'life according to the flesh' to 'life according to the Spirit' (cf., Rom. 8:1-13). Conversion means accepting by a personal decision, the saving sovereignty of Christ and becoming his disciple" (*Redemptoris Missio*, December 7, 1990).

everyone had to have the same intensely dynamic conviction with no room for doubting, otherwise he could not be saved. The person who did not exhibit this intense, firm, and undaunted faith could not claim to be saved by then appealing to the graces of the Church. The individual, without depending on his Church's graces to progress him in faith, had to experience that crucial moment when he personally recognized his total corruption, that his own efforts at restitution were worthless, and subsequently throw himself on the mercies of God by seizing Christ, more or less outside the confines of the Church.

Luther's View of Sin and Predestination

In light of his view of sin, perhaps the area of Luther's thought that had the greatest influence on his theology, and one that appears over and over again in his writings, is his anthropology. One can best understand this by comparing Luther's anthropology to that of one of the most prominent spokesman for the Catholic Church, St. Augustine (354-430). Augustine, and the Catholic Church following him, believed that after the fall of Adam, man was *not* totally corrupted.[50] Guided and prompted by grace, man retained the ability to respond to God's call. The flesh would strive against the spirit but the spirit had the ability to overcome the flesh. The more the man was victorious with his spirit, the more he would become justified in God's eyes. Conversely, Luther believed that man was totally corrupted by the fall of Adam, retaining no ability to respond to God once he transgressed. His flesh *and* his spirit were corrupt. Thus it was not a matter of gaining victory over the flesh to become

---

[50] Echoing Augustine's view, the Council of Trent stated: "Whereas all men have lost their innocence in the prevarication of Adam, 'having become unclean,' and as the Apostle says, 'by nature children of wrath' as it [the Council] has set forth in the decree on original sin, to that extent were they the servants of sin, and under the power of the devil and of death, that not only the Gentiles by the force of nature, but not even the Jews by the very letter of the law of Moses were able to be liberated or to rise therefrom, although free will was not extinguished in them, however weakened and debased in its powers" (Session 6, Chapter 1, DS, 792a). For Augustine's acknowledgment of free will both before and after the fall of Adam, see **Appendix 9**. See also article by Catholic theologian Thomas Molar in *Christian News*, Nov. 4, 1985, 19

justified, simply because the spirit of man had no power to do so. He writes: "...nothing good or upright is left in man, while he is unjust, ignorant of God, a contemptor of God, adverse and useless before God."[51] The consequence of this radical anthropology was the need for an equally radical and decisive justification to take man out of this total corruption. To accomplish this, Luther invented the notion of the *alien righteousness of Christ* which is *imputed* to the individual, a concept heretofore unheard of in the Church. Since Christ's righteousness is a total righteousness, it can work effectively to bring man out of total corruption. For Luther, man was either totally under grace or totally under wrath.

If man is totally corrupt after the fall of Adam, how does one have the ability to "seize" Christ? Alongside of his teaching that the individual had to have a firm faith in order to be justified, Luther believed that the faith was a gift of God. He writes: "...faith itself is a gift of God, a work of God in our hearts, which justifies us because it takes hold of Christ in the Savior."[52] Hence, on the one hand, Luther saw that faith has its source in God, but on the other hand, he taught that the individual had to generate a firm conviction of his salvation in faith.[53] The individual was given such a

---

51 WA 18, 762, 31-32 (Latin: "nec quicquam boni aut honesti in homine relinqui, dum iniustus, ignarus Dei, contemptor Dei, aversus et inutilis coram Deo definitur").

52 LW 26, 88.

53 Lutheran theologian Carl Braaten summarizes this tension in Luther's thought — a tension remaining in modern Lutheranism: "The inward reconciliation of the heart of God with sinners occurs not because of the connection we initiate with Christ, but because of the connection Christ establishes with us. The free and full forgiveness of sins is proclaimed as an objective gift of God, on account of Christ, to sinners, not because they repent and believe but in order that they may believe and repent. But, of course, one must personally believe. One must repent and believe in order that one may personally experience the forgiveness of sins and enjoy the benefit of fellowship with God. Luther never tired of stressing that each one must do one's own confessing, believing, and repenting, even as one must do one's own dying. No one can do it for another. But here is where a certain unclarity in Luther's own manner of expressing himself could open the very door which Luther was trying to shut and keep shut against the specters of Pelagianism, semi-pelagianism, synergism, humanism, and nominalistic libertarianism. Luther frequently said that faith justifies and faith alone. "Allein der Glaube macher gerecht." A tension could arise between the role of God and the human role which then must be systematically balanced in an ordo salutis" (*Justification: The Article Upon Which the Church Stands or Falls*, op. cit., pp. 24-25).

high degree of responsibility in this endeavor of faith that Luther believed if one lost this conviction he would necessarily lose his salvation. Unlike his Calvinistic colleagues, in this regard Luther was close to his Catholic predecessors.

So what was the real problem with Luther's thought that raised such ire among the Catholic hierarchy? Essentially, in an overreaction to what he perceived to be corrupting influences in the Church of his day, Luther went off the track in two separate yet related vectors. First, as noted above, at the one extreme was his overemphasis on the reflexive nature of faith. Faith became so subjective, 'psychologized,' and independent of the Church's channel of graces that the individual took precedence over the Church, making the Church merely a necessary evil, as it were. According to the Catholic hierarchy, this reduction of the Church's importance in matters of salvation was not the picture portrayed by the New Testament and the consensus of sixteen centuries of Tradition. Second, at the other extreme, Luther veered off the accepted path in his extreme views of predestination. Luther developed his initial ideas of predestination as he read the anti-Pelagian writings of Augustine, writings in which Augustine had condemned the idea, as did the Council of Orange in 529 after him, that man had no original sin and could consequently come to God by his own power.[54] The problem was that Luther went far beyond the teach-

54 Pelagius (d. 420) denied original sin and man's hereditary guilt from Adam. He said that physical death, whether in the case of Adam or his descendants, is not caused by sin, but is necessarily involved in nature. Spiritual death is not the inherited consequence of Adam's sin, but afflicts each individual who misuses his power of free choice by choosing to sin. All men by virtue of their reason and free will have the power to avoid making this unrighteous choice. If in the exercise of his free and morally responsible will man so chooses, he may grasp the eternal aid of divine grace which is bestowed according to man's merit. The unassisted human will takes the determining initiative in the matter of salvation. Writing on Pelagius, Augustine remarks: "He [Pelagius] parries their question when they ask him, 'Why do you affirm that man without the help of God's grace is able to avoid sin?' by saying, 'The actual capacity of not sinning lies not so much in the power of will as in the necessity of nature.' Here the opinion is express which all along was kept in the background...The reason why he attributes to the grace of God the capacity of not sinning is, that God is the Author of nature, in which, he declares, this capacity of avoiding sin is inescapably implanted" (*On Natrue and Grace*, NPNF, Vol. 5, p. 141).

ing of Augustine on this issue, a fact not readily admitted or sometimes even known by Protestants either then or now. Among his more extreme convictions, Luther believed that all things that occur in the world happen by *absolute necessity*, including the sin of man. In Luther's view, God was the first cause for the sin of man and in turn predestined some of these to eternal perdition, a view whose precursor was John Wycliffe (1320-1384) who was eventually condemned by the Church at the Council of Constance. In this regard, Luther states his position in *Assertio omnium articulorum* of 1520 directed against Pope Leo X:

> Do you have anything to growl at here you miserable Pope? It is necessary to revoke this article. For I have incorrectly said that free will before grace exists in name only. I should have said candidly: "Free will is a fiction, a name without substance." Because no one indeed has the free power to think good or evil, but (as the article of Viglephi [Wycliffe] condemned at [the Council of] Constance correctly teaches) all things happen by absolute necessity. This is what the Poet [Virgil] meant when he said: "All thing are determined by a fixed law." And Christ says in Matthew 10: "The leaf of a tree does not fall to the ground without the will of your Father in heaven, and even the hairs of your head are all numbered." And in Isaiah 41 he insults them saying, "Do good or evil if you can."[55]

Before we analyze this quote, we need to understand the possible reasons for Luther's extreme views. This can best be done by investigating some of the major schools of thought prior to him.

[55] WA 7, 146, 3-12 (Latin: "Habes, miserande Papa, quid hic oggannias? Unde et hunc articulorum necesse est revocare. Male enim dixi, quod liberum arbitrium ante gratiam sit res de solo titulo, sed simpliciter debui dicere 'liberum omnia (ut Viglephi articulus Constantiae damnatus recte docet) de necessitate absoluta eveniunt. Quod et Poeta voluit, quando dixit 'certa stant omnia lege,' Et Christus Matth. x. 'Folium arboris non cadit in terram sine voluntate patris vestri qui in celis est et capilli capitis vestri omnes numerati sunt.' Et Esa. xli. Eis insultat dicens 'Bene quoque aut male si potestis facite'" (see also WA 18, 615, 12-17 in chapter 7). Luther maintained these extreme views throughout his career, beginning in 1525 with his work *De Servo Arbitrio* ("The Bondage of the Will") written against Erasmus which he later in 1537 called one of his best works.

On the one hand, Luther maintained that he was combating the Nominalist school of theology propagated by medieval theologians William of Ockham (1280-1349) and Gabriel Biel (d. 1495).[56] Luther had first been introduced to theological study by Biel. Educated at Tübingen, Biel was a very popular and admired theologian of the day. Like many of the medieval theologians, Biel had attempted to solve the age-old problem between God's foreknowledge of events in history with man's free will to make his own choices, or, between God's grace that provided salvation and man's free will to move man toward that salvation. To this day the problem has not been solved. But in Luther's opinion, Ockham and Biel had assigned too much power to the free will side of the equation. Luther concluded that Biel and others were retreating to Pelagianism. Luther's diatribe expanded as he confronted the writings of Desiderius Erasmus (1466-1536). Luther is pleased that Erasmus understands the real issue at stake, but he disagrees vehemently with Erasmus' defense of free will. Erasmus had engaged Luther in a debate on one particular point of Pope Leo's 41 disputations against Luther — proposition 36, which represented Luther's view as: "Free will after sin is a matter of title only; and as long as one does what is in him, one sins mortally."[57]

In the estimation of the Catholic hierarchy, Luther overreacted to the problem and thereby erred in producing the above retort opting for "free will as a fiction" in which "no one has the power to think good or evil" but that "all things happen of necessity." Luther

---

[56] Nominalism is the philosophic view that universal terms are mere words and have no counterpart in the mind or in reality. Contrary to popular opinion among Evangelicals that nominalism was a distinct theological school of thought in the medieval period, Alister McGrath makes quite a convincing case that nominalism was a philosophical perspective of many thinkers of that day. McGrath uses the term *via moderna* to describe this pervasive thought form. McGrath further postulates that the tendency among Protestants to equate nominalism with Pelagian theology is misleading. Of the *via moderna* McGrath writes: "[it] is to be interpreted in a sense which allows a man to play a positive role in his own justification, without elevating that role to Pelagian proportions. In this way, the theologians of the *via moderna* were able to maintain the teaching of both the early and later Franciscan schools concerning man's meritorious disposition towards justification, while establishing a conceptual framework within which this teaching could be safeguarded from the charge of Pelagianism..." (*Iustitia Dei*, II, pp. 170-171).

[57] DS #776.

further enraged the Church by supporting his thesis with a quote from the pagan poet Virgil, suggesting latent within him a deep-rooted affinity to the pagan notion of fatalism. Luther exacerbated this outrage by speculative theological reasoning. Luther went so far as to say that the free will of man is automatically excluded by the mere fact of man's creatureliness, rather than by his sinful state, thus implying, to many of his critics, that God was the author of sin. What the Catholic hierarchy saw in this extreme position of Luther's was a resurrection of the old Manichean heresy of the 3rd century. To them, Luther appeared as a *bona fide* fatalist or determinist.[58]

On the other side, though Erasmus rightly attacked Luther's stand on *absolute necessity,* he perhaps did not do the best job in defending the Church's official stand on the relationship between grace and free will, a formulatory synthesis which would only come at the Council of Trent almost fifty years later.[59] Erasmus' apparent inadequacy to handle the issue further repelled Luther from the Church.[60] He accused Erasmus of Pelagianism. Other

---

58 Historian Philip Schaff says of Luther: "The Reformer held the most extreme view on divine predestination and in his book on the Slavery of the Human Will, against Erasmus, he went further than Augustin before him and Calvin after him" (Schaff, *History of the Christian Church*, Vol. IV, p. 524). In some places Luther spoke of a weakened free will ("*liberum arbitrium in inferioribus,*" cf., WA 56, 385; 1, 365; 18, 638, 4-11; LW 31, 58; 26, 174) but in light of the newer concept of the enslaved will (*"servum arbitrium"*), free will is totally masked or rendered meaningless. Though some have come to Luther's defense, maintaining that he did not intend to teach such extreme views (e.g., Althaus, Barth, Bornkamm), these authors do not address the main passages from which Luther is accused of such views, (viz., WA 7, 146, 6-12 and WA 18, 615, 12-17; see chapter 7 for details). In any case, intended or not, Luther left himself open for condemnation by the Church for appearing very much like a determinist. In the words of Cardinal Ottaviani, "it is not what he thought but what he wrote that we judge; the possible harm to souls is caused by that which has been printed, not from that which the author in question may have intended to say" (KNAK, No. 89, Dec. 4, 1963, p. 9).

59 Erasmus' main response to Luther is titled *De Libero Arbitrio* ("On Free Will"). Unfortunately for Erasmus, most of the estimations of his debate with Luther do not take into account his great work titled *Hyperaspistes*, which critics say is much more to the point and in line with Catholic teaching. The Council of Trent reaffirmed the anti-Pelagian and anti-semi-Pelagian teaching of Augustine and the Council of Orange of 529.

60 At other places, however, Luther said this of Erasmus: "But neither Erasmus nor any of the others took the matters seriously. Only Latomus has written excellently against me. Mark this well: Only Latomus wrote against Luther; all the rest, even Erasmus, were croaking toads" (LW 54, 77).

critics have also maintained that though Erasmus believed in grace, he failed to speak specifically of grace undergirding free will. The Council of Orange in 529 had condemned free will without grace yet Erasmus did not seem to be aware of it, nor did he reference the citation of Orange appearing in the writings of Anselm (1033-1109), Bernard of Clairvaux (1090-1153), Thomas Aquinas (1224-1274), and Gregory of Rimini (d. 1358), who all recognized Augustine and his anti-Pelagian theology as the norm for the Church. These theologians recognized that man could do nothing except by the grace of God, a grace that was properly called "prevenient." Consequently, Luther is often accused of not really knowing, or perhaps not being fair, to the Scholastic theology he repudiated. Ockham, Biel, and Erasmus were certainly not the most informed or orthodox spokesman for Catholicism.[61] However, once Luther overreacted to Erasmus by denying a dialectic between grace and free will, speaking rather of the human will moved by the *absolute necessity* of the divine will, his voice was never listened to again in Catholic ears. Thus, Pope Leo's proposition 36, among others, sealed Luther's fate and his excommunication.[62] On June

---

[61] In light of this evidence, we take issue with the statement by Alister McGrath that "the important rulings of the Second Council of Orange (529) on justification were quite unknown to the Middle Ages" (*ARCIC II and Justification,* p. 10). But in the next paragraph McGrath admits: "But the possibility that Luther may have passed judgment upon the entire church of the period on the basis of his experience of a single school of thought (the *via moderna*) cannot be excluded completely" (Ibid). Modern Catholic theologians such as Louis Bouyer and Joseph Lortz agree that Luther was struggling against un-Catholic elements left over from the medieval period.

[62] The following incident reveals something of Luther's character. He had remarked previously that he had not held to all 41 articles with conviction, regarding some as only debating points. When the Pope condemned all of them, however, Luther replied to the Pope as if he was convinced of the absolute truth of all 41 (See Herbert Rix, *Martin Luther: The Man and the Image*, pp. 222-223). Johannes Meister Eckhart (c. 1260-1327), a German Dominican theologian and mystic, had been excommunicated a few centuries earlier for beliefs very similar to Luther. Eckhart did not believe God's determinations were based on secondary causes or contingencies. He taught that God is a necessary being and as such there is no distinction between his being and his operations, therefore, all God's operations are absolutely necessary, thus, all things happen with the same necessity as God's very existence. Eckhart had used this argumentation to assert that the Incarnation had to occur of necessity, because it was just as necessary as God's divine being. Luther is

15, 1520, The Pope issued the bull *Exsurge Domine* to excommunicate Luther.[63]

Luther's View of Works

Once the individual possessed faith, Luther taught that he was responsible to maintain and increase his faith. If he did not, he might lose his faith and eventually lose his salvation. Works were said to be the *fruits* of firm faith and Luther was quite fond of using the analogy of a tree and its fruits to prove his point, especially in his Galatian commentary. To show the variances in his theology, however, in some places Luther seemed to come close to the Catholic position. He writes in one place "good works are necessary for salvation."[64] In light of the rest of his theology, precisely what he meant by such a statement is anyone's guess. In his general theology Luther believed that the individual could do nothing good in himself. Sin always emasculated any good that man attempted to do. God merely tolerated a believer's works, provided his faith was firm. Instead of becoming better in his person through works of love and obedience, Luther believed that the more Christ became a part of the individual's life the more he would recognize that sin permeated his every action, thus showing his dire need for the "alien" righteousness of Christ. Contrary to today's Protestantism, however, Luther did not believe in a separation of justification and sanctification but understood the former both as an event

---

62 cont. essentially saying the same thing as Eckhart, that is, because of God's unchangeable nature, he is thus unchangeable in knowing whatever he knows. In other words, God foreknows whatever he foreknows and therefore, by his very essence as God, unchangeably decrees whatever comes to pass, without contingency or consideration from secondary causes.

63 Other matters addressed in *Exsurge Domine* were Luther's view of the sacraments, e.g., his claim that even though baptized, sin remains in the infant (#2); that contrition is not required in penance and actually makes one more of a sinner; that only belief is required for forgiveness (#5-#15); that indulgences are only useful and effective in extreme cases, e.g., public crimes (#17-#22); that the Pope does not have final authority in the Church (#23-#28); that Councils have erred (#29-#30); that even in doing good works, man sins (#31-#32); that purgatory cannot be proved from Scripture, and that those in purgatory are not assured of salvation (#37-#41); (DS 741-781).

64 WA 39I, 96, 6 (Latin: "quod bona opera sint etiam necessaria ad salutem").

and a process. Hence, in this respect, he is much closer to the Council of Trent than to contemporary Protestantism or even traditional Lutheranism.[65] Luther also distinguished between a legal and moral righteousness. This distinction appears in his 1529 work *Two Kinds of Righteousness*.

In some instances, Luther was so adamant against works contributing anything to the individual's status with God that he wrote statements like the following:

> This shall serve you as a true rule, that whenever the Scriptures order and command to do good works, you must so understand it that the Scriptures forbid good works." [66] "If you should not sin against the Gospel, then be on your guard against good works; avoid them as one avoids a pest." [67]

---

65 Evangelicals Geisler and MacKenzie remind today's Evangelicals that Luther believed in a "progressive sense" of the word justification as he showed by these words: "For we understand that a man who is justified is not already righteous but moving toward righteousness (WA 39I, 83; Ch. 34, 152)." Geisler and MacKenzie then say that his "progressive" justification is what Protestants call "sanctification," and they conclude, "What later Protestants were to divide, Luther kept together" (op. cit., p. 224). See also Alister McGrath, *Iustitia Dei*, II, p. 18 for a similar evaluation of Luther's progressive justification. We should note, however, that one of Geisler's and MacKenzie's purposes for pointing out this feature of Luther's theology is to support their notion that *sanctification* is by faith alone, not works, a view not readily accepted by modern Evangelical conceptions of sanctification.

66 WG 2, 171.

67 JN 1, 318. In his commentary on Galatians 3:10, written from 1535-1538 toward the end of his career, and in the midst of the controversy between the nomian and antinomian Protestant sects that had become prevalent by this time, Luther admits to the diverse ways Scripture speaks of faith and works: sometimes "outside of works;" at other times "along with good works." To find a precedent for this duality, Luther makes faith without works analogous to the divinity of Christ, i.e., the superior part of his nature. Faith with works is made analogous to the conjoining of Christ's divinity with his humanity. Thus, Luther can say, "Everything is...attributed to the man on account of the divinity," and analogously say, "Everything that is attributed to works belongs to faith" (LW 26, 265-266). Here we see an almost desperate attempt to salvage *faith alone* theology by subordinating works to faith through an appeal to an even more enigmatic subject, the hypostatic union in Christ. Not only is this a wrong view of the relationship between faith and works, but Cardinal Yves Congar, O. P. postulates that this reveals a defect in Luther's understanding of Christology. In the same vein, Paul Hacker has pinpointed what he feels are several instances in Luther's writings in which not only are his Christological views suspect of heterodoxy, but also his Trinitarian views (*The Ego in Faith*, pp. 129-133).

Luther's View of Love

Luther's view of love was affected by his understanding of works. In giving works a role secondary to faith in the individual's relationship with God, Luther treated love as a theological afterthought — something done in this life only to prove that one had faith in God sufficient enough for salvation. Luther was suspicious that the Church was using love as a mask for works righteousness. He reasoned that love and law were identical because law commands nothing else but love. Since the law commanding love conflicts with faith, Luther concludes, "therefore love too is not from faith."[68] Hence Luther's view forces love over to the side of law and works. Luther's comment on the relationship between love and the flesh makes this especially evident:

> As we have said, therefore, the apostle imposes an obligation on Christians through this law about mutual love in order to keep them from abusing their freedom. Therefore the godly should remember that for the sake of Christ they are free in their conscience before God from the curse of the Law, from sin, and from death, but that according to the body they are bound; here each must serve the other through love, in accordance with this commandment of Paul.[69]

This comment connects the practice of love directly to fleshly bondage and indirectly to the curse of death itself. It reduces the eternal, all-pervasive dimension of love to a mere temporary medicine for the present plight of man. Luther forces Paul to decide between faith and love, concluding in favor of justification by faith alone, which is distinguished wholly from law and love. Luther claimed that the popes erred when in the name of love they set up a law and "therefore made of the Gospel a law of love."[70] It is no surprise that after 1518 there is a marked absence from Luther's writings regarding love and its place in the Christian faith. For

---

68 LW 26, 270-271.
69 LW 27, 49.

Catholicism, however, love was the pinnacle of the Christian faith and from which everything else flowed. In the relationship between love and faith, love is superior not only because it is an eternal virtue, but also because, as Paul says, it is "love that *believes* all things,"[71] not necessarily faith, in itself.

How then did Luther explain the direct command from God to love Him? First, Luther made love an exclusive exchange between a man and his neighbor, not an offering from man to God.[72] Faith remains as the only virtue that man gives to God. In his commentary on Galatians 5:6, Luther writes:

> Paul is describing the whole of the Christian life in this passage: inwardly it is faith toward God, and outwardly it is love or works towards one's neighbor. Thus a man is a Christian in a total sense: inwardly through faith in the sight of God, who does not need our works; outwardly in the sight of men, who do not

---

[70] LW 26, 73. Of the relationship between law and gospel, Luther remarked in *Table Talk*: "There is no man living on earth who knows how to distinguish between the law and the gospel...Even the man Christ was so wanting in understanding when he was in the vineyard that an angel had to console him [John 12:27-29]; though he was a doctor from heaven he was strengthened by the angel" (LW 54, 127).

[71] 1 Corinthians 13:7 — (Ἡ ἄλαπη... πάντα πιστεύει). This may be a profound truth — a truth beyond the common understanding of simply adding love to faith. Essentially, love of God is what motivates one to have faith in him. Love is supreme because it is the catalyst that breeds faith. This also ties in with the Council of Trent's insistence that justification is the infusion of not only faith, but also of love and hope: "man...receives the said justification together with the remission of sins all these gifts infused at the same time: faith, hope and love" and speaks highly of the Catholic concept of "faith formed by love." Paul also says in 1 Corinthians 13:7 that "love hopes for all things" showing that even hope is directed and initiated by love.

[72] Paul Hacker points out that in 1515-1516, Luther's lectures on Romans and Galatians were in perfect conformity to Augustine's view of love. Luther speaks of works as "the sole motive of love for God" and that "love makes works meritorious" (WA 56, 248, 8; and 57II, 97, 28). By 1518, however, Luther had come to the point of denying the possibility of contrition out of love for God. He then stated, "Love God in his creatures: he does not will that you love him in his majesty." Melanchthon also noticed this radical transformation in Luther's conception of love (*The Ego in Faith*, pp. 70-71).

derive any benefit from the faith but do derive benefit from works of our love.[73]

Second, Luther had to grapple with Scriptural declarations that love was the fulfillment of the law (Romans 13:10; Galatians 5:14) ultimately forcing him to conclude that love, as part of the law, had no association with justification. One who failed in one point of love thus failed in one point of law, forcing the law to condemn him. Moreover, to Luther, if love fulfilled the law and thereby justified the individual, this made grace superfluous. Hence Luther postponed the fulfillment of the law through love until the eternal state. Rather than seeing the fulfillment of love as dependent on God's grace and God's viewing man through grace, Luther is trapped in *opposing* love to grace and can only reconcile them in the afterlife.[74] What Luther failed to recognize is that love, just

---

[73] LW 27, 30. Luther maintains this position in spite of numerous passages which require and encourage love of God (e.g., Matthew 22:37; John 14:15, 21; 16:27; Romans 5:5; 1 Cor. 2:9; 16:22; James 1:12; 2:5; 1 John 4:10, 19; 5:3; 2 John 6). Not until the Pietist movement in the late seventeenth century would Protestant thought emphasize the love of man towards God. Reformed theologians still maintain that man cannot love God with his whole heart, mind, and soul as commanded in Matthew 22:37.

[74] As Catholic theologian Peter Manns has stated: "An exaggerated fear of works righteousness and a legitimate concern for the grace of justification prevented Luther from taking the last intellectual step toward openly expressing in paradoxical unity both the necessity for salvation and the total gratuity of charity, as entailed in his principles...We go beyond Luther — however, following his basic principles — by simply expanding the simul of "sin and righteousness" by means of this other simul: our effort as necessary for salvation *and* pure grace, servitude *and* freedom, purposeful striving *and* spontaneity. Thus we come to a doctrine of justification in which absolute faith truly becomes incarnate faith through active charity" (Ibid., pp. 155-156). Manns also points out that although Luther at times appeared to divorce love from grace and gospel, putting it on the side of law and works, his theology is not consistent in that he: (1) speaks of love as one with the gospel (LW 27, 51, 113); (2) opposes love against works (LW 26, 273f, 329, 345f; 27, 65); (3) affirms the unity of love of God and love of neighbor (LW 26, 133, 161, 257, 275, 329, 345f; 27, 65); (4) understands love not as a facultative addition to faith but as the fruit of faith (LW 26, 145, 153, 155, 161, 169, 220, 376). Luther also has no problem with adding hope to faith in the statement, "Without hope faith is nothing, because hope bears and overcomes evil" (WA 40I, 21, 33 — Latin: "Ita fides sine spe est nihil, quia spes fert et vincit mala"). Luther says in effect that hope carries the faith that initiated justification, yet he cannot say the same of love, which he sees only as an instrument.

exactly like faith, is a gift of God, and is manifested with man's cooperation through God's grace.

In his concept of "taking hold" or "seizing" Christ, Luther passionately opposed the Catholic idea of "faith formed by love." In his commentary on Galatians 5:6, the famous verse of Paul in which he gives the formula, "faith working through love," Luther writes:

> They say that we must believe in Christ and that faith is the foundation of salvation, but they say that this faith does not justify unless it is "formed by love." This is not the truth of the Gospel; it is a falsehood and pretense...For faith that takes hold of Christ, the Son of God, and is adorned by Him is the faith that justifies, not a faith that includes love. For if faith is to be sure and firm, it must take hold of nothing but Christ alone...Just as our opponents refuse to concede to us the freedom that faith in Christ alone justifies, so we refuse to concede to them, in turn, that faith formed by love justifies.[75]

Later, Luther added:

> But this love or the works that follow faith do not form or adorn my faith but my faith forms and adorns my love.[76] FAITH [sic] is the principal point and the highest commandment which includes all others in itself.[77] Rather, faith shall be the master over love, and love shall yield to it.[78] Faith has confidence in God; therefore it cannot be deceived. Love has confidence in men; therefore it is often deceived.[79]

In saying these things, it was obvious that Luther was absolutely reversing the traditional doctrine, making faith supreme over love rather than love supreme over faith. However, though faith to

---

75 LW 26, 88-90.
76 LW 26, 161.
77 WA 36, 365, 8.
78 WA 39I, 23, 11-12 (German: "Sondern der glaub fol herr fein uber liebe, und im fol die liebe meicken...").
79 LW 27, 39.

Luther was absolutely alone in justification, in commenting on Galatians 5:6 he was careful to say:

> "...faith working through love," that is, a faith that is neither imaginary nor hypocritical but true and living. This is what proves and motivates good works through love. This is the equivalent of saying: He who wants to be a true Christian or to belong to the kingdom of Christ must be truly a believer. But he does not truly believe if works of love do not follow his faith.[80]

Another of Luther's comments illuminates his main objection:

> They read this passage through a colored glass, and they distort the text to suit their own dreams. For Paul does not speak of "faith which justifies through love," or of "faith which makes acceptable through love."...He says that works are done on the basis of faith through love, not that a man is justified through love...It is an obvious trick when they suppress the true and genuine meaning of Paul and interpret "working" to mean "justifying" and "works" to mean "righteousness."[81]

---

[80] LW 27, 30. This contrasts with Luther's 1519 work, *Small Commentary on Galatians*, in which he says, "Behold this is walking in the Spirit and not fulfilling the desires of the flesh, to be led by the Spirit, not to be under the law, for the whole law to be embraced in the one point of charity, that is if these are not done. Faith alone does not suffice, yet faith alone justifies, because if it is real faith it beseeches the Spirit of love. But the Spirit of love flees all these things and thus fulfills the law and attains the kingdom of God. Hence the whole thing is attributed to faith..." (WA 2, 591, 26 — Latin: Ecce hoc est spiritu ambulare et non perficere carnis desyderia, spiritu duci, non esse sub lege atque omnem legem in uno charitatis capitulo complecti, scilicet si haec non fiant. Iam vides, quam non sufficiat sola fides, et legem implet et regnum dei consequitur. Proinde totum fidei tribuendum..."). Hacker notes that the early Luther spoke of freedom manifesting itself in works alone under the Spirit of Love. The later Luther speaks of freedom only in terms of a free conscience not worried about the wrath of God (*The Ego in Faith*, p. 71).

[81] LW 27, 28. As Protestant Anri Morimoto has rightly said, however, "Luther's criticism is pertinent only insofar as he lines up conversion, justification, and sanctification in his own context" (*Jonathan Edwards and the Catholic View of Salvation*, p. 128). Similarly, Catholic theologian George Tavard states that Luther's objections, specifically his attack on *fides formata* (informed faith) was "particularly disastrous" since "this concept had originally no other purpose than to embody the concern that faith must be a living faith — Luther's very concern" *(Justification: An Ecumenical Study,* p. 103).

At times, Luther seems to come very close to the Catholic understanding. In 1535 he wrote: "Justification is in reality a kind of rebirth in newness." This understanding echoes his 1517 teaching, (which is considered by many to be the high point of his career), of the "healing" or "transforming power" of grace in justification. In his sermon of February 24, 1517, Luther maintained that Christ is *actuosissimus* (active) in our lives, working with his grace to transform our lives.[82] After 1518, however, Luther is consumed with vengeance against the Pope and there is little concern to enhance his teaching on transforming grace. Except for glimpses about the "newness" provided by grace in the later Galatians commentary, references to transforming grace are rare in Luther's teaching. His concentration slips to the ego asserting its own certitude of faith, which, in the end, reduces Christ's work to that of salving troubled consciences; relativizes the patient cleansing work of grace through love; turns the Christian's gaze from Christ to himself; and excludes penance from the life of the Christian.[83] Later Lutheran theology, especially that guided by Philip Melanchthon, saw grace more as a forensic non-imputation of sin, yet still retained some remnants of transformation.[84]

---

82 LW 34, 113. Though Luther exhibited less and less a theology of "healing grace" as he progressed in his career, we catch glimpses of his earlier theology in such references as "newness" in regard to justification. Jared Wicks points out that Luther's theology of 1517, considered by many to be the high point of his career, spoke of a healing and transforming grace which he called the "living, moving, operative spirit." (*Man Yearning For Grace*, pp. 268-269).

83 Ibid., pp. 272-273. The exclusion of penance is in sharp contrast to Luther's 1517 work *Treatise on Indulgences.* Hence Luther not only denied the sacramental nature of penance, but he also developed an aversion to personal penance.

84 In the *Apology of the Augsburg Confession*, Melanchthon writes: "And to be justified means to make unrighteous men righteous or to regenerate them, as well as to be pronounced or accounted righteous. For Scripture speaks both ways." Where Melanchthon held his ground, however, is evident in the next sentence: "Therefore, we want to show first that faith alone makes a righteous man out of an unrighteous one, that is, that it [faith alone] receive the forgiveness of sins" (*Book of Concord*, ed. Theodore Tappert, p. 117). It is no surprise that Melanchthon and Cardinal Contarini could almost come to agreement at the Diet of Regensburg in 1541 on the nature of justification. Unfortunately, the tide of emotion was too great to overcome. A version of this compromise, under the name "double justification" was presented by Bishop Seripando at the Council of Trent but it was eventually rejected.

When we witness such diverse opinions in Luther regarding the nature of justification, we wonder whether Luther had ever settled the issue in his mind, was confused, or was admitting that the problem was indeed more complex than he at first imagined. In the end, however, it becomes clearer that the real issue for Luther was the *kind* of faith the individual possessed, rather than understanding love and works as truly causing and truly necessary for justification. Though Luther showed some glimpses of transforming grace in the progression of justification, the overwhelming evidence shows that Luther avoids connecting faith and love in any direct manner, especially as his polemics against the papacy went into full swing. In another place he writes: "The true Gospel, however, is this: Works or love are not the ornament or perfection of faith; but faith itself is a gift of God, a work of God in our hearts, which justifies us because it takes hold of Christ in the Savior."[85] It was the attempt to make faith the exclusive instrument of justification that the Council of Trent, referring to the phrase in Galatians 5:6 (i.e., "faith working through love"), categorically denied in the theology of Luther.[86] The high Scholastic theologians of earlier centuries had used the same formula to encapsulate their concept of justification, and it was this medieval concept that Luther originally opposed.[87] Luther writes of the scholastics: "Such are the dreams of the scholastics. But where they speak of love we speak

---

[85] LW 26, 88.

[86] Session 6, Chapter 7; DS 800.

[87] "Fides quae per charitatem operatur" as used by Thomas Aquinas (II-II, Q. 4, A. 3). Protestant Anri Morimoto defends Aquinas' view against false charges: "It may sound as if there are two kinds of faith, one formed and the other unformed. Yet the reader must be reminded that faith in Thomas' conception, too, is a joint act of the intellect and will. Faith is 'an act of the intellect, it asserts to the Divine truth' but unlike other acts of the intellect, it asserts to the truth 'at the command of the will.' Moreover, it is charity, as a preeminent act of the will, that commands, determines, and disposes the intellect to the particular object of faith. When Thomas says that charity 'perfects' and 'forms' faith in the above definition, therefore, he means that the act of the asserting intellect is now 'directed' and 'guided' by charity to its proper object. There are neither two kinds of faith nor is the nature of faith altered by charity. Faith, whether formed or unformed, is of one kind; and the Reformers, under different terminology, tried to affirm — namely, faith, if it is genuine, is an act that involves the whole human personality, not just the intellect or will. Whether this is tantamount to the elimination of "by faith alone,' as some suspect, is a question to be discussed within the context in which the statement occurs" (*Jonathan Edwards*, op. cit., pp 125-127).

of faith. And while they say that faith is the mere outline...we say in opposition that faith takes hold of Christ."[88] It is precisely Luther's separation of love from faith that, even among some Lutheran scholars, exposed the inadequacy of his theology.[89] Augustine and the Church following him insisted that hope and love be added to faith for justification. Luther made love of God unattainable in this life and replaced it rather, with an ego-centered affirmation of salvation. Though both Augustine and Luther would decry the mere faith of demons, Augustine writes:

> "That ye believe on Him" not, that ye believe Him. But if ye believe on Him, ye believe Him; yet he that believes Him does not necessarily believe *on* Him. For even the devils believed Him, but they did not believe *on* Him...For, "to him that believeth *on* Him that justifieth the ungodly, his faith is counted unto him for righteousness." What then is "to believe *on* Him"? By believing to love Him, by believing to esteem highly, by believing to go into Him and to be incorporated in His members...Not any faith of what kind soever, but "faith that worketh by love."[90] This cannot happen unless hope and love are added.[91]

Scripture's axiom in regard to the relationship between faith and love is clear: "faith without love is nothing;" "love believes all things;" and "faith working through love."[92] Scripture teaches through these and other passages that one must love God in order to truly believe *on* Him. Loving God for who he is compels the

---

[88] LW 26, 88, 129. To show the extent of Luther's positioning of faith over love, Hacker points out that in interpreting the Song of Songs, which according to traditional understanding extolls the deep love between the bridegroom and the bride, Luther used this intimate relationship to describe faith. By the 1531-1535 Commentary on Galatians, he had totally excluded love from the relationship (*The Ego in Faith*, op. cit., p. 85).

[89] Hacker points out, for example, that Lutheran theologian Paul Althaus admits that Luther's view of love "involved a problem for Luther in view of the central tenet of his theology." Hacker concludes, "Unfortunately, the scholar [Althaus] failed to realize that a theological system whose central tenet is at variance with a central theme of the New Testament must for this very reason miss the essential intention of Holy Scripture" (Ibid., p. 76).

[90] *Homilies on John*, 29, 6.

[91] *Sermons*, 144, 2.

[92] 1 Corinthians 13:2, 7; Galatians 5:6.

true seeker to believe in him, even though he cannot see him and even though he may be surrounded by circumstances that tempt him to deny God's love and integrity. Unless love of God is the basis for faith in him, the mental effort required to believe *firmly* is simply too much for the individual mind to sustain. The mental exercise of raw faith, without love, results in a distortion of and revulsion towards the personality or thing believed. Moreover, when the individual's justification is only made effective by the constant self-assertion of faith, faith becomes a laborious effort, a work, if you will, that the believer must consistently keep on the surface of his consciousness in order to be justified. Though there is not room in this study to explain all these ramifications, such was the plight of the Protestant scholastic and liberal theology which followed Luther's footsteps in the seventeenth and eighteenth centuries, wherein faith in God without personally loving him became the plight of the modern Christian.

Disillusionment in Luther

Even in Luther's time, the honeymoon of his theology soon gave way to the realities of life, of sin, and of man. Luther laments:

> Since the downfall of Popery and the cessations of excommunications and spiritual penalties, the people have learned to despise the word of God. They no longer care for the churches; they have ceased to fear and honor God...After throwing off the yoke of the Pope, everyone wishes to live as he pleases. [They say] 'we will spend the day like Lutherans. Drunkenness has come upon us like a deluge.'[93] If God had not closed my eyes, and if I had foreseen these scandals, I would never have begun to teach the gospel.[94]

---

[93] WL 12, 788.

[94] WL 6, 920. This was not only true among the laity in Luther's time, but in Lutheranism itself. After the death of Luther in 1546, and the military defeat of the German-Lutheran princes in 1547, there arose a series of controversies concerning the "pure doctrine" of Luther. The Gnesio-Lutheran party who claimed to adhere to the original teachings of Luther, accused the "Philippist" party, comprised of followers of Philip Melanchthon, of taking Luther's views to the extreme. Attempts to bring these parties together resulted in several "formulas," the last of which was the *Formula of Concord* in 1577 (*Book of Concord*, op. cit., p. 463).

Of his own spiritual growth under his "new Gospel" Luther confesses: "I confess...that I am more negligent than I was under the Pope and there is now nowhere such an amount of earnestness under the Gospel, as was formerly seen among monks and priests."[95]

Regarding the doctrinal confusion of his day, Luther wrote in a letter to James Propst: "I — an exhausted old man, tired out from so many labors — constantly become younger from day to day; that is, new sects always rise up against me, and renewed youth is necessary to fight them."[96] In a letter to Zwingli, he writes: "If the world last long it will be again necessary, on account of the different interpretations of Scripture which now exist, that to preserve the unity of faith we should receive the Councils and decrees and fly to them for refuge."[97] Yet we must remember that it was Luther who caused much of this confusion when he told his followers: "For to each one God is such as he is believed to be."[98]

John Calvin (1509-1564)

Though Luther seems to have come to some degree of reevaluation about his theology, later in the same century John Calvin produced an even stronger wave of dissension from the Church. Of Luther's addition of the word *alone* to Romans 3:28, Calvin writes:

> The Law, therefore, has no part in it, and their objection to the exclusive word *alone* is not only unfounded, but is obviously absurd. Does he not plainly enough attribute everything to faith alone when he discounts it with works?"[99]

Although it is obvious that Calvin did not object to Luther's addition of the word alone to the New Testament text, he, and the

---

95 WL 9, 1311.

96 *Letters*, September 15, 1538; LW 182-183.

97 Contra Zuingli et Oecol. Cited in "Sola Scriptura: A Blueprint For Anarchy" by Patrick Madrid (*Catholic Dossier*, 1996).

98 WA 5, 248, 12 (Latin: "Talis enim est deus, qualis creditur cuique").

99 *Institutes* 3:11:19.

Reformation theologians who followed him,[100] did not welcome Luther's attempt to "make rubble" of the epistle of James. They were aware of the severe repercussions sure to result from taking a dim view of the canonicity of James.[101] To defend one's belief about the nature of salvation by eliminating or disparaging a book of the historically accepted canon of the New Testament would not sit well in the minds of future critics. It was one thing to reject the Deutero-canonical books of the Old Testament, which all the Reformers had done; but to reject a New Testament book was unthinkable. If one could reject James, could he not eventually reject other books of the accepted canon that seemed to contradict his own understanding of doctrine? Luther intensified this danger when he also expressed contempt for the epistle to the Hebrews and the book of Revelation since they delineate some of the same theological principles as the epistle of James.[102]

---

[100] Luther's protégé, Philip Melanchthon, writes: "If they dislike the exclusive particle 'alone,' let them remove the other exclusive terms from Paul, too, like 'freely,' 'not of works,' 'it is a gift,' etc., for these terms are also exclusive" *(Book of Concord*, op. cit., p. 117). Similar to Melanchthon, Evangelical Alister McGrath oversimplifies the controversy, saying: "Even as late as 1535, Luther was prepared to grant the pope his power and authority, on condition that the latter conceded that sinners are freely forgiven through the grace of God" (*ARCIC II and Justification*, p. 8). As we have seen in this entire study, Melanchthon's "exclusive" terminology, and McGrath's emphasis on "grace" was and still is recognized by Rome, but in the traditional way.

[101] Melanchthon, one of the chief counselors to Luther, who advised him not to reject the book of James, turns the tables and attempts to use James against Rome. He writes in the Apology of the Augsburg Confession: "The words of James will cause us no trouble if our opponents do not read into them their opinion about the merit of works...First, we must note that this text is more against our opponents than against us. They teach that a man is justified by love and works but say nothing about the faith by which we take hold of Christ...How much better is James' teaching. For he does not omit faith nor exalt love in preference to it, but keeps it, lest Christ, the propitiator, be excluded from justification...James did not hold that by our good works we merit grace and the forgiveness of sin. He is talking about the works of the justified, who have already been reconciled and accepted and have obtained the forgiveness of sins" (*Book of Concord*, op. cit., p. 142).

[102] Luther had rejected the Deutero-canonical books, e.g., Maccabees, Judith, Tobit, Sirach (Ecclesiasticus), Wisdom and Baruch, and additions to Esther, Daniel and Jeremiah. He also showed contempt for such Old Testament books as Job, Esther, Ecclesiastes, etc. In the New Testament he either questioned or outrightly rejected the books of James, Hebrews, Revelation, and the epistles of John.

Rejecting the suggestion of "throwing Jimmy into the stove," Protestant interpretations of Scripture subsequent to Luther had to face the epistle of James squarely. It was the first time in history that those going by the name of "Christian" were forced to give an alternative interpretation to the epistle of James — an interpretation that would have to dispute the clear and unambiguous language that one was "not justified by faith alone." Since Luther saw the epistle of James as a problem which could only be solved by ignoring or eliminating the book, choosing to keep James in the canon meant that subsequent Reformers had a lot of explaining to do. In attempting to establish an alternative interpretation, they took many and varied approaches to say that James did not really mean to deny justification by faith alone even though the text seems to say, verbatim, that he did. One explanation offered by John Calvin was that James was not using the word "justified" in the same sense as Paul was. He postulates the following:

> If you would make James consistent with the other Scriptures and with himself, you must give the word justify, as used by him, a different meaning from what it has with Paul...What then? It appears certain that he [James] is speaking of the manifestation, not of the imputation of righteousness...[103]

Here Calvin asserts that James uses the word justification to refer to a mere "manifestation" of Abraham's righteousness, whereas he allows Paul's use of the same word to refer to an "imputation" of righteousness. What Calvin means is that Paul is using the word justification to refer to a single event in the life of Abraham that once for all granted him salvation, and that James is referring to the subsequent act or acts whose only purpose is to demonstrate that Abraham already received this prior justification. Much of contemporary Protestantism has used Calvin's explanation to understand the book of James.[104]

Before we examine the rest of Calvin's conception of justification, it would be helpful to see the other theological movements

[103] *Institutes* 3:17:11, 12.

[104] The reader is asked to refer to the discussion of the book of James in chapter 2 for a refutation of Calvin's teaching.

and perspectives occurring during this time in history. As noted in the study of Luther, a dramatic tension surfaced in the nature of justification between the concept of imputation and the concept of infusion or transformation. This tension was exposed as the differences between the theologies of the German and Swiss theologians became more prominent. As opposed to Martin Luther and Philip Melanchthon (1497-1560) who represented the German view, Swiss theologians such as Martin Bucer (1491-1551) understood justification in two phases, a primary justification that was acquired by faith but a secondary justification by works.[105] Huldreich Zwingli (1484-1531) went a step further by defining justification in primarily moral and ethical terminology. Johannes Œcolampadius (1482-1531) spoke of justification not in forensic terminology but as regenerating the individual's interior life. Heinrich Bullinger (1504-1575), succeeding Zwingli in Switzerland, likewise spoke of justification as an actualization of righteousness. We see that within the space of a few years, the Swiss theologians seemed to be paving a road back to the Catholic concept wherein justification is understood as a transformation of the inner self, not as a forensic imputation of alien righteousness.[106]

Even on the German side, however, consensus between Luther and Melanchthon began to break down. Though Luther laid the

---

[105] Schaff records Luther's attitude toward Bucer: "Luther spoke a kind word to Œcolampadius; but when he first met his friend Bucer, who now sided with Zwingli, he shook his hand, and said, smiling, and pointing his finger at him, 'You are a good-for-nothing knave" (*History of the Christian Church*, Vol. VII, p. 636).

[106] Alister McGrath notes that these "strongly moralist doctrines of justification associated with the early Reformed writers such as Zwingli and Bucer actually threatened Luther's insights into the doctrine" (*ARCIC II and Justification*, p. 13). McGrath notes of Zwingli: "In his understanding of justification, Zwingli departs considerably from Luther...which led Melanchthon to hint darkly at Marburg of the works righteousness of the Swiss Reformers" *(Iustitia Dei*, II, p. 33). We must emphasize, however, that not only did they threaten Luther's doctrine but it must also be admitted that they were more Catholic than Lutheran in their concept of justification. Ironically, in other doctrines, Luther was more Catholic than the Swiss. For example, in regard to the Eucharist, Luther and Zwingli fought bitterly for years. Luther believed, similar to Catholicism, that the Eucharist, at least momentarily, became the actual body of Christ. Zwingli held that the Eucharist was purely symbolic. These differences created such tension that, speaking of Zwingli, Luther stated in *Table Talk*: "If God has saved him, he has done so above and beyond the rule"

ground work in his theory of imputation, Melanchthon is the first to apply forensic terminology to justification. In doing so, however, Melanchthon created a rift between justification and sanctification that much of Luther's writings sought to keep together. It was inevitable that once the moral element was divorced from justification, as was true in Melanchthon's theology, sanctification could no longer be joined with it.[107] Moreover, Melanchthon formulated his conception of justification at the expense of discarding other cher-

106 cont. (LW 54, 152). Countering such statements, Zwingli called Lutherans "flesh-eater, blood drinkers," and the communion bread "a baked God." Of Zwingli's writings Luther says: "How true it is that the Devil is a master of a thousand arts...How he can turn and twist and throw all sorts of obstacles in the way to prevent men from being saved and abiding in the Christian truth!" Luther's diatribes were so fierce that Bucer later wrote to him: "Dear Dr. Luther, I humbly beseech you not to be so furious in this matter as heretofore. If you are Christ's, so are we. It behooves us to contend only with the Word of God, and to observe Christian self-control...God grant unto you the knowledge of truth, and of thyself, that you remain *Luther*, and not become *loutrion* [Greek for water used in washing]. The truth will prevail. Amen." Luther retorted that Zwingli's writings were "a mask of the Devil" and "nothing but an inspiration of the Devil" (*History of the Christian Church*, Vol. VII, p. 620-628).

107 Reinhold Seeberg remarks that Melanchthon broke "...the inseparable connection, which is in Luther always maintained between regeneration, justification and sanctification" (cited in *Justification and Sanctification* by Peter Toon, p. 87). In this regard, Lutheran theologian Carl Braaten, citing the works of Lutheran Karl Holl *[The Cultural Significance of the Reformation* (1959); *The Reconstruction of Morality* (1979); and *What Did Luther Understand by Religion* (1977)] states: "Holl distinguished between analytic and synthetic justification. Synthetic justification was defined as a declarative judgment of God whereby the sinner was justified solely on the basis of the work of Christ. Holl maintained that Luther rejected this view of justification, as did Holl himself. It was Melanchthon who made the great mistake of narrowing justification down to the declaration that sinners are righteous on account of the external merits of Christ, whereas Luther allegedly understood justification as a real transformation of persons from the state of sinfulness to that of righteousness. For Holl God does not only declare a person righteous, he literally makes a person righteous. If God were to declare a person righteous who is in fact unrighteous, God would be a liar, trading on a legal fiction. God would be dealing with sinners as though they were perfectly righteous. Holl called this the fatal 'as though.'" (Braaten, op. cit., pp. 13-14). Braaten goes on to explain how Holl's view was pitted against the view of Theodosius Harnack [*Luther's Theologie mit besonderer Beziehung auf seine Versohnungs-und Erlosungslehre*, I, 1862, 1865, reissued 1927] at the 1963 Lutheran World Federation meeting in Helsinki with no resolution to this day.

ished beliefs of Luther. The early Melanchthon believed, like Luther, in the concept of the *absolute necessity of all things.* Eventually, however, Melanchthon could not accept what later appeared to him to be a fatalistic theology. In a vehement reaction against Luther's views, he concluded that the individual was not passive in justification; rather, alone with the 'Word and the Holy Spirit,' the individual could come to the faith of justification by the facility of his own free will, even apart from grace.[108] Melanchthon proposed that no one is drawn to God unless he wishes to be drawn. Perhaps to save face he added that the individual did not gain any merit from God in this process. Many other theologians followed Melanchthon's teaching on free will, among them Johann Pfeffinger, Georg Major, and Andreas Osiander. After many years of controversy, the Lutheran *Formula of Concord* in 1577 rejected Melanchthon's teaching on free will before grace, but it also rejected Luther's fatalistic view of predestination and absolute necessity. Interestingly, similar to the Council of Trent's formulation in 1563, the Formula of Concord concluded that under the influence of grace, an individual can assent to faith by his own free will.[109]

Seeing all the theological permutations developing, Calvin attempted both to take justification out of the realm of the moral life and to reassert the doctrines of absolute predestination and the causal necessity of all things. Calvin sought to plug the leak, as it were, to prevent the Reformation from ending up Catholic. In the process, however, he showed his own tendencies toward Catholic theology. With regard to justification this was evident in a crucial difference between Luther's understanding of the relationship of faith and regeneration and Calvin's understanding. Luther insisted that jus-

---

[108] Showing that he understood the ramifications of Luther's and Calvin's views on 'absolute necessity,' in a letter to Calvin, Melanchthon writes: "As regards the question treated in your book, the question of predestination...I maintain the proposition that God is not the author of sin, and therefore cannot will it. David was by his own will carried into transgression." Schaff notes that this new position of Melanchthon is in "direct opposition to the assertion in the first edition of his *Loci* (1521), and his commentary on the Romans (1524), that God does all things not *permissive*, but *potenter*, and that he foreordained and wrought the adultery of David, and the treason of Judas, as well as the vocation of Paul" (*History of the Christian Church*, Vol. VIII, p. 392).

[109] *Book of Concord*, op. cit., pp. 616-631.

tifying faith came *before* regeneration.[110] In Luther's view, man would first "seize" Christ by faith and then God would regenerate him to live a holy life. Though the "seizing" itself was considered a gift of God, nevertheless the man was not regenerate in the act of faith. Calvin, and the Reformed faith after him, reversed the order and put regeneration prior to faith. Calvin reasoned that Luther's primacy of faith over regeneration would lean toward the Pelagian conception of salvation. Calvin wanted the events of justification to be totally in the hand of God, not dependent on man's volition. Apparently, Calvin foresaw the problem in Lutheranism between faith being a gift of God and faith being an act required of man's will. Hence, to Calvin, regeneration must precede faith since the former is a change by divine fiat, not dependent on the will of man, which in turn allows him to reach out in faith and apprehend Christ. In short, while Luther stressed the "seizing" of Christ through faith, Calvin stressed that Christ irresistibly "seized" the individual.[111]

[110] This Lutheran distinctive was recognized by the 1577 *Formula of Concord*, which stated: Frequently, the word 'regeneration' means sanctification or renewal which follows the righteousness of faith, as Dr. Luther used the term in his book *On the Councils and the Church* and elsewhere (WA 50:599; 625ff)."

[111] Some claim that Calvinism, not Calvin, is responsible for the belief that regeneration precedes faith/justification (Robert Brinsmead, *Present Truth,* "The Order of Justification and Regeneration," Sept. 1976, p. 17). It is said that Calvin did not wish to separate justification from regeneration, as the sun's heat is not separated from its light (cf., *Institutes* 3:11:6). Though such a defense is pleaded, it is difficult not to see Calvin being opposed to faith preceding regeneration considering such statements as: "But faith is the principal work of the Holy Spirit ... faith itself has no other source than the Spirit... 'he baptizes us in the Holy Spirit and fire' bringing us into the light of faith in his gospel and so regenerating us that we become new creatures" (3:1:4); "As if the Holy Spirit, by illumining our hearts unto faith" (3:2:8); "For the Spirit is not only the initiator of faith..." (3:2:33); "Christ, when he illumines us into faith by the power of his Spirit..." (3:2:35). It was these kinds of statements, said in the context of his opposition to the Catholic doctrine of "formed" and "unformed" faith, that Calvin sought to make faith the product solely of the Spirit's regeneration, thereby securing the individual's adoption and election (3:2:8, 11, 12).

This eliminated the subjective element in Luther's theology.[112] Ironically, subsequent Lutheran theology sided more with Calvin than Luther. Whereas Luther had believed that justification came immediately upon the "seizing" by faith, Lutheranism sided with Calvin in affirming that faith was prompted by the internal regeneration of the individual. By the same token, however, Lutheranism maintained Luther's view that the believer could reject his faith and thus lose his justification.[113] Calvin, of course, saw things differently. Once justified, the individual could never lose his status with God, and if it seemed as if he did, it logically meant that he never actually possessed it originally.[114] However, in claiming that regeneration preceded faith and resulted in a secure justification, this meant that the regeneration which produced justification would be very similar to or identical with the Catholic concept that justification entailed an internal transformation or regeneration of the individual.[115] Not surprisingly, Calvin and Calvinistic confessions

---

[112] In this regard, Alister McGrath points out, "Indeed, most Reformed theologians regarded Luther's preoccupation with the doctrine of justification as hopelessly subjective — what was required was an objective basis, as provided in scripture, upon which reform might proceed, rather than an unhealthy obsession with existential subjectivity" *(ARCIC II and Justification*, p. 13). We must interject upon McGrath's statement and say that appeals to the objectivity "as provided by scripture," are somewhat ironic when one remembers that Luther's theology, as subjective as it was, purported to take us back to the *objective* study of "scripture alone," without the Church or Tradition to bother us.

[113] In 1520 Luther wrote: "A Christian or one baptized...can never, even though he wants to, forfeit his salvation even through ever so many sins, unless he decides not to believe" (WA 6, 529, 11). The Augsburg Confession stated: "Rejected here are those who teach that persons who have once become godly cannot fall again" (Art. XII, 9).

[114] Of Luther's view Calvin writes: Those who answer that men's condemnation properly arises from unbelief alone, not from particular sins, do not satisfy me...But because in weighing righteousness and unrighteousness, they seem to apply the same reckoning to good and evil works, in this I am constrained to disagree with them" (*Institutes* 3:18:10).

[115] "Man...receives in the said justification together with the remission of sins all these infused at the same time: faith, hope and charity" (CT, Session 6, Chapter 7).

found themselves using the word "infusion" in reference to justification, a term hitherto reserved for Catholicism.[116]

Regarding Luther's view of "absolute necessity," Lutheranism had forthrightly rejected this view. Calvin reintroduced the concept by appealing, as Luther did, to the writings of Augustine. Calvin writes: "I shall not hesitate, then, simply to confess with Augustine that 'the will of God is the necessity of things,' and that what he has willed will of necessity come to pass, as those things which he has foreseen will truly come to pass."[117] In another place Calvin writes: "Augustine everywhere speaks of this necessity; and...did not hesitate to affirm it in these words: 'Through freedom man came to be in sin, but the corruption which followed as punishment turned freedom into necessity.'" Calvin concludes this section with: "But if this is true, then it is clearly expressed that man is surely subject to the necessity of sinning."[118] Since Calvin, opposed to Augustine, denied free will in man, this made his view of "necessity" seem all the more extreme — a view which would not be accepted by the Council of Trent.[119]

Since Calvin purports to be battling the Pelagian ideas of Ockham, Biel, and Erasmus that Luther claimed to be debating, there is much overlap between the Reformation theologians and Augustine — an overlap that Reformed theology often transposes into an inseparable kinship between Augustine and Calvin. As we have seen with Luther, however, the problem with comparing Calvin

---

[116] Calvin used the word "infused" [Latin: *perfundo*] in the statement: "Rather, we ought first to cleave unto him so that, infused with his holiness, we may follow whither he calls," and "The first is that the love of righteousness, to which we are otherwise not at all inclined by nature, may be instilled and established in our hearts..." (*Institutes* 3:6:2). Francis Turretin also used "infusion" [Latin: *infundo*] in *Institutes of Elenctic Theology* (15:4:13). The Canons of Dort in 1618, which was a synod called to respond to the Arminian Remonstrance in 1610 that held to the free will of man in salvation, stated: "Faith is therefore a gift of God in this way: not that it is merely offered by God to the free will of man, but that it is actually conferred on man, implanted and *infused* in him" [Latin: *infundo*] ("The Third and Fourth Heads of Doctrine," Art. 11, 14, *Creeds of Christendom*, 3:590, 591).

[117] *Institutes* 3:23:8. The editor, John McNeil, references Augustine's work *On the Literal Interpretation of Genesis*, PL 34, 350, as the source. See **Appendix 19** for a refutation of Calvin's citing of Augustine on this issue.

[118] *Institutes* 2:3:5

[119] Session 6, Canons 4, 5, 6.

and Augustine is two-fold: (1) Although Augustine's soteriology was solidified toward the end of his theological career in his anti-Pelagian writings, (many of which were used at the Council of Orange in 529 AD and became the official teaching of the Catholic Church), he never modified his ecclesial or sacramental theology, a theology which Luther radically altered and which Calvin totally obliterated. Thus, there is a strong tendency among Protestant theologians to establish a link with Augustine through grossly selective citation of his voluminous writings.[120] Calvin is no exception. He quotes from Augustine *ad nauseam*, but usually only those passages which agree with his particular theological bent, especially those dealing with necessity and causality.[121] (2) Although there is much overlap between Calvin's and Augustine's anti-Pelagian views, still Augustine did not share many of Calvin's teachings in this regard. All in all, Augustine had a much more balanced soteriological view than Calvin. For example, though Augustine was strongly predestinarian, he also insisted that man retained free will. Calvin explicitly denied free will.[122] Calvin believed that God predestined the fall of Adam, a view that was further advanced by Theodore Beza and the Puritans.[123] Neither Augustine, the Council

---

[120] Among current evangelicals, a good example of this tendency is evident in the books *A View of Rome* by John H. Armstrong, pp. 26, 32-34; and *Chosen By God* by R. C. Sproul, p. 65.

[121] Calvin either quotes from or alludes to Augustine over one thousand times in the *Institutes* alone, and several thousand times in the remainder of his writings.

[122] Calvin writes: "From this, too, we see how mad is the confidence of the Papists, relying on free will..." (*Commentary on St. John*, op. cit., p. 273).

[123] In the Reformed tradition, this view was further subdivided into "supralapsarianism" and "infralapsarianism," the former being the stronger of the two. In view of some of his statements, Calvin seems to side with the supralapsarian view: "The Father has chosen us in Christ before the foundation of the world...Here, surely, the fall of Adam is not presupposed as preceding God's decree in time; but it is what God determined before all ages that is shown, when he willed to heal the misery of mankind" (*Institutes* 2:12:5). Editor John McNeil comments in the footnote: "this passage briefly shows Calvin as favouring the supralapsarian as opposed to the infralapsarian view of the decrees of God" (Ibid). Alister McGrath remarks: "Predestination, for Augustine, refers only to the divine decision to redeem, not to the act of abandoning the remainder of fallen humanity. For Calvin, logical rigour demands that God actively chooses to redeem or to damn. God cannot be thought of as doing something by default: he is active and sovereign in his actions. Therefore God actively wills the salvation of those who will be saved and the damnation of those who will not" (*Reformation Thought*, 2nd edition, 1993, p. 125).

of Orange (529) nor the Council of Valence (855) which followed Augustine's teaching, ever allowed such an idea.[124] Augustine taught that Adam needed God's infused grace in order to avoid the temptation of the devil in the Garden of Eden.[125] Calvin speaks of Adam having only external graces or endowments from the created world.[126] Augustine understood justification as a process whereby the Holy Spirit initially and continually infuses grace into the individual thereby transforming him into a righteous person. Calvin taught that justification was external to man and imputed to him, and did not include a moral transformation of the individual. Augustine believed in Purgatory; Calvin did not. Augustine believed in the subjective uncertainty of salvation; Calvin did not.[127] Space does not permit a more detailed elaboration of the extensive differences between these two theologians.

Calvin's View of Faith and Works

In speaking of the relationship between faith and works, Calvin's language is somewhat evasive. We notice this more in what he admits than in what he is willing to debate. In his commentary on Galatians, completed in 1548, Calvin writes:

---

124 Council of Orange, Canon 25: "We not only do not believe that some have been truly predestined to evil by divine power, but also with every execration we pronounce anathema upon those, if there are such, who wish to believe so great an evil." Council of Valence, Canon 3: "...in regard to evil men, however, we believe that God foreknew their malice, because it is from them, but that He did not predestine it, because it is not from Him."

125 *De correptione et gratia*, PL 11, 29; 11, 31; 11, 32; *Admonition and Grace*, JR 1952, 1954, 1955).

126 Calvin writes: "Man in his first condition excelled in these pre-eminent endowments, so that his reason, understanding, prudence, and judgment not only sufficed for the direction of his earthly life, but by them men mounted up even to God eternal bliss...In this integrity man by free will had the power, if he so willed, to attain eternal life...Therefore, Adam could have stood if he wished, seeing that he fell solely by his own will...his choice of good and evil was free, and not that alone, but the highest rectitude was in his mind and will, and all the organic parts were rightly composed to obedience..." (*Institutes* 1:15:8). See chapter 7 for further detail.

127 *The Gift of Perseverance*, ch. 33: "To which calling there is no man that can be said by men with any certainty of affirmation to belong, until he has departed from this world; but in this life of man, which is a state of trial upon the earth, he who seems to stand must take heed lest he fall" (NPNF, Vol. 5, p. 538).

> It is not our doctrine that the faith which justifies is alone. We maintain that it is always joined with good works. But we contend that faith avails by itself for justification...When we debate justification, however, we exclude all works...when you discuss justification beware of allowing any mention of love or of works but resolutely hold on to the exclusive adverb.[128]

On the one hand, Calvin admits quite candidly that "faith" should not be qualified by the word "alone" in the statement, "It is not our doctrine that the faith which justifies is alone." On the other hand, he craftily tells his readers that they must make an absolute break between faith and works when debating the issue with [Catholic] opponents. He tells them to "hold on the exclusive adverb [or adjective]," i.e., the word "alone." It is only logical to assume that Calvin feared that unless he insisted on the "exclusive adverb," common sense might prevail in intellectual discussion and reveal that faith could not be alone in justification.

Shortly before his death in 1564, Calvin wrote his last words on the relationship between faith and works. In his commentary on Ezekiel, he admitted:

> ...for this proposition that faith without works justifies is true and yet false, according to the different senses which it bears. The proposition, that faith without works justifies by itself is false because faith without works is void. But if the clause "without works" is joined with the word "justifies," the proposition will be true. Therefore, faith cannot justify when it is without works, because it is dead, and a mere fiction.[129]

Though Calvin remained a true Reformer who was not about to bend to the Papists he despised, this excerpt shows a marked movement away from the strict *aloneness* of faith espoused by Luther. It also and demonstrates a continuing evolution in Calvin's

---

[128] *Calvin's New Testament Commentary*, op. cit., p. 96.
[129] *Commentary on the Prophet Ezekiel*, Vol. 2 (Grand Rapids: Baker, 1979), p. 238.

thinking on this issue. We see the same dichotomy in this 1564 quote as we do in the previous quote from 1548. The fact that Calvin wrote the 1564 piece near his death suggests that he struggled with the issue of the relationship between faith and works all his life.

As Calvin makes his departure from key points in Luther's theology, one way he attempts to explain his view is in the use of the term "double grace":

> By partaking of him, we principally receive double grace: namely, that being reconciled to God through Christ's blamelessness, we may have in heaven instead of a Judge a gracious Father. And secondly, that sanctified by Christ's spirit we may cultivate blamelessness and purity of life. Of regeneration, indeed, the second of these gifts, I have said what seemed sufficient.[130]

We see the following in Calvin's statement: First, through grace, a way of reconciliation to God has been established. Second, the reconciliation is one in which God turns from "Judge" to "Father."[131] Third, the individual is able to live a life of purity due to the grace that God gives him. Here Calvin equates the second distribution of grace with being "sanctified by Christ's spirit." That he further describes this second grace as "regeneration" shows that to Calvin grace is in some sense substantive. The substantive nature of grace seems especially relevant since, as we discovered earlier, regeneration precedes faith and justification in Calvin's theology. We

---

130 *Institutes* 3:6:11.

131 Calvin uses the principle of the *leniency* of a father in other places: "But sons, who are more generously and candidly treated by their fathers, do not hesitate to offer the incomplete and half-done and even defective works, trusting that their obedience and readiness of mind will be accepted by their fathers, even though they have not quite achieved what their fathers intended. Such children we ought to be, trusting that our services will be approved by our most merciful Father, however small, rude, and imperfect these may be..." (*Institutes* 3:19:5). "This tenderness in overlooking and tolerating vices is a sign of God's fatherly favor" (Ibid., 3:3:2). The reader should note that this perspective in Calvin is very similar to that of Charles Hodge about which we remarked in chapters 1 and 5 in connection with the Catholic understanding of justification.

are forced to conclude that perhaps Calvin did not realize how close he came to the Catholic teaching of "infused" grace.[132]

To explain his view of "justification by works," Calvin writes:

> He is said to be justified in God's sight who is both reckoned righteous in God's judgment and has been accepted on account of his righteousness...Thus, justified before God is the man who, freed from the company of sinners, has God to witness and affirm his righteousness...which deserves a testimony of righteousness before God's throne will be said to be justified by works, or else he who, by the wholeness of his works, can meet and satisfy God's judgment.[133]

Here we see that by the reference to "God's throne" Calvin reserves the "justification by works" (as part of his "double justification" theology) to the end time judgment. Hence, what Catholicism applies to the progressive nature of justification, Calvin limits to the end. In reality, though, Calvin's concept of being "accepted by God...on account of his [the individual's] righteousness" is merely a formality due to the fact that the individual had *already been* "reckoned righteous" by imputation. This previous "reckoning" was total and complete, which necessarily makes the individual's own righteousness of no real consequence. Calvin's "justification by works," then, is not really a justification at all, it is more a rite of passage. Calvin reveals his real interest on the nature of justification in the next series of statements, revealing that he holds two entirely different concepts within his "double justification":

> On the contrary, justified by faith is he who, excluded from the righteousness of works grasps the righteousness of Christ through faith, and clothed in it, appears in God's sight not as a sinner but as a righteous man. Therefore we explain justification simply as

---

132 This analysis of Calvin is said in respect of his multifaceted view of regeneration, a view which also allowed him to understand regeneration as an ongoing process in the individual Christian. Today's Reformed theologians, however, speak more of "sanctification" rather than "regeneration" for events after justification, and understand regeneration as that which occurs before justification and sanctification (cf., R. C. Sproul, *Chosen By God*, p. 72).

133 *Institutes* 3:11:1.

> the acceptance with which God receives us into his favor as righteous men. And we say that it consists in the remission of sins and the imputation of Christ's righteousness.[134]

In the same context, however, Calvin says something that seems remarkably Catholic — a statement similar to Augustine's explanation as to the rationale in Catholic theology as to why God accepts and gives merit to our works:[135]

> For the Lord cannot fail to love and embrace the good things that he works in them through his Spirit. But we must always remember that God "accepts" believers by reason of works *only because he is their source and graciously*, by way of adding to his liberality, deigns also to show "acceptance" toward the good works he has himself bestowed.[136] (emphasis mine)

When the question surfaced in his deliberations with Andreas Osiander over the significance of faith for justification, Calvin wrote:

> I willingly concede Osiander's objection that faith of itself does not possess the power of justifying, but only in so far as it receives Christ. For if faith justified of itself or through some intrinsic power, so to speak, as it is always weak and imperfect it would effect this only in part; thus the righteousness that conferred a fragment of salvation upon us would be defective...We compare faith to a kind of vessel; for unless we come empty and with the mouth of our soul open to seek Christ's grace, we are not capable of receiving Christ.

Here we see Calvin attempting to maintain the proposition that only Christ's righteousness justifies the individual. But no matter how much he stresses Christ's righteousness, he cannot escape the fact that the faith of the individual must be of a *specific quality* in order to receive this divine righteousness. Calvin says faith is a "vessel" and that we must "come empty and with the mouth of our

---

[134] *Institutes* 3:11:2.

[135] cf., Augustine's famous saying in his letter to Sixtus: "God, crowning our merits, crowns nothing else but his own gifts" (*Letter to Sixtus*, PL 194, 3, 9).

[136] *Institutes* 3:17:5.

soul open," but he does so without admitting that this requires the individual to prepare and manifest the proper spiritual disposition in order to receive Christ's righteousness. Unless the individual provides the "emptying" and "opening the mouth of the soul," there can be no application of justification, and thus faith, as weak or as strong as it is calculated to be, nevertheless becomes the ultimate determinant of whether the individual is justified or not. This is the same trap that modern Evangelicals fall into when they speak of the "quality of faith" or "saving faith" that is required to receive Christ's righteousness. As soon as one introduces such a variable, and by this requires the individual to possess a certain quality of faith prior to justification, then the determination of whether the individual receives the justification falls squarely on his own shoulders.

As we have seen earlier in our study, Calvin previously claimed that the individual could not be justified by works because works could not stand before the "tribunal of God."[137] Conversely, we must remember from the above discussion that Calvin also insisted that works, in the context of his "justification by works," were judged at "God's throne" [*viz.*, "tribunal"]. At the "throne," Calvin says the individual "will be said to be justified by works, or else he who, by the wholeness of his works, can meet and satisfy God's judgment." Calvin also said that at the "throne" God can be satisfied "only because he is their source and *graciously*, by way of adding to his liberality, deigns also to show 'acceptance'" (emphasis mine). Apparently, then, Calvin believed that God does not give "acceptance" to the individual on the basis of strict standards that one would normally associate with a *throne*, but rather he offers it out of his "graciousness." Consequently, in the judgment of works, Calvin mixes and matches "God's tribunal" with his "graciousness" — at some points treating the tribunal in strict legal terms, without mercy and grace [i.e., "...since at God's tribunal they must draw back"], but at other times as the place where "mercy" and "acceptance" are freely given. In respect of this contradiction, Calvin simply has no room left from which to criticize the Catholic theology of works. Moreover, we must insist that what Calvin holds as necessary with respect to God's judging of our works, in

[137] Calvin writes: "We agree that good works are required of righteousness, but we do not allow them the power of conferring it, since at God's tribunal they must draw back" (*Commentary on James*, op. cit., p. 287).

turn, should also be applied to God's judgment of our faith. Since only God can be the ultimate judge of the *kind* of faith that is required of the individual in order to receive Christ's righteousness, whether the judgment of this faith is made from Calvin's "tribunal of God" or from God's "graciousness," or both, there must be some criterion from which God judges the quality of the faith required for justification, and only God can be its determiner. If this is true of faith, then it can also be true of works, and thus there can be no room for Calvin to claim the existence of erroneous doctrine within Catholicism since she holds that faith and works are required for justification, *both* of which are judged by the same divine criteria — God's graciousness.

Other Issues and Controversies

Like Luther, Calvin trained for the priesthood and was thus very familiar with everything Catholic. As he departed from the Church, he had various opportunities to converse with the Catholic hierarchy. In one of these instances, Calvin was confronted by a letter Cardinal Jacopo Sadolet had written to the people of Geneva, Calvin's model city of Reformation theology. Remarking on the unity of Catholic belief, as opposed to the variety of Protestant beliefs that had already permeated Europe, Sadolet appeals to the Genevans to reconsider Catholicism:

> Truth is always one, while error is varied and multiform; that which is straight is simple, that which is crooked has many turns. Can anyone who confesses Christ fail to perceive that such a teaching of the holy Church is the proper work of Satan, and not of God? What does God demand of us? What does Christ enjoin? That we be all one in him.[138]

Calvin took up the challenge by writing a lengthy letter in return. His tactic was both theological and ethical, pointing out the corruptions of the Church not only in his time, but also of past centuries. He buttressed his accusations against some of the corrupt Catholic hierarchy by citing the condemnations given by the

[138] Schaff, *History of the Christian Church*, Vol. VIII, op. cit., p. 401.

Old Testament prophets against the corrupt Levitical priests of that period. In comparing 16th century priests with Levitical priests, Calvin writes: "I had before my eyes the examples of Thy prophets, who I saw had a similar contest with the priests and false prophets of their day, though these were undoubtedly the rulers of the Church among the Israelitish people." Then, from a theological basis, he complained of "false teachings" in the Catholic Church such as the views on Baptism and the Eucharist. He writes: "The true meaning of Baptism and the Lord's Supper, also, was corrupted by numerous falsehoods."[139] In this double-fisted response to Sadolet, Calvin won back many of the Genevans.

Let us examine the merits of Calvin's accusations. Though everyone recognizes that anyone who understands himself as a man of God should not tolerate corruption in the Church, the issue is: who among those claiming allegiance to God have the right to administer that judgment? It is one thing to compare the corruptions of the Church with the corruptions of the Levitical priests, but it is quite another for a man to claim that the priesthood is illegitimate and should be abolished because of those corruptions. The prophets of the Old Testament never called for the abolition of the priestly or prophetic office but only sought the reform of these institutions. They simply did not have the right or power to abolish something that God had ordained. Eventually, if the false priests and prophets did not heed the warnings of God, God himself would come in judgment upon the perpetrators, but still maintain the institution. Because it is God's Church to do with as he pleases, it is precisely the presumptions of men to act in ways that only belong to God that are no less immoral than the acts of those whom these men would condemn. Old Testament prophets had similar temptations but did not succumb to them. Habakkuk, for example, lived in a time when the nation of Israel was very wicked. Habakkuk earnestly wanted God to judge Israel for her sins and complained that God was refraining from doing so. God assured him that some day he would bring judgment upon them, but in the meantime Habakkuk had to trust that God knew what was best. In the end, Habakkuk realized that he could not demand that God come in judgment when Habakkuk thought it should happen but must wait on God, no matter how long

139 Ibid., pp. 406-408. Calvin, as opposed to Luther, believed that Baptism and the Eucharist were symbolic.

it seemed to take. In the same way, if the Reformers were concerned about the corruptions in the Church, they should have waited on God to bring his judgment upon the perpetrators rather than take it upon themselves to abolish the offices of the Church.

We must also take issue with Calvin's claim that Baptism and the Lord's Supper "suffered from corruption." Though Calvin would not accept what he called the "wafer god," he was aware, as were his contemporaries, that the unanimous consent of the early Fathers held views of Baptism and the Eucharist that were diametrically opposed to his views. Even Luther, as much as he disagreed with the Church on certain issues, never relinquished the Church's teaching on these two important sacraments. Anglican doctrine concurred. We cannot help but conclude that Calvin set himself up not only as the moral judge of the Church, but also as the sole judge of Church doctrine. From the Catholic perspective, it is precisely in such physically unprovable matters as Baptism and the Eucharist that God catches men in their own craftiness, who, not accepting the traditional doctrine by faith in Christ's preservation of truth, have taken it upon themselves to be wiser than God. As Paul said to the Corinthians: "Did the word originate with you? Or are you the only people it has reached? If anyone thinks he is a prophet or spiritually gifted, let him acknowledge that what I am writing to you is the Lord's command. If he ignores this, he himself will be ignored" (1 Cor. 14:36-38); and again, "Do not deceive yourselves. If any one of you thinks he is wise by the standards of this age, he should become a 'fool' so that he may become wise...As it is written: 'He catches the wise in their craftiness,' and again: 'The Lord knows that the thoughts of the wise are futile'" (1 Cor. 3:18-20). Though it was hard for Calvin to accept that a "wafer" could be transubstantiated into God himself, and that water could effectuate one's salvation, it is precisely in these seemingly "foolish things" that God chooses "to shame the wise" (1 Cor. 1:27-31). As Wisdom 12:17 states, "For you show your strength when people doubt the completeness of your power."

Andreas Osiander and Jacobus Arminius

Contrary to popular opinion, it was not the Catholic Church that gave Luther and Calvin the most difficult challenge to their respective theologies. Many voices from within the Reformation itself were in bitter dispute right from the beginning. Although they agreed in theory that salvation was not confined to the Church, they disagreed vehemently as to how the individual acquired his salvation directly from God. As we can surmise from the study of Reformation history already presented, the two most controversial issues concerning the doctrine of justification were: (1) to what degree, if any, man's free will was involved in justification, and (2) whether to understand justification as an internal transformation or as a forensic event totally external to the individual.[140] On the second issue, Andreas Osiander (1498- 1552), a Reformed theologian from Germany, explicitly opposed the concept of forensic justification first introduced by Luther and developed later by Melanchthon and Calvin. Identical to Augustine, Osiander held that God acts as a physician, not as a judge, who cures man of his spiritual sickness, thus "making" a man just rather than merely "imputing" him just.[141] Osiander insisted that any notion of external or forensic justification was alien to Scripture, especially to those passages in the gospel of John that spoke of the indwelling Christ. Ironically, Osiander had borrowed Luther's and Calvin's concept of "union with Christ" but discarded their theory of the imputation of righteousness.[142] Even before Osiander, however, Andreas von Karlstadt, who in 1517 while preparing for a debate with Luther had reread the works of Augustine, became convinced that justification was indeed an interior transformation of the individual in which one

---

[140] Catholic theologian Albert Pighius of Holland (d. 1542), in his debates with Luther and Calvin, concluded that the Reformation concepts of the total slavery of the human will, and the absolute necessity of all events, were the two principal errors of the period.

[141] Calvin writes of Osiander: "Osiander laughs at those men who teach that 'to be justified' is a legal term; because we must actually be righteous. Also, he despises nothing more than that we are justified by free imputation...Osiander objects that it would be insulting to God and contrary to his nature that he should justify those who actually remain wicked" (*Institutes* 3:11:11). Calvin then uses 2 Cor. 5:19 as proof of legal imputation. Ironically, this is the same verse Reformed theologian Charles Hodge (1841) would use to support the Protestant concept of sanctification (see chapter 5 of this book). Protestant historian Philip Schaff supports Calvin, but with an interesting admission in favor of the Catholic view: "Modern exegesis has justified this view of δικαιόω and δικαίωσις, according to Hellenistic usage, although etymologically the verb may mean *to make just*, i.e., to sanctify, in accordance with verbs in όω, e.g. δηλόω φανερόω τυφλόω, *to make manifest*, etc." (Schaff, *History of the Christian Church*, Vol. VII, p. 123, n. 2).

[142] *Encyclopedia of Religion*, ed. Virgilius Ferm, 1959, p. 553.

was made righteous. In making this discovery, Karlstadt was following Johannes von Staupitz (d. 1524), the very person who a few years earlier had encouraged Luther to read the Scriptures in order to awaken from his "dogmatic slumbers."[143] In fact, Luther's ideas of justification met considerable resistance among the German and Swiss Reformers, culminating in Germany with the *Formula of Concord* which modified and dismissed many of his views.

A few years after Osiander, Jacobus Arminius[144] (1560-1609), a Dutch Reformed theologian, along with his followers called "Remonstrants," had attacked Luther's and Calvin's other doctrinal arm: the notion of absolute predestination. As noted previously, Luther spoke of the *absolute necessity of all things*, including God's causal connection to the sin of man. Calvin developed this line of thinking, claiming that God had predestined the fall of Adam.[145] Arminius and the Remonstrants had rejected all the tenets of Calvinism, e.g., limited atonement, unconditional election, irresistible grace, and espe-

---

143 This contrasts with the claim made by Evangelical Michael Horton that the "Augustinian abbot [Staupitz] argued that faith was the sole criterion of God's acceptance of the believing sinner" (*Roman Catholicism*, op. cit., pp. 265-266). Contrary to the impression Horton conveys, Staupitz remained a faithful Catholic, supporting all the doctrines of his Church and denouncing Lutheranism as a heresy in 1523 (Ferm, p. 734). See also, McGrath, *Iustitia Dei*, II, pp. 20-21 supporting Staupitz's transformational understanding of justification. Similar to Horton, N. Geisler and R. MacKenzie, in dedicating their book *Roman Catholics and Evangelicals: Agreements and Differences* to Staupitz, give the false impression that Staupitz had renounced Catholicism for the Lutheran version of justification.

144 His native Dutch name was Jacob Hermann, but the Latinized form was Jacobus Arminius.

145 In addition to Calvin's statement in INT 2:12:5, n. 121, Calvin writes: " They say it is not stated in so many words that God decreed that Adam should perish for his rebellion. As if, indeed, that very God, who, Scripture proclaims, 'does whatever he pleases' would have created the noblest of his creatures to an uncertain end...And it ought not to seem absurd for me to say that God not only foresaw the fall of the first man, and in him the ruin of his descendants, but also meted it out in accordance with his own election." Editor McNeil notes: "Calvin affirms Adam's original free will (cf. 1:15:8), yet insists that Adam's fall was willed by God..." (3:23:7, f. 18). In spite of this, McGrath insists that Calvin did not teach the doctrine of 'limited atonement,' but that it was later added by Theodore Beza and those following Calvin as they abandoned Calvin's stress on "union with Christ" and opted for an emphasis on divine election (*Iustitia Dei*, II, p. 40).

cially "double-predestination."[146] Arminius did believe, however, that grace came before the decision of the will, but with the stipulation that the grace was resistible. Arminian doctrine had wide influence in Europe and became the base upon which much of Protestant and Evangelical doctrine would be built.[147]

---

[146] Calvinism's basic doctrine is often summarized using the acronym TULIP (T = total depravity, i.e., the whole of man is depraved, there is no good in him, and he has no free will to chose for God. Some Reformed theologians teach that 'total depravity' is not 'utter depravity' and thus prefer the term 'radical depravity,' that is, that man is not as bad as he could be (e.g., Sproul, *Chosen By God*); U = unconditional election, i.e., God did not foresee anything good in man to elect him to salvation; L = limited atonement, i.e., God desired and planned to save only a limited number of individuals, and it is only to them that the atonement of Christ was designed; the rest were predestined, reprobated, or passed over into damnation; I = irresistible grace, i.e., that the predetermined end of regenerating grace cannot be thwarted. An elected individual may resist grace, but eventually grace will win out and he will be saved; P = perseverance of the saints, i.e., once elected and justified, the individual cannot lose their salvation. If he falls away, it proves he was never elected or justified originally. Arminius and the Remonstrants opposed each of these points with the natural opposite. No acronym, however, has been assigned to them. In the *Conference of Remonstrants* 11/7 it was stated: "Persons truly regenerate, by neglecting grace and grieving the Holy Spirit with sin, fall away totally, and at length finally, from grace into eternal reprobation." Calvin also debated heatedly over his views of predestination with other Reformed theologians such as Hierosme Bolsec, Sebastian Castellio, and Faustus Socinius, the latter attempting to answer Calvin by proposing a doctrine of man's free will within a limitation of divine foreknowledge wherein God foreknows or foreordains only the necessary future, which became known as *Socinianism*. Michael Servetus was Calvin's most ardent opponent. Though Calvin had banished Bolsec from Geneva, he was not so kind to Servetus. Becoming harsher than the popes he despised, and putting himself above the freedom of conscience and worship which had originally attracted Protestantism's followers, Calvin wrote to his friend Farel in 1546 concerning Servetus: "But I am unwilling to pledge my word for his safety; for if he does come, and my authority be of any avail, I shall never suffer him to depart alive" (Schaff, *History of the Christian Church*, VIII, p. 692). Servetus was in fact executed, an incident Calvin never publically regretted or repented of.

[147] In Reformation circles there were so many other dissenters from Luther's and Calvin's ideas that there is not enough space to list them all. Some of the more prominent names were Pirkheimer, Rubeanus, Rufus, Zasius, Amerpach, Wizel, Strauss, Wildenauer, Haner, Clareanus, and Billicanus. Pirkheimer, like Erasmus, supported Luther in the beginning; his name was even included in the papal bull which excommunicated Luther, but by the late 1520s Pirkheimer was saying of Luther: "In earlier years almost all men applauded the name of Luther, but nowadays nearly all are overcome with disgust upon hearing this name. The good report of his notable virtues has not only waned,

As time went on, Calvin's slant on predestination became the central issue among many of the subsequent Reformed theologians, especially Theodore Beza (1519-1605). Theology became a highly esoteric exercise of attempting to plumb the depths of the secret plan of election. Elaborate systems of covenants, either between God and man or among the persons of the Trinity, soon overshadowed the simple faith of the original formulators.[148] The Reformed faith began to move in two opposite directions. On the one hand, as predestination began to subsume most of Reformed theology, its adherents eventually became a cloistered community of enigmatic theoreticians who had a difficult time assimilating into society.[149] On the other hand, Reformation theology began to make its presence felt in the universities of Europe, mixing the secular with the theological. Reintroduced by Philip Melanchthon, Theodore Beza incorporated the Aristotelian method into Reformation theology in an effort to systematize its beliefs. Ironically, the very Aristotelian thought of the medieval period that Luther had rejected, in a few short years became pervasive in Post-Reformation thought. Breakthroughs in the sciences and arts, and a sea of competing ideologies and economies, dwarfed theological concerns. Continuing the process begun in the Italian Renaissance and boosted by the Enlightenment, theologians debated every twist and wrinkle concerning how the individual was accepted by his Maker without the mediation of and the grace within the Church. By the late 17th century, literally hundreds of Protestant denominations had spanned Europe and were spilling over into the Americas. And be-

---

147 cont. but practically died out. In addition to his insults and his audacity, impudence, arrogance and abusive language, he puts on such a bold front that he will stop at no lie. What he asserts today, without any shame he dares to deny tomorrow" (WA 26, 514; cited in Rix, *Martin Luther: The Man and the Image*, p. 214). Catholic theologian Dollinger thoroughly analyzes such contentions in *The Reformation* (Regensburg, 1846); cited in Schaff, *History of the Christian Church*, pp. 435-440). With his poem titled, "The Wonderful 'One-Hoss Shay," Protestant Oliver Wendell Holmes, who rebelled against the Calvinism of his father-pastor, is well-known for claiming that Calvinism officially died in America on November 1, 1855. Much of the turning from Calvinism was due to the teaching of evangelist Charles Finney.

148 The aspect of "covenant" became a highly debated issue between the Amyraldians and the Sulmarians.

149 Calvinism soon developed into a dogmatic legalism whose failure first become evident in Calvin's inability to make the city of Geneva a model of state-sponsored religion. Later, Calvinistic Puritans in New England, after a few generations, failed in the same way.

cause theology seemed ever more esoteric and remote, thus scientific, ethical, political and economic concerns began to replace theological concerns. From the many competing voices spawned by the Reformation, with its internecine wars and persecutions, the average man reasoned that while theology divides, science unites.

Anabaptism, Pietism, and Methodism

In reaction to what was regarded as the mechanical and esoteric views of Lutheranism and Calvinism, other movements spawned by the Reformation produced even more variations on the nature of salvation. The Anabaptists of the early 1500s rejected both Lutheran and Calvinistic views of forensic justification, calling the notion "utterly foreign."[150] Anabaptist Hans Hut is quoted as saying, "if man is to be justified by God he must prepare himself that God may accomplish his work in him" and "it [faith] alone does not save man."[151] The Anabaptists also differed from Luther and Calvin regarding infant baptism. On this doctrine, Anabaptists are forerunners of today's Baptists. The understanding of baptism with respect to justification is significant in that both Catholic and Lutheran theology understand baptism as the means of grace for salvation, otherwise known as *baptismal regeneration*.[152] If baptis-

---

150 Friedmann, Robert. *The Theology of Anabaptism*, p. 87; as cited in "Deviations From Historic Solafideism in the Reformed Community" by Andrew Sandlin in *The Chalcedon Report*, 1995, p. 21.

151 Ibid., pp. 88-89. Friedmann concludes that the Anabaptist understanding of justification was "a change in the nature or quality of the person who first was, but no longer is — at least in intention — a sinner...it does not mean merely an acquittal in court but an actual change in man's nature...A forensic view of grace, in which the sinner is forgiven, and undeservedly justified, is simply unacceptable to the existential faith of the Anabaptists" (p. 91).

152 The doctrine of baptismal regeneration was so firm in the mind of Luther that not only did he severely castigate his Reformation peer Huldreich Zwingli for his repudiation of the view, but when the Catholic hierarchy posed the ultimate question as to how Luther knew, objectively, that he was justified, Luther attributed such knowledge to his water baptism rather than to his "firm" faith. Despite this view, however, it was difficult theologically for Luther to incorporate the necessity of baptism into his concept of justification by *faith alone*. Nevertheless, Luther writes: "So they have become nothing but legalists and Mosaists, defecting from Christ to Moses and calling the people back from Baptism, faith and the promises of Christ to the Law and works, changing grace into the Law and the Law into grace" (LW 26, 143).

mal regeneration is true, then denying baptism to infants would necessarily involve denying them salvation, and thus their eternal destiny would be in jeopardy if they died in infancy. Hence, one's understanding of baptism directly affects one's understanding of salvation and its recipients.

The Anabaptists also taught a form of "Christian perfection" as well as social reform by civil law. Whereas Luther stressed a *faith alone* gospel that led to antinomianism, the Anabaptists stressed a neonomian gospel.[153] The Calvinists, on the other hand, who purported to strike a middle ground between Luther and the Anabaptists, soon fell into esoteric theories and dogmatic legalism which gave impetus in the 17th century to the hollowness of what came to be known as "Protestant scholasticism."

In reaction to the antinomianism of Luther and the dogmatic legalism of Calvinism, Philip Spener gave birth to the Pietist movement in the late 17th century. This developed into the Moravian movement under von Zinzendorf (1700-1760), and finally the Methodist movement under John Wesley (1703-1791). These movements rejected the Calvinist concept of predestination; stressing, rather, the exercise of free will and personal piety. In addition, Pietism's emphasis on "active" faith left no room for the concept of forensic imputation of righteousness. Like the Swiss theologians before him, the English Quaker, Robert Barclay (1648-1690), though retaining elements of Calvinism, maintained that justification must be understood as making one righteous.[154] As with the Anabaptists, excesses in some of these denominations became apparent. Concepts such as "Christian perfection" (i.e., attaining the status of no personal sin) became the goal of the individual and reached new heights in Methodism (so named for the "method" of attaining godly perfection), further complicating the issue of how one is ultimately saved. Regarding predestination, Wesley stated that it

[153] Thomas Munzer, founder of the Anabaptists, is said to have despised Luther more than he despised the Popes (Schaff, VII, p. 442). Similarly, the citizens of Geneva, after experiencing Calvin's state-sponsored Christianity, expelled Calvin, remarking that they "hated him worse than the Pope." Papyrius Masso reported of the Genevans: "They would rather be with Beza in hell than with Calvin in heaven" (Ibid., p. 496).

> ...makes vain all preaching, and tending to destroy holiness, the comfort of religion and zeal for good works, yea, the whole Christian revelation by involving it in fatal contradictions...It is a doctrine of blasphemy...it represents our blessed Lord as a hypocrite, a deceiver of the people, a man void of common sincerity, as mocking his helpless creatures by offering what he never intends to give, by saying one thing and meaning another...It destroys all the attributes of God, his justice, mercy, and truth, yea, it represents the most holy God as worse than the devil, as both more false, more cruel and more unjust.[155]

After reading Luther's 1535 *Commentary on Galatians*, the work, more than any other, which expressed Luther's *faith alone* theology, Wesley had these critical words to say:

> I was utterly ashamed. How have I esteemed this book, only because I heard it so commended by others; or, at best, because I had read some excellent sentences occasionally quoted from it! But what shall I say?...Why, not only that the author makes nothing out, clears up not one considerable difficulty; that he is quite shallow in his remarks on many passages, and muddy and confused almost on all; that he is deeply tinctured with mysticism throughout, and hence often dangerously wrong...as an irreconcilable enemy to the gospel of Christ!...Again, how blasphemously does he speak of good works and of the law of God!...But who are thou that 'speakest evil of the law and judgest the law'?[156]

---

[154] Ferm, *Encyclopedia of Religion*, op. cit., p. 56.

[155] Sermon on *Free Grace*, preached at Bristol, England, vol. I, p. 482. In his work, *The Decline and Fall of the Roman Empire*, Gibbon concludes of Calvinism: "...many a sober Christian would rather admit that a wafer is God than that God is a cruel and capricious tyrant" (p. 151). Gibbon's comment is significant in light of the fact that at the Diet of Regensburg in 1541 Catholic and Protestants had come close to an agreement on the issues of justification and the doctrine of the Real Presence, but when Calvin would not accept what he called "the wafer god," the Diet disbanded without resolution on any topic.

[156] *The Journal of John Wesley,* London, 1938, Vol. II, p. 467 (cited in George Tavard's, *Justification: An Ecumenical Study*, p. 88.)

Other Reformed Theologians

Jonathan Edwards and Hermann Bavinck

One of Puritan New England's more prominent personalities, Jonathan Edwards, who other Reformed theologians admit departed significantly from certain key points of the Reformed faith,[157] said the following:

> That we should take the word [justification] in such a sense and understand it as the judge's accepting a person as having both a negative and positive righteousness belonging to him, and looking on him therefore as not only quit or free from any obligation to punishment, *but also as just and righteous...is not only most agreeable to the etymology and natural import of the word, which signifies to make righteous...but also manifestly agreeable to the force of the word as used in Scripture.*[158] (emphasis mine).

Perhaps some Reformed theologian will want to come to the defense of Edwards since Charles Hodge, the source of this quote, seems not to notice, or purposely glosses over, the evident Catholicity of this language. Although what Edwards means by "negative and positive righteousness" is not in itself clear, he seems to suggest its real meaning when he adds that the word *justification* "signifies to make righteous." Edwards supports this view by appealing both to the lexical etymology of justification and to the manner in which it is used in Scripture. Here we have one of the leading Puritan Calvinists speaking in language that many Catholics of his day would have welcomed as a turn in the right direction.

That Edward's language implies the Catholic concept of transformational righteousness is made clear by Tryon Edward's later expunging of 14 references to the word "infusion" from his forebear's work *Charity and Its Fruits*.[159] Protestant Arthur Crabtree

---

[157] Cited in Charles Hodge's, *Justification by Faith Alone*, ed. John Robbins, 1995, p. 41.

[158] Ibid., p. 41.

[159] Cited in Anri Morimoto's, *Jonathan Edwards and the Catholic Vision of Salvation,* 1995, p. 105.

concludes: "...by faith alone, apart from works of love, Edwards never makes his meaning clear, and his whole doctrine remains shrouded in obscurity."[160] Other teachings of Edwards, for example, "love is the essence of faith," which he uses several times in his writings, substantiate Crabtree's criticism but bring Edwards very close to the Catholic view.[161] We witness Edwards confirming this notion as he wonders why his Reformation predecessors thought that the concept of "faith formed by love" was "wicked" and "wretched."[162]

Following Jonathan Edwards' thought and echoing Calvin's apparent manipulation of faith and works, Hermann Bavinck, the famous Dutch theologian of the last century, stated in his classic work *Gereformeerde Dogmatiek*:

> ...the distinction mentioned makes it possible for us to conceive of faith at the same time as a receptive organ and as an active power. If justification in every respect comes about after faith, faith becomes a condition, an activity, which must be performed by man beforehand, and it cannot be purely receptive...But if this faith is saving faith, then it cannot be 'historical knowledge' or 'bare assent,' it is at bottom a living and active faith, and it *does not stand opposed to all work in every respect...In this sense, faith itself is a work, John 6:29, the best work and principle of all good works...the more lively and the more powerful faith is, so much the more does it justify us.*[163] (emphasis mine).

What exactly Bavinck means by "it does not stand opposed to all work in every respect" is not clear, but it certainly suggests that he does not regard works as an either/or issue. Further, his specifying that, "faith itself is a work" seems to coalesce faith and works in a way that Luther certainly would not have accepted and which

---

160 *The Restored Relationship: A Study in Justification and Reconciliation*, 1963.

161 Cf., *Charity and Its Fruits*, WY, 8:139, 330; *Treatise on Grace*, 40; *Concerning Faith*, 617, 619, 623; *Notes on the Bible*, WD, 9:5111; *Miscellanies*, no. 820.

162 *Concerning Faith*, p. 625.

163 *Gereformeerde Dogmatiek*, 4th ed. (Kampen: J. H. Kok, 1930), p. 206.

is much to the right of Calvin's thought.[164] Yet Bavinck's analysis make sense. After all, we could easily assert that as God gives man the command to believe in him, man does a work of obedience by believing.[165] Man does not merely have the choice to believe; rather, he is obligated to believe. A refusal to believe would be considered disobedience to God's command and cause for judgment. Bavinck's third statement "the more powerful faith is, so much more does it justify us," seems to distance itself from the strict Calvinist view that faith only apprehends, and does not increase, our justification. Calvinists of the 16th century would never have said that one is justified *more and more* as he lives his Christian life of faith, and if he did he would be thoroughly Catholic.[166] Yet Bavinck seems to be implying such a condition.

In other writings we find Bavinck further distancing himself from Calvin, while pointing out the alarming ramifications of Calvin's views. In the work cited above, Bavinck writes:

> Calvin did not resolve the problems which arise with this article of faith [justification]. In particular...with respect to the relation in which justification stands to election and atonement on the one hand, and to sanctification and glorification on the other. When justification occupies a place between these pairs, then there is always a tendency to connect it more with either the first or second pair of benefits; and to the degree that this happens, the same degree the doctrine itself acquires a different meaning...With Calvin we still find both representations united

---

164 In his pre-Protestant days, however, Luther believed that faith was a work (WA 6, 204, 25). Other Protestants had also viewed faith as a work, among them Anglican Harry Hammond of England. In fact, the English Reformation as a whole had gone through the same phases as those of the German and Swiss Reformations — a stress on forensic imputation in the early stages of the theology, which then gave way to infused righteousness and viewing faith as a work (see McGrath, *Iustitia Dei*, II, pp. 109-110). John Henry Newman (1801-1890), who later converted to Catholicism, came from this latter phase of the English Reformation. See also, *The Rise of Moralism* by C. F. Allison.

165 Cf., Acts 16:31: "Believe on the Lord Jesus and you shall be saved" and Acts 17:30: "God...now commands all men everywhere to repent."

166 Council of Trent, Session 6, Chapter 10: "...faith cooperating with good works, they increase and are further justified, as it is written: 'He that is just, let him be justified still,' and again: 'Be not afraid to be justified even to death,' and again, 'you see, that by works a man is justified and not by faith alone.'"

with one another, but they are soon separated in Reformed theology and each developed in a one-sided direction.[167]

What Bavinck is describing as a flaw in Calvin's theology centers around whether one should understand justification as merely a result of God's election of an individual so that God is totally responsible for the justification, or as being intimately involved with man's response to come to God and subsequently live an obedient life. Bavinck is saying that if one perspective is chosen over the other (e.g., choosing the election perspective over the free will perspective), then there is a distortion of the doctrine of justification. Various theologians have faulted the Calvinistic view in much the same way. One of Lutheranism's most lauded conservative voices, R. C. H. Lenski, refers to the "false Calvinistic exegesis" in this regard.[168] (Lenski's critique of Calvin, however, is based on

---

[167] Bavinck, op. cit., p. 471.

[168] *Interpretation of Saint Paul's Epistle to the Romans*, 1936, p. 9. Current Reformed theologians attempt to make Calvinism a 'middle-of-the-road' position between Luther's antinomianism and Anabaptist neonomianism. D. Clair Davis, for example, maintains that the Calvinistic view of absolute predestination is the antidote for the Lutheran/Anabaptist controversy, as well as a surety of salvation against the so-called nominalistic theology of Aquinas and the medieval theologians ("How Did the Church in Rome Become Roman Catholicism" in *Roman Catholicism: Evangelicals Analyze What Unites and Divides Us*, ed. John Armstrong, 1994, pp. 55-61). Davis attempts to take election out of the speculative realm and make it a practical certainty — "a personal relationship with God, one not dependent on the offices of the church" — almost as if the Christian had seen his name written in the Bible as one of God's elect. Donald Bloesch attempts to do the same when he says, "A holy life is a sign of our election by God to eternal life, but it is not a means by which we merit eternal life (as in the Catholic view)" (Ibid., p. 156). Calvin had used the same argument against Osiander (*Institutes* 3:11:11). As nice as certainty in one's election would be, it is neither realistic nor biblical. An individual can *think* all he wants that he is elect, whether it is termed or seen through a "personal relationship" or "holiness," but in an absolute sense this will not make him any more sure of his salvation than someone who sees election in a different way. In reality, it is the Calvinist who lives under the oppressive cloud of uncertainty, for it is he who teaches that if one falls away from the faith one was never saved originally (*Institutes* 3:24:7; see also R. C. Sproul in *Chosen By God*, p. 181). This makes each Calvinist's salvation as uncertain as anyone else's — he simply cannot know if in the future he will end up falling away and then be told he was never saved, and thus, never elected, in the first place. Ironically, according to Calvin's view of "double predestination," he would have actually been elected to eternal damnation (*Institutes* 2:12:5; 3:23:1, 7).

Lutheran theology stemming from the Lutheran *Formula of Concord*; whereas Luther himself held to an absolute predestination).

Even some of today's staunch Reformed Evangelicals who follow in the line of Calvin and Bavinck, though they would probably never admit it, show hints here and there in their writings of Catholic soteriology.[169] John H. Gerstner, in his recently written *A Primer on Roman Catholicism,*[170] comments:

> We do insist that the Holy Spirit unites the regenerate soul with Christ and produces faith and all virtues along with it forever, which is the very substance of infused grace...Justification does not refer to the state of man, but it does not exclude it...if nothing were done to the man, God would not look at him as justified.[171]

Here Gerstner agrees with the Calvinist doctrine that regeneration produces faith and good works. But then he adds the clause, "which is the very substance of infused grace." By his sentence structure, the word "which," referring to the entire main clause of the sentence, includes both all virtues *and* faith, hence infused grace is said to produce both faith and works. Normally, infused grace is a Catholic term used in direct opposition to the Reformation concept of imputed righteousness that Gerstner supposedly maintains.

---

[169] Reformed theologian Andrew Sandlin writes: "Especially troubling is the modification of the Protestant dictum of solafideism within the Reformed community, devoted as this faith community has been historically to the preservation and perpetuation of Reformation theology, and, specifically, soteriology" ("Deviations From Historic Solafideism in the Reformed Community" in *The Chalcedon Report*, February, 1995, p. 18).

[170] Soli Deo Gloria Publications, 1995. Gerstner also wrote a chapter in the recent book *Justification by Faith Alone*, ed. John Armstrong, titled *Rome Not Home* which critiqued former Reformed Presbyterians Scott and Kimberly Hahn's account of their conversion to Roman Catholicism in the book *Rome Sweet Home* (San Francisco: Ignatius, 1993).

[171] "Aquinas was a Protestant" in *Tabletalk*, May, 1994, p. 14. Citing the same source, Reformed theologian Andrew Sandlin critiques Gerstner's view by saying, "John Gerstner posits a view of justification mirroring in some ways that of Tridentine Romanism, despite his stated intention to avoid the collapse of justification into sanctification as understood by Rome on the one hand, and the severing of justification from sanctification as in modern antinomian evangelicalism on the other. The key flaw in Gerstner's thesis is his insistence that justification comprehends infused righteousness" (Sandlin, *The Chalcedon Report*, op. cit., p. 23-24).

Yet in the above statement Gerstner is saying that faith itself is the product of infused grace, a purely Catholic concept. To add more fuel to the fire, Gerstner then says, "justification does not refer to the state of man."[172] This statement is problematic since the legal

[172] To say the least, Gerstner's comments are confusing. We wonder if he is really speaking for the classic Reformed position. A century and a half earlier, Charles Hodge had written: "justification...does not produce any subjective change in the person justified...That is done in regeneration and sanctification" (*Justification By Faith Alone*, ed., John Robbins, p. 43). In light of Gerstner's confusing theological analysis, it is ironic that in commenting on Scott Hahn's departure from Reformed Protestantism into Catholicism, Gerstner states no less than 14 times in 19 pages that Hahn "didn't understand the Reformed faith which he left" (*Justification By Faith Alone*, ed. John Armstrong, pp. 166-185). Though I know personally that Hahn does understand the Reformed faith, and quite thoroughly, one wonders how Gerstner expects anyone to understand clearly the lines of demarcation between Calvinism and Catholicism considering the contradictory and ambiguous statements he makes above. R. C. Sproul remarks on Gerstner's statement in his book *Faith Alone*. Sproul refers to Anglican theologian Alister McGrath's statement in *Justification by Faith: What It Means For Us Today* (1988, p. 61) that "justification...involves a change in status rather than in nature" as a "slip of the pen," since it seems to be the goal of both Sproul and Gerstner to include a change in nature in justification. Sproul tries to counteract McGrath's statement by adding: "Justification, technically considered, may not mean a change of human nature, but it certainly *implies* a change in nature" (*Faith Alone*, p. 110). We wonder how such a monumental change as a change in the nature of a man could be realized only by *implication*? Such statements are characteristic of the ambivalent nature of the Reformed arguments. To help in smoothing this problem over, Sproul invents the terminology "complex or nexus of justification," as if wrapping the ambiguity up in a word package will solve the quandary posed by McGrath's opposing language and the contradictions in the Reformed position as a whole (Ibid., p. 111). Andrew Sandlin notes the same contradiction in Sproul. He writes: "the inventive expression 'complex of justification' seems to imply that justification involves more than God's forensic act declaring sinners righteous on account of Christ's atonement...one thus cannot be certain of just what role infused righteousness plays in Sproul's complex of justification." Sandlin concludes his analysis of Gerstner's and Sproul's viewpoint by stating: "In laudable efforts to combat the pervasive spirit of modern antinomianism, Gerstner and Sproul have jeopardized the historic Reformed conception of *sola fide*" (*The Chalcedon Report*, 1995, pp. 24, 26). Perhaps Sandlin is correct, but he must also admit that if stalwarts of the Reformed faith such as Gerstner and Sproul cannot see or clearly state the distinction, how, indeed, can the doctrine of *faith alone* survive or even be comprehended? Ambivalence on the doctrine of justification, such as that displayed by Gerstner and Sproul, pervades Evangelical thought. Take for example, the analysis of justification by two other stalwarts of the Evangelical faith, Norman Geisler and Ralph MacKenzie, in their latest work, *Roman Catholics and Evangelicals:*

framework within which Reformed theology operates appeals exclusively to the forensic model when speaking of justification rather than associating any element of transformation or nature to justification. Gerstner's final statement confirms that justification is associated with the personal change in the nature of the individual: "If nothing were done to the man, God would not look at him as justified." This again is very problematic because forensic imputation in traditional Reformed thought does not include "God looking for something" within the man to determine or confirm his justification. In the Reformed view, justification is supposed to be a totally external event, something settled in God's law court, as it were, without reference to the individual's personal disposition. Gerstner's statements therefore, reveal fundamental flaws in the whole system of Reformed theology.[173]

[172 cont.] *Agreements and Differences*. They state: "Of course, at the moment of forensic justification one is also *made righteous* in an *ontological* sense (cf., 2 Cor. 5:17, 21)" (p. 240, n. 68, emphasis mine). Not only do they use the Catholic language of "made righteous," but they reinforce this by the addition of "ontological" — a word that is normally used in philosophy to denote the actual existence or essence of something. Six pages later, to support an argument for forensic justification, they commandeer Calvin and conclude: "Man is *not made righteous* in justification, but is accepted as righteous..." (p. 246, emphasis mine). We find this contrast even more puzzling when we discover that Geisler, being an avowed Dispensational Arminian, is anti-Calvinist in most of his theology, believing, for example, that "God will save the greatest number actually achievable without violating their free choice" ("God, Evil and Dispensations" in *Walvoord: A Tribute*, ed. Donald Campbell (Moody Press, 1980), pp. 102-103). Geisler and MacKenzie also attempt to impress the reader of their kinship with Luther by siding with Luther's "progressive" sense of justification; yet they fail to alert the reader that Luther absolutely repudiated Geisler's and MacKenzie's doctrine of free will; a doctrine, Luther said, which was the greatest heresy of the church (*Roman Catholics and Evangelicals*, pp. 221-226). This is common in the eclecticism of Evangelical theology — drawing support for a particular point of doctrine from an opponent who is at odds with one's larger body of doctrine.

[173] Gerstner makes similar statements in his work, *Jonathan Edwards: Evangelist*, 1995, pp. 127-131. At least in some circles, there seems to be an unadmitted shift away from the traditional Reformed concept of justification. We glimpse this from time to time. Another example is Reformed theologian Louis Berkhof's reaction to the 1946 book by Edward Boehl. Boehl had proposed that Calvin's concept that regeneration was prior to justifying faith was "Romish" and was tantamount to denying *sola fide*. Berkhof, who wrote the preface to Boehl's book, states: "Some of his errors [Boehl's] are directly connected with his presentation of the doctrine of justification. His zeal for

Changing Times: Confusion and Ecumenism

As Protestantism moved on, differences in the theology of salvation separated it into more and more denominations. At times the differences were minor; at other times they were crucial to the understanding of the gospel itself. Yet whether Calvinist, Lutheran, Methodist, or Pentecostal, Protestants had one thing in common — an animosity toward Rome and anything Catholic. With rare exceptions, productive dialogue between Rome and Protestantism was nonexistent. They were finally free from Roman rule and were happy to interpret the Bible for themselves. The Council of Trent (1545-1563), which anathematized anyone holding a view of salvation contrary to Rome's, had opened the coffin and Vatican I (1870), which formalized the Pope's infallibility, closed the lid. Dogmatic papal pronouncements, as far as Protestants were concerned, only served to alienate the two groups. As late as the 20th century, Pius X's encylical *Editae Saepe*, pejoratively known as the Borromeo encyclical among Protestants (in remembrance of staunch counter-Reformation theologian St. Charles Borromeo) lavished praise on Borromeo for his fight against "the proud and rebellious [Protestant] men and enemies of the cross of Christ...who were corruptors."[174] Since Pius X had much to say in condemnation of the modernist movements in Protestantism, the atmosphere

---

173 cont. salvation merely by imputation, without allowing for anything good in man, sometimes carries him to unwarranted lengths and leads to precarious positions...According to him the regenerate man is himself just as wicked as the unregenerate man" (Boehl, Edward. *The Reformed Doctrine of Justification,* p. 10). I thank my Catholic colleague, Richard White, for this information and the following insightful observation of Berkhof's comments: "Thus, he [Berkhof] implies that justification involves something more than imputation; it also involves the endowment of 'new spiritual qualities.' But once this is admitted, Boehl's criticism [of Calvin's *ordo salutis* which Boehl feels denies *sola fide*] would seem to apply" (The Sola Fide in Lutheran and Calvinist Soteriology, nd). Berkhof's only saving grace here may be his switch from "justification" to "salvation" from the first sentence to the second sentence, implying that Reformed thought can limit imputation to justification but not extend it into other areas of salvation, namely, sanctification and glorification.

174 Pope St. Pius X; date: May 26, 1910. Just four years later, Reformed theologian George Salmon wrote of Roman Catholicism: "...they are the devil's apostles, evangelists and prophets. The true apostles, evangelists and prophets preach God's word, not against God's word" (*The Infallibility of the Church*, 1914, p. 347).

of conservative Tridentine theology persisted among Catholic theologians up until at least World War II. Afterward, certain prominent Catholics took liberties, due in part to their misunderstanding of one of the next great encyclicals, *Divino Afflante Spiritu*,[175] which spoke of opening the Catholic hermeneutic up to investigate critical theories of historical and theological research.[176]

With the advent of Vatican II (1962-1965), a new dimension was added to the appeal of the Catholic Church — ecumenism. Although Vatican II reaffirmed papal infallibility and even confirmed that the Magisterium and the Church at large were infallible,[177] the

---

175 Pope Pius XII; date: September 30, 1943.

176 The notorious Hans Küng is probably the best example of a wayward Catholic theologian. Heavily influenced by the Protestant liberal theologian Karl Barth, Küng maintained that there was really no difference between the Catholic view of justification and that of Protestantism typified by Barth. To prove this, Küng made a surprising assertion in his book *Justification: The Doctrine of Karl Barth and a Catholic Reflection* in 1964. Küng said that the transformational view of Trent presupposed a declaratory verdict of God (p. 221). Barth, who wrote the Introduction to Küng's book, wondered how this could be so, stating: "How do you explain the fact that all this could remain hidden for so long and from so many, both outside and inside the church?" (Ibid., p. xxi). Other Catholic theologians played their own variations on Küng's theme. Catholic liberal and semi-liberal theologians such as Edward Schillebeeckx, Pierre Teilhard de Chardin, Karl Rahner, and Richard McBrien have much more in common with their Protestant liberal counterparts such as Karl Barth, Emil Brunner, Rudolph Bultmann and Paul Tillich than they do with the theologians and doctrines of their own Catholic Church. As John Macquarrie of Union Seminary pointed out, Catholic liberals have taken the torch from Protestant liberals. For a detailed critique of Catholic liberal theology from an Evangelical perspective, see "Roman Catholic Theology Today" by Robert Strimple, in *Roman Catholicism: Evangelical Protestant Analyze What Divides and Unites Us*, 1994, pp. 85-118). Strimple's only fault is that he fails to distinguish properly between statements of Catholic liberal theologians and the official statements of the Catholic Magisterium, the latter of which has not veered one iota from historic Catholic doctrine. In effect, by overemphasizing the liberal element, Strimple, writing in such a one-sided way that only the astute reader is able to recognize his bias, builds a scary strawman that is not at all representative of the Catholic Church. Conversely, Evangelical J. I. Packer has opted for more optimistic thinking: "While it is true that the Magisterium has not actually made any statements that indicate a change of heart in the Vatican, we must observe that it has also not uttered any statement which has condemned this shift in interpretation" *(Here We Stand: Justification by Faith Today*, 1986, p. 125).

Council also carried with it the atmosphere of *aggiornamento*.[178] This opening of the windows for fresh air, as understood by informal statements of Pope John XXIII, sought to communicate Catholic truths in a new and better way, with new approaches to ecumenical dialogue that up till then had been virtually nonexistent for the 400 years since the Reformation. Some Catholic traditionalists would later assert that Vatican II went too far by setting aside cherished rites and customs of the ancient Church. Modern theologians took the open air of Vatican II as a license to delve into more esoteric theological areas, with the result that previously nonexistent liberal thinking attained a high concentration, if not performance, in the Church. No one could deny, however, that the Council did create a platform for dialogue with those of other faiths. It was introducing a kinder, gentler Catholic Church. A major move in this direction was evident in the lifting of the mutual "excommunication" between Rome and the Eastern Orthodox Churches in 1967.

As Catholicism was opening its doors for dialogue, notwithstanding having to handle its own heretics and renegades, Protestantism, and more particularly Evangelicalism (a term which distinguishes conservative Protestants from liberal Protestants), was seeing many of its cherished ideas and beliefs begin to deteriorate. Divisions over charismatic gifts, women in ministry, contraception and abortion, divorce and remarriage, inspiration and inerrancy, sociopolitical concerns, Christian "psychology," theonomy, fiscal responsibility, pastoral impropriety, televangelist shysters, 'health and wealth' gospels, failed end-time predictions, and many other events and trends, began to create a kind of Orwellian nightmare for Evangelicalism.[179]

---

177 Vatican II, *Lumen Gentium*, n. 25.

178 Italian for "updating."

179 Literature describing this phenomenon is just starting to appear, e.g., David Wells, *No Place for Truth: Or Whatever Happened to Evangelical Theology?*; Iain Murray, *Revival and Revivalism: The Making and Marring of American Evangelicalism;* Mark Noll, *The Scandal of the Evangelical Mind*; Michael Horton, *Made in America: The Shaping of Modern American Evangelicalism*; *Power Religion: The Selling Out of the Evangelical Church*; John Armstrong, ed., *The Coming Evangelical Crisis;* Donald Bloesch, *The Future of Evangelical Christianity*; Stephan Ulstein, *Growing Up Fundamentalist*; James Hunter, *Evangelicalism: The Coming Generation*; Carl F. H. Henry, *Twilight of a Great Civilization: The Drift Toward Neo-Paganism.*

The confusion and uncertainty left over from the Reformation began to seep through the cracks in the halls of Protestant theology. European Protestant liberals, a product of Protestant scholasticism which began in the 17th century, eventually migrated to America and undertook to destroy Protestant Fundamentalism's reliance on inspired Scripture. Eventually they turned the mainline Protestant denominations into mere purveyors of a social gospel. These liberal Protestants explicitly rejected the traditional doctrines of salvation passed down from the Reformation. Astute conservative Protestants began to break away from the liberals, little knowing that within a few years they would have to contend within their own ranks with major disagreements regarding cherished fundamental beliefs.[180]

The Norman Shepherd Controversy

In the late 1970s and early 1980s, a new and ominous crack appeared in the Reformed/Evangelical foundation. After almost 20 years of teaching systematic theology at Westminster Theological Seminary, Professor Norman Shepherd began to teach that "works are necessary for justification" in his classroom lectures.[181] Shepherd documented his views in a 1979 piece titled *The Grace of Justification*.[182] The tension created by his views became unbearable and in 1981 Shepherd was called before the board and faculty for examination. Amazingly, much support for Shepherd surfaced in the faculty, the student body, and many churches across the coun-

---

[180] J. Gresham Machen was one of the first to break away from the increasingly liberal Princeton Theological Seminary, who then formed Westminster Theological Seminary. Machen is noted as saying, "Far more serious still is the division between the Church of Rome and evangelical Protestantism in all its forms. Yet how great is the common heritage that unites the Roman Catholic Church...to devout Protestants today!...it seems almost trifling compared to the abyss which stands between us and many ministers of our own church" (*Christianity and Liberalism*, 1923, p. 52). Seventy five years later, Westminster Seminary was shaken to the core by the "Shepherd issue" — a movement that seemed to "unite the Roman Catholic Church...to devout Protestants today" much more than the Westminster professors desired.

[181] I have firsthand knowledge of these events since I was a student at Westminster at the time.

[182] Westminster Theological Seminary, Philadelphia, PA, February 8, 1979.

try which were affiliated with the seminary.[183] Not surprisingly, many of the supporters came from the ranks of Protestant "theonomists" who believed that Old Testament civil laws were also to be applied in the present Christian era.[184] They thought to use Shepherd's stress on works as a platform for applying God's justice through civil mandate. The tide of opposition among some influential personalities at Westminster became too great and it eventually forced Shepherd from his teaching post. Westminster Seminary produced a subsequent document castigating Shepherd and refuting his views. In a writing style reminiscent of the Canons of the Council of Trent, this Westminster Statement enumerated and refuted each wrinkle of Shepherd's views.[185]

As expected, Shepherd spent considerable time on the epistle of James to defend his views. His 1979 paper is filled with references to James, numerous citations of Jesus' teaching about salva-

---

183 The Board of Trustees of Westminster Seminary confirmed this support in the following statement: "Statements endorsing Mr. Shepherd's position have been issued by a majority of the Faculty and by a majority of the Board of Trustees."

184 Such noted theologians as Greg Bahnsen, Gary North, and R. J. Rushdooney disputed bitterly with anti-theonomists such as Robert Godfrey, Meredith Kline, and most of the staff of Westminster Seminary, each side writing books over a period of fifteen years condemning the other's views. It is no surprise that Reformed theologian Andrew Sandlin critiques Gary North's views on justification by seeing tendencies in North's writings "a la Shepherd" of "a process contingent on human activity." North makes such wide-ranging statements as, "We are continually in God's court of law. As we work out our salvation with fear and trembling, God continually brings judgment on our activities...God continually evaluates our actions, and He declares us progressively righteous, as we mature as spiritually regenerated creatures" (Sandlin, *The Chalcedon Report*, p. 26). This is one of the first times a Reformed Evangelical theologian has coupled forensic imputation with progressive justification, and is thus a precedent setting idea in Reformed thought. We have already seen the seeds of North's view in Luther's amalgamation of the forensic and the progressive aspects of justification, as well as Calvin's merging of the judgment at "God's throne" with the "graciousness" and "acceptance" of man by God. What North fails to see, however, is that, strictly speaking, God cannot evaluate us from the perspective of law, since law must, by its very nature, condemn us for the slightest fault. Only when we understand that God views our faith and works within the realm of grace — a grace that seeks to please God *personally* not *judicially* — can there be any gratuity given to man or righteousness deemed to him. This is the Catholic view.

185 *The Westminster Statement on Justification*, approved by the Faculty and Board, May 27, 1980.

tion, and many passages from the book of Hebrews. Shepherd postulated that Reformed theologians, in their continual attempt to treat James's view of justification as a mere afterthought in relation to Paul's view, had watered down the epistle of James and misdirected its full teaching. In addition, Shepherd placed the burden of proof upon his Protestant brethren to show why there is such a consistent emphasis on works of obedience in the New Testament, pointing out that no book in Scripture refrained from suspending the results of one's eternal destiny upon the presence or absence of obedience.[186]

Theologically, Shepherd argued quite cogently that if the Reformed view held that regeneration precedes justification, a position, we will recall, that distinguished Calvin from Luther, then, since it is equally true that regeneration precedes and produces sanctification, then justification must also be the result, in some way, of regeneration (a view of which we have already seen leanings in the writings of John Gerstner). Since works flow from the fact that one has been regenerated, then both justification and sanctification must incorporate works into their respective dimensions of salvation.[187] Shepherd further argued that the context of justifi-

[186] *The Grace of Justification*, p. 13.

[187] Other Reformed theologians say almost the same thing as Shepherd but without following their reasoning to its logical conclusion. For example, R. C. Sproul writes, "All who are regenerated are changed...Faith is the fruit of regeneration...The necessity, inevitability, and immediacy of good works are linked to the work of regeneration" (*Justification By Faith Alone*, ed. John Armstrong, p. 26). Hence, we ask: If faith and good works are the fruit of regeneration, then how can faith be separated from good works in justification? Perhaps Luther anticipated this contradiction and thus insisted, in opposition to Calvin, on faith preceding regeneration. Interestingly, one of Shepherd's original supporters at Westminster, Professor of New Testament Richard Gaffin, wrote a book in 1978 (around the time the Shepherd controversy was brewing) titled the *Centrality of the Resurrection*, which was republished under the title *Resurrection and Redemption: A Study in Paul's Soteriology*, in 1987. In the book, Gaffin argues that Reformed theology's entire concept of the *ordo salutis* is a misapplication of Paul's thought. Gaffin draws support for his thesis from two prominent figures of the Reformed faith, Geerhardus Vos (*The Pauline Eschatology*, 1930); and Hermann Ridderbos (*Paul: An Outline of His Theology*, 1966, 1975). In place of the *ordo salutis*, Gaffin proposes that Paul's soteriology is essentially eschatological with specific reference to the resurrection of Christ, and to the believer's union with him both spiritually and physically as the unifying theme of the New Testament. Gaffin points out the failure

cation by works mentioned in James 2:24 was purely a salvation context, noted by James' rhetorical question "Can faith save him?" in James 2:14, which is also prefaced by a reference to God's final judgment in James 2:13. Hence, it seemed obvious to Shepherd, and his growing supporters, that the works of an individual play an integral part in his justification and in determining whether God will save or damn him on judgment day.

The Lutheran/Catholic Dialogue

Around the same time that the Shepherd controversy was springing up at the Calvinistic seminary of Westminster, Lutherans and Catholics in Europe were beginning to converse in official meetings in an attempt to smooth out their doctrinal differences. The product of this venture is known as the Lutheran/Catholic Dialogue (1978-1983). It would have been unthinkable a few decades prior that such a dialogue would conclude, "The Tridentine decree on justification, with its own way of insisting on the primacy of grace...is not necessarily incompatible with the Lutheran doctrine of *sola fide*, even though Trent excluded this phrase."[188] Though the Dialogue did recognize some "irreconcilable differences" concerning forensic justification, merit and various Catholic practices, one of the truly mollifying efforts was the fifth material convergence: "By justification we are both declared and made righteous. Justification

---

[187 cont.] of the traditional *ordo salutis* in several respects: (1) it treats justification, adoption, and sanctification as separate acts rather than distinct aspects of a single act, at the same time, attempting to dismiss the confusion by appealing to the "temporal," "logical," or "causal" connection between the items of the *ordo salutis*; (2) its failure to explain how the items of the *ordo salutis* are related to the act of being joined existentially to Christ. Gaffin writes: "If at the point of inception this union is prior (and therefore involves the possession in the inner man of all that Christ is as resurrected), what need is there for the other acts?" (Ibid., pp. 138-139). Gaffin's first objection regarding the "temporal" and "logical" distinction in the *ordo salutis* is frequently used in current Reformed polemic in an attempt to smooth over its inherent contradictions (e.g., Michael Horton in *What Still Divides Us: A Protestant and Roman Catholic Debate*, audio tape #7 titled "Cross Examination: Sola Fide"; available through Basilica Press, San Diego, CA. Participants include: Michael Horton, W. Robert Godfrey, and Rod Rosenbladt versus Patrick Madrid, William Marshner, and Robert Sungenis, March 3-4, 1995).

[188] *Lutheran/Catholic Dialogue*, 1978-1983, p. 35.

therefore, is not a legal fiction. God, in justifying, effects what he promises; he forgives sin and makes us truly righteous."[189] The conclusion of the Dialogue says as much: "...That work [God's saving work] can be expressed in the imagery of God as judge who pronounces sinners innocent and righteous...and also in a transformed view which emphasizes the change wrought in sinners by infused grace." In other words, in an effort to reach an agreement, the Lutheran/Catholic dialogue attempted to solve the problem of justification by the various ways men conceptualize biblical truth.[190] Though such statements would probably make Luther, Melanchthon or Calvin turn over in their respective graves, the Vatican interprets such exchange as certainly a move in the right direction.[191]

Anglicans and Catholics

Following the Lutheran/Catholic dialogue, Anglicans and Catholics met in an international commission and produced a joint statement in 1987 titled *Salvation and the Church*. It asserted, as did the Lutheran/Catholic Dialogue, "God's grace effects what he declares; his creative word imparts what it imputes. By pronouncing us righteous, God also makes us righteous."[192] The commission concluded with: "...We are agreed that this is not an area where any remaining differences of theological interpretation or ecclesiological emphasis either within or between our Communions, can justify our continuing separation. We believe that our two Communions are agreed on the essential aspects of the doctrine of salvation and on the Church's role within it."[193] With con-

[189] Ibid., p. 69.

[190] See Peter Böckmann in *Dialogue and Alliance* 2 (1988) for a worthy critique.

[191] In 1991, Pope John Paul II is quoted as saying: "There is no one who is not aware that the Protestant reformation arose out of the doctrine of justification and that it breached the unity of western Christians...A shared understanding — and we believe we are very close to this goal — will help, we are certain, to resolve the other controversies which are directly or indirectly linked to it" (cited in: "Augustine and Christian Unity," *30 days*, by Lucio Brunelli, No. 12, 1994, pp. 21-22). The Dialogue met again in Geneva in 1995. For a description and analysis of the dialogue, see **Appendix 16.**

[192] *ARCIC II*, p. 17.

[193] Ibid., p. 26.

clusions such as this, there is no telling what the future may bring in regard to reconciliation. Given the rise of radical and liberal movements in the Anglican church (e.g., opening the episcopate to women), many Anglican clergy have left their churches and made their conciliation and membership in the Catholic Church official. In the last few years, over three hundred Anglican priests have joined the Catholic Church as a refuge from the feminist agenda in their homeland.

The "Lordship Salvation" Controversy

Concurrent with the above events, more fissures began to appear in the Evangelical foundation of justification. Zane Hodges, professor at the conservative Dallas Theological Seminary, published a book in 1981 titled *The Gospel Under Siege*.[194] It was Hodges' contention that the pure gospel of *faith alone* was under siege — not under siege by avid Roman Catholic scholars, but by some of the most prominent stalwarts of the Evangelical faith to date. Along with his Dallas associates, Hodges claimed that one should accept Jesus as Savior but one does not necessarily have to accept him as Lord. What Hodges meant was that faith, only and absolutely faith alone, is all that is required for salvation. Works of obedience may or may not come but they have nothing whatsoever to do with the salvation of the individual. One who insists on works as a requirement for salvation in any sense, Hodges asserts, reverts to the works gospel condemned by Paul. One can say this much for Hodges — at least he followed his Protestant dictum of *faith alone* to its logical conclusion rather than capitulating to the dichotomous view that started with Calvin and that many Evangelicals perpetuate today in the adage "justification is by faith alone but by a faith that is not alone."[195] Hodges, like Luther before him, realized the full implications of *faith alone* theology — it meant that faith *was* alone. Luther followed his convictions to their logical conclusion and ended up "throwing Jimmy into the stove," but at least he was honest with his own theology.

---

[194] Hodges wrote a further response titled *Absolutely Free! A Biblical Reply to Lordship Salvation*, in 1989.

[195] *Acts of the Council of Trent*, 3:152.

Hodges' view did not just pop on the scene in 1981. It was undergirded by the Dispensational theology of Dallas Theological Seminary, which was a product of the theology of C. I. Scofield and propagated by the famed *Scofield Reference Bible* of 1909. Other theologians of this mold were Lewis Sperry Chafer and Charles Ryrie[196] who both taught at Dallas Theological Seminary. In 1948 Chafer wrote: "to impose a need to surrender the life to God as an added condition of salvation is most unreasonable. God's call to the unsaved is never said to be unto the Lordship of Christ."[197]

In response to the Chafer/Ryrie/Hodges onslaught, other prominent Evangelicals banded together and wrote scathing critiques of their Protestant brethren. One of the more popular is John F. MacArthur.[198] In order to combat what he called

---

[196] Ryrie wrote of similar views to Scofield in the book *Balancing the Christian Life* in 1969.

[197] *Systematic Theology*, 3:385.

[198] *The Gospel According to Jesus: What Does Jesus Really Mean When He Says Follow Me?* 2nd ed., 1988, 1994. J. I. Packer and James Montgomery Boice wrote the respective Forewords of the two editions. These men, along with R. C. Sproul of Ligonier Ministries; D. James Kennedy of Coral Ridge Presbyterian Church; and Michael Horton of Christians United for Reformation, and James Boice of Tenth Presbyterian Church in Philadelphia, form the inner circle of the Calvinistic polemic against the Dispensational, Arminian theology of Chafer, Ryrie, Hodges, and most of present-day Evangelicalism. J. I. Packer, however, has had somewhat of a falling out with his peers because of his recent signing of the ECT document stating his willingness to work with Catholics. In the reprint of Charles Hodge's 1841 work, *Justification By Faith Alone*, editor John Robbins comments on the back cover: "The Bible's teaching on justification has come under renewed attack by well-known religious figures including Charles Colson, Bill Bright, Pat Robertson, and J. I. Packer, and Christians are in great danger at being deceived today than they have been in several centuries." Robbins also makes it clear that he has somewhat of an axe to grind in doing the reprint of Hodge's work by his critique of one of Hodge's conciliatory efforts in the book. Hodge wrote, "Indeed it is a matter of devout thankfulness to God that underneath the numerous grievous and destructive errors of the Romish Church, the great truths of the Gospel are preserved...Every true worshiper of Christ must in his heart recognize as a Christian brother, wherever he may be found, anyone who loves, worships, and trusts the Lord Jesus Christ as God manifest in the flesh and the only Saviour of men." Robbins then makes the following comment on Hodge: "Hodge errs because any man or church which denies justification by faith alone cannot be said to preserve the great truths of the Gospel" (Ibid., p. 69). Robbins also wrote the article, "The Counterfeit Gospel of Charles Colson, Part 2" in *The Trinity Review* (February, 1994) 4. Recently, some of the aforementioned Reformed spokesmen met at

"antinomianism" among his opponents, MacArthur spent almost all of his 300-page work exegeting passages from the Gospels, systematically going through many of the teachings of Jesus which specified that works indeed play a large part in our standing and relationship with God. This is not surprising. Catholic theology has always maintained that the Gospels deny *faith alone* theology most emphatically. Yet from another perspective it is quite ironic that MacArthur chose Jesus's teachings as his best attack against the *faith alone* theology of Zane Hodges. The attack on Hodges is in direct contrast to MacArthur's most recent joint venture, *Justification By Faith Alone*, which in a mere 20 pages attempts to refute Catholic theology by pointing out various passages in the Gospels that teach a *faith alone* theology.[199] In this attempt, MacArthur cites only four passages which he feels illustrate his point. We find it quite contradictory that MacArthur can amass a 300 page volume emphasizing Jesus's teaching on works of obedience against those, like Zane Hodges, who separate works from faith, yet refrain from calling such teaching heresy.[200] Yet he and his colleagues do not hesitate to affirm that Rome's joining of faith and works, even under the auspices of God's grace, is "another gospel" deserving of anathema.[201] Ironically, Zane Hodges has called MacArthur's view "heresy."[202] Like most Reformed theologians, MacArthur has found himself trying to walk the razor-thin edge between the gospel of Hodges and the gospel of Rome. For them it is easier to live in the dichotomous world of "faith alone but not a faith that is alone," yet

[198 cont.] Harvard University and formulated "The Cambridge Declaration of Alliance of Confessing Evangelicals," April 20, 1996, which is a five page document stating clearly what it is to be a "Reformed Evangelical" and denouncing anything as heretical that did not hold to the strict "Lutheran/Calvinist" tenets of the Reformation.

[199] Editor Don Kistler, op. cit., pp. 1-20. We deal with MacArthur's interpretation of these passages in Chapter 3.

[200] MacArthur's own assessment in *The Gospel According to Jesus*, p. xii.

[201] So stated in *Justification By Faith Alone*, ed. Don Kistler, pp. 12-13. See also *Faith Alone* by R. C. Sproul for a similar assessment, op. cit., pp. 175-192.

[202] MacArthur, *The Gospel According to Jesus*, p. xii.

we find that many of them are accused by their Reformed brethren of falling off the edge.[203]

Ironically, though they probably would not claim to be siding with Zane Hodges, Evangelicals Norman Geisler and Ralph MacKenzie come in the back door, as it were, and claim a message curiously similar to Hodges. They show this in their interpretation of Philip Melanchthon's statement in the Apology of the Augsburg Confession. From Protestant George Anderson's work *Justification By Faith*, Geisler and MacKenzie extract Melanchthon's statement that "the importance of faith not be restricted to the beginning of justification" (Article IV, 71). Geisler and MacKenzie then use this statement as a precedent for their belief that:

> You are not only justified by faith alone, but you are being sanctified by faith alone. For without faith it is impossible to please [God] (Heb. 11:6)...We call the error of Galatianism (namely, works are necessary for sanctification) a "serious error." If it is a heresy, then many Protestants are heretical at this point too, since at least in practice if not in theory, they too teach works are a condition for progressive sanctification...We are saved by grace

---

[203] As cited earlier in *The Chalcedon Report* by Andrew Sandlin. MacArthur's longtime critic, Michael Horton, in his editorial work, *Christ the Lord: The Reformation and Lordship Salvation*, showed MacArthur's early "Catholic" leanings. Horton quotes MacArthur as saying: "And we've been learning that justification, then, or God imputing to us his righteousness, God putting his righteousness to our account, must be seen in two ways. First of all, it is a forensic declaration, that is, it is a statement of God relative to judicial reality...I heard recently that a preacher said, 'When we are saved, it is only a legal pronouncement; there's no change at all. It is simply that God declares us righteous, contrary to the real fact, but based on the death of Jesus Christ.' That is not true. There is a declaration, there is a legal statement, but there is a second aspect, and theologians would call this the ontology of justification, or the reality of it. And it is this: that God not only declares us to be righteous, based on the satisfying work of Christ, but in Christ *he makes us righteous. We are made righteous*...And so you must see, then, in justification by faith, both of those elements. That which is declared about us, that we are from now on right with God, can only be declared because in fact it is true that we have been recreated in his image" (emphasis mine). Horton asserts that MacArthur has since "corrected" his position, thus attempting to plug another "Catholic" leak in the Reformed polemic.

and sanctified by grace (Titus 2:11-13). Also, we are justified by faith alone as well as sanctified by faith alone.[204]

In one fell swoop, Geisler and MacKenzie have categorized many, if not most, Evangelical Protestants as "heretical," since it is a fact that most of them believe that works are a necessary and distinguishing feature of sanctification.[205] As Luther attempted to do, Geisler and MacKenzie prop up *faith alone* as the quintessential criterion for orthodoxy, the *sine qua non* of the Christian religion. This theology subsumes or destroys anything that comes in its path, no matter how viable it seems to be.[206] It would be interesting to see which side of the equation Geisler and MacKenzie will eventually endorse: Hodges or MacArthur. At any rate, they have introduced quite a novel understanding of sanctification that has heretofore not been used by anyone in Protestant history.

ECT: Evangelicals and Catholics Together

Further evidence of a breakup in the Evangelical stance on *faith alone* justification is the recent document signed by major Evangelical and Catholic spokesmen.[207] Evangelicals such as Chuck

---

[204] *Roman Catholics and Evangelicals: Agreements and Differences*, pp. 237, 239.

[205] Some Evangelicals maintain that works are "necessary" for justification, but to escape the practical ramifications of this position shift the argument against Catholicism to one concerning the "ground" of justification, e.g., Norman Shepherd, Roger Wagner, John Murray, et al., which we covered in chapter 5. Some speak of works as being necessary to qualify the faith that justifies, e.g., R. C. Sproul, *Faith Alone*, pp. 88, 171.

[206] Despite their appeal to Melanchthon for a precedent, there is no substantiation for Geisler's and MacKenzie's elevation of *faith alone* to the area of sanctification. Perhaps because they did not go to the primary source, i.e., the *Apology of the Augsburg Confession*, but instead quote from George Anderson concerning Melanchthon's statement, they have misconstrued what Melanchthon actually said. Melanchthon does not say that *faith alone* sanctifies. He does not even use the word "sanctification" in the paragraph cited by Geisler and MacKenzie. Moreover, the entire context of the preceding and subsequent paragraphs is confined to the discussion of *justification*, not sanctification (*Apology*, op. cit., ed. Theodore Tappert, pp. 116-117).

[207] *Evangelicals and Catholics Together: The Christian Mission in the Third Millenium*, March 29, 1994.

Colson, Pat Robertson, J. I. Packer, and Bill Bright, to name a few, signed the document knowing that the words *faith alone* were not included in the joint statement on justification. The signers agreed on the biblical language of Paul, "we are justified through faith," rather than adding the infamous addendum "alone" of Luther.[208] As expected, the voices of the Geneva theologians railed against their Evangelical brothers for stooping to such depths. To sign a document that on the surface purported to iron out the theological difficulties between the two faiths in order to work together on social concerns was to them crossing the line into compromise.[209] Though most of the Evangelical signers of the ECT document would probably not be ready to capitulate to a full-blown Catholic soteriology, their willingness to reach some sort of consensus with amenable Catholic theologians shows either that they are not clear in their own minds on the meaning or implication of *faith alone* theology, or that they do not deem such differences with Rome to be as crucial as they once were in the 16th century. In any case, the cracks in *faith alone* theology continue to become increasingly evident.

---

208 This was not the first time Catholics had agreed to the language "justified by faith" without the addendum "alone." At the Diet of Regensburg of 1541, Catholic theologians, including John Eck, Cardinal Contarini and Bishop Marone met with John Calvin, Philip Melanchthon, and Martin Bucer. Historian Philip Schaff claims that "the Catholics agreed to the evangelical view of justification by faith (without the Lutheran *sola*)..." (op. cit., VIII, p. 382). In contrast, Alister McGrath states that the Diet "seemed to compromise both the evangelical and catholic positions on justification in order to reach what was basically a diplomatic settlement" (*ARCIC II and Justification*, p. 15).

209 R. C. Sproul personally contacted one of the signers, noted Reformed theologian, J. I. Packer, in order to change his mind about signing the document. Packer subsequently defended himself in an article "Why I Signed It," published in *Christianity Today* 12-12-94. Sproul also says he contacted Chuck Colson. To this day, Colson and Packer maintain their signature on the document. Sproul's conclusion: "The Colson-Neuhaus document did not cause disunity but exposed a serious rift within evangelicalism" ("Coram Deo" in *Tabletalk*, Nov. 1994, 2). John MacArthur strongly opposes any collaboration with Catholics (See *Reckless Faith: When the Church Loses Its Will To Discern*, 1994; as does Dave Hunt who says that "the document represents the most devastating blow against the gospel in at least 1,000 years" ("Current Issues" in *Voice, Journal of the Independent Fundamentalist Churches of America*, July/August 1994, 21-24).

Five Views of Sanctification

Still another sign of the deterioration of faith alone theology can be seen in two recent books which delineate the differences among Evangelicals on a related topic. In a 1987 book titled *Five Views of Sanctification*, each of five Evangelical theologians presented their views of sanctification and were subsequently critiqued by the other four.[210] After reading the various contrasting views and counter views, one's head swims in a sea of confusion. The book is one of the most amazing testimonials to the havoc private interpretation has wrought upon Christendom. Even more revealing than the confusion about Sanctification is that the book could just as well be titled *Five Views of Justification* since the critique of each other's work invariably enters into the whole area of how one is saved. Another book appearing just one year later with the almost identical title, *Christian Spirituality: Five Views of Sanctification* confirmed that the issue of justification is just as much at the forefront of these discussions as sanctification. One of the major topics of discussion in the book was deciding on what *faith alone* really meant, as well as how to understand sin and obedience in the Christian life. The five authors represented some well-known yet very diverse seminaries and denominations.[211] Though the title of the book purports to be about sanctification, inside one finds an altogether different story. The astute reader realizes after the first few pages that the doctrine of justification is

---

[210] Melvin Dieter (Wesleyan View); Anthony Hoekema (Reformed View); Stanley Horton, (Pentecostal View); J. Robertson McQuilkin (Keswick View); and John F. Walvoord ("Augustinian-Dispensationalist").

[211] Russell Spittler (Fuller Seminary); Lawrence Wood (Asbury Seminary); Glenn Hinson (Southern Baptist); Sinclair Ferguson (Westminster Seminary); and Gerhard Forde (Luther-Northwestern Seminary). Books of this type are common in Evangelicalism. Others include, e.g., *Four Views on Salvation in a Pluralistic World* (1996); *Five Views on Law and Gospel* (1996); *Are Miraculous Gifts for Today: Four Views* (1996); *Women in Ministry: Four Views* (1989); *The Meaning of the Millenium: Four Views* (1977); *Predestination and Free Will: Four Views of Divine Sovereignty and Human Freedom* (1986).

on the line. Three of the five authors show clear tendencies toward Catholic soteriology.[212]

Another View of Justification

Evangelicals are still not done trying to unravel the biblical concept of justification. After a development that began a few decades ago, James Dunn brought to the forefront of the discussion a somewhat radical approach. Suggesting as much in the title "The Justice of God: A Fresh Look at the Old Doctrine of Justification by Faith," Dunn first praises Luther for releasing Europe from the grip of medieval Catholicism, but postulates that there were two crucial errors in Luther's theology. The first is Luther's unjustified projection of his own scrupulosity and feeling of wretchedness upon the apostle Paul.[213] The second is Luther's conclusion that the Ju-

---

212 R. C. Sproul notes in his book *Faith Alone* some of the comments from Russell Spittler of Fuller Theological Seminary. Remarking on Luther's teaching on justification, Spittler says, "...it looks wrong to me...I hope it's true...I simply fear it's not" (op. cit., p. 193). Michael Horton notices the same of Spittler with a longer quote, "'But can it really be true — saint and sinner simultaneously? I wish it were true...Is this correct: I don't need to work at 'becoming.' I'm already declared to be holy? No sweat needed? Still, I'm grateful for Luther's phrase [simul iustus et peccator, simultaneously justified and sinful] and for his descendants. Their earthiness has called me away from my superspirituality. But simul iustus et peccator? I hope it's true! I simply fear it's not'" (*Five Views*, pp. 42-43). In the same book, the Wesleyan representative, Lawrence W. Wood, defines justification as "freedom from the acts of sin" and "an *infusion* of divine love" (Ibid., pp. 37-38, emphasis mine). Horton also points out the aberrations of once-staunch Reformed theologian Clark Pinnock who has totally reversed his Calvinistic beliefs *(A Wilderness in God's Mercy*, 1992). Pinnock is famous for stating: "Calvinism makes God some kind of terrorist who goes around handing out torture or disaster and even is willing people to do things the Bible says God hates." But in repudiating his Reformed theology, Pinnock has gone so far as to say that God does not know the future ("God Limits His Knowledge" in *Predestination and Free Will*, eds. David and Randall Basinger, 1986, pp. 143-162).

213 This idea did not originate with Dunn, however. In 1897, William Werde published *Uber Aufgabe und Methode der sogennanten nertestamentlichen Theologie* (Gottingen: Vandenhoeck and Ruprecht) which was translated by Robert Morgan into "The Task and Methods of New Testament Theology" in *The Nature of New Testament Theology* (Naperville, IL: Allenson) which argued that Paul's sole purpose in stressing justification by faith was to counter the imposition of Jewish customs on Gentile converts. A couple of decades ago, Krister Stendahl, in "The Apostle Paul and the Introspective Conscience

daism of Paul's day taught a narrow legalistic religion, which Luther had equated with medieval Catholicism. Dunn points out that Judaism originated and functioned within God's grace and was not legalistic. His conclusion is that Paul was not reacting to a legalistic justification by good works. He further concludes that the main problem for which Paul admonishes the Jews was ethnic pride against the Gentiles. Dunn says that Paul really taught not the denial of works for justification but that God accepted Gentiles without their having to take on a Jewish lifestyle or change their nationality. All in all, Dunn maintains that both Protestants and Catholics have had the wrong focus when examining the writings of Paul.[214] Dunn's purpose is to globalize the concept of justification by emphasizing justice and denationalizing salvation. He concludes:

> Luther needed to discover justification by faith at the individual level. Just as much today we need to rediscover Paul's original teaching on the subject. God accepts all who believe and trust in him: Gentile as well as Jew, black and white, Palestinian and Israelite, central American and U.S. citizen, Roman Catholic and Protestant, Orthodox and Muslim...[215]

---

213 cont. of the West" challenged the prevailing view of Paul which, he said, had been adopted from Augustine and Luther, that Paul suffered from a scrupulous conscience and terrible feelings of guilt and anxiety before his conversion. Stendahl said, as Dunn later did, that Paul's main emphasis was not himself but salvation history and the inclusion of the Gentiles into the community of God once dominated by the Jews. Stendahl's work is now reprinted in *Paul Among the Jews and Gentiles*, see pp. 78-96. The Lutheran/Catholic dialogue also pointed out Luther's "over-scrupulosity."

214 Dunn's social emphasis has already been addressed by Catholic theology, however. The Catholic Church has developed distinct social directives for the Christian in the world, buttressed by traditional soteriological doctrines. The recent encyclicals by Pope John Paul II are some of the most powerful social critiques ever presented to the Church, for example, *Centesimus Annus*, which denies such social movements as liberation theology and critiques aspects of both capitalism and socialism. Other encyclicals and official statements include *Laborem Exercens, Sollicitudo Rei Socialis, Veritatis Splendor, Evangelium Vitae, Ut Unum Sint, Familiaris Consortio, Mulieris Dignitatem, Redemptoris Missio*, showing deep concern for social and family issues. Other papal encyclicals, Pope Paul VI: *Populorum Progressio, Nostra Aetate, Dignitatis Humanae, Evangelii Nuntiandi*; John XXIII: *Mater et Magistra*; Pius XI: *Quas Primas, Social Reconstruction*; and Leo XIII: *Rerum Novarum*, have all made extensive statements on social issues.

215 Dunn, op. cit., p. 29.

This is certainly a challenge to classic and modern Protestant thinking. Dunn forces the Evangelical to escape from the cocoon of his own self-importance. From a Catholic perspective, however, there are many oversights and exegetical flaws in the means Dunn uses to arrive at his final point.[216] Like many in Protestantism, Dunn emphasizes the points he likes of Paul's teaching to the exclusion of others he does not find palatable with his own theology. Suffice it to say, however, that Evangelicals have yet another theory to contend with in their understanding of justification by *faith alone*.

---

[216] See **Appendix 3** for further discussion and critique of Dunn's view. For a thorough critique of Dunn, Werde, Stendahl and E. P. Sanders, from a Protestant perspective, see *Justification By Faith* by Mark A. Seifrid (Leiden, New York, Koln: E. J. Brill, 1992) pp. 42-65.

Epilogue

Peter M. J. Stravinskas, Ph.D

Robert Sungenis has honored me by dedicating this work to me, along with two other Catholics committed to the apologetics apostolate. Inviting me to write the Epilogue is a distinct pleasure for many reasons, not the least of which is that I shall not have to convince you of the value of the work, for you will have already apprehended that. Secondly, making prognostications cannot be proved wrong for the present moment. Thirdly, nowadays it is a rare treat for a cleric to be offered the opportunity to have the "last word" on anything!

As our author has amply demonstrated, *sola fide* presents insurmountable obstacles from scriptural, theological, historical and anthropological points of view. Of course, one of the major difficulties with *sola fide* is that it attempts to create a dichotomy where none is necessary. Indeed, the Catholic way is always catholic, which is to say, whenever possible, inclusive rather than exclusive. Hence, the Catholic Tradition does not pit Scripture against Tradition (*sola Scriptura*) or grace against merit (*sola gratia*) — two other Reformation rallying cries. No, the Church of the Ages sees paradox where others might see contradiction in realities like a Virgin Mother or a God-man. Similarly, faith, by all means, but not in opposition to works nor works in isolation from faith.

At this point in your odyssey through the faith/works controversy, I trust you have had what is called "a good read," even if it has not been an easy one. Thomas à Kempis once quipped that he would rather be able to experience compunction than to define it. There is a charm in the sentiment, but we must admit that it does not truly reflect the Catholic way of doing things, which engages the intellect as part of the pilgrimage of faith. While this present work is clearly scholarly, it must be distinguished from many other efforts along these lines over the past five centuries. Previous volumes often exhibited an acerbic tone; yet others lacked passion because they had reduced the discussion to blandly academic. Robert Sungenis is not only a competent theologian but a convinced believer who, with the sacred author, holds that God wants all men to be saved, precisely by coming to know the truth (cf., 1 Timothy 2:4). But being an intelligent person and one desirous of fulfilling the Second Vatican Council's hope for Christian unity, he has refrained from polemics even while defending and explaining in the most articulate way possible the Church's position on this topic.

However, one might ask, "Why even raise the question?" Because Luther himself asserted the central character of this teaching — and a man has a right to be taken seriously and on his own terms. More than three decades after Vatican II, with the movement toward Christian unity now a permanent part of the landscape, and with some of the worst hostilities between Christians put aside, we need not walk on eggshells, avoiding difficult subjects, so as to preserve the peace. That would be the "false irenicism" condemned by the Council (*Unitatis Redintegratio*, n. 11). On the contrary, friends and "brethren" (even if separated) should be able to speak honestly to each other; otherwise, our ecumenism is little more than a shallow exercise in "tea and sympathy," unworthy of either human or Christian dignity.

Pope John Paul II has charted out the course for the Catholic Church for many years to come. In regard to ecumenical relations, following Vatican II, he has called for the removal of all unnecessary obstacles to full communion. At the very same time, however, he has noted the critical importance of the forging of a unity grounded not in wishful thinking but in fidelity to the full-throated and complete proclamation of the Gospel: "The unity willed by God can be attained only by the adherence of all to the content of revealed faith in its entirety. In matters of faith, compromise is in contradiction with God Who is truth" (*Ut Unum Sint*, n. 18). And so, if a theological stance is neuralgic, it cannot be swept under the carpet but must be engaged in the process we call dialogue. In the same document, he reminds us that "dialogue puts before the participants real and genuine disagreement in matters of faith" — an essential step along the road to unity. Attitudes, however, are equally significant, as we read that "above all, these disagreements should be faced in a sincere spirit of fraternal charity, of respect for the demands of one's own conscience and of the conscience of the other party, with profound humility and love for the truth" (n. 39).

Returning to the Reformation principle of sola fide is particularly worthwhile as the Christian community is poised to cross the threshold of the third millennium. Pope John Paul II has made evangelization and re-evangelization the keynotes of this period of preparation. Interestingly enough, he has identified 1997 as specially dedicated to the Jesus Who brings us salvation. A book on this issue, then, is most apropos. Beyond that, he has written intensely of the need for this kind of work to be carried out by the laity (cf., *Tertio Millennio Adveniente*, n. 21) and "from an ecumenical point of view" (n. 41). Robert Sungenis has heard the invitation and responded to the challenge; in doing so, he paves the way for others to follow.

What could gladden the Heart of Christ more than to have His brothers and sisters reach across the theological divide of centuries to share their insights on how they have experienced the salvation He has won for them and in which He wants them to participate in the most profound manner possible? Needless to say, that means being united not only in Him but to one another.

May Mary, Mother of Christ and Mother of the Church, be for us the very best of mothers who always wishes harmony among her children. Dr. Luther himself asserted in his homily for Christmas 1530: "I shall not fail to love the Mother Mary." So, may she whom he invoked as "O Mary, noble, tender Virgin," pray her Son to pour out upon us all a double portion of His Spirit to understand the powerful truth of justification and thus to live from it, indeed to live it.

Appendix 1

History of Catholic Views on Martin Luther

Starting with the 1549 work of John Cochlaus, *Commentaria de actis et scriptis Martini Lutheri*, and promoted by the suggestions of John Eck, Luther was viewed as a wretched human being. Cochlaus' work was to influence many Catholic biographies on Luther. In 1904, the German Dominican, Heinrich Denifle, wrote an 860 page biography of Luther which attacked the character of Luther. This was followed in 1911 by the Jesuit, Hartmann Grisar, in a 2,600 page volume of more attacks on Luther. Although a little more subtle than Denifle, Grisar introduced the suggestion that Luther had a mental neurosis. In the *Catholic Encyclopedia*, the article by H.G. Ganss, owing much to the work of Denifle, similarly attacked the character of Luther. Hilaire Belloc added similar thoughts in his work *Europe and the Faith* a few years later. Next, Patrick O'Hare's work, *The Facts About Luther*, presented Luther as a sick man, one who rejected the doctrine of works because he simply did not have the character to do them. O'Hare concludes by labeling Luther the "Antichrist," the same accusation the latter had leveled against the papacy of his day. H. Evennett's work, *The Reformation,* offered a different slant suggesting that Luther's theology was merely a product of the Teutonic psyche and "thoroughly typical of German psychology," crystallizing the German discontent with being the economic, political, and intellectual slaves of Europe, and mobilizing them in order to quell their feelings of inferiority to the Italians who controlled the Roman Church. In 1937, Joseph Clayton in *Luther and His Work* developed Evennett's viewpoint, adding excerpts of Denifle's attack on Luther's character. Clayton also contrasted the subjective individualism of Luther's theology with the corporate understanding emphasized in Catholicism.

In 1917, however, a shift began in the assessment of Luther. German theologian F.X. Kiefl with his article, *Martin Luther's Religiose Psyche* published in the Roman Catholic review, *Hochland,* suggested that Luther's emphasis on faith alone was justified; the doctrine does not imply any moral slackening, since faith normally shows itself in works. Kiefl sympathized with what he understood as Luther's genius and his respect for the transcendent God. In 1929, Anton Fisher stressed the emphasis on prayer in Luther's life. In 1931, Hubert Jedin critcized the views of Denifle, suggesting instead that any Catholic who truly wants to understand the real Luther should disregard the image of him handed down by the Church.

After these reinterpretations of Luther, Roman Catholic historian Joseph Lortz in 1939 published *Die Reformation in Deutschland.* His premise was that the Church of the medieval period needed some kind of reformation. To Lortz, Luther was a complex genius who is misunderstood to this very day. He attributes much of this misunderstanding to Luther's modifications, paradoxes, and exaggerations as well as the extreme vulgarity of his accusations. He concludes that Luther was a "religious man" who though fervent in prayer and immersed in Scripture, nevertheless mistakenly oversimplified the Scriptural message of which the Roman Catholic Church possessed the fullness. Lortz further suggests that the heavy influence of Ockham's nominalism rendered Luther incapable of understanding Biblical revelation in its fullness. He therefore rejected a Catholicism that was not Catholic, attributing teachings to a Church that it never taught. Seeking assurance, Luther, by interpreting texts according to his conscience, became a prisoner of his personal interpretation. Lortz, however, was known as a Nazi sympathizer and it was the latter who honored Luther as both a good German and an anti-Semite hero. In 1943, Adolf Herte supported Lortz's approach by denouncing the 1549 work of John Cochlaus.

In 1946, J. Hessen's theological assessement in *Luther in katholischer Sicht* rejected Lortz's critique of Luther, saying that the subjective elements in his theology were only formal. To Hessen, Luther's theology was very objective since, by the mediation of

Christ, it was a genuine meeting with God. Hessen believed Luther was a true prophet, like those in the Old Testament, stressing Luther's original desire to reform the Church, not to separate from it. Hessen stresses Luther's emphasis on morality in the face of his antinomian critics, his preservation of sacramental grace in Baptism and the Eucharist, and his attack on the Church's intellectualism, moralism, pervasive sacramentalism, and institutionalism.

In 1947, Karl Adam of Tubingen produced *Una Sancta in Katholischer Sicht,* praising what he understood as Luther's genius, gifts, heroism, passion, literary style, scholarship, and personal piety. Adam faulted Luther, however, for using these qualities against the Church instead of for her, asserting that by 1512 Luther had already rebelled and intended to separate from the Church. Further, Adam held that Luther was not the first to discover the passive sense of the righteousness of God. This understanding was already prevalent among the medieval exegetes before him. Adam maintained that where Luther went off track was in his theological innovation that man was "sin, nothing but sin." Adam sided with Lortz in saying that Luther's understanding of the Scriptural message was too narrow and not able to satisfy all the needs and nuances of the Christian faith. Adam courageously confesses the Church's scandals, but he faults Luther for going so far beyond eliminating these abuses as to separate himself from the Church. If he had remained, Adam estimates that Luther would have been a reformer comparable to Thomas Aquinas and St. Francis of Assisi.

In 1954, Friedrich Richter, a convert from Lutheranism, although rejecting Denifle's caricatures, reintroduced the emphasis on subjectivism in Luther and explained that Luther's temperament and inability to master his passions led him to separate from the Church. Richter also held that Luther did not fully understand the Thomistic doctrine of justification. In 1961, Fr. Thomas Sartory, O.S.B., also rejected Denifle's thesis and the so-called "subjectivism" of Luther, suggesting that psychoanalysis by subsequent critics could not do justice to Luther's acute view of divine wrath which disrupted his life. Interestingly, Sartory suggested that because the Council of Trent broke with tradition by not condemning the Reformers by name, it left open the door for future dialogue with Protestantism. Sartory concludes: "Nevertheless, in spite of our reservations, in spite of the "No" spoken against him by the Church, we Catholics wish to hear his word in so far as it is a witness to the Gospel, so that we too may be inflamed with the love of God which burns in him." Sartory received high praise from Lutheran scholars for his fair treatment of Luther, among them Paul Althaus, and from some Catholic theologians, among them Karl Rahner. Rahner affirms the "No" given to Luther but reiterates that the Catholic Church has therefore given no official judgment of him since Trent did not mention Luther by name. (Details and further commentary can be found in Richard Stauffer's *Luther As Seen By Catholics* (Richmond, VA: John Knox Press, 1967), pp. 13-55). George H. Tavard shows much sympathy for Luther, portraying him as one who has been misunderstood, even, as he says, St. Augustine was misunderstood (see "Luther in Catholic Thought" in *Justification: An Ecumenical Study* (New York: Paulist Press, 1990) pp. 95-111; See also *Interpreters of Luther*, ed. Jaroslav Pelikan (Philadelphia: Fortress Press, 1968).

A recent writing by popular Catholic writer Peter Kreeft states: "How do I resolve the Reformation? Is it faith alone that justifies, or is it faith and good works? Very simple. No tricks. On this issue I believe Luther was simply right; and this issue is absolutely crucial...Much of the Catholic Church has not yet caught up with Luther; and, for that matter, much of Protestantism has regressed from him" (*Fundamentals of the Faith: Essays in Christian Apologetics* (San Francisco, Ignatius, 1988), p. 290). The reader should note, however, that in a letter to me, Kreeft wrote that he should not have used such language in describing Luther's views (letter on file, dated October 22, 1993). In another work, Kreeft states: "The faith-works controversy that sparked the Protestant Reformation was due largely to an equivocation on the word *faith*. If we use faith as Catholic theology does...that is, if we mean intellectual faith — then faith alone is not sufficient for salvation, for 'even the demons believe and shudder.' Hope, and above all love, need to be added to faith. But if we use faith as Luther did, and as Paul did in Romans and Galatians, that is, as heart-faith, then this is saving faith. It is sufficient for salvation, for it necessarily produces the good works of love just as a good tree necessarily produces good fruit. Protestants and Catholics agree on this" (*Hand-*

book of Christian Apologetics (Downer's Grove, IL: Intervarsity Press, 1994), p. 31). Using the same Scriptural reference, Evangelical Alister McGrath states: "Luther does not, as is frequently represented, reject the necessity of good works in justification: opera sunt necessaria ad salutem, sed non causant salutem, quia fides sola dat vitam." He frequently appeals to the biblical image of the good tree which bears good fruit, thus testifying to, rather than causing, its good nature" *(Iustitia Dei*, (London: Cambridge University Press, 1986), Vol. 2, p. 16). (NB: As noted in chapters 2 and 5 of this book, "saving faith" is not the crux of the issue in justification). As a final remark, it is worth noting that in Luther's exegesis of the parable of the tree and its fruits he leaves uninterpreted the concluding statement of Jesus, "Every tree that does not bear good fruit is cut down and thrown into the fire (Matt. 7:19) (See Peter Manns, "Absolute and Incarnate Faith — Luther on Justification in the Galatian Commentary of 1531-1535" in *Catholic Scholars Dialogue With Luther*, ed. Jared Wicks, S.J. (Chicago: Loyola University Press, 1970) f. 55-56, p. 130). Though Luther saw good works as a necessary product of faith, he was in no way ready to admit the Catholic teaching that love and good works held a specific causality and necessity in salvation that if not consciously added to faith would be cause for judgment.

Appendix 2

Analysis of the Latin word *iustificare*

In his work, *Iustitio Dei*, McGrath maintains that in Augustine's translations, his Latin meanings were not faithful to the Hebrew meanings. This echoes the assertion of the German Lutheran, Martin Chemnitz (1522-1586), a student of Melanchthon, who said that Augustine misrepresented the Greek word *dikaioun* (δικαιοῦν) to refer to "making righteous" instead of "declaring righteous." McGrath cites Chemnitz's view on page 29, and elsewhere in the book attempts to show through the etymology and usage of the Hebrew that *tsedaqah* (צדקה) is a more general word than the Latin *iustificare*. Hence, McGrath says Augustine's Latin translation missed the "soteriological overtones" associated with the Hebrew *tsedaqah* (p. 8). McGrath says these kinds of problems were further complicated by the Greek word *dikaiosune* (δικαιοσύνη) which was also limited in scope due to its Aristotelian origins. To support this position, McGrath cites several usages of the Greek *eleemosune* (ἐλεημοσύνη — "mercy, alms") by the LXX to translate the noun *tsedaqah* rather than the normal insertion of *dikaiosune.* McGrath also cites the anomalies of where LXX uses *dikaiosune* to translate *tsedaqah* in Lev. 19:36; Deut. 25:15; and Ezk. 45:10; in these instances the Hebrew merely carries the sense of "accurate" not, as translated, "just." In another example, McGrath cites the translation in Deut. 33:19 which should be "correct sacrifices" instead of "righteous sacrifices." Similarly, McGrath sees a weakness in *dikaiosune* to translate the general scope of the Hebrew verb *tsadaq* (צדק). He cites the LXX translation of Isaiah 5:22-23 and 43:26 as proof. As a result, McGrath is of the opinion that the semantic range of the root *dikaioun* was expanded to accommodate *tsedaqah.* McGrath suggests that the difficulty comes to the fore when the "post-classical" Latin term *iustificare* is used to translate the "expanded" forms of the *dikaioo* cognates. More importantly, McGrath also asserts that Greeks and Latins had decisively different ideas of the concept of merit, and that this was the main cause for the Latin church's emphasis on merit and the prevalence of merit in medieval theology. According to McGrath, in Greek culture *merit* was only a matter of "estimation" which is not inherent in its object, i.e., considering an entity to be something that it is not in itself. McGrath asserts that *merit,* in the Latin culture, refers to the quality inherent in the object or person. Representative of these two meanings, according to McGrath, is the Greek passive *axiousthai* (ἀξιουσθαι — "to deem worthy") and the Latin equivalent, *mereri*. The Greek word that would have denoted "inherent merit" is *meroma*, from which the Latin *meritum* is derived. McGrath's conclusion: the disjunction between *axiousthai* and *mereri* is similar to the disjunction between *dikaiosune* and *iustificare*. Hence the Greek word has the primary sense of being *considered righteous,* whereas the Latin word denotes *being righteous* or the reason one is considered righteous. All in all, McGrath concludes that the initial transference of a Hebrew concept, to a Greek concept, to a Latin concept, led to a fundamental alteration in the concepts of justification and righteousness as the gospel spread from Palestine to the Western world (p. 15).

Biblical Critique of McGrath's Theory

McGrath's linguistic analysis and conclusion appear to read into history what his theology dictates. Despite the anomalies that always occur in translating a word from one language to another, it is a matter of certain faith that inspired Scripture, which translates Hebrew text into Greek text, cannot err, and does not envision the problem McGrath proposes. First, without reservation, the New Testament authors use the *dikaioo* cognates to translate the Hebrew and Septuagint cognates. These translations occur in many non-justification contexts (i.e., "non-imputation" contexts). For example, in 2 Cor. 9:9 Paul cites a quotation from Psalm 112:9 and uses the Greek *dikaiosune* to translate the Hebrew feminine noun *tsadaqah* (צדקה — which the LXX also translates as *dikaiosune*). The context of 2 Cor. 9:9-10 concerns liberal giving, both of God and men, to those in need. Thus, contrary to McGrath's thesis, *dikaiosune* is understood as that which is *inherent* within both God and man due to the good they have done. Similarly, Hebrews 1:9 uses *dikaiosune* to translate the Hebrew male noun *tsadaq* (צדק) in Psalm 45:7 (of which the LXX uses *dikaiosune*) and speaks of the *inherent* righteousness of Christ. (The relevance of the LXX may be even more significant here since Hebrews 1:6 is quoted by Paul directly from the LXX). In addition, 1 Peter 3:12 uses *dikaioo* to translate the Hebrew adjective *tsadeek* of Psalm 34:15 (of which the LXX uses *dikaious*). The context of 1 Peter 3:12 regards righteous individuals as *inherently* righteous, for it is they who "turn from evil to do good" and "seek peace and pursue it." Similarly, Hebrews 11:7 uses *dikaiosune* to describe the righteousness of Noah, translating the Hebrew adjective *tsadeek* in Genesis 7:1 which refers to God seeing Noah as inherently righteous for his goodness in the midst of the wicked people of his day.

We should also add that Scripture does not support McGrath's assessment of the Greek word *axioo* (ἄξιοω) to refer only to the *estimation* of an individual rather than his merit (which he distinguishes from the Latin notion of merit that gives the individual the "right" of the third party estimation, i.e., because he is deserving of it). The New Testament uses *axioo* not only in considering someone worthy but also in recognizing someone worthy because he is *actually* worthy. For example, Hebrews 3:3 uses *axioo* in reference to Christ's worthiness: "Jesus has been counted worthy of greater honor than Moses..." This is a common usage of *axioo* and its cognates in the New Testament (cf., 1 Thess. 1:11; 1 Tim. 5:17; Col 1:10; et al).

Appendix 3

Analysis of "Works of the Law"

Augustine writes:

> Although, therefore, the apostle seems to reprove and correct those who were being persuaded to be circumcised, in such terms as to designate by the word "law" circumcision itself and other similar legal observances, which are now rejected as shadows of a future substance by Christians who yet hold what those shadows figuratively promised; he at the same time, nevertheless, would have it to be clearly understood that the law, by which he says no man is justified, lies not merely in those sacramental [ceremonial] institutions which contained promissory figures, but also in those works by which whosoever has done them lives holily, and amongst which occurs this prohibition: "Thou shalt not covet."...Is it possible to contend that it is not the law which was written on those two tables that the apostle describes as "the letter that killeth," but the law of circumcision and the other sacred rites which are now abolished? But then how can we think so, when in the law occurs this precept, "Thou shalt not covet," by which very commandment, notwithstanding it being holy, just, and good, "sin," says the apostle, "deceived me, and by it slew me?" What else can this be than "the letter" that "killeth."? Augustine, *On the Spirit and the Letter* (AD 412), The NFPF, Vol. 5, Augustin: Anti-Pelagian Writings (Peabody, MA: Hendrickson Publishers, Inc, 1994), p. 93.

Luther and Calvin, in their Galatian commentaries, respectively, attempted to limit the Catholic rejoinder to holding that "works of law" referred to the ceremonial law. Luther writes:

> Hence the opinion of Jerome and others is to be rejected when they imagine that here Paul is speaking about the works of the Ceremonial Law, not about those of the Decalogue (LW, Commentary on Galatians 2:16, op. cit., p. 123).

Calvin writes:

> The question now is, what is meant by *the works of the law?* The Papists, misled by Origen and Jerome, think, and in fact assert definitely, that the dispute relates to shadows and accordingly interpret the works of the law as ceremonies...In short, they hold that this does not refer to moral works. (Calvin's New Testament Commentaries, *Galatians*, trans., T.H.L. Parker, eds., David Torrence and Thomas Torrence (Grand Rapids, Eerdmans, 1965, 1980), p. 38).

At one point in his theology, Thomas Aquinas made a linguistic distinction between the ceremonial law and the moral law in reference to "works of law," as noted in his statement: "It should be known, therefore, that some works of the Law were moral and some ceremonial. The moral, although they were contained in the Law, could not, strictly speaking, be called 'works of law,' for man is induced to them by natural instinct and by the natural law. But the ceremonial works are properly called the 'works of law,'" (*Commentary on Saint Paul's Epistle to the Galatians* (Albany, NY: Magi, 1966)). Thomas' formulation does not clarify to what extent the phrases, "strictly speaking" and "properly" divorce the moral law from "works of law." This is true of most formulations that seek to emphasize the ceremonial law over the moral law. The commentator attempts to qualify the extent of the ceremonial law, but the remaining portion of the law, e.g., the moral law, is never clearly set aside, defined, shown how it relates to the ceremonial law, or how it fits into the general category of how works of law cannot justify.

Even some modern Catholic theologians have revived Jerome's view. In his commentary on Galatians, Frank Matera cites some current thought on the issue. He writes:

> While Jerome understood the phrase to refer to circumcision, the Sabbath, and other ceremonial laws, Luther and Calvin insisted that Paul was speaking of the whole Law, and not just its ceremonial aspects, and so do most modern commentators. . . The context of this letter and the recent research of E. P. Sanders and J. Dunn, however, suggest that the expression primarily envisions circumcision, dietary laws, and the observance of Jewish feast days, all of which were viewed as identity markers that distinguished Jews from Gentiles . . . Thus ἐξ ἔργων νόμου, is a technical phrase akin to a code word and has a precise meaning for Paul and the Galatians. It also occurs in 3:2, 5, 10 and Rom. 4:2, 6; 9:12, 32; 11:6 (*Galatians* (Collegeville, MN: Michael Glazier, 1992) p. 93).

A few points need to be said about this view. First, Matera fails to reveal that the view concerning "works of law" as applying to both the ceremonial law and the moral law originated with Augustine who lived at the same time as Jerome. Luther and Calvin were not the first. Second, there is an obvious ambivalence in Matera's definition (as well as Sanders' and Dunn's definition) of ἐξ ἔργων νόμου, because one statement says that it "*primarily* envisions circumcision," but the next statement says it is "a code word and has a *precise* meaning for Paul." The use of "primarily" is ambiguous, since the reader does not know whether the authors are saying that the primacy of the ceremonial law is such that it essentially neutralizes or nullifies other dimensions of the law, or that in being only a primary concern it still leaves room to include another or secondary concern into the discussion of the meaning of ἐξ ἔργων νόμου,. Third, the view of Dunn, et al., that "works of law" refers only to the ceremonial law is based on a new Protestant understanding of Justification. This thesis purports that Paul's main concern is global justice, not necessarily individual justification. (See *The Justice of God: A Fresh Look at the Old Doctrine of Justification by Faith*, by James Dunn and Alan Suggate (Grand Rapids: Eerdmans Publishing, 1993)). In Paul's teaching on justification, Dunn, et al., maintain that the overriding concern is to teach Jews that they are no longer "set apart" for God. Rather, they must come to accept the Gentiles as part of God's covenant community. Since the ceremonial aspects of the Mosaic law, e.g., circumcision, dietary laws, etc., were the most prominent aspects of the Mosaic law that separated Jews from Gentiles, it is concluded that "works of law" can only refer to the ceremonial law, not the moral law. Since the moral law is common to both ethnic groups, the authors maintain that it cannot be a distinguishing aspect between Jew and Gentile. Hence Dunn and Suggate conclude: "Justification by faith is Paul's fundamental objection to the idea that God has limited his saving goodness to a particular people." Although there is some truth to this dimension of justification, elevating this dimension to be the fundamental concern of Paul is a distortion of the concept of justification. While Paul has great concern that as a group the Gentiles should not be impeded from the Christian faith by obsolete cultic practices, the question still remained whether each Gentile would avail himself of the justification God had offered to him, how he would avail himself of it, and more so, whether he would persevere in that justified state. Paul focuses on this latter responsibility in Galatians 5:13-6:10. In this sense, justification becomes intensely individualistic. The inspired writers teach the Gentile to seek for justification by modeling his faith and obedience on those individuals in the Old Testament who became and remained justified despite belonging to a nation that was in large part faithless (cf., Rom. 2:4-10; 4:12-25; 5:12-14; 7:1-25; 11:13-22; 1 Cor. 10:1-13; 2 Cor. 3:12-6:2; 12:20-13:10; Heb. 3:12-4:16; 10:19-13:14; James 1:1-5:20). In each case, whether Old or New Testament, the individual had to struggle with whether or not he, within his own person, was being faithful and obedient to God, and hence he struggled with his own justification. Each individual had to come to the point at which he recognized that his own works, whether from natural law or codified law, could not procure his justification. Dunn's view ignores Paul's concern of legal obligation that Paul so strenuously teaches in Romans 4:4 and 11:35. Dunn also ignores or does not do justice to Paul's all-inclusive condemnation of the law (i.e., law as a concept, which included moral, religious, natural, and any other kind of law) in Romans 3:19-20; 4:15; 7:7-12; Galatians 3:19, et al. Paul had to reeducate the Galatians, tempted as they were by the Judaizers to base their justification on extraneous works, that only through grace could they be saved (Gal. 6:12-15). Performing works from an obsolete law in an effort to secure their justification was certainly wrong, but not merely because it attempted to ostracize Gentiles; rather, because it made the mistake of putting God in a position of obligation to man.

Critiquing the view of Dunn, as well as similar ideas advanced by E. P. Sanders [*Paul and Palestinian Judaism*], Bruce Longenecker [*Eschatology and the Covenant*] and Lloyd Gaston ["Paul and the Torah" in *Antisemitism and the Foundations of Christianity*], Mark Seifrid comments:

> Thus the false dichotomy which Dunn draws between universalism (Paul) and particularism (Judaism) obscures the issues at stake...It is true that Paul does not regard his opponents as seeking to secure salvation solely by their own efforts, but that does not mean that 'merit theology' is thereby excluded...If Paul was fundamentally concerned with nationalistic sentiment, why does he begin by addressing the human being, not the Jew? Why does he begin with personal soteriological implications of passing moral judgments on others [Rom. 2:1-11]? Even when Paul speaks rhetorically to the Jew, he does not deal with simple ethnic pride, but with the assumption that the knowledge of God's will mediated by the Law brings moral superiority [Rom. 2:17-24]...Circumcision was indeed a 'national boundary marker,' but Paul here assumes that it also was a claim to religious preeminence mediated by the Law, and consequently constituted an assurance of salvation. It is this claim which he attacks in Rom 2.

Prior to Dunn and Sanders, Protestant William Wrede advanced a similar line of thinking. Wrede proposed that Paul's sole purpose in employing the theme of justification by faith was to oppose the imposition of Jewish customs on Gentile converts. (William Wrede, "The Tasks and Method of New Testament Theology" in The Nature of New Testament Theology SBT 2nd series, ed. and trans. Robert Morgan (Naperville, IL: Allenson, 1973) p. 100). Critiquing Wrede's thesis, Mark A. Seifrid states:

> This reduction of "works of the Law" to Jewish customs is not at all convincing. Wrede's dichotomization of ritual and ethics runs against the grain of virtually all early Judaism, including the Hellenistic variety attested by Philo, since even for him ritual demands serve to teach ethical lessons [Philo: *De Specialibus Legibus*, 1.1-2.12]. The close connection between purity and transgression which appears in the Qumran materials is indicative of the essential unity of the issue in the minds of most first-century Jews. Moreover, as Douglas Moo has observed, the expression 'works of the Law' never means anything more precise than 'works done in obedience to the Law' ["'Law,' 'Works of the Law,' and Legalism in Paul," WTS 45 (1983): 73-100]. Wrede already had 4 Ezra available to him, where in an admittedly strict form of Judaism 'works' were accorded salvific value [4 Ezra 7:77]. And it now appears that a fragment of a letter discovered in Cave 4 at Qumran attests a connection between (anticipated) deeds of obedience ('works') and the attribution of righteousness by God...It is therefore difficult to believe that no connection existed between Paul's postconversion conception of 'grace' and his earlier righteousness 'obtained through the Law.' Boasting in the Law, which expresses itself in a confidence in circumcision, includes a commitment to high moral standards [Rom. 2:17-29]. The appeal to David as a witness to righteousness...in Rom 4:6-8, also presumes a broader conception of 'works' than 'mere' ritual practices, since here 'justification' is understood as the forgiveness of transgression. Nor is it possible to reduce the theme of 'justification by faith' to a mere opposite of 'works of the Law.' The phrase ἔργα νόμου, does not appear in Phil [Philippians] 3 where the concept of a righteousness through Christ is contrasted with righteousness through the Law.

In light of this controversy, Catholics must make careful note that the Council of Trent, in deliberating on the nature of justification in Session 6, never reduced the argument to, or posited a distinction between, the ceremonial and moral law. The ceremonial law is alluded to only once in the 6th Session of Trent. There, it is merely quoting Paul's statement in Gal. 5:6, "neither circumcision avails anything, nor uncircumcision, but faith, which works by charity" (Chapter 7). As noted above in the excerpt from Calvin, during the heat of the Reformation, there were apparently some in the Catholic hierarchy who were using the argument that "works of law" referred to the ceremonial law in order to explain the kind of works that did not justify the individual. To clear up the issue, the Council of Trent did not hesitate to take the discussion to its highest level in asserting the total antithesis of justification by law as opposed to justification by grace. They did not debate whether "works of law" referred to ceremonial laws or moral laws. This was immediately made clear in the very first Canon of the Sixth Session: "If anyone shall say that man can be justified before God by his own works which are done either by his *own natural powers*, or through the *teaching of the Law*, and without divine grace through Jesus Christ: let him be anathema." Trent's approach to the subject was not to dissect the different aspects of law but to make a blanket statement that law, as a system in itself, could not justify the individual. Working on the principle that God, because he is transcendent and perfect, could not be put in a position of obligation to man, Trent maintained this high level of analysis and recognized that even faith, because it is a gift of God, could not merit justification. In this way, they went beyond the Reformers by stating in Session 6, Chapter 8: "...because *none* of those things which precede justification, *whether faith or works*, merit the grace of justification." Trent understood and emphasized that all must come through grace and thus law, as a system in itself, which is antithetical to grace and which attempts to obligate God, can never justify. Trent made it clear that it was siding with Augustine's view, cited above, as opposed to the limited view of Jerome. Hence, we must conclude, with Trent, that Paul is not saying that things such as circumcision and dietary laws are not required merely because they are obsolete; rather, on a higher level of argumentation, he is using these as representatives to show that law, as a system in itself, cannot justify the individual. This is clarified in Paul's thesis that one is required "to obey the whole law" if he insists on basing his relationship to God on any part of the Mosaic law (cf., Galatians 3:10; 5:3; Romans 4:14-15). In the specific situation at Galatia, requiring Christians to perform obsolete laws of ceremony in order to secure justification made their relationship with God one of obligation rather than grace, and thus made them obligated to obey the whole law perfectly.

In many instances where Paul contrasts grace against works, there is little or no concern that Jewish ceremonial laws were being imposed on Gentiles, rather, Paul's focus is on developing a total antithesis between the system of law and the system of grace (cf., Romans 7:1-10; 9:10-13; 11:5-6; 3:19-20; 4:13-17; Ephesians 2:8-9; Titus 3:5; Galatians 3:19-25). As the Council of Trent appealed to Romans 11:6 (Session 6, Chapter 8: "And if by grace then it is no longer by works") it did so not merely in regard to the first century A.D. problem of Jews judaizing Gentiles, but in reference to the ninth century B.C. religious contentions between one Jew and another. As described in the context of Romans 11:1-5, there were many Jews in Elijah's time who self-righteously claimed to be following God but who bowed the knee to Baal, in opposition to the righteous Jews who numbered among the remnant of seven thousand and did not worship Baal. It is in this setting that Paul concludes with the final dictum in Romans 11:6 that salvation comes by grace, not works. Apparently, he understood that those who were "doing works" outside of grace were the Jews who, although possessing the words and works of Torah like their righteous brothers, bowed the knee to a false god. It was the stark contrast between their life-style and their religious heritage, not a contention between Jew and Gentile over circumcision, that caused Paul to conclude that grace, not works, saves. In short, it was the Jews' erroneous understanding of the *entire* concept and purpose of works and law that Paul wanted to expose, not merely there insistence on ethnic distinctives such as circumcision. Hence, we must insist that the Catholic Church does not believe in an "artificial distinction between 'works of law' and 'works'" (Geisler and MacKenzie, *Roman Catholics and Evangelicals*, p. 234), rather, she believes in a God who despises *any* self-righteous works but is pleased with selfless obedience within his arms of grace.

Appendix 4

Analysis of Condign and Congruent Merit

Strict merit denotes a contractual relationship between two parties in which one party performs work for the other party and thus is owed a compensation for the work done. The paying party is under legal obligation to pay the working party. *Condign* or *congruent* merit denotes a non- contractual relationship between two parties in which neither the party doing the work demands payment from the party for whom the work is done, nor can the party for whom the work is performed be under obligation to pay for the work. Whatever is given to the first party for the work done is only by the sheer gratuity of the second party. In other words, the party for whom work is done may pay the worker out of kindness, but he is not obligated to do so. Specifically, condign merit (Latin: *meritum de condigno*) is that which is gratuitously rewarded to an individual in keeping with his obedience. The reward only applies to the just. It can be an increase in sanctifying grace or an increase in heavenly glory (cf., Hebrews 6:10; 1 Timothy 6:18-19; 2 Timothy 4:8). Congruent merit (Latin: *meritum de congruo*) is merit given in accord with the act performed but far outweighing the act itself, either to the just or the unjust (cf., Psalm 50:19; Luke 18:9-14; 1 Timothy 1:13-14).

Evangelical R. C. Sproul gives a false impression of Catholicism's concept of condign merit by stating: "Condign merit imposes a legal obligation for reward, whereas congruous merit does not" (*Faith Alone*, p. 147). By this assessment Sproul does a severe injustice to Catholic theology. Catholic theology does not teach that condign merit "imposes a legal obligation." It is precisely because it is not a strict legal obligation upon God that merit can be understood as condign, i.e., a reward that is fitting but not legally required. God gives what is just but he is not contractually obligated to do so. Section 2007 of the *Catholic Catechism* (1994) confirms this distinction: "With regard to God, there is no strict right to merit on the part of man" (Section 2007, p. 486). The 1566 Catechism, titled *Catechismus Romanus* and subtitled *Catechismus ex decreto Tridentini* which was issued following the Council of Trent and thereby sought to explain the Council, stated that grace always precedes, accompanies, and follows man's good works, and that merit is impossible apart from grace. Although one could argue that condign merit may, in one sense, require God to follow through with what he promised as a reward for obedience, this is not equivalent to the notion of strict merit. Moreover, the mere fact that he can offer condign merit for obedience stems ultimately from his benevolence, not from a law overruling God that mandates him to do so. Thus we should not understand condign merit as legally obligating God outside of the realm of grace.

Thomas Aquinas, who advanced the concept of *meritum de condigno* that had first been introduced by Bonaventure, insisted that, in the strict sense, God is never a debtor to man. He is, rather, in debt to himself insofar as he has pledged himself to fulfill his promises. Aquinas writes:

> Note the difference between meritum de condigno and that which is said to be merit in strict justice. Even though both bespeak some right to a reward, they do so in different ways. Merit in strict justice implies an absolute equality without any grace given to the person who merits. But merit de condigno involves an equality which arises from grace which has been given to the one meriting (*Summa Theologica*, I-II, Q. 114, a. 1, ad 3).

As R. C. Sproul gave a false impression of this Catholic teaching, evangelical Michael Horton gives the same distorted impression by failing to make the proper distinction between strict contractual merit and gratuitous condign merit. He writes: "Here, the Roman church distinguished between condign merit, which is *an outright payment for that which was truly earned*, and congruent merit, which is not really earned in the truest sense of the term, but which God graciously accepts 'as if' it had been merited truly" (*Roman Catholicism: Evangelical Protestants Analyze What Unites and Divides Us*, p. 266, n. 9, emphasis mine). The statement "outright payment for that which was truly earned" wrongly puts condign merit in terms of debt paid under legal contract, i.e., that which is owed to the party who works without regard to the benevolence of the one for whom the work is done. This distorted notion of condign merit perpetuated by today's evangelicals is nothing new, however — it began with Luther. Attempting to explain the difference between congruent merit and condign merit, Luther writes in his Galatian commentary:

> They attribute the merit of grace and the forgiveness of sins to the mere performance of the work. For they say that a good work performed before grace can earn a "merit of congruity"; but once grace has been obtained, the work that follows deserves eternal life by the "merit of condignity." If a man outside a state of grace and in mortal sin performs a good work by his own natural inclination — such as reading or hearing Mass, giving alms, etc. — this man deserves grace "by congruity." Once he has obtained grace this way, he goes on to perform a work that merits eternal life "by condignity." Now in the first case God is not indebted to anyone. But because He is good and righteous, it is proper for Him to approve such a good work, even though it is performed in mortal sin, and to grant grace for such a deed. But once grace has been obtained, *God has become a debtor and is obliged by right to grant eternal life*. (LW, Galatians 2:16, op. cit., p. 124) emphasis mine.

Laying aside the matter of the application of "merit of congruity" in Scripture, which is briefly covered in Chapter 4 of this book, Luther, in the above passage, distorts the meaning of condign merit by holding that in such a case God is a "debtor" to man and is "obliged" to grant eternal life. Since Luther is using these terms in the context of Law, (which is evident in the immediately preceding paragraphs as he points out that the Law which does not justify includes both the ceremonial and moral aspects of law), indicates that in Catholic theology condign merit obligates God, *under law*, to grant eternal life by right. Moreover, even under grace God is not a "debtor by right to grant eternal life" simply because God can take away the gift. If there is any obligation it is because God has put himself in that position, not because man has obliged God to assume such. Scripture gives us many instances in which God obligates himself but at the same time it sees no infringement on the principles of grace (e.g., Hebrews 6:13-18). In this regard, Catholic theologian Peter Manns has rightly said that Luther did not understand the Thomistic theology he castigated. That the concept of condign merit is one of the chief irritants of Catholic theology to Luther is noted in his extensive reference to condign merit throughout the Galatian commentary. But as many have discovered, Luther's polemic merely attacks a caricature of the Catholic faith, not the real Catholic faith.

Unfortunately, even some Catholic authors have confused the issue of strict merit versus condign merit by referring to the latter as "merit in the true and proper sense." This is at best misleading and certainly apt to be misunderstood by Protestants looking for any clue of "salvation by merit" in Catholicism. For example, in a recent work it was stated: "Merit de condigno... is a type of merit that can be obtained only by Jesus Christ in light of his divine nature. The redemptive act by Jesus Christ on the cross was both satisfactory (removing the relationship of guilt between the human race and God) and meritorious (establishing a right to reward from Almighty God, which is always at the same time presupposing a gift of grace from God). Cf. Council of Trent, D 799, D 809, 810..." (*Mary: Coredemptrix, Mediatrix, Advocate: Theological Foundations Towards a Papal Definintion,* ed. Mark I. Miravalle, (Santa Barbara, CA: Queenship Publishing, 1995), p. 262). In response, we must point out that the Council of Trent does not even mention the phrase *merit de condigno*, let alone define it as something exclusively attributable to Christ. The addition of "which is always at the same time presupposing a gift of grace from God" may include the essence of *merit de condigno,* but this cannot be applicable to Christ, especially to the exclusion of man.

Some evangelicals show at least show recognition of the true understanding of merit in Catholic theology, though not consistently. For example, Norman Geisler and Ralph MacKenzie describe condign merit as follows: "Of course, this demand is not intrinsic; it is only because God has placed himself in this situation because of his promise to reward good works" *(Roman Catholics and Evangelicals,* p. 227). Geisler and MacKenzie, rather than speak of the principle as an "outright payment" as Michael Horton does, add that the principle of condign merit is an arrangement in which God himself decides, in his own person, to reward man for his works, not because a law is obligating God to do such. In other instances, Geisler and MacKenzie portray the Catholic doctrine of gracious merit as erroneous. This is noted, for example, in their continual reference (pp. 222, 226-228, 232) to Ludwig Ott's statement, "By his works the justified man really acquires a claim to supernatural reward from God" (*Fundamentals of Catholic Dogma*, p. 264). Because Ott's phrase "acquires a claim" seems rather strong, Geisler and MacKenzie infer (though Ott does not intend to convey anything beyond what Trent proposed) that Catholic doctrine puts God in a position of strict legal obligation. Without citing Ott's full paragraph, Geisler and MacKenzie leave the false impression that Catholic theology teaches strict merit by legal obligation, and unfortunately they use this as a major point of contention between Protestants and Catholics. As noted above, however, neither the Council of Trent nor the Catholic Catechism teach this. We would suggest, however, that Ott's language is perhaps too strong for Protestant sensitivities to this issue. This tendency is seen in another of Ott's statements: "...he [Paul] thereby shows that the good works of the just establish a legal claim (meritum de condigno) to reward on God. Cf. Hebr. 6, 10." Though knowledgeable Catholics understand the intent and the context in which Ott makes this statement, we also understand how such language could be misleading and hence be the object of criticism among Protestants. To be fair to both sides, we must reiterate that the Council of Trent did not use the language of Ott (i.e., either "legal claim" or "meritum de condigno"); rather, the Council chose to remain with the biblical language that God gives reward "...as a recompense which is...to be faithfully given to their good works and merit" (Section 809), and in interpreting this language the Catholic Catechism insists, "With regard to God, there is no strict right to merit on the part of man" (Section 2007, p. 486).

Geisler and MacKenzie also attempt to nullify the Catholic concept of gracious merit by such statements as:

> Catholics...overlook the fact that Scripture teaches that grace and meritorious works are mutually exclusive...Often the problem seems to stem from a fallacious inference that simply because something is prompted by grace it is not obtained by merit. Just because the previous graciousness of a friend may prompt one to do a job for him that one would not otherwise have accepted does not mean that the wages earned from it were not at least partly merited, even if they were higher wages that one deserved. Thus, neither merit in the strict sense of what is justly earned nor merit which is based in part on what is earned but goes beyond that by God's goodness is compatible with grace (*Roman Catholics and Evangelicals*, p. 230).

There are several problems with this analysis. First, in saying that "grace and meritorious works are mutually exclusive" Geisler and MacKenzie fail to make the proper distinction — a distinction that Scripture itself makes. On the one hand, Scripture is clear in Romans 11:6, "And if by grace, then it is no longer by works." On the other hand, Scripture also says in Romans 2:6-8, "God will give to each person according to what he has done. To those who persist in doing good, seek glory, honor and immortality, he will give eternal life." Here it is clear that God gives "eternal life" (not just a personal reward in heaven) for those who have done good and sought immortality. In light of this, it comes as no surprise that Geisler and MacKenzie make no reference to Romans 2:6-8 in their discourse on justification. No passage in Scripture teaches the mutual relationship between grace and merit better than Romans 2:6-8. Second, the reason Geisler and MacKenzie fail to see this distinction is that they have not incorporated the difference between contractual obligation and non-contractual gratuity into the discussion. The best they can do to acknowledge a difference is to say "...wages earned from it were not *at least partly* merited" or "since the payment is owed (*at least in part*) for work done" (Ibid. p. 230, emphasis mine). By the addition of "at least in part" Geisler and MacKenzie recognize that it is not a full-fledged payment made from strict contractual obligation, yet they refuse to consider that anything less than a full-fledged payment is something outside the realm of contractual obligation. Under a legal framework, the worker is either contractually owed for all that is due for his work, or he is not. There is no quasi realm of obligation wherein he is owed "at least in part" for his work. Rather than create a quasi-contract which is ambiguously defined as "at least in part," we insist that work not fully performed under a contractual obligation must be placed in a different category, that is, a category of non-contractual gratuity. The payment of one who performs work under a non-contractual gratuity is not guaranteed nor legally binding. Although a mutual agreement can be established between the payor and the payee, unless the agreement is legally formalized, the payment to the payee is dependent solely on the payor's integrity and sense of justice. If there is no legally binding document witnessed and validated by a third party which states that the payor must pay the payee, he is not bound, except by his own word, and thus he could renege on his promise to pay. In other words, it is a non-contractual gratuity that can be taken away at the whim of the payor. We all agree that man cannot place God in a position of contractual obligation but we must also agree that God does not "at least pay in part" from contractual obligation. God gives only through non-contractual gratuity. If in the course of this arrangement God becomes bound it is only because he bound himself to be gracious, not because a law of contractual obligation had forced him into that situation. Geisler and MacKenzie seem to recognize the distinction between man placing God in the position of obligation and God putting himself in a position of obligation by the statement "Of course, this 'legal' claim is not intrinsic but only because God has promised it" (Ibid. p. 232). It is precisely because they do not fully address this particular point, however, that Geisler's and MacKenzie's argument falls short and becomes inadequate to answer all the information Scripture provides. Scripture teaches that there is no incompatibility between God obligating himself to give reward or inheritance and the concept of grace. As Paul says in Romans 4:16, "Therefore, the promise comes by faith, so that it may be by grace and may be guaranteed to all Abraham's offspring..." We see that God's promise to reward is made from his grace. In speaking of the same promise under grace, Hebrews 6:13-14 states: "When God made a promise to Abraham, since there was no one greater for him to swear by, he swore by himself, saying, 'I will surely bless you and give you many descendants.'" The law is not obligating God; rather, God is obligating himself. The relationship between the promise of God and gracious merit becomes all the more evident when we realize that Paul's reference to the swearing by an oath is taken from Genesis 22 when Abraham's *work* of sacrificing Isaac was manifested to God, not in Genesis 15 which centers on his faith. It is the same passage from which James concludes that Abraham was justified by his works (James 2:24). God did not contractually owe anything to Abraham, yet from an arrangement of non-contractual gratuity God promised, based on his personal divine nature, a reward to Abraham. Although at times he may have wondered why he made such a commitment (e.g., Exodus 32:9-14), he did not renege on his oath that he swore to himself.

In another light, if we follow Geisler's and MacKenzie's principle to its logical conclusion we can also maintain that the very atonement offered in Christ must likewise fit into the category of not being an "intrinsic demand" on the part of God, but one in which God obligated himself to save man because he, uncoerced by any law, simply desired to do so. Because of his integrity as God, he will follow through with the salvation of individuals. Only with respect to his personal integrity as God can it be said that he has obligated himself. By the same token, even if one were to classify *condign* merit as that which is "earned" by the individual due to the fact that God obligated himself to reward him, it must be understood that God obligated himself out of his grace and benevolence, not because he was forced or required to do so by any law. Donald Bloesch makes a somewhat disguised recognition of this principle in the statement, "Merit in the strict sense — works that truly deserve God's favor (de condigno)..." (*Roman Catholicism: Evangelical Protestants Analyze What Unites and Divides Us*, p. 151). Though Bloesch's statement is somewhat misleading due to the use of the word "strict," nevertheless, he at least recognizes by the phrase "deserve God's favor" that the reward comes from "favor" (i.e., grace), rather than from a legal and contractual obligation imposed by man.

Alister McGrath also admits the distinction between man imposing a contractual obligation on God and God placing himself under obligation, by the statement, "in the former case [condign merit], God is under an obligation (a self-imposed obligation, of course) to reward a human act" (*ARCIC II and Justification*, p. 19). Similar to the analysis of Geisler and MacKenzie, the problem with McGrath's explanation is that he fails to address the distinction between God's "self-imposed obligation" being administered through grace and a contractual obligation outside the realm of grace. In a glib sort of way, he parenthetically refers to "self-imposed obligation" and thereby treats this dimension of the issue as a mere afterthought, projecting into the reader's mind that such a condition on the nature of merit should really make no significant difference in the discussion, yet it is one of the most crucial distinctions in all of Catholic theology. As noted above, in accord with Catholic theology, Scripture is clear that God can place himself under obligation without any infringement on the nature of grace (cf. Hebrews 6:13-18; Romans 4:16-17).

At other times, McGrath takes liberties with the medieval term *meritum de condigno*. In reference to the deliberations at the Council of Trent, McGrath states: "the Latin verbs *mereri* and *promereri* were used with the sense 'merit in the strict and proper sense of the term' (in other words, condign merit)" (Ibid). He makes a similar statement a little later in the words: "'The Council unquestionably teaches that it is impossible to merit justification in the strict sense of the term — in other words, merit de condigno'"(ibid., p. 21). This, again, is very misleading. The Council of Trent did not use the medieval language of *meritum de condigno* in its chapters and canons. In fact, a deliberate resolution was made at the Council not to use such terminology. Yet McGrath takes it upon himself to equate "'merit in the strict and proper sense of the term'" with "in other words, condign merit." This equation again fails to recognize the crucial distinction in Catholic theology between strict merit, (i.e., merit imposed on God under legal obligation), and gracious merit, (i.e, condign merit in the medieval use of the term). McGrath covers himself, somewhat, by a previous statement: "The assertion that justification cannot be merited — found at several points in the Tridentine decree on justification — must be understood to mean that justification cannot be merited in the *full sense of the word* (proprie et vere mereri)" (emphasis mine). Though this statement indicates that McGrath has at least some recognition of the major distinction Trent made between strict merit and gracious merit, the ambiguity of the language "full sense of the word" does not do enough justice to the distinction. Apparently, McGrath feels there is a distinction worthy of mention, but such a cursory description as "full sense," especially without a proper and precise explanation which McGrath fails to do with this language, simply does not help in understanding Trent's intent; rather, it leaves the reader with an ambiguous and undefined understanding of what Trent was attempting to accomplish in this very complicated yet decisive area of theology.

Appendix 5

Analysis of Early Bible Translations Using "Faith Alone"

Historian Philip Schaff also finds 'Nur durch den glauben' in what he calls "pre-Lutheran Bibles" (*History of the Christian Church*, Vol. VII (Grand Rapids: Eerdmans, 1910), p. 362). Catholic theologian Michael Schmaus mentions the 1483 edition as well as the Italian versions (*Dogma: Justification and the Last Things*, 1977, p. 29). The facts behind these translations, however, do not allow for the impression Sproul is trying to give his readers. Of the 18 editions of the German Bible published before Luther, 14 were in High German, the last 5 were dependent on a revision published by Anthonius Koburger, otherwise known as the Nuremberg Bible of 1483. German editions are earlier and much more numerous than those of other countries because of the number and vigor of printing presses which had multiplied in the Rhine towns. Many of these large publishers, including Koburger, were suspected of sympathizing with the Reformation. In most editions, the printer's name was absent so as to avoid censorship by Catholic authorities. Quoting the historian Wather, Deanesly notes that it is quite certain that none of these printed Bibles was an official edition, was approved of, or could pass the censor of the Catholic Church at that time. Deanesly also notes that the Catholic Church did not favor issuing *any* German editions. The Catholic archbishop in Mainz, in the edict of 1486, forbade the making of any more German translations unless approved by the Church.

Regarding the Italian versions, Brucioli undertook one of the first translations, the New Testament being published first by Giunti in 1530. Brucioli's sympathy with the Reformation caused Rome to condemn his Venice edition, which was put on the *Index of Forbidden Books*. Later Italian versions produced by the Dominican, Marmochino, and Diodati brought Brucioli's edition into conformity with the Latin Vulgate and produced an acceptable Italian version.

These facts sho that the Catholic Church certainly did not approve any versions containing *allein* or *sola* in Romans 3:28. Sources for the above analysis: Margaret Deanesly, *The Lollard Bible: And Other Medieval Biblical Versions* (Cambridge University Press, 1920), pp. 122-124. Geddes MacGregor, *A Literary History of the Bible* (New York: Abingdon Press, 1968), pp. 68, 99-100. A. Vaccari, S.J., "Bibbe Protestanti E Bibbie Cattolica" in *La Civilta Cattolica* (Roma: Direzione E Amministrazione, 1923), pp. 343-351. Charles Hodge also maintains that "The Fathers also often use the expression 'man is justified by faith alone.'" James Buchanan (*The Doctrine of Justification* (Edinburgh: Banner of Truth, 1991, reprint) also made the same claim. See Chapter 1 for further refutation. (We should also add, that contrary to the criticism that Protestants levy against the Latin Vulgate for being obscure, the Vulgate derives its name from the Latin "vulgáris," (from which we get the word "vulgar" in English) which was the term used to describe the common or plain speech of the day).

Appendix 6

Critique of Protestant Views Denying Eternal Punishment

On this question, Fudge draws together the thoughts of the most prominent Evangelical scholars, many of the early fathers, and Middle Age and Reformed theologians in a heavily footnoted and bibliographical treatise. His view differs from that of the Jehovah's Witnesses who believe in instantaneous annihilation of the wicked without temporal punishment. Though Fudge's theory is beyond the scope of this book to critique, suffice it to say that the traditional Christian teaching is that Hell involves *eternal* separation and punishment from God. The sins of the individual will determine the degree of punishment. The Catholic Catechism states:

> The teaching of the Church affirms the existence of hell and its eternity. Immediately after death the souls of those who die in a state of mortal sin descend into hell, where they suffer the punishment of hell, "eternal fire." The chief punishment of hell is eternal separation from God, in whom alone man can possess the life and happiness for which he was created and for which he longs. (Paragraph 1035, p. 270).

This is in accord with the traditional teaching of the Fathers and Councils, e.g., The Athanasian Creed, c. 4th - 5th century, states: "...but those who have done evil into eternal fire"; the Council of Arles, 475 states: "the eternal fires and the infernal flames have been prepared in advance for capital deeds..."; the Council of Constantinople, 553, Canon 9 states: "If anyone says or holds that the punishment of the demons and of impious men is temporary, and that it will have an end at some time, that is to say, there will be a complete restoration of the demons or of impious men, let him be anathema" (This was directed mainly against Origen's idea of hell being a "purifying fire," or the *Apocatastasis*); The Fourth Lateran Council, 1215, chap. 1 states: "...that they may receive according to their works...the latter everlasting punishment with the devil, and the former everlasting glory with Christ." The Council of Lyons, 1247, #24, states: "Moreover, if anyone without repentance dies in mortal sin, without a doubt he is tortured forever by the flames of eternal hell." The Council of Florence, 1438-1445, states: "...cannot become participants in eternal life, but will depart into everlasting fire which was prepared for the devil and his angels." John XXII, 1316-1334, states: "...the souls of those who die in mortal sin, or with only original sin, descend immediately into hell; however, to be punished with different penalties and in different places." See also Ignatius (110), *Letter to the Ephesians*, which states: "the unquenchable fire;" Polycarp (155) in *The Martyrdom of Polycarp* refers to: "the eternal and unquenchable fire;" Papias (130) states: "will be condemned to the everlasting fire;" Clement of Rome (150) states: "will rescue us from eternal punishment...by their deeds are punished with terrible torture in unquenchable fire;" Justin Martyr (100-165) states, "every man will receive the eternal punishment or reward...they who live wickedly and do not repent will be punished in everlasting fire...but the wicked, clothed in eternal sensibility, He will commit to the eternal fire;" Irenaeus (140-202) states, "lawless and blasphemous among men into everlasting fire...they will be damned forever;" Tertullian (155-240) states: "and the godless equally perpetual and unending...will be punished in fire equally unending;" Hippolytus (235) states: "the lovers of evil shall be given eternal punishment. The unquenchable and unending fire awaits these latter, and a certain firey worm which does not die and which does not waste the body, but continually bursts forth from the body with unceasing pain. No sleep will give them rest, no night will soothe them;" Clement of Alexandria (150-211) states: "and for this the penalty is punishment in eternal fire;" Cyprian (252) states: "Too late will they believe in eternal punishment, who would not believe in eternal life;" Lactantius (250-317) states: "It will be similar to the earthly flesh, but indestructible and lasting forever, so that it will be able to hold together under torture and under eternal fire, the nature of which is different from the common fire we use for the necessities of life;" Cyril of Jerusalem (315-386) states: "But if a man is sinful, he shall receive an eternal body fitted to endure the penalties of sins, so that he may burn in the eternal fire without ever being consumed;" Basil (370) states: "it is one of the artifices of the devil, that many men, as if forgetting these and other such statements and utterances of the Lord, ascribe an end to punishment, so that they can sin the more boldly. If, however, there were going to be an end to eternal punishment, there would likewise be an end to eternal life...The qualification of eternal is ascribed to both of them...'he shall be flogged with many...with few stripes' refer not to an end but to a distinction of punishment;" Gregory of Nyssa (335-394) states: "while the incessant and inconsolable wailing takes vengeance forever;" Jerome (386) "There are many who say there are no future punishments for sins nor any torments extrinsically applied...these arguments and fraudulent fancies are but inane and empty words...and if they give them credence they only add to the burden of eternal punishment which they will carry with them." Augustine (354-430) states: "But in the life to come the soul will be connected in such a way to the body that the bond between them will be dissolved by no length of time nor broken by pain...These will go into eternal fire; the just, however, into eternal life. In both instances the Greek has *aionion*. If mercy calls us to believe that the future punishment of the impious will not be punishment without end, what are we to believe about the reward of the righteous, when eternity is specified in both clauses in the same passage, in the same sentence, and with the same word?...Both, for the reason that they are without end, are called eternal, that is, *aionion*....the latter will be enduring unhappily in eternal death without the power to die; for both shall be without end;" Fulgentius of Ruspe (467-527) states: "and for this reason they will not be extinguished even by death, so that the never-ending torment to body and soul will be a punishment of eternal death." All citations are from Denzinger and Jurgens.

Appendix 7

Excerpts from the Council of Valence (855 AD)

Canon 1: ...For concerning the foreknowledge of God, and predestination, and other questions in which the minds of the brethren are proved not a little scandalized, we believe that we must firmly hold that only which we are happy to have drawn from the maternal womb of the Church.

Canon 2: We faithful hold that "God foreknows and has foreknown eternally both the good deeds which good men will do, and the evil which evil men will do," because we have the word of Scripture which says: "Eternal God, who are the witness of all things hidden, who knew all things before they are" [Daniel 13:42]; and it seems right to hold "that the good certainly have known that through His grace they would be good, and that through the same grace they would receive eternal rewards; that the wicked have known that through their own malice they would do evil deeds, and that through His justice they would be condemned by eternal punishment....Certainly neither (do we believe) that the foreknowledge of God has placed a necessity on any wicked man, so that he cannot be different, but what that one would be from his own will, as God, who knew all things before they are, He foreknew from His omnipotent and immutable Majesty. Neither do we believe that anyone is condemned by a previous judgment on the part of God but by reason of his own iniquity. Nor (do we believe) that the wicked thus perish because they were not able to be good; but because they were unwilling to be good, they have remained by their own vice in the mass of damnation either by reason of original sin or even by actual sin.

Canon 3: ...faithfully we confess the predestination of the elect to life, and the predestination of the impious to death; in the election, moreover, of those who are to be saved, the mercy of God precedes the merited good. In the condemnation, however, of those who are to be lost, the evil which they have deserved precedes the just judgment of God. In predestination, however, (we believe) that God has determined only those things which He Himself either in His gratuitous mercy or in His just judgment would do according to Scripture which says: "Who has done the things which are to be done" [Isaiah 45:11 LXX]; in regard to evil men, however, we believe that God foreknew their malice, because it is from them, but that He did not predestine it, because it is not from Him. (We believe) that God, who sees all things, foreknew and predestined that their evil deserved the punishment which followed, because He is just, in whom, as Saint Augustine says, there is concerning all things everywhere so fixed a decree as a certain predestination...Concerning this unchangeableness of the foreknowledge of the predestination of God, through which in Him future things have already taken place, even in Ecclesiastes the saying is well understood: "I know that all the works which God has made continue forever. We cannot add anything, nor take away those things which God has made that He may be feared" [Eccl 3:14]. "But we do not only not believe the saying that some have been predestined to evil by divine power," namely as if they could not be different, "but even if there are those who wish to believe such malice, with all detestation," as the Synod of Orange, "we say anathema to them."

Canon 5: Likewise we believe that we must hold most firmly that all the multitude of the faithful, regenerated "from the water and the Holy Spirit"...that neither for these could there have been true regeneration unless there were true redemption; since in the sacraments of the Church there is nothing false...Moreover, from this very multitude of the faithful and the redeemed some are preserved in eternal salvation, because through the grace of God they remain faithfully in their redemption, bearing in their hearts the voice of their God Himself: "Who...perseveres even unto the end, he will be saved" [Matt. 10:22; 24:13]; that others, because they were unwilling to remain in the safety of faith, which in the beginning they received, and because they choose by wrong teaching or by a wrong life to void rather than to preserve the grace of redemption, came in no way to the fullness of salvation and to the reception of eternal beatitude...

Canon 6: Likewise concerning grace, through which those who believe are saved, and without which never has a rational creature lived happily, and concerning free will weakened through sin in our first parents, but reintegrated and healed through the grace of our Lord Jesus for His faithful, we most constantly and in complete faith confess the same, which the most Holy Fathers by the authority of the Sacred Scriptures have left for us to hold, which the Synod of Africa and the Synod of Orange have professed, which the most blessed Pontiffs of the Apostolic See in the Catholic faith have held; but also concerning nature and grace, we presume in no manner to change to another way.

Appendix 8

Patristic Evidence for Purgatory and Prayers for the Dead

Augustine was the chief spokesman for the doctrine of Purgatory, yet allusions to it are evident in many works of the early Fathers. One of the more frequent allusions to Purgatory is evident in the common practice of prayers for the dead. 2 Maccabees 12:45f. shows a prevalent belief among the Jews in this regard. In the early church, inscriptions on catacomb walls include prayers for the dead, as did all the major liturgies of the early church. Early Fathers who made reference to prayers for the dead or some type of purgation after death include: **Tertullian** (212) in *The Soul,* writes: "...and if we interpret the last farthing to be the light offense which is to be expiated there before the resurrection, no one will doubt that he should undergo some punishments in Hades, without prejudice to the fullness of the resurrection, after which recompense will be made through the flesh also;" In *On Monagomy* Tertullian writes: "...Indeed, she prays for his soul and asks that he may, while waiting, find rest; and that he may share in the first resurrection. And each year, on the anniversary of his death, she offers the sacrifice;" **Cyril of Jerusalem** (350) in the *Catechetical Lectures,* writes: "...we call upon God for...those who have already fallen asleep...for we believe that it will be of very great benefit to the souls of those for whom the petition is carried up, while this holy and most solemn sacrifice is laid out...For I know that there are many who are saying this: 'If a soul departs from this world with sins, what does it profit it to be remembered in the prayer?' Well, if a king were to banish certain persons who had offended him, and those intervening for them were to plait a crown and offer it to him on behalf of the ones who were being punished, would he not grant a remission of their penalties? In the same way we too offer prayers to Him for those who have fallen asleep, though they be sinners...and thereby propitiate the benevolent God for them as well as for ourselves;" **Ephraim** (306) "I conjure you, my brethren and friends, in the name of God who commands me to leave you, to remember me when you assemble to pray. Do not bury me with perfumes. Give them not to me, but to God. Me, conceived in sorrows, bury with lamentations, and instead of perfumes assist me with your prayers; for the dead are benefited by the prayers of living Saints" (Gibbons, p. 177). **Ambrose** (333) "Blessed shall both of you be [deceased Gratian and Valentinian], if my prayers can avail anything. No day shall pass you over in silence. No prayer of mine shall omit to honor you. No night shall hurry by without bestowing on you a mention in my prayers. In every one of the oblations will I remember you" (Ibid). **Basil** (370) in *Homilies on the Psalms,* writes: "...and if they are found to have any wounds from their wrestling, any stains or effects of sin, they are detained. If, however, they are found unwounded and without stain, they are, as unconquered, brought by Christ into their rest;" **Gregory of Nyssa** (385) in *Sermon on the Dead,* writes: "...he is not able to partake of divinity until he has been purged of the filthy contagion in his soul by purifying fire;" **Epiphanius** (374) in *Panacea Against All Heresies,* writes: "Furthermore, as to mentioning the names of the dead, how is there anything very useful in that? What is more timely or more excellent than that those who are still here should believe that the departed do live...who are praying for the brethren as if they were but sojourning in a foreign land? Useful too, is the prayer fashioned on their behalf, even if it does not force back the whole of guilty charges laid to them;" **Chrysostom** (398) in *Homilies on Philippians*, writes: "Let us weep for them, let us assist them to the extent of our ability, let us think of some assistance for them, small as it may be, yet let us somehow assist them. But how, and in what way? By praying for them and by entreating others to pray for them, by constantly giving alms to the poor on their behalf...Not in vain was it decreed by the Apostles that in the awesome Mysteries remembrance should be made of the departed...For when the entire people stands with hands uplifted, a priestly assembly, and that awesome sacrificial Victim is laid out, how, when we are calling upon God, should we not succeed in their defense?. But this is done for those who have departed in the faith...;" **Augustine** (392) in *Explanations of the Psalms*, writes: "Yet plainly, though, we be saved by fire, that fire will be more severe than anything a man can suffer in this life."; in *Genesis Defended Against the Manicheans*, writes: "But the man who perhaps has not cultivated the land and has allowed it to be overrun with brambles has in this life the curse of his land on all his works, and after this life we will have either purgatorial fire or eternal punishment;" in *The City of God*, Augustine writes: "Temporal punishments are suffered by some in this life only, by some after death, by some both here and hereafter; but all of them before that last and strictest judgment. But not all who suffer temporal punishment after death will come to eternal punishment, which are to follow after that judgment" (JR); "For some of the dead, indeed, the prayer of the Church or of pious individuals is heard; but it is for those who, having been regenerated in Christ, did not spend their life so wickedly that they can be judged unworthy of such compassion, nor so well that they can be considered to have no need of it. As also, after the resurrection, there will be some of the dead to whom, after they have endured the pains proper to the spirits of the dead, mercy shall be accorded, and acquittal from the punishment of the eternal fire. For were there not some whose sins, though not remitted in this life, shall be remitted in that which is to come, it could not be truly said, 'They shall not be forgiven, neither in this world, neither in that which is to come' (*City of God*, Book 21, Chap. 24. See also Chaps. 25-27; Schaff, Vol. 3, pp. 470-475).

The Councils of the Church also confirmed the doctrine of Purgatory:

Council of Lyons (1274): "Because if they die truly repentant in charity before they have made satisfaction by worthy fruits of penance for (sins) committed and omitted, their souls are cleansed after death by purgatorial or purifying punishments..."

Council of Florence (1439): "It is likewise defined, that, if those truly penitent have departed in the love of God, before they have made satisfaction by worthy fruits of penance for sins of commission and omission, the souls of these are cleansed after death by purgatorial punishments..."

Council of Trent (1563): "Since the Catholic Church, instructed by the Holy Spirit, in conformity with the sacred writings and the ancient tradition of the Fathers in sacred councils, and very recently in this ecumenical Synod, has taught that there is a purgatory, and that the souls detained there are assisted by the suffrages of the faithful and especially by the acceptable sacrifice of the altar, the holy Synod commands the bishops that they insist that the sound doctrine of purgatory, which has been transmitted by the holy Fathers and the holy Councils, be believed by the faithful of Christ, be maintained, taught, and everywhere preached."

Council of Trent, Session 6, Canon 30: "If anyone shall say that after the reception of the grace of justification, to every penitent sinner the guilt is so remitted and the penalty of eternal punishment so blotted out that no penalty of temporal punishment remains to be discharged either in this world or in the world to come in purgatory before the entrance to the kingdom of heaven can be opened: let him be anathema."

Vatican Council II, *Lumen Gentium* 49: "Others have died and are being purified, while still others are in glory, contemplating "in full light, God himself triune and one, exactly as he is.""

Catholic Catechism, Section 958: "Communion with the dead. In full conscioiusness of this communion of the whole Mystical Body of Jesus Christ, the Church in its pilgirm members, from the very earliest days of the Christian religion, has honored with great respect the memory of the dead; and 'because it is a holy and a wholesome thought to pray for the dead that they may be loosed from their sins' she offers her suffrages for them (f. 498: LG 50; cf. 2 Macc 12:45.)"

Appendix 9

Augustine's View on Predestination, Grace and Free Will

Augustine wrote of more developed and mature viewpoints in his work "*Retractationes.*" One of his more famous changes in interpretation concerned his view of Romans 7. The early Augustine had understood the passage as referring to a Jew under the law, while the later Augustine, in breaking with tradition, understood it as a Christian struggling against concupiscence. Augustine also had several views of the difficult verse, 1 Tim. 2:4. He writes in one place: "That of all those who are saved, none would be saved unless he will it...we see that so many men are not saved because God does not will it, even if men do" (*Letter of Augustine to Vitalis*, Layman of Carthage, 427 AD, JR 1457); in another place: "God, however, 'wills all men to be saved and to come to a knowledge of the truth but not in such a way that He would take away their free choice..." (*The Spirit and The Letter*, 412 AD, JR 1735); in another place as: "but in such a way that by 'all men' we are to understand every kind of man, by whatever grouping they be classified: kings and private persons, noblemen and base-born..." (*Enchiridion of Faith, Hope, and Love*; JR 1927).

Regarding predestination and free will, on the one hand, Augustine wrote such things as: "I speak thus of those who are predestined to the kingdom of God, whose number is so certain that one can neither be added to them nor taken from them" (*On Rebuke and Grace*, NPNF, V, xiii, 39, 487); he also writes: "It is not to be doubted, therefore, that human wills are unable to resist the will of God, who, 'did all things whatsoever He willed, in heaven and on earth...even with the very wills of men, He does what He wills...bending human hearts as he pleases'" (*Admonition and Grace*,

426 AD, JR 1963). On the other hand, he also wrote: "But because the will is prepared by the Lord we must ask Him to give our wills such a strength as will suffice for putting our will into action. It is certain that in willing anything, it is we that do the willing; but it is He that enables us to will what is good...It is certain that in doing anything, it is we that act but it is he that enables us to act, by His bestowing efficacious powers upon our will...I remind you to understand, for someone who denies that God brings about the desire for grace into the hearts of men, should not believe that God does this with unwilling men, which would be most absurd, but they become willing after having been unwilling" (*Against Julian*, Opus imperfectum, II, 157, CSEL, 85.1, 279). Or he makes such statements as, "For if it [a decision] is forced, it is not willing" (Ibid., I, 101, CSEL 85, 119). Since *Against Julian* is one of Augustine's last works, begun first in 421 and produced in unfinished form between 428-430 AD, this shows that Augustine maintains a dialectic between grace and free will that was consistent with Catholic tradition. Augustine made reference to the "enslaved will" ("servum arbitrium") only once in his disputations with Julian ("sed vos festinatis et praesumptionem vestram festinando praecipiatis. Hic enim vultis hominem perfici atque utinam die dono, et non libero, vel potius servo proprie voluntatis arbitrio (CSEL II, 8, 23). Luther noticed this single reference and promptly used it against Erasmus in his 1516 *Disputatio* (WA, I, 148), but showing from his context and other writings it is apparent that Augustine did not mean the same thing as Luther. To Augustine there was a distinction between freedom and free will, only the former was lost at the fall. Contrary to some zealous Reformed writers who wished to see a rejection of free will in Augustine's *Retractationes,* many of his beliefs in "*Free Choice*" ("*De libero arbitrio*"), written between 388-395, are reiterated in the *Retractiones* (e.g., *De libero arbitrio*: "Quapropter nihil tam in nostra potestate, quam ipsa voluntas est" (PL 32, 3, 3, 7), cf., *Retractationes:* "Voluntas igitur nostra nec voluntas esset, nisi esset in nostra potestate. Porro, qui est in potestate, libera est nobis. Non enim est nobis liberum, quod in potestate non habemus, aut potest non esse quod habemus" (PL 32, 1, 22), in which Augustine reiterates, as noted above in *Against Julian*, that a will would not be a will unless it was free, that is, in our power.

Early on, Augustine did make one change. Prior to his seating as bishop of Hippo, Augustine was a semi-Pelagian since he assumed that the initiative to accept God's offer of salvation still belonged to fallen man. The change in this position came in the work he wrote to Simplicianus, the successor of Ambrose, *De diversis quaestionibus VII ad Simplicianum* (396- 397). Augustine now taught that God had to inspire the very response of faith in man. By 412, Augustine in *Forgiveness and the Just Deserts of Sins, and the Baptism of Infants*, shows a good balance between grace and free will, not wishing to assert one at the expense of the other: "Let us take care not to defend grace in such a way that we would seem to take away free choice; nor again can we insist so strongly on free choice that we could be judged in our proud impiety, ungrateful for the grace of God" (PL 44, 2, 18, 28). Also in 412 AD, in *The Spirit and the Letter*, Augustine shows the same dialectic between grace and free will. He writes: "Without free will there can be neither good or bad living" (PL 44, 5, 7); along with: "God, however, wills all men to be saved and to come to a knowledge of the truth; but not in such a way that He would take away their free choice; for the good or evil use of which it is most just that they be judged" (PL 44, 33, 58); and: "Grace does not make free will void but establishes it...faith itself, in which seems to be the beginning either of salvation, or of that series leading to salvation which I have just mentioned, is placed in our power" (NFPF, V, 106); and: "Certainly, it is likewise God who works in man the will to believe, and in all things anticipates us with His mercy. But to consent to God's summons or to dissent from it, as I said before, belongs to our own will (PL 44, 34, 60). In *The City of God* (413-426) Augustine writes: "We are, therefore, in no way compelled, if we retain the foreknowledge of God, to discard our choice of will, or, if we retain choice of will, to deny — which were shocking — God's foreknowledge of future events. Rather, we embrace both...Man, therefore, does not sin because God foreknew that he would sin" (PL 41, 5, 10, 2). In *Nature and Grace* (415), Augustine does not side with the Reformed doctrine of "total depravity" but speaks of fallen man as *sick* in need of a physician: "...natura...hominis...iam medico indiget, quia sana non est" (CSEL 3, 3). In *Against Julian* he says: "Adam was given free will by the Creator, was vitiated by the deceiver and was healed by the Savior" (*Opus imperfectum*, 3, 110). Augustine never uses the term "vitiated" (Latin: "vitiatum") in the sense of total depravity. He assures his readers he is not taking away man's free will when he speaks of grace: "For, when we say these things we are not taking away free will but praising the grace of God" (Latin: "Non enim, cum ista commemoramus, arbitrium voluntatis tollimus, sed Dei gratiam praedicamus"). He also states that God does not command what is impossible for man to do: "non igitur Deus impossibilia iubet; sed iubendo admonet et facere quod possis, et petere quod non possis." In *Grace and Original Sin* (417), Augustine writes: "But because that question which discusses the choice of the will and the grace of God has such difficulty in its distinctions that when free choice is defended it seems to be a denial of God's grace and when God's grace is asserted free choice may seem to be taken away, Pelagius is able so to involve himself in the concealments of this obscurity that he can even declare that he agrees with these findings that we have quoted from the writings of Saint Ambrose" (PL 44, 1, 47, 52). In *Grace and Free Choice* (426- 427), Augustine sought to address some confusion that had been created over his views. Augustine begins by saying: "But because there are some persons who defend grace to such an extent that they deny man's free will or who think that, when grace is defended, free will is denied, I have decided to write something to you, brother Valentinus" (PL 44, 1, 1). He continues: "God has revealed to us through his holy Scripture that there is free will in man" ("Revelavit autem nobis per Scripturas suas sanctus, esse in homine liberum voluntatis arbitrium" (PL 44, 2, 2)). Augustine then says that God's commandments would have no value for man unless he had free will to follow them: "ipsa divina praecepta homini non prodessent, nisi haberet liberum voluntatis arbitrium, quo ea faciens ad promissa praemia perveniret" (Ibid). He writes: "...all these precepts of love would be given to men to no purpose at all if men did not have free will" (PL 44, 18, 37). Augustine cites Ecclesiasticus (Sirach) 15:11-18; James 1:13f. and Proverbs 19:3 to support his argument for free will, saying, "See how clearly free will is taught here" ("Ecce apertissime videmus expressum liberum humanae voluntatis arbitrium" (PL 44, 2, 3)). Augustine also cites Proverbs 1:8; 3:7,

11, 27, 29; 5:2; Psalms 35:4; Matthew 6:19; 10:28; 1 Cor. 15:34; 1 Timothy 4:14; James 2:1; 4:11; 1 John 2:15 for more support of free will (PL 44, 2, 4). He also includes the indicative and conditional statements on the activity of the will (Matthew 16:24; Luke 2:14; 1 Cor. 7:56f; 9:17; 1 Timothy 5:11). Augustine points out that Scripture speaks of self-control as a matter of free will (1 Timothy 5:22; 1 Cor. 7:37, (PL 44, 4, 7).

All in all, Augustine maintains that whenever Scripture requires man to do or not do something, free will is sufficiently demonstrated: "For where one is said to 'not will this' and 'not will that' and where an act of the will is required to do or not do something in respect to God's commandments, free will is sufficiently demonstrated" (Latin: "Nempe ubi dicitur 'Noli hoc et noli illud' et ubi ad aliquid faciendum vel non faciendum in divinis monitis opus voluntatis exigitur, satis liberum demonstratur arbitrium" (PL 44, 2, 4)). He points out the aid of grace to the free will in Matthew 26:41 and Luke 22:32 (PL 44, 4, 9), and especially in 1 Cor. 15:10: "It is not the grace of God alone, nor Paul alone, but the grace of God along with him" (PL 44, 5, 12), and 2 Cor. 6:1: "Why does he entreat them if the reception of grace means that they lose their own will." As is clearly evident in the corpus of Augustine's writings, he is very careful to preserve the dialectic between grace and free will. Of the best works available, one which exhaustively demonstrates this principle in Augustine is Eugene Portalie's, *Augustine*. Originally in French, it is also available in English, translated by R. J. Bastian, under the title: *A Guide to the Thought of St. Augustine* (Chicago: 1960), cf., pp. 219-233.

Appendix 10

Analysis of the Word "Alone" in Modern Translations

The word "alone" derives from the Greek μόνον or μόνος which are used 113 times in the New Testament and usually translated as "alone" or "only." The only time *monon* is used in reference to faith or justification is in James 2:24, preceded by the words οὐκ ἐκ ("not by"). Paul was certainly aware of the word μόνον since more than half of the occurrences of the word are in his epistles, most appearing in the book of Romans, e.g., Romans 3:29; 4:12,16,23: 11:3.

The same scholars who see no problem with adding *alone* to Paul's words, rail against groups like the Jehovah's Witnesses who add the word "*a*" to John 1:1 (i.e., "and the word was *a* god"). Historically, we would have denounced the Arians if they had added *like* to the same verse (i.e., "and the word was like God") on the pretense that it was "implied" in John's language, or the Docetists if they had added the words *"only seemed"* to 1 Thess. 4:14 (i.e., "Jesus only seemed to die"), or the Pelagians if they had added *only some* to 1 Cor. 15:22 (i.e., "as in Adam only some die") on the same pretense of "implication."

Protestants, when it is to their advantage, castigate these sorts of additions. In a recent broadcast of *The Bible Answer Man*, produced by the Christian Research Insititute (February 23, 1996), Norman Geisler, a prominent Evangelical and outspoken critic of Catholicism, in reference to a caller's comment that liberal theologians added the word "only" to some biblical texts in an attempt to prove that Jesus did not rise from the dead, asserted: "if they have to add the word "only" in order to avoid a contradiction, they have a problem." Interestingly, Geisler implies elsewhere that Catholic theologian Louis Bouyer believes in *faith alone* theology. Citing Bouyer's book, *The Spirit and Forms of Protestantism*, Geisler and co-author MacKenzie comment: "Bouyer argues that the Lutheran doctrine of justification by faith alone is not a heresy but is consistent with Catholic tradition and in harmony with the teachings of Augustine, Anselm, and Aquinas." Curiously, Geisler and MacKenzie do not cite a specific statement from Bouyer to this effect; rather, they refer the reader to "chaps. 1 through 6 [of Bouyer's book] covering such topics as salvation as a free gift, justification by faith..." (Geisler, Norman and MacKenzie, Ralph. *Evangelicals and Catholics: Agreements and Differences*, p. 98; Bouyer, Louis, *The Spirit and Forms of Protestantism*, trans., A.V. Littledale, 1955). Geisler and MacKenzie cannot cite a specific statement from Bouyer asserting that Luther's doctrine of "faith alone" is consistent with Catholic tradition for the simple reason that he never says such. Bouyer speaks only of *justification by faith*, and he even titles Chapter 5 of his book by this title without the addendum "alone." Perhaps a fairer treatment is given by Geisler and MacKenzie on page 221 when they state: "Bouyer...notes that, for Catholics, faith is necessary for salvation but not totally sufficient; works prompted by grace are also necessary for salvation." One wonders, however, how they could admit this on page 221 in view of their contradictory assertion on page 98.

Evangelical Robert Zins, in an attempt similar to that of R. C. Sproul cited in chapter 1 and Appendix 5, tries to make a case in the publication *Theo~Logical* (2nd Quarter, 1996), that Catholicism is not consistent in its aversion to the word *only* since even Catholic Bibles, namely, the New American Bible of 1970, which renders Galatians 5:5 as: "It is in the Spirit that we eagerly await the justification we hope for, and only faith can yield it." To Zins this rendering shows that

> ...the Roman Catholic translators of the NAB knew and understood that justification by faith alone could be logically deduced from the book of Galatians, and were convinced enough by this that they were willing to add the word 'only' in order to bring out what is clearly being taught. Although they corrected this blunder in a later translation, pointing it out may prevent other Roman apologists from presenting such an obvious red herring.

Zins's analysis exhibits a classic example of turning circumstantial evidence into fact. One must consider several factors before concluding, as Zins does, that these Roman Catholic translators "were convinced enough" of justification by faith alone "that they were willing to add the word 'only' in order to bring out what is clearly being taught." First, we should point out that these 1970 translators 'were *not* convinced enough' to add the word *alone* or *only* to the classic passage of Romans 3:28, as Luther did, nor did they add it to Galatians 2:16. If the concept of the "aloneness" of faith were on their mind, and if this doctrine were, as Zins claims, "clearly being taught" in the context, they had a perfect opportunity to add such language to these important passages. Second, with the first reason above as background, there is a perfectly plausible explanation why these 1970 translators used *only* in Galatians 5:5. This can be seen in the 1970 NAB translator's rendering of the next verse, Galatians 5:6, which if understood correctly should remove all doubt as to their intentions regarding the use of *only* in Galatians 5:5. The 1970 NAB translation of Galatians 5:6 reads: "In Christ Jesus neither circumcision nor the lack of it counts for anything, *only* faith which expresses itself through love." Here we see that the 1970 NAB used the word *only* in both Galatians 5:5 and 5:6 — a fact which Zins does not reveal to his reader. With a little more thoughtful analysis, one would see that since in Galatians 5:6 *only* precedes not just *faith* but *faith working through love,* then the addition of *only* (a word that does not appear in the Greek text of either Galatians 5:6 or Galatians 5:5), has an obvious purpose: to quantify the specific clause "faith working through love," rather than, as Zins claims, to describe *faith* apart from love. In other words, the NAB translators treated "faith working through love" as a specific theological unit and thus they preceded the clause with the word *only* in order to point out this indivisible connection between faith and love. The context supports this connection, since by its numerous references to the "law" it indicates that the focus of contrast is between the "law" which cannot justify and faith and love which jointly produces justification. The context, then, shows us that the original 1970 NAB's addition of *only* in Galatians 5:5 not only does not teach a *faith alone* theology, but, in fact, does precisely the opposite — it emphasizes the Catholic concept that only faith working through love, not faith alone, can justify. Without knowing the original intent of the translators, as proven by their usage of *only* in Galatians 5:6, a biased critic would be predisposed to accuse the 1970 translators of betraying Catholic theology. Consequently, it was, no doubt, for false assumptions like those of Robert Zins that the revised edition of the NAB in 1986 removed the word *only* from Galatians 5:5. They wished to avoid the impression that their addition of *only* was for the purpose of teaching a *faith alone* theology. This makes sense, only in light of the constant and consistent Catholic apologetic that has denied justification by *faith alone* since the time of the Reformation, without deviation. To refer to a translation that the Catholic Church no longer uses, and then not to address the context in which the word *only* is added, is very short-sighted critical analysis.

Appendix 11

Analysis of the phrase "dead in sins"

The Reformed/Calvinistic persuasion puts an unbearable weight on the word "dead" in Ephesians 2:1,5 so as to make the metaphor support the gargantuan doctrine of "total depravity" — the teaching which asserts that after the fall of Adam man was *totally* incapable of responding to God. We must insist, however, that Paul did not intend or suggest that the weight of "total depravity" be placed on the simple analogy of a dead body. Paul does not suggest in the context of Ephesians 2 that the individual is totally incapable of coming out of his dead state and responding to God; rather, it is clear that one who is "dead in sins" is in a spiritually estranged state, under the wrath of God. To support their view of the word "dead" in Ephesians 2:5, many Reformed theologians cite the example of Jesus raising Lazarus from the dead in John chapter 11. They reason from this story that because Lazarus, being dead, was totally incapable of responding to the call of Jesus to rise, then, analogously, the spiritually dead to which Paul refers in Ephesians 2:1,5 and Colossians 2:13 are similarly incapable of responding. Such a comparison presents several problems. First, the primary concern in John 11 is the physical resurrection, a resurrection which points to the final physical resurrection of all men at the end of time on the "last day." Martha confirms this primary focus in John 11:24 by saying, "I know he will rise again in the resurrection at the last day." The phrase "last day" (Greek: ἐσχάτῃ ἡμέρᾳ) is used only 6 times in the New Testament (as opposed to the plural "last days" which is used much more frequently and which encompasses an indefinite time period rather than one day). In each reference of the "last day," only the physical resurrection of the body is in view (cf., John 6:39, 40, 44, 54; 11:24; 12:48). Jesus confirms Martha's understanding of the future physical resurrection and makes it the primary focus of his action in raising Lazarus with the words, "I am the resurrection and the life. He who believes in me will live, even though he dies..." Nothing in the context of John 11 speaks to a spiritual resurrection. Within the parameters of respectable hermeneutics, it is highly inappropriate to use the physical death and resurrection of John 11 to support the spiritual death and resurrection of Ephesians 2:1-5.

We can confirm that the physical death and resurrection in John 11 is incompatible with the spiritual death and resurrection of Ephesians 2:1-5 (and the interpretation of "total depravity") by investigating the various ways Scripture uses the metaphor of spiritual death. For example, the parable of the Prodigal Son in Luke 15 portrays an image of spiritual death precisely opposite the Reformed concept. This story's primary concern is to illustrate the initial spiritual salvation of an individual (as opposed to the physical resurrection in the story of Lazarus). Hence, we see a context in which the New Testament author's meaning of spiritually "dead" can be gleaned much more appropriately. In the story of the Prodigal Son, the son leaves his father's house with his share of the wealth. After squandering the wealth, the son finally comes to his senses and returns by his own free will to the father. The father, in turn, greets his son with compassion and invites him back into the home. This sequence of events becomes very significant in our present discussion on the meaning of the metaphor "dead" since the father describes the son's return specifically in Luke 15:24 as, "For this my son was *dead* and is alive again; he was lost and is found." Not without significance, verse 32 repeats verbatim the father's description of his son's return: "...because this brother of yours was *dead* and is alive again; he was lost and is found." In light of the fact that the son himself came to his senses and subsequently made his way home, Jesus's use of the metaphor "dead" to describe the father's understanding of the son's previous spiritual state connotes a state not of "total depravity," but rather of cooperation by the son with the father's will. Moreover, since the story of the Prodigal Son is surrounded by other parables in Luke 15-16 which illustrate the nature of initial salvation, (e.g., "The Lost Sheep" in Luke 15:1-7; "The Lost Coin" in Luke 15:8-10; and "The Shrewd Manager" in Luke 16:1-3), this medley of parables does far more to help us understand the extent and limitations of spiritual death in regard to conversion than does the story of the physical death and resurrection of Lazarus.

Another dimension that will help us understand the meaning of spiritual death is the particular theological perspective from which the teaching of "total depravity" is derived. Those of the Reformed/Calvinistic persuasion view Adam's fall as the beginning of mankind's totally depraved nature, mainly because they believe that Adam acted of his own free will, apart from the guiding grace of God, in his decision to sin. Calvinists believe that God "endowed" Adam with the capability of free will and then more or less left him on his own to utilize this untainted dimension of his humanness in order to make the right decision. Since God instilled no grace in Adam, his fall cannot afterwards have retained any residual grace through which he could respond to God in the future. Since Adam did not possess infused grace before the fall, the Reformed perspective requires a total and radical transformation of man's spiritual state after the fall. In Reformed doctrine, this decisive transformation occurs in "regeneration." Many Reformed writers speak of God *infusing* his grace into man at this point, a view not without its difficulties because it is opposed to the Lutheran view of "faith prior to regeneration" and closer to the Catholic view wherein prevenient grace precedes faith. (See chapters 7 and 9 for further discussion concerning this aspect of Calvinism.) The Augustinian/Catholic perspective views Adam's pre- and postlapsarian states in quite a different manner. It understands Adam to possess the grace of God in his soul prior to his fall — grace which is present to a degree sufficient to give him the power to resist the temptation to sin. Adam chooses to ignore this grace and subsequently sins. But God does not totally abandon Adam; Adam retains sufficient grace after his fall — a degree of grace whereby, though he is spiritually estranged from God and is under the eternal wrath of God (i.e., "dead"), he is nonetheless not "totally depraved," and thus he is able to respond to God. He must now cooperate with God by using the residual grace he possesses which will lead, if he responds correctly, to the salvific grace of God.

Appendix 12

Analysis of the Greek *dia* in the Accusative Case

Beeke's contention can be refuted in several ways, one general and a few specific. First, Beeke confuses *meritorious cause* with the *faith* of the individual, the latter being only the *instrumental cause*. Catholic theology has always maintained that the atonement of Christ is the meritorious cause of justification (Council of Trent: Session 6, Chapter 7).

Second, Beeke's grammatical analysis is misleading. The word διὰ is used 615 times in the New Testament: 61%, or 376, are in the genitive; 39%, or 239, are in the accusative. Though not used with the word justify, διὰ is used in the accusative case in reference to faith. For example, Hebrews 3:19 states, "καὶ βλέπομεν ὅτι οὐκ ἠδυνήθησαν εἰσελθεῖν δι' ἀπιστίαν" ("and we see that they were not able to enter *because of disbelief*"). Hebrews 4:6 adds a further commentary on this fact and states, "καὶ οἱ πρότερον εὐαγγελισθέντες οὐκ εἰσῆλθον δι' ἀπείθειαν" ("and the ones formerly having the gospel preached to them did not enter *because of disobedience*"). Joining these two verses together we understand that the Jews in the Old Testament received the *gospel* (cf., Hebrews 4:2) but were not blessed by God and thus they underwent his judgment ***because of*** (διά in the accusative) their disbelief (ἀπιστίαν) and disobedience (ἀπείθειαν) (cf., 1 Cor. 10:1-12). (See also Matthew 13:58 and 17:20 which also use διὰ in the accusative in relation to faith).

Third, though διὰ in the accusative is never again associated with faith in the New Testament, which would seem to add at least some credibility to the claim of Beeke, what Beeke does not recognize is that the accusative case of διὰ is ***never used of any redemp-***

tive act in the New Testament, including the meritorious cause of justification, i.e., the atonement of Christ. Scripture uses διὰ in the accusative case only in reference to non-redemptive acts (e.g., Rom. 2:24; 1 Cor. 4:17; Eph. 5:6; Phil. 1:24; James 4:2; 1 Pet. 2:13).

Fourth, the New Testament writers prefer to use διὰ in the ***genitive*** case to describe the acts of redemption, *even* the meritorious cause of justification itself (cf., John 1:7; Acts 3:16; Acts 10:43; Acts 15:11; Rom. 5:5, 9, 10, 11, 17, 21; Gal. 1:15; 3:18; Eph. 3:12; Heb. 2:14; 6:18; 13:21; 1 Peter 1:3; 3:21, 1 John 4:9, et al).

Fifth, only three verses even remotely speak in redemptive terms using διὰ in the accusative: 2 Cor. 9:14; Eph. 2:4; Heb. 2:9. The first says only that the hearts of one set of Christians long for others *because of* the grace given to the latter; the second says only that God has mercy *because o*f his love; the third refers to benefits only Jesus receives *because of* what God did for him (cf., John 6:57). None of these speaks of the cause of justification as the apprehending of Christ's righteousness.

Appendix 13

Analysis of the word "draw" in John 6:44

In regard to the meaning of "draw" in John 6:44, R. C. Sproul cites two passages which use the Greek word ἑλκύσῃ ("draw") in a context in which the obvious meaning is "to drag" (e.g., James 2:6; Acts 16:19). By limiting his biblical references to these two passages, however, Sproul ignores the other possible meanings of ἑλκύω used in Scripture. The New Testament uses ἑλκύω 6 places and its cognate ἕλκω 2 places. Of the former, John 18:10; 21:6,11, and Acts 16:19 use ἑλκύω in the sense of "dragging" a person or object. Other verses use it in a different sense. In John 12:32 Jesus says, "But I, when I am lifted up from the earth will *draw* all men to myself." Jesus is certainly not saying, "I will drag all men to me." Rather, a universal drawing is denoted by the word "all" (Greek: πάντας), and this is reinforced by the previous verse as Jesus refers twice to the whole "world." The implication is that as the whole world is judged and its prince, Satan, driven out, Jesus will then *draw* all the men of that world to him. The power of Satan will have been vanquished at the cross so that men can freely come to God (cf., John 16:11; Hebrews 2:14; 1 John 3:8; 2 Timothy 2:25-26; 2 Corinthians 4:4; Romans 16:20; Revelation 12:1-17). Since it is well-known, however, that not all the men in the world come to Jesus, then the "drawing" of John 12:32 certainly cannot be viewed as "irresistible." Similarly, according to lexical sources, ἑλκύω can mean "to drag" or "to draw" (cf., Bauer, op. cit., p. 251; Liddell and Scott, op. cit., p. 216).

The Septuagint frequently uses the Greek word ἑλκύω. The uses include: Deut. 21:3-4 in which an animal is led, not dragged, to a certain location; Nehemiah 9:30 as "to bear long;" Job 20:28

as "to bring;" Ecclesiastes 2:3 as "to excite;" Song of Solomon 1:4 as "to entice;" Jeremiah 38:3 (LXX) as "to draw out of love." The cognate ἑλκύω can mean "a movement to" as used in Ecclesiastes 1:5; "to lift up" as in Isaiah 10:15; or "to rush forth" as in Daniel 7:10. We see, then, that both ἑλκύω and ἕλκω have quite a range of meanings that does not connote the "irresistibility" that Reformed theology imposes on the words.

Appendix 14

Analysis of Thomist vrs. Molinist Views on Predestination

Augustine and Aquinas espoused the view, to one degree or another, that God did not take into account man's response to grace (e.g., *Summa Theologica* I, 23.5 — "Yet why [God] chooses some for glory and reprobates other has no reason except the divine will"). Spanish Jesuit Luis Molina espoused the opposite view. Robert Bellarmine and Francisco Suarez, attempting to strike a balance between the Augustinian and Molinist views, held a view known as *Congruism.* Alphonsus Ligouri also attempted to balance the two sides. The Church, as yet, has not made a definitive judgment on any of these views. Aquinas attempted to boil the problem down to the following: "If it is true that God's love causes all goodness, then does it not follow that one thing will be better than another if God wills greater good for one than for another?" Others maintain that it is not that simple, for neither the premise nor the conclusion is properly defined, let alone capable of being proven.

For a good overview of these contentions see the work by Rev. Reginald Garrigou-Lagrange, titled "La predestination des saints et la grace" (Belgium: Desclee, De Brouwer & Cie). The English title is "Predestination." Aside from his historical analysis, Garrigou-Langrange defends the Augustinian/Thomist view as opposed to the Molinist view. Fr. William Most in *Grace, Predestination, and the Salvific Will of God* (Christendom Press, 1996) presents an alternative view. For a balanced commentary see Michael Schmaus, *Dogma: Justification and the Last Things*, pp. 39-41.

The Reformed persuasion admits that it does not know the criterion God used to save one individual as opposed to another. For example, R. C. Sproul states: "Why does God only save some?...The only answer I can give to this question is that I don't know. I have no idea why God saves some but not all" (*Chosen By God*, pp. 36-37). For Catholicism, this is an open question waiting for resolution. Although Augustine believed that one could be regenerate yet still not persevere (*Admonition and Grace*, PL 44, 6, 9), he still stated: "If you ask me why God did not give perseverance to those to whom He gave that love by which they might live in a Christian manner, I can only answer that I do not know" (ibid., PL 44, 7, 16). This unanswered question of Augustine is some of what is being addressed by the Molinist view.

If some version of the Molinist view is correct, a possible solution to this controversy could be, on the one hand, to affirm that, categorically or strictly speaking, God does not base his election on who we are or what we have done. On the other hand we can affirm God's right to elect those who *please* him. As we have noted throughout this study, under the strict system of law and God's standard of perfection, all men are sinners deserving of God's wrath. This is why God describes his choice of Jacob over Esau as: "Yet, before the twins were born or had done anything good or bad — in order that God's purpose in election might stand: *not of works* but by him who calls..." Under the strict standards of law, no one can be saved. God cannot be placed in a position of legal obligation. However, within the system of grace which stems from the *personal* nature of God rather than the rigid, legal rudiments of law, the criterion for whom he will choose can be justly based on what he *personally* admires or values in the individual despite the individual's condition of sin. God's personal "liking" of an individual through his eyes of grace, then, could be the chief substance of his "good pleasure" noted in some New Testament predestination passages (cf., Eph. 1:5,9; Luke 11:13; 12:31-32; Romans 11:1-10). On a *personal* level, it is possible to love a person for what we know and treasure about him intrinsically even though that person has sinned or will sin against us, especially if the person is repentant, or we expect they will come to repentance. We have seen earlier the case of Paul who specified without reserve that he was chosen and shown mercy by God *because* of his ignorance (cf., 1 Timothy 1:13; Galatians 1:13-16). Once shown the right path, Paul followed God with his whole heart. Similarly, David is called a "man after God's own heart" whom God admired very much even though David fell into serious sin (Acts 13:22; 1 Sam. 13:14). God "loves" Jacob while he "hates" his brother Esau. Understanding the personal nature of God, we should not refrain from assigning emotional quality to God's "love" and "hate." As we have noted earlier, this passionate aspect of God's personality permeates the Old and New Testaments. We saw an outstanding example of this in the account of Exodus 32 which portrays God as so emotionally angry against the sins of Israel that Moses, in an attempt to appease God, has to "remind" God of his covenant promise to Abraham. Later in Exodus 33:17- 19 God says to Moses, "I will do the very thing you have asked, because I am *pleased* with you and I know you by name." Again, it is God's "pleasure" in Moses and his personal relationship with him which gives Moses favor in God's eyes. For our present discussion, it is even more remarkable that God's pleasure in Moses is followed in verse 19 with the words, "...I will have mercy on whom I will have mercy, and I will have compassion on whom I will have compassion" showing that God's mercy and compassion are tied in with how the individual has pleased God. This is the same passage that Paul quotes in Romans 9:14-16 when he is speaking in the context of God's election, which shows that election is intimately related to the individual's pleasing of God and God's personal nature. God's love is not to be pictured as a mechanical and unemotional attribute but as a passionate and intense divine quality that God does not hesitate to describe in human terms (e.g., Hosea 11:4; Psalm 103:13; Deuteronomy 5:9). Hence "love" indicates that God has a personal liking of Jacob, even though Jacob sometimes sinned. We can understand God's personal liking of Jacob since Scripture portrays his life as one of love and service to God, while Esau is portrayed as godless and despicable from the beginning. Though all men are sinners, it is the arrogant, hateful, and unrepentant whom God resists and in whom he has *no pleasure* (cf., James 4:6-10; 1 Peter 5:5; 2 Timothy 3:8; John 8:44; Acts 13:46-48; Matthew 13:11-15). Hence, God's viewing of man through God's own personal and gracious nature would allow him to base his decision on "good pleasure," i.e., what he sees through grace, despite the sin of the individual. In this way, God's decision would not be impersonal and arbitrary. It would be based on what he *personally* likes and dislikes of those he views, even in the face of their sin and imperfection, thus preserving his integrity as a just God in his ultimate decision on whom he will save and not save. All in all, it is the *personal* nature of God that is the key to understanding his relationship with man and man's eventual salvation or damnation.

Appendix 15

Analysis of "Faith" in Hebrews 11:1

Protestant translations give various translations of Hebrews 11:1, e.g., NIV: "Now faith is being sure of what we hope for and certain of what we do not see;" NEB: "Faith gives substance to our hopes, and makes us certain of realities we do not see;" ASV, RSV, NRSV, NASB: "Now faith is the assurance of things hoped for, the conviction of things not seen;" KJV: "Now faith is the substance of things hoped for, the evidence of things not seen;" Moffatt: "Now faith means that we are confident of what we hope for, convinced of what we do not see;" Goodspeed: "Faith means the assurance of what we hope for; it is our conviction about things that we cannot see;" Phillips: "Now faith means putting our full confidence in the things we hope for, it means being certain of things we cannot see." As Lutheran theologian Robert G. Hoerber points out:

> In Hebrews 1:3 we read that the Son is "an exact representation of his (= God's) real being" (χαρακτὴρ τῆς υποστάσεως). The sense of "confidence" or "assurance" must be eliminated, since examples of this meaning cannot be found. Therefore this translation must be ruled out in Hebrews 11:1, although it has enjoyed much favor since Luther. According to Bauer-Arndt-Gingrich-Danker (p. 847), Hebrews 11:1 should be rendered: "In faith things hoped for become realized" or "In faith things hoped for become reality." So the renderings of Hebrews 11:1 by NRSV, NASB, NIV, Phillips, Moffatt, and Goodspeed miss the point, while NKJV and NEB come closer to the meaning of ὑπόστασις (in this verse (*Concordia Journal* / January 1995, pp. 78-79).

Hoerber continues by quoting Kittel as saying:

It should also be noted that ὑπόστασις (here is parallel to ἔλεγχος ["proof" or "evidence"] and that it occurs in a sentence full of central theological concepts. Now as regards ἔλεγχος it is evident that this does not mean subjective non- doubting nor does it have anything at all to do with conviction: it bears the objective sense "demonstration"...the ἔλεγχος πραγμάτων οὐ βλεπομένων ["the proof or evidence of things not seen"] is the proof of things one cannot see, i.e., the heavenly world which alone has reality, whereas in Hebrews everything visible has only the character of the shadowy and frontal. If one follows the meaning of ὑπόστασις in Hb. 1:3, then ὑπόστασις ἐλπιζομένων bears a similar sense: it is the reality of the goods hoped for, which have by nature a transcendent quality. Primarily, then, ἔλεγχος and ὑπόστασις do not describe faith but define the character of the transcendent future things, and do so in the same sense as Philo...and other representatives of Middle Platonism...speak of the reality and actuality of God and the world of Ideas. In a formulation of incomparable boldness Hb. 11:1 identifies πίστις (with this transcendent reality: Faith is the reality of what is hoped for in exactly the sense in which Jesus is called the χαρακτήρ of the reality of the transcendent God in 1:3. The one formulation is as paradoxical as the other to the degree that the presence of the divine reality is found in the one case in the obedience of a suffering and dying man (cf. Hb 5:7) and in the other in the faith of the community. But this is the point of Hebrews. Only the work of this Jesus and only participation in this work (= faith) are not subject to the corruptibility of the merely shadowy and prototypical.

Appendix 16

Excerpts from the Joint Declaration on the Doctrine of Justification between The Lutheran Federation and the Pontifical Council for Promoting Christian Unity (Geneva 1995)

The Preamble of the Declaration states:

> "...Justification was regarded as the crux of all the disputes, and resulted in the mutual doctrinal condemnations both in the Lutheran Confessions and by the Roman Catholic Church's Council of Trent. These condemnations are still operative today and thus have a church-dividing effect."
>
> "(4) In their discussions of the doctrine of justification, all the dialogue reports as well as the responses show a high degree of agreement in their approach and conclusions. . .(5) The present document has this intention: namely, to show that on the basis of their dialogue Lutherans and Roman Catholics are now able to articulate and advocate a common understanding of the faith content of the doctrine of justification."
>
> "(7). . .the churches and the doctrinal condemnations which have so far existed neither takes the condemnation lightly nor disavows the history and tradition of one's own church. On the contrary, this declaration rests on the conviction that our churches are in a historical process guided by God in which they gain new insights.

> Developments take place which not only make it possible, but also require them to examine the divisive questions and mutual condemnations of the past and see them in a new light."

3. The Common Understanding of Justification

> "(14) Together we confess: 'It is solely by grace and by faith in Christ's saving work and not because of any merit in us that we are accepted by God and receive the Holy Spirit who renews our hearts and equips us for and calls us to good works'"

Author's comment: Here we see a statement quoted from a previous document ("All Under One Christ" 14, in *Growth in Agreement*, pp. 241- 247). This statement is not unlike that contained in the 1995 ECT document between Evangelicals and Catholics. The Declaration uses the biblical relationship between grace and faith to the exclusion of works or "merit." The word "merit" is obviously taken in the strict sense of the term, that is, in the sense of legal obligation as defined earlier in this book. This intention seems to be verified by a following statement: "...bestowed on us and receive in faith, but — in any form whatever — can never earn" (#16, p. 5), or the statement: "All persons stand under God's judgment and are by themselves unable to earn justification before God or even to turn to God for salvation" (#18, p. 6). The Catholic doctrine of "cooperation" is then described as, "When Catholics say that people "cooperate" by consenting to God's justifying action, they do not mean by this an action stemming from one's own power, but see such personal consent as itself the effect of justifying grace" (#19, p. 6). The statement "we are accepted by God" is somewhat vague yet it implies that the basis for this "acceptance" is by grace. We notice also that the Declaration does not include the controversial addendum "alone" in relation to faith.

> "(15) All people are called by God to respond in faith to God's justifying action in Christ, whereby alone they are declared and made righteous. They are to make their own what is proclaimed and imparted to them in word and sacrament in the community of believers..."

Author's comment: The amalgamation between *declared* and *transformational* righteousness is the same here as it was in the 1983 joint Declaration. What neither this nor the 1983 Declaration does, however, is define "declared righteousness" as to whether it is an external forensic/courtroom declaration with only legal imputation in view, or, simply a declaration in the sense of God verbalizing the existence of the righteousness in man, such as the verbalization in Genesis 1:3: "Let there be light." The latter does not necessarily have a forensic element. The closest the Declaration comes to the concept of imputation appears in the statement: "God both declares and makes believers righteous. Their sins are not *imputed* to them and through the Holy Spirit God creates in them an active love" (#21, p. 6). The Declaration does not say that Christ's righteousness is imputed to the believer but confines itself to the language that "sins are not imputed." The Declaration does not define, however, what it means by "imputed." We have seen in our study that the Greek word λογίζομαι or its Hebrew equivalent חשב from which the translation "imputed" is often derived, preponderantly refers to declaring an entity or state to exist that in reality exists, and that that definition is in opposition to the historic Protestant notion of imputing a righteousness to the believer that in fact does not reside in him personally. The phrase "*creates* in them an active love" shows by the word "creates" that the Declaration understands that a transformation is occurring in the individual at the moment of justification. We also notice that the phrase "word and sacrament" implies the natural affinity between Lutheran and Catholic doctrine in sacramental life that is not natural to most other Protestant denominations.

> "(30) This difference in Lutheran and Catholic understanding of justification represents different concerns and emphases. The difference has been described with the conceptual pair "forensic" and "effective," or more recently with "proclamatory" and "transformational." But these are not mutually contradictory terms which 'cut through everything we have in common, and make mutual condemnation compellingly necessary,' for both sides do affirm the concerns of the other side and seek to preserve the whole gospel including forgiveness of sins and the renewal of

> life, while holding that justification is both unmerited and unconditional."

Author's comment: Once again, the Declaration attempts to amalgamate declaratory and transformational righteousness but without explaining how the legal dimension fits into the transformational. Catholicism would have an easier task in joining the declaratory and the transformational since the former does not necessitate a purely forensic element, or, because the legal, when joined with the concept of divine sonship through the biblical concept of covenant relations, is not treated as an extrinsic or separate entity that must first be satisfied in order to, and only then, make room for sonship. Lutheranism, at least from its historic roots, would have a much more difficult time in joining declaratory and transformational aspects simply because the forensic element was historically propounded with the express purpose of denying a transformational aspect to the decisive moment of extrinsic justification.

> "(32) When according to Catholic understanding the renewal of life through the grace of justification is emphasized, then this renewal in faith, hope, and love is nothing else than the response to God's unfathomable gift of grace. It contributes nothing to justification on the basis of which one could make an appeal before God."

Author's comment: The statement, "make an appeal before God" is vague and misleading. Similar statements appear in earlier documents: "Catholic doctrine knows itself to be at one with the Protestant concern in emphasizing that the renewal of the human being does not 'contribute' to justification, and is certainly not a contribution to which he could make any appeal before God" (p. 15, LV:E 52f.); and "'the renewal of the human being does not contribute to justification, and is certainly not a contribution to which a person could make any appeal before God' our objection no longer applies" (p. 15, VELKD 89, 12-21). Because the Declaration has not defined what it means by the vague and ambiguous language "make an appeal before God" it runs into danger when it then says, "...does not contribute to justification." Historic Catholic theology holds that justification is a process, not a one-time event. Because it is a process, in that sense, works do contribute to justification. If the Declaration is using the phrase "make an appeal before God" in the strict sense of a legal obligation between God and man such that man earns and God owes, then it is correct to say that the "inner renewal does not contribute to justification." However, Catholic theology teaches that one can make a gracious appeal to God, or make an appeal based on God's benevolence which does not legally obligate God but which appeals to his character as a personal being who seeks graciously to reward us for our efforts to please him.

> "(37) - This was emphasized in a particular way by the Reformers: in the midst of temptation, believers should not look to themselves but, in faith, look solely to Christ and trust only him. In this way they are assured of their salvation, but cannot be secure."

Author's comment: Though this statement acknowledges both the Catholic and Lutheran belief that the individual, through his own lack of continuance in faith, can lose his salvation, it does not address the divergence of opinion among the Reformation theologians in this regard, e.g., John Calvin, Theodore Beza, et al, who believed that the Christian could not lose his salvation.

> "(39) Catholic and Lutherans confess together that good works - a Christian life lived in faith, hope and love - follow justification and are its fruits. The justified are to live and act in the grace they receive - in biblical terms, to bring forth fruit."

Author's comment: Though it is true that the Bible uses the term "fruit" in reference to the works of the believer, it does not use this analogy to teach that works will automatically or inevitably flow from one who is justified. In the same way that Scripture teaches that one must make a continual and conscious effort to avoid sin, Scripture also teaches that one must make a conscious effort to add works to faith, or, make a conscious effort to continue in works once one claims to have faith. It teaches this with the proviso that many decide not to continue in obedience and good works and subsequently fall away. The statement "follow justification and are its fruits" is misleading in the sense that it fails to distinguish the Catholic distinctive that justification is not a one-time event (though it is initiated at baptism at a decisive moment) but a process in which works continue the justification once started.

Appendix 17

The Official Interpretation of "extra ecclesiam nulla salus"

Regarding the Church's official interpretation of the decree of Pope Benedict VIII: "extra ecclesiam nulla salus," the Supreme Sacred Congregation of the Doctrine of the Faith, in a letter to the Archbishop of Boston in 1949, wrote: "Now, among those things which the Church has always preached and will never cease to preach is contained also that infallible statement by which we are taught that there is no salvation outside the Church. However, this dogma must be understood in that sense in which the Church herself understands it. For, it was not to private judgments that Our Savior gave for explanation those things that are contained in the deposit of faith, but to the teaching authority of the Church...Therefore, no one will be saved who, knowing the Church to have been divinely established by Christ, nevertheless refuses to submit to the Church or withholds obedience from the Roman Pontiff, the Vicar of Christ on earth...Therefore, that one may obtain eternal salvation, it is not always required that he be incorporated into the Church *actually* as a member, but it is necessary that at least he be united to her by desire and longing. However, this desire need not always be explicit, as it is in catechumens; but when a person is involved in invincible ignorance, God accepts also an implicit desire, so called because it is included in that good disposition of soul whereby a person wishes his will to be conformed to the will of God..." The Catholic Catechism, introducing the question with: "Outside the Church there is no salvation," goes on to say, "How are we to understand this affirmation, often repeated by the Church Fathers? Reformulated positively, it means that all salvation comes from Christ the Head through the Church which is his Body:" Quoting

Lumen Gentium 14 from Vatican II, the Catechism continues: "Basing itself on Scripture and Tradition, the Council teaches that the Church, a pilgrim now on earth, is necessary for salvation: the one Christ is the mediator and the way of salvation; he is present to us in his body which is the Church. He himself explicitly asserted the necessity of faith and Baptism, and thereby affirmed at the same time the necessity of the Church which men enter through Baptism as through a door. Hence, they could not be saved who, knowing that the Catholic Church was founded as necessary by God through Christ, would refuse either to enter it or to remain in it" (Section 846). The Catechism continues in Section 847: "This affirmation is not aimed at those who, through no fault of their own, do not know Christ and his Church:" and quoting from *Lumen Gentium* 16 of Vatican Council II: "Those who, through no fault of their own, do not know the Gospel of Christ or his Church, but who nevertheless seek God with a sincere heart, and, moved by grace, try in their action to do his will as they know it through the dictates of their conscience — those too may achieve eternal salvation." The infallible nature of "extra ecclesiam nulla salus" is pointed out here to contend with various opinions, among both Catholics and Protestants, that the statement is not infallible, including the remarks made by evangelical Donald Bloesch in *Roman Catholicism: Evangelical Protestants Analyze What Divides and Unites Us*, ed. John Armstrong, 1994), pp. 164-165,167.

Appendix 18

Analysis of Anselm's Satisfaction Theory of the Atonement

Anselm pointed out that the atonement served as a satisfaction to God for the damage done to his honor. Adding to the concept of Irenaeus, Athanasius, and Augustine, wherein the atonement was considered a *ransom* paid to God, Anselm taught that infinite satisfaction was necessary since: (1) man could do nothing in himself to restore God's honor, (2) man owes every good work to God in any case, and (3) divine justice required either eternal punishment for sin or an infinite satisfaction of the divine honor (*Cur Deus Homo*, I, xi and II, vi). Thus, the death of a God-man was required for atonement. Thomas Aquinas developed the objective dimension in the *Summa Theologica* (III, qq. 46-50). Peter Abelard (b. 1079) had earlier advanced a more subjective view in that the cross draws man to recognize the power of God and his infinite love, which leads man to repentance. The Council of Trent uses the following language: "...merited justification for us by His most holy passion on the wood of the Cross, and made satisfaction for us to God the Father" (Session 6, Chapter 7); "...through the merit of his passion, the grace, whereby they are made just, is bestowed upon them" (Chapter 3); "...gratuitously by divine mercy for Christ's sake..." (Chapter 9). In reference to the Council of Trent, the Catholic Catechism uses Anselm's and Aquinas's language of objective "satisfaction" (Sections 614-617), and also refers to subjective satisfaction between God and man (Sections 1459-1460). Catholic theology retains and employs the term "ransom" to describe the redemptive principle, as noted in the Catholic Catechism, Section 601: "...as a ransom that would free men from slavery of sin" (cf., Isaiah 53:11-12; John 8:34-36) and Section 605: "...to give his life a ransom for many." Conversely, Catholic theologian Joseph Fitzmeyer argues that even though the Old Testament imagery speaks to appeasement of anger, this was not Paul's intent, rather, Fitzmeyer sees *expiation* as the primary effect of Christ's atonement, citing the use of the Greek word ἱλάσκομαι in the LXX of God's forgiveness of sins. The problem with expiation, however, is that it can either be strictly defined (i.e., as a payment for sin), or loosely defined (e.g., to make amends, pacify, apologize, etc.). Fitzmeyer does not specify which he is using *(The Jerome Biblical Commentary*, op. cit., p. 302). In any case, appeasing God's anger against sin and the subsequent forgiveness for those sins that issues forth from the appeasement are certainly overlapping concepts, neither negating the other. As Fitzmeyer limits his analysis to ἱλάσκομαι he fails to address the numerous cognates of the word in the LXX and the various Hebrew words that are behind these cognates which suggest an alternative meaning.

Appendix 19

Augustine's Views on Necessity and Contingency

Calvin quotes the last words of a very long sentence from Augustine in Migne 34, 350 (*De Genesi Ad Litteram*, Chapter 15, Section 26) which in Latin reads: "...cujus voluntas rerum necessitas est," which the editor correctly translates into English as "the will of God is the necessity of things." Calvin's use of this quote to support his concept of necessity without free will totally ignores the context of Augustine's quote, which is not talking, at all, about the will but of natural causes and propensities. Chapter 14 of the same work, titled *Rationes causales mundo primum inditae, cujus generis fuerint*, begins a discussion of the causal reasons, or 'seeds,' that God put into the world when he first created it. Augustine raises two possibilities: Did God put into created things a natural seed in which things would work as we now see them work, such that everything takes time to reach its maturity, or, did God put different causal 'seeds' into the creation at first, namely, that things would appear originally at their full maturity. This is similar to the "chicken or egg" argument common in modern science. This question is germane to Augustine's discussion, since he is speaking about the six days of creation. Augustine concludes that Adam was created as a fully-grown young man, rather than from the 'dust of the earth' acting as a surrogate womb, as it were. Augustine believes that God put into the nature of created things certain directive laws that would determine how things would develop. Augustine then proposes two possibilities how this may be worked out: (1) God puts into the nature of created things reasons or causes sufficient to account for how they *actually* develop; or (2) God puts into the nature of created things merely enough reasons or causes so that they *may* develop, reserving to his will the exact determination as to how they *actually* turn out. Of these two possibilities, Augustine does not resolve which one is true. In posing these two questions, Augustine shows that he may be way ahead of his time, for the same questions appear in modern discussion between deterministic views of nature (e.g., macrophysic equilibrium in closed systems) and a 'quantum' view of nature (e.g., microphysic possibilities as demonstrated, for example, by the Heisenberg 'uncertainty principle,' or what we may call "loaded propensities") which does not allow us to calculate, with certainty, how things will turn out. What Augustine does conclude, however, is that in either theory, things turn out consonant with the divine will, i.e., things happen as God desires and knew they would. The phrase that Calvin quotes ("the will of God is the necessity of things") merely comes at the end of Augustine's discussion of the second theory.

In the same paragraph from which Calvin takes Augustine's quote, Augustine says, "If, however, he put into the world only the force of possibility, so that man would come to be in whatever way he would come to be, and he could come to be this way and that way, then, he kept back in his own will the precise manner in which he [Adam] would come to be, and did not put it into the constitution of the world. But obviously, even in this theory, man was not made contrary to what was existent in the first condition of his causes, because what was there in his cause was that he could come to be this way [as a mature adult] from the dust of the earth. But not that he would, of necessity, come to be that way, because this is not in the constitution of creation but in the will of the Creator whose will is the necessity of things."[1] In this final statement Augustine is saying that if the second theory is correct, God is the necessary supplier of the concrete outcome of things, or, that God's will can make the possibilities go one way or the other. Augustine,

[1] Latin: "...si autem vim tantum ibi posuit possibilitatis, ut homo fieret quoquo modo fieret, ut et sic et sic posset, id est ut id quoque ibi esset, quia et sic et sic posset; unum autem ipsum modum quo erat facturus in sua voluntate servavit, non mundi constitutioni contexuit: manifestum est etiam sic non factum esse hominem contra quam erat in illa prima conditione causarum; quia ibi erat etiam sic fieri posse, quamvis non ibi eratita fieri necesse esse: hoc enim non erat in conditione creaturae, sed in placito Creatoris, cujus voluntas rerum necessitas est."

then, is speaking about the same thing that the medieval theologians had theorized concerning "contingent causes."

In Chapter 16, Augustine gives a further example to explain how he is applying this second theory, if it is valid. Under the title *In rei natura est, ut quid esse possit; ut futurum sit, nonnisi in Dei voluntate*, he says, "We, despite the infirmity of our understanding, can know from things that have already come to be in time, what is in the nature of each because we learn it by experience, but what will exactly come to pass we do not know. For example, it is in the nature of a youth that he will grow old, but whether it is also in God's will, we do not know. But in any case, it would not be in nature unless it had already been God's will who established all things. When one sees a child, he can see the childhood in him, but the capacity to become an old man is hidden. But from my mind it is not hidden; I can see from the nature of things that the child has the capacity to become an old man. Whether the child also has, in his makeup, a determinate reason that he will become an old man, I cannot learn from inspecting his nature."

In Chapter 17, he writes: "Perhaps there is in the world a necessary reason that this man should grow old. All I care about is if it is not in the world, then it is in God." In other words, if it is not naturally worked out, God himself will work it out. In this way, God is the caretaker or the one who makes the final package as we see it eventually displayed in the world. Augustine continues: "For things will necessarily come to be which He wills, and those things are truly future which he has foreknown."

In conclusion, we must understand that Augustine's entire discussion in Chapters 14-18 is about nature, not about will; terms and ideas that were further discussed and enhanced by medieval theologians. There is nothing in his discussion that says anything against free will. Moreover, the entire discussion concerns things that are in themselves contingent, (e.g., will this particular youth live to be 80 years old or not?). Medieval theologians would say that such a question is left insufficiently determined by its causes, and thus, they would side with Augustine's second theory (our "quantum" theological theory of causality). In terms of secondary or contingent causes, that is, causes at work in the world, such matters are not fully determined, but once they come to pass, they are, of course, unchangeable (e.g., once the child has reached his 80th birthday, there is no more contingency). The matter is contingent in itself, but it is no longer contingent in status once it is completed. This is all Augustine is trying to say. He is not talking about things in themselves, and thus is not saying that the will of God converts contingent matters into necessary events, but that he makes them no longer contingent in status, i.e., they are now complete and irreversible — the past cannot be changed. In a word, Augustine and the medieval theologians are saying that it is the divine will that determines the concrete outcome of things that are left undetermined by natural causes. Neither Augustine nor the medieval theologians, however, are denying free will.

Appendix 20

Canons of the Council of Trent: Session VI, Justification

Canon 1) If anyone shall say that man can be justified before God by his own works which are done either by his own natural powers, or through the teaching of the Law, and without divine grace through Christ Jesus: let him be anathema.

Canon 2) If anyone shall say that divine grace through Christ Jesus is given for this only, that man may more easily be able to live justly and merit eternal life, as if by free will without grace he were able to do both, though with difficulty and hardship: let him be anathema.

Canon 3) If anyone shall say that without the anticipatory inspiration of the Holy Spirit and without His assistance man can believe, hope and love or be repentant, as he ought, so that the grace of justification may be conferred upon him: let him be anathema.

Canon 4) If anyone shall say that man's free will moved and aroused by God does not cooperate by assenting to God who rouses and calls, whereby it disposes and prepares itself to obtain the grace of justification, and that it cannot dissent, if it wishes, but that like something inanimate it does nothing at all and is merely in a passive state: let him be anathema.

Canon 5) If anyone shall say that after the sin of Adam man's free will was lost and destroyed, or that it is a thing in name only, indeed a title without a reality, a fiction, moreover, brought into the Church by Satan: let him be anathema.

Canon 6) If anyone shall say that it is not in the power of man to make his ways evil, but that God produces the evil as well as the good works, not only by permission, but also properly and of Himself, so that the betrayal of Judas is no less His own proper work than the vocation of Paul: let him be anathema.

Canon 7) If anyone shall say that all works that are done before justification, in whatever manner they have been done, are truly sins or deserving of the hatred of God, or that the more earnestly anyone strives to dispose himself for grace, so much the more grievously does he sin: let him be anathema.

Canon 8) If anyone say that the fear of hell, whereby by grieving for sins we flee to the mercy of God or refrain from sinning, is a sin or makes sinners worse: let him be anathema.

Canon 9) If anyone shall say that by faith alone the sinner is justified, so as to understand that nothing else is required to cooperate in the attainment of the grace of justification, and that it is in no way necessary that he be prepared and disposed by the action of his own will: let him be anathema.

Canon 10) If anyone shall say that men are justified without the justice of Christ by which He merited for us, or that by that justice itself they are formally just: let him be anathema.

Canon 11) If anyone shall say that men are justified either by the sole imputation of the justice of Christ, or by the sole remission of sins, to the exclusion of grace and charity, which is poured forth in their hearts by the Holy Spirit and remains in them, or even that the grace by which we are justified is only the favor of God: let him be anathema.

Canon 12) If anyone shall say that justifying faith is nothing else than confidence in the divine mercy which remits sins for Christ's sake, or that it is this confidence alone by which we are justified: let him be anathema.

Canon 13) If anyone shall say that it is necessary for every man in order to obtain the remission of sins to believe for certain and without any hesitation due to his own weakness and indisposition that his sins are forgiven him: let him be anathema.

Canon 14) If anyone shall say that man is absolved from his sins and justified, because he believes for certain that he is absolved and justified, or that no one is truly justified but he who believes himself justified, and that by this faith alone absolution and justification are perfected: let him be anathema.

Canon 15) If anyone shall say that a man who is born again and justified is bound by faith to believe that he is assuredly in the number of the predestined: let him be anathema.

Canon 16) If anyone shall say that he will for certain with an absolute and infallible certainty have that great gift of perseverance up to the end, unless he shall have learned this by a special revelation: let him be anathema.

Canon 17) If anyone shall say that the grace of justification is attained by those only who are predestined unto life, but that all others, who are called, are called indeed, but do not receive grace, as if they are by divine power predestined to evil: let him be anathema.

Canon 18) If anyone shall say that the commandments of God are even for a man who is justified and confirmed in grace impossible to observe: let him be anathema.

Canon 19) If anyone shall say that nothing except faith is commanded in the Gospel, that other things are indifferent, neither commanded nor prohibited, but free, or that the ten commandments in no way pertain to Christians: let him be anathema.

Canon 20) If anyone shall say that a man who is justified and ever so perfect is not bound to observe the commandments of God and the Church, but only to believe, as if indeed the Gospel were a mere absolute promise of eternal life, without the condition of observation of the commandments: let him be anathema.

Canon 21) If anyone shall say that Christ Jesus has been given by God to men as a Redeemer in whom they should trust, and not also as a legislator, whom they should obey: let him be anathema.

Canon 22) If anyone shall say that he who is justified can either persevere in the justice received without the special assistance of God, or that with that assistance he cannot: let him be anathema.

Canon 23) If anyone shall say that a man once justified can sin no more, nor lose grace, and that therefore he who falls and sins was never truly justified; or, on the contrary, that throughout his whole life he can avoid all sins even venial sins, except by a special privilege of God, as the Church holds in regard to the Blessed Virgin: let him be anathema.

Canon 24) If anyone shall say, that justice received is not preserved and also not increased in the sight of God through good works but that those same works are only the fruits and signs of justification received, but not a cause of its increase: let him be anathema.

Canon 25) If anyone shall say that in every good work the just one sins at least venially, or (what is more intolerable) mortally, and therefore deserves eternal punishments, and that it is only because God does not impute those works unto damnation that he is not damned, let him be anathema.

Canon 26) If anyone shall say that the just ought not to expect and hope for an eternal recompense from God and the merit of Jesus Christ for the good works which have been performed in God, if by doing well and in keeping the divine commandments they persevere even to the end: let him be anathema.

Canon 27) If anyone shall say that there is no mortal sin except that of infidelity, or that grace once received is not lost by any other sin however grievous and enormous, except the sin of infidelity: let him be anathema.

Canon 28) If anyone shall say that together with the loss of grace by sin faith also is always lost, or that the faith that remains is not a true faith, though it be not a living one, or that he, who has faith without charity, is not a Christian: let him be anathema.

Canon 29) If anyone shall say that he who has fallen after baptism cannot by the grace of God rise again; or that he can indeed recover lost justice, but by faith alone without the sacrament of penance, contrary to what the holy Roman and universal Church, taught by Christ the Lord and His apostles, has hitherto professed, observed, and taught: let him be anathema.

Canon 30) If anyone shall say that after the reception of the grace of justification, to every penitent sinner the guilt is so remitted and the penalty of eternal punishment so blotted out that no penalty of temporal punishment remains to be discharged either in this world or in the world to come in purgatory before the entrance to the kingdom of heaven can be opened: let him be anathema.

Canon 31) If anyone shall say that the one justified sins, when he performs good works with a view to an eternal reward: let him be anathema.

Canon 32) If anyone shall say that the good works of the man justified are in such a way the gifts of God that they are not also the good merits of him who is justified, or that the one justified by the good works, which are done by him through the grace of God and the merit of Jesus Christ (whose living member he is), does not truly merit increase of grace, eternal life, and the attainment of that eternal life (if he should die in grace), and also an increase of glory: let him be anathema.

Canon 33) If anyone shall say that because of this Catholic doctrine of justification as set forth by the holy Synod in this present decree, there is in some degree a detraction from the glory of God or from the merits of Jesus Christ our Lord, and that the truth of our faith, and in fact the glory of God and of Jesus Christ are not rather rendered illustrious: let him be anathema.

NB: The "anathemas" of the Council of Trent do not mean that the Roman Catholic Church condemns one to hell for believing points contrary to these Canons. Those who hold to points opposed to these Canons, through no fault of their own, are placed in the category of "invincible ignorance." However, the Church stipulates that those who, knowing these Canons to be true, and deliberately teach doctrines contrary to them, are either excommunicated from the Church or prohibited from joining the Church.

Appendix 21

Further Study on Adoption

In this appendix, I want to take the opportunity to commend the work of Richard A. White, whose doctoral dissertation was presented to me after this manuscript was completed and typeset. The Dissertation is titled: *Justification in Ecumenical Dialogue: An Assessment of the Catholic Contribution*, presented to and accepted by Marquette University, May 1995. White makes substantial contributions to the study of justification, in particular to the relationship of filiation and justification. White first analyzes the strengths and weakness of the three major ecumenical dialogues on justification: The Lutheran/Catholic Dialogue, The Anglican/Catholic Dialogue, and The German Ecumenical Working Group: Lehverurteilungen — kirchentrennend. He also critiques Hans Küng's work, *Justification: The Doctrine of Karl Barth and a Catholic Reflection*. In summation, White rightly points out that all of these efforts failed to address adequately the major point of contention between Catholics and Protestants, that is, the formal cause of justification. White insists that attempts to coalesce the Protestant notion of forensic imputation with the Catholic concept of infused grace have been very weak. As I have also suggested in *Not By Faith Alone*, White proposes that one possible bridge of unity in this ongoing controversy can be built by incorporating the concept of filiation as one of the main planks in the understanding of justification. White does an excellent job of showing how this can be done. White begins by showing how the early Fathers, both East and West, incorporated filiation in their interpretation of justification. He then shows how the biblical record supports this concept, and finally, how the Council of Trent used filiation as a unifying theme in its decrees on justification. Especially attractive for our study is White's work on the concept of adoption. We transcribe in full this section of his dissertation:

"While making use of the filiation theme, he [Paul] preferred the idea of *huiothesia* [Greek: υἱοθεσία] (usually translated "adoption") over divine begetting; the former appears five times in the Pauline literature (Gal. 4:5; Rom. 8:15; 8:23; 9:4; Eph. 1:5).[1]

i. Background Question

A major question asked by interpreters of these texts is whether or not Paul was influenced by any particular area of his background when he employed the term *huiothesia*. Did he look primarily towards the Old Testament, or was he arguing from an analogy based on a particular Greek or Roman legal practice? Many scholars reject the former view because of the apparent absence of adoption in the OT. Moreover, the term *huiothesia* does not appear in the Septuagint, nor in any Hellenistic Jewish literature. On the other hand, the term dates from the 2nd century B.C. in Greek literature,[2] and perhaps even as early as the 5th century B.C.[3] Furthermore, adoption was a common practice in Greco-Roman legal systems. These facts have led a number of scholars to posit a Greek and/or Roman background for Paul's use of *huiothesia.*[4]

But there are good reasons to challenge this. It is questionable, to begin with, to say that adoption was unknown in the OT; in fact, numerous examples have been suggested by OT scholars.[5] More

---

1 Other Pauline filiation texts include Gal 3:26; Rom. 9:8; 9:26-27; Phil. 2:15; II Cor. 6:18; Titus 3:7.

2 For references, see W.V. Martitz, "huiothesia," in *Theological Dictionary of the New Testament*, vol. 8, ed. G Friedrich and G. Kittel (Grand Rapids: Eerdmans, 1972), pp. 387-88.

3 Martin W. Schoenberg, "Huiothesia: The Word and the Institution," *Scripture* 14 (1962): 116.

4 For a defense of the Greek background, see T. Rees, "Adoption," in *The International Standard Bible Encyclopedia*, vol. 1, ed. Geoffrey W. Bromiley (Grand Rapids: Eerdmans, 1979), p. 58. Exponents of the Roman background view include Francis Lyall, *Slaves, Citizens, Sons: Legal Metaphors in the Epistles* (Grand Rapids: Zondervan, 1984), pp. 67-99; J.D. Hester, *Paul's Concept of Inheritance*, SJT Occasional Papers 14 (Edinburgh: Oliver and Boyd, 1968), pp. 57-62.

5 See Samuel Feigin, "Some Cases of Adoption in Israel," Journal of Biblical Literature 50 (1931): 186-200; William H. Rossell, "New Testament Adoption— Greco-Roman or Semitic?" Journal of Biblical Literature 71 (1952): 233-34. The following are suggested examples of adoption in the Old Testament; The two children of Bilhah (Gen. 30:3-8); Ephraim and Manasseh (Gen. 48:5); Moses (Ex. 2:10); Jephthah (Judges 11); the child of Ruth (Ruth 4:16); Genubath (1 Kings 11:20); Esther (Est. 2:7); and Ezra (Ezra 10:44).

importantly, Paul himself places *huiothesia* in an OT context, naming the "adoption of sons" as a privilege belonging to Israel (Rom. 9:4).[6] This, as Byrne points out, "would seem to align him very closely to the 'sonship of God' tradition of the Jewish background."[7] Furthermore, the use of the Aramaic phrase "Abba" in the context of *huiothesia* (Gal. 4:6; Rom. 8:15) also points to a semetic background. It is reasonable to suppose, therefore, as James I. Cook comments, "that the Apostle borrowed *huiothesia* from the language of the Greco-Roman world, but poured into it a fundamentally Old Testament content."[8]

This conclusion is supported by an examination of the sonship/adoption passages. Just as in the OT Israel's sonship is presented as a liberation from slavery in Egypt (Ex. 4:22-23), so in both Galatians and Romans Christian filiation is presented as a liberation from various forms of bondage, e.g., sin, death and the law (Rom. 8:2; Gal. 4:5).[9]

Continuity with Israel's sonship is demonstrated in another way too. In both epistles, Paul is concerned with delineating the true nature of Abrahamic sonship, and further, the criteria for this sonship. Physical descent from the patriarch is not enough (Rom. 9:6-7). The true children of Abraham are those who belong to Christ through faith (Gal. 3:29) and are symbolized in Isaac understood spiritually (Gal. 4:21-31; Rom. 9:7-8).

ii. Galatians

These themes are developed in separate ways in the two epistles. In Galatians, Paul was combating Judaizers who, through a dis-

---

6 See Martin W. Schoenberg, "Huiothesia: The Adoptive Sonship of the Israelites," *American Ecclesiastical Review* 143 (1960): 261-273.

7 Byrne, *Sons of God*, p. 84.

8 James I. Cook, "The Concept of Adoption in the Theology of Paul," in *Saved By Hope: Essays in Honor of Richard C. Oudersluys*, ed. James I. Cook (Grand Rapids, Michigan: Eerdmans, 1978), p. 137. Herman Ridderbos adds, "The term [*huiothesia*] stems from the Hellenistic world of law; its content, however, must not be inferred from the various Roman or Greek legal systems...but must rather be considered against the Old Testament, redemptive-historical background of the adoption of Israel as Son of God." Herman Ridderbos, *Paul: An Outline of His Theology* (Grand Rapids: Eerdmans, 1975), pp. 197-198. This is Scott's conclusion as well. Scott, *Adoption as Sons of God*, p. 267.

9 Scott finds Exodus typology in both passages. Ibid., pp. 267-269.

torted understanding of the "works of the law," were apparently insisting upon the necessity of circumcision.[10] Paul's argument in Gal. 3 was intended to counter this and to prove that the "works of the law" are in fact unnecessary;[11] the true children of Abraham are those who belong to Christ through faith and baptism. He concluded his argument as follows:

> For you are all sons of God through faith in Christ Jesus. For all of you who were baptized into Christ have clothed yourselves with Christ. There is neither Jew nor Greek, there is neither slave nor free man, there is neither male nor female; for you are all one in Christ Jesus. And if you belong to Christ, then you are Abraham's offspring, heirs according to the promise (Gal. 3:26-29).

In short, the Galatian believers are already "sons of God" and "heirs" to the promise of Abraham through faith and baptism in Christ; the "works of the law" are superfluous.

In Gal. 4:1-7, Paul reiterated in an abbreviated form the same themes of chapter three: slavery under the law, the redemption worked out by Christ, and the sonship which results from this. Now, however, the sonship is explained in terms of the *huiothesia* idea:

But when the fullness of the time came, God sent forth His Son, born of a woman, born under the law, in order that He might redeem those who were under the law, that we might receive the adoption as sons (*ten huiothesian*). And because you are sons, God has sent forth the Spirit of His Son into our hearts, crying, "Abba! Father!" Therefore you are no longer a slave, but a son; and if a son, then an heir through God (Gal. 4:4-7).

Galatian believers become adopted sons through their relationship with Christ, the unique Son. But the *huiothesian* has several

[10] According to G. Walter Hansen, the opponents may have argued on the basis of Gen. 17 that circumcision would lead the Galatian Christians to perfection; for in that text, the command to be perfect is followed by the command to circumcise. Paul counters this argument with his own interpretation of the Abraham narrative. G. Walter Hansen, *Abraham in Galatians: Epistolary and Rhetorical Contexts* (Sheffield: Sheffield Academic Press, 1989), pp. 172-174.

[11] Hansen points out that the phrase "works of the law" refers in large part to "circumcision and the Jewish laws of ritual purity." Ibid., p. 102.

nuances of meaning here. On the one hand, Paul had already spoken of the heir as not differing from the slave until the date set by the Father (Gal. 4:2). Thus, the *huiothesian* is that sonship realized by faithful Jews; it is not adoption strictly speaking because faithful Jews were already sons, but the full status of sonship that comes only through Christ. On the other hand, as Byrne writes:

> the Galatian Christians are heirs because the way to the inheritance depended not on the simple growth to maturity of those who from the beginning were sons, but on a sonship conferred at a later time in response to a promise — a promise directed specifically to 'Gentiles' (3:8,14). They are heirs because God has faithfully kept his promise to call all to sonship and inheritance.[12]

Jews and Gentiles then, are both sons and heirs through Christ, receiving the *huiothesian*. And as Paul continued, "Because you are sons, God has sent forth the Spirit of His Son into our hearts, crying 'Abba! Father!'" (Gal. 4:6). In this way, the "Abba" cry characteristic of Christ's relationship to the Father as Son of God "becomes available to all believers through the agency of the Spirit."[13] It is a privilege of the spirit-filled children of God and attests to their filial status.

iii. Romans

Moving on to the parallel text in Romans 8:14-17, we find many of the same themes:

> For all who are led by the Spirit of God, these are sons of God (*hoioi theou*). For you did not receive a spirit of slavery leading to fear again, but you have received a spirit of adoption as sons (*pneuma huiothesias*) by which we cry out, "Abba! Father!" The Spirit Himself bears witness with our spirit that we are children of God (*tekna theou*), and if children, heirs also,

[12] Byrne, *Sons of God*, pp. 185-186.

[13] Frank J. Matera, *Galatians* (Collegeville, Minnesota: The Liturgical Press, 1992), p. 151. Byrne points out that the phrase "Abba, Father" may suggest a liturgical context. *Sons of God*, p. 100.

> heirs of God (*kleronomoi theou*) and fellow heirs with Christ, if indeed we suffer with Him, in order that we may also be glorified with Him (Rom. 8:14-17).[14]

The similarities between this passage and Gal. 4:4-7 are evident. In the latter, for example, Paul emphasized the contrast between the 'condition' of slavery and the 'condition' of *huiothesia* as an abiding status. He makes a similar contrast in this text between the "spirit of slavery" (*pneuma douleias*) and the "spirit of adoption" (*pneuma huiothesias*). James Dunn comments that "the contrast is once again primarily epochal, between the old epoch from whose dominance they have emerged and the new...[15] Thus, the "spirit of adoption" is not simply a filial sentiment, but an actual state or condition 'effected' by the Holy Spirit. It is the Spirit which brings about *huiothesia*, in contrast to the slavish spirit which was the lot of Israel under the law.[16]

Despite the similarities between these two texts, we find, as Vellanickal observes, an increased emphasis in Rom. 8 on "our participation of the Spirit and on the causal role of the Spirit in our sonship."[17] He explains:

> In Gal God sends the Spirit while in Rom we receive the Spirit. In Gal the Spirit cries 'Abba, Father,' while in Rom we cry in the Spirit which we received. In Rom the Spirit testifies with our Spirit. So there is an intimate relation between the activity of the Spirit and our activity as sons of God under the influence of the Spirit.[18]

---

[14] Note that Paul used four different terms in so many verses to express the Christian's divine filiation. Most commentators agree that the change from *huioi* (sons) in verse 14 to *tekna* (children) in verses 16 and 17 is inconsequential. See, for example, C.E.B. Cranfield, *A Critical and Exegetical Commentary on the Epistle to the Romans*, vol. 1 (Edinburgh: T. & T. Clark, 1975), p. 396.

[15] James D. G. Dunn, *Romans 1-8* (Dallas: Word Books, 1988), p. 452.

[16] In fact, Byrne identifies a connection between *pneuma douleias* and the law. Byrne, *Sons of God*, p. 99.

[17] Vellanickal, *The Divine Sonship*, p. 80.

[18] Ibid.

The Spirit is in fact a major theme throughout Rom. 8, and is again associated with our divine filiation in Rom. 8:18-25.[19] In this passage, Paul placed *huiothesia* in an eschatological context: "And not only this, but also we ourselves, having the first fruits of the Spirit, even we ourselves groan within ourselves, waiting eagerly for our adoption as sons, the redemption of our body."[20] According to Scott, "the present and future aspects of *huiothesia* in Rom. 8 reflect successive stages of participation in the Son by the Spirit and, as such, constitute ways that believers share with the Son in the Davidic promise."[21]

d. Summary

To sum up, divine filiation is a dynamic soteriological theme throughout the NT, but especially in the Johannine and Pauline writings. The children of God are those who share in Christ's sonship by becoming one with Him through faith and baptism. Furthermore, the distinctive mark of sonship in Christ is a real communication of the Spirit as a new principle of life. In the Johannine material this was presented as a divine begetting, whereas Paul emphasized adoption in Christ through the Spirit. In both cases,

---

19 The familial imagery of 8:12-17 is continued in this passage: the creation itself waits for the "revealing of the sons of God" (8:19), attains to the "glory of the children of God" (8:21), and "groans and suffers the pains of childbirth" (8:22).

20 According to Byrne, this refers to the "glorious existence manifest in the resurrection" so that "the revelation of our glory and the revelation of our sonship are opposite sides of...one coin." Byrne, *Sons of God*, p. 215, 105. On this basis, Byrne thinks *huiothesia* is best translated as 'sonship' or 'instatement as sons,' present now but "properly in force only in the risen state that follows upon physical death" (Ibid., p. 217).

21 Scott, *Adoption as Sons of God*, p. 269. "In the present aspect (v. 15), believers receive the Spirit of *huiothesia*, by which they appropriate the "Abba" - cry of the earthly Jesus and thus begin to participate in the Son's Spirit-led sonship at baptism...Likewise, just as Jesus as the seed of David was set as messianic Son of God in power by the Holy Spirit at the proleptic resurrection of the dead (Rom. 1:4; cf. 2 Sam. 7:12, 14), so also believers, who have the Spirit as the means of resurrection (Rom. 8:11), eagerly await their predestined resurrection/adoption into the glorified image of the resurrected Son (vv. 23, 29; cf. Eph 1:5), when the Son will be the Firstborn among many brothers (v. 29; cf. Ps. 89:27)." Ibid., pp. 265, 269.

divine childhood expresses in a special way the believer's familial intimacy with the Father and the total gratuitousness of his or her salvation.[22]

[22] It is noteworthy that in his overview of the experience of grace in the NT, Edward Schillebeeckx identifies filiation as a first and basic interpretative element. He argues that filiation along with the gift of the Holy Spirit "form the basis for all other expostions." Schillebeeckx, *Christ: The Experience of Jesus as Lord*, p. 468.

Selected Bibliography

Abbot, Walter M. ed. *The Documents of Vatican II* (New York: America Press, 1966).

Adam, Karl. *Una Sancta in Katholischer Sicht* (Dusseldorf: Patmos Verlag, 1948).

Akin, James. "The 'if only' interpretation of Romans 2" unpublished paper on file, 1995.

idem, "A Tiptoe through TULIP" in *This Rock*, September 1993.

Aland, Kurt, et al, eds., *The Greek New Testament* (New York: American Bible Society, 1975).

Allison, C.F. *The Rise of Moralism: The Proclamation of the Gospel from Hooker to Baxter* (London: Society for Promotion of Christian Knowledge, 1966).

Althaus, Paul. *The Theology of Martin Luther.* Trans. Robert Schultz (Philadelphia: Fortress Press, 1966).

Anderson, George H. and Austin J. Murphy, Joseph Burgess, eds., *Justification By Faith: Lutherans and Catholics in Dialogue* (Minneapolis: Augsburg Publishing, 1985).

Aquinas, Thomas. *Summa Theologiae* (New York: McGraw Hill Book Co., 1963, 1976).

Armstrong, John, ed. *Roman Catholicism: Evangelical Protestants Analyze What Divides and Unites Us* (Chicago: Moody Press, 1994).

idem, ed., *Justification by Faith Alone* (Morgan, PA: Soli Deo Gloria, 1995). Contributors include: John MacArthur, R. C. Sproul, Joel Beeke, John Gerstner, John Armstrong.

idem, *A View of Rome: A Guide to Understanding the Beliefs and Practices of Roman Catholics* (Chicago: Moody Press, 1995).

idem, *The Coming Evangelical Crisis* (Chicago: Moody Press, 1995).

Arminius, Jacobus. *The Works of James Arminius*, reprinted edition (Grand Rapids: Baker Books House, 1956).

Augustin, Aurelius. *A Select Library of the Nicene and Post-Nicene Fathers of the Christian Church*, ed. Philip Schaff (New York: Christian Literature Co, 1886-90; reprinted edition., Grand Rapids: Eerdmans Publishing, 1974).

Bahnsen, Greg L. *Theonomy in Christian Ethics* (Phillipsburg, NJ: Presbyterian and Reformed Publishing, 1984).

Bainton, Roland H. Here I Stand — A Life of Martin Luther (New York: The New American Library, 1950).

Barrett, C. K. *Commentary on the Second Epistle to the Corinthians* (New York: Harper and Row 1973).

Barth, Karl. *Church Dogmatics*, eds., Geoffrey Bromiley and Thomas Torrence (Edinburgh: T & T Clark, 1936-1969).

Barth, Markus. *Justification.* Trans. A.N. Woodruff III (Grand Rapids: Eerdmans Publishing, 1971).

Basinger, David and Basinger, Randall, eds., *Predestination and Free Will* (Downers Grove: Intervarsity Press, 1986).

Bauer, Walter. *A Greek-English Lexicon of the New Testament and Other Early Christian Literature*, 2nd ed. Revised by Gingrich, F. W. & Danker, F. W. (Chicago and London: The University of Chicago Press, 1979).

Bavinck, Herman. *Gereformeerde Dogmatiek* (Kampen: J. H. Kok, 1928-1930).

idem, *Our Reasonable Faith.* Trans. Henry Zylstra (Grand Rapids: Baker Book House, 1956).

idem, *The Doctrine of God*. Trans. William Hendriksen (Edinburgh: Banner of Truth Trust, 1977).

Beeke, Joel R. *Assurance of Faith: Calvin, English Puritanism, and the Dutch Second Reformation* (New York: Peter Lang, 1991).

Bellarmin, Robertus. *Opera omnia,* reprinted edition (Paris: L. Vives, 1870-74).

Belloc, Hilaire. *Europe and the Faith* (New York: Paulist Press, 1920).

Belting, Natalia M. "Calvin and Justification by Faith." *The Christian Scholar* 45 (1972): 198-205.

Berkhof, Hendrikus. "The Act of Faith in the Reformed Tradition" in *Faith: Its Nature and Meaning*, ed. Paul Surlis (Dublin: Gill and MacMillan, 1972, pp. 99-115).

Berkhof, Louis. *The Assurance of Faith* (Grand Rapids: Smitter, 1928).

idem, *Systematic Theology,* reprinted ed. (London: Banner of Truth Trust, 1977).

idem, *The History of Christian Doctrine* (Grand Rapids: Baker Book House, 1937).

Berkouwer, Gerrit C. *Faith and Justification.* Trans. Lewis Smedes (Grand Rapids: Eerdmans Publishing, 1954).

idem, *The Conflict with Rome* (Philadelphia: Presbyterian and Reformed, 1958).

Beza, Theodore. *Confessio Christianae fidei, et eiusdem collation cum Papisticis haeresibus. Genevae apud Eustathium Vignon,* 1587, translated from French by Robert Fyll (London: Roger Ward, 1639).

Bloesch, Donald G. *Essentials of Evangelical Theology*, vol. 1 (New York: Harper and Row, 1978).

idem, *The Future of Evangelical Christianity* (Garden City, NY: Doubleday, 1983).

Boehl, Edward. *The Reformed Doctrine of Justification.* Trans. C.H. Riedesel, reprinted edition (Grand Rapids: Eerdmans, 1946).

Boettner, Loraine. *Roman Catholicism* (Philadelphia: Presbyterian and Reformed, 1962).

Boice, James Montgomery. *Standing on the Rock: Biblical Authority in a Secular Age* (Grand Rapids: Baker Book House, 1994).

idem, et al. *The Cambridge Declaration of the Alliance of Confessing Evangelicals*, April 20, 1996.

Bok Den, N.W. "Freedom of the Will: A Systematic and Biographical Sounding of Augustine's Thoughts on Human Willing" in *Augustiniana* 44 (1994).

Böckmann, Peter. "Justification by Faith: Lutheran and Roman Catholic," *Dialogue and Alliance* 2 (1988).

Boudreau, Albert H. *The Born-Again Catholic* (Locust Valley: Living Flame Press, 1983).

Bouyer, Louis. *The Spirit and Forms of Protestantism.* Trans. A.V. Littledale (London: Harvill Press, 1956).

idem, *Eucharist: Theology and Spirituality of the Eucharistic Prayer* (Notre Dame: University of Notre Dame Press, 1968).

idem, *Liturgical Piety* (Notre Dame: University of Notre Dame Press, 1955).

Boyer, Charles S. I. *Luther Sa doctrine* (Rome: Presses De L'Universite Gregorienne, 1970).

Braaten, Carl E. *Justification: The Article By Which the Church Stands or Falls* (Minneapolis: Fortress Press, 1990).

idem, "No Breakthrough Whatever on the Lutheran-Catholic and Roman Catholic on 'Justification and Faith,'" *Dialog*, 23 (1984) 246.

Bradwardine, Thomas. *De causa Dei contra pelagium, et de virtute causarum, ad suos Mertonenses, libri tres*, reprint ed. (Frankfurt am Main: Minerva, 1964).

Bray, John S. "The Value of Works in the Theology of Calvin and Beza." *Sixteenth Century Journal* 4, 2 (October 1973): 77-86.

idem, *Theodore Beza's Doctrine of Predestination* (Nieuwkoop: B. De Graaf, 1975).

Brinsmead, Robert. "Further Observations on the Order of Justification and Regeneration." *Present Truth* 5/6 (September, 1976).

Bromiley, Geoffrey W. "The Doctrine of Justification in Luther." *Evangelical Quarterly* 24 (1952): 91-100.

Brown, Harold O. J. "What Do Catholics Believe?" *Christianity Today*, Nov. 1993.

Brown, Peter. *Augustine of Hippo* (Berkely and Los Angeles: University of California Press, 1967).

Brown, Raymond and Joseph Fitzmeyer and Roland Murphy, Roland. *The Jerome Biblical Commentary* (New Jersey: Prentice Hall, 1968).

Brunelli, Lucio. "Augustine and Christian Unity" *30 Days*, No. 12, 1994.

Buchanan, James. *The Doctrine of Justification,* reprinted ed. (Grand Rapids: Baker Book House, 1977).

Burton, Ernest. *Syntax of the Moods and Tenses in New Testament Greek,* reprinted ed. (Grand Rapids: Kregal Publications, 1978).

Buttrick, George ed., *The Interpreter's Bible* (New York: Abingdon Press, 1954).

Byrne, Brendan. *'Sons of God' - 'Seed of Abraham': A Study in the Idea of the Sonship of God of all Christians in Paul Against the Jewish Background.* (Rome: Biblical Institute Press, 1979).

Calvin, John. "Acts of the Council of Trent with the Antidote." in *Tracts and Treatises* (reprinted ed., Grand Rapids: Baker Book House, 1979).

idem, *Commentaries of Calvin*, 22 vols., reprinted ed. (Grand Rapids: Baker Book House, 1979).

idem, *Institutes of the Christian Religion*, ed. John T. McNeil (Philadelphia: Westminster Press, 1960).

idem, *A Reformation Debate: Sadoleto's Letter to the Genevans and Calvin's Reply,* reprinted ed. (Grand Rapids: Baker, 1976).

Canons and Decrees of the Council of Trent, trans. H. J. Schroeder, O. P. (Rockford, IL: Tan Books, 1978).

Carson, Donald A., ed. *Right With God: Justification in the Bible and the World* (Grand Rapids: Baker Book House and Paternoster Press, 1992)

idem, *Exegetical Fallacies* (Grand Rapids: Baker Book House, 1984).

idem, *Divine Sovereignty and Human Responsibility* (Atlanta: John Knox, 1981).

Catechism of the Catholic Church, United States Catholic Conference, Inc. — Libreria Editrice Vaticana, 1994.

Catholic Encyclopedia (Washington D.C. The Catholic University of America, 1967.

Companion to the Catechism of the Catholic Church (San Francisco: Ignatius Press, 1994).

Chadwick, Henry. "Justification by Faith: A Perspective." *One in Christ* 20 (1984).

Chafer, Lewis S. *Systematic Theology* (Dallas: Dallas Theological Seminary, 1948).

Chemnitz, Martin. *Examination of the Council of Trent.* trans., Fred Kramer (St. Louis: Concordia, 1971).

Chilton, David. *Days of Vengeance* (Ft. Worth, Texas: Dominion Press, 1987).

Clark, Gordon H. *Biblical Predestination* (Nutley, NJ: Presbyterian and Reformed Publishing, 1969).

Clayton, Joseph. *Luther and His Work* (Milwaukee: Bruce Publishing Co., 1937).

Clouse, Robert. *The Meaning of the Millennium: Four Views* (Downers Grove, IL: InterVarsity Press, 1977).

Colacci, Mario. *The Doctrinal Conflict between Roman Catholic and Protestant Christianity* (Minneapolic: T. S. Denison and Co., 1962).

Cook, James I. "The Concept of Adoption in the Theology of Paul." *Saved by Hope: Essays in Honor of Richard C. Oudersluys,* ed. James I. Cook (Grand Rapids, MI: 1978).

Cosgrove, C.H. "Justification in Paul: A Linguistic and Theological Reflection." *Journal of Biblical Literature* 106 (1987): 653-70.

Crabtree, Arthur B. *The Restored Relationship: A Study in Justification and Reconciliation* (Valley Forge, PA: Judson, 1963).

Cross, F. L. *Oxford Dictionary of the Christian Church*, revised edition (Oxford University Press, 1983).

Currie, David. *Born Fundamentalist, Born Again Catholic* (San Francisco: Ignatius Press, 1995).

Dantine, Wilhelm. *Justification of the Ungodly*. Trans. Eric and Ruth Gritsch (St. Louis: Concordia, 1968).

Daujat, Jean. *The Theology of Grace* (New York: Hawthorne Books, 1959).

Deanesly, Margaret. *The Lollard Bible and Other Medieval Biblical Versions* (Cambridge University Press, 1920).

De Lubac, Henri. *The Splendor of the Church* (San Francisco: Ignatius Press, 1986).

idem, *Augustinianism and Modern Theology.* Trans. Lancelot Sheppard (New York: Herder and Herder, 1969).

Dempsey, Douglas, E. *Justification in Late Medieval Preaching: A Study of John Geiler of Keisersberg* (New York: E.J. Brill, 1989).

Denifle, Heinrich. *Luther und Luthertum,* translated into French by Abbe J. Paquier (1910-1913).

Denzinger, Henry. *Enchiridion Symbolorum.* 13th edition. Trans. Roy J. Deferrari (St. Louis: B. Herder Books, 1957).

DeSales, Francis. *The Catholic Controversy* (Illinois: Tan Publishing, 1989).

Dieter, Melvin., Anthony Hoekema, Stanley Horton, J. Robertson McQuilkin, John F. Walvoord. *Five Views of Sanctification* (Grand Rapids: Zondervan Publishing, 1987).

Djuth, Marianne. "Stoicism and Augustine's Doctrine of Human Freedom after 396" in *Collectanea Augustiniana - Augustine: Second Founder of the Faith*, ed., Joseph Schnaubelt & Frederick Van Fleteren (NY: Peter Lang (1990).

Douglass, Jane Dempsey. "The Image of God in Humanity: A Comparison of Calvin's Teaching in 1536 and 1559" in *In Honor of John Calvin*, 1509- 1564, ed., E.J. Furcha (Montreal: McGill University, 1987) 175-203.

Duggins, Davis. "Across the Divide: How Can evangelicals and Catholics relate to one another?" *Christianity Today*, November 1993.

Duggan, G. H. *Beyond Reasonable Doubt* (Boston: Daughters of St. Paul, 1987).

Dulles, Avery. "Justification in Contemporary Catholic Theology" in *Justification by Faith: Lutherans and Catholics in Dialogue VII*, ed., H. George Anderson (Minneapolis: Augsburg, 1985).

Dunn, J. D. G. "The New Perspective on Paul." *Bulletin of the John Rylands Library* 65 (1983): 95-122; also in *Jesus, Paul and the Law: Studies in Mark and Galatians* (Louisville, KY: Westminster/John Knox, 1990).

Dunn, James D. G. and Alan M. Suggate. *The Justice of God: A Fresh Look at the Old Doctrine of Justification by Faith.* (Grand Rapids: Eerdmans Publishing, 1993).

Dupuis, Jacques. *The Christian Faith in the Doctrinal Documents of the Catholic Church*, 6th ed (New York: Alba House, 1996).

Eadie, John. *The English Bible* (London: MacMillian, 1876).

Edwards, Jonathan. *Justification by Faith Alone,* reprinted ed. (Edinburgh: Banner of Truth Trust, 1974).

Ellicott, John. *Commentary on the Whole Bible* (Grand Rapids: Zondervan Publishing).

Elliger, K. and W. Rudolph, eds. *Biblia Hebraica Stuttgartensia* (Deutsche Bibelstiftung Stuttgart, 1967/77).

Engel, Mary Potter. *John Calvin's Perspectival Anthropology* (Atlanta: Scholar Press, 1988).

England, R. G. *Justification Today: The Roman Catholic and Anglican Debate* (Oxford: Latimer House, 1979).

Farrar, Frederic W. *History of Interpretation* (Grand Rapids: Baker Book House, 1886, 1961).

Ferm, Virgilius. *Encyclopedia of Religion* (New Jersey: Littlefield, 1959).

Flannery, Austin. *Vatican Council II: The Conciliar and Post Conciliar Documents* (New York: Costello Publishing Co., 1975).

Forde, Gehard O. *Justification By Faith: A Matter of Death and Life* (Philadelphia: Fortress Press, 1982).

Fournier, Keith A. *House United? Evangelicals and Catholics Together: A Winning Alliance for the 21st Century* (Colorado: NavPress, 1994).

idem, *Evangelical Catholics: A Call for Christian Cooperation to Penetrate the Darkness with the Light of the Gospel* (Nashville: Nelson, 1990).

Frame, John M. *Evangelical Reunion: Denominations and the Body of Christ* (Grand Rapids: Baker Book House, 1991).

Friedmann, Robert. *The Theology of Anabaptism* (Scottsdale, PA: Herald Press, 1973).

Fudge, Edward. *The Fire That Consumes: A Biblical and Historical Study of the Doctrine of Final Punishment* (Texas: Providential Press, 1982).

Fung, Ronald Y. K. "The Forensic Character of Justification." *Themelios* 3 (1977): 16-21.

idem, "Righteousness and Faith in the Thought of Paul." Ph.D. dissertation, Manchester, 1975.

Gaffin, Richard. *Resurrection and Redemption: A Study in Paul's Soteriology* (New Jersey: Presbyterian and Reformed, 1987).

Garrigou-Langrange, Reginald. *Predestination.* Translated from *La predestination des saints et la grace* (Belgium: Desclee, De Brouwer and Cie).

idem, *Providence*. Translated by Dom Bede Rose, O.S.B. (St. Louis: Herder Book Co, 1937).

Geddes, MacGregor. *A Literary History of the Bible* (New York: Abingdon Press, 1968).

Geisler, Norman and Ralph MacKenzie. *Roman Catholics and Evangelicals: Agreements and Differences* (Grand Rapids: Baker Book House, 1995).

Geisler, Norman. *Thomas Aquinas: An Evangelical Appraisal* (Grand Rapids, Baker Books, 1991).

George, A. C. "Martin Luther's Doctrine of Sanctification with Special Reference to the Formula 'Simul Iustus Et Peccator': A Study in Luther's Lectures on Romans and Galatians." Th.D. dissertation, Wesminster Theological Seminary, 1982.

Gerrish, Brian A. "The Mirror of God's Goodness: Man in the Theology of Calvin" in *Concordia Theological Quarterly* 45 (1981): 211-222.

idem, *Grace and Gratitude* (Minneapolis: Fortress Press, 1993).

Gerstner, John H. *A Primer on Justification* (Morgan, PA: Soli Deo Gloria Publications, 1995).

idem, *Jonathan Edwards: Evangelist* (Morgan, PA: Soli Deo Gloria Publications, 1995).

idem, *Jonathan Edwards: A Mini-Theology* (Wheaton, IL: Tyndale House, 1987).

idem, "Aquinas was a Protestant" in *Tabletalk*, published by Ligonier Ministries, May 1994.

Gibbons, James. *The Faith of Our Fathers* (Illinois: Tan Publishing, 1876, 1980).

Gleason, Robert W. *Grace.* (New York: Sheed and Ward, 1962).

Gore, Ralph J. "The Lutheran Ordo Salutis with Special Reference to Justification and Sanctification: A Reformed Analysis." Master's thesis, Faith Theological Seminary, 1983.

Green, Lowell C. *How Melanchthon Helped Luther Discover the Gospel: The Doctrine of Justification in the Reformation* (Fallbrook, CA: Verdict Publications, 1979).

Grisar, Hartmann. *Luther* (Freibourg-im-Breisgau, 1911-1912).

Gutherie, Donald. *New Testament Introduction* (Downers Grove, IL: Inter-Varsity Press, 1968).

idem, "The Influence of Erasmus upon Melanchthon, Luther and the Formula of Concord in the Doctrine of Justification." *Church History* 43 (1974).

Hacker, Paul. *The Ego in Faith: Martin Luther and the Origin of Anthropocentric Religion* (Chicago: Franciscan Herald Press, 1970).

idem, "Martin Luther's Notion of Faith" in *Catholic Scholars Dialogue with Luther*, ed., Jared Wicks (Chicago: Loyola University Press, 1970):85-105.

Hagglund, Bengt. *The Background of Luther's Doctrine of Justification in Late Medieval Theology* (Philadelphia: Fortress Press, 1971).

Hahn, Scott & Kimberly. *Rome Sweet Home* (San Francisco: Ignatius, 1993).

Hahn, Scott. "The Authority Justification Debate." Participants: Scott Hahn of The University of Steubenville versus Robert Knudsen of Westminster Theological Seminary, 1990.

Hahn, Scott. "Kinship By Covenant: A Biblical Theological Study of Covenant Types and Texts in the Old and New Testaments" Ph.D. Dissertation, 1995 for Marquette University.

Hall, Basil. "Calvin against the Calvinists." *John Calvin*, ed. Ford L. Battles, et al. (Appleford: Sutton Courtenay Press, 1966) pp. 19-37.

Hardon, John. *The Catholic Catechism* (New York: Doubleday and Co., 1975).

Harnack, Adolph. *History of Dogma*. Trans. N. Buchanan, et al. (Boston: Roberts Brothers, 1897).

Haydock, G. Leo. ed. The Douay-Rheims New Testament with Comprehensive Catholic Commentary (Monrovia, CA: Catholic Treasures, 1991).

Hays, R. B. *Echoes of Scripture in the Letters of Paul* (New Haven, CT: Yale University Press, 1989).

Headley, John M. *Luther's View of Church History* (New Haven: Yale University Press, 1963).

Heinz, Johann. *Justification and Merit: Luther vs. Catholicism* (Berrien Springs, MI: Andrews University Press, 1981).

Hendriksen, William. *Romans* (Grand Rapids: Baker Book House, 1982).

Henry, Carl, F. H. *Twilight of a Great Civilization: The Drift Toward Neo- Paganism* (Westchester: Crossway, 1988).

Hesselinks, John. *On Being Reformed: Distinctive Characteristics and Common Misunderstandings* (Ann Arbor, MI: Servant Books, 1983).

Hessen, J. *Luther in okumenischer Sicht*, 1946, cited in Stauffer, f. 51.

Hodge, Alexander A. *The Doctrine of Justification* (London: Banner of Truth Trust, 1961).

Hodge, Charles. *Justification by Faith Alone*, ed. John Robbins. (New Mexico: Trinity Foundation, 1995).

idem, *Systematic Theology* (New York: Scribner, Armstrong and Co., 1877); abridged edition, ed. Edward N. Gross (Grand Rapids: Baker Book House, 1988).

idem, *Commentary on Romans* (London: Banner of Truth Trust, 1909, 1972).

idem, *An Exposition of the Second Epistle to the Corinthians* (Grand Rapids: Eerdmans Publishing, 1973).

Hodges, Zane. *The Gospel Under Siege* (Dallas: Redencion Viva, 1981).

idem, *Absolutely Free! A Biblical Reply to Lordship Salvation* (Grand Rapids: Zondervan, 1989).

Hoerber, Robert G. (*Concordia Journal* / January 1995).

Hoekema, Anthony A. *Saved By Grace* (Grand Rapids: Eerdmans, 1989).

Hoeksema, Jomer. *The Voice of our Fathers: An Exposition of the Canons of Dordrecht* (Grand Rapids: Reformed Free Publishing Ass., 1980).

Holl, Karl. *The Cultural Significance of the Reformation*, trans. Karl and Barbara Hertz and John Lichtblau (New York: Meridian Books, 1959).

idem, *The Reconstruction of Morality.* Trans. Fred Meuser and Walter Wietzke (Philadelphia: Fortress Press, 1979).

idem, *What Did Luther Understand by Religion*? Trans. Fred Meuser and Walter Wietzke (Philadelphia: Fortress Press, 1977).

Horton, Michael S. "Evangelicals and Catholics Together." *Evangelical Times* (July 1994):10

idem, *Made in America: The Shaping of Modern American Evangelicalism* (Grand Rapids: Baker Book House, 1991).

idem, *Power Religion: The Selling Out of the Evangelical Church* (Grand Rapids: Baker Book House, 1993).

idem, *Putting Amazing Back into Grace* (Grand Rapids: Baker Book House, 1991, 1994).

Horton, Michael S. and James I. Packer. "Resolutions for Roman Catholic & Evangelical Dialogue." *Modern Reformation* (July-August, 1994): 28-29.

Horton, Michael S. "What Still Divides Us." A Debate between Protestants: Horton, W. Robert Godfrey, Rod Rosenbladt versus Catholics: Patrick Madrid, William Marshner, Robert Sungenis. (March, 1995).

Howard, Thomas. *Evangelical is Not Enough: Worship of God in Liturgy and Sacrament* (San Francisco: Ignatius, 1984).

idem, "Witness for the Faith: What Catholics Can Learn from Billy Graham." *Crisis* (April 1991).

Hughes, Philip E. "Justification by Faith: Distortions of the Doctrine." *Evangelical Quarterly* 24 (1952):78-90.

idem, *The Second Epistle to the Corinthians* (Grand Rapids: Eerdmans Publishing, 1962).

Hunt, Dave. "Current Issues" in *Voice, Journal of the Independent Fundamentalist Churches of America*, July/August 1994, 21-24.

Hunter, James D. *Evangelicalism: The Coming Generation* (Chicago: University of Chicago Press, 1987).

Jedin, Hubert. *A History of the Council of Trent*. trans., Dom Ernest Graf (St. Louis: B Herder, 1957-1961).

Jenning, Robert. *Extra-Sacramental Justification* (Catholic University Press, 1944).

Jeremias, Joachim. *The Central Message of the New Testament* (New York: Charles Scribner's Sons, 1965).

Johnson, Kevin O. *Why Do Catholics Do That? A Guide to the Teachings and Practices of the Catholic* Church (New York: Ballentine Books, 1994).

Jones, Douglass, ed. "Non Est: Real Legal Fictions." *Credenda Agenda*, Vol. 8, No. 3, 1996.

idem, "An Exchange of Ideas: Election." *Credenda Agenda*, Vol. 8, No. 3, 1996).

Jordan, James B. "Christian Piety: Deformed and Reformed" *Geneva Papers* (New Series), No. 1 (September 1985).

Jurgens, William. *Faith of the Early Fathers* (Minnesota: Liturgical Press, 1979).

Karlberg, Mark W. "The Original State of Adam: Tensions Within Reformed Theology" in *Evangelical Quarterly* 59 (1987): 291-309.

Keating, Karl. *What Catholics Really Believe — Setting the Record Straight* (Ann Arbor, MI: Servant Publications, 1992).

idem, *Catholicism and Fundamentalism* (San Francisco: Ignatius Press, 1988).

Kelly, J. N. D. *Early Christian Doctrines* (New York: Harper and Row, 1978).

Kittel, Gerhard, and Geoffrey Bromiley, eds. Theological Dictionary of the New Testament (Grand Rapids: Erdmans, 1964).

Kiefl, F. X. "Martin Luther's Religiose Psyche." *Hochland*, 1917.

Kistler, Don ed., *Sola Scriptura: The Protestant Position on the Bible* (Morgan, PA: Soli Deo Gloria, 1995).

Kline, Meredith G. *By Oath Consigned: A Reinterpretation of the Covenant Signs of Circumcision and Baptism* (Grand Rapids: Eerdmans Publishing, 1968).

Klooster, Fred H. Calvin's Doctrine of Predestination, 2nd edition, (Grand Rapids: Baker Book House, 1977).

Knox, David Broughton. *The Doctrine of Faith in the Reign of Henry VIII* (London: James Clarke, 1961).

Knox, John. *The Works of John Knox,* reprinted ed. (New York: AMS Press, 1966).

Kreeft, Peter. *Fundamentals of the Faith: Essays in Christian Apologetics* (San Francisco: Ignatius Press, 1988).

Kreeft, Peter and Ronald K. Tacelli. *Handbook of Christian Apologetics* (Downers Grove, IL: InterVarsity Press, 1994).

Kuiper, Herman. *By Grace Alone: A Study in Soteriology* (Grand Rapids: Eerdmans, 1955).

Kuyper, Abraham. *Lectures on Calvinism* (Grand Rapids: Eerdmans Publishing, 1931).

Kümmel, W.G. *The New Testament: The History of its Investigation and Problems.* Trans. S. M. Gilmour and H. C. Kee (Nashville: Abingdon Press, 1972).

Küng, Hans. *Justification: The Doctrine of Karl Barth and a Catholic Reflection* (New York: Thomas Nelson and Sons, 1964).

Ladd, George Eldon. *A Theology of the New Testament* (Grand Rapids: Eerdmans Publishing, 1974).

Lamberigts, Mathijs. "Julian of Aeclanum: A Plea for a Good Creator." *Augustiniana* 38 (1988):5-24.

idem, "Augustine, Julian of Aeclanum and E. Pagels' *Adam, Eve and the Serpent.*" *Augustiniana* 39 (1989): 393-435.

Lambrecht, Jan and Richard Thompson. *Justification By Faith: The Implications of Romans 3:27-31* (Wilmington, DE: M. Glazier, 1989).

Lampe, G. W. H. ed. *The Doctrine of Justification by Faith* (London: A.R. Mowbray and Co., 1954).

Lane, A. N. S. "Did Calvin Believe in Freewill?" *Biblical and Historical Essays* (Liverpool Bible College (1981): 72-90).

idem, "Calvin's Use of the Fathers and Medievals." *Calvin Theological Journal* 16 (1981): 149-203.

Leaver, Robin A. *Luther on Justification* (St. Louis: Concordia: 1975).

Lehmann, Karl. *Justification By Faith* (New York: Contynuum, 1996).

Lehmann, Karl and Wolfhart Pannenberg. *The Condemnations of the Reformation Era: Do They Still Divide?* Trans. Margaret Kohl (Minneapolis: Fortress Press, 1990).

Lenski, R. C. H. *Interpretation of St. Paul's Epistle to the Romans* (Minneapolis: Augsburg Publishing, 1936).

idem, *Interpretation of the Gospel According to John* (Minneapolis: Augsburg Publishing, 1943).

Liberto, David. "Augustine, Calvin and Free Choice" unpublished paper on file, 1995.

idem, "Augustine, Freedom and Grace" unpublished paper on file, 1995.

Liddell and Scott. *Greek-English Lexicon* (Oxford: Clarendon Press, 1977).

Logan, Samuel T., Jr. "The Doctrine of Justification in the Theology of Jonathan Edwards." *Westminster Theological Journal* 46 (1984):26-52.

Lortz, Joseph. "The Basic Elements of Luther's Intellectual Style." *Catholic Scholars Dialogue with Luther* (Chicago: Loyola University Press, 1970):3-33.

idem, *Die Reformation in Deutschland*, vol. 1 (Freiburg: Herder, 1949); *The Reformation in Germany,* translated by Ronald Walls (New York: Herder and Herder, 1968).

Louw, Johannes P. and Eugene A. Nida. Greek-English Lexicon of the New Testament Based on Semantic Domains (United Bible Society, 1988).

Luther, Martin. *D. Martin Luthers Werke: Kritische Gesamtausgabe.* 103 vols. ed., J. C. F. Knaake, et al. Weimar edition: Herman Bohlaus, 1883f).

idem, Briefwechsel edition, 1930ff.

idem, Teschreden edition, 1912ff.

idem, *Lectures on Romans*, ed. W. Pauck (Philadelphia: Westminster Press, 1961).

idem, *Luther's Works*, ed. and trans. Jaroslav Pelikan, et al. (St. Louis: Concordia Publishing House (vols. 1-30); Philadelphia: Fortress Press (vols. 31-55), 1955-1979).

Lutheran World Federation. *Justification Today* (New York: National Lutheran Council, 1965).

Lutzer, Erwin. *All One Body — Why Don't We Agree?* (Wheaton, IL: Tyndale Publishers, 1989)

MacArthur, John F. Jr. *The Gospel According to Jesus* (Grand Rapids: Zondervan, 1988, 1994).

idem, *Justification by Faith* (Chicago: Moody Press, 1985).

idem, *Reckless Faith: When the Church Loses Its Will To Discern* (Wheaton: Crossway, 1994).

idem, "Grace to You" (National radio program, May 3, 1996).

MacGregor, Geddes. *A Literary History of the Bible* (New York. Abingdon Press, 1968).

Machen, J. Gresham. *The New Testament: An Introduction to its Literature and History* (London: Banner of Truth Trust, 1977).

idem, *Machen's Notes on Galatians*, "Faith and Works," ed. John Skilton (Phila, PA: Presbyterian and Reformed Publishing, 1972).

Madrid, Patrick, ed. *Surprised By Truth* (San Diego: Basilica Press, 1994).

Manns, Peter. "Absolute and Incarnate Faith — Luther on Justification in the Galatians' Commentary of 1531-1535." *Catholic Scholars Dialogue with Luther* (Chicago: Loyola University Press, 1970): 121-156.

Marshner, William. "Justification by Faith." *Reasons for Hope: Catholic Apologetics* (Front Royal, VA: Christendom College Press, 1978).

Martin, Ralph P. *Reconciliation: A Study of Paul's Theology* (Atlanta: John Knox, 1980).

Martin, Robert P. *Accuracy of Translation and the New International Version: The Primary Criterion in Evaluating Bible Versions* (Carlisle, PA: Banner of Truth Trust, 1989).

Martitz, W.V. "huiothesia." *Theological Dictionary of the New Testament.* Vol. 8, ed. G. Freidrich and G. Kittel, (Grand Rapids, MI: Eerdmans, 1972).

Matera, Frank J. *Galatians* (Collegeville, Minnesota: Liturgical Press, 1992).

Matheson, Peter. *Cardinal Contarini at Regensberg* (New York: Oxford University Press, 1972).

McCarthy, James G. *The Gospel According to Rome: Comparing Catholic Tradition and the Word of God* (Oregon: Harvest House Publishers, 1995).

McDonough, Thomas M. *The Law and the Gospel in Luther: A Study in Martin Luther's Confessional Writings* (Oxford University Press, 1963).

McGrath, Alister. *Iustitia Dei: A History of the Christian Doctrine of Justification.* 2 vols. (Cambridge: Cambridge University Press, 1986).

idem, "ARCIC II and Justification: Some Difficulties and Obscurities relating to Anglican and Roman Catholic Teaching on Justification." *Anvil* 1 (1984).

idem, *ARCIC II and Justification: An Evangelical Anglican Assessment of "Salvation and the Church"* (Oxford: Latimer House, 1987).

idem, "Augustinianism? A Critical Assessment of the So-Called 'Medieval Augustinian Tradition' on Justification." *Augustiniana* 31 (1981):247-267.

idem, *Christian Theology: An Introduction* (Oxford: Blackwell Publishers, 1994).

idem, "Do We Still Need a Reformation?" *Christianity Today*, December, 1994.

idem, "John Henry Newman's 'Lectures on Justification:' The High Church Misrepresentation of Luther." *Churchman* 97 (1983):37-60.

idem, "Justification: Barth, Trent and Küng." *Scottish Journal of Theology* 34 (1981):517-529.

idem, *Justification By Faith: What it Means for us Today* (Grand Rapids: Academie Books, 1988).

idem, "Justification — 'Making Just' or 'Declaring Just.'" *Churchman* 96, 1 (1982).

idem, *A Life of John Calvin* (Oxford: Blackwell, 1990).

idem, *Luther's Theology of the Cross: Martin Luther's Theological Breakthrough* (Oxford, UK; New York: Blackwell, 1985).

idem, *Reformation Thought*, 2nd edition (Grand Rapids, Baker Books, 1993).

McNeill, John T. ed. and trans. *Calvin: Institutes of the Christian Religion* (Philadelphia: Westminster Press, 1960).

idem, *The History and Character of Calvinism* (New York: Oxford University Press, 1973).

McSorley, Harry J. "Erasmus versus Luther — Compounding the Reformation Tragedy" *Catholic Scholars Dialogue with Luther*, ed., Jared Wicks (Chicago: Loyola University Press, 1970)107-117.

idem, *Luther: Right or Wrong?: An Ecumenical-theological study of Luther's Major Work, The Bondage of the Will* (New York: Newman Press, 1968, c1969).

Melanchthon, Philip. *Melanchthon on Christian Doctrine: Loci Communes*, trans. and ed. Clyde L. Manschreck, reprinted ed. (Grand Rapids: Baker Book House, 1982).

Metzger, Bruce Manning. *A Textual Commentary on the Greek New Testament* (New York: United Bible Society, 1975).

Miel, Jan. *Pascal and Theology* (Baltimore and London: The John Hopkins Press, 1969).

Miravalle, Mark I. ed. *Mary: Coredemptrix, Mediatrix, Advocate: Theological Foundations Towards a Papal Definition* (Santa Barbara, CA: Queenship Publishing, 1995).

Montgomery, John W. *Ecumenicity, Evangelicals and Rome* (Grand Rapids: Zondervan, 1969).

Moo, Douglas J. "'Law,' 'Works of the Law,' and Legalism in Paul," *Westminster Theological Journal* 45 (1983).

Morimoto, Anri. *Jonathan Edwards and the Catholic Vision of Salvation* (University Park: Pennsylvania State University Press, 1995).

Most, William G. *Catholic Apologetics Today* (Rockford, IL: Tan Publishing, 1986).

idem, *Grace, Predestination, and the Salvific Will of God* (Front Royal, VA: Christendom Press, 1996).

Murray, Iain. *Revival and Revivalism: The Making and Marring of American Evangelicalism* (London: Banner of Truth, 1994).

Murray, John. *Collected Writings* (Edinburgh: Banner of Truth Trust, 1978-1983).

idem, *The Epistle to the Romans* (Grand Rapids: Eerdmans Publishing, 1959, 1965).

idem, *Redemption Accomplished and Applied* (Grand Rapids: Eerdmans Publishing, 1955).

Nash, Ronald H., ed. *Evangelical Renewal in the Mainline Churches* (Westchester, IL: Crossway, 1987).

Neuhaus, Richard John, and Charles Colson, et al. "Evangelicals and Catholics Together: The Christian Mission in the Third Millennium," paper: March 29, 1994.

Neuhaus, Richard John. *The Catholic Moment: The Paradox of the Church in the Postmodern World* (San Francisco: Harper and Row, 1987).

idem, "The Reformation Ante: A Response to Carl Braaten." *Dialog* 29 (1990).

Newman, John Henry. *Sermons*, 1824-1843 (Oxford: Clarendon Press, 1991).

idem, *Lectures on the Doctine of Justification,* (London: Rivingstone, 1874; reprinted ed. New York: Longmans, Green, and Co., 1990).

idem, *Conscience, Consensus and the Development of Doctrine* (New York: Doubleday, 1992).

Nicoll, W. Robertson ed. *The Expositor's Bible* (New York: A. C. Armstrong, 1907).

idem, *The Expositor's Greek Testament* (Grand Rapids: Eerdmans Publishing, 1980).

Noll, Mark. "John Wesley and the Doctrine of Assurance." *Bibliotheca Sacra* 132 (April 1975):161-177.

idem, *The Scandal of the Evangelical Mind* (Grand Rapids: Eerdmans, 1994).

North, Gary. *Backward Christian Soldiers? An Action Manual for Christian Reconstruction* (Tyler, TX: Institute for Christian Economics, 1984).

Oberman, Heiko Augustinus. "Archbishop Thomas Bradwardine: A Fourteenth Century Augustinian." Ph.D. dissertation, Utrecht University, 1957).

idem, "'Iustitia Christi' and 'Iustitia Dei': Luther and the Scholastic Doctrines of Justification." *Harvard Theological Review* 59 (1966):1-26.

O'Brien, John A. *The Faith of Millions* (Huntington, IN: Our Sunday Visitor, 1974).

O'Connell, Robert J. *St. Augustine's Early Theory of Man, A.D. 386-391* (Cambridge, Mass: Belknap Press of Harvard University, 1968).

O'Hare, Patrick F. *The Facts About Luther,* reprinted ed. (Rockford, IL: Tan Books and Publishing, 1987).

Olin, John C. ed. *A Reformation Debate:John Calvin and Jacob Sadoleto* (New York: Harper & Row, 1966).

Osborne, Kenan B. *Reconciliation and Justification: The Sacrament and its Theology* (New York: Paulist Press, 1990).

Ott, Ludwig. *Fundamentals of Catholic Dogma* (Rockford, IL: Tan Books and Publishing, 4th ed. 1960).

Owen, John. *An Exposition of the Epistle to the Hebrews.* 7 vols. ed., W. H. Goold (Grand Rapids: Baker Book House, 1980).

Packer, James I., et al. *Here We Stand: Justification by Faith Today* (London: Hodder and Stoughton, 1986).

idem, "Why I Signed It." *Christianity Today*, December 1994.

Palm, David. "Current Roman Catholic Teaching on Sanctification." Midwest Baptist Conference Theological Workshop, February, 1996.

Palmer, Edwin H. *The Five Points of Calvinism.* (Grand Rapids: Baker Book House, 1972).

Parker, T.H.L. "Calvin's Doctrine of Justification." *Evangelical Quarterly* 24 (1952):101-107.

Payne, Gordon R. "Augustinianism in Calvin and Bonaventure" in *Westminster Theological Journal* 44 (1982):1-30.

Pelikan, Jaroslav. ed. *Interpreters of Luther* (Philadelphia: Fortress Press, 1968).

idem, *Reformation of Church and Dogma* (University of Chicago Press, 1984).

Perrota, Kevin. "The U.S. Catholic Church." *Evangelical Renewal in the Mainline Churches*, ed. Ronald Nash (Westchester, IL: Crossway, 1987).

Pesch, Otto. *Theologie der Rechtfertigung bei Martin Luther und Thomas von Aquin* (Mainz: M. Grünewald, 1967).

Peter, Carl J. "Justification by Faith Alone: The Article by which the Church Stands or Falls? A Reply." *Dialog* 29 (1990).

Pinnock, Clark. *A Wilderness in God's Mercy* (Grand Rapids: Zondervan Publishing, 1992).

idem, "God Limits His Knowledge" in *Predestination and Free Will*, eds. David Basinger and Randall Basinger (Illinois: Intervarsity, 1986).

Plantinga, Jacob. "The Time of Justification." Th.M. thesis, Westminster Theol. Seminary, 1977.

Plass, Edward. ed. *What Luther Says: An Anthology* (St. Louis: Concordia, 1959).

Portalie, Eugene. *A Guide to the Thought of Augustine.*, Trans. Ralph. J. Bastian (Chicago: H. Regnery Co. 1960).

Preus, Robert D. *The Theology of Post-Reformation Lutheranism* (St. Louis: Concordia, 1970).

Preus, Rolf. "An Evaluation of Lutheran/Roman Catholic Conversations of Justification." Unpublished M.A. Thesis. Fort Wayne, Indiana: Concordia Theological Seminary, 1987.

Rahner, Karl and Herbert Vorgrimler. *Dictionary of Theology*. 2nd ed. (New York: Crossroad, 1981).

Rahner Karl. "Justified and Sinner at the Same Time," in *Theological Investigations VI: Concerning Vatican Council II*, (New York: Crossroad Publishing Co., 1982).

idem, "Some Implications of the Scholastic Concept of Uncreated Grace." *Theological Investigations I: God, Christ, Mary and Grace.* Trans. by Cornelius Ernst. (Baltimore: Helicon Press, 1961).

Ramm, Bernard. *Protestant Biblical Interpretation* (Grand Rapids: Baker Book House, 1970).

Ratzinger, Joseph Cardinal. *Introduction to Christianity* (San Francisco: Ignatius, 1990).

Reid, G. ed. *The Great Acquittal: Justification by Faith and Current Christian Thought* (London: Collins, 1992).

Ridderbos, Hermann. *Paul: An Outline of His Theology.* Trans. John R deWitt (Grand Rapids: Eerdmans, 1975, reprinted from the Dutch original of 1966).

Rist, John. "Augustine on Free Will and Predestination." *Doctrines of Human Nature, Sin and Salvation in the Early Church*, ed. Everett Ferguson (New York and London: Garland Publishing, 1993):180-207.

Rix, Herbert D. *Martin Luther: The Man and the Image* (New York: Irvington Press, Inc., 1983).

idem, *Augustine: Ancient Thought Baptized* (Cambridge: Cambridge University Press, 1994).

Robbins, John W. "The Counterfeit Gospel of Charles Colson" part II, in *Trinity Review*, February 1994.

idem, ed. *Justification by Faith Alone by Charles Hodge* (NM: Trinity Foundation, 1995).

idem, "The Relationship between Justification and Sanctification" Parts I & II. *The Trinity Review* (September 1996, No. 139 & 140).

Rohr, John von. *The Covenant of Grace in Puritan Thought* (Atlanta: Scholars Press, 1986).

Rolston, Holmes III. *John Calvin versus the Westminster Confession* (Atlanta: John Knox Press, 1977).

Roman Catholic Bishops of the United States. "An Evaluation of the Lutheran-Catholic Statement Justification by Faith." *Lutheran Quarterly* 5 (1991).

Rupp, Ernst Gordon. *The Righteousness of God: Luther Studies* (London: Hodder and Stoughton, 1953).

Rupp, Ernst Gordon, ed. *Luther and Erasmus: Free Will and Salvation* (Library of Christian Classics)

Ryrie, Charles. *Balancing the Christian Life* (Chicago: Moody Press, 1969).

Saarinen, Risto. *Weakness of the Will in Medieval Thought: From Augustine to Buridan* (Leiden and New York: E. J. Brill, 1994).

Salmon, George. *The Infallibility of the Church* (London: John Murray Publishing, 1914).

Sanders, E.P. *Paul and Palestinian Judaism: A Comparison of Patterns of Religion* (Philadelphia: Fortress Press, 1977).

idem, *Paul, the Law, and the Jewish People* (Philadelphia: Fortress Press, 1983).

Sandlin, Andrew. "'Justification' The Principal Hinge of Religion." *The Chalcedon Report* 351 (October 1994):14-17.

idem, "Deviations From Historic Solafideism in the Reformed Community" *The Chalcedon Report* (February, 1995).

Santmire, H. Paul. "Justification in Calvin's 1540 Romans Commentary." *Church History* 33 (1964):294-305.

Sartory, Thomas. *The Oecumenical Movement and the Unity of the Church.* Trans. Hilda Graef (Westminster, MD: Newman Press, 1963).

Schaff, Philip. *History of the Christian Church,* 8 volumes, reprinted ed. (Grand Rapids: Eerdmans Publishing, 1985).

idem, *The Principle of Protestantism.* Trans. John W. Nevin (Philadelphia: United Church Press, 1964).

Schaff, Philip, ed. *A Select Library of the Nicene and Post-Nicene Fathers of the Christian Church.* 14 vols. (Grand Rapids: Eerdmans Publishing, 1969).

Schaff, Philip, and Henry Wace, eds. *A Select Library of Nicene and Post-Nicene Fathers of the Christian Church: Second Series.* 14 vols. (Grand Rapids: Eerdmans Publishing, 1971).

Schillebeeckx, Edward. *Christ: The Experience of Jesus as Lord.* Trans. by John Bowden (New York: Crossroad Publishing Company, 1989).

Schmaus, Michael. *Dogma:6 Justification and the Last Things* (Kansas City and London: Sheed and Ward, 1977).

Schreck, Alan. *Catholic and Christian: An Explanation of Commonly Misunderstood Catholic Beliefs* (Ann Arbor, MI: Servant Books, 1984).

Schultz, Samuel and Morris Inch. *Interpreting the Word of God* (Chicago: Moody Press, 1976)

Schurb, Ken. "Sixteenth-Century Lutheran-Calvinist Conflict on the Protevangelium"*Concordia Theological Quarterly* (January 1990):25-47.

Schweitzer, Alexander. *Die protestantishen Centraldogmen* (Zurich: Orell, Fussli, 1854).

Schweizer, Albert. *Paul and His Interpreters.* Trans. William Montgomery (London: A & C Black, 1912).

Scofield, C. I. *The New Scofield Reference Bible,* reprinted ed. (New York: Oxford University Press, 1967).

Seeburg, Reinhold. *Text-Book of the History of Doctrines,* reprinted ed., trans. Charles E. Hay (Grand Rapids: Baker Book House, 1977).

Seifrid, Mark A. *Justification By Faith: The Origin and Development of a Central Pauline Theme* (New York: E.J. Brill, 1992).

Sharp, Larry D. "The Doctrines of Grace in Calvin and Augustine." *Evangelical Quarterly* 52 (1980):84-96.

Shea, Mark P. *By What Authority: An Evangelical Discovers Catholic Tradition* (Huntington, IN: Our Sunday Visitor Publications, 1996).

Shedd, W.G.T. *Dogmatic Theology,* reprinted (Grand Rapids: Zondervan, 1971).

Sheed, Frank. *Theology and Sanity* (Huntington, IN: Our Sunday Visitor, 1978).

Sheen, Fulton. *Peace of Soul* (New York: McGraw Hill, 1949).

Shepherd, Norman. "The Grace of Justification." Paper submitted to Westminster Theological Seminary, February 8, 1979.

idem, "34 Theses Discussed at the Meeting of the Presbytery." (Philadelphia, December 16, 1978).

Sheridan, Thomas. *Newman on Justification: A Theological Biography* (New York: Alba House, 1967).

Silva, Moises. *Has the Church Misread the Bible* (Grand Rapids: Academie Books, 1987).

idem, *Biblical Words and Their Meaning* (Grand Rapids, Academie Books, 1983).

Skilton, John ed., *Machen's Notes on Galatians, "Faith and Works"* (Presbyterian and Reformed Publishing, 1972).

Smyth, Herbert W. *Greek Grammar* (Cambridge, MA: Harvard University Press, 1920, 1980).

Smyth, Martin. "Differences between the Roman and Reformed Doctrines of Justification." *Evangelical Quarterly* 36 (1964):42-48.

Soards, M.L. "The Righteousness of God in the Writings of the Apostle Paul." *Biblical Theology Bulletin* 15 (1985): 104-109.

Spicq, C. *Theological Lexicon of the New Testament.* Trans. J. D. Ernest (Peabody, MA: Hendrikson Publishers, 1995).

Spittler, Russell., Lawrence Wood, Glenn Hinson, Sinclair Ferguson, and Gerhard Forde. *Christian Spirituality: Five Views of Sanctification* (Downers Grove: Intervarsity Press, 1987).

Sproul, R.C. *Faith Alone: The Evangelical Doctrine of Justification* (Grand Rapids: Baker Book House, 1995).

idem, *Chosen by God* (Illinois: Tyndale House Publishers, 1986).

idem, *Knowing Scripture* (Illinois: InterVarsity Press, 1977).

idem, et al. *Classical Apologetics* (Grand Rapids: Academie Books, 1984).

Stauffer, Richard. *Luther as Seen by Catholics* (Richmond, VA: John Knox Press, 1967).

Stendahl, Kristar. *Paul Among Jews and Gentiles* (Birmingham, England: SCM, 1977).

Steurmann, W.E. "A Critical Study of Calvin's Concept of Faith." Ph.D. dissertation, University of Tulsa, OK 1952.

Stevens, P. Gregory, O.S.B. *The Life of Grace* (Englewood Cliffs, NJ: Prentice-Hall, 1963).

Stibbs, A. M. "Justification by Faith: The Reinstatement of the Doctrine Today." *Evangelical Quarterly* 24 (1952): 156-167.

Strehle, Stephen. *Calvinism, Federalism, and Scholasticism: A Study of the Reformation Doctrine of Covenant* (Bern: Peter Lang, 1988).

Stravinskas, Peter, M. J. ed. *The Catholic Encyclopedia* (Huntington, Indiana: Our Sunday Visitor, 1991).

Tappert, Theodore G. *The Book of Concord* (Philadelphia: Fortress Press, 1959).

Tavard, George H. *Justification: An Ecumenical Study* (New York: Paulist Press, 1983).

idem, *Protestant Hopes and The Catholic Responsibility* (Notre Dame, Indiana: Fides Publishers, 1960).

Terry, Milton S. *Biblical Hermeneutics* (Grand Rapids: Zondervan, 1974).

Teselle, Eugene. "Nature and Grace in Augustine's Expositions of Genesis 1, 1-5." *Recherches augustiniennes V* (1968):95-137.

Thomas, Geoffrey. "Evangelicals and Catholics Together." *The Founders Journal* 17 (Summer 1994):27-29.

Toon, Peter. *The Emergence of Hyper-Calvinism in English Nonconformity*, 1689- 1765 (London: The Olive Tree, 1967).

idem, *Justification and Sanctification* (Westchester, IL: Crossway, 1983).

idem, *Born Again: A Biblical and Theological Study of Regeneration* (Grand Rapids: Baker Book House, 1986).

idem, *Protestants and Catholics: A Guide to Understanding the Differences Among Christians* (Ann Arbor: Servant Books, 1983).

Torrance David and Thomas Torrance, eds. *Calvin's New Testament Commentaries.* Trans. A.W. Morrison (Grand Rapids: Eerdmans Publishing, 1972).

Torrance, Thomas F. *The School of Faith: The Catechisms of the Reformed Church* (London: James Clarke, 1959).

idem, *Calvin's Doctrine of Man* (London: Lutterworth Press, 1949).

Turretin, Francis. *Institutes of Elenctic Theology.* Trans. George Giger. James Dennison, Jr. ed. (Phillipsburg, NJ: Presbyterian and Reformed Publishing, 1992).

Ulstein, Stephen. *Growing Up Fundamentalist* (Downers Grove, IL: Intervarsity Press, 1995).

Vaccari, A. "Bibbe Protestanti E Bibbie Cattolica" in *La Civilta Cattolica* (Roma: Direzione E Amministrazione, 1923).

Van Til, Cornelius. *Introduction to Systematic Theology* (Philadelphia: Presbyterian and Reformed Publishing, 1974).

idem, *Common Grace and the Gospel* (Nutley, NJ: Presbyterian and Reformed Publishing, 1972).

idem, *The Defense of the Faith* (Philipsburg, NJ: Presbyterian and Reformed Publishing, 1967).

Via, D. O. "The Right Strawy Epistle Reconsidered: A Study in Biblical Ethics and Hermeneutics" *Journal of Religion* 49 (1969):255-257.

Vos, Arvin. *Aquinas, Calvin and Contemporary Protestant Thought: A Critique of Protestant Views on the Thought of Thomas Aquinas* (Grand Rapids: Eerdmans, 1985).

Vos, Geerhardus. *The Pauline Eschatology* (Princeton, NJ. Princeton University Press, 1930).

Wagner, Roger. "New Confusions for Old: Rome and Justification." *Antithesis,* vol. 1, no. 5, Sept./Oct. 1990.

Walker, Williston. *John Calvin* (New York: Schocken Books, 1906, 1969).

Warfield, Benjamin B. *Biblical and Theological Studies* (Philadelphia: Presbyterian and Reformed, 1968).

idem, *The Plan of Salvation* (Grand Rapids: Eerdmans Publishing, n.d.).

idem, *Calvin and Augustine*, ed. Samuel G. Craig (Philadelphia: Presbyterian and Reformed, 1956).

idem, "A Review of 'De Zekerheid des Geloofs' [by Hermann Bavinck]." *Selected Shorter Writings of Benjamin B. Warfield,* II, pp. 106-123, ed., John E. Meeter (Nutley, NJ: Presbyterian and Reformed, 1973).

Watson, P. S. "Luther and Sanctification." *Concordia* 30 (1959):243-259.

Webster, William. *Roman Catholicism at the Bar of History* (Banner of Truth, 1995).

Wells, David. "The Protestant Perspective on Human Nature" *The Human Condition in the Jewish and Christian Traditions*, ed. Frederick E. Greenspahn (Hoboden: KTAV Publishing, 1986) 73-100.

idem, *No Place for Truth: Or Whatever Happened to Evangelical Theology*? (Grand Rapids: Eerdmans Publishing, 1993).

Wendel, Francois. *Calvin: The Origins and Development of His Religious Thought.* Trans. Philip Mairet (New York: Harper and Row, 1963).

Werde, William. *Uber Aufgabe und Methode der sogennanten neutertamentlichen Theologie* (Gottingen: Vandenhoeck and Ruprecht, 1987), trans. Robert Morgan: "The Task and Methods of New Testament Theology" in The Nature of New Testament Theology (Naperville, IL: Allenson).

Wesley, John. *The Works of the Reverend John Wesley*, ed. Thomas Jackson, reprinted ed. (Grand Rapids: Baker Book House, 1983).

Westcott, Frederick Brooke. *The Doctrine of Justification.* reprinted ed. (Minneapolis: Klock & Klock, 1983).

Westminster Theological Seminary Board of Trustees. *Westminster Statement on Justification* (Philadelphia: May 27, 1980).

White, James R. *The Roman Catholic Controversy: Catholics and Protestants — Do the Differences Still Matter* (Minneaopolis: Bethany House, 1996).

idem, *The Fatal Flaw* (Southbridge, MA: Crowne Publications, 1990).

idem, "Whatever Happened to the Gospel? A Review of And Reponse to 'Evangelicals and Catholics Together: The Christian Mission in the Third Millenium.'" *Christian Renewal* (August 1994):10-11, 13-14.

idem, *Answers to Catholic Claims* (Southbridge, MA: Crowne Publications, 1990).

White, Richard. "Sola Gratia, Solo Christo: The Roman Catholic Doctrine of Justification" unpublished paper, for Trinity Evangelical Divinity School, December, 1987.

idem, "The Sola Fide in Lutheran and Calvinist Soteriology with Special Reference to the Placement of Justification in the Ordo Salutis" unpublished paper, 1987.

idem, *Justification in Ecumenical Dialogue: An Assessment of the Catholic Contribution.* A Dissertation submitted to Marquette University, May1995.

Whitefield, George. *The Works of George Whitefield* (London: Printed for Edward and Charles Dilly, 1771).

Wicks, Jared ed. *Catholic Scholars Dialogue with Luther* (Chicago: Loyola University Press, 1970).

idem, *Luther and His Spiritual Legacy* (Wilmington, DE: Michael Glazier Inc., 1983).

idem, *Man's Yearning for Grace: Luther's Early Spiritual Teaching* (Washington: Corpus Books, 1968).

Williams, S. K. "'The Righteousness of God' in Romans." *Journal of Biblical Literature* 99 (1980):241-290.

Wrede, William. "The Task and Method of New Testament Theology" in The Nature of New Testament Theology SBT Second Series 25, ed. and trans. Robert Morgan (Naperville, IL: Allenson, 1973).

Ziesler, J.A. *The Meaning of Righteousness in Paul* (Cambridge University Press, 1972).

Zins, Robert M. *Romanism: The Relentless Roman Catholic Assault on the Gospel of Jesus Christ* (Hunstville, AL: White Horse Publications, 1994, 1995).

idem, "The Marketing of Merit in the Roman Catholic Religion." *Theo~Logical*, 2nd quarter, 1996.

Final Prayers

St. Augustine, blessed of God regarding the truth of the gospel, pray for us that God will grant to your earthly brethren in these turbulent times the same knowledge and wisdom he gave to you. Look down on us in pity and pray that we may be strengthened to bring forth truth in the face of all the opposition of the Devil.

St. Gregory the Great, noble and courageous successor of St. Peter, please obtain for us the graces necessary to adequately proclaim and defend God's revealed truth.

St. Thomas Aquinas, pray for us that we may be as diligent in our study of Scripture as once you were. Help us to answer all inquiries regarding the faith in the most effective and complete manner.

St. Francis de Sales, valiant defender of the faith, we beseech your intercession on behalf of our writing and teaching. May it always be faithful to Sacred Tradition, charitable, and efficacious in bringing souls closer to Christ and His Church.

St. Michael the Archangel, defend us in battle, be our protection against the wickedness and snares of the devil. May God rebuke him, we humbly pray; and do thou, Oh Prince of the heavenly host, by the power of God, thrust into hell Satan and all evil spirits who wander through the world for the ruin of souls.

Mary, Mother of God, we pray that you will beseech your Son, who alone provides grace and wisdom, to help us in our efforts to further the cause of the Church. May your holiness and faithfulness be brought to God on our behalf, so that he may have mercy and patience with us as we endeavor to honor his name.

Glorious Lord Jesus, we pray that your great prayer to God the Father for unity among all Christian brethren be realized before your return.

"We could say more but could never say enough; let the final word be: 'He is the all.'" (Ecclesiasticus 43:27).

Amen

Index of Authors and Significant Persons

Index of Scripture

Numbers

1 Corinthians